MACROECONOMICS

PRINCIPLES AND POLICY

SIXTH EDITION
MACROECONOMICS

PRINCIPLES AND POLICY

WILLIAM J. BAUMOL
C.V. STARR CENTER
FOR APPLIED ECONOMICS,
NEW YORK UNIVERSITY

ALAN S. BLINDER
PRINCETON UNIVERSITY

THE DRYDEN PRESS
HARCOURT BRACE COLLEGE PUBLISHERS

FORT WORTH PHILADELPHIA SAN DIEGO NEW YORK ORLANDO AUSTIN SAN ANTONIO
TORONTO MONTREAL LONDON SYDNEY TOKYO

Publisher	Liz Widdicombe
Senior Acquisitions Editor	Rick Hammonds
Senior Developmental Editor	Daryl Fox
Manuscript Editor	Margie Rogers
Production Manager	Mandy Manzano
Designer	Linda Miller
Director of Editing, Design, and Production	Diane Southworth
Literary Permissions	Shirley Webster
Photo Editor	Elizabeth Banks
Indexer	Leslie Leland Frank
Compositor	Monotype Composition Company, Inc.
Text Type	Palatino 10/12

About the Cover   The curve in the left-hand corner represents a production possibilities frontier. As Chapter 3 tells us, any point on or inside this frontier is attainable. Notice that the icons representing the *Twelve Ideas for Beyond the Final Exam* are outside the frontier. It is the mission of this text to help each student move these important ideas into his or her frontier. Within this text, students will find the resources and technology to master core economic concepts and expand their frontier.

COVER SOURCE: All copyright © Tommy Flynn/Photonica

Address for Editorial Correspondence
The Dryden Press, 301 Commerce Street, Suite 3700, Fort Worth, TX 76102

Address for Orders
The Dryden Press, 6277 Sea Harbor Drive, Orlando, FL 32887
1-800-782-4479, or 1-800-433-0001 (in Florida)

ISBN: 0-03-097454-2

Library of Congress Catalog Card Number: 93-74231

Printed in the United States of America

3 4 5 6 7 8 9 0 1 2   048   9 8 7 6 5 4 3 2 1

The Dryden Press
Harcourt Brace College Publishers

Illustration credits appear on page **C-1**, which constitutes a continuation of the copyright page.

ABOUT THE AUTHORS

William J. Baumol was born and raised in New York City. He received his undergraduate degree in economics with a minor in art from the City University of New York and his Ph.D. in economics from the London School of Economics.

He taught at Princeton University for over forty years, and he is now at New York University where he is the director of the C. V. Starr Center for Applied Economics.

Professor Baumol has published over five hundred scholarly articles and more than twenty books that have been translated into a dozen languages.

He has been president of four professional societies, including the American Economic Association. He is also a member of the Board of Trustees of the Joint Council on Economic Education and a member of the National Academy of Sciences.

He is married and has two children and two grandchildren. Besides courses in economics, Professor Baumol also taught wood sculpture at Princeton University.

Alan S. Blinder was born in New York City and earned his A.B. at Princeton University, his M.Sc. at the London School of Economics, and his Ph.D. at Massachusetts Institute of Technology—all in economics.

Since 1971, he has taught at Princeton University, where he is now the Gordon S. Rentschler Memorial Professor of Economics. Professor Blinder chaired the department of economics from 1988 to 1990, and he is also the founder and director of Princeton's Center for Economic Policy Studies.

Professor Blinder is the author of ten books and scores of scholarly articles. He is currently a member of the Council of Economic Advisers and president-elect of the Eastern Economic Association.

Professor Blinder is married, has two sons, and currently lives in Washington, D.C.

THE DRYDEN PRESS SERIES IN ECONOMICS

ASCH AND SENECA
Government and the Marketplace
Second Edition

BAKER
An Introduction to International Economics

BAUMOL AND BLINDER
Economics: Principles and Policy
Sixth Edition (Also available in micro and macro paperbacks)

BAUMOL, PANZAR, AND WILLIG
Contestable Markets and the Theory of Industry Structure
Revised Edition

BERCH
The Endless Day: The Political Economy of Women and Work

BREIT AND ELZINGA
The Antitrust Casebook: Milestones in Economic Regulation
Second Edition

BRUE
The Evolution of Economic Thought
Fifth Edition

CAMPBELL, CAMPBELL, AND DOLAN
Money, Banking, and Monetary Policy

CLAUDON AND OLSEN
Eco Talk

DEMMERT
Economics: Understanding the Market Process

DOLAN AND LINDSEY
Economics
Seventh Edition (Also available in micro and macro paperbacks)

ECKERT AND LEFTWICH
The Price System and Resource Allocation
Tenth Edition

EDGMAND, MOOMAW, AND OLSON
Economics and Contemporary Issues
Second Edition

ESTEY
The Unions: Structure, Development, and Management
Third Edition

FRIEDMAN
Milton Friedman Speaks (Video)

GARDNER
Comparative Economic Systems

GLAHE
Microeconomics: Theory and Application
Second Edition

GREEN
Macroeconomics: Analysis and Applications

GWARTNEY AND STROUP
Economics: Private and Public Choice
Sixth Edition (Also available in micro and macro paperbacks)

GWARTNEY AND STROUP
Introduction to Economics: The Wealth and Poverty of Nations

HEILBRONER AND SINGER
The Economic Transformation of America: 1600 to the Present
Second Edition

HIRSCH AND RUFOLO
Public Finance and Expenditure in a Federal System

HIRSCHEY AND PAPPAS
Fundamentals of Managerial Economics
Fourth Edition

HIRSCHEY AND PAPPAS
Managerial Economics
Seventh Edition

HOERNEMAN, HOWARD, WILSON, AND COLE
CAPER: Computer Assisted Program for Economic Review

HYMAN
Public Finance: A Contemporary Application of Theory to Policy
Fourth Edition

JOHNSON AND ROBERTS
Money and Banking: A Market-Oriented Approach
Third Edition

KAUFMAN
The Economics of Labor Markets
Fourth Edition

KEATING AND WILSON
Fundamentals of Managerial Economics

KEATING AND WILSON
Managerial Economics
Second Edition

KENNETT AND LIEBERMAN
*The Road to Capitalism: The Economic Transformation
of Eastern Europe and the Former Soviet Union*

KIDWELL, PETERSON, AND BLACKWELL
Financial Institutions, Markets, and Money
Fifth Edition

KOHN
Money, Banking, and Financial Markets
Second Edition

KREININ
International Economics: A Policy Approach
Sixth Edition

LANDSBURG
Price Theory and Applications
Second Edition

LINK, MILLER, AND BERGMAN
EconoGraph II: Interactive Software for Principles of Economics

LOTT AND RAY
Applied Econometrics with Data Sets

NICHOLSON
Intermediate Microeconomics and Its Application
Sixth Edition

NICHOLSON
Microeconomic Theory: Basic Principles and Extensions
Fifth Edition

ORMISTON
Intermediate Microeconomics

PUTH
American Economic History
Third Edition

RAGAN AND THOMAS
Principles of Economics
Second Edition (Also available in micro and macro
paperbacks)

RAMANATHAN
Introductory Econometrics with Applications
Second Edition

RUKSTAD
*Corporate Decision Making in the World Economy:
Company Case Studies*

RUKSTAD
*Macroeconomic Decision Making in the World Economy:
Text and Cases*
Third Edition

SAMUELSON AND MARKS
Managerial Economics

SCARTH
Macroeconomics: An Introduction to Advanced Methods
Third Edition

SMITH AND SPUDECK
Interest Rates: Principles and Applications

THOMAS
Economics: Principles and Applications
(Also available in micro and macro paperbacks)

WACHTEL
Labor and the Economy
Third Edition

WALTON AND ROCKOFF
History of the American Economy
Seventh Edition

WELCH AND WELCH
Economics: Theory and Practice
Fourth Edition

YARBROUGH AND YARBROUGH
The World Economy: Trade and Finance
Third Edition

ZIMBALIST, SHERMAN, AND BROWN
Comparing Economic Systems: A Political-Economic Approach
Second Edition

THE HARCOURT BRACE COLLEGE OUTLINE SERIES

Emery
Principles of Economics: Macroeconomics

Emery
Principles of Economics: Microeconomics

Emery
Intermediate Microeconomics

To my four children,
Ellen, Daniel,
and now Sabrina and Jim

W.J.B.

For Scott, who is now
Beyond the Final Exam,
and William, who is on his way

A.S.B.

P R E F A C E

Economic analysis has continued to progress since the writing of the previous edition; but it has produced no revolutionary upheavals requiring major changes in this book. However, the world about us has changed in ways that were beyond belief just a few years ago. Who would have dreamed five years ago that the Berlin Wall would be chopped up and sold as souvenirs in shops throughout the world, that the Soviet Union would disintegrate, and that Europe—and even Russia itself—would be headed by leaders eager to declare their commitment to the market mechanism?

For us, the fundamental importance of these events stems not only from their negative verdict on the workability of central planning, nor from the fact that the free market has won the competitive struggle with "Marxism," sensational though that victory clearly is. Perhaps equally important for the long run is the fact that these cataclysmic developments are sure to affect our economy in a variety of ways. U.S. military spending is being cut substantially, under powerful public pressure. The reunification of Germany has implications for the U.S. balance of payments and for American competitiveness in world markets. U.S. business is now offered substantial marketing and investment opportunities in the newly reopened economies of Eastern Europe that competition does not permit it to ignore.

These and other related developments hammer home the fact that American workers and American firms carry out their economic activities *in a market that is fundamentally international.* Half a century ago, the rest of the world mattered far less to the U.S. economy than it does today. Back then, General Motors was primarily concerned with competition from Ford and Chrysler; foreign cars were hardly worth worrying about. In almost all industries, the bulk of U.S. production was sold to other Americans. Imports and exports constituted a far smaller share of GDP than they do today. But all this has changed. American producers of computers, airplanes, and TV programs make a large proportion of their sales and profits outside our borders. Television sets in U.S. homes come almost entirely from abroad, and Japanese cars are the primary competitive threat to our automobile industry.

For these reasons, it made sense in the past for most of the pages of an *American* textbook to treat the U.S. economy as an isolated world complete in itself, and, for the sake of expository simplicity, that is how most books were written. Only in later chapters were international economic linkages introduced as a necessary but troublesome complication, modifying somewhat the isolated-country analysis of the remainder of the volume.

Accordingly, in this Sixth Edition, our book continues the reorientation introduced in the Fifth Edition, seeking to provide the reader with a depiction of the workings of an economy firmly intertwined with many others. The international interconnections of our economy are embedded throughout the book rather than appended as an afterthought. Illustrative cases, descriptive factual materials, analytic tools, and end-of-chapter problems have all been modified in this way. We trust the result will give the reader an enhanced sense of pertinence, and offer him or her more illuminating insights into the way the economy really works.

This edition, however, continues the basic philosophy of its predecessors. In particular, we avoid the fiction, so popular among textbook writers, that everything is of the utmost importance—a pretense that students are sufficiently intelligent to see through in any event. We try, instead, to highlight those important ideas that are likely to be of lasting significance—principles that students will want to remember long after the course is over because they offer insights that are far from obvious, because they are of practical importance, and because they are widely misunderstood by intelligent laymen. A dozen of the most important of these ideas are selected as **12 Ideas for Beyond the Final Exam** and are called to the reader's attention when they occur through the use of the book's logo.

All modern economics textbooks abound with "real world" examples. We try to go beyond this by elevating the examples to preeminence for, in our view, the policy issue or everyday economic problem ought to lead the student naturally to the economic principle, not the other way around. For this reason, many chapters start with a real policy issue or a practical problem, sometimes drawn from our own experience, that may seem puzzling or paradoxical to noneconomists. We then proceed to describe the economic analysis required to remove the mystery.

In so doing, we use technical terminology and diagrams only where there is a clear need for them, never for their own sake. Still, economics is a technical subject and so this is, unavoidably, a book for the desk, and not for the bed. We make, however, strenuous efforts to simplify the technical level of the discussion as much as possible without sacrificing content. Fortunately, almost every important idea in economics can be explained in plain English, and this is what we try to do.

Finally, in addition to a host of minor changes throughout the volume, we have, with some invaluable help (see below) gone over the book with considerable care, seeking to emphasize issues related to discrimination against minority groups and women. It should be emphasized that this is no attempt to impart political correctness into the book. We frankly do not care whether what we have written is or is not deemed "politically correct" by any particular observer. Moreover, we are deeply dedicated to academic freedom, meaning that we are prepared to defend the right of any writer on economics to take positions, political and economic, very different from our own. However, we also believe that the economic issues raised by discrimination against women or the members of any minority group are of profound significance and, in addition, our own value judgments emphatically call for the devotion of effort to the elimination of all such discrimination. We have sought to act accordingly in the revision of the book, while meticulously seeking to avoid any attempt to foist our own political views or value judgments upon anyone.

As a last personal note, we must mention that completion of the work has had to be carried out under the handicap of a divorce between the coauthors. Happily, their separation entails neither disagreement nor rancor, and there is every reason to expect it to be temporary. However, when Alan Blinder left for Washington to join President Clinton's Council of Economic Advisers, though that undoubtedly contributed to the relevance of this book's materials to the real world, it made communication between us far more challenging. Besides, we simply miss one another.

However, there is a silver lining to this inconvenience. Blinder reports renewed and enhanced respect for Herb Stein's observation that "most of the economics that is usable for advising on public policy is at about the level of the introductory undergraduate course."

NOTE TO THE STUDENT

We would like to offer one suggestion for success in your macroeconomics course. Unlike some of the other courses you may be taking, macroeconomics is cumulative—each week's lesson builds on what you have learned before. You will save yourself both a lot of frustration and a lot of work by keeping up on a week-to-week basis. To help you do this, there is a chapter summary, a list of important terms and concepts, and a selection of questions to help you review at the end of each chapter. Making use of these learning aids will increase your success in your macroeconomics course. For additional assistance, see the following list of ancillary materials.

ANCILLARIES

As economic education incorporates new technologies, our extensive learning package has been expanded to accommodate the needs of students and instructors. Each of the following items can be ordered through your bookstore or your local Dryden representative.

Study Guide by Craig Swan, University of Minnesota (for students)

- Available in macro or micro splits, as well as a combined version.
- Chapter reviews and "Basic Exercises" have been updated and revised.
- More multiple-choice questions in "Self Test for Understanding."
- New "Economics in Action" sections in all chapters.
- New "Supplementary Exercises" based on external reading that emphasize critical thinking.

Instructor's Manual by John Isbister, University of California–Santa Cruz

Each chapter corresponds to a text chapter and opens with a brief summary, pointing out highlights and principal goals. Each chapter contains the following instructional elements:

- The "Chapter Outline" section contains major and minor headings. Instructors can use this to get a quick and comprehensive overview.
- Two "Major Ideas" are listed and explained.
- "On Teaching the Chapter" contains ideas for presenting the material. It helps the instructor think about new pedagogical strategies.
- An additional set of "Problems" requires numerical, graphical or theoretical answers.
- "Discussion Questions" are available which may be assigned for written responses or for classroom discussion.
- Available in micro, macro, and combined versions.

New Test Bank A by Peter Schwarz and Julia Mobley, University of North Carolina–Charlotte

■ Consists of 2,700+ questions of True/False, Multiple Choice, and 10 essay questions per chapter with an emphasis on problem solving.

■ Combined micro/macro versions are available.

Computerized Test Bank A by Peter Schwarz and Julia Mobley, University of North Carolina–Charlotte

■ Appears in combined version.

■ Available in IBM 3.5, 5.25, and Mac versions.

■ EXAMASTER⁺ allows you to add and edit your own questions, create and edit graphics, print scrambled versions of tests, convert multiple-choice questions to open-ended questions, plus much more.

New Test Bank B by John Dodge, Sioux Falls College

■ Available in micro and combined versions.

■ For instructors who want additional questions.

■ Consists of 2,700+ questions of True/False, Multiple Choice, and 10 essay questions per chapter with an emphasis on problem solving.

Computerized Test Bank B by John Dodge, Sioux Falls College

■ Available in IBM 3.5, 5.25, and Mac versions.

Transparency Acetates and Masters

■ Full color acetates provide exact graphics from the text.

■ One color Transparency Masters for all text figures can be duplicated for students.

■ "Sequenced" acetates allow the instructor to build in curve shifts and changes, facilitating student understanding.

Economics in Focus Videos by Media Solutions

■ Facilitate multi-level learning and critical thinking through its up-to-date coverage of current events in our society, while focusing on economic issues important to students and their understanding of the economy.

■ Recent segments from MacNeil/Lehrer's *News Hour* program are updated quarterly.

■ **Economics in Focus** looks at three major themes:

  ▪ *International Economic Scene* covers free trade, foreign policy, and other related issues.

  ▪ *Economic Challenges and Problems* explores such topics as declining incomes, the budget deficit, and inflation.

  ▪ *The Political Economy* looks at the role of the government, free enterprise, and economic stabilization.

  ▪ Each issue of **Economics in Focus** closes with a special feature story or one-to-one interview with a noted economist.

Laser Discs

This package contains both a microeconomics disc and a macroeconomics disc. Each focuses on the core principles and presents the information interactively. A brief 5–7 minute video from CBS begins each learning section. Related animated graphics then follow. With an understanding of the concepts, the student is challenged with critical thinking questions. A printed *Media Instructor's Manual* explains how the laser discs coordinate with *Macroeconomics: Principles and Policy, Sixth Edition*.

TAG Software (Tututorial and Graphing) Software by Todd Porter and Teresa Riley, Youngstown State University (for students)

■ This award-winning software has been significantly enhanced to contain an extensive chapter-by-chapter tutorial, a hands-on graphing section where students are actually required to draw curves (with key strokes or a mouse) and a practice exam for each section. Students receive feedback on their answers. Available in IBM versions.

Macintosh Tutorial Software (for students)

■ This user-friendly interface allows students to revisit and apply concepts from the text.

Lecture Presentation Software

■ Menu-driven presentation software.
■ Each video clip and still frame image on laser disc has a specific page and/or figure reference to the text.
■ Allows instructor to add lecture notes, video, and laser disc material.
■ Available in IBM Windows and Apple Macintosh formats, with supporting documentation.

Mathematics Supplement by Denise Kummer, St. Louis Community College–Meramec

■ Walks the student through basic math and algebra.
■ Structured lessons allow for review and practice with variables, averages, ratios, percentages, and simple equations.
■ A real help to students with varied math backgrounds.

Dryden's *News-by-Fax* by John Isbister, University of California–Santa Cruz

■ Provides instructors with updates regarding current issues on a monthly basis.
■ Includes source of the article under discussion, a brief summary of the article, and questions for classroom discussion.
■ Establishes close links to the text by providing page / topic references to the text.

NOTE TO THE INSTRUCTOR

This book contains about half of the chapters found in our book, *Economics: Principles and Policy*, Sixth Edition. Throughout *Macroeconomics* we occasionally refer to chapters in *Microeconomics*, which contains the other half of the materials in *Economics*.

In trying to improve the book from one edition to the next, we rely heavily on our experiences as teachers. But our experience using the book is minuscule compared with that of the hundreds of instructors who use it nationwide. If you encounter problems, or have suggestions for improving the book, we urge you to let us know by writing to either one of us in care of The Dryden Press, 301 Commerce Street, Suite 3700, Fort Worth, TX 76102. Such letters are invaluable, and we are glad to receive them, even if they are critical (but not *too* critical!). Many such suggestions accumulated over the past three years found their way into the Sixth Edition.

What follows are suggested course outlines for a one-semester and a one-quarter course in macroeconomics.

OUTLINE FOR A ONE-SEMESTER COURSE IN MACROECONOMICS

CHAPTER NUMBER	TITLE
1	What Is Economics?
2	A Profile of the U.S. Economy
3	Scarcity and Choice: *The* Economic Problem
4	Supply and Demand: An Initial Look
5	The Realm of Macroeconomics
6	Unemployment and Inflation: The Twin Evils of Macroeconomics
7	Income and Spending: The Powerful Consumer
8	Demand-Side Equilibrium: Unemployment or Inflation?
9	Changes on the Demand Side: Multiplier Analysis
10	Supply-Side Equilibrium: Unemployment *and* Inflation?
11	Managing Aggregate Demand: Fiscal Policy
12	Money and the Banking System
13	Monetary Policy and the National Economy
14	The Debate over Monetary Policy
15	Budget Deficits and the National Debt: Fact and Fiction
16	The Trade-Off between Inflation and Unemployment
17	Productivity and Growth in the Wealth of Nations
18	International Trade and Comparative Advantage
19	The International Monetary System: Order or Disorder?
20	Macroeconomics in a World Economy
21	Growth in Developed and Developing Countries

OUTLINE FOR A ONE-QUARTER COURSE IN MACROECONOMICS

CHAPTER NUMBER	TITLE
1	What Is Economics?
2	A Profile of the U.S. Economy
3	Scarcity and Choice: *The* Economic Problem
4	Supply and Demand: An Initial Look

5   The Realm of Macroeconomics
6   Unemployment and Inflation: The Twin Evils of Macroeconomics
7   Income and Spending: The Powerful Consumer
8   Demand-Side Equilibrium: Unemployment or Inflation?
9   Changes on the Demand Side: Multiplier Analysis
10 Supply-Side Equilibrium: Unemployment *and* Inflation?
11 Managing Aggregate Demand: Fiscal Policy
12 Money and the Banking System
13 Monetary Policy and the National Economy
14 The Debate over Monetary Policy
15 Budget Deficits and the National Debt: Fact and Fiction
16 The Trade-Off between Inflation and Unemployment

WITH THANKS

Finally, and with great pleasure, we turn to the customary acknowledgments of indebtedness. Ours have been accumulating now through six editions. In these days of specialization, not even a pair of authors can master every subject that an introductory text must cover. Our friends and colleagues Albert Ando, Charles Berry, Rebecca Blank, William Branson, the late Lester Chandler, Gregory Chow, Avinash Dixit, Robert Eisner, Stephen Goldfeld, Claudia Goldin, Ronald Grieson, Daniel Hamermesh, Yuzo Honda, Peter Kenen, Melvin Krauss, Herbert Levine, the late Arthur Lewis, Burton Malkiel, Edwin Mills, Janusz Ordover, Uwe Reinhardt, Harvey Rosen, Laura Tyson, and Martin Weitzman have all given generously of their knowledge in particular areas over the course of six editions. We have learned much from them, and only wish we had learned more.

In this Sixth Edition we owe a particularly heavy debt to Professor Susan Feiner of Hampton University who went over the book with terrifyingly meticulous and thoughtful care, catching errors, pointing out expository shortcomings, and suggesting fundamental revisions. She was also enormously helpful in suggesting places where the book did not deal adequately or appropriately with issues relating to discrimination by sex or ethnic group. In all matters we have adopted most of her suggestions. Perhaps it would have been a better book if we had adopted all of them.

Many economists and students at other colleges and universities offered useful suggestions for improvements, many of which we have incorporated into the Sixth Edition. We wish to thank Robert C. Stuart, Rutgers University; David Aschaur, Bates College; Tom Beveridge, North Carolina State University; Ivan Keith Cohen, Trinity College; Norman L. Dalsted, Colorado Sate University; Larry DeBrock, University of Illinois–Urbana-Champaign; John Edgren, Eastern Michigan University; Robert Eisner, Northwestern University; Chris Ellis, University of Oregon; Shelby Gerking, University of Wyoming; Ami Glazer, University of California–Irvine; Doug Greenley, Moorhead State University; Harry Holzer, Michigan State University; Michael Kupilik, University of Montana; Woo Bong Lee, Bloomsburg University; Charles Okeke, Community College of Southern Nevada; Kevin Rask, Colgate University; Bob Sharp, Eastern Kentucky University; Ernst Stromsdorfer, Washington State University; Roy Van Til, University of Maine at Farmington; Walter Wessels, North Carolina State University; Louise Wolitz, University of Texas at Austin; Prof. Wong, California State University–Fullerton; Ali Zadeh, Susquehanna University; and Michael Zweig, SUNY–Stony Brook.

We also wish to thank the many economists who responded to our questionnaire; their responses were invaluable in planning this revision: Peter Adelsheim, St. Martin's College; Carlos Aguilar, El Paso County Community College; Carolyn Ahern, Monterey Peninsula College; Samuel Kojo Andoh, Southern Connecticut State University; M. Aokoi, University of Rhode Island; K. Arakelian, University of Rhode Island; Roger Atkins, Marshall University; Chris Austin, Normandale Community College; John Azer, Normandale Community College; Robert A. Baade, Lake Forest College; Mohsen Bahmani-Oskooee, University of Wisconsin at Milwaukee; Donald Baum, University of Nebraska; Prof. Baye, Penn State; D.V.T. Bear, University of California–San Diego; Klaus Becker, Texas Tech University; Dallas Blevins, University of Montevallo; Scott Bloom, North Dakota State Univesity; Prof. Brent, Fordham University; John Bungum, University of Minnesota; Evert Campbell, Point Loma Nazarene College; Michael Carter, University of Lowell (MA); Prof. Ceyhun, University of North Dakota; Anthony Chan, Woodbury University; Dan Cobb, St. Louis Community College; Steven Cobb, Xavier University; Joyce Cooper, Boston University; Claude Cox, St. Louis Community College; Ward Curran, Trinity College; Prof. Diulio, Fordham University; Cliff Dobitz, North Dakota State University; Robert Dunn, George Washington University; John C. Dutton, North Carolina State University; Prof. Dziadosz, St. Joseph's University; Alfredo Esposto, Eastern Michigan University; Prof. Fardminash, Temple University; Michael Ferrantino, Southern Methodist University; Prof. Fesmeire, University of Tampa; Rudy Fichtenbaum, Wright State University; Prof. Field-Hendry, CUNY–Queens; Warren Fisher, Susquehanna University; Nancy R. Fox, St. Joseph's University; Richard Fryman, West Georgia College; Yilma Gebremariam, Southern Connecticut State University; Prof. George, LaSalle University; Prof. Ghosh, Tulane University; Prof. Gimmell, Gettysburg College; Leon Graubard, Worcester Polytechnic Institute; John Green, University of Northern Colorado; Robert Gustavson, Washburn University of Topeka; Rick Hafer, Southern Illinois University; Rebecca Havens, Point Loma Nazarene College; Mark Herander, University of South Florida; Roger Hinderliter, Ithaca College; Dennis Hoffman, Arizona State University; Shane Hunt, Boston University; Beth Ingram, University of Iowa; Walter Johnson, University of Missouri; Prof. Jones, McNeese State University; Frederick Joutz, George Washington University; Prof. Kane, Fordham University; Robert Kerchner, Washington University of Topeka; Jerry Kingston, Arizona State University; Evan Kraft, Salisbury State University; Prof. Kreider, Beloit University; Dale Kuntz, Bentley College; Tae-Hwy Lee, Louisiana State University; Jon G. Lindgren, North Dakota State University; Adam Lutzker, Albion College; Diane Macunovich, Williams College; Michael Manove, Boston University; Robert Marcott, University of St. Thomas; Jeff Marin, Boston University; Jay Martin, Longwood College; John McDowell, Arizona State University; Erica McGrath, Monterey Peninsula College; Ron McNamara, Bentley College; A. Mead, University of Rhode Island; B. Nahata, University of Louisville; Thomas A. Odegaard, Baylor University; Ronald Oldson, University of Kansas; Prof. O'Niel, University of North Dakota; Prof. O'Reilley, North Dakota State University; Theodore Paulos, Wallace State Community College; Prof. Pavlivls, Pennsylvania State University; Helen Popper, Santa Clara University; A. T. Powell, Los Angeles Southwest College; Ali Pyarali, University of South Carolina–Salkehatchie; Prof. Rahman, McNeese State University; Prof. Railing, Gettysburg College; G. Ramsay, University of Rhode Island; John Rappaport, Mount Holyoke College; Prof. Ratkus, LaSalle University; Steven Resnick, University of Massachusetts; Greg Rhodus, Bentley College; Nancy Roberts, Arizona State University; John E. L. Robertson, Paducah Community College; Malcolm Robinson, University of Cincinnati; Gary Rourke, Lakewood Community College; Thomas Sav, Wright State University; Elizabeth Savoca, Smith College; John Schorn, Georgetown University; Steven Shapiro, University of North Florida; John Shaw, California State University–Fresno; John Shea, University of Wisconsin; Earl Shinn, University of Montevallo; Harlan Smith, Marshall University; Janet Smith, Arizona State University; Stephen Smith, Bakersfield College; Paul Snoonian, University of Lowell; Prof. Solon, CUNY–Queens; Steven Spartan, Kansas City, Kansas Community College; J. Starkey, University of Rhode Island; James A. Stephenson, Iowa State University; William Stolte, Berea College; Scott Stradley, University of North Dakota; Richard Sutch, University of California–Berkeley; Prof. Thomas, University of South Florida; James Thornblade, Bentley College; Robert Turner, Colgate University; Lynn

Usher, University of Louisville; Prof. Vaz, CUNY–Queens; Lori Warner, University of the Pacific; Rob Wassner, Wayne State University; George Wasson, St. Louis Community College; Art Woolf, University of Vermont; and Dirk Yandell, University of San Diego.

Obviously, the book you hold in your hand was not produced by us alone. An essential role was played by the fine people at The Dryden Press including Rick Hammonds, Daryl Fox, Linda Miller, Mandy Manzano and Elizabeth Banks. In particular, our very capable manuscript editor, Margie Rogers, who has, we feel, become a friend, again worked hard and well to turn our manuscript into the book you see. We appreciate all their efforts.

We also thank our intelligent and delightful secretaries and research co-workers at Princeton and New York University. Phyllis Durepos and Janeece Roderick struggled successfully with the chaos of manuscript exchange, management of proofs, and the simple but difficult task of keeping track of the myriad and all too easily scattered pieces of the uncompleted work. Above all, one of us owes an unrepayable debt to his longstanding partner in crime, Sue Anne Batey Blackman, who carried out much of the updating of materials and who contributed draft paragraphs, illustrative items, and far more with her usual insight and diligence. By now, she undoubtedly knows more about the book than the authors do.

And finally there are our wives, Hilda Baumol and Madeline Blinder. They have now participated and helped in this project for eighteen years. Over that period, if possible, our affection has grown.

WILLIAM J. BAUMOL
ALAN S. BLINDER

BRIEF CONTENTS

Preface   ix

PART I

GETTING ACQUAINTED WITH ECONOMICS   1

1	WHAT IS ECONOMICS?	2
2	A PROFILE OF THE U.S. ECONOMY	27
3	SCARCITY AND CHOICE: *THE* ECONOMIC PROBLEM	55
4	SUPPLY AND DEMAND: AN INITIAL LOOK	74

PART II

THE MACROECONOMY: AGGREGATE SUPPLY AND DEMAND   103

5	THE REALM OF MACROECONOMICS	104
6	UNEMPLOYMENT AND INFLATION: THE TWIN EVILS OF MACROECONOMICS	123
7	INCOME AND SPENDING: THE POWERFUL CONSUMER	150
8	DEMAND-SIDE EQUILIBRIUM: UNEMPLOYMENT OR INFLATION?	181
9	CHANGES ON THE DEMAND SIDE: MULTIPLIER ANALYSIS	207
10	SUPPLY-SIDE EQUILIBRIUM: UNEMPLOYMENT *AND* INFLATION?	227

PART III

FISCAL AND MONETARY POLICY   249

11	MANAGING AGGREGATE DEMAND: FISCAL POLICY	250
12	MONEY AND THE BANKING SYSTEM	273
13	MONETARY POLICY AND THE NATIONAL ECONOMY	298
14	THE DEBATE OVER MONETARY POLICY	321
15	BUDGET DEFICITS AND THE NATIONAL DEBT: FACT AND FICTION	353
16	THE TRADE-OFF BETWEEN INFLATION AND UNEMPLOYMENT	381

PART IV

THE UNITED STATES IN THE WORLD ECONOMY 411

17 PRODUCTIVITY AND GROWTH IN THE WEALTH OF NATIONS   412

18 INTERNATIONAL TRADE AND COMPARATIVE ADVANTAGE   432

19 THE INTERNATIONAL MONETARY SYSTEM: ORDER OR DISORDER?   460

20 MACROECONOMICS IN A WORLD ECONOMY   485

PART V

ALTERNATIVE ECONOMIC SYSTEMS 509

21 GROWTH IN DEVELOPED AND DEVELOPING COUNTRIES   510

GLOSSARY   G-1

INDEX   I-1

CONTENTS

Preface **ix**

PART I

GETTING ACQUAINTED WITH ECONOMICS 1

1 WHAT IS ECONOMICS? 2

Ideas for Beyond the Final Exam 3

Idea 1: The Trade-Off between Inflation and Unemployment 3

Idea 2: The Illusion of High Interest Rates 3

Idea 3: Do Budget Deficits Burden Future Generations? 4

Idea 4: The Overwhelming Importance of Productivity Growth in the Long Run 4

Idea 5: Mutual Gains from Voluntary Exchange 5

Idea 6: The Surprising Principle of Comparative Advantage 5

Idea 7: Attempts to Repeal the Laws of Supply and Demand: The Market Strikes Back 6

Idea 8: Externalities: A Shortcoming of the Market Cured by Market Methods 6

Idea 9: Rational Choice and True Economic Costs: The Role of Opportunity Cost 7

Idea 10: The Importance of Marginal Analysis 8

Idea 11: The Cost Disease of the Personal Services 8

Idea 12: The Trade-Off between Output and Equality 9

Epilogue 9

Inside the Economist's Tool Kit 10

Economics as a Discipline 10

The Need for Abstraction 10

The Role of Economic Theory 13

What Is an Economic "Model"? 15

Reasons for Disagreements: Imperfect Information and Value Judgments 15

Last Word: Common Sense Is Not Always Reliable 17

Summary 18

Key Concepts and Terms 18

Questions for Review 18

APPENDIX: THE GRAPHS USED IN ECONOMIC ANALYSIS 19

Two-Variable Diagrams 19

The Definition and Measurement of Slope 20

Rays through the Origin and 45° Lines 23

Squeezing Three Dimensions into Two: Contour Maps 23

Summary 26

Key Concepts and Terms 26

Questions for Review 26

2 A PROFILE OF THE U.S. ECONOMY   27

The American Economy: A Thumbnail Sketch 28

A Growing Economy . . . But with Inflation 31

The Inputs: Labor and Capital 35

The Outputs: What Does America Produce? 39

The Central Role of Business Firms 40

What's Missing from the Picture? Government 42

Conclusion: The Mixed Economy 47

Summary 47

Key Concepts and Terms 48

Questions for Review 48

APPENDIX: FURTHER PERILS IN THE INTERPRETATION OF GRAPHS 49

Distorting Trends by Choice of the Time Period 49

Dangers of Omiting the Origin 51

Unreliability of Steepness and Choice of Units 52

Summary 54

Questions for Review 54

3 SCARCITY AND CHOICE: *THE* ECONOMIC PROBLEM   55

Scarcity, Choice, and Opportunity Cost 56

Opportunity Cost and Money Cost 58

Production, Scarcity, and Resource Allocation 58

Scarcity and Choice for a Single Firm 59

The Principle of Increasing Costs 61

Scarcity and Choice for the Entire Society 62

Scarcity and Choice Elsewhere in the Economy 64

The Concept of Efficiency 66

The Three Coordination Tasks of Any Economy 68

Specialization, Division of Labor, and Exchange 68

Markets, Prices, and Three Coordination Tasks 70

Radical and Conservative Goals Can Both Be Served by the Market Mechanism 71

Summary 72

Key Concepts and Terms 73

Questions for Review 73

4 SUPPLY AND DEMAND: AN INITIAL LOOK   74

Fighting the Invisible Hand 75

Demand and Quantity Demanded 76

Supply and Quantity Supplied   78

Equilibrium of Supply and Demand   80

Shifts of the Demand Curve   84

Shifts of the Supply Curve   87

Restraining the Market Mechanism: Price Ceilings   91

Restraining the Market Mechanism: Price Floors   93

A Can of Worms   95

A Simple but Powerful Lesson   98

Summary   98

Key Concepts and Terms   99

Questions for Review   99

PART  II

THE
MACROECONOMY:
AGGREGATE SUPPLY
AND DEMAND   103

5   THE REALM OF MACROECONOMICS   **104**

Drawing a Line between Macroeconomics and Microeconomics   105

Supply and Demand in Macroeconomics   107

Gross Domestic Product   109

Limitations of the GDP: What GDP Is Not   111

The Economy on a Roller Coaster   113

From World War II to 1973   116

The Great Stagflation, 1973–1980   117

Reaganomics and Its Aftermath   118

The Problem of Macroeconomic Stabilization: A Sneak Preview   119

Summary   121

Key Concepts and Terms   122

Questions for Review   122

**6   UNEMPLOYMENT AND INFLATION: THE TWIN EVILS OF
MACROECONOMICS**   **123**

The Costs of Unemployment   124

Counting the Unemployed: The Official Statistics   128

Types of Unemployment   128

How Much Employment Is "Full Employment"   129

Unemployment Insurance: The Invaluable Cushion   130

The Costs of Inflation   131

Inflation: The Myth and the Reality   132

Inflation as a Redistributor of Income and Wealth   135

Real versus Nominal Interest Rates   136

Inflation and the Tax System   137

Usury Laws, Interest Rate Ceilings, and Other Impediments   138

Other Costs of Inflation   140

Creeping versus Galloping Inflation   141

The Costs of Creeping versus Galloping Inflation   143

Creeping Inflation Does Not Necessarily Lead to Galloping Inflation   143

Summary   144

Key Concepts and Terms   144

Questions for Review   145

APPENDIX: HOW STATISTICIANS MEASURE INFLATION   146

Index Numbers for Inflation   146

The Consumer Price Index   146

How to Use a Price Index to "Deflate" Monetary Figures   147

The GDP Deflator   148

Summary   148

Key Concepts and Terms   149

Questions for Review   149

7   INCOME AND SPENDING: THE POWERFUL CONSUMER   **150**

Aggregate Demand, National Product, and National Income   151

The Circular Flow of Spending, Production, and Income   152

Demand Management and the Powerful Consumer   155

Consumer Spending and Income: The Important Relationship   156

The Consumption Function and the Marginal Propensity to Consume   160

Movements Along versus Shifts of the Consumption Function   162

Other Determinants of Consumer Spending   162

Why Tax Policy Failed in 1975   165

The Predictability of Consumer Behavior   166

Summary   167

Key Concepts and Terms   167

Questions for Review   168

APPENDIX A: THE SAVING FUNCTION AND THE MARGINAL PROPENSITY TO SAVE   169

Summary   170

Key Concepts and Terms   171

Questions for Review   171

APPENDIX B: NATIONAL INCOME ACCOUNTING   172

Defining GDP: Exceptions to the Rules   172

GDP as the Sum of Final Goods and Services   172

GDP as the Sum of All Factor Payments   173

GDP as the Sum of Values Added   176

Alternative Measures of the Income of the Nation   177

Summary   179

Key Concepts and Terms   179

Questions for Review   179

8 DEMAND-SIDE EQUILIBRIUM: UNEMPLOYMENT OR INFLATION?   **181**

The Extreme Variability of Investment   182

The Determinants of Net Exports   184

The Meaning of Equilibrium GDP   185

Equilibrium on the Demand Side of the Economy   187

Constructing the Expenditure Schedule   187

The Mechanics of Income Determination   189

The Aggregate Demand Curve   191

Demand-Side Equilibrium and Full Employment   193

The Coordination of Saving and Investment   196

Summary   199

Key Concepts and Terms   200

Questions for Review   200

APPENDIX A: THE "LEAKAGE" AND "INJECTIONS" APPROACH   202

Graphical Analysis   202

Induced Investment   203

Variable Imports   204

Summary   204

Key Concepts and Terms   204

Questions for Review   204

APPENDIX B: THE SIMPLE ALGEBRA OF INCOME DETERMINATION   205

Questions for Review   205

9 CHANGES ON THE DEMAND SIDE: MULTIPLIER ANALYSIS   **207**

The Magic of the Multiplier   208

Demystifying the Multiplier: How It Works   210

Algebraic Statement of the Multiplier   211

The Multiplier Effect of Consumer Spending   213

The Multiplier Effect of Government Purchases   214

The Multiplier Effect of Net Exports   215

The Multiplier in Reverse   217

The Paradox of Thrift   218

The Multiplier and the Aggregate Demand Curve   218

Summary   220

Key Concepts and Terms   220

Questions for Review   221

APPENDIX A: THE SIMPLE ALGEBRA OF THE MULTIPLIER   222

APPENDIX B: THE MULTIPLIER IN THE PRESENCE OF FOREIGN TRADE   223

Summary   226

Questions for Review   226

10 SUPPLY-SIDE EQUILIBRIUM: UNEMPLOYMENT *AND* INFLATION?   227

The Aggregate Supply Curve   228

Shifts of the Aggregate Supply Curve   230

The Shape of the Aggregate Supply Curve   232

Equilibrium of Aggregate Demand and Supply   233

Recessionary and Inflationary Gaps Revisited   234

Adjusting to an Inflationary Gap: Inflation   235

Demand Inflation and Stagflation   238

An Example from Recent History: 1988 to 1990   239

Adjusting to a Recessionary Gap: Deflation or Unemployment?   239

Does the Economy Have a Self-Correcting Mechanism?   241

Stagflation from Supply Shifts   243

Inflation and the Multiplier   244

A Role for Stabilization Policy   247

Summary   247

Key Concepts and Terms   247

Questions for Review   248

PART III

FISCAL AND MONETARY POLICY   249

11 MANAGING AGGREGATE DEMAND: FISCAL POLICY   250

Income Taxes and the Consumption Schedule   251

The Multiplier Revisted   254

Multipliers for Tax Policy   256

Government Transfer Payments   258

Planning Expansive Fiscal Policy   259

Planning Restrictive Fiscal Policy   260

The Choice between Spending Policy and Tax Policy   260

Some Harsh Realities   261

The Idea Behind Supply-Side Tax Cuts   262

Some Flies in the Ointment   264

Toward Assessment of Supply-Side Economics   264

Clintonomics as Supply-Side Economics   268

Summary   268

Key Concepts and Terms   269

Questions for Review   269

APPENDIX: ALGEBRAIC TREATMENT OF FISCAL POLICY AND AGGREGATE DEMAND   270

Questions for Review   271

12 MONEY AND THE BANKING SYSTEM   273

Policy Issue: Should We Deregulate or Reregulate the Banks?   274

Barter versus Monetary Exchange   275

The Conceptual Definition of Money 277

What Serves as Money? 277

How the Quantity of Money Is Measured 279

How Banking Began 282

Principles of Bank Management: Profits versus Safety 283

Bank Regulation 284

How Bankers Keep Books 286

The Limits to Money Creation by a Single Bank 287

Multiple Money Creation by a Series of Banks 289

The Process in Reverse: Multiple Contractions of the Money Supply 292

Why the Deposit Creation Formula Is Oversimplified 294

The Need for Monetary Control 295

Summary 295

Key Concepts and Terms 296

Questions for Review 296

13 MONETARY POLICY AND THE NATIONAL ECONOMY   **298**

Money and Income: The Important Difference 299

The Federal Reserve System: Origins and Structure 299

The Independence of the Fed 301

Controlling the Money Supply: Open-Market Operations 302

Open-Market Operations, Bond Prices, and Interest Rates 303

Controlling the Money Supply: Reserve Requirements 304

Controlling the Money Supply: Lending to Banks 306

Proposals for Tightening Monetary Control 307

The Money Supply Mechanism 308

The Demand for Money 309

Equilibrium in the Money Market 311

Interest Rates and Total Expenditure 312

Monetary Policy and Aggregate Demand in the Keynesian Model 313

Money and the Price Level in the Keynesian Model 316

From Models to Policy Debates 318

Summary 319

Key Concepts and Terms 319

Questions for Review 320

14 THE DEBATE OVER MONETARY POLICY   **321**

Velocity and the Quantity Theory of Money 322

The Determinants of Velocity 323

Monetarism: The Quantity Theory Modernized 326

Fiscal Policy, Interest Rates, and Velocity 328

Debate: Should Stabilization Policy Rely on Fiscal or Monetary Policy? 329

Debate: Should the Fed Control the Money Supply or Control Interest Rates? 331

Debate: The Shape of the Aggregate Supply Curve   335

Debate: Should the Government Intervene?   339

Debate: Rules or Discretion?   341

Techniques of Economic Forecasting   342

The Accuracy of Economic Forecasts   346

Other Dimensions of the Rules-versus-Discretion Debate   347

Conclusion: What Should Be done?   349

Summary   350

Key Concepts and Terms   351

Questions for Review   351

15 BUDGET DEFICITS AND THE NATIONAL DEBT: FACT AND FICTION   **353**

The Partisan Political Debate over the Budget Deficit   354

Should the Budget Be Balanced?   354

Deficits and Debt: Some Terminology   355

Some Facts about the National Debt   356

Interpreting the Budget Deficit   359

Bogus Arguments about the Burden of the Debt   365

Budget Deficits and Inflation   367

Deficits, Interest Rates, and Crowding Out   370

The True Burden of the National Debt   374

The Economic Effects of Budget Deficits: Causation versus Correlation   375

Conclusion: The Economics and Politics of the Budget Deficit   377

Summary   379

Key Concepts and Terms   380

Questions for Review   380

16 THE TRADE-OFF BETWEEN INFLATION AND UNEMPLOYMENT   381

Demand-Side Inflation versus Supply-Side Inflation: A Review   382

Applying the Model to a Growing Economy   384

Demand-Side Inflation and the Phillips Curve   385

Supply-Side Inflation and the Collapse of the Phillips Curve   390

What the Phillips Curve Is Not   392

Fighting Unemployment with Fiscal and Monetary Policy   394

What Should Be Done?   396

Inflationary Expectations and the Phillips Curve   398

The Theory of Rational Expectations   401

Why Economists (and Politicians) Disagree   403

The Dilemma of Demand Management   404

Attempts to Improve the Trade-Off Directly   404

Wage–Price Controls   405

Indexing   407

Summary   408

Key Concepts and Terms   409

Questions for Review   410

PART IV

THE UNITED STATES IN THE WORLD ECONOMY   411

17 PRODUCTIVITY AND GROWTH IN THE WEALTH OF NATIONS   412

Life in the "Good Old Days"   413

The Magnitude of Productivity Growth   415

Significance of the Growth of Productivity   419

The Second Major Development: Convergence   420

Why International Equalization?   420

Are All Countries Participating in Equalization?   421

The U.S. Productivity Slowdown: Is American Economic Leadership Doomed?   422

The U.S. Productivity Growth Lag behind Other Industrial Countries   424

Productivity and the Deindustrialization Thesis   425

Unemployment and Productivity Growth   428

Concluding Comment   430

Summary   430

Key Concepts and Terms   431

Questions for Review   431

18 INTERNATIONAL TRADE AND COMPARATIVE ADVANTAGE   432

Why Trade?   433

Mutual Gains from Trade   434

International versus Intranational Trade   435

The Law of Comparative Advantage   436

The Arithmetic of Comparative Advantage   437

The Graphics of Comparative Advantage   440

Comparative Advantage and Competition of "Cheap Foreign Labor"   442

Supply–Demand Equilibrium and Pricing in World Trade   443

Tariffs, Quotas, and Other Interferences with Trade   445

How Tariffs and Quotas Work   447

Tariffs versus Quotas   448

Why Inhibit Trade?   449

Other Arguments for Protection   452

What Import Prices Most Benefit a Country?   454

Conclusion: A Last Look at the "Cheap Foreign Labor" Argument   455

Summary   457

Key Concepts and Terms   457

Questions for Review   458

19 THE INTERNATIONAL MONETARY SYSTEM: ORDER OR DISORDER? 460

What Are Exchange Rates? 461

Exchange Rate Determination in a Free Market 462

The Purchasing-Power Parity Theory: The Long Run 465

Economic Activity and Exchange Rates: The Medium Run 467

Interest Rates and Exchange Rates: The Short Run 467

Market Determination of Exchange Rates: Summary 468

Fixed Exchange Rates and the Definition of the Balance of Payments 469

Defining the Balance of Payments in Practice 472

The U.S. Balance of Payments Accounts 472

A Bit of History: The Gold Standard 474

The Bretton Woods System and the International Monetary Fund 475

Adjustment Mechanisms under the Bretton Woods System 476

Why Try to Fix Exchange Rates? 478

The Current Mixed System 479

Recent Developments in International Financial Markets 480

Summary 482

Key Concepts and Terms 483

Questions for Review 484

20 MACROECONOMICS IN A WORLD ECONOMY 485

International Trade and Aggregate Demand: A Quick Review 487

Relative Prices, Exports, and Imports 488

The Effects of Changes in Exchange Rates 489

Lags in International Trade and the J Curve 490

Aggregate Supply in an Open Economy 492

The Macroeconomic Effects of Exchange Rates 492

Interest Rates and International Capital Flows 494

Fiscal Policy in an Open Economy 495

Monetary Policy in an Open Economy 497

International Aspects of Reaganomics 498

The Link between the Budget Deficit and the Trade Deficit 500

Is the Trade Deficit a Problem? 502

On Curing the Trade Deficit 502

Conclusion: We Are Not Alone 505

Summary 506

Key Concepts and Terms 507

Questions for Review 507

PART  V

**ALTERNATIVE
ECONOMIC
SYSTEMS 509**

21 GROWTH IN DEVELOPED AND DEVELOPING COUNTRIES   510

Some Basic Principles of Growth Analysis   511

How to Measure Growth: Total Output or Output per Capita?   511

On Growth in Population: Is Less Really More?   512

The Crowded Planet: Exponential Population Growth   513

Requirements for Increased Growth   515

Accumulating Capital by Sacrificing Consumption: The Case of Soviet Russia   516

The Payoff to Growth: Higher Consumption in the Future   518

Growth without Sacrificing Consumption: Something for Nothing?   518

Is More Growth Really Better?   519

Problems of the Less Developed Countries   522

Living in the LDCs   522

Recent Trends   524

Impediments to Development in the LDCs   526

Help from Industrialized Economies   532

Loans and Grants by the United States and Others   533

Can LDCs Break Away from Poverty?   534

Summary   535

Key Concepts and Terms   535

Questions for Review   536

GLOSSARY   **G-1**

CREDITS   **C-1**

INDEX   **I-1**

PART I

Getting

Acquainted

with

Economics

WHAT IS ECONOMICS?

*Why does public
discussion of economic
policy so often show
the abysmal ignorance
of the participants?
Why do I so often
want to cry at what
public figures, the
press, and television
commentators say
about economic
affairs?*

ROBERT M. SOLOW

 Economics is a broad-ranging discipline, both in the questions it asks and the methods it uses to seek answers. Rather than try to define the discipline in a single sentence or paragraph, we will instead introduce you to economics by letting the subject matter speak for itself. ¶ The first part of the chapter is intended to give you some idea of the sorts of issues economic analysis helps clarify and the kinds of solutions that economic principles suggest. Many of the world's most pressing problems are economic in nature. So a little knowledge of basic economics is essential to anyone who wants to understand the world in which we live. ¶ The second part briefly introduces the methods of economic inquiry and the tools that economists use. These are tools you may find useful in your career, personal life, and role as an informed citizen, long after the course is over. ¶ A good deal of economic analysis is carried out with the help of graphs, and so this book is replete with them. For those of you who are unfamiliar with graphs and their properties, the appendix to this chapter provides a brief introduction that will enable you to follow the discussion in the remainder of this volume.

IDEAS FOR BEYOND THE FINAL EXAM

As college professors, we realize it is inevitable that you will forget much of what you learn in this course—perhaps with a sense of relief—soon after the final exam. There is not much point bemoaning this fact; elephants may never forget, but people do.

Nevertheless, some economic ideas are so important that you will want to remember them well beyond the final exam, for if you do not, you will have shortchanged your education. To help you pick out a few of the most crucial concepts, we have selected 12 from among the many contained in this book. Some offer critical and enduring insights into the workings of the economy. Others bear on important policy issues that appear in newspapers. Others point out common misunderstandings that occur among even the most thoughtful lay observers. As the opening quotation of this chapter suggests, many learned judges, politicians, business leaders, and university administrators who failed to understand or misused these economic principles could have made wiser decisions than they did.

Each of the **12 Ideas for Beyond the Final Exam** will be discussed in depth as it occurs in the course of the book, so you should not expect to master them after reading this opening chapter. Nonetheless, it is useful to sketch them briefly here, both to introduce you to economics and to provide a selective preview of what is to come.

THE TRADE-OFF BETWEEN INFLATION AND UNEMPLOYMENT

Inflation these days is running a bit below 3 percent per year. In 1990, it was just over 5 percent. What made the inflation rate fall? Most economists believe the answer is simple: In mid-1990, the U.S. economy entered a recession that proved to be deeper and longer than policymakers anticipated. The unemployment rate rose from a low of 5.2 percent in June 1990 to a peak of 7.8 percent in June 1992, and then receded only slowly.

Economists maintain that this conjunction of events—falling inflation and high unemployment—was no coincidence. Owing to features of our economy that we will study in Parts 2 and 3, there is an agonizing *trade-off between inflation and unemployment*, meaning that most policies that lower inflation also cause higher unemployment for a while.

Since this trade-off poses one of the fundamental dilemmas of national economic policy, we will devote all of Chapter 16 to examining it in detail. And we shall also consider some suggestions for escaping from the trade-off, such as supply-side economics (Chapter 10) and wage–price controls (Chapter 16).

THE ILLUSION OF HIGH INTEREST RATES

Is it more costly to borrow money at 12 percent interest or at 8 percent? That would seem an easy question to answer, even without a course in economics. But, in fact, it is not. An example will show why.

In 1992, banks were lending money to home buyers at annual interest rates as low as 8 percent. In 1981, these rates had been over 12 percent. Yet economists maintain that it was actually cheaper to borrow in 1980 than in 1992. Why? Because inflation in 1980 was running at about 10 percent per year while it was down to about 3 percent by 1992.

But why is information on inflation relevant for deciding how costly it is to borrow? Consider the position of a person who borrows $100 for one year at a 12 percent rate of interest while prices are rising at 10 percent per year. At the end of the year the borrower pays back her $100 plus $12 interest. But over that same year her indebtedness declines by $10 *in terms of what that money will buy*. Thus, in terms of *purchasing power*, the borrower really pays only $2 in interest on her $100 loan, or 2 percent.

Now consider someone who borrows $100 at 8 percent interest when inflation is only 3 percent. This borrower pays back the original $100 plus $8 in interest and sees the purchasing power of his debt decline by $3 due to inflation—for a net payment in purchasing-power terms of $5, or 5 percent. Thus, in the economically relevant sense, the 8 percent loan at 3 percent inflation is actually more expensive than the 12 percent loan at 10 percent inflation.

As we will learn in Chapter 6, the failure to understand this principle has caused troubles for our tax laws, for the financial system, and for the housing and public utility industries. In Chapter 15 we will see that it has even led to misunderstanding of the size and nature of the government budget deficit.

DO BUDGET DEFICITS BURDEN FUTURE GENERATIONS?

Large federal budget deficits have been in the news for more than a decade now. Congress has struggled continually to cut the deficit and has failed to comply with several deficit-reduction laws that it set for itself (the Gramm-Rudman-Hollings Act). First President Reagan and then President Bush argued that raising taxes is worse than tolerating the deficit, a claim disputed by many. Critics have objected that deficits hold dire consequences—including higher interest rates, more inflation, a stagnant economy, and an irksome burden on future Americans.

The conflicting claims and counterclaims that have marked this debate are bound to confuse the layperson. Who is right? Are deficits really malign or benign influences on our economy? The answers, economists insist, are so complicated that the only correct short answer is: it all depends. The precise factors on which the answers depend, and the reasons why, are sufficiently important that they merit an entire chapter (Chapter 15). There we will learn that a budget deficit may or may not burden future generations, depending on its size and on the reasons for its existence.

THE OVERWHELMING IMPORTANCE OF PRODUCTIVITY GROWTH IN THE LONG RUN

In Geneva, a worker in a watch factory now turns out roughly one hundred times as many mechanical watches per year as her ancestors did three centuries earlier. The **productivity** of labor (output per hour of work) in cotton production has probably gone up more than a thousandfold in two hundred years. It is estimated that rising labor productivity has increased the standard of living of a typical American worker about sevenfold in the past century. This means that Americans now enjoy about seven times as much clothing, housewares, and luxury goods as did a typical inhabitant of the United States one hundred years ago.

Economic issues such as inflation, unemployment, and monopoly are important to us all, and will receive much attention in this book. But in the long run nothing has as great an effect on our material well-being and the amounts society can afford to spend on hospitals, schools, and social amenities as the rate of growth of productivity. Chapter 17 points out that what appears to be a small increase in productivity growth can have a huge effect on a country's standard of living over a long period of time because productivity compounds like the interest on savings in a bank.

Similarly, a slowdown in productivity growth that persists for a substantial number of years can have a devastating effect on standards of living. After 1973, productivity growth in the United States, *like that of other industrial countries,* suffered a serious decline. Between 1950 and 1973, the productivity of American workers rose at an annual rate of about 1.9 percent, but since then that growth rate has averaged only about 0.6 percent per year. If productivity growth in the latter period had matched that of the earlier period, average income per person in the United States would now be about 27 percent greater than it actually is!

 **MUTUAL GAINS FROM VOLUNTARY EXCHANGE**

One of the most fundamental ideas of economics is that in a voluntary exchange *both* parties must gain something, or at least expect to gain something. Otherwise why would they both agree to trade? This principle may seem self-evident, and it probably is. Yet it is amazing how often it is ignored in practice.

For example, it was widely believed for centuries that governments should interfere with international trade because one country's gain from a swap must be the other country's loss (Chapter 18). Analogously, some people feel instinctively that if Mr. A profits handsomely from a deal with Ms. B, then Ms. B must have been exploited. Laws sometimes prohibit mutually beneficial exchanges between buyers and sellers—as when a loan transaction is banned because the interest rate is "too high" (Chapter 6), or when a willing worker cannot be hired because the wage rate is "too low", or when the resale of tickets to sporting events ("ticket scalping") is outlawed even though the buyer is happy to pay the high price (Chapter 4).

In every one of these cases, and many more, well-intentioned but misguided reasoning blocks the mutual gains that arise from voluntary exchange—and thereby interferes with one of the most basic functions of an economic system (see Chapter 3).

 **THE SURPRISING PRINCIPLE OF COMPARATIVE ADVANTAGE**

The Japanese economy produces many products that Americans buy in huge quantities—including cars, TV sets, cameras, and electronic equipment. American manufacturers often complain about the competition and demand protection from the flood of imports that, in their view, threatens American standards of living. Is this view justified?

Economists think not. They maintain, as suggested in the last Idea, that both sides must gain from international trade. But what if the Japanese were able to produce *everything* more cheaply than we can? Would it not then be true that Americans would be thrown out of work and that our nation would be impoverished?

A remarkable result, called the law of **comparative advantage**, shows that even in this extreme case the two nations can still benefit by trading and that each can gain as a result! We will explain this principle fully in Chapter 18, where we will also note some potentially valid arguments in favor of providing special incentives for particular domestic industries. But for now a simple parable will make the reason clear.

Suppose Sally grows up on a farm and is a whiz at plowing, but is also a successful country singer who earns $4000 a performance. Should Sally turn down singing engagements to leave time for plowing? Of course not. Instead she should hire Alfie, a much less efficient farmer, to do the plowing for her. Sally may be a better farmer. But she earns so much more by specializing in singing that it makes sense to leave the farming to Alfie. Alfie, though a less skilled farmer than Sally, is an even worse singer. Thus Alfie earns a living by specializing in the job at which he at least has a *comparative* advantage (his farming is not as bad as his singing), and both Alfie and Sally gain. The same is true of two countries. Even if one of them is more efficient at everything, both countries can gain by producing the things they do best *comparatively*.

ATTEMPTS TO REPEAL THE LAWS OF SUPPLY AND DEMAND: THE MARKET STRIKES BACK

When a commodity is in short supply, its price naturally tends to rise. Sometimes disgruntled consumers badger politicians into "solving" the problem by imposing a legal ceiling on the price. Similarly, when supplies are abundant—say, when fine weather produces extraordinarily abundant crops—prices tend to fall. This naturally dismays producers, who often succeed in getting legislation to prohibit low prices by imposing price floors.

But such attempts to repeal the laws of supply and demand usually backfire and sometimes produce results virtually the opposite of those that were intended. Where rent controls are adopted to protect tenants, housing grows scarce because the law makes it unprofitable to build and maintain apartments. When price floors are placed under agricultural products, surpluses pile up.

History provides some spectacular examples of the free market's ability to strike back at attempts to interfere with it. In Chapter 4, we will see that price controls contributed to the hardships of George Washington's army at Valley Forge. Two centuries earlier, when the armies of Spain surrounded Antwerp in 1584, hoping to starve the city into submission, profiteers kept Antwerp going by smuggling food and supplies through enemy lines. However, when the city fathers adopted price controls to end these "unconscionable" prices, supplies dried up and the city soon surrendered.

As we will see in Chapter 4 and elsewhere in this book, such consequences of interfering with the price mechanism are no accident. They follow inevitably from the way free markets work.

EXTERNALITIES: A SHORTCOMING OF THE MARKET CURED BY MARKET METHODS

Markets are very efficient at producing just the goods that consumers want, and in the quantities they desire. They do so by rewarding those who respond to what consumers want and who produce these products economically. Similarly, the market mechanism ferrets out waste and inefficiency by seeing to it that inefficient producers lose money.

This works well as long as an exchange between a seller and a buyer affects only those two parties. But often an economic transaction affects uninvolved third parties. Examples abound. The electric utility that generates power for the Midwest also produces pollution which kills freshwater fish in New York State. A farmer sprays crops with toxic pesticides, but the poison seeps into the ground water and affects the health of neighboring communities.

Such social costs—called **externalities** because they affect parties *external* to the economic transaction that causes them—escape the control of the market mechanism. As we will learn in *Microeconomics*, there is no financial incentive to motivate polluters to minimize the damage they do. Hence, business firms make their products as cheaply as possible, disregarding externalities that may damage the quality of life.

Yet, in *Microeconomics*, we point out a way for the government to use the market mechanism to control undesirable externalities. If the electric utility and the farmer are charged for the harm they cause the public, just as they are charged when they use tangible resources such as coal and fertilizer, then they will have an incentive to reduce the amount of pollution they generate. Thus, in this case, economists believe that market methods are often the best way to cure one of the market's most important shortcomings.

RATIONAL CHOICE AND TRUE ECONOMIC COSTS: THE ROLE OF OPPORTUNITY COST

Despite dramatic improvements in our standard of living since the Industrial Revolution, we have not come anywhere near a state of unlimited abundance, and so we must constantly make choices. If you purchase a new home, you may not be able to afford to eat at expensive restaurants as often as you used to. If a firm decides to retool its factories, it may have to postpone plans for new executive offices. If a government expands its defense program, it may be forced to reduce its outlays on roads or school buildings.

Economists say that the true costs of such decisions are not the number of dollars spent on the house, the new equipment, or the military establishment, but rather *the value of what must be given up in order to acquire the item*—the restaurant meals, the new executive offices, the improved roads, and new schools. These are called **opportunity costs** because they represent the *opportunities* the individual, firm, or government must forgo to make the desired expenditure. Economists maintain that rational decision-making requires that opportunity costs be considered (see Chapter 3).

The **OPPORTUNITY COST** of some decision is the value of the next best alternative which you have to give up because of that decision (for example, working instead of going to school).

The cost of a college education provides a vivid example that is probably close to your heart. How much do you think it *costs* to go to college? Most likely you would answer this question by adding together your expenditures on tuition, room and board, books, and the like, and then deducting any scholarship funds you may receive. Economists would not. They would first want to know how much you could be earning if you were not attending college. This may sound like an irrelevant question; but because you give up these earnings by attending college, they must be added to your tuition bill as a cost of your education. Nor would economists accept the university's bill for room and board as a measure of your living costs. They would want to know by how much this exceeds what it would have cost you to live at home, and only this extra cost would be counted as an expense. On balance, a college education probably costs more than you think.

I d e a 10

THE IMPORTANCE OF MARGINAL ANALYSIS

Many pages in this book will be spent explaining, and extolling the virtues of, a type of decision-making process called **marginal analysis** (see especially Chapters 5 and 6 in *Microeconomics*), which can best be illustrated by an example.

Suppose an airline is told by its accountants that the full cost of transporting one passenger from Los Angeles to New York is $300. Can the airline profit by offering a reduced rate of $200 to students who fly on a standby basis? The surprising answer is: probably yes. And the reason is that most of the costs will be paid whether the plane carries 20 passengers or 120 passengers.

Marginal analysis points out that costs such as maintenance, landing rights, and ground crews are irrelevant to the decision whether to carry standby passengers for reduced rates. The only costs that *are* relevant are the *extra* costs of writing and processing additional tickets, the food and beverages these passengers consume, the additional fuel required, and so on. These costs are called **marginal costs** and are probably quite small in this example. Any passenger who pays the airline more than its marginal cost will add something to the company's profit. So it probably is more profitable to let the students ride at low fares than to let the plane fly with empty seats.

There are many real cases in which decision makers, not understanding marginal analysis, have rejected such advantageous possibilities as the reduced fare in our hypothetical example. These people were misled by calculating in terms of *average* rather than *marginal* cost figures—an error that can be quite costly.

I d e a 11

THE COST DISEASE OF THE PERSONAL SERVICES

A distressing phenomenon is occurring throughout the industrialized world. Many community services have been deteriorating—fewer postal deliveries and garbage pickups, larger classes in public schools—even though the public is paying more for them. The costs of providing many services have risen consistently faster than the rate of inflation.

Perhaps the most prominent examples are medical care and education, which constitute a large percentage of many government and household budgets, and which many consider to be indispensable products for society. For example, over the 44-year period since 1948 the daily cost of a stay at a hospital outstripped the rate of inflation by more than 700 percent! A natural response is to attribute the problem to greed, inefficiency, and political corruption. But this cannot be the whole story, because the scenario has been repeated in virtually every other industrialized country, despite great differences in the way these services are provided.

One of the major causes of the problem is economic. And it has nothing to do with either corruption or inefficiency; rather, it stems from the dazzling growth in efficiency of private manufacturing industries! Because technological improvements make workers more productive in manufacturing, costs go down and wages rise. But wages rise not only for the manufacturing workers but also for postal workers, teachers, and other service workers (because, otherwise these workers would leave their low-paying service jobs and compete for jobs in high-paying industries). But the technology of labor-intensive personal services is not easily changed. Since it still takes one person to drive a postal truck and one teacher to teach a class, the cost of these services is forced to rise in step with wage increases. This is what has been called the "cost disease" of the personal services, a malady that affects many services, including medical care, university teaching, restaurant cooking, retailing, and automobile repairs.

This is important to understand not because it excuses the financial record of our governments, but because an understanding of the problem suggests what we should expect the future to bring and, perhaps, indicates what policies should be advocated to deal with it.

I d e a 12 THE TRADE-OFF BETWEEN OUTPUT AND EQUALITY

"Supply-side" economics was one of the cornerstones of the so-called Reagan revolution, and was embraced by President Bush. The basic idea behind supply-side tax cuts (Chapter 11) is to spur productivity and efficiency by providing greater incentives for working, saving, and investing. Often, that means lowering tax rates. There are important elements of truth in this position. No one doubts that proper economic incentives are critical.

Yet many people feel that the unequal distribution of income in our society is unjust; that it is inequitable for the super rich to sail yachts while poor people go homeless. Such people are disturbed by the fact that supply-side tax cuts are likely to make the distribution of income even more unequal than it already is. During the 1992 presidential campaign, challenger Bill Clinton attacked the strategy as "trickle down" economics, meaning that it offered mere crumbs to working people while serving heaping portions to the rich. This position, too, has elements of truth.

In fact, we have a genuine dilemma. To provide stronger incentives for success in the economic game, the gaps between the "winners" and the "losers" must necessarily be widened. It is these gaps, after all, that provide the incentives to work harder, to save more, and to invest productively. But such programs also breed inequality. Thus, economists say there is a *trade-off* between the *size* of a nation's output and the degree of *equality* with which that output is distributed. Supply-side tax cuts are one example. Another is anti-poverty programs. Many policies designed to divide the proverbial economic pie more equally inadvertently cause the size of the pie to shrink.

EPILOGUE

These, then, are a dozen of the more fundamental concepts to be found in this book—ideas that we hope you will retain **Beyond the Final Exam**. There is no need to master them right now, for you will hear much more about each as the book progresses. Instead, keep them in mind as you read—we will point them out to you as they occur by the use of the book's logo ◕—and look back over this list at the end of the course. You may be amazed to see how natural, or even obvious, they will seem then.

INSIDE THE ECONOMIST'S TOOL KIT

Now that you have some idea of the kinds of issues economists deal with, you should know something about the way they grapple with these problems.

ECONOMICS AS A DISCIPLINE

Economics has something of a split personality. Although clearly the most rigorous of the social sciences, it nevertheless looks decidedly more "social" than "scientific" when compared with, say, physics. An economist must be a jack of several trades, borrowing modes of investigation from numerous fields. Usefulness, not methodological purity, is the criterion for inclusion in the economist's tool kit.

Mathematical reasoning is used extensively in economics, but so is historical study. And neither looks quite the same as when practiced by a mathematician or a historian. Statistical inference plays a major role in modern economic inquiry; but economists have had to modify standard statistical procedures to fit the kinds of data they deal with. In 1926, John Maynard Keynes, the great British economist, summed up the many faces of economic inquiry in a statement that still rings true today.

> *The master-economist . . . must understand symbols and speak in words. He must contemplate the particular in terms of the general, and touch abstract and concrete in the same flight of thought. He must study the present in the light of the past for the purposes of the future. No part of man's nature or his institutions must lie entirely outside his regard. He must be purposeful and disinterested in a simultaneous mood; as aloof and incorruptible as an artist, yet sometimes as near the earth as a politician.*[1]

An introductory course in economics will not make you a master-economist; but it should help you approach social problems from a pragmatic and dispassionate point of view. You will not find solutions to all society's economic problems in this book. But you should learn how to pose questions in ways that will help produce answers that are both useful and illuminating.

THE NEED FOR ABSTRACTION

Some students find economics unduly abstract and "unrealistic." The stylized world envisioned by economic theory seems only a distant cousin to the world they know. There is an old joke about three people—a chemist, a physicist, and an economist—stranded on an isolated island with an ample supply of canned food but no implements to open the cans. In debating what to do, the chemist suggested lighting a fire under the cans, thus expanding their contents and causing the cans to burst. The physicist doubted that this would work. She advocated building a catapult with which they could smash the cans against some nearby boulders. Then they turned to the economist for his suggestion. After a moment's thought, he announced his solution: "Let's assume we have a can opener."

---

[1]See his *Essays in Biography* (New York: Norton, 1951), pages 140–141.

Economic theory *does* make unrealistic assumptions; you will encounter many of them in the pages that follow. But this propensity to abstract from reality results from the incredible complexity of the economic world, not from any fondness economists have for sounding absurd.

Compare the chemist's simple task of explaining the interactions of compounds in a chemical reaction with the economist's complex task of explaining the interactions of people in an economy. Are molecules motivated by greed or altruism, by envy or ambition? Do they ever emulate other molecules? Do forecasts about them influence their behavior? People, of course, do all these things, and many, many more. It is therefore immeasurably more difficult to predict human behavior than to predict chemical reactions. But, if economists tried to keep track of every aspect of human behavior, they would never get anywhere. Thus:

ABSTRACTION means ignoring many details in order to focus on the most important elements of a problem.

Abstraction from unimportant details is necessary to understand the functioning of anything as complex as the economy.

To appreciate why economists **abstract** from details, imagine the following hypothetical situation. You have just arrived, for the first time in your life, in Los Angeles. You are now at the Los Angeles Civic Center. This is the point marked *A* in Figures 1–1 and 1–2, which are alternative maps of part of Los Angeles. You

---

Figure 1-1   MAP 1

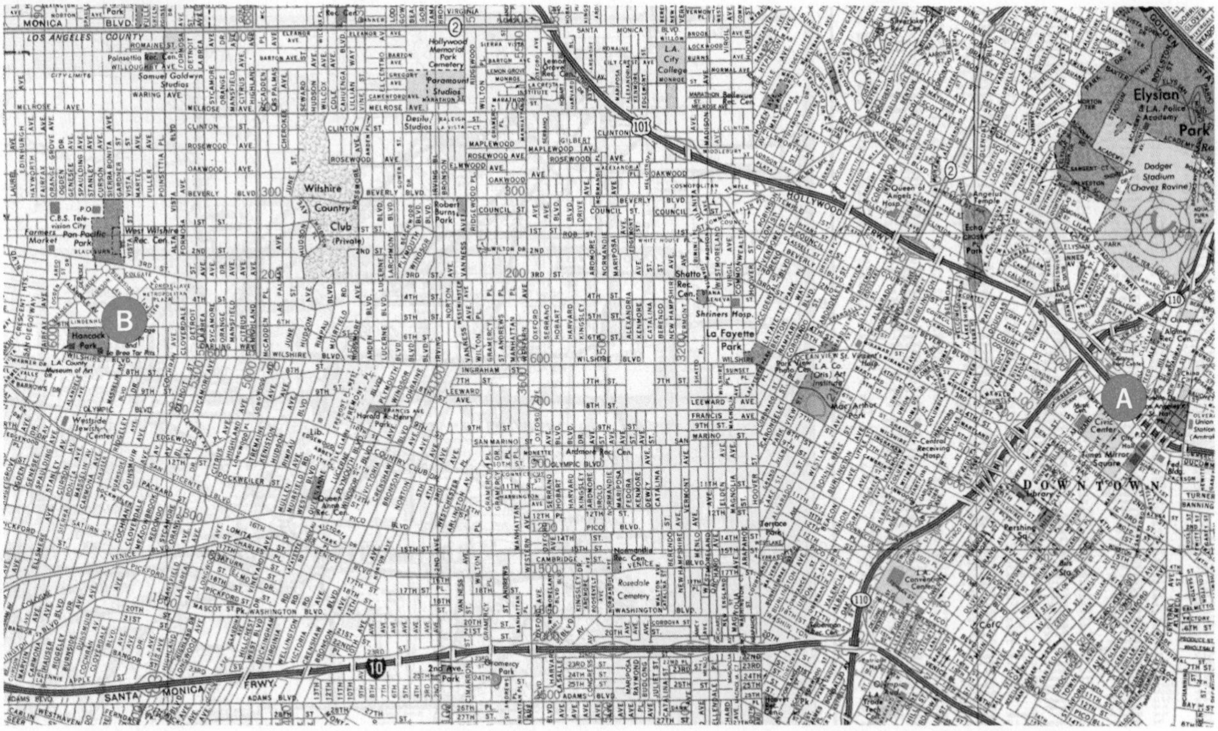

Map 1 gives complete details of the road system of Los Angeles. If you are like most people, you will find it hard to read and not very useful for figuring out how to get from the Civic Center (point *A*) to the La Brea tar pits (point *B*). For this purpose, the map carries far too much detail, though for some other purposes (for example, locating some small street in Hollywood), it may be the best map available.

Figure **1–2**   **MAP 2**

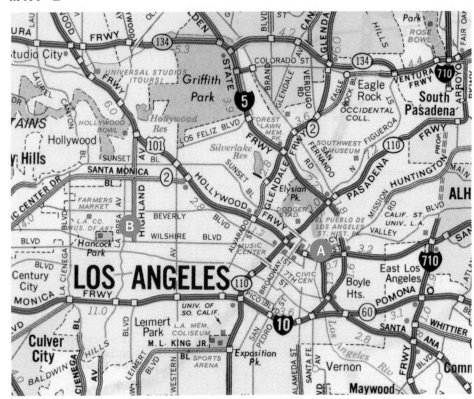

Map 2 shows a different perspective of Los Angeles. Minor roads are eliminated—we might say, *assumed away*—in order to present a clearer picture of where the major arteries and freeways go. As a result of this simplification, several ways of getting from the Civic Center (point *A*) to the La Brea tar pits (point *B*) stand out clearly. For example, we can take the Hollywood freeway west to Alvarado Blvd south, then west on Wilshire Blvd. The Tar Pits are on the right. While we might find a shorter route by poring over the details of Map 1, most of us will feel more comfortable with Map 2.

want to drive to the famous La Brea tar pits, marked *B* on each map. Which map would you find more useful? You will notice that Map 1 (Figure 1–1) has the full details of the Los Angeles road system. Consequently, it requires a major effort to read it. In contrast, Map 2 (Figure 1–2) omits many minor roads so that the freeways and major arteries stand out more clearly.

Most strangers to the city would prefer Map 2. With its guidance they are likely to find the tar pits in a reasonable amount of time, even though a slightly shorter route might have been found by careful calculation and planning using Map 1. Map 2 seems to *abstract* successfully from a lot of confusing details while retaining the essential aspects of the city's geography. Economic theories strive to do the same thing.

Map 3 (Figure 1–3), which shows little more than the major interstate routes that pass through the greater Los Angeles area, illustrates a danger of which all theorists must beware. Armed only with the information provided on this map, you might never find the La Brea tar pits. Instead of a useful idealization of the Los Angeles road network, the map makers have produced a map that is oversimplified for our purpose. Too much has been assumed away. Of course, this map was never intended to be used as a guide to the La Brea tar pits, which brings us to an important point:

There is no such thing as one "right" degree of abstraction for all analytic purposes. The proper degree of abstraction depends on the objective of the analysis. A model that is a gross oversimplification for one purpose may be needlessly complicated for another.

MAP 3

Map 3 strips away still more details of the Los Angeles road system. In fact, only major trunk roads and freeways remain. This map may be useful for passing through the city or getting around it, but it will not help the tourist who wants to see the sights of Los Angeles. For this purpose, too many details are missing.

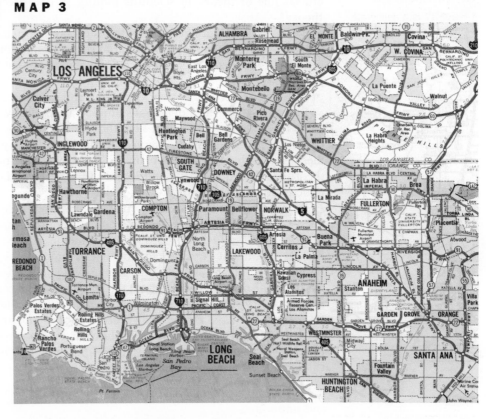

Economists are constantly treading the thin line between Map 2 and Map 3, between useful generalization about complex issues and gross distortions of the pertinent facts. How can they tell when they have abstracted from reality just enough? There is no objective answer to this question, which is why applied economics is as much art as science. One of the things distinguishing good economics from bad economics is the degree to which analysts are able to find the factors that constitute the equivalent of Map 2 (rather than Maps 1 or 3) for the problem at hand. It is not always easy to do.

For example, suppose you want to learn why different people have different incomes, why some are fabulously rich while others are abjectly poor. People differ in many ways, too many to enumerate, much less to study. The economist must ignore most of these details in order to focus on the important ones. The color of a person's hair or eyes is probably unimportant to the problem at hand, but the color of his or her skin certainly is. Height and weight may not matter, but education probably does. Proceeding in this way, we pare Map 1 down to the manageable dimensions of Map 2. But there is a danger of going too far, stripping away some of the crucial factors, and winding up with Map 3.

THE ROLE OF ECONOMIC THEORY

A person "can stare stupidly at phenomena; but in the absence of imagination they will not connect themselves together in any rational way." These words of the renowned American philosopher-scientist C.S. Peirce succinctly express the

A **THEORY** is a deliberate simplification of relationships whose purpose is to explain how those relationships work.

crucial role of theory in scientific inquiry. What, precisely, do we mean by a **theory**?

To an economist or natural scientist, the word *theory* means something different from what it means in common parlance. In scientific usage, a theory is *not* an untested assertion of alleged fact. The statement that oat bran provides protection from heart disease is not a theory; it is a *hypothesis*, which will prove to be true or false once the right sorts of experiments have been completed.

Instead, a theory is a deliberate simplification (abstraction) of factual relationships that attempts to explain how those relationships work. It is an *explanation* of the mechanism behind observed phenomena. Thus, gravity forms the basis of theories that describe and explain the paths of the planets. Similarly, Keynesian theory (discussed in Parts 2 and 3) seeks to describe and explain how government policies affect the path of the national economy.

Economic theory has acquired an unsavory public image in recent years—partly because of inaccurate predictions by some economists, partly because doctrinal disputes have spilled over into the news media, and partly because some politicians have found it expedient to scoff at economists. This bad image is unfortunate because theorizing is essential to provide a logical structure for organizing and analyzing economic data. Without theory, economists could only "stare stupidly" at the world. With theory, they can attempt to understand it.

People who have never studied economics often draw a false distinction between *theory* and *practical policy*. Politicians and business people, in particular, often reject abstract economic theory as something that is best ignored by "practical" people. The irony of these statements is that:

It is precisely the concern for policy that makes economic theory so necessary and important.

If we could not change the economy through public policy, economics could be a historical and descriptive discipline, asking, for example, what happened in the United States during the Great Depression of the 1930s or how is it that industrial pollution got to be so serious in the twentieth century. But deep concern about public policy forces economists to go beyond historical questions. To analyze policy options, they are forced to deal with possibilities *that have not actually occurred*.

For example, to learn how to prevent depressions, they must investigate whether the Great Depression of the 1930s could have been avoided by more astute government policies. Or to determine what environmental programs will be most effective, they must understand how and why a market economy produces pollution and what might happen if government placed taxes on industrial waste discharges and automobile emissions. As Peirce suggested, not even a lifetime of ogling at real-world data will answer such questions.

Two variables are said to be **CORRELATED** if they tend to go up or down together. But correlation need not imply causation.

Indeed, the facts can sometimes be highly misleading. Data often indicate that two variables move up and down together. But this statistical **correlation** does not prove that either variable *causes* the other. For example, people drive their cars more slowly when it rains, and there are also more traffic accidents. But this correlation does not mean that slow driving causes accidents. Rather, we understand that both phenomena are caused by a common underlying factor—more rain. How do we know this? Not just by looking at the correlation (the degree of similarity) between data on accidents and driving speeds. Data alone tell us little about cause and effect. We must use some simple theory as part of our analysis.

Similarly, most economic issues hinge on some question of cause and effect. So simply observing correlations in data is not enough. Only a combination of theoretical reasoning and data analysis can hope to provide meaningful answers. We must first proceed deductively from assumptions to conclusions and then test the conclusions against data. In that way, we may hope to understand *how*, if at all, different government policies will lead to a lower unemployment rate or *how* a tax on emissions will reduce pollution.

Statistical correlation need not imply causation. Some theory is usually needed to interpret data.

WHAT IS AN ECONOMIC "MODEL"?

An **ECONOMIC MODEL** is a simplified, small-scale version of some aspect of the economy. Economic models are often expressed in equations, by graphs, or in words.

An **economic model** is a representation of a theory or a part of a theory, often used to gain insight into cause and effect. The notion of a "model" is familiar enough to children; and economists—like other scientists—use the term in much the same way that children do.

A child's model automobile or airplane looks and operates much like the real thing, but it is much smaller and much simpler, and so it is easier to manipulate and understand. Engineers for General Motors and Boeing also build models of cars and planes. While their models are far bigger and much more elaborate than a child's toy, they use them for much the same purposes: to observe the workings of these vehicles "up close," to experiment with them in order to see how they might behave under different circumstances. ("What happens if I do this?") From these experiments, they make educated guesses as to how the real-life version will perform.

Economists use models for similar purposes. A.W. Phillips, the famous engineer-turned-economist who discovered the "Phillips curve" (discussed in Chapter 33), was talented enough to construct a working model of the determination of national income in a simple economy, using colored water flowing through pipes. For years this contraption, depicted in Figure 1–4, has graced the basement of the London School of Economics. However, most economists lack Phillips's manual dexterity, so economic models are generally built with paper and pencil rather than with hammer and nails.

Because many of the models used in this book are depicted in diagrams, we explain the construction and use of various types of graphs in the appendix to this chapter. But sometimes economic models are expressed only in words. The statement "Business firms produce the level of output that maximizes their profits," is the basis for a behavioral model whose consequences are explored in some detail in Parts 2 through 5 in *Microeconomics*. Don't be put off by seemingly abstract models. Think of them as useful road maps. And remember how hard it would be to find your way around Los Angeles without one.

REASONS FOR DISAGREEMENTS: IMPERFECT INFORMATION AND VALUE JUDGMENTS

"If all the earth's economists were laid end to end, they could not reach an agreement," or so the saying goes. Politicians and reporters are fond of pointing out that economists can be found on both sides of many issues of public policy. If economics is a science, why do economists quarrel so much? After all, astronomers do not debate whether the earth revolves around the sun or vice versa.

The question reflects a misunderstanding of the nature of science. Disputes are normal at the frontier of any science. For example, astronomers once did argue,

| *F i g u r e* | **1–4** | **THE PHILLIPS MACHINE** |

The late Professor A.W. Phillips, while teaching at the London School of Economics in the early 1950s, built this machine to illustrate Keynesian theory. This is the same theory that we will explain with words and diagrams later in the book; but Phillips's background as an engineer enabled him to depict the theory with the help of tubes, valves, and pumps. Because economists are not very good plumbers, few of them try to build models of this sort; most rely on paper and pencil instead. But the two sorts of models fulfill precisely the same role. They simplify reality in order to make it understandable.

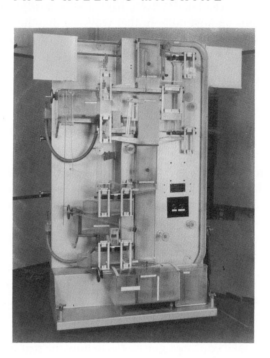

and quite vociferously, over whether the earth revolves around the sun. Nowadays, they argue about black holes, gamma-ray bursts, neutrinos, and other esoterica. These arguments go mostly unnoticed by the public because few of us understand what they are talking about. But economics is a *social* science, so its disputes are aired in public. All sorts of people are eager to join economic debates about inflation, pollution, poverty, and the like. Sometimes it seems as if anyone who has ever bought or sold anything fancies himself an amateur economist.

Furthermore, the fact is that economists agree on much more than is commonly supposed. Virtually all economists, regardless of their politics, agree that taxing polluters is one of the best ways to protect the environment, that rent controls can ruin a city (Chapter 4), and that free trade among nations is preferable to the erection of barriers through tariffs and quotas (see Chapter 18). The list could go on and on. It is probably true that the issues about which economists agree *far* exceed the subjects on which they disagree.

Finally, many disputes among economists are not scientific disputes at all. Sometimes the pertinent facts are simply unknown. For example, you will learn in Chapter 21 of *Microeconomics* that the proper tax to levy on industrial wastes depends on quantitative estimates of the harm done by the pollutant. Unfortunately, for most waste products, good estimates are not yet available. This makes it difficult to agree on a concrete policy proposal.

Another important source of disagreements is that economists, like other people, come in all political stripes: conservative, middle-of-the-road, liberal, radical. Each may have different values and a different view of what constitutes the good society. So each may hold a different view of the "right" solution to a public policy problem, even if they agree on the underlying analysis.

For example, we noted early in this chapter that anti-inflation policies are likely to cause recessions. Using tools we will describe in Part 3, many economists believe they can even measure how deep a recession we must endure to reduce inflation by a given amount. Is it worth having 2.6 million more people out of work for a year to cut the inflation rate by 1 percent? An economist cannot answer this any more than a nuclear physicist could have determined whether dropping the atomic bomb on Hiroshima was a good idea. The decision rests on judgments about the moral trade-off between inflation and unemployment, judgments that can be made only by the citizenry through its elected officials.

While economic science can contribute the best theoretical and factual knowledge there is on a particular issue, the final decision on policy questions often rests either on information that is not currently available or on tastes and ethical opinions about which people differ (the things we call "value judgments"), or on both.

Earlier in this chapter, we said that economics cannot provide all the *answers* but can teach you how to ask the right *questions*. Now you know some reasons why. By the time you finish studying this book, you should have a good understanding of when the right course of action turns on disputed facts, when on value judgments, and when on some combination of the two.

LAST WORD: COMMON SENSE IS NOT ALWAYS RELIABLE

Many people think sound decisions are just a matter of "common sense." If that were so—if untrained but intelligent observers could reach the right economic decisions using only their instincts and intuition—there would be little reason to study economics. Unfortunately, common sense is not always a reliable guide in economics.

True, there are many cases where it is not misleading. Most people undoubtedly realize, for example, that a surge in demand for a product is likely to raise its price, at least for a while. They also understand that increases in the prices of American goods will reduce the quantity we can export to foreign countries.

But many economic relationships are counterintuitive. Try your intuition on this one, for example. You own a widget manufacturing company that rents a warehouse. Your landlord raises your rent by $10,000 per year. Should you raise the price of your widgets to try to recoup some of your higher costs? Or should you lower your price to try to sell more and "spread your overhead?" We shall see in Chapter 6 that both answers are probably wrong!

When intuition fails, common sense will lead to error—sometimes serious error. We have seen, for example, that an interest rate of 8 percent under some circumstances may make borrowing more expensive than a 12 percent interest rate under other circumstances. We have seen that the fact that the costs of public services keep rising faster than inflation may have nothing to do with mismanagement or wrongdoing by government officials but may, instead, be a side effect of technological improvement. We will see later that rent controls on low-rent apartments may make the lives of the poor more miserable, not less.

All these and many more counterintuitive economic relationships will be explained in this book. By the end, you will have a better sense of when common sense works and when it fails. You will be able to recognize common fallacies that are all too often offered as pearls of wisdom by public figures, the press, and television commentators.

Summary

1. To help you get the most out of your first course in economics, we have devised a list of 12 important ideas that you will want to remember **Beyond the Final Exam**. Here we list them briefly, indicating where each idea occurs in the book.

   (1) Most government policies that reduce inflation are likely to intensify the unemployment problem, and vice versa. (Chapter 16)

   (2) Interest rates that appear very high may actually be very low if they are accompanied by high inflation. (Chapter 6)

   (3) Budget deficits may or may not be advisable, depending on the circumstances. (Chapter 15)

   (4) In a **voluntary exchange**, both parties must expect to benefit. (Chapters 3 and 18)

   (5) Two nations can gain from international trade, even if one is more efficient at making everything. (Chapter 18)

   (6) In the long run, **productivity** is almost the only thing that matters for a nation's material well-being. (Chapter 17)

   (7) Lawmakers who try to repeal the "law" of supply and demand are liable to open a Pandora's box of troubles they never expected. (Chapter 4)

   (8) **Externalities** cause the market mechanism to misfire, but this defect of the market can be remedied by market-oriented policies. (*Microeconomics* Chapters 13 and 21)

   (9) To make a rational decision, the opportunity cost of an action must be measured, because only this calculation will tell the decision maker what she has given up. (Chapter 3)

   (10) Decision-making often requires the use of **marginal analysis** to isolate the costs and benefits of that particular decision. (Chapter 5)

   (11) The operation of free markets is likely to lead to rising prices for public and private services. (*Microeconomics* Chapter 13)

   (12) Most policies that equalize income will exact a cost by reducing the nation's output. (*Microeconomics* Chapter 17)

2. Economics is a broad-ranging discipline that uses a variety of techniques and approaches to address important social questions.

3. Because of the great complexity of human behavior, economists are forced to **abstract** from many details, to make **generalizations** that they know are not quite true, and to organize what knowledge they have according to some theoretical structure.

4. **Correlation** need not imply **causation**.

5. Economists use simplified models to understand the real world and predict its behavior, much as a child uses a **model** railroad to learn how trains work.

6. While these models, if skillfully constructed, can illuminate important economic problems, they rarely can answer the questions that policymakers are confronted with. For this purpose, value judgments are needed, and the economist is no better equipped to make them than is anyone else.

7. Common sense is often an unreliable guide to the right economic decision.

Key Concepts and Terms

Voluntary exchange	Marginal analysis	Correlation versus causation
Comparative advantage	Marginal costs	Economic model
Productivity	Abstraction and generalization	Opportunity cost
Externalities	Theory	

Questions for Review

1. Think about how you would construct a "model" of how your college is governed. Which officers and administrators would you include and exclude from your model if the objective were

   a. to explain how decisions on financial aid are made?
   b. to explain the quality of the faculty?

   Relate this to the map example in the chapter.

2. Relate the process of "abstraction" to the way you take notes in a lecture. Why do you not try to transcribe every word the lecturer utters? Why do you not just write down the title of the lecture and stop there? How do you decide, roughly speaking, on the correct amount of detail?

3. Explain why a government policymaker cannot afford to ignore economic theory.

Appendix	**THE GRAPHS USED IN ECONOMIC ANALYSIS**[2]

Economic models are frequently analyzed and explained with the help of graphs; and this book is full of graphs. But that is not the only reason for you to study how they work. Most of you will deal with graphs in the future, perhaps frequently. They appear in newspapers. Doctors use graphs to keep track of patients' progress. Governments use them to keep track of the amount of money that they owe to foreign countries. Business firms use them to check their profit and sales performance. Persons concerned with social issues use them to examine trends in ethnic composition of cities and the relation of felonies to family income.

Graphs are invaluable because of the way they facilitate interpretation and analysis of both data and ideas. They enable the eye to take in at a glance important relationships that would be far less apparent from prose descriptions or long lists of numbers. But badly constructed graphs can confuse and mislead.

In this appendix we show, first, how to read a graph that depicts a relationship between two variables. Second, we define the term *slope* and describe how it is measured and interpreted. Third, we explain how the behavior of three variables can be shown on a two-dimensional graph. More detail on graphs of statistical data are provided in the appendix to Chapter 2.

TWO-VARIABLE DIAGRAMS

Much of the economic analysis to be found in this and other books requires that we keep track of two **variables** simultaneously. For example, in studying the operation of markets, we will want to keep one eye on the *price* of a commodity and the other on the *quantity* that is bought and sold.

For this reason, economists frequently find it useful to display real or imaginary figures in a *two-dimensional graph*, which simultaneously represents the behavior of two economic variables. The numerical value of one variable is measured along the bottom of the graph (called the *horizontal axis*), starting

from the **origin** (the point labeled "0"), and the numerical value of the other is measured up the side of the graph (called the *vertical axis*), also starting from the origin.

Figures 1–5(a) and 1–5(b) are typical graphs of economic analysis. They depict an (imaginary) *demand curve*, represented by the blue dots in Figure 1–5(a) and the heavy blue line in Figure 1–5(b). The graphs show the price of natural gas on their vertical axes and the quantity of gas people want to buy at each such price on the horizontal axes. The dots in Figure 1–5(b) are connected by the continuous blue curve labeled DD.

Economic diagrams are generally read as one reads latitudes and longitudes on a map. On the demand curve in Figure 1–5, the point marked *a* represents a hypothetical combination of price and quantity demanded in St. Louis. By drawing a horizontal line leftward from that point to the vertical axis, we learn that the average price for gas in St. Louis is $3 per thousand cubic feet. By dropping a line straight down to the horizontal axis, we find that 80 billion cubic feet are wanted by consumers at this price, just as the statistics in Table 1–1 show. The other points on the graph give similar information. For example, point *b* indicates that if natural gas in St. Louis cost only $2 per thousand cubic feet, quantity demanded would be higher—it would reach 120 billion cubic feet.

Notice that information about price and quantity is *all* we can learn from the diagram. The demand curve will not tell us about the kinds of people who live in St. Louis, the size of their homes, or the condition of their furnaces. It tells us about the price and the quantity demanded at that price; no more, no less. Specifically, it does tell us that when price declines there is an increase in the amount of gas consumers are willing and able to buy.

A diagram abstracts from many details, some of which may be quite interesting, in order to focus on the two variables of primary interest—in this case, the price of natural gas and the amount of gas that is demanded at each price. All the diagrams used in this book share this basic feature. They cannot tell the reader the "whole story" any more than a map's latitude and longitude figures for a particular city can make someone an authority on that city.

---

[2]Students who have a nodding acquaintance with geometry and feel quite comfortable with graphs can safely skip this appendix. See page 25 for appendix definitions.

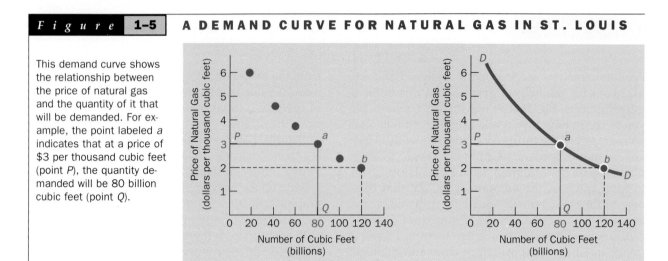

| Figure | 1–5 | A DEMAND CURVE FOR NATURAL GAS IN ST. LOUIS |

This demand curve shows the relationship between the price of natural gas and the quantity of it that will be demanded. For example, the point labeled *a* indicates that at a price of $3 per thousand cubic feet (point *P*), the quantity demanded will be 80 billion cubic feet (point *Q*).

THE DEFINITION AND MEASUREMENT OF SLOPE

One of the most important features of the diagrams used by economists is the pace with which the line, or curve, being sketched runs uphill or downhill as we move to the right. The demand curve in Figure 1–5 clearly slopes downhill (the price falls) as we follow it to the right (that is, if more gas is to be demanded). In such instances we say that *the curve has a negative slope, or is negatively sloped, because one variable falls as the other one rises.*

The **slope of a straight line** is the ratio of the vertical change to the corresponding horizontal change as we move to the right along the line, or as it is often said, the ratio of the "rise" over the "run."

The four panels of Figure 1–6 show all the possible slopes for a straight-line relationship between two unnamed variables called *Y* (measured along the vertical axis) and *X* (measured along the horizontal axis). Figure 1–6(a) shows a negative slope,

much like our demand curve. Figure 1–6(b) shows a positive slope, because variable *Y* rises (we go uphill) as variable *X* rises (as we move to the right). Figure 1–6(c) shows a *zero* slope, where the value of *Y* is the same irrespective of the value of *X*. Figure 1–6(d) shows an *infinite* slope, meaning that the value of *X* is the same irrespective of the value of *Y*.

Slope is a numerical concept, not just a qualitative one. The two panels of Figure 1–7 show two positively sloped straight lines with different slopes. The line in Figure 1–7(b) is clearly steeper. But by how much? The labels should help you compute the answer. In Figure 1–7(a) a horizontal movement, *AB*, of 10 units (13–3) corresponds to a vertical movement, *BC*, of 1 unit (9 − 8). So the slope is $BC/AB = \frac{1}{10}$. In Figure 1–7(b), the same horizontal movement of 10 units corresponds to a vertical movement of 3 units (11 − 8). So the slope is $\frac{3}{10}$, which is larger.

By definition, the slope of any particular straight line is the same no matter where on that line we choose to measure it. That is why we can pick any

| Table | 1–1 | QUANTITIES OF NATURAL GAS DEMANDED AT VARIOUS PRICES |

Price ($ per thousand cubic ft.)	$2	3	4	5	6
Quantity Demanded (billions of cubic feet)	120	80	56	38	20

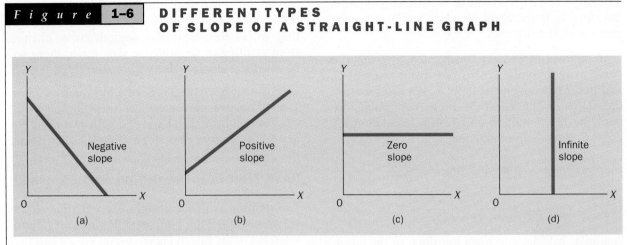

Figure 1-6 DIFFERENT TYPES OF SLOPE OF A STRAIGHT-LINE GRAPH

In Figure 1–6(a), the curve goes downward as we read from left to right, so we say it has a negative slope. The slopes in the other figures can be interpreted similarly.

horizontal distance, *AB,* and the corresponding slope triangle, *ABC,* to measure slope. But this is not true of lines that are curved.

Curved lines also have slopes, but the numerical value of the slope is different at every point.

The four panels of Figure 1–8 provide some examples of slopes of curved lines. The curve in Figure 1–8(a) has a negative slope everywhere, while the curve in Figure 1–8(b) has a positive slope every-

where. But these are not the only possibilities. In Figure 1–8(c) we encounter a curve that has a positive slope at first but a negative slope later on. Figure 1–8(d) shows the opposite case: a negative slope followed by a positive slope.

It is possible to measure the slope of a smooth curved line numerically *at any particular point.* This is done by drawing a *straight* line that *touches,* but does not *cut,* the curve at the point in question. Such a line is called a tangent to the curve.

Figure 1-7 HOW TO MEASURE SLOPE

Slope indicates how much the graph rises per unit move from left to right. Thus, in Figure 1–7(b), as we go from point *A* to point *B,* we go 13 − 3 = 10 units to the right. But in that interval, the graph rises from the height of point *B* to the height of point *C*; that is, it rises 3 units. Consequently, the slope of the line is *BC/ AB* = 3/10.

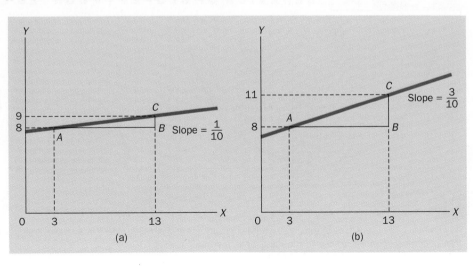

The slope of a curved line at a particular point is the slope of the straight line that is tangent to the curve at that point.

In Figure 1–9 we have constructed tangents to a curve at two points. Line *tt* is tangent at point *C*, and line *TT* is tangent at point *F*. We can measure the slope of the curve at these two points by applying the definition above. The calculation for point *C*, then, is the following:

$$\text{Slope at point } C = \text{Slope of line } tt = \frac{(\text{Distance } BC)}{(\text{Distance } BA)}$$

$$= \frac{(3 - 6)}{(3 - 2)} = \frac{(-3)}{(1)} = -3.$$

A similar calculation yields the slope of the curve at point *F*, which, as we can see from Figure 1–9, must be numerically smaller:

$$\text{Slope at Point } F = \text{Slope of line}$$

$$TT = \frac{(1.5 - 2)}{(8 - 5)} = \frac{(-0.5)}{(3)} = -0.16.$$

EXERCISE

Show that the slope of the curve at point *G* is between −0.16 and −3.

What would happen if we tried to apply this graphical technique to the high point in Figure 1–8(c) or to the low point in Figure 1–8(d)? Take a ruler and try it. The tangents that you construct should be horizontal, meaning that they should have a slope exactly equal to zero. It is always true that where the slope of a smooth curve changes from positive to negative, or vice versa, there will be at least a single point with a zero slope.

Curves that have the shape of a hill, such as Figure 1–8(c), have a zero slope at their *highest* point. Curves that have the shape of a valley, such as Figure 1-8(d), have a zero slope at their *lowest* point.

RAYS THROUGH THE ORIGIN AND 45° LINES

The point at which a straight line cuts the vertical (*Y*) axis is called the *Y-intercept*. For example, the *Y*-intercept of the line in Figure 1–7(a) is a bit less than 8. Lines whose *Y*-intercept is zero have so many special uses that they have been given a special name, a **ray through the origin**, or a **ray**.

Figure 1–10 contains three rays through the origin, and the slope of each is indicated in the diagram. The ray in the center—whose slope is 1—is particularly useful in many economic applications because it marks off points where *X* and *Y* are equal (as long as *X* and *Y* are measured in the same units). For example, at point *A* we have *X* = 3 and *Y* = 3, at point *B*, *X* = 4 and *Y* = 4, and a similar relation holds at any other point on that ray.

How do we know that this is always true for a ray whose slope is 1? If we start from the origin

---

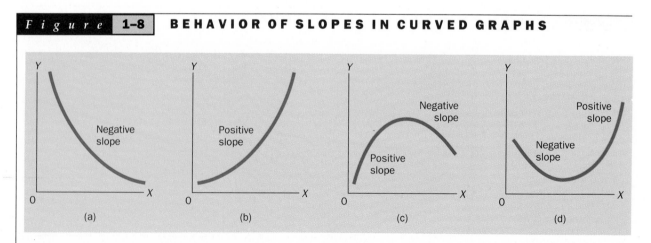

F i g u r e **1–8** **BEHAVIOR OF SLOPES IN CURVED GRAPHS**

As Figures 1–8(c) and 1–8(d) indicate, where a graph is not a straight line it may have a slope that starts off as positive but that becomes negative farther to the right, or vice versa.

F i g u r e **1–9** | **HOW TO MEASURE SLOPE AT A POINT ON A CURVED GRAPH**

To find the slope at point *F*, draw the line *TT*, which is tangent to the curve at point *F*; then measure the slope of the straight-line tangent *TT*, as in Figure 1–7. The slope of the tangent is the same as the slope of the curve at point *F*.

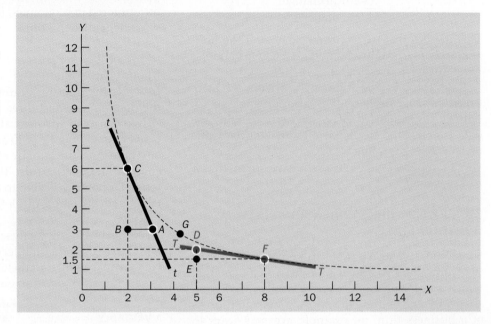

F i g u r e **1–10** | **RAYS THROUGH THE ORIGIN**

Rays are straight lines drawn through the zero point on the graph (*the origin*). Three rays with different slopes are shown. The middle ray, the one with slope = +1, has two properties that make it particularly useful in economics: (1) it makes a 45° angle with either axis, and (2) any point on that ray (for example, point *A*) is exactly equal in distance from the horizontal and vertical axes (length *DA* = length *CA*). So if the items measured on the two axes are in equal units, then at any point on that ray, such as *A*, the number on the *X*-axis (the abscissa) will be the same as the number on the *Y*-axis (the ordinate).

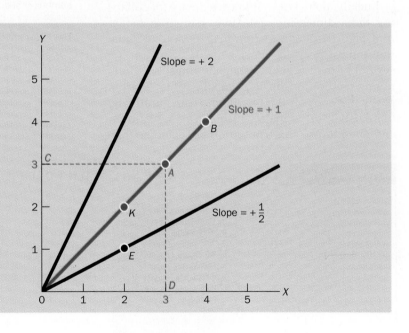

(where both X and Y are zero) and the slope of the ray is 1, we know from the definition of slope that:

$$\text{Slope} = \frac{\text{(Vertical change)}}{\text{(Horizontal change)}} = 1.$$

This implies that the vertical change and the horizontal change are always equal, so the two variables must always remain equal.

Rays through the origin with a slope of 1 are called **45° lines** because they form an angle of 45° with the horizontal axis. If a point representing some data is above the 45° line, we know that the value of Y exceeds the value of X. Conversely, whenever we find a point below the 45° line, we know that X is larger than Y.

SQUEEZING THREE DIMENSIONS INTO TWO: CONTOUR MAPS

Sometimes, because a problem involves more than two variables, two dimensions just are not enough, which is unfortunate since paper is only two dimensional. When we study the decision-making process of a business firm, for example, we may want to keep track simultaneously of three variables: how much labor the firm employs, how much raw material it imports from foreign countries, and how much output it creates.

Luckily, there is a well-known device for collapsing three dimensions into two, namely a *contour map*. Figure 1–11 is a contour map of Mount Rainier, the highest peak in the state of Washington. On several of the irregularly shaped "rings" we find a number indicating the height above sea level at that particular spot on the mountain. Thus, unlike the more usual sort of map, which gives only latitudes and longitudes, this contour map exhibits three

pieces of information about each point: latitude, longitude, and altitude.

Figure 1–12 looks more like the contour maps encountered in economics. It shows how some third variable, called Z (think of it as a firm's output, for example), varies as we change either variable X (think of it as a firm's employment) or variable Y (think of it as the use of imported raw material). Just like the map of Mount Rainier, any point on the diagram conveys three pieces of data. At point A, we can read off the values of X and Y in the conventional way (X is 30 and Y is 40), and we can also note the value of Z by checking to see on which contour line point A falls. (It is on the $Z = 20$ contour.) So point A is able to tell us that 30 hours of labor and 40 yards of cloth produce 20 units of output.

While most of the analyses presented in this book will be based on the simpler two-variable diagrams, contour maps will find their applications, especially in the appendixes to Chapters 6 and 8.

A **VARIABLE** is something, such as price, whose magnitude is measured by a number; it is used to analyze what happens to other things when the size of that number changes (varies).

The lower left-hand corner of a graph where the two axes meet is called the **ORIGIN**. Both variables are equal to zero at the origin.

A straight line emanating from the origin, or zero point on a graph, is called a **ray** through the origin or, sometimes, just a **RAY**.

A **45° LINE** is a ray through the origin with a slope of +1. It marks off points where the variables measured on each axis have equal values.[3]

---

[3]The definition assumes that both variables are measured in the same units.

F i g u r e 1–11   **A GEOGRAPHIC CONTOUR MAP**

All points on any particular contour line represent geographic locations that are at the same height above sea level.

SOURCE: U.S. Geological Survey.

Figure 1–12   AN ECONOMIC CONTOUR MAP

In this contour map, all points on a given contour line represent different combinations of labor and raw materials capable of producing a given output. For example, all points on the curve Z = 20 represent input combinations that can produce 20 units of output. Point A on that line means that the 20 units of output can be produced using 30 labor hours and 40 yards of cloth. Economists call such maps *production indifference maps*.

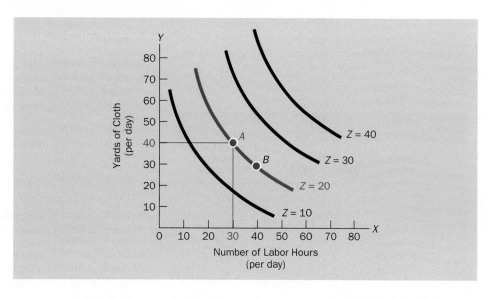

Summary

1. Because graphs are used so often to portray economic models, it is important for students to acquire some understanding of their construction and use. Fortunately, the graphics used in economics are usually not very complex.

2. Most economic models are depicted in **two-variable diagrams**. We read data from these diagrams just as we read the latitude and longitude on a map: each point represents the values of two **variables** at the same time.

3. In some instances, three variables must be shown at once. In these cases, economists use contour maps, which, as the name suggests, show "latitude," "longitude," and "altitude" all at the same time.

4. Often, the most important property of a line or curve drawn on a diagram will be its slope, which is defined as the ratio of the "rise" over the "run," or the vertical change divided by the horizontal change. Curves that go uphill as we move to the right have **positive slopes**, while curves that go downhill have **negative slopes**.

5. By definition, a **straight line** has the same **slope** wherever we choose to measure it. The **slope of a curved line** changes, but the slope at any point on the curve can be calculated by measuring the slope of a straight line **tangent to the curve** at that point.

Key Concepts and Terms

Variable
Two-variable diagram
Horizontal and vertical axes
Origin (of a graph)

Slope of a straight (or curved) line
Negative, positive, zero, and infinite slope
Tangent to a curve

Y-intercept
Ray through the origin, or ray
45° line
Contour map

Questions for Review

1. Look for a graph in your local newspaper, on the financial page or elsewhere. What does the graph try to show? Is someone trying to convince you of something with this graph?

2. Portray the following hypothetical data on a two-variable diagram:

ENROLLMENT DATA: UNIVERSITY OF NOWHERE		
ACADEMIC YEAR	TOTAL ENROLLMENT	ENROLLMENT IN ECONOMICS COURSES
1990–1991	3000	300
1991–1992	3100	325
1992–1993	3200	350
1993–1994	3300	375
1994–1995	3400	400

Measure the slope of the resulting line, and explain what this number means.

3. From Figure 1–9, calculate the slope of the curve at point G.

4. Sam believes that the number of job offers he will get depends on the number of courses in which his grade is B+ or better. He concludes from observation that the following figures are typical:

Number of grades of B+ or better   0 1 2 3 4

Number of job offers   1 3 4 5 6

Put these numbers into a graph like Figure 1–5(a). Measure and interpret the slopes between adjacent dots.

5. In Figure 1–10, determine the values of X and Y at point K and at point E. What do you conclude?

6. In Figure 1–12, interpret the economic meaning of points A and B. What do the two points have in common? What is the difference in their economic interpretation?

Chapter 2

A PROFILE OF THE U.S. ECONOMY

E pluribus unum.

MOTTO ON U.S. CURRENCY

This chapter introduces you to the U.S. economy. It might seem that no such introduction is necessary, for you have probably lived your entire life in the United States. Every time you work at a summer or term-time job, pay your college bills, or buy a hot dog, you not only participate in the American economy but observe something factual about it. ¶ But the casual impressions we acquire in our everyday lives, while sometimes correct, are at other times quite misleading. Experience shows that most Americans—not just students—are either unaware of, or harbor grave misconceptions about, some of the most basic facts about our economy. For example, one popular myth holds that America is inundated with imported goods, mostly from Japan. According to another myth, business profits account for something like a third of the price we pay for a typical good or service. Also, "everyone knows" that federal civilian employment has grown rapidly over the last few decades. In fact, none of these things are true. ¶ So, before we begin to construct elaborate theories about how the economy works, it is useful to get a clear—*and accurate*—picture of just what our economy looks like. What *is* the U.S. economy?

THE AMERICAN ECONOMY: A THUMBNAIL SKETCH

An **ECONOMY** is a collection of markets in a defined geographical area.

A logically prior question is: What is an **economy**? An economy is a collection of markets in a defined geographical area. Usually, that area is a nation-state; so we speak, for example, of the U.S. economy or the Japanese economy. But sometimes the area is considerably smaller—such as the economy of the Northeast, or of New York City. And sometimes the area is bigger than a nation, such as the European Community or the economy of South America.

The markets that comprise an economy generally number in the hundreds or even thousands, and cover a bewildering variety of goods and services. Some of these markets are closely related—such as those for automobiles and tires. But others may be almost totally unrelated—such as the markets for lawyers and breakfast cereals.

A BIG, RICH COUNTRY

The U.S. economy is the biggest national economy on earth, but for two very different reasons.

First, there are a lot of us. The population of the United States is nearly 260 million—making it, now that the former Soviet Union has split apart, the third most populous nation on earth. That vast total includes children, retirees, full-time students, institutionalized people, and the unemployed, none of whom produce much output. But even the working population of the United States numbers over 120 million. As long as they are reasonably productive, that many people are bound to produce a vast outpouring of goods and services. And they do.

But population is not the main reason why the U.S. economy is the biggest in the world by far. After all, India has about three and a half times the population of the United States but an economy smaller than that of Texas. The second reason why the U.S. economy is so large is that we are a very rich country. Because American workers are among the most productive in the world, our economy produces more than $24,000 worth of goods and services for every living American. If each of the 50 states was a separate country, California would be the eighth largest national economy on earth!

OUTPUTS are the goods and services that consumers want to acquire. **INPUTS** or **FACTORS OF PRODUCTION** are the labor, machinery, buildings, and natural resources used to make these outputs.

Understanding why some countries (like the United States) are so rich and others (like India) are so poor is one of the central questions of economics. It is useful to think of an economic system as a *social mechanism*—a machine, if you like—which takes as **inputs** labor and other things we call **factors of production** and transforms them into **outputs**, the things people want to consume. The American economic machine performs this task with extraordinary efficiency, while the Indian machine runs quite inefficiently. Learning why is one of the chief reasons to study economics.

Thus what makes the American economy the center of world attention is our unique combination of prosperity and population. There are other rich countries in the world. At current exchange rates, Germany and Switzerland, among others, have higher per capita outputs than we do.[1] And there are other countries with huge populations, like China and Indonesia. But no nation combines huge popula-

---

[1]Many economists caution that we should not simply use exchange rates in making international comparisons, but should adjust for the different purchasing power of money within each country. On a purchasing-power basis, German per capita income was estimated to be 21 percent below U.S. per capita income in 1989 (the most recent year available for international comparisons).

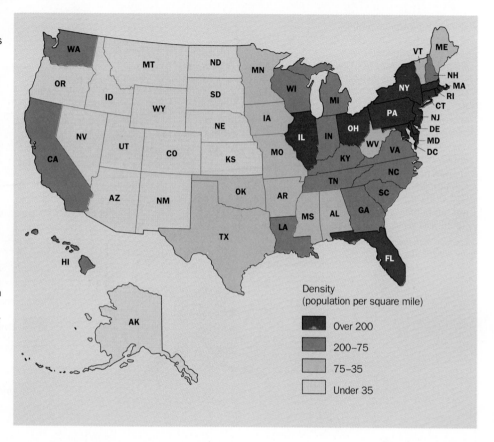

F i g u r e **2–1**   **POPULATION DENSITIES BY STATE, 1991**

This map divides the states of the United States into four groups according to population density. The most densely populated states (over 200 people per square mile) are displayed in dark blue; they are clearly concentrated in the Northeast. States with intermediate population densities (75–200 people and 35–75 people per square mile, respectively) are shown in medium blue and light blue. They are found all over the nation, but especially in the Midwest and South. The most sparsely populated states, shown in tan, are mainly in the West.

SOURCE: *Statistical Abstract of the United States, 1992.*

Density
(population per square mile)

■	Over 200
▨	200–75
░	75–35
□	Under 35

tion with high per capita income the way the United States does. Japan, with an economy about 60 percent as large as ours, is the only nation that comes close.

While we are a rich and populous country, the 50 states certainly have not been created equal. Population density varies enormously across the country—from a high of more than 1000 people per square mile in crowded New Jersey to a low of just one person per square mile in Alaska. Figure 2–1 shows where population density is highest and lowest. Income variations are much less pronounced. But, still, average incomes in Mississippi are less than half that of Connecticut. Figure 2–2 shows how per capita income varies among the 50 states.

A PRIVATE ENTERPRISE ECONOMY

Part of the secret of America's economic success is that free markets and private enterprise have flourished here. America is not unique in these respects. These days more than ever, private enterprise and capitalism are the rule, not the exception, around the globe. But the United States has taken the idea of the free market further than almost any other country.[2] It remains "the land of opportunity."

[2]The tiny city-state of Hong Kong is often held up as an even more extreme example than the United States.

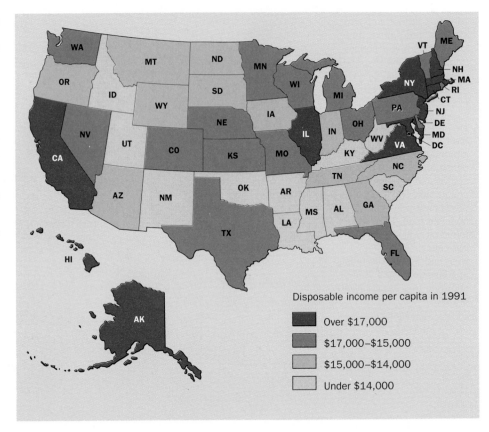

F i g u r e **2–2** **DISPOSABLE INCOME PER CAPITA BY STATE, 1991**

Although the United States is a unified economy, per capita income nonetheless differs substantially from state to state. The richest states (incomes over $17,000 per capita), shown in dark blue, are concentrated in the Northeast, but also include California, Alaska, and Hawaii. The poorest states (per capita incomes under $14,000), indicated in tan, are found mainly in the South and West.

SOURCE: *Statistical Abstract of the United States, 1992.*

Disposable income per capita in 1991

- Over $17,000
- $17,000–$15,000
- $15,000–$14,000
- Under $14,000

GROSS DOMESTIC PRODUCT (GDP) is a measure of the size of an economy. It is, roughly speaking, the money value of all the goods and services produced in a year.

Every country has a mixture of public and private ownership of property. Even in the darkest days of communism, people owned their own personal possessions. In our country, the post office and Tennessee Valley Authority are enterprises of the federal government, and many cities and states own and operate mass transit facilities and sports stadiums. But the United States stands out among the world's nations as among the most "privatized." Hardly any industrial assets are publicly owned in America. Even many city bus companies, and almost all utilities (such as electricity, gas, and telephones), are run as private companies in the United States; in Europe, they are normally government enterprises.

We are also one of the most "marketized" economies on earth. The standard measure of the total output of an economy is called **Gross Domestic Product (or GDP)**, a term which appears frequently in the news. The share of GDP that passes through markets in the United States is enormous. While government purchases of goods and services amount to almost 20 percent of GDP, much of that is purchased from private businesses. Direct government *production* of goods is extremely rare in our society, and government services amount to only about 11 percent of GDP.

A RELATIVELY "CLOSED" ECONOMY

All nations trade with other nations, and we are no exception. Our annual exports exceed $650 billion and our annual imports exceed $700 billion. That's a lot of money. But America's international trade often gets more attention than it deserves. The fact is that we produce most of what we consume and consume most of what we produce.

Among the most severe misconceptions about the U.S. economy is the myth that this country no longer manufactures anything, but rather imports everything from, say, Japan. In fact, only about 11 percent of America's GDP is imported, and only about a fifth of that comes from Japan. Contrary to a second myth, once we include *services* as well as *goods* in the total, America's exports—at about 10.5 percent of our GDP—are almost (but not quite) as large as our imports.

Economists use the terms *open* and *closed* to indicate how important international trade is to a nation. A common measure of "openness" is the average of exports and imports, expressed as a share of GDP. Thus, the Netherlands is considered an extremely **open economy** because it imports and exports about 53 percent of its GDP. (See Table 2–1.) On the other hand, the old Soviet Union was a relatively **closed economy**; it exported and imported merely 7 percent of its production. By this criterion, the United States stands out as among the most closed of the advanced, industrial nations (see Table 2–1). We export and import a smaller share of GDP than most of the countries listed in the table.

Yes, it's a small world and growing smaller. But the United States—with its vast size and geographical isolation—remains relatively insular by world standards, even today. Nonetheless, it is important to realize that this insularity is receding from the peak it attained just after World War II. Exports rose from just 5.5 percent of GDP in 1972 to 9.0 percent in 1982 and 10.7 percent in 1992. We are a great trading nation, and increasingly so.

An economy is called relatively **OPEN** if its exports and imports constitute a large share of its GDP. An economy is considered relatively **CLOSED** if they constitute a small share.

A GROWING ECONOMY . . . BUT WITH INFLATION

The next salient fact about the U.S. economy is its growth; it gets bigger almost every year. Gross domestic product in 1992 was $5950 billion, more than ten times as much as in 1962. Figure 2–3 charts the upward march of GDP in the United States since 1950. The rise looks impressive indeed; GDP increased more than

T a b l e **2–1**	**OPENNESS OF VARIOUS NATIONAL ECONOMIES** (average of exports and imports, as share of GDP)
The Netherlands	53%
Germany	35%
Canada	25%
United Kingdom	24%
Mexico	11%
United States	11%
Japan	9%
Soviet Union (1990)	7%

SOURCE: IMF, World Bank, and CIA.

| Figure | 2–3 | **THE GDP OF THE UNITED STATES SINCE 1950** |

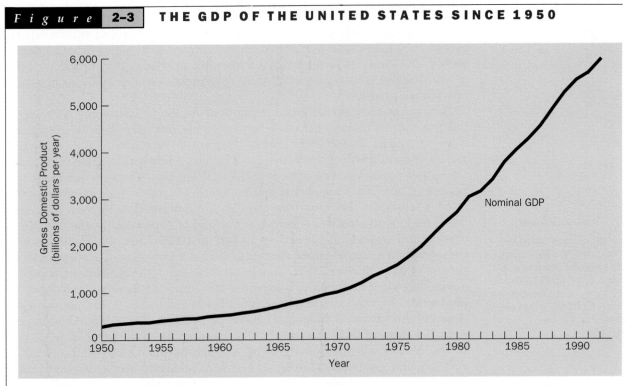

This time-series graph shows that the gross domestic product (GDP) of the United States, measured in dollars, has grown about twenty-fold since 1950.

SOURCE: Department of Commerce.

twenty-fold over the period. But the impression left by the graph is misleading. There is less here than meets the eye, and we need to understand why.

SOME PERILS IN READING GRAPHS: A DIGRESSION[3]

A **TIME SERIES GRAPH** is a type of two-variable diagram in which time is the variable measured along the horizontal axis. It shows how some variable changed as time passed.

Charts like Figure 2–3, in which time is measured horizontally and some economic variable (in this case GDP) is measured vertically, are used all the time to portray economic data. They are called **time series graphs**. You will find many of them in this book and many more in newspapers and magazines. Quite a number of you will wind up reading time series charts routinely in your work after college. So it is vital to understand what they do and do not show.

By summarizing an immense amount of data in compact form, time series graphs can be invaluable—offering an instant visual grasp of the course of events. However, if misused, such graphs are very dangerous. They can easily mislead persons who are not experienced in dealing with them. Perhaps even more dangerous are the lies perpetrated accidentally and unintentionally by people who draw graphs without sufficient care and who may innocently mislead themselves as well as others. Consider Figure 2–3 as an example.

[3]Some further problems, beyond those discussed in the text, are dealt with in an appendix to this chapter.

INFLATION refers to a sustained increase in the average level of prices.

Most of the spectacular growth in GDP over this 42-year period was a reflection of two rather mundane facts. First, the price of almost everything rose between 1950 and 1992 because of **inflation**; in fact, average prices in 1992 were about six times higher than in 1950. Since each dollar in 1992 bought only about one-sixth of what it did in 1950, the dollar makes a rather poor measuring rod for comparing *production* in the two years. Most of the "growth" of GDP depicted in Figure 2–3 reflects inflation, not increases in output.

REAL GDP is the value of all the goods and services produced by an economy in a year, evaluated in dollars of constant purchasing power. Hence, inflation does not raise real GDP.

Economists correct for inflation by a process called *deflating by a price index*, which is explained fully in the appendix to Chapter 6. Proper deflation leads to the blue line in Figure 2–4, which shows the growth of GDP *in dollars of constant purchasing power*. Economists call this **real GDP**. By this truer measure, we find that output in 1992 was about 3.4 times as high as in 1950, not twenty times as high.

Second, there were many more Americans alive in 1992 than in 1950—69 percent more to be exact. So output *per person* rose by considerably less than even the blue line in Figure 2–4 indicates. The brown line corrects for *both* inflation *and* population growth by charting the time series behavior of GDP *per capita* in dollars of constant purchasing power. Americans were indeed richer in 1992 than

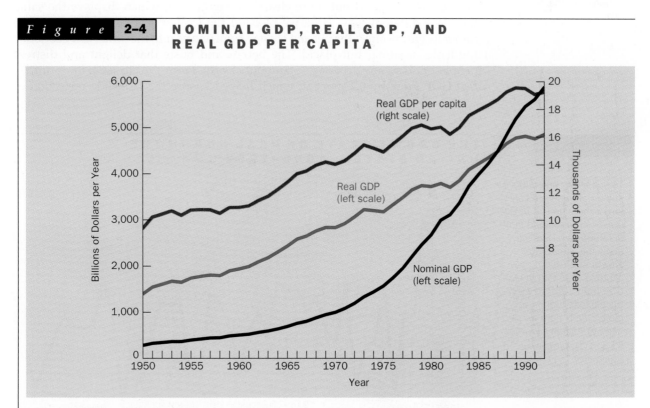

Figure **2–4**   **NOMINAL GDP, REAL GDP, AND REAL GDP PER CAPITA**

The blue line shows that real GDP, that is GDP measured in dollars of constant purchasing power, has grown much less than GDP in current dollars (black line). Thus most of the "growth" indicated by Figure 2–3 was just inflation. The brown line takes the next step and corrects for the fact that America was a much bigger place—in terms of population—in 1992 than in 1950. It therefore gives a more accurate picture of the increase in standards of living.

SOURCE: Department of Commerce.

in 1950, but not by nearly as much as a naive look at Figure 2–3 suggested. In fact, the American standard of living roughly doubled over this period, rather than rising twenty-fold. How misleading it can be simply to "look at the facts!" There is a general lesson to be learned from this example:

The facts, as portrayed in a time series graph, most assuredly do not "speak for themselves." Because almost everything grows in a growing economy, one must use judgment in interpreting growth trends. Depending on what kind of data are being analyzed, and for what purpose, it may be essential to correct for population growth, for rising prices, or for other distorting or misleading influences.

BUMPS ALONG THE GROWTH PATH: RECESSIONS

The bird's-eye view offered by Figure 2–4 conceals one more important fact: When you inspect the data more closely, America's economic growth has been quite irregular. We experience alternating periods of good and bad times which are called *economic fluctuations* or sometimes just *business cycles*. In some years—eight since 1950, to be exact—GDP actually declines. Such periods of *declining* economic activity are called **recessions**.

The bumps along the American economy's historic growth path are visible in Figure 2–4 but stand out more clearly in Figure 2–5, which displays the same data in a different way. Here we plot not the *level* of real GDP each year, but rather its *growth rate*—the percent change from one year to the next. Now economic life looks anything but placid. The booms and busts that delight and distress people—and swing elections—stand out clearly. From 1983 to 1984, for example, real GDP grew by 6.2 percent, which helped ensure the landslide reelection of

A **RECESSION** is a period of time during which the total output of the economy falls.

F i g u r e **2–5**

THE GROWTH RATE OF REAL GDP IN THE UNITED STATES, 1950–1992

This diagram takes the same data used to construct the blue line in Figure 2–4, but uses it in a different way. Here we show the year-to-year growth rate (that is, percentage increase) in real GDP from 1950 to 1992. Recessions stand out more clearly here as periods of *negative* growth.

SOURCE: Department of Commerce.

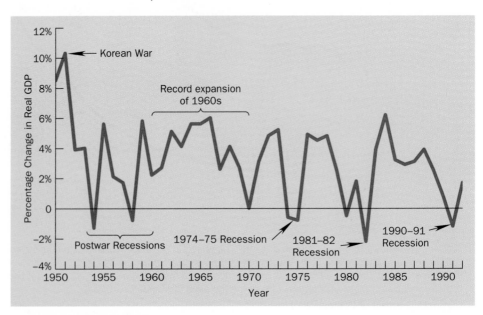

THE UNEMPLOYMENT RATE IN THE UNITED STATES, 1929–1992

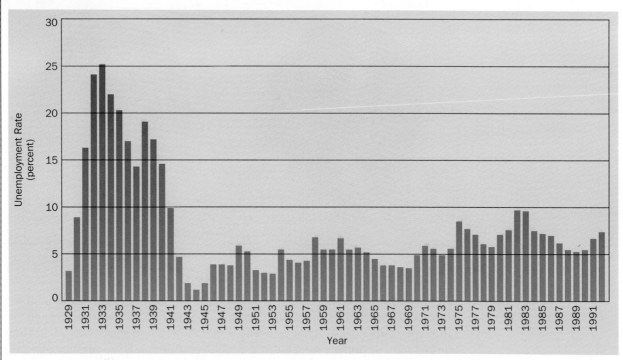

This time series chart shows the ups and downs of the U.S. civilian unemployment rate, annually since 1929. The Great Depression and World War II stand out as most unusual events.

SOURCE: Bureau of Labor Statistics.

Ronald Reagan. But from 1990 to 1991, real GDP actually fell by 1.2 percent, which helped Bill Clinton defeat George Bush.

One important consequence of these ups and downs in economic growth is that *unemployment* varies considerably from one year to the next. (See Figure 2–6.) During the Great Depression of the 1930s, unemployment ran as high as 25 percent of the work force. But it fell to barely over 1 percent during World War II. Just within the last few years, the national unemployment rate has been as low as 5.2 percent (in June 1990) and as high as 7.8 percent (in June 1992). In human terms, that 2.6 percentage point difference meant about 3.5 million *more* jobless workers. Understanding why joblessness varies so dramatically, and what we can do about it, is another major reason for studying economics.

THE INPUTS: LABOR AND CAPITAL

Let us now return to the analogy of an economy as a machine turning inputs into outputs. The most important input is human labor: the men and women who run the machines, work behind the desks, and serve you in the stores.

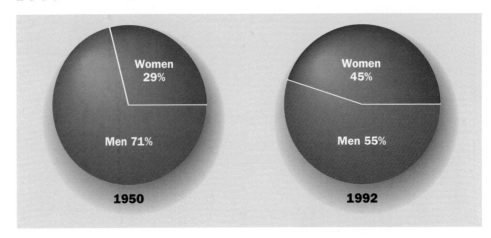

Figure **2-7** **THE COMPOSITION OF EMPLOYMENT BY SEX, 1950 AND 1992**

In 1950, just 29 percent of jobs were held by women. By 1992, this share had risen to 45 percent.

SOURCE: Bureau of Labor Statistics.

THE AMERICAN WORKFORCE: WHO IS IT?

We have already mentioned that more than 120 million Americans hold jobs. Roughly 55 percent of these workers are men and 45 percent are women. This ratio represents a drastic change from a generation or two ago, when most women worked only at home. (See Figure 2–7.) Indeed, the massive entrance of women into the paid labor force has been one of the major social transformations of American life during the second half of the twentieth century. In 1950, just 29 percent of women worked in the marketplace; now more than 45 percent do. In truth, we are probably still adapting to this change. The expanding role of women in the labor market has raised many controversial questions—such as whether they are discriminated against (the evidence suggests that they are), whether employers should be compelled to provide maternity leave, and so on.

In contrast to women, teenagers represent a dwindling share of the American workforce. (See Figure 2–8.) Young men and women aged 16–19 accounted for 8.6 percent of employment in 1974 but only 4.6 percent in 1992. As the baby boom gave way to the baby bust, people under 20 became scarce resources! Still, about 6 million teenagers hold jobs in the U.S. economy today. Most of them are in low-wage jobs like working in fast-food restaurants, amusement parks, and the like. Relatively few teenagers can be found in the nation's factories.

THE AMERICAN WORKFORCE: WHAT IT DOES

What do these 120 million people do? The only real answer is: Almost anything you can imagine. In 1991, America had 772,000 lawyers, 481,000 bank tellers, 685,000 private security guards, and 77,000 professional athletes. Figures 2–9 and 2–10 look at the data somewhat more systematically.

Figure 2–9 shows the breakdown by sector. It holds some surprises for most people. The majority of American workers—like workers in all advanced nations—are engaged in producing services, not goods. In 1992, about 85 million people were employed by service industries, including 25 million in retail and wholesale trade, while only 23.5 million produced goods. The popular image of the typical American worker as a factory hand—Homer Simpson, if you will—

Figure **2–8** **TEENAGE EMPLOYMENT AS A SHARE OF TOTAL EMPLOYMENT, 1960–1992**

The share of teenagers (ages 16–19) in total employment rose from 1960 to a peak in 1974. Since then, it has generally been falling.

SOURCE: *Economic Report of the President, 1993.*

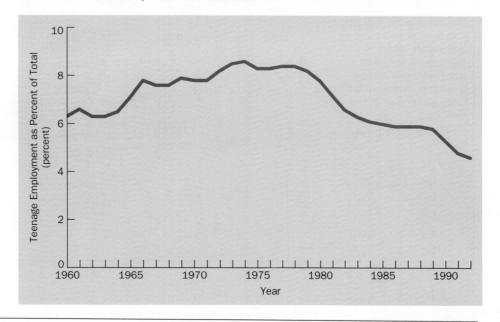

is really quite misleading. Manufacturing companies employ only about 18 million people, and more than a third of them work in offices rather than in the factory. Governments at all levels employ about 21.5 million people. Contrary to another popular misconception, few of these civil servants work for the *federal* government. Federal *civilian* employment is just under 3 million—and has barely grown in two decades. Finally, about 3.2 million Americans work on farms, and the armed forces employ about 1.5 million soldiers.

Most Americans engage in *physical* labor only incidentally. Figure 2–10 breaks down the workforce by occupation. We see that the biggest category is "technical,

Figure **2–9** **CIVILIAN EMPLOYMENT BY SECTOR, 1992**

More Americans produce services than goods. In fact, all levels of government now employ more workers than the manufacturing sector, and almost as many as the entire goods-producing sector.

SOURCE: Bureau of Labor Statistics.

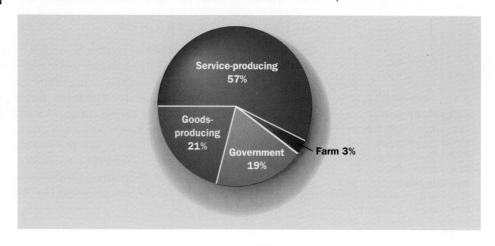

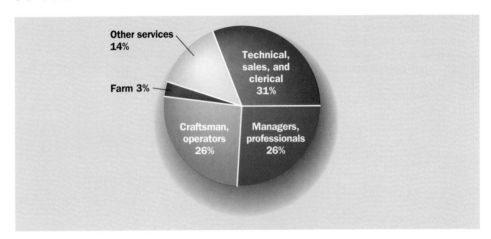

Figure 2–10 THE OCCUPATIONAL BREAKDOWN OF THE WORKFORCE

Blue-collar production jobs now account for only about one-quarter of U.S. employment. There are about as many managers and professionals, and more technical, sales, and clerical workers.

SOURCE: Bureau of Labor Statistics.

sales, and clerical" workers, a diverse group that includes, among other occupations, secretaries and sales people. About 26 percent of Americans are managers or professionals—a category that includes doctors, lawyers, and college professors. Other service workers comprise another 14 percent, leaving just 26 percent in the traditional blue-collar occupations: craftsmen and operators.

THE AMERICAN WORKFORCE: WHAT IT EARNS

All together, these workers earn almost three-quarters of the income generated by the production process. That figures up to an average hourly wage of about $11—plus fringe benefits like health insurance and pensions, which can add an additional 30–40 percent for people holding what are often called "good jobs." Since the average work week is about 35 hours long, a typical weekly pay check is about $385 before taxes. That is hardly a princely sum, and most college graduates can expect to earn more.[4] But that is what wage rates are like in a rich country. Wages in Japan and throughout northern Europe are similar.

CAPITAL AND ITS EARNINGS

After deducting the tiny sliver of income that goes to land and natural resources, most of the remainder accrues to the owners of *capital*—the machines and buildings that make up the nation's industrial plant. Sometimes the ownership of capital is obvious: Edna's Sub Shop is owned by Edna. But the great majority of business assets are owned *indirectly*, via **corporations**. When Phil Ballard buys 100 shares of AT&T stock for $4300, he becomes the owner of a tiny fraction of the company's vast assets. Phil probably will never see the switching systems and fiber optic lines that he "owns," but he is entitled to a share of the company's profits.

The total market value of American business assets—a tough number to estimate—is believed to be in the neighborhood of $11 trillion. Since that capital

A **CORPORATION** is a firm that has the legal status of a fictional individual. This fictional individual is owned by a number of persons, called its stockholders, and is run by a set of elected officers (usually headed by a president) and a board of directors.

[4]These days, college graduates typically earn about 70 percent more than those with only a high school diploma.

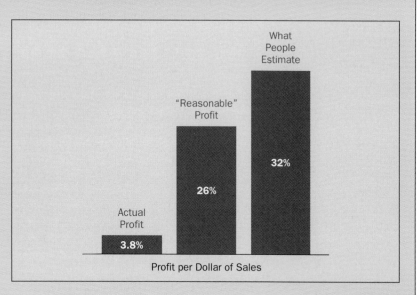

Public Opinion on Profits

Most Americans think corporate profits are much higher than they actually are. A recent public opinion poll, for example, found that the average citizen thought that corporate profits *after tax* amounted to 32 percent of sales for the typical manufacturing company. The actual profit rate at the time was closer to 4 percent! Interestingly, when a previous poll asked how much profit was "reasonable," the response was 26 cents on every dollar of sales— over six times as large as profits actually were.

SOURCE: "Public Attitudes Toward Corporate Profits," Opinion Research Corporation, *Public Opinion Index*, Princeton, N.J., June 1986.

earns an average rate of return of about 10 percent before taxes, the total earnings of capital come to about $1100 billion. Of this, profits are less than half; the rest is mainly interest.

Public opinion polls routinely show that Americans have a distorted view of the level of business profits in our society. The man and woman in the street believes that profits account for 30 percent or so of the price of a typical product. In fact, when you spend a dollar in our economy, about 66 cents is for labor costs, 11 cents goes to cover the wear and tear on the capital stock,[5] 13 cents is for taxes, and 4 cents is for interest. That leaves about 6 cents for after-tax profits.

THE OUTPUTS: WHAT DOES AMERICA PRODUCE?

What does all this labor and capital produce? Consumer spending accounts for more than two-thirds of GDP. And what an amazing variety of goods and services that is! American households spend roughly 45 percent of their budgets on goods—ranging from $112 billion per year on new cars to $50 billion on tobacco products. Expenditures on services absorb the other 55 percent of household budgets, of which housing commands the largest share. But Americans also spend $61 billion annually on their telephone bills, $29 billion on air tickets, and $36 billion on dentists.

---

[5]Economists and accountants call this *depreciation*. It is a well-known cost of doing business.

This leaves roughly a third of GDP for all nonconsumption uses. The government buys almost 20 percent: such things as airplanes, guns, and the services of soldiers, teachers, and bureaucrats. The rest is mainly business purchases of machinery and industrial structures (about 10 percent of GDP) and household purchases of new houses (about 4 percent).

THE CENTRAL ROLE OF BUSINESS FIRMS

Calvin Coolidge once said that "the business of America is business." He was largely right. When we peer inside the economic machine that turns inputs into outputs, we see mainly private companies—literally millions of them. We mentioned earlier that the United States has about 260 million people and 120 million workers. Astonishingly, it also has about 19 million business firms—about one for every 14 people!

The owners and managers of these businesses hire people, acquire or rent capital goods, and arrange for the production of the things people want to buy. Sound simple? It isn't. About 50,000–60,000 businesses fail every year. A few succeed spectacularly. Some do both. Wang Laboratories, an early entrant into the calculator and word processing business, was founded by a brilliant Chinese immigrant in the 1950s and grew to have annual sales of $3 billion and 30,000 employees by 1984. Eight years later, it was bankrupt. Fortunately for the U.S. economy, however, the lure of riches induces hundreds of thousands of people to start new businesses every year—against the odds.

A **PROPRIETORSHIP** is a business firm owned by a single person.

Most business firms are very small. If we simply count firms, the greatest number are what are called **sole proprietorships**—businesses owned by a single individual or family. There are more than 14 million of them in the United States, including most farms and small retail establishments. (Sometimes called "Mom and Pop" stores.) But the average annual sales of a proprietorship is about $50,000—less than the salary of most college professors! Altogether, these 14 million companies account for just 6 percent of total business sales.

A **PARTNERSHIP** is a firm whose ownership is shared by a fixed number of partners.

There are also about 1.7 million **partnerships** in America. Most of them are also very small; the average partnership has under $300,000 in annual revenue. But a few, such as the nation's biggest law and accounting firms, are enormous. The giant law firm of Baker & McKenzie has annual revenues of about $500 million.

Finally, of course, we have the nation's *corporations*—about 4 million of them. Many of these companies are also small; about three-quarters have annual sales under $1 million. But all of America's largest companies—including such household names as Exxon, IBM, General Motors, Proctor & Gamble, and Merck—are corporations. Corporations account for about 90 percent of America's output.

A number of these giant firms do business all over the world, just as foreign-based *multinational corporations* do business here. Indeed, some people claim that it is now impossible to determine the true "nationality" of a multinational corporation—which may have factories in ten or more countries, sell its wares all over the world, and have stockholders in dozens of nations. (See the accompanying boxed insert.) Most of General Motors' profits are generated abroad, for example. And the Honda you drive was probably made in Ohio.

Firms compete with other companies in their *industry*. Many economists believe that this *competition* is the key to industrial efficiency. The sole supplier of a commodity will find it easy to make money, and may therefore fail to innovate or control costs. Its management is liable to become relaxed and sloppy. But a

Is That an American Company?

Robert Reich, who is currently serving as Secretary of Labor to President Clinton, has argued that it is almost impossible to define the nationality of a multinational company these days. While many scholars think Reich exaggerates the point, no one doubts that he has one. Here are some examples:

What's the difference between an "American" corporation that makes or buys abroad much of what it sells around the world and a "foreign" corporation that makes or buys in the United States much of what it sells? . . . The mind struggles to keep the players straight. In 1990, Canada's Northern Telecom was selling to its American customers telecommunications equipment made by Japan's NTT at NTT's factory in North Carolina.

If you found that one too easy, try this: Beginning in 1991, Japan's Mazda would be producing Ford Probes at Mazda's plant in Flat Rock, Michigan. Some of these cars would be exported to Japan and sold there under Ford's trademark.

A Mazda-designed compact utility vehicle would be built at a Ford plant in Louisville, Kentucky, and then sold at Mazda dealerships in the United States. Nissan, meanwhile, was designing a new light truck at its San Diego, California, design center. The trucks would be assembled at Ford's Ohio truck plant, using panel parts fabricated by Nissan at its Tennessee factory, and then marketed by both Ford and Nissan in the United States and in Japan. Who is Ford? Nissan? Mazda? . . .

SOURCE: Robert B. Reich, *The Work of Nations* (New York: Knopf), 1991, pages 131, 124.

company besieged by dozens of competitors eager for its business must keep alert at all times. The rewards for success in business can be magnificent. But the punishment for failure is severe.

American industries differ substantially in how competitive they are. One commonly used measure is the four-firm **concentration ratio**, that is, the fraction of an industry's output produced by its four largest firms. Table 2–2 shows this figure for a selection of American industries. The range is enormous. At one extreme, four firms control 90 percent of the market for manufacturing new cars; at the other extreme, the four largest firms account for barely 1 percent of the retail sales of those cars.

Many economists, however, feel that the concentration ratio is a misleading indicator of competitiveness in a *global* economy. General Motors, Ford, and Chrysler together may produce virtually all the cars that carry American nameplates. But the managements of these companies know very well that they face ferocious competition from Toyota, Honda, and Volkswagen, to name just a few. As long as a national economy is *open to trade*, its goods-producing industries are bound to be highly competitive.[6]

The **CONCENTRATION RATIO** is the percentage of an industry's output produced by its *four* largest firms. It is intended to measure the degree to which the industry is dominated by a few large firms.

---

[6]International competition in services is more difficult. A Russian barber would gladly cut your hair for $1. But try getting to his shop!

Table 2-2	CONCENTRATION RATIOS IN SELECTED INDUSTRIES, 1987
INDUSTRY	**FOUR-FIRM RATIO**
Motor vehicles	90%
Malt beverages	87%
Photographic equipment	77%
Tires and inner tubes	69%
Department stores	44%
Computers	22%
Men's and boy's clothing	19%
Chemicals	14%
Travel agencies	8%
New and used car dealers	1%

SOURCE: Bureau of the Census.

WHAT'S MISSING FROM THE PICTURE? GOVERNMENT

Thus far we have the following capsule summary of how the U.S. economy works:

■ About 19 million private businesses, energized by the profit motive, employ about 120 million workers and about $11 trillion of capital. A theory of how they make these decisions will be presented in *Microeconomics* Chapters 5 and 6.

■ These firms bring their enormously diverse wares to market, where they try to sell them to about 260 million consumers. The theory of how consumers decide what to buy is the subject of *Microeconomics* Chapters 7 and 8.

■ Households and businesses are linked together in a tight circle, depicted in Figure 2–11. Firms use their receipts from sales to pay wages to their employees and interest and profits to the people who provide them with capital. These income flows, in turn, enable consumers to purchase the goods and services that companies produce. This circular flow of money and goods is central to the analysis of how the national economy works—the main subject of this book.

■ All these activities are linked together by a series of interconnected markets, some of which are highly competitive and others of which are less so. Various market forms are studied in *Microeconomics* Chapters 9–12.

All very well and good. But the story leaves out something important: the role of *government*, which is pervasive even in our decidedly free-market economy. Just what does government do in the U.S. economy—and why?

While an increasing number of tasks seem to get assigned to the state each year, the traditional role of government in a market economy revolves around five jobs: providing certain goods and services such as national defense, raising taxes to pay for these services, redistributing income, regulating business, and making and enforcing the rules. Every one of these is steeped in controversy and surrounded by intense political debate. Each will be discussed at length later in the book. But we conclude this chapter with a brief look at the role of government, nonetheless.

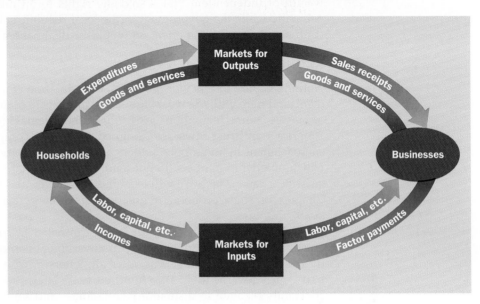

Figure **2-11** THE CIRCULAR FLOW OF GOODS AND MONEY

This diagram depicts the ways in which households and firms interact in markets. The upper half signifies the markets for outputs—the goods and services that firms produce and households purchase. The lower half illustrates the markets for inputs like labor and capital that households sell (or rent) to businesses. In each case, the outer loop indicates the flow of money while the inner loop signifies the flow of physical goods and services.

THE GOVERNMENT AS REFEREE

The economic game can be thought of as a contest. Businesses want to sell their wares for the highest possible prices; consumers want to buy them as cheaply as possible. Each firm wants to gain some advantage over its competitors. For the most part, power is diffused in our economy, and people "play by the rules." But, in the scramble for competitive advantage, disputes are bound to arise. Did Company A live up to its contract? Who owns that disputed piece of property? In addition, some unscrupulous businesses are liable to step over the line now and then—via misleading advertising, attempts to monopolize markets, employment of child labor, and the like.

Enter the government as rulemaker, referee, and arbitrator. Congress and state and local legislatures pass the laws that define the rules of the economic game. The executive branches of all three levels of government have the responsibility for enforcing them. And the courts interpret the laws and adjudicate disputes. All this is familiar.

One particular aspect of the government's rulemaking function is, in fact, *so* familiar that Americans are apt to forget it entirely. But it is proving to be a crushing burden to the formerly socialist economies as they try to make the transition to capitalism. We refer to the *definition and enforcement of property rights*. The answer to the question, *Who owns that?* is usually clear and unambiguous in our country. Your mother and father probably own your family house, Edna owns Edna's Sub Shop, and the shareholders of IBM own the company.

Now think about Russia, where almost everything until recently belonged to the state. Who now owns all the apartment buildings, trucks, industrial machinery, and factories? Is it the tenants, the truck drivers, and the workers? Or is it the managers who ran the enterprises? Or the government? Or the people as a whole? Until such questions are answered, and property rights are clearly defined, it will be difficult or impossible to conduct business in these countries. For example, in one infamous incident a few years ago, the central government of the Common-wealth of Independent States sold the rights to an oilfield to one Western oil company while the government of the local republic sold them to another! Such confusion has a chilling effect on would-be dealmakers.

REGULATING BUSINESS

Nothing is pure in this world of ours. Even in "free-market" economies, govern-ments interfere with the workings of free markets in many ways and for a myriad of reasons. Some regulations grow out of the rulemaking function. For example, America's **antitrust laws** are designed to protect competition against possible encroachment by monopoly. Others are aimed at promoting social objectives to which unfettered markets do not tend. Environmental regulations are a particu-larly clear case, which we will examine in Chapter 21. Finally, as we shall see in Chapter 18, some economic regulations have *no* persuasive economic rationale at all!

We mentioned earlier that the American belief in free enterprise runs deep. For this reason, the regulatory role of government is more contentious here than in most other countries. It was, after all, Jefferson who said that government is best which governs least. Two hundred years later, Presidents Reagan and Bush constantly pledged to dismantle regulations—and sometimes did.

GOVERNMENT EXPENDITURES

During the 1992 presidential election, incumbent George Bush incessantly attacked challenger Bill Clinton's plans as more "tax and spend." He had a point. Taxing and spending are the government's most prominent roles.

During fiscal year 1993, the federal government spent about $1.5 *trillion*—a sum that is literally beyond comprehension. Figure 2–12 shows where the money went. Over one-third went for *pensions and income security* programs, which include both social insurance programs, like social security and unemployment compensa-tion, and programs designed to assist the poor. About 19 percent went for *national defense*. Another 16 percent was absorbed by *health care* expenditures, mainly on Medicare and Medicaid. Adding in *interest on the national debt*, these four functions alone accounted for about 84 percent of federal spending. The rest went for a miscellany of other purposes including education, transportation, agriculture, housing, and foreign aid.

Government spending at the state and local levels was over $1 trillion. Educa-tion claimed the biggest share of state and local government budgets (30 percent), with health and public welfare programs in second place (19 percent).

Despite this vast outpouring of public funds, many observers believe that serious social needs remain unmet. Critics claim that our public infrastructure (such as bridges and roads) is inadequate, that our educational system is lacking, that we do not do enough for the poor and homeless, and so on. Many of these claims were echoed during the 1992 presidential campaign. Other critics argue that government tries to do too much—and does it too inefficiently.

TAXES IN AMERICA

To finance this array of goods and services, taxes are required. Sometimes it seems that the tax collector is everywhere. We have income and payroll taxes withheld from our paychecks, sales taxes added to our purchases, property taxes levied on our homes; we pay gasoline taxes, liquor taxes, and telephone taxes.

F i g u r e **2–12** **THE ALLOCATION OF GOVERNMENT EXPENDITURES**

These graphs show how the government dollar is spent. The federal government spends most of its money on national defense (19 percent) and on transfer payments to retirees, the poor, the unemployed, and veterans (35 percent). The biggest share of state and local government spending goes for education (30 percent), with health and welfare expenditures (19 percent) in second place.

SOURCE: *Economic Report of the President, 1993* and *Statistical Abstract of the United States, 1992.*

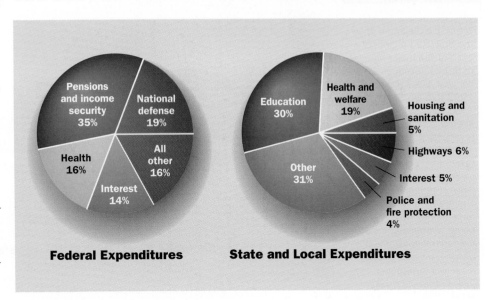

Federal Expenditures   **State and Local Expenditures**

Americans, it seems, have always felt that there are too many taxes and that they are too high. In the 1970s and 1980s, anti-tax sentiment became a dominant feature of the U.S. political scene. The old slogan "no taxation without representation" gave way to the new slogan "no new taxes." Yet by international standards, Americans are among the most lightly taxed people in the world. Figure 2–13

F i g u r e **2–13** **THE BURDEN OF TAXATION IN SELECTED COUNTRIES, 1989**

Americans are lightly taxed in comparison with the citizens of other advanced industrial countries. The Swedes and the Dutch, for example, pay far higher taxes than we do. Even the Japanese and the Swiss, two countries traditionally noted for their low taxes, pay lower average tax rates than the Americans.

SOURCE: *Statistical Abstract of the United States, 1992.*

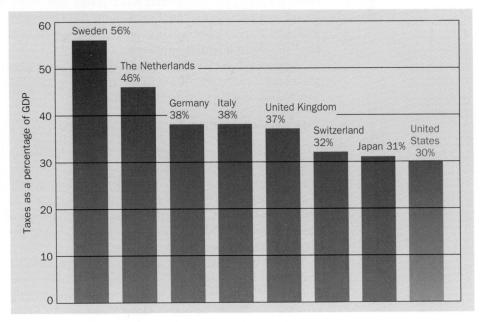

Figure 2–14 · SOURCES OF GOVERNMENT REVENUE

These pie diagrams show the projected shares of each of the major sources of federal revenues for fiscal year 1993 (October 1992 through September 1993) and the actual shares for state and local revenues in fiscal year 1990. Personal income taxes and payroll taxes clearly account for the majority of federal revenues. The states and localities raise money from a potpourri of sources, including the federal government.

SOURCE: Office of Management and Budget and *Statistical Abstract of the United States, 1992.*

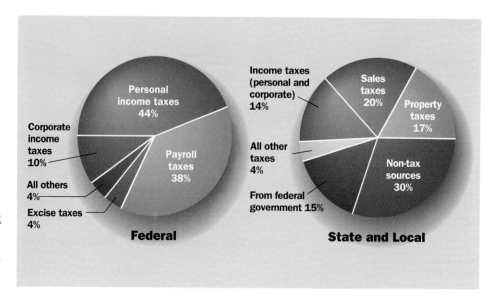

compares the fraction of income paid in taxes in the United States with that paid by residents of other wealthy nations. Americans shoulder the lowest tax burdens in the industrialized world.

How is this money raised? The *personal income tax* is the federal government's biggest revenue source, though the *payroll tax*—a flat-rate tax on wages and salaries up to a certain limit—is not far behind. The rest of federal revenue comes mainly from the *corporate income tax.* Most states and many large cities levy a broad-based *sales tax* on retail purchases, with certain specific exemptions (such as food and rent). Local governments generally raise revenue by levying *property taxes* on homes and business properties.

Figure 2–14 shows the breakdown of revenue sources at both the federal and state and local levels. We will have much to say about the economic effects of these taxes in *Microeconomics* Chapter 20.

THE GOVERNMENT AS REDISTRIBUTOR

In a market economy, people earn incomes according to what they have to sell. The details of this process are examined in *Microeconomics* Chapters 15–17. Unfortunately, many people have nothing to sell but unskilled labor, which commands a paltry price. Others lack even that. Such people are bound to fare poorly in unfettered markets. In extreme cases, they will go homeless, hungry, and ill. Robin Hood transferred money from rich to poor. Some people think the government should do the same; others disagree.

If poverty amidst riches offends your moral sensibilities—a personal judgment that each of us must make—there are two basic approaches. The socialist idea is to force the distribution of income to be more equal by overriding the workings of markets. "From each according to his ability to each according to his needs" was Marx's ideal. In practice, things were not quite so noble under socialism. But there is little doubt that incomes in the old Soviet Union were more equally distributed than in the United States.

The liberal idea is to let free markets determine the distribution of *before-tax* incomes, but then to use the tax system and **transfer payments** to reduce inequality—just as Robin Hood did. This is the rationale for, among other things, **progressive taxation** and the anti-poverty programs colloquially known as "welfare." Americans who support redistribution line up solidly behind the liberal approach. But which ways are the best, and how much is enough? These highly contentious questions will be addressed in *Microeconomics* Chapter 17.

TRANSFER PAYMENTS are sums of money that certain individuals receive as outright grants from the government rather than as payments for services rendered.

A tax is **PROGRESSIVE** if the ratio of taxes to income rises as income rises.

CONCLUSION: THE MIXED ECONOMY

A **MIXED ECONOMY** is one in which there is some public influence over the workings of free markets. There may also be some public ownership mixed in with private property.

Ideology notwithstanding, all nations at all times blend public and private economic ownership of property in some proportions. All rely on markets for some purposes; but all also assign some role to government. Hence people speak of the ubiquity of **mixed economies**. But mixing is not homogenization; different countries can and do blend state and market in different ways. Even today, the Russian economy is a far cry from the Italian economy, much less from that of Hong Kong.

While most of you were in high school, communism collapsed all over Europe. It was one of the most stunning events in world history. Now the formerly socialist economies are in the midst of a painful transition from a system in which private property, free enterprise, and markets played subsidiary roles to one in which they are central. These nations are changing the mix, if you will—and dramatically so. To understand why this transformation is at once so difficult and so important, we need to explore the main theme of this book: **What does the market do well, and what does it do poorly**? This task begins in the next chapter.

Summary

1. An **economy** is a collection of markets in a defined geographical area. It can be thought of as a social mechanism for transforming **inputs (factors of production)** into **outputs**.

2. The U.S. economy is the biggest national economy on earth both because Americans are rich by world standards and because we are a populous nation. Relative to most other advanced countries, our economy is also exceptionally "privatized" and **closed**.

3. The U.S. economy has grown dramatically over the years. But this growth is exaggerated by looking at dollar figures, which are distorted by both **inflation** and population growth. To get a better understanding of the growth of living standards, we must look at **real GDP** *per capita*.

4. The growth path of the United States economy has

been interrupted by periodic **recessions**, during which unemployment rises.

5. America has a big, diverse workforce whose composition by age and sex has been changing substantially. Relatively few workers these days work in factories or on farms; most work in service industries.

6. Employees take home most of the nation's income. Most of the rest goes, in the forms of interest and profits, to those who provide the capital.

7. There are about 19 million businesses in the United States. Most of these are small **sole proprietorships** or **partnerships**. But most of the output is produced by **corporations**, some of which are gigantic and operate on a global scale.

8. Governments at the federal, state, and local levels employ almost a fifth of the America workforce and

produce about a fifth of the GDP. They finance their expenditures by taxes, which account for about 30 percent of GDP. This percentage is the lowest in the industrialized world.

9. In addition to raising taxes and making expenditures, the government in a market economy serves as referee and enforcer of the rules, regulates business in a variety of ways, and redistributes income through taxes and **transfer payments**. For all these reasons, we say that we have a **mixed economy** which blends private and public elements.

Key Concepts and Terms

Economy
Inputs (factors of production)
Outputs
Gross Domestic Product (GDP)
Real GDP

Open economy
Closed economy
Inflation
Recession
Sole proprietorship

Partnership
Corporation
Transfer payments
Mixed economy

Questions for Review

1. Which are the two biggest national economies on earth? Why are they so much bigger than the others?

2. What is meant by a "factor of production?" Have you ever sold any on a market?

3. Do you have any ideas why per capita income in Connecticut is roughly double that of Mississippi?

4. What is the difference between nominal gross domestic product and real gross domestic product? Why is this distinction important?

5. Roughly speaking, what fraction of American labor works in factories? In service businesses? In government?

6. It sounds paradoxical to say that most American businesses are small, but most of the output is produced by large businesses. How can this be true?

7. What is the role of government in a mixed economy?

FURTHER PERILS IN THE INTERPRETATION OF GRAPHS

The chapter warned you against certain dangers that arise in interpreting time series graphs. But there are others. This appendix deals with three of them.

DISTORTING TRENDS BY CHOICE OF THE TIME PERIOD

Users of statistical data must be on guard for distortions of trends caused by unskillful or unscrupulous choice of the beginning and ending periods for the graph. This is best explained by an example.

Figure 2–15 shows the behavior of average stock market prices over the period January 1966–June 1982. The numbers have been corrected for inflation; that is, they are expressed in dollars of constant purchasing power. The graph displays a clear down-hill movement that would suggest to anyone not familiar with other information that stocks are a terrible investment.

However, an unscrupulous seller of stocks could use similar stock market statistics for a different group of years to tell exactly the opposite story. Figure 2–16 shows the behavior of average stock in 1989 and 1990. Stocks now look like a superb investment.

A much longer and less-biased choice of period (Figure 2–17) gives a less distorted picture. It indicates that investments in stocks are sometimes profitable, sometimes unprofitable. The lesson is that:

The deliberate or inadvertent distortion resulting from an unfortunate or unscrupulous choice of time period for a graph must constantly be watched for.

While no ironclad rules can give absolute protection from this difficulty, several precautions can be helpful.

1. Make sure the first date on the graph is not an exceptionally high or low point. By comparison with 1966, a year of unusually high stock prices, the years immediately following are bound to give the impression of a downward trend.

Figure **2-15** **STOCK PRICES, JANUARY 1966–JUNE 1982**

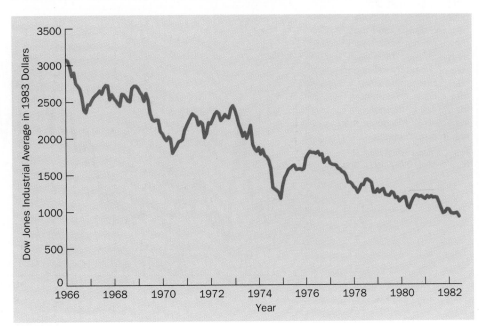

This graph seems to show that stock market prices generally go down.

Figure | 2-16 | STOCK PRICES, JANUARY 1988–JULY 1990

This graph seems to indicate that the value of stocks is steadily climbing.

SOURCE: *Economic Report of the President 1991.*

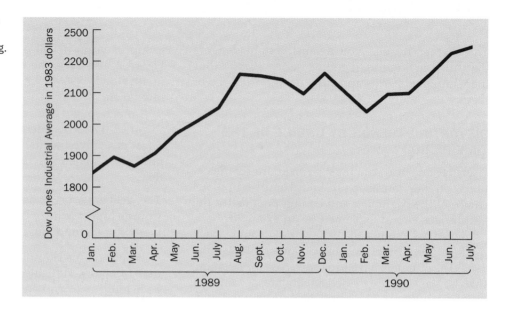

Figure | 2-17 | FULL HISTORY OF STOCK PRICES, CORRECTED FOR INFLATION, 1925–1992

Here we see that stock prices have lots of *both* ups and downs, and that they have not risen nearly as much, over three quarters of a century, as is popularly supposed—after they have been corrected for the fall in the purchasing power of the dollar that resulted from inflation.

SOURCE: *Economic Report of the President 1990, 1991,* and *1992.*

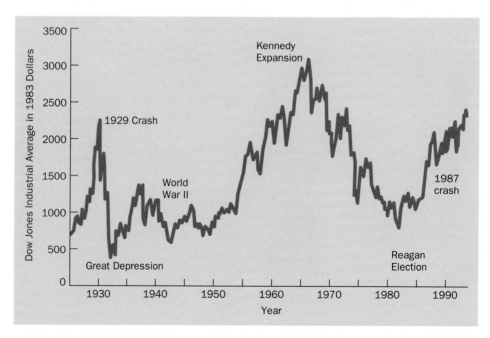

2. For the same reason, make sure the graph does not end in a year that is extraordinarily high or low (although this may be unavoidable if the graph simply ends with the most recent data).

3. Make sure that (in the absence of some special justification) the graph does not depict only a very brief period of time, which can easily be atypical—like Figure 2–16.

DANGERS OF OMITTING THE ORIGIN

Frequently, the value of an economic variable described by a graph does not fall anywhere near zero during the period under consideration. For example, between 1988 and 1992 the civilian unemployment rate never fell below 5 percent. This means that a time series graph showing unemployment over time would have much wasted space between the horizontal axis (where the unemployment rate is zero) and the level of the graph representing 5 percent. There are simply no data points to plot in that range. It is therefore tempting to eliminate this wasted space by beginning the graph at 5 percent, as the magazine *The International Economy* did when it published Figure 2–18 in 1992.

What is wrong with the drawing? Nothing, if you read carefully. But a hasty glance would vastly exaggerate the rise in unemployment. Figure 2–18 makes it look like the United States experienced an economic catastrophe from 1990 to 1992, with

unemployment exploding. A less misleading graph, which includes the origin as well as all the "wasted space" in between, is shown in Figure 2–19. Note how this alternative presentation gives a dramatically different visual impression.

Omitting the origin in a graph is dangerous because it exaggerates the magnitudes of the changes that have taken place.

Sometimes, it is true, the inclusion of the origin would waste so much space that it is undesirable to include it. In that case, a good practice is to put a clear warning on the graph to remind the reader that this has been done. Figure 2–20 shows one way to do so.

UNRELIABILITY OF STEEPNESS AND CHOICE OF UNITS

The last pitfall we will consider has consequences similar to the one we have just discussed. The problem is that we can never trust the visual impression we get from the steepness of a graph. A graph of stock market prices that moves uphill sharply (has a large positive slope) appears to suggest that prices are rising rapidly, while another graph in which the rate of climb is much slower seems to imply that prices are going up sluggishly. Yet, depending on how one draws the graph, exactly the same statistics can produce a graph that is rising quickly or slowly.

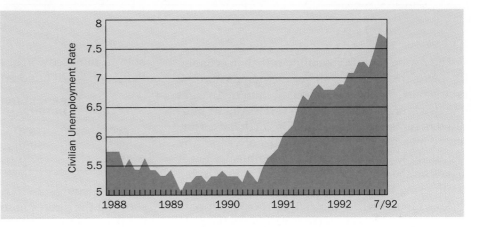

F i g u r e **2–18**   **A GRAPH DISTORTED BY OMISSION OF THE ORIGIN**

A hasty glance at this figure seems to show that, from mid-1990 to mid-1992, unemployment in the United States soared to disastrous heights.

SOURCE: *The International Economy,* September/October 1992, p. 10.

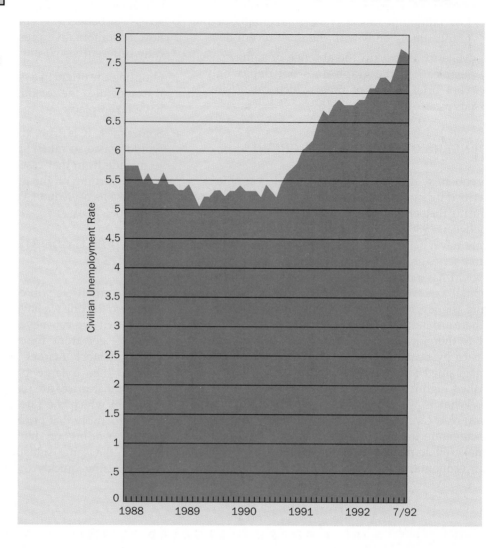

Figure **2–19** **THE SAME GRAPH WITH ORIGIN POINT INCLUDED**

Extending the previous graph all the way to zero unemployment shows that the rise in unemployment, while significant, was not so enormous as the previous graph suggested.

The reason for this possibility is that, in economics, there are no fixed units of measurement. Coal production can be measured in hundredweight (hundreds of pounds) or in tons. Prices can be measured in cents or dollars or millions of dollars. Time can be measured in days or months or years. Any one of these choices is perfectly legitimate, but it makes all the difference to the speed with which a graph using the resulting figures rises or falls.

An example will bring out the point. Suppose we have the following imaginary figures on daily production from a coal mine, which we measure both in hundredweight and in tons (remembering that 1 ton = 20 hundredweight):

YEAR	PRODUCTION IN TONS	PRODUCTION IN HUNDREDWEIGHT
1980	5000	100,000
1985	5050	101,000
1990	5090	101,800

Look at Figures 2–21(a) and 2–21(b), one graph showing the figures in tons and the other showing the figures in hundredweight. The line looks quite flat in one panel, but quite steep in the other.

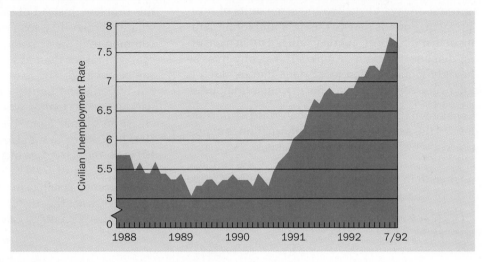

Figure **2-20**

THE SAME GRAPH WITH A WARNING BREAK

An alternative way to warn the reader that the zero point has been left out is to put a break in the graph, as illustrated here.

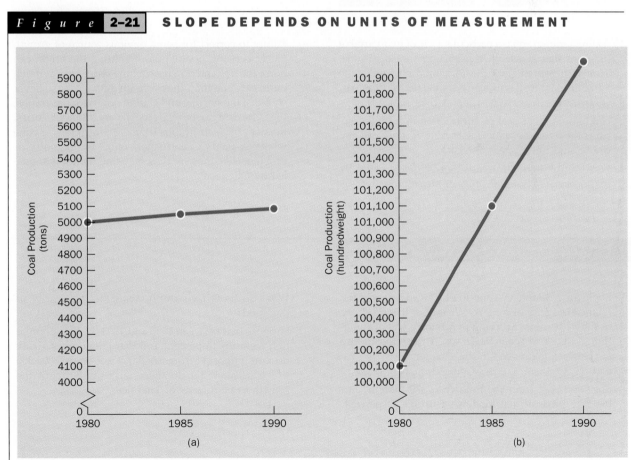

Figure **2-21**

SLOPE DEPENDS ON UNITS OF MEASUREMENT

In part (a), coal production is measured in tons, and production seems to be rising very slowly. In part (b), production is measured in hundredweight (hundred-pound units) so the same facts now seem to say that production is rising spectacularly.

Unfortunately, we cannot solve the problem by agreeing always to stick to the same units of measurement. Pounds may be the right unit for measuring demand for beef, but they will not do in measuring demand for cloth or for coal. A penny may be the right monetary unit for postage stamps, but it is not a very convenient unit for pricing automobiles.

A change in units of measurement stretches or compresses the axis on which the information is represented, which automatically changes the visual slope of a graph. Therefore, we must never place much faith in the apparent implications of the slope of an ordinary graph in economics.

Chapter 7 on demand analysis will offer a useful approach that economists have adopted to deal with this problem. Instead of calculating changes in "absolute" terms—like tons of coal—they use as their common unit the *percentage* increase. By using percentages rather than absolute figures, the problem can be avoided. The reason is simple. If we look at our hypothetical figures on coal production again, we see that no matter whether we measure the increase in output from 1980 to 1985 in tons (from 5000 to 5050) or in hundredweight (from 100,000 to 101,000), the *percentage* increase was the same. Fifty is one percent of 5000, and 1000 is one percent of 100,000. Since a change in units affects both numbers *proportionately*, the result is a wash; it does not change the percentage calculation.

Summary

1. A time series graph is a particular type of two-variable diagram that is useful in depicting statistical data. Time is measured along the horizontal axis, and some variable of interest is measured along the vertical axis.

2. While time series graphs are invaluable in helping us condense a great deal of information in a single picture, they can be quite misleading if they are not drawn and interpreted with care.

3. For example, growth trends can be exaggerated by inappropriate choice of units of measurement or by failure to correct for some obvious source of growth (such as rising population). Omitting the origin can make the ups and downs in a time series appear much more extreme than they actually are. Or, by a clever choice of the starting and ending points for the graphs, the same data can be made to tell very different stories. Readers of such graphs—and this includes anyone who ever reads a newspaper—must be on guard for problems like these or they may find themselves misled by "the facts."

Questions for Review

1. Look for a graph in your local newspaper, on the financial page or elsewhere. What does the graph try to show? Is someone trying to convince you of something? Check to see if the graph is distorted in any of the ways mentioned in this chapter.

2. Suppose that between 1992 and 1993 expenditures on dog food rose from $60 million to $70 million, and that the price of dog food went up by 20 percent. What do these facts imply about the popularity of dog food?

3. Suppose that between 1983 and 1993 the U.S. population went up 10 percent and that the number of silk neckties imported from Thailand rose from 3,000,000 to 3,600,000. What do these facts imply about the growth in popularity of Thai ties?

Chapter 3

SCARCITY AND CHOICE: *the* ECONOMIC PROBLEM

Our necessities are few but our wants are endless.

INSCRIPTION FOUND IN A FORTUNE COOKIE

The market—what it does well, and what it does badly—is, as we noted in concluding the previous chapter, the central issue of this book. But before we delve into the details of this complex subject, we must first ask a preliminary question: What is the basic task that economists expect the market to carry out? ¶ The answer economists most frequently give is that the market resolves *the* fundamental problem of the economy: the fact that all decisions are constrained by the scarcity of available resources. A science-fiction writer can depict a world in which everyone travels about in a petroleum-powered yacht, but the earth almost certainly lacks the resources needed to make that dream come true. The scarcity of resources, both natural and man-made, makes it vital that we stretch our limited resources as far as possible. Even millionaires, monarchs, and wealthy nations constantly find them-selves frustrated by the fact that they lack sufficient purchasing power, labor, and natural resources to do everything they would like. So they, like you and we, must constantly make hard choices. ¶ Because of scarcity, every economic decision involves a trade-off. Should you use that $5 bill to buy a hoagie or some new diskettes for your computer files? Should Chrysler Corporation invest more money in assembly lines or in research on auto design and fuel efficiency? The key role of the market is to facilitate and guide such decisions, assigning each hour of labor and each kilowatt-hour of electricity to the task where, it is hoped, input will serve the public most effectively. Scarcity, then, is the fundamental fact with which the market (or the central planner) must grapple.

The chapter introduces a way to analyze the limited choices available to any decision maker. The same sort of analysis, based on the concept of *opportunity cost*, will be shown to apply to the decisions of business firms, of governments, and of society as a whole. Many of the most basic ideas of economics—such as *efficiency, division of labor, exchange,* and the *role of markets*—are introduced here for the first time. These concepts are useful in analyzing the unpleasant choices forced upon us by scarcity.

PROBLEM: THE "INDISPENSABLE NECESSITY" SYNDROME

It is natural, but not rational, for people to try to avoid facing up to the hard choices that scarcity makes necessary. This happened, for example, when countries such as Russia and Poland were forced by extreme scarcity of foreign currency to tighten their belts sharply during the 1990s. Shortages of foreign currency meant that these governments and their people had to cut down severely on consumer goods and productive inputs purchased from abroad. But most proposals for cuts were met with demonstrations and the cry that each item slated for reduction was *absolutely* essential.

In the same period, something similar went on in the United States. Taxpayers' revolts made it impossible, politically, for federal, state, and local revenues to increase very much while government services were growing more expensive because of inflation and for other reasons. Belt-tightening was the order of the day. But as politicians and administrators struggled with these decisions, they learned that their constituents often were unwilling to accept *any* reductions. Whether the proposal was to reduce payments to the elderly, expenditure on libraries, outlays on schools, or even defense spending, protest groups argued that the cut in question would destroy American society.

Yet, regrettable as it is to have to give up anything, reduced budgets mean that *something* must go. If everyone reacts by declaring *everything* to be indispensable, the decision maker is in the dark and is likely to end up making cuts that are bad for everyone. When the budget must be reduced, it is critical to determine which cuts are likely to prove *least damaging* to the people affected.

It is nonsense to assign top priority to everything. No one can afford everything. An optimal decision is one that chooses the most desirable alternative *among the possibilities permitted by the quantities of scarce resources available.*

SCARCITY, CHOICE, AND OPPORTUNITY COST

One of the basic themes of economics is that the **resources** of decision makers, no matter how large they may be, are always limited, and that as a result everyone has some hard decisions to make. The U.S. government has been agonizing over difficult budget decisions for years, though it spends about a trillion and a half

RESOURCES are the instruments provided by nature or by people that are used to create the goods and services humans want. Natural resources include minerals, the soil (usable for agriculture, building plots, and so on), water, and air. Labor is a scarce resource partly because of time limitations (the day has only 24 hours), and partly because the number of skilled workers is limited. Factories and machines are resources made by people. These three types of resources are often referred to as "land," "labor," and "capital." They are also called the inputs used in production processes or **FACTORS OF PRODUCTION** .

dollars annually! Even Philip II, of Spanish Armada fame, ruler of one of the greatest empires in history, frequently had to cope with rebellion on the part of his troops, whom he was often unable to pay or to supply with even the most basic provisions. His government actually went bankrupt about a half-dozen times.

But far more fundamental than the scarcity of funds is the scarcity of physical resources. The supply of fuel, for example, has never been limitless, and some environmentalists claim that we should now be making some hard choices, such as keeping our homes cooler in winter and warmer in summer, living closer to our jobs, or giving up such fuel-using conveniences as dishwashers. While energy is the most widely discussed scarcity these days, the general principle of scarcity applies to all the earth's resources—iron, copper, uranium, and so on.

Even goods that can be produced are in limited supply because their production requires fuel, labor, and other scarce resources. Wheat and rice can be grown. But nations have nonetheless suffered famines because the land, labor, fertilizer, and water needed to grow these crops were unavailable. We can increase our output of cars, but the increased use of labor, steel, and fuel in auto production will mean that something else, perhaps the production of refrigerators, will have to be cut back. This all adds up to the following fundamental principle of economics, one we will encounter again and again in this text.

Virtually all resources are *scarce*, meaning that humanity has less of them than we would like. So choices must be made among a *limited* set of possibilities, in full recognition of the inescapable fact that a decision to have more of one thing means we will have less of something else.

In fact, one popular definition of economics is that it is the study of how best to use limited means in the pursuit of unlimited ends. While this definition, like any short statement, cannot possibly cover the sweep of the entire discipline, it does convey the flavor of the type of problem that is the economist's stock in trade.

A **RATIONAL DECISION** is one that best serves the objective of the decision maker, whatever that objective may be. Such objectives may include a firm's desire to maximize its profits, a government's desire to maximize the welfare of its citizens, or another government's desire to maximize its military might. The term "rational" connotes neither approval nor disapproval of the objective itself.

The **OPPORTUNITY COST** of any decision is the forgone value of the next best alternative that is not chosen.

THE PRINCIPLE OF OPPORTUNITY COST

Economics examines the options available to households, business firms, governments, and entire societies given the limited resources at their command, and it studies the logic of how **rational decisions** can be made from among the competing alternatives. One overriding principle governs this logic—a principle we have already introduced in Chapter 1 as one of the **12 Ideas for Beyond the Final Exam**. With limited resources, a decision to have more of something is simultaneously a decision to have less of something else. Hence, the relevant *cost* of any decision is its **opportunity cost**—the value of the next best alternative that is given up. Rational decision making, be it in industry, government, or households, must be based on opportunity-cost calculations.

To illustrate opportunity cost, we continue the example in which production of additional cars requires the production of fewer refrigerators. While the production of a car may cost $15,000 per vehicle, or some other money amount, *its real cost to society is the refrigerators it must forgo to get an additional car*. If the labor, steel, and fuel needed to make a car are sufficient to make twelve refrigerators, we say that the opportunity cost of a car is twelve refrigerators. The principle of opportunity cost is of such general applicability that we devote most of this chapter to elaborating it.

OPPORTUNITY COST AND MONEY COST

Since we live in a market economy where (almost) everything "has its price," students often wonder about the connection between the opportunity cost of an item and its market price. What we just said seems to divorce the two concepts. We stressed that the true cost of a car is not its market price but the value of the other things (like refrigerators) that could have been made instead. This *opportunity cost* is the true sacrifice the economy must incur to get a car.

But isn't the opportunity cost of a car related to its money cost? The answer is that the two are often closely tied because of the way a market economy sets the prices of the steel and electricity that go into the production of cars. Steel is valuable because it can be used to make other goods. If the items that steel can make are themselves valuable (that is, if those items are valued highly by consumers), the price of steel will be high. But if the goods that steel can make have little value, the price of steel will be low. Thus, if a car has a high opportunity cost, then a well-functioning price system will assign high prices to the resources that are needed to produce cars, and therefore a car will also command a high price. In sum:

If the market is functioning well, goods that have high opportunity costs will tend to have high money costs, and goods whose opportunity costs are low will tend to have low money costs.

Yet it would be a mistake to treat opportunity costs and explicit monetary costs as identical. For one thing, there are times when the market does not function well and hence does not assign prices that accurately reflect opportunity costs. Many such examples will be encountered in *Microeconomics*, especially in Chapters 13 and 21.

Moreover, some valuable items may not bear explicit price tags at all. We have already encountered one such example in Chapter 1, where we contrasted the opportunity cost of going to college with the explicit money cost. We learned that one important item typically omitted from the money-cost calculation is the *market* value of your time; that is, the wages you could be earning by working instead of attending college. These forgone wages, which you give up in order to acquire an education, are part of the opportunity cost of your college education just as surely as are tuition payments.

Other common examples are goods and services that are given away "free." You incur no explicit monetary cost to acquire such an item. But you may have to pay implicitly by waiting in line. If so, you incur an opportunity cost equal to the value of the next best use of your time.

PRODUCTION, SCARCITY, AND RESOURCE ALLOCATION

Consumers do not obtain all the goods and services they would want to acquire if those goods and services were provided free; that is what we mean when we say that outputs are scarce. Scarcity forces consumers to make choices. If Fred buys a motorboat, he may be unable to replace his old coat. The scarcity of goods and services, in turn, is attributed to the scarcity of the land, labor, and capital needed to produce them.

The scarcity of such input resources, then, means that the economy cannot produce all the bread, hats, cars, and computers that consumers would want if they were available at a zero price. Somehow it must be decided whether or not to assign more fuel to the production of refrigerators, which will mean there is less fuel to use in the production of airplanes or washing machines.

The **ALLOCATION OF RESOURCES** refers to the decision on how to divide up the economy's scarce input resources among the different outputs produced in the economy and among the different firms or other organizations that produce those outputs.

The decision on how to **allocate resources** among the production of different commodities is made in different ways in different types of economies. In a centrally controlled economy such as the former Soviet Union, many such decisions were made by government bureaus. In a market economy such as the United States, Canada, or Great Britain, no one group or individual makes such resource allocation decisions explicitly. Rather, they are made automatically, often unobserved, by what are called the "forces of supply and demand." For example, if consumers want more beef than ranchers now supply, that will make it profitable for ranchers to hire more labor to increase their cattle herds, thus reallocating labor and other inputs away from other production activities and into increased production of beef.

SCARCITY AND CHOICE FOR A SINGLE FIRM

The nature of opportunity cost is perhaps clearest in the case of a single business firm that produces two outputs from a fixed supply of inputs. Given the existing technology and the limited resources at its disposal, the more of one good the firm produces, the less of the other it will be able to produce. And unless management carries out an explicit comparison of the available choices, weighing the desirability of each against the others, it is unlikely that it will make rational production decisions.

Consider the example of a farmer whose available supplies of land, machinery, labor, and fertilizer are capable of producing the various combinations of soybeans and wheat listed in Table 3–1. Obviously, the more land and other resources she devotes to production of soybeans, the less wheat she will be able to produce. Table 3–1 indicates, for example, that if she produces only soybeans, she can harvest 40,000 bushels. But, if soybean production is reduced to only 30,000 bushels, the farmer can also grow 38,000 bushels of wheat. Thus the opportunity

Table	3–1	PRODUCTION POSSIBILITIES OPEN TO A FARMER	

BUSHELS OF SOYBEANS	BUSHELS OF WHEAT	LABEL IN FIGURE 3-1
40,000	0	A
30,000	38,000	B
20,000	52,000	C
10,000	60,000	D
0	65,000	E

cost of obtaining 38,000 bushels of wheat is 10,000 fewer bushels of soybeans. Or, put another way, the opportunity cost of 10,000 more bushels of soybeans is 38,000 bushels of wheat. The other numbers in Table 3–1 have similar interpretations.

Figure 3–1 is a graphical representation of this same information. Point *A* corresponds to the first line of Table 3–1, point *B* to the second line, and so on. Curves similar to *AE* appear frequently in this book; they are called **production possibilities frontiers**. Any point *on or inside* the production possibilities frontier is attainable. Points outside the frontier cannot be achieved with the available resources and technology.

The production possibilities frontier always slopes downward to the right. Why? Because resources are limited. The farmer can *increase* her wheat production (move to the right in Figure 3–1) only by devoting more of her land and labor to growing wheat, meaning that she must simultaneously *reduce* her soybean production (move downward) because less of her land and labor remain available for growing soybeans.

Notice that in addition to having a negative slope, our production possibilities frontier *AE* has another characteristic—it is "bowed outward." Let us consider a bit carefully what this curvature means.

Suppose our farmer is initially producing only soybeans, so that she uses for this purpose even land that is much more suitable for wheat cultivation (point *A*). Now suppose she decides to switch some of her land from soybean production to wheat production. Which part of her land will she switch? Obviously, if she is sensible, she will use the part best suited to wheat growing. If she shifts to point *B*, soybean production falls from 40,000 bushels to 30,000 bushels as wheat production rises from zero to 38,000 bushels. A sacrifice of only 10,000 bushels of soybeans "buys" 38,000 bushels of wheat.

Imagine now that the farmer wants to produce still more wheat. Figure 3–1 tells us that the sacrifice of an additional 10,000 bushels of soybeans (from 30,000

A **PRODUCTION POSSIBILITIES** frontier shows the different combinations of various goods that a producer can turn out, given the available resources and existing technology.

| *Figure* 3–1 | **PRODUCTION POSSIBILITIES FRONTIER FOR PRODUCTION BY A SINGLE FIRM** |

With a given set of inputs, the firm can produce only those output combinations given by points in the shaded area. The production possibilities frontier, *AE*, is not a straight line but one that curves more and more as it nears the axes. That is, when the firm specializes in only one product, those inputs that are especially adapted to the production of the other good lose at least part of their productivity.

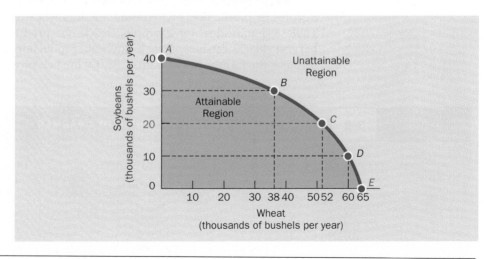

down to 20,000) will yield only 14,000 more bushels of wheat (see point *C*). Why? The main reason is that inputs tend to be specialized. As we noted, at point *A* the farmer was using resources for soybean production that were much more suitable for growing wheat. Consequently, their productivity in soybeans was relatively low, and when they were switched to wheat production, the yield was very high. But this cannot continue forever. As more wheat is produced, the farmer must utilize land and machinery that are better suited to producing soybeans and less well-suited to producing wheat. This is why the first 10,000 bushels of soybeans forgone "buys" the farmer 38,000 bushels of wheat while the second 10,000 bushels of soybeans "buys" her only 14,000 bushels of wheat. Figure 3–1 and Table 3–1 show that these returns continue to decline as wheat production expands: the next 10,000-bushel reduction in soybean production yields only 8000 bushels of additional wheat, and so on.

We can now see that the *slope* of the production possibilities frontier represents graphically the concept of *opportunity cost*. Between points *C* and *B*, for example, the opportunity cost of acquiring 10,000 additional bushels of soybeans is 14,000 bushels of forgone wheat; and between points *B* and *A*, the opportunity cost of 10,000 bushels of soybeans is 38,000 bushels of forgone wheat. In general, as we move upward to the left along the production possibilities frontier (toward more soybeans and less wheat), the opportunity cost of soybeans in terms of wheat increases. Or, putting the same thing differently, as we move downward to the right, the opportunity cost of acquiring wheat by giving up soybeans increases.

| THE PRINCIPLE OF INCREASING COSTS

The **PRINCIPLE OF INCREASING COSTS** states that as the production of a good expands, the opportunity cost of producing another unit generally increases.

We have just described a very general phenomenon, which is applicable well beyond farming. The **principle of increasing costs** states that as the production of one good expands, the opportunity cost of producing another unit of this good generally increases.

This principle is not a universal fact; there can be exceptions to it. But it does seem to be a technological regularity that applies to a wide range of economic activities. As our example of the farmer suggests, the principle of increasing costs is based on the fact that resources tend to be specialized, at least in part, so that some of their productivity is lost when they are transferred from doing what they are relatively good at to what they are relatively bad at. In terms of diagrams such as Figure 3–1, the principle simply asserts that the production possibilities frontier is bowed outward.

Perhaps the best way to understand this idea is to contrast it with a case in which there are no specialized resources. Figure 3–2 depicts a production possibilities frontier for producing black shoes and brown shoes. Because the labor and capital used to produce black shoes are just as good at producing brown shoes, the frontier is a straight line. If the firm cuts back its production of black shoes by 10,000 pairs, it always gets 10,000 additional pairs of brown shoes. No productivity is lost in the switch because resources are not specialized.

More typically, however, as a firm switches more and more of its productive capacity from commodity X to commodity Y, it will eventually be forced to employ in Y production more and more inputs that are better suited to making X. This

| Figure | 3-2 | PRODUCTION POSSIBILITIES FRONTIER WITH NO SPECIALIZED RESOURCES |

Resources that produce black shoes are just as good at producing brown shoes. So there is no loss of productivity when black shoe production is decreased in order to increase brown shoe production. For example, if the firm moves from point *A* to point *B*, black shoe output falls by 10,000 pairs and brown shoe output rises by 10,000 pairs. The same would be true if it moved from point *B* to point *C*, or from point *C* to point *D*. The production possibilities frontier is therefore a straight line.

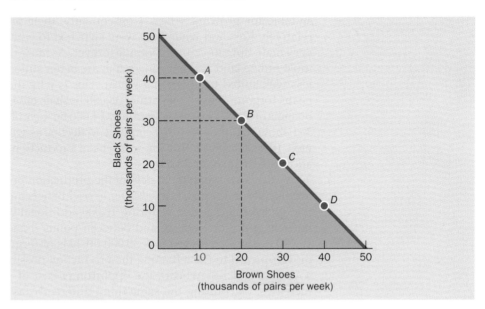

variation in the *proportions* in which inputs are used is forced on the firm by the limited quantities of some of the inputs it uses. It explains the typical curvature of the firm's production possibilities frontier.

SCARCITY AND CHOICE FOR THE ENTIRE SOCIETY

Like an individual firm, the entire economy is also constrained by its limited resources and technology. If society wants more aircraft and tanks, it will have to give up some boats and automobiles. If it wants to build more factories and stores, it will have to build fewer homes and sports arenas. In general:

The position and shape of the production possibilities frontier that constrains the choices of the economy are determined by the economy's physical resources, its skills and technology, its willingness to work, and how much it has devoted in the past to the construction of factories, research, and innovation.

Since the debate over reducing military strength has been so much on the agenda of several nations recently (see box on page 64), let us illustrate the nature of society's choices by the example of choosing between military might (represented by missiles) and civilian consumption (represented by automobiles). Just like a single firm, the economy as a whole has a production possibilities frontier for missiles and automobiles determined by its technology and the available resources of land, labor, capital, and raw materials. This production possibilities frontier may look like curve *BC* in Figure 3–3.

F i g u r e **3-3** **THE PRODUCTION POSSIBILITIES FRONTIER FOR THE ENTIRE ECONOMY**

This production possibilities frontier is curved because resources are not perfectly transferable from automobile production to missile production. The limits on available resources place a ceiling, *C*, on the output of one product and a different ceiling, *B*, on the output of the other product.

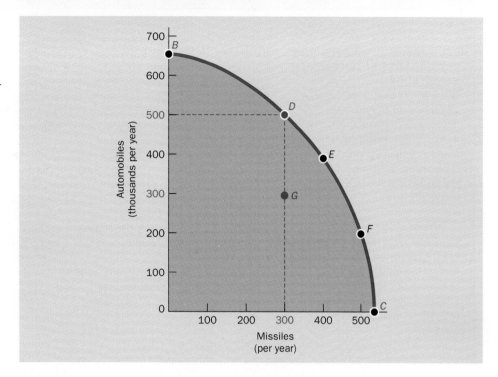

If most workers are employed in auto manufacturing, the production of automobiles will be large but the output of missiles will be small. If resources are transferred in the other direction, the mix of output can be shifted toward increased production of missiles at some sacrifice of automobiles (the move from *D* to *E*). However, something is likely to be lost in the transfer process—the seat fabric that went into the cars will not help much in missile production. As summarized in the principle of increasing costs, physical resources tend to be specialized, so the production possibilities frontier probably curves downward toward the axes.

We may even reach a point where the only resources left are items that are not very useful outside auto building facilities. In that case, even a very large additional sacrifice of automobiles will enable the economy to produce very few more missiles. That is the meaning of the steep segment, *FC*, on the frontier. At point *C* there is very little more output of missiles than at *F*, even though at *C* *automobile* production has been given up entirely.

The downward slope of society's production possibilities frontier implies that hard choices must be made. Our civilian consumption ("automobiles") can be increased only by decreasing military expenditure, not by rhetoric nor by wishing it so. The curvature of the production possibilities frontier implies that, as defense spending increases, it becomes progressively more expensive to "buy" additional military strength ("missiles") by sacrificing civilian consumption.

A Military–Civilian Output Trade-Off in Reality

"KONVERTSIA": SWORDS INTO PLOWSHARES IN THE FORMER SOVIET UNION

The effort to convert large chunks of the massive Soviet military armaments industry into production for the civilian economy is proceeding in fits and starts, as the following excerpts illlustrate:

Izhevsk, Russia—Guns have always been Izhevsk's business, even when this city on the western edge of the Ural Mountains was a ramshackle outpost of the czar's empire. In 1947, the city produced the first AK-47 rifle, which became perhaps the world's most popular automatic and arguably one the best known products of the Soviet Union's vaunted and secretive military-industrial complex . . . .

So far, the evidence is that conversion [of such arms manufacturing centers], pushed by Moscow since 1988, is proceeding with considerable difficulty . . . . 20 percent of military production [has] switched over to consumer products in the last two years, but that still [has] left the economy heavily dependent on both the military and the space program.

Some factory directors have tried hard to find new niches for their workers. Motozavod, a plant with 20,000 employees specializing in sophisticated electronic equipment, is now turning out a grab bag of 60 different goods, from stereo tape players to clothing labels, from disposable syringes to cardiograms to an apparatus that helps men overcome impotence.

At Radiozavod, another large plant, which produced sophisticated [satellite] tracking systems, the most profitable business these days is in high-quality, high-priced bricks, a commodity which, unlike military hardware, is in both high demand and short supply.

SOURCE: Celestine Bohlen, "Arms Factory Can Make Bricks, But, Russia Asks, Is That Smart?," *The New York Times*, February 24, 1992, pp. A1 and A10.

SCARCITY AND CHOICE ELSEWHERE IN THE ECONOMY

We have stressed that limited resources force hard choices upon business managers and society as a whole. But the same type of choices arise elsewhere—in households, in universities and other nonprofit organizations, as well as the government.

The nature of opportunity cost is perhaps most obvious for a household that must decide how to divide its income among the goods and services that compete for the family's trade. If the Simpson family buys an expensive new car, it may be forced to cut back sharply on some of its other purchases. This does not make it unwise to buy the car. But it does make it unwise to buy the car until the full implications of the purchase for the family's overall budget are considered. If the Simpson family is to use its limited resources most effectively, it must explicitly acknowledge that the opportunity costs of the car are the things it will actually choose to forgo as a result; for example, a shorter vacation and making do with the old TV set.

Even a rich and powerful nation like the United States or Japan must cope with the limitations implied by scarce resources. The necessity for choice imposed on the governments of these nations by their limited budgets is similar in character to the problems faced by business firms and households. For the goods and services it buys from others, a government has to prepare a budget similar to that of a very large household. For the items it produces itself—education, police protection, libraries, and so on—it faces a production possibilities frontier much like that of a business firm. Even though the U.S. government will spend about $1.5 trillion in 1993, some of the most acrimonious debates between *every* U.S. president and his critics have been over how to allocate the government's limited resources among competing uses.

APPLICATION: ECONOMIC GROWTH IN THE UNITED STATES AND JAPAN

Among the economic choices that any society must make, there is one extremely important choice that illustrates well the concept of opportunity cost. This choice is embodied in the question "How fast should the economy grow?"[1] At first, the question may seem ridiculous. Since **economic growth** means, roughly speaking, that the average citizen gets larger and larger quantities of goods and services, is it not self-evident that faster growth is always better?

Again, the fundamental problem of scarcity intervenes. Economies do not grow by magic. Scarce resources must be devoted to the process of growth. Cement and steel that could be used to make swimming pools and stadiums must be diverted to the construction of more machinery and factories. Wood that could have been used to make furniture and skis must be used for hammers and ladders instead. Grain that could have been eaten must be used as seed to plant additional acres. By deciding how large a quantity of resources to devote to future needs rather than to current consumption, society in effect *chooses* (within limits) how fast it will grow.

In diagrammatic terms, economic growth means that the economy's production possibilities frontier shifts outward over time—like the move from *FF* to *GG* in Figure 3–4(a). Why? Because such a shift means that the economy can produce more of both of the outputs shown in the graph. Thus, in the figure, after growth has occurred, it is possible to produce the combination of products represented by points like *N*. Before growth had occurred, point *N* was beyond the economy's means because it was outside the production possibilities frontier.

How does growth occur? That is, what shifts an economy's production frontier outward? There are many ways. For example, workers may acquire greater skill and learn to produce more output in an hour. Such increases in labor's productivity are discussed in Chapter 17. Perhaps even more important, the economy may construct more capital goods, temporarily giving up some consumption goods to provide the resources to build the factories and machines. Finally, inventions like the steam engine, AC electricity, and industrial robots can and do increase the economy's productive capacity, thereby shifting its production frontier outward.

Figure 3–4 illustrates, for two different countries, the nature of the choice by depicting production possibilities frontiers for **consumption goods** that are consumed today (like food and electricity) versus **capital goods** that can produce larger outputs for future consumption (like drill presses and electricity-generating plants). Figure 3–4(a) depicts a society, such as the United States, that devotes a relatively small quantity of resources to growth, preferring current consumption instead. It chooses a point like *A* on this year's production possibilities frontier, *FF*. At *A*, consumption is relatively high and production of capital is relatively low, so the production possibilities frontier shifts only to *GG* next year. Figure 3–4(b) depicts a society, such as Japan, much more enamored of growth. It selects a point like *B* on its production possibilities frontier, *ff*. At *B*, consumption is

ECONOMIC GROWTH occurs when an economy is able to produce more goods and services for each consumer.

A **CONSUMPTION GOOD** is an item that is available for immediate use by households, and that satisfies wants of members of households without contributing directly to future production by the economy.

A **CAPITAL GOOD** is an item that is used to produce other goods and services in the future, rather than being consumed today. Factories and machines are examples.

---

[1]Economic growth will be studied in detail in Chapter 21.

F i g u r e **3-4**   **GROWTH IN TWO ECONOMIES**

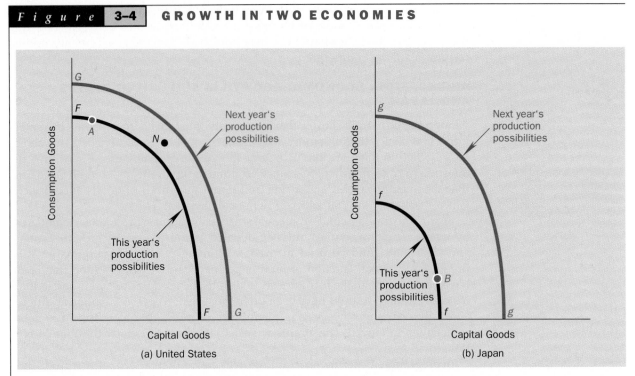

Growth shifts the black production possibilities frontiers *FF* and *ff* outward to the blue frontiers *GG* and *gg*, meaning that each economy can produce more of both goods than it could before. If the shift in both economies occurs in the same period of time, then the Japanese economy [part (b)] is growing faster than the U.S. economy [part (a)] because the outward shift in (b) is much greater than the one in (a).

much lower and production of capital goods is much higher, so its production possibilities frontier moves all the way to *gg* by next year. Japan grows faster than the U.S. But the more rapid growth has a price—an *opportunity cost*: The Japanese must give up some of the current consumption that Americans enjoy.

An economy grows by giving up some current consumption and producing capital goods for the future instead. The more capital it produces, the faster will its production possibilities frontier shift outward over time.

It should be noted that the production of capital goods is not the only way to shift the economy's production possibilities frontier outward. New technology—the process of invention and innovation—is probably the primary means by which economies have increased the output they can produce with a given quantity of resources. Increased education and training of the labor force is generally believed to yield a similar result.

THE CONCEPT OF EFFICIENCY

So far in our discussion of scarcity and choice, we have assumed that either the single firm or the whole economy always operates on its production possibilities frontier rather than *below* it. In other words, we have tacitly assumed that, whatever it decides to do, the firm or economy does so *efficiently*. Economists define *efficiency* as the absence of waste. An efficient economy utilizes all of its available resources and produces the maximum amount of output that its technology permits.[2]

To see why any point on the economy's production possibilities frontier in Figure 3–3 represents an efficient decision, suppose for a moment that society has decided to produce 300 missiles. According to the production possibilities frontier, if 300 missiles are to be produced, then the maximum number of automobiles that can be made is 500,000 (point *D* in Figure 3–3). The economy is therefore operating efficiently if it actually produces 500,000 automobiles rather than some smaller amount such as 300,000 (as at point *G*). While point *D* is efficient, point *G* is not. This is so because the economy is capable of moving from *G* to *D*, thereby producing 200,000 more automobiles without giving up any missiles (or anything else). Clearly, failure to take advantage of the option of choosing point *D* rather than point *G* constitutes a wasted opportunity.

Note that the concept of efficiency does not tell us which point on the production possibilities frontier is *best*; it only tells us that no point that is *not* on the frontier can be best, because any such point represents wasted resources. For example, should society ever find itself at point *G*, the necessity of making hard choices would (temporarily) disappear. It would be possible to increase production of *both* missiles *and* automobiles by moving to a point such as *E*.

Why, then, would a society ever find itself at a point below its production possibilities frontier? There are a number of ways in which resources are wasted in real life. The most important of them, unemployment, is an issue that will take up a substantial part of this book (especially in Parts 2 and 3). When many workers are unemployed, the economy finds itself at a point like *G*, below the frontier, because by putting the unemployed to work in both industries, the economy could produce more missiles *and* more automobiles. The economy would then move from point *G* to the right (more missiles) and upward (more automobiles) toward a point like *E* on the production possibilities frontier. Only when no resources are wasted by unemployment or misuse is the economy on the frontier.

Inefficiency occurs in other ways as well. One prime example is when inputs are not assigned to the right task—as when wheat is grown on land best suited to soybean cultivation, while soybeans are grown on land more appropriate for wheat production. Another important type of inefficiency occurs where large firms produce goods or services that are best turned out by small enterprises that can pay closer attention to detail, or when small firms produce outputs best suited to large-scale production. Other examples are the outright waste that occurs because of favoritism (e.g., promotion of an incompetent brother-in-law) or restrictive labor practices (e.g., union rules that require a railroad to keep a fireman on a diesel locomotive where there is nothing for a fireman to do).

A particularly serious form of waste is caused by discrimination against African-American, Hispanic, or female workers. When a job is given to a white male in preference to a more qualified African-American woman, output is sacrificed and the entire community is apt to be affected adversely. Every one of these inefficiencies means that the community obtains less output than it could have, given the available inputs.

---

[2]A more formal definition of *efficiency* is offered in *Microeconomics* Chapter 10.

THE THREE COORDINATION TASKS OF ANY ECONOMY

In deciding how to use its scarce resources, society must somehow make three sorts of decisions. First, as we have just emphasized, it must figure out **how to utilize its resources efficiently**; that is, it must find a way to get *on* its production possibilities frontier. Second, it must decide **what combination of goods to produce**—how many missiles, automobiles, and so on; that is, it must select one specific point on the production possibilities frontier. Finally, it must decide **how much of each good to distribute to each person**, doing so in a sensible way that does not assign meat to vegetarians and wine to teetotalers.

Certainly, each of these decisions—*which are often referred to as "how?" "what?" and "to whom?"*—can be made in many ways. For example, a central planner can tell people how to produce, what to produce, and what to consume, as used to be done, at least to some extent, in the former Soviet Union and the other countries of Eastern Europe.[3] But these decisions also can be made without central direction, through a system of prices and markets *whose directions are dictated by the demands of consumers and by the costs of producers.* As the formerly socialist countries have learned, markets can do an impressively effective job in carrying out these tasks. To see how markets can do this, let us consider each task in turn.

SPECIALIZATION, DIVISION OF LABOR, AND EXCHANGE

Efficiency in production is one of the economy's three basic tasks. Many features of society contribute to efficiency; others interfere with it. While different societies pursue the goal of economic efficiency in different ways, one source of efficiency is so fundamental that we must single it out for special attention: the tremendous gains in productivity that stem from **specialization** and the consequent **division of labor**.

DIVISION OF LABOR means breaking up a task into a number of smaller, more specialized tasks so that each worker can become more adept at a particular job.

Adam Smith, the founder of modern economics, first marveled at this mainspring of efficiency and productivity on a visit to a pin factory. In a famous passage near the beginning of his monumental book, *The Wealth of Nations* (1776), he described what he saw:

> *One man draws out the wire, another straightens it, a third cuts it, a fourth points it, a fifth grinds it at the top for receiving the head; to make the head requires two or three distinct operations; to put it on is a peculiar business, to whiten the pins is another; it is even a trade by itself to put them into the paper . . . .*[4]

Smith observed that by dividing the work to be done in this way, each worker became quite skilled in a particular specialty, and the productivity of the group of workers as a whole was enhanced enormously. As Smith related it:

> *I have seen a small manufactory of this kind where ten men only were employed . . . . Those ten persons . . . could make among them upwards of forty-eight thousand pins in a day . . . . But if they had all wrought separately and independently . . . they certainly could not each of them have made twenty, perhaps not one pin in a day . . . .*[5]

---

[3]Central planning will be considered in some detail in *Microeconomics* Chapter 23.
[4]Adam Smith, *The Wealth of Nations* (New York: Random House, Modern Library Edition, 1937), page 4.
[5]*Ibid.*, page 5.

Adam Smith, the philosopher of the market system, was born the son of a customs official in 1723 and ended his career in the well-paid post of collector of customs for Scotland. He received an excellent education at Glasgow College, where, for the first time, some lectures were being given in English rather than Latin. A fellowship to Oxford University followed, and for six years he studied there mostly by himself, since, at that time, teaching at Oxford was virtually nonexistent.

After completing his studies, Smith was appointed professor of logic at Glasgow College and, later, professor of moral philosophy, a field which then included economics. Fortunately, he was a popular lecturer because, in those days, a professor's pay in Glasgow depended on the number of students who chose to attend his lectures. At Glasgow, Smith was responsible for helping young James Watt find a job as an instrument maker. Watt later invented a key improvement in the steam engine that made its use possible in factories, trains, and ships. So in this and many other respects, Smith was present virtually at the birth of the Industrial Revolution, whose prophet he was destined to become.

After 13 years at Glasgow, Smith accepted a highly paid post as a tutor to a young Scottish nobleman with whom he spent several years in France, a customary way of educating nobles in the eighteenth century. Primarily because he was bored during these years, Smith began working on *The Wealth of Nations*. Several years after his return to England, in 1776, the book was published and rapidly achieved popularity.

The Wealth of Nations was one of the first systematic treatises in economics, contributing to both theoretical and factual knowledge about the subject. Among the main points made in the book are the importance for a nation's prosperity of free trade and the division of labor; the dangers of tariffs and government-protected monopolies; and the superiority of self-interest—the instrument of the "invisible hand"—over altruism as a means of making the economy serve the public interest.

The British government was grateful for the ideas for new tax legislation Smith proposed, and to show its appreciation appointed him to the lucrative sinecure of collector of customs. The salary from this post together with the lifetime pension awarded him by his former pupil left him very well-off financially, although he eventually gave away most of his money to charitable causes.

The intellectual world was small in the eighteenth century, and Smith's acquaintances included David Hume, Samuel Johnson, James Boswell, Jean Jacques Rousseau, and (probably) Benjamin Franklin. Smith got along well with everyone except Samuel Johnson, who was noted for his dislike of Scots. Smith was absent-minded and apparently timid with women, being visibly embarrassed by the public attention of the eminent ladies of Paris during his visits there. He never married, and he lived with his mother most of his life. When he died, the Edinburgh newspapers recalled only that Smith was kidnapped by gypsies when he was four years old. But thanks to his writings, he is remembered for a good deal more than that.

In other words, through the miracle of division of labor and specialization, ten workers accomplished what would otherwise have required thousands. This was one of the secrets of the Industrial Revolution, which helped lift humanity out of the abject poverty that had for so long been its lot.

But specialization created a problem. With division of labor, people no longer produced only what they wanted to consume themselves. The workers in the pin factory had no use for the thousands of pins they produced each day; they wanted to trade them for things like food, clothing, and shelter. Specialization thus made it necessary to have some mechanism by which workers producing pins could **exchange** their wares with workers producing such things as cloth and potatoes.

Without a system of exchange, the productivity miracle achieved by the division of labor would have done society little good. With it, standards of living rose enormously. As we observed in Chapter 1, such exchange benefits *all* participants.

**MUTUAL GAINS
FROM VOLUNTARY
EXCHANGE**

Unless there is deception or misunderstanding of the facts, a *voluntary* exchange between two parties must make both parties better off. Even though no additional goods are produced by the act of trading, the welfare of society is increased because each individual acquires goods that are more suited to his or her needs and tastes. This simple but fundamental precept of economics is one of our **12 Ideas for Beyond the Final Exam.**

While goods can be traded for other goods, a system of exchange works better when everyone agrees to use some common item (such as pieces of paper with unique markings printed on them) for buying and selling goods and services. Enter *money*. Then workers in pin factories, for example, can be paid in money rather than in pins, and they can use this money to purchase cloth and potatoes. Textile workers and farmers can do the same.

These two phenomena—specialization and exchange (assisted by money)—working in tandem led to a vast improvement in the well-being of humanity. But what forces induce workers to join together so that the fruits of the division of labor can be enjoyed? And what forces establish a smoothly functioning system of exchange so that each person can acquire what she or he wants to consume? One alternative is to have a central authority telling people what to do. But Adam Smith explained and extolled another way of organizing and coordinating economic activity—the use of markets and prices.

MARKETS, PRICES, AND THE THREE COORDINATION TASKS

A **MARKET SYSTEM** is a form of organization of the economy in which decisions on resource allocation are left to the independent decisions of individual producers and consumers acting in their own best interests without central direction.

Smith noted that people are adept at pursuing their own self-interest, and that a **market system** is a fine way to harness this self-interest. As he put it—with pretty clear religious overtones—in doing what is best for themselves, people are "led by an invisible hand" to promote the economic well-being of society as a whole.

People who live in a well-functioning market economy like ours tend to take the achievements of the market for granted, much like the daily rising and setting of the sun. Few bother to think about, say, what makes Florida oranges show up daily in South Dakota supermarkets. While the process by which the market guides the economy and leads it to work in such an orderly fashion is far from obvious to most of the public, the general principles are not exceedingly complex.[6]

---

[6]This topic is studied in detail in *Microeconomics* Chapter 10.

Firms are encouraged by the profit motive to use inputs efficiently. Valuable resources (such as energy) command high prices, and so producers have a strong incentive not to use them wastefully. The market mechanism also guides firms' output decisions, and hence those of society. A rise in the price of wheat, for example, will persuade farmers to produce more wheat and to devote less of their land to soybeans. Finally, a price system uses a series of voluntary exchanges to determine what goods go to which consumers. Consumers use their income to buy the things they like best among those they can afford. But the ability to buy goods is not divided equally. Workers with valuable skills and owners of scarce resources are able to sell what they have at attractive prices. With the incomes they earn, they can then purchase the goods and services they want most, within the limits of their budgets. Those who are less successful in selling what they own receive lower incomes, and so cannot afford to buy much. In some cases, they suffer severe deprivation.

This, in broad terms, is how a market economy solves the three basic problems facing any society: how to produce any given combination of goods efficiently, how to select an appropriate combination of goods, and how to distribute these goods sensibly among the people. As we proceed through the following chapters, you will learn much more about these issues. You will see that they constitute the central theme that permeates not only this text, but the work of economists in general. As you progress through the book, keep in mind the following two questions: **What does the market do well, and what does it do poorly?** There are numerous answers to both questions, as you will learn in subsequent chapters.

1. Society has many important goals. Some of them, such as producing goods and services with maximum efficiency (minimum waste), can be achieved extraordinarily well by letting markets operate more or less freely.

2. Free markets will not, however, achieve all of society's goals. For example, they often have trouble keeping unemployment and inflation low. And there are even some goals—such as protection of the environment—for which the unfettered operation of markets may be positively harmful. Many observers also believe that markets do not necessarily lead to an equitable distribution of income.

3. But even in cases where the market does not perform at all well, there may be ways of harnessing the power of the market mechanism to remedy its own deficiencies.

RADICAL AND CONSERVATIVE GOALS CAN BOTH BE SERVED BY THE MARKET MECHANISM

Since economic debates often have political and ideological overtones, we think it important to close this chapter by emphasizing that the central theme that we have just outlined is neither a defense of nor an attack on the capitalist system. Nor is it a "conservative" position. One does not have to be a conservative to recognize that the market mechanism can be an extraordinarily helpful instrument for the pursuit of economic goals. Most of the formerly staunch socialist countries of Europe are now working hard to "marketize" their economies, and even the People's Republic of China now seems to be moving in that direction.

The point is not to confuse means and ends in deciding on how much to rely on market forces. Radicals and conservatives surely have different goals, and they may also differ in the means they advocate to pursue these goals. But means should be chosen on the basis of how effective they are in achieving the adopted goals, not on some ideological prejudgments.

Even Karl Marx recognized, indeed emphasized, that the market is a remarkably efficient mechanism for producing an abundance of goods and services unparalleled in pre-capitalist history. Such wealth can be used to promote conservative goals, such as reducing tax rates. Or it can be used to facilitate the achievement of the goals of liberals or even radicals, such as more generous public support of the impoverished, the construction of more public schools and hospitals, and the provision of amenities such as national parks and museums.

Certainly, there are economic problems with which the market cannot deal. Indeed, we have just noted that the market is the *source* of a number of significant problems. But the evidence leads economists to believe that many economic problems are best handled by market techniques. The analysis in this book is intended to help you identify the objectives which we can rely upon the market mechanism to achieve, and those which it will fail to promote, or at least not promote very effectively. We urge you to forget the slogans you have heard—whether from the left or from the right—and make up your own mind after you have learned the materials covered in this book.

Summary

1. Supplies of all **resources** are limited. Because resources are **scarce**, a **rational decision** is one that chooses the best alternative among the options that are possible with the available resources.

2. It is irrational to assign highest priority to everything. No one can afford everything, and so hard choices must be made.

3. With limited resources, a decision to obtain more of one item is also a decision to give up some of another. What we give up is called the **opportunity cost** of what we get. The opportunity cost is the true cost of any decision. This is one of the **12 Ideas for Beyond the Final Exam**.

4. The allocation of resources refers to division of the economy's scarce **inputs** (fuel, minerals, machines, labor, and so on) among the economy's alternative uses for them.

5. When the market is functioning effectively, firms are led to use resources efficiently and to produce the things that consumers want most. In such cases, opportunity costs and money costs (prices) correspond closely. When the market performs poorly, or when important costly items do not get price tags, opportunity costs and money costs can be quite different.

6. A firm's **production possibilities frontier** shows the combinations of goods the firm can produce with a designated quantity of resources, given the state of

technology. The frontier usually is not a straight line, but is bowed outward because resources tend to be specialized.

7. The principle of increasing costs states that as the production of one good expands, the opportunity cost of producing another unit of this good generally increases.

8. The economy as a whole has a production possibilities frontier whose position is determined by its technology and by the available resources of land, labor, capital, and raw materials.

9. If a firm or an economy ends up at a point below its production possibilities frontier, it is using its resources inefficiently or wastefully. This is what happens, for example, when there is unemployment.

10. **Economic growth** means there is an outward shift in the economy's production possibilities frontier. The faster the growth, the faster this shift occurs. But growth requires a sacrifice of current consumption, and this is its opportunity cost.

11. **Efficiency** is defined by economists as the absence of waste. It is achieved primarily by gains in productivity brought about through **specialization**, **division of labor**, and a **system of exchange**.

12. If an exchange is voluntary, both parties must benefit even though no new goods are produced. This is another of the **12 Ideas for Beyond the Final Exam**.

13. Every economic system must find a way to answer three basic questions: How can goods be produced most efficiently? How much of each good should be produced? How should goods be distributed?

14. The market system works very well in solving some of society's basic problems, but it fails to remedy others and may, indeed, create some of its own. Where and how it succeeds and fails constitute the theme of this book and characterize the work of economists in general.

Key Concepts and Terms

Resources
Scarcity
Choice
Rational decision
Opportunity cost
Outputs
Inputs (means of production)

Production possibilities frontier
Allocation of resources
Principle of increasing costs
Economic growth
Consumption goods
Capital goods
Efficiency

Specialization
Division of labor
Exchange market system
Three coordination tasks

Questions for Review

1. Discuss the resource limitations that affect
   a. the poorest person on earth
   b. the richest person on earth
   c. a firm in Switzerland
   d. a government agency in China
   e. the population of the world.

2. If you were president of your college, what would you change if your budget were cut by 10 percent? By 25 percent? By 50 percent?

3. If you were to drop out of college, what things would change in your life? What, then, is the opportunity cost of your education?

4. A person rents a house for which she pays the landlord $8000 a year. The house can be purchased for $100,000, and the tenant has this much money in a bank account that pays 4 percent interest per year. Is buying the house a good deal for the tenant? Where does opportunity cost enter the picture?

5. Construct graphically the production possibilities frontier for the Grand Republic of Glubstania, using the data given in the following table. Does the principle of increasing cost hold in the Glubstanian economy?

6. Consider two alternatives for Glubstania in the year 1994. In case (a), its inhabitants eat 60 million pork muffins and build only 12,000 noodle-making machines. In case (b), the population eats only 15 million pork muffins but builds 36,000 noodle machines. Which case will lead to a more generous production possibilities frontier for Glubstania in 1995? (*Note*: In Glubstania, noodle machines are used to produce pork muffins.)

GLUBSTANIA'S 1994 PRODUCTION POSSIBILITIES

PORK MUFFINS (millions per year)	NOODLE MACHINES (thousands per year)
75	0
60	12
45	22
30	30
15	36
0	40

7. Sarah's Snack Shop sells two brands of potato chips. Brand X costs Sarah 75 cents per bag, and Brand Y costs Sarah $1. Draw Sarah's production possibilities frontier if she has $60 budgeted to spend on potato chips. Why is it not "bowed out"?

8. To raise chickens, it is necessary to use many types of feed, such as corn and soy meal. Consider a farm in the former Soviet Union, and try to describe how decisions on the number of chickens to be raised, and the amount of each feed to use in raising them, was made under the old communist regime. If the farm is now a private enterprise, how does the market guide the decisions that used to be made by the central planning agency?

9. The United States is one of the world's wealthiest countries. Think of a recent case in which the decisions of the U.S. government were severely constrained by scarcity. Describe the trade-offs that were involved. What was the opportunity cost of the decisions that were actually made?

Chapter 4

SUPPLY AND DEMAND: AN INITIAL LOOK

The free enterprise system is absolutely too important to be left to the voluntary action of the marketplace.

CONGRESSMAN RICHARD KELLY
OF FLORIDA (1979)

If the issues of scarcity, choice, and coordination constitute the basic *problem* of economics, then the mechanism of supply and demand is its basic investigative *tool*. Whether your course concentrates on macroeconomics or microeconomics, you will find that the so-called law of supply and demand is the fundamental tool of economic analysis. Supply and demand analysis is used in this book to study issues seemingly as diverse as inflation and unemployment, the international value of the dollar, government regulation of business, and protection of the environment. So careful study of this chapter will pay rich dividends. ¶ The chapter describes the rudiments of supply and demand analysis in steps. We begin with demand, then add supply, and finally put the two sides together. *Supply and demand curves*—graphs that relate price to quantity supplied and quantity demanded, respectively— are explained and used to show how prices and quantities are determined in a free market. Influences that shift either the demand curve or the supply curve are catalogued briefly, and the analysis is used to explain why airlines often run "sales" and how computers found their way into the home.

One major theme of the chapter is that governments around the world and throughout recorded history have attempted to tamper with the price mechanism. We will see that these bouts with Adam Smith's invisible hand often have produced undesired side effects that surprised and dismayed the authorities. These unfortunate effects were no accidents, but were inherent consequences of interfering with the operation of free markets. The invisible hand fights back!

Finally, a word of caution. This chapter makes heavy use of graphs such as those described in the appendix to Chapter 1. If you encounter difficulties with these graphs, we suggest you review pages 19–26 before proceeding.

FIGHTING THE INVISIBLE HAND

Adam Smith was a great admirer of the price system. He marveled at its intricacies and extolled its accomplishments—both as a producer of goods and a guarantor of individual freedom. Many people since Smith's time have shared his enthusiasm, but many others have not. His contemporaries in the American colonies, for example, were often unhappy with the prices produced by free markets and thought they could do better by legislative decree. (They could not, as the accompanying boxed insert shows.) And there have been countless other instances in which the public's sense of justice was outraged by the prices charged on the

---

Price Controls at Valley Forge

George Washington, the history books tell us, was beset by many enemies during the winter of 1777–1778—including the British, their Hessian mercenaries, and the merciless winter weather. But he had another enemy that the history books ignore, an enemy that meant well but almost destroyed his army at Valley Forge. As the following excerpt explains, that enemy was the Pennsylvania legislature.

In Pennsylvania, where the main force of Washington's army was quartered . . . the legislature . . . decided to try a period of price control limited to those commodities needed for use by the army. . . . The result might have been anticipated by those with some knowledge of the trials and tribulations of other states. The prices of uncontrolled goods, mostly imported, rose to record heights. Most farmers kept back their produce, refusing to sell at what they regarded as an unfair price. Some who had large families to take care of even secretly sold their food to the British who paid in gold.

After the disastrous winter at Valley Forge when Washington's army nearly starved to death (thanks largely to these well-intentioned but misdirected laws), the ill-fated experiment in price controls was finally ended. The Continental Congress on June 4, 1778, adopted the following resolution:

"Whereas . . . it hath been found by experience that limitations upon the prices of commodities are not only ineffectual for the purposes proposed, but likewise productive of very evil consequences . . . resolved, that it be recommended to the several states to repeal or suspend all laws or resolutions within the said states respectively limiting, regulating or restraining the Price of any Article, Manufacture or Commodity."

SOURCE: Robert L. Schuettinger and Eamonn F. Butler, *Forty Centuries of Wage and Price Controls* (Washington, D.C.: Heritage Foundation, 1979), page 41. Reprinted by permission.

open market, particularly when the sellers of the expensive items did not enjoy great popularity—landlords, moneylenders, and oil companies are good examples.

Attempts to control interest rates (which may be thought of as the price of borrowing money) go back hundreds of years before the birth of Christ, at least to the code of laws compiled under Hammurabi in Babylonia about 1800 B.C. Our historical legacy also includes a rather long list of price ceilings on foods and other products imposed in the reign of Diocletian, emperor of the declining Roman Empire. More recently, Americans have been offered the "protection" of a variety of price controls. Ceilings have been placed on some prices (such as rents) to protect buyers, while floors have been placed under other prices (such as farm products) to protect sellers. Many if not most of these measures were adopted in response to popular opinion, and there was a great outcry whenever it was proposed that any of them be weakened or eliminated.

Yet, somehow, everything such regulation touches seems to end up in even greater disarray than it was before. Despite rent controls, rents in New York City soared. Despite laws against ticket "scalping," tickets for popular shows and sports events sell at tremendous premiums—tickets to the Super Bowl, for example, are often scalped for $1000 or more. Taxis cost much more in New York City (where they are tightly regulated) than in Washington, D.C. (where they are not). And the list could go on.

Still, legislators continue to turn to controls whenever the economy does not work to their satisfaction, just as they did in 1777. The 1970s and 1980s saw a return to rent controls in many American cities, a brief experiment with overall price controls by a Republican administration that had vowed never to turn to them, a web of controls over energy prices, and a revival of agricultural price supports.

INTERFERENCES WITH THE "LAW" OF SUPPLY AND DEMAND

Public opinion frequently encourages legislative attempts to "repeal the law of supply and demand" by controlling prices. The consequences usually are quite unfortunate, exacting heavy costs from the general public and often aggravating the problem the legislation was intended to cure. This is another of the **12 Ideas for Beyond the Final Exam**, and it will occupy our attention throughout this chapter.

To understand what goes wrong when markets are tampered with, we must first learn how they operate when they are unfettered. This chapter takes a first step in that direction by studying the machinery of supply and demand. Then, at the end of the chapter, we return to the issue of price controls, illustrating the problems that can arise by case studies of rent controls in New York City and price supports for milk.

Every market has both buyers and sellers. We begin our analysis on the consumers' side of the market.

DEMAND AND QUANTITY DEMANDED

Noneconomists are apt to think of consumer demands as fixed amounts. For example, when the production of a new model of computer is proposed, management asks "What is its market potential? How many will we be able to sell?" Similarly, government bureaus conduct studies to determine how many engineers will be "required" in succeeding years.

Economists respond that such questions are not well posed—that there is no *single* answer to such a question. Rather, they say, the "market potential" for computers or the number of engineers that will be "required" depends on a great number of things, *including the price that will be charged for each.*

The **QUANTITY DEMANDED** is the number of units consumers want to buy over a specified period of time.

The **quantity demanded** of any product normally depends on its price. Quantity demanded also has a number of other determinants, including population size, consumer incomes, tastes, and the prices of other products.

Because of the central role of prices in a market economy, we begin our study of demand by focusing on the dependence of quantity demanded on price. Shortly, we will bring the other determinants of quantity demanded back into the picture.

Consider, as an example, the quantity of milk demanded. Almost everyone purchases at least some milk. However, if the price of milk is very high, its "market potential" may be very small. People will find ways to get along with less milk, perhaps by switching to tea or coffee. If the price declines, people will be encouraged to drink more milk. They may give their children larger portions or switch away from juices and sodas. Thus:

There is no *one* demand figure for milk, for computers, or for engineers. Rather, there is a different quantity demanded for each possible price.

THE DEMAND SCHEDULE

A **DEMAND SCHEDULE** is a table showing how the quantity demanded of some product during a specified period of time changes as the price of that product changes, holding all other determinants of quantity demanded constant.

Table 4–1 displays this information for milk in what we call a **demand schedule**, which indicates how much consumers are willing and able to buy at different possible prices during a specified period of time. The table shows the quantity of milk that will be demanded in a year at each possible price ranging from $1 to 40¢ per quart. We see, for example, that at a relatively low price, like 50¢ per quart, customers wish to purchase 70 billion quarts per year. But if the price were to rise to, say, 90¢ per quart, quantity demanded would fall to 50 billion quarts.

Common sense tells us why this should be so.[1] First, as prices rise, some customers will reduce their consumption of milk. Second, higher prices will induce

T a b l e **4–1**	DEMAND SCHEDULE FOR MILK	
PRICE (dollars per quart)	QUANTITY DEMANDED (billions of quarts per year)	LABEL IN FIGURE 4–1
1.00	45	*A*
0.90	50	*B*
0.80	55	*C*
0.70	60	*E*
0.60	65	*F*
0.50	70	*G*
0.40	75	*H*

[1]This common-sense answer is examined more fully in Chapters 7 and 8.

Figure 4-1	DEMAND CURVE FOR MILK

This curve shows the relationship between price and quantity demanded. To sell 70 billion quarts per year, the price must be only 50¢ (point *G*). If, instead, price is 90¢, only 50 billion quarts will be demanded (point *B*). To sell more milk, the price must be reduced. That is what the negative slope of the demand curve means.

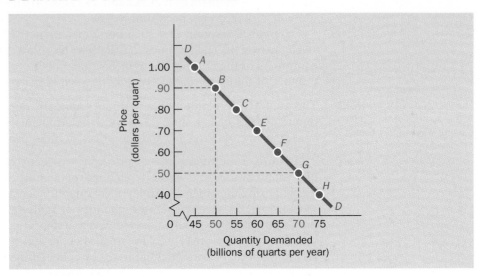

some customers to drop out of the market entirely—for example, by switching to soda or juice. On both counts, quantity demanded will decline as the price rises.

As the price of an item rises, the quantity demanded normally falls. As the price falls, the quantity demanded normally rises.

THE DEMAND CURVE

A **DEMAND CURVE** is a graphical depiction of a demand schedule. It shows how the quantity demanded of some product during a specified period of time will change as the price of that product changes, holding all other determinants of quantity demanded constant.

The information contained in Table 4–1 can be summarized in a graph like Figure 4–1, which we call a **demand curve**. Each point in the graph corresponds to a line in the table. For example, point *B* corresponds to the second line in the table, indicating that at a price of 90¢ per quart, 50 billion quarts per year will be demanded. Since the quantity demanded declines as the price increases, the demand curve has a negative slope.[2]

Notice the last phrase in the definitions of the demand schedule and the demand curve: "holding all other determinants of quantity demanded constant." These "other things" include consumer incomes and preferences, the prices of soda and orange juice, and perhaps even advertising by the dairy association. We will examine the influences of these factors later in the chapter. First, however, let's look at the sellers' side of the market.

SUPPLY AND QUANTITY SUPPLIED

Like quantity demanded, the quantity of milk that is supplied by dairy farmers is not a fixed number; it also depends on many things. Obviously, we expect

---

[2]If you need to review the concept of *slope*, refer back to the appendix to Chapter 1, especially pages 20–23.

The **QUANTITY SUPPLIED** is the number of units sellers want to sell over a specified period of time.

more milk to be supplied if there are more dairy farms, or more cows per farm. Or cows may give less milk if bad weather deprives them of their feed. As before, however, let's turn our attention first to the relationship between **quantity supplied** and one of its major determinants—the price of milk.

Economists generally suppose that a higher price calls forth a greater quantity supplied. Why? Remember our analysis of the principle of increasing cost in Chapter 3 (page 61). According to that principle, as more of any farmer's (or the nation's) resources are devoted to milk production, the opportunity cost of obtaining another quart of milk increases. Farmers will therefore find it profitable to raise milk production only if they can sell the milk at a higher price—high enough to cover the additional costs incurred to expand production.

Looked at the other way around, we have just concluded that higher prices normally will be required to persuade farmers to raise milk production. This idea is quite general and applies to the supply of most goods and services.[3] As long as suppliers want to make profits and the principle of increasing costs holds:

A **SUPPLY SCHEDULE** is a table showing how the quantity supplied of some product during a specified period of time changes as the price of that product changes, holding all other determinants of quantity supplied constant.

As the price of an item rises, the quantity supplied normally rises. As the price falls, the quantity supplied normally falls.

THE SUPPLY SCHEDULE AND THE SUPPLY CURVE

The relationship between the price of milk and its quantity supplied is recorded in Table 4–2. Tables like this are called **supply schedules**; they show how much sellers are willing to provide during a specified period at alternative possible prices. This particular supply schedule shows that a low price like 50¢ per quart will induce suppliers to provide only 40 billion quarts, while a higher price like 80¢ will induce them to provide much more—70 billion quarts.

A **SUPPLY CURVE** is a graphical depiction of a supply schedule. It shows how the quantity supplied of some product during a specified period of time will change as the price of that product changes, holding all other determinants of quantity supplied constant.

As you might have guessed, when information like this is plotted on a graph, it is called a **supply curve**. Figure 4–2 is the supply curve corresponding to the supply schedule in Table 4–2. It slopes upward because quantity supplied is higher when price is higher.

Notice again the same phrase in the definition: "holding all other determinants of quantity supplied constant." We will return to these "other determinants" a bit later in the discussion. But first we are ready to put demand and supply together.

T a b l e **4–2**	**SUPPLY SCHEDULE FOR MILK**	
PRICE (dollars per quart)	**QUANTITY SUPPLIED** (billions of quarts per year)	**LABEL IN FIGURE 4–2**
1.00	90	*a*
0.90	80	*b*
0.80	70	*c*
0.70	60	*e*
0.60	50	*f*
0.50	40	*g*
0.40	30	*h*

[3]This analysis is carried out in much greater detail in the next two chapters.

| Figure | 4-2 | SUPPLY CURVE FOR MILK |

This curve shows the relationship between the price of milk and the quantity supplied. To stimulate a greater quantity supplied, price must be increased. That is the meaning of the positive slope of the supply curve.

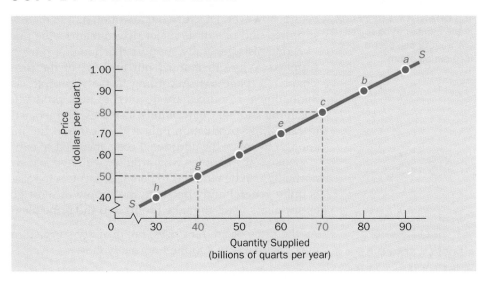

EQUILIBRIUM OF SUPPLY AND DEMAND

To analyze how price is determined in a free market, we must compare the desires of consumers (demand) with the desires of producers (supply) and see whether the two plans are consistent. Table 4–3 and Figure 4–3 help us do this.

Table 4–3 brings together the demand schedule from Table 4–1 and the supply schedule from Table 4–2. Similarly, Figure 4–3 puts the demand curve from Figure 4–1 and the supply curve from Figure 4–2 on a single graph. Such a graphic device is called a **supply–demand diagram**, and you will encounter many of them in this book. Notice that, for reasons already discussed, the demand curve has a negative slope and the supply curve has a positive slope. Most supply–demand diagrams are drawn with slopes like these.

| Table | 4-3 | DETERMINATION OF THE EQUILIBRIUM PRICE AND QUANTITY OF MILK |

PRICE (dollars per quart)	QUANTITY DEMANDED (billions of quarts per year)	QUANTITY SUPPLIED (billions of quarts per year)	SURPLUS OR SHORTAGE?	PRICE WILL
1.00	45	90	Surplus	Fall
0.90	50	80	Surplus	Fall
0.80	55	70	Surplus	Fall
0.70	60	60	Neither	Remain the same
0.60	65	50	Shortage	Rise
0.50	70	40	Shortage	Rise
0.40	75	30	Shortage	Rise

Figure 4–3 · SUPPLY–DEMAND EQUILIBRIUM

In a free market, price and quantity are determined by the intersection of the supply curve and the demand curve. In this example, the equilibrium price is 70¢ and the equilibrium quantity is 60 billion quarts of milk per year. Any other price is inconsistent with equilibrium. For example, at a price of 50¢, quantity demanded is 70 billion (point *G*), while quantity supplied is only 40 billion (point *g*), so that price will be driven up by the unsatisfied demand.

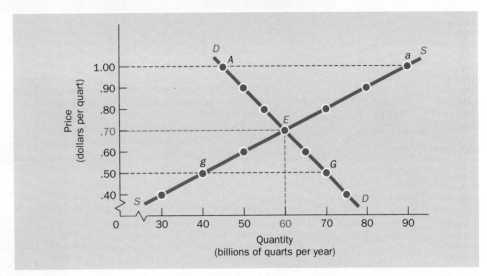

There is only one point in Figure 4–3, point *E*, at which the supply curve and the demand curve intersect. At the price corresponding to point *E*, which is 70¢ per quart, the quantity supplied and the quantity demanded are both 60 billion quarts per year. This means that, at a price of 70¢ per quart, consumers are willing to buy just what producers are willing to sell.

At any lower price, such as 50¢, only 40 billion quarts of milk will be supplied (point *g*) whereas 70 billion quarts will be demanded (point *G*). Thus quantity demanded will exceed quantity supplied. There will be a **shortage** equal to 70 − 40 = 30 billion quarts. Alternatively, at a higher price like $1, quantity supplied will be 90 billion quarts (point *a*) while quantity demanded will be only 45 billion (point *A*). Quantity supplied will exceed quantity demanded, so there will be a **surplus** equal to 90 − 45 = 45 billion quarts.

Since 70¢ is the price at which quantity supplied and quantity demanded are equal, we say that 70¢ per quart is the **equilibrium price** in this market. Similarly, 60 billion quarts per year is the **equilibrium quantity** of milk. The term "equilibrium" merits a little explanation, since it arises so frequently in economic analysis.

An **equilibrium** is a situation in which there are no inherent forces that produce change; that is, a situation that does not contain the seeds of its own destruction. Think, for example, of a pendulum at rest at its center point. If no outside force (such as a person's hand) comes to push it, the pendulum will remain where it is; it is in *equilibrium*. But if you give the pendulum a shove, its equilibrium will be disturbed and it will start to move upward. When it reaches the top of its arc, the pendulum will, for an instant, be at rest again. But this is not an equilibrium position, for a force known as gravity will pull the pendulum downward. Thereafter, its motion from side to side will be governed by gravity and friction. Eventually, we know, the pendulum will return to the point at which it started, which is its only equilibrium position. At any other point, inherent forces will cause the pendulum to move.

A **SHORTAGE** is an excess of quantity demanded over quantity supplied. When there is a shortage, buyers cannot purchase the quantities they desire.

A **SURPLUS** is an excess of quantity supplied over quantity demanded. When there is a surplus, sellers cannot sell the quantities they desire to supply.

An **EQUILIBRIUM** is a situation in which there are no inherent forces that produce change. Changes away from an equilibrium position will occur only as a result of "outside events" that disturb the status quo.

EXPERIMENTAL ECONOMICS

In theory, supply and demand curves determine prices. But does reality work the way the theory claims? Physicists use experiments to help answer such questions. However, for a long time it was believed that economists could not perform laboratory experiments. After all, people are not guinea pigs. Can economists recreate an entire economy, or even a single market, in a laboratory? And, even if this is done, how can the experimenter get the "guinea pigs" to act as they would in making real decisions—with real money at stake?

For a long time, economists felt that experimental methods were beyond their reach. So they relied almost exclusively on statistical inference to test their theories. But the statistical approach is an imperfect solution because it does not allow us to isolate just *one* influence at a time, as a scientifically controlled experiment does.

Lately, this view of experimentation in economics has begun to change. While economists still rely mainly on statistical analysis, they have also begun to experiment. Market experiments are now conducted to test theories about the behavior of large firms, about government programs that provide financial assistance to poor people, and about a wide variety of other subjects.

Who are the subjects of these experiments? You guessed it. They are often college students who volunteer to participate. Some may volunteer because the experiments are interesting; but there is also money to be earned. In fact, that is what motivates participants to act as they would in a real market. One such experiment was conducted at

UCLA and Los Angeles City College*. The objective was to see whether demand and supply curves do in fact determine price in the way the theory claims.

Students were divided into two groups: sellers and buyers. Each was given some money to start. Sellers purchased fictitious "goods" from the experimenter (who acted like a wholesaler), and then tried to sell them to buyers. If they could sell them at higher prices than they paid, sellers got to pocket the difference. Similarly, buyers could resell their purchases to the experimenter, who would pay according to a fixed schedule. They, too, got to keep any profits they made.

For example, seller A was able to buy from the wholesaler at the following prices:

Unit	1st	2nd	3rd	4th	5th	6th	7th	8th
Price	$2.30	2.30	2.30	2.31	2.31	2.36	2.50	2.70

That is, she could purchase up to three units of the commodity at a price of $2.30 per unit. However, if she bought a fourth unit, the price would go up to $2.31, and so on. It is clear that, if the market price was, say $2.35, seller A should want to supply five units, because she can obtain this many units from the wholesaler at lower prices. But seller A would be irrational to acquire the sixth unit from the wholesaler for $2.36 and then sell it for $2.35.

So the experimenters knew that, at a price of $2.35, seller A's theoretical quantity supplied was five units. And they could reach a similar conclusion for every other price and every other seller. Analogously, the experimenters were able to calculate the theoretical quantities demanded for each buyer. The theoretical price at which the supply and demand curves intersected was $2.44.

How did the actual prices turn out in the experiment? The experiment was repeated five times, each repetition involving about 20 transactions. The average actual price was slightly lower than the theoretical equilibrium price of $2.44, but the experimental price almost always fell in the $2.40–$2.50 range. And the price came closer and closer to $2.44 as students acquired more experience. In the last two experiments, the average prices were $2.418 and $2.434—within 2.2 percent of the predicted equilibrium. Apparently, the experiments do work, and so does the theory—as a reasonable *approximation* to reality.

*See C.R. Plott, "Externalities and Corrective Policies in Experimental Markets," *The Economic Journal*, vol. 93, March 1983, pages 106–127.

The concept of equilibrium in economics is similar and can be illustrated by our supply and demand example. Why is no price other than 70¢ an equilibrium price in Table 4–3 or Figure 4–3? What forces will change any other price?

Consider first a low price like 50¢, at which quantity demanded (70 billion) exceeds quantity supplied (40 billion). If the price were this low, many frustrated customers would be unable to purchase the quantities they desired. In their scramble for the available supply of milk, some would offer to pay more. As customers sought to outbid one another, the market price would be forced up. Thus a price below the equilibrium price cannot persist in a free market because a shortage sets in motion powerful economic forces that push price upward.

Similar forces operate if the market price is *above* the equilibrium price. If, for example, the price should somehow get to be $1, Table 4–3 tells us that quantity supplied (90 billion) would far exceed quantity demanded (45 billion). Producers would be unable to sell their desired quantities of milk at the prevailing price, and some would find it in their interest to undercut their competitors by reducing price. Such competitive price-cutting would continue as long as the surplus persisted, that is, as long as quantity supplied exceeded quantity demanded. Thus a price above the equilibrium price cannot persist indefinitely.

We are left with only one conclusion. The price 70¢ per quart and the quantity 60 billion quarts per year is the only price-quantity combination that does not sow the seeds of its own destruction. It is the only *equilibrium*. Any lower price must rise, and any higher price must fall. It is as if natural economic forces place a magnet at point *E* that attracts the market just like gravity attracts a pendulum.

The analogy to a pendulum is worth pursuing further. Most pendulums are more frequently in motion than at rest. However, unless they are repeatedly buffeted by outside forces (which, of course, is exactly what happens to pendulums used in clocks), pendulums gradually return to their resting points. The same is true of price and quantity in a free market. Markets are not always in equilibrium, but, if they are not interfered with, experience shows that they normally *move toward equilibrium*.

THE LAW OF SUPPLY AND DEMAND

In a free market, the forces of supply and demand generally push the price toward its equilibrium level, the price at which quantity supplied and quantity demanded are equal.

The **LAW OF SUPPLY AND DEMAND** states that, in a free market, the forces of supply and demand generally push the price toward the level at which quantity supplied and quantity demanded are equal.

Like most economic "laws," the **law of supply and demand** is occasionally disobeyed. Markets sometimes display shortages or surpluses for long periods of time. Prices sometimes fail to move toward equilibrium. But the "law" is a fair generalization that is right far more often than it is wrong.

The last interesting aspect of the pendulum analogy concerns the "outside forces" of which we have spoken. A pendulum that is blown by the wind or pushed by a hand does not remain in equilibrium. Similarly, many outside forces can disturb equilibrium in a market. In 1990–1991, the world oil market was disturbed by a war in the Persian Gulf. In 1992, Hurricane Andrew struck Florida and disturbed equilibrium in the market for oranges.

Often these outside influences *change the equilibrium price and quantity* by shifting either the supply curve or the demand curve. If you look again at Figure 4–3, you can see clearly that any event that causes *either* the demand curve *or* the supply curve to shift will also change the equilibrium price and quantity. Such events constitute the "other things" that were held constant in our definitions of supply and demand curves. We are now ready to analyze how these outside forces affect the equilibrium of supply and demand, beginning on the demand side.

SHIFTS OF THE DEMAND CURVE

Returning to our example of milk, we noted earlier that the quantity of milk demanded is influenced by a variety of things other than the price of milk. Changes in population, consumer income, and the prices of alternative beverages such as soda and orange juice presumably change the quantity of milk demanded even if the price of milk is unchanged.

Since the demand curve for milk depicts only the relationship between the quantity of milk demanded and the price of milk, holding all other factors constant, a change in any of these other factors produces a *shift of the entire demand curve*. More generally:

A change in the price of a good produces a **movement along a fixed demand curve**. By contrast, a change in any other variable that influences quantity demanded produces a **shift of the entire demand curve**. If consumers want to buy *more* at any given price than they wanted previously, the demand curve shifts to the right (or outward). If they desire *less* at any given price, the demand curve shifts to the left (or inward).

Figure 4–4 shows this distinction graphically. If the price of a quart of milk falls from 80¢ to 60¢ and quantity demanded rises accordingly, we move *along demand curve D_0D_0 from point C to point F*, as shown by the blue arrow. If, on the other hand, consumers suddenly decide that they like milk better than they did formerly, *the entire demand curve shifts outward from D_0D_0 to D_1D_1*, as indicated by the blue arrows. To make this general idea more concrete and to show some of its many applications, let us consider some specific examples.

1. *Consumer incomes*. If average incomes increase, consumers will purchase more of most foods, including milk, even if the price of milk remains the same. That is, *increases in income normally shift demand curves outward to the right*, as depicted in Figure 4–5(a). In this example, the quantity demanded at the old equilibrium price of 70¢ increases from 60 billion quarts per year (point E on demand curve D_0D_0) to 75 billion (point R on demand curve D_1D_1). We know that 70¢ is no longer the equilibrium price, since at this price quantity demanded (75 billion) exceeds quantity supplied (60 billion). To restore equilibrium, price will have to rise. The diagram shows the new equilibrium at point T, where the price is 80¢ per quart and both quantities demanded and supplied are 70 billion quarts per year. This illustrates a general result.

   Any factor that causes the demand curve to shift outward to the right, and does not affect the supply curve, will raise the equilibrium price and the equilibrium quantity.[4]

---

[4]This statement, like many others in the text, assumes that the demand curve is downward-sloping and the supply curve is upward-sloping.

| F i g u r e | 4-4 | **MOVEMENTS ALONG VERSUS SHIFTS OF A DEMAND CURVE** |

If quantity demanded increases because the price of a commodity falls, the market moves along a fixed demand curve such as D_0D_0 (see the movement from C to F). If, on the other hand, quantity demanded increases due to a change in one of its other determinants (such as consumer tastes or incomes), the entire demand curve shifts outward, as shown here by the shift from D_0D_0 to D_1D_1.

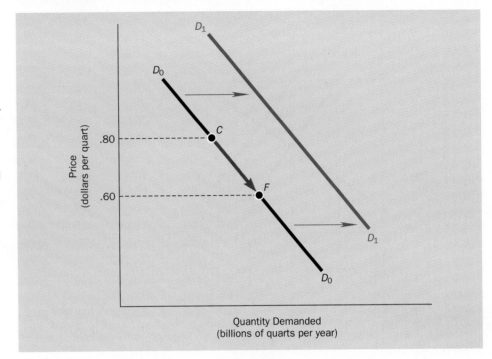

Everything works in reverse if consumer incomes fall. Figure 4–5(b) depicts a leftward (inward) shift of the demand curve that results from a decline in consumer incomes. For example, the quantity demanded at the previous equilibrium price (70¢) falls from 60 billion quarts (point E) to 45 billion (point L on demand curve D_2D_2). At the initial price, quantity supplied must begin to fall. The new equilibrium will eventually be established at point M, where the price is 60¢ and both quantity demanded and quantity supplied are 50 billion. In general:

Any factor that shifts the demand curve inward to the left, and does not affect the supply curve, will lower both the equilibrium price and the equilibrium quantity.

2. *Population.* Population growth affects quantity demanded in more or less the same way as increases in average incomes. A larger population will presumably wish to consume more milk, even if the price of milk and average incomes are unchanged, thus shifting the entire demand curve to the right as in Figure 4–5(a). The equilibrium price and quantity both rise. Similarly, a decrease in population should shift the demand curve for milk to the left, as in Figure 4–5(b), causing equilibrium price and quantity to fall.

3. *Consumer preferences.* If the dairy industry mounts a successful advertising campaign extolling the benefits of drinking milk, families may decide to raise their quantities demanded. This would shift the entire demand curve

Figure 4-5 THE EFFECTS OF SHIFTS OF THE DEMAND CURVE

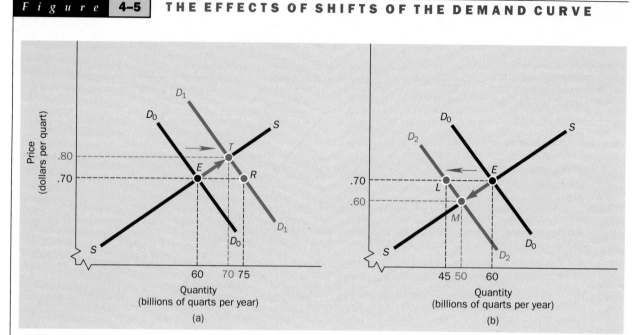

(a)

(b)

A shift of the demand curve will change the equilibrium price and quantity in a free market. In part (a), the demand curve shifts outward from D_0D_0 to D_1D_1. As a result, equilibrium moves from point E to point T; both price and quantity rise. In part (b), the demand curve shifts inward from D_0D_0 to D_2D_2, and equilibrium moves from point E to point M; both price and quantity fall.

for milk to the right, as in Figure 4–5(a). Alternatively, a medical report on the dangers of kidney stones may persuade consumers to drink less milk, thereby shifting the demand curve to the left, as in Figure 4–5(b). Again, these are general phenomena.

If consumer preferences shift in favor of a particular item, that item's demand curve will shift outward to the right, causing both equilibrium price and quantity to rise (Figure 4–5[a]). Conversely, if consumer preferences shift against a particular item, that item's demand curve will shift inward to the left, causing equilibrium price and quantity to fall (Figure 4–5[b]).

4. *Prices and availability of related goods.* Because soda, orange juice, and coffee are popular drinks that compete with milk, a change in the price of any of these beverages can be expected to shift the demand curve for milk. If any of these alternative drinks become cheaper, some consumers will switch away from milk. Thus the demand curve for milk will shift to the left, as in Figure 4–5(b). Other price changes shift the demand curve for milk in the opposite direction. For example, suppose that cookies, a commodity that goes well with milk, become less expensive. This may induce some consumers to drink more milk and thus shift the demand curve for milk to the right, as in Figure 4–5(a).

Increases in the prices of goods that are substitutes for the good in question (as soda is for milk) move the demand curve to the right, thus raising both the equilibrium price and quantity. Increases in the prices of goods that are normally used together with the good in question (such as cookies and milk) shift the demand curve to the left, thus lowering both the equilibrium price and quantity.

While the preceding list does not exhaust the possible influences on quantity demanded, enough has been said to indicate the principles involved. Let us therefore turn to a concrete example.

APPLICATION: WHY AIRLINES RUN SALES

Anyone who travels knows that airline companies reduce fares sharply to attract more customers at certain times of the year—particularly in winter (excluding the holiday period), when air traffic is light. There is no reason to think that air transportation gets cheaper in winter. Why, then, do airlines run such "sales"? A simple supply and demand diagram (see Figure 4–6) holds the answer.

Given the number of planes in airlines' fleets, the supply of seats is relatively fixed, as indicated by the steep supply curve SS in Figure 4–6, and is more or less the same in summer and winter. During seasons when people want to travel less, the demand curve for seats shifts leftward from its normal position, D_0D_0, to a position such as D_1D_1. Hence, equilibrium in the air-traffic market shifts from point E to point A. Thus both price and quantity decline at certain times of the year, not because flying gets cheaper or airlines get more generous, but because of the discipline of the market.

SHIFTS OF THE SUPPLY CURVE

Like quantity demanded, the quantity supplied on a market typically responds to a great number of influences other than price. The weather, the cost of feed,

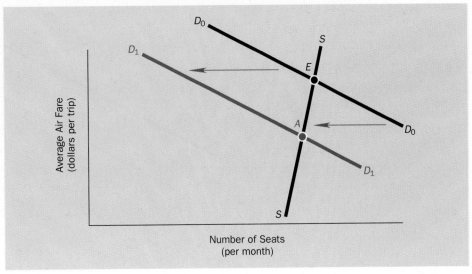

| *F i g u r e* | **4-6** | **SEASONAL CHANGES IN AIRLINE FARES** |

During seasons of slack demand for air travel, the demand curve shifts leftward from D_0D_0 to D_1D_1. In consequence, the market equilibrium point shifts from E to A, causing both price and quantity to decline.

y-axis: Average Air Fare (dollars per trip)

x-axis: Number of Seats (per month)

the number and size of dairy farms, and a variety of other factors all influence how much milk will be brought to market. Since the supply curve depicts only the relationship between the price of milk and the quantity of milk supplied, holding all other factors constant, a change in any of these other factors will cause the entire supply curve to shift. That is:

A change in the price of the good causes a **movement along a fixed supply curve**. But price is not the only influence on quantity supplied. And, if any of these other influences changes, the **entire supply curve shifts**.

Figure 4–7 once again depicts the distinction graphically. A rise in price from 60¢ to 80¢ will raise quantity supplied by *moving along supply curve* S_0S_0 from point f to point c. But any rise in quantity supplied attributable to a factor other than price will *shift the entire supply curve outward to the right* from S_0S_0 to S_1S_1, as shown by the blue arrows. Let us consider what some of these other factors are, and how they shift the supply curve.

1. *Size of the industry.* We begin with the most obvious factor. If more farmers enter the milk industry, the quantity supplied at any given price will increase. For example, if each farm provides 600,000 quarts of milk per year when the price is 70¢ per quart, then 100,000 farmers provide 60 billion quarts, but 130,000 farmers provide 78 billion. Thus, when more farms are in the industry, the quantity of milk supplied will be greater at any given price—and hence the supply curve will be farther to the right.

   Figure 4–8(a) illustrates the effect of an expansion of the industry from 100,000 farms to 130,000 farms—a rightward shift of the supply curve from S_0S_0 to S_1S_1. Notice that at the initial price of 70¢, the quantity supplied after

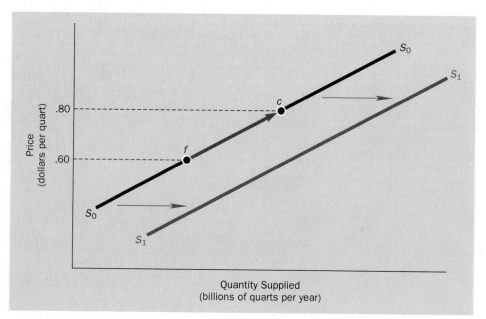

F i g u r e   4–7

MOVEMENTS ALONG VERSUS SHIFTS OF A SUPPLY CURVE

If quantity supplied rises because the price increases, we move along a fixed supply curve such as S_0S_0 (see the red arrow from point f to point c). If, on the other hand, quantity supplied rises because some other factor influencing supply improves, the entire supply curve shifts outward to the right from S_0S_0 to S_1S_1 (see the blue arrows).

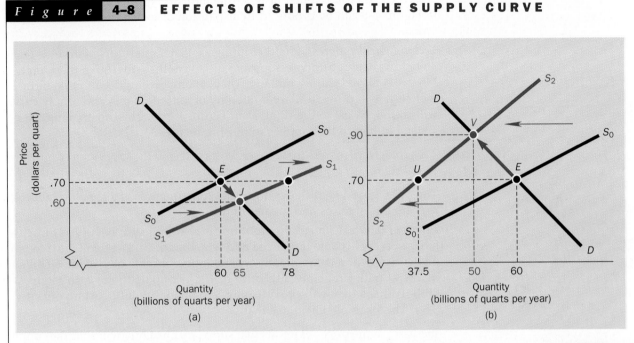

Figure **4–8** **EFFECTS OF SHIFTS OF THE SUPPLY CURVE**

A shift of the supply curve will change the equilibrium price and quantity in a market. In part (a), the supply curve shifts outward to the right, from S_0S_0 to S_1S_1. As a result, equilibrium moves from point E to point J; price falls as quantity increases. Part (b) illustrates the opposite case—an inward shift of the supply curve from S_0S_0 to S_2S_2. Equilibrium moves from point E to point V, which means that price rises as quantity falls.

the shift is 78 billion quarts (point I on supply curve S_1S_1), which exceeds the quantity demanded of 60 billion (point E on supply curve S_0S_0).

We can see in the graph that the price of 70¢ is too high to be the equilibrium price; so the price must fall. The diagram shows the new equilibrium at point J, where the price is 60¢ per quart and the quantity is 65 billion quarts per year. The general point is that:

Any factor that shifts the supply curve outward to the right, and does not affect the demand curve, will lower the equilibrium price and raise the equilibrium quantity.

This must *always* be true if the industry's demand curve has a negative slope, because the greater quantity supplied can be sold only if price is decreased to induce customers to buy more.[5]

Figure 4–8(b) illustrates the opposite case: a contraction of the industry from 100,000 farms to 62,500 farms. The supply curve shifts inward to the left and equilibrium moves from point E to point V, where price is 90¢ and quantity is 50 billion quarts per year. In general:

Any factor that shifts the supply curve inward to the left, and does not affect the demand curve, will raise the equilibrium price and reduce the equilibrium quantity.

[5]Graphically, whenever a positively sloped curve shifts to the right, its intersection point with a negatively sloping curve must always move lower. Just try drawing it yourself.

Even if no farmers enter or leave the industry, results like those depicted in Figure 4–8 can be produced by expansion or contraction of the existing farms.

2. *Technological progress*. Another influence that shifts supply curves is technological change. Suppose someone discovers that cows give more milk if Mozart is played during milking. Then, at any given price of milk, farmers will be able to provide a larger quantity of output; that is, the supply curve will shift outward to the right, as in Figure 4–8(a). This, again, illustrates a general influence that applies to most industries:

Technological progress that reduces costs will shift the supply curve outward to the right.

Thus, as Figure 4–8(a) shows, the usual consequences of technological progress are lower prices and greater output.

3. *Prices of inputs*. Changes in input prices also shift supply curves. Suppose farm workers become unionized and win a raise. Farmers will have to pay higher wages and consequently will no longer be able to provide 60 billion quarts of milk profitably at a price of 70¢ per quart (point E in Figure 4–8[b]). Perhaps they will provide only 37.5 billion (point U on supply curve S_2S_2). This example illustrates that:

Increases in the prices of inputs that suppliers must buy will shift the supply curve inward to the left.

4. *Prices of related outputs*. Dairy farms produce more than milk. If cheese prices rise sharply, farmers may decide to use some raw milk to make cheese, thereby reducing the quantity of milk supplied. On a supply-demand diagram, the supply curve would shift inward, as in Figure 4–8(b).

Similar phenomena occur in other industries, and sometimes the effect goes the other way. For example, suppose the price of beef goes up, which increases the quantity of meat supplied. That, in turn, will raise the number of cowhides supplied even without any change in price of leather. Thus, a rise in the price of beef will lead to a rightward shift in the supply curve of leather. In general:

A change in the price of one good produced by a multiproduct industry may be expected to shift the supply curves of all the other goods produced by that industry.

APPLICATION: A COMPUTER IN EVERY HOME?

Twenty years ago, no one owned a home computer. Now there are tens of millions of them, and enthusiasts look forward to the day when computers will be as commonplace as television sets. What brought the computer from the laboratory into the home? Did Americans suddenly develop a craving for computers?

Hardly. What actually happened is that scientists in the 1970s invented the microchip—a stunning technological breakthrough that sharply reduced both the size and cost of computers. Within a few years, microcomputers were in commercial production. And, as the technology continued to improve, the cost of computers fell and fell and fell. Today, $1500 will buy you more computing power than a multi-million dollar computer could deliver two decades ago—and the machine will play games, too!

| Figure | 4-9 | THE EFFECTS OF RAPID TECHNOLOGICAL CHANGE ON THE COMPUTER MARKET |

The invention of the microchip and other technological breakthroughs caused the supply curve of computers to shift outward to the right—moving from S_0S_0 to S_1S_1. Consequently, equilibrium shifted from point E to point A. The price of microcomputers fell from $10,000 to $1500, and the quantity increased from 100,000 to 3 million per year.

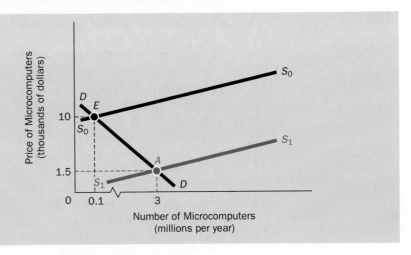

In terms of our supply and demand diagrams, the rapid technological improvement in computer manufacturing shifted the supply curve dramatically to the right. As Figure 4–9 shows, a large outward shift of the supply curve should lower the equilibrium price and raise the equilibrium quantity—which is just what happened to the computer industry. It was not the *demand curve* that shifted out, but the *supply curve*.

RESTRAINING THE MARKET MECHANISM: PRICE CEILINGS

As we have noted already, lawmakers and rulers have often been dissatisfied with the outcomes of free markets. From Rome to Pennsylvania and from biblical times to the space age, they have battled the invisible hand. Sometimes, rather than trying to make adjustments in the workings of the market, governments have sought to raise or lower the prices of specific commodities *by decree*. In many of these cases, those in authority felt that the prices set by the market mechanism were, in some sense, immorally low or immorally high. Penalties were therefore imposed on anyone offering the commodities in question at prices lower or higher than those determined by the authorities.

But the market has proven itself a formidable foe that strongly resists attempts to circumvent its workings. In case after case where legal **price ceilings** are imposed, virtually the same set of consequences ensues:

A **PRICE CEILING** is a legal maximum on the price that may be charged for a commodity.

1. A persistent shortage develops. Queuing, direct rationing, or any of a variety of other devices, usually inefficient and unpleasant, have to be substituted for the distribution process provided by the price mechanism. *Example*: Rampant shortages in Eastern Europe and the former Soviet Union helped precipitate the revolts that ended communism.

2. An illegal, or "black," market often arises to supply the commodity. There are usually some individuals who are willing to take the risks involved in

meeting unsatisfied demands illegally, if legal means will not do the job. *Example*: Although most states ban the practice, ticket "scalping" occurs at most popular sporting events and rock concerts.

3. The prices charged on illegal markets are almost certainly higher than those that would prevail in free markets. After all, lawbreakers expect some compensation for the risk of being caught and punished. *Example*: Goods that are smuggled illegally into a country are normally quite expensive.

4. In each case, a substantial portion of the price falls into the hands of the illicit supplier instead of going to those who produce the good or who perform the service. *Example*: A constant complaint in the series of hearings that marked the history of theater ticket price controls in New York City was that the "ice" (the illegal excess charge) fell into the hands of ticket scalpers rather than going to those who invested in, produced, or acted in the play.

5. Investment in the industry generally dries up. Because price ceilings reduce the potential returns that investors can earn, less capital will be invested in industries subject to price controls. Even fear of impending price controls can have this effect. *Example*: Tight limits on the prices that public utilities could charge for power led to underinvestment in power-generating stations in the late 1970s and early 1980s, and thus to power shortages in the 1980s.

These points and others are best illustrated by considering a concrete example of price ceilings.

A CASE STUDY: RENT CONTROLS IN NEW YORK CITY

New York is the only major city in the United States that has had rent controls continuously since World War II. The objective of rent control is, of course, to protect the consumer from high rents. But most economists believe that rent control does not help the cities or their inhabitants and that, in the long run, it makes almost everyone worse off. Elementary supply–demand analysis shows us what actually happens.

Figure 4–10 is a supply–demand diagram for rental units in New York. Curve *DD* is the demand curve and curve *SS* is the supply curve. Without controls, equilibrium would be at point *E*, where rents average $1200 per month and 3 million units are occupied. If rent controls are effective, they must set a ceiling price *below* the equilibrium price of $1200. But with a low rent ceiling, such as $800, the quantity of housing demanded will be 3.5 million (point *B*) while the quantity supplied will be only 2.5 million (point *C*).

The diagram shows a shortage of 1,000,000 apartments. This theoretical concept of a "shortage" manifests itself in New York City as an abnormally low vacancy rate—typically about half the national urban average.

As we expect, rent controls have spawned a lively black market in New York. The black market raises the effective price of rent-controlled apartments in many ways, including bribes, "key money" paid to move up on the waiting list, and requiring prospective tenants to purchase worthless furniture at inflated prices.

According to the diagram, rent controls reduce the quantity supplied from 3 million to 2.5 million apartments. How does this show up in New York? First, some property owners, discouraged by the low rents, have converted apartment buildings into office space or other uses. Second, some apartments have been inadequately maintained. After all, rent controls create a shortage which makes

| Figure | 4–10 | SUPPLY–DEMAND DIAGRAM FOR RENTAL HOUSING |

When market forces are permitted to set rents, the quantity of dwellings supplied will equal the quantity demanded. But when a rent ceiling forces rent below the market level, the number of dwellings supplied (point *C*) will be less than the number demanded (point *B*). Thus, rent ceilings induce housing shortages.

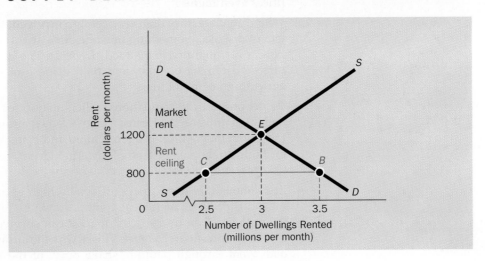

even dilapidated apartments easy to rent. Third, some landlords have actually abandoned their buildings rather than pay rising tax and fuel bills. These abandoned buildings rapidly become eyesores and eventually pose threats to public health and safety.

With all these problems, why do rent controls persist in New York City? And why are some other cities moving in the same direction? Part of the explanation is that most people simply do not understand the problems that rent controls create. Another part is that landlords are unpopular politically. But a third, and important, part of the explanation is that not everyone is hurt by rent controls. Those who benefit from controls fight hard to preserve them. In New York, for example, many tenants pay rents that are only a fraction of what their apartments would fetch on the open market. They are, naturally enough, quite happy with this situation. This last point illustrates another very general phenomenon:

Virtually every price ceiling or floor creates a class of people with a vested interest in preserving the regulations because they benefit from them. These people naturally use their political influence to protect their gains, which is one reason why it is so hard to eliminate price ceilings or floors.

RESTRAINING THE MARKET MECHANISM: PRICE FLOORS

A **PRICE FLOOR** is a legal minimum on the price that may be charged for a commodity.

Interferences with the market mechanism are not always designed to keep prices *low*. Agricultural price supports and minimum wages are two notable examples in which the law keeps prices *above* free-market levels. **Price floors** are typically accompanied by a standard set of symptoms:

1. A surplus develops as sellers cannot find enough buyers. *Example*: Surpluses of various argicultural products have been a persistent—and costly—problem for the U.S. government. The problem is even more severe in the Euro-

pean Community, where the so-called common agricultural policy holds prices even higher.

2. Where goods, rather than services, are involved, the surplus creates a problem of disposal. Something must be done about the excess of quantity supplied over quantity demanded. *Example*: The government has often been forced to purchase, store, and then dispose of large amounts of surplus agricultural commodities.

3. To get around the regulations, sellers may offer discounts in disguised—and often unwanted—forms. *Example*: When airline fares were regulated by the government, airlines offered more and better food and stylish uniforms for flight attendants instead of lowering fares. Today, the food is worse but tickets cost much less.

4. Regulations that keep prices artificially high encourage overinvestment in the industry. Even inefficient businesses whose high operating costs would doom them in an unrestricted market can survive beneath the shelter of a generous price floor. *Example*: This is why the airline and trucking industries both went through painful "shake outs" of the weaker companies in the 1980s.

Once again, a specific example is useful.

A CASE STUDY: MILK PRICE SUPPORTS

America's extensive program of farm price supports began in 1933 as "a temporary method of dealing with an emergency"—farmers were going broke in droves. It is with us still today, even though the farm population of the United States is less than a sixth of what it was then.

One of the more absurd legacies of that "temporary emergency" is a maze of milk-marketing orders covering the pricing and distribution of milk in 44 milk-producing regions of the country. By setting the prices of milk, butter, and cheese as high as three times those on world markets, the government ensures that America will suffer from chronic overproduction—as Figure 4–11 shows.

In the diagram, the equilibrium price for milk is 70¢ per quart, but we assume that the government sets a *price floor* at 90¢. At this high price, farmers produce 80 billion quarts per year—20 billion above the equilibrium quantity. But consumers want to purchase only 50 billion—10 billion below the equilibrium quantity. The result is a huge *surplus* of milk—30 billion quarts per year in the example.

In a market economy like ours, Congress cannot simply set prices by decree; it must do something to enforce the price floor. Normally, that "something" is buying up the surplus, that is, adding 30 billion quarts per year in *government demand* to the private demand shown in Figure 4–11.[6] That, of course, requires a lot of the taxpayers' money. In addition, all the surplus milk must be stored somewhere—usually as cheese, for milk does not keep well. That creates another bill for the taxpayer to pick up. But there is more. We pay again as consumers in the form of higher prices for milk—90¢ rather than 70¢ in the example. According to current estimates, milk price supports cost American taxpayers and consumers together about $10–$12 billion a year.

---

[6]Draw a new demand curve into Figure 4–11 which includes this government demand. It must be parallel to DD but 30 billion quarts farther to the right. If you draw it accurately, it will pass exactly through point *B*.

F i g u r e **4–11** **ANALYSIS OF MILK PRICE SUPPORTS**

In this diagram, which repeats the supply and demand curves from Figure 4–3, the support price for milk (90¢ per quart) exceeds the equilibrium price (which is 70¢). Quantity supplied at the support price is 80 billion quarts per year (point *B*) while quantity demanded is only 50 billion (point *A*). To keep the price at 90¢, the government must buy up the 30-billion-quart surplus each year.

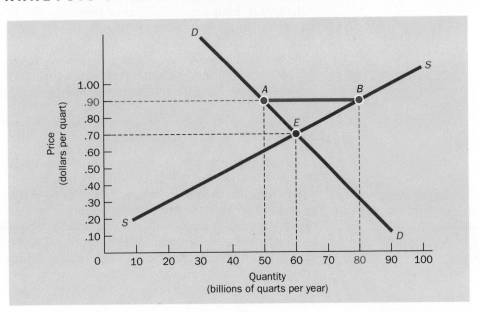

Sometimes the government tires of all this and tries something else. For example, in 1986 it offered to pay dairy farmers to slaughter 1.6 million cows. The result? An uproar from beef raisers as meat prices collapsed.[7] As we said earlier, those who would flaunt the will of the market had better be prepared for unforeseen consequences.

A CAN OF WORMS

Our two case studies—rent controls and milk price supports—illustrate some of the major side effects of price floors and ceilings, but barely hint at others. There are difficulties that we have not even mentioned, for the market mechanism is a tough bird that imposes suitable retribution on those who seek to circumvent it by legislative decree. Here is a partial list of other problems that may arise when prices are controlled.

FAVORITISM AND CORRUPTION

When price ceilings or floors create shortages or surpluses, someone must decide who gets to buy or sell the limited quantity that is available. This can lead to discrimination along racial or religious lines, political favoritism, or corruption in government. For example, it has been argued that the high U.S. support price for sugar has led to widespread corruption in Caribbean nations, as foreign producers vie for the valuable right to export sugar cane to the United States.

[7]See Review Question **8** at the end of the chapter.

UNENFORCEABILITY

Attempts to limit prices are almost certain to fail in industries with numerous suppliers, simply because the regulating agency must monitor the behavior of so many sellers. Ways will be found to evade or violate the law, and something akin to the free-market price will generally reemerge. But there is an important difference: since the evasion mechanism, whatever its form, will have some operating costs, those costs must be borne by someone. Normally, that someone is the consumer.

AUXILIARY RESTRICTIONS

Fears that a system of price controls will break down invariably lead to regulations designed to shore up the shaky edifice. Consumers may be told when and from whom they are permitted to buy. The powers of the police and the courts may be used to prevent the entry of new suppliers. Occasionally, an intricate system of market subdivision is imposed, giving each class of firms a protected sphere in which others are not permitted to operate. Laws banning conversion of rent-controlled apartments to condominiums are one example. Milk-marketing orders are another. A few years ago, milk cost so much less in New Jersey than in New York that people were actually smuggling milk into New York State!

LIMITATION OF VOLUME OF TRANSACTIONS

To the extent that controls succeed in affecting prices, they can be expected to reduce the volume of transactions. Curiously, this is true regardless of whether the regulated price is *above* or *below* the free-market equilibrium price. If it is set above the equilibrium price, quantity demanded will be below the equilibrium quantity. On the other hand, if the imposed price is set below the free-market level, quantity supplied will be cut down. Since sales volume cannot exceed either the quantity supplied or the quantity demanded, a reduction in the volume of transactions is the result.[8]

MISALLOCATION OF RESOURCES

Departures from free-market prices are likely to produce misuse of the economy's resources because the connection between production costs and prices is broken. For example, Russian farmers used to feed their farm animals bread, instead of unprocessed grains, because price ceilings kept the price of bread ludicrously low. In addition, just as more complex locks lead to more sophisticated burglary tools, more complex regulations lead to the use of yet more resources for their avoidance. New jobs are created for executives, lawyers, and economists. It may well be conjectured that at least some of these expensive professionals could be put to better use elsewhere.

Economists put it this way. Free markets are capable of dealing with the three basic coordination tasks outlined in Chapter 3: deciding *what* to produce, *how* to produce it, and *to whom* the goods should be distributed. Price controls throw a monkey wrench into the market mechanism. Though the market is surely not flawless, and government interferences often have praiseworthy goals, good intentions are not enough. Any government that sets out to repair what it sees as a

---

[8]See Review Question **9** at the end of the chapter.

Economic Aspects of the War on Drugs

POLICY

DEBATE

For years now, the U.S. government has engaged in a highly publicized "war on drugs." At part of this effort, billions of dollars have been spent on trying to stop illegal drugs at the border. In some sense, interdiction has succeeded: literally tons of cocaine and other drugs have been seized by federal agents. Yet all these efforts have made barely a dent in the flow of drugs to America's city streets. Simple economic reasoning explains why.

When drug interdiction works, it shifts the supply curve of drugs to the left, thereby driving up street prices. But that, in turn, raises the rewards for potential smugglers and attracts more criminals into the "industry," which shifts the supply curve back to the right. The net result is that increased shipments of drugs to our shores replace much of what the authorities confiscate. This is why many economists believe that any successful anti-drug program must

concentrate on reducing *demand*, which would lower the street price of drugs, not on reducing *supply*, which can only raise it.

Some economists—and some noneconomists as well—would go even further and advocate *legalization* of many drugs. While this remains a highly controversial position which few are ready to endorse, the reasoning behind it is straightforward. A stunningly high fraction of all the violent crimes committed in America—especially robberies and murders—are drug-related. One major reason is that street prices of drugs are so high that addicts must steal to get the money and drug traffickers are all too willing to kill to protect their highly profitable "businesses."

How would things differ if drugs were legal? Since Colombian farmers earn pennies for drugs that sell for hundreds of dollars on the streets of Los Angeles and New York, we may safely assume that drugs would be vastly cheaper under legalization. And that, proponents point out, would reduce drug-related crimes dramatically. When, for example, was the last time you heard of a gang killing connected with the distribution of cigarettes or alcoholic beverages?

The argument against legaliza-

tion of drugs is largely moral: Should the state sanction potential lethal substances? But there is also an economic aspect. The vastly lower street prices of drugs that would surely follow legalization would increase drug use. Thus, while legalization would almost certainly reduce crime, it would also produce more addicts. The key question here—to which no one has a good answer—is: How many more addicts? If you think the increase in quantity demanded would be large, you are unlikely to find legalization an attractive option.

defect in the market mechanism must take care lest it cause even more serious damage elsewhere. As a prominent economist once quipped, societies that are too willing to interfere with the operation of free markets soon find that the invisible hand is nowhere to be seen—a point that the formerly communist nations grew to understand in a very painful way.

A SIMPLE BUT POWERFUL LESSON

The lessons you have learned in this chapter may seem elementary, even obvious. In many respects, they are. But they are also very important, indeed, indispensable. Although the law of supply and demand is one of the simplest principles in economics, it is also one of the most powerful. Astonishing as it may seem, many people in authority, even highly intelligent people, fail to understand the law of supply and demand or cannot apply it to concrete situations.

For example, a few years ago the *New York Times* carried a dramatic front page picture of the president of Kenya setting fire to a large pile of elephant tusks that had been confiscated from poachers. The accompanying story explained that the burning was intended as a symbolic act to persuade the world to halt the ivory trade.[9] Economists claim no expertise on the likely psychological effect of burning elephant tusks, though one may doubt that it touched the hearts of criminal poachers. However, one economic effect was clear. By reducing the supply of ivory on the world market, the burning of tusks forced up the price of ivory, which raised the illicit rewards reaped by those who slaughter elephants. That could only encourage more poaching—precisely the opposite of what the Kenyan government sought to accomplish.

---

[9]The *New York Times*, July 19, 1989.

Summary

1. The quantity of a product that is demanded is not a fixed number. Rather, **quantity demanded** depends on such factors as the price of the product, consumer incomes, and the prices of other products.

2. The relationship between quantity demanded and price, holding all other things constant, can be displayed graphically on a **demand curve**.

3. For most products, the higher the price, the lower the quantity demanded. So the demand curve usually has a negative slope.

4. The quantity of a product that is supplied also depends on its price and many other influences. A **supply curve** is a graphical representation of the relationship between **quantity supplied** and price, holding all other influences constant.

5. For most products, the supply curve has a positive slope, meaning that higher prices call forth greater quantities supplied.

6. A market is said to be in **equilibrium** when quantity supplied is equal to quantity demanded. The equilibrium price and quantity are shown by the point on a graph where the supply and demand curves intersect. The **law of supply and demand** states that price and

quantity tend to gravitate to this point in a free market.

7. A change in quantity demanded that is caused by a change in the price of the good is represented by a **movement along a fixed demand curve**. A change in quantity demanded that is caused by a change in any other determinant of quantity demanded is represented by a **shift of the demand curve**.

8. This same distinction applies to the supply curve: Changes in price lead to **movements along a fixed supply curve**; changes in other determinants of quantity supplied lead to **shifts of the whole supply curve**.

9. Changes in consumer incomes, tastes, technology, prices of competing products, and many other influences cause shifts in either the demand curve or the supply curve and produce changes in price and quantity that can be determined from **supply–demand diagrams**.

10. An attempt by government regulations to force prices above or below their equilibrium levels is likely to lead to **shortages** or **surpluses**, black markets in which goods are sold at illegal prices, and to a variety of other problems. This is one of the **12 Ideas for Beyond the Final Exam.**

Quantity demanded
Demand schedule
Demand curve
Quantity supplied
Supply schedule
Supply curve

Supply–demand diagram
Shortage
Surplus
Equilibrium price and quantity
Equilibrium
Law of supply and demand

Shifts in vs. movements along supply
    and demand curves
Price ceiling
Price floor

1. How often do you go to the movies? Would you go more often if a ticket cost half as much? Distinguish between your demand curve for movie tickets and your "quantity demanded" at the current price.

2. What would you expect to be the shape of a demand curve

    a. for a medicine that means life or death for a patient?
    b. for gasoline at an intersection with four gas stations?

3. The following are the assumed supply and demand schedules for footballs in Anytown, USA:

DEMAND SCHEDULE		SUPPLY SCHEDULE	
PRICE	QUANTITY DEMANDED (per year)	PRICE	QUANTITY SUPPLIED (per year)
$13	6,000	$13	71,000
11	13,000	11	63,000
9	29,000	9	29,000
7	50,000	7	11,000
5	61,000	5	0

    a. Plot the supply and demand curves and indicate the equilibrium price and quantity.
    b. What effect will an increase in the price of leather (a factor of production) have on the equilibrium price and quantity of footballs, assuming all other things remain constant? Explain your answer with the help of a diagram.
    c. What effect will a decrease in the price of soccer balls (a substitute commodity) have on the equilibrium price and quantity of footballs, assuming again that all other things are held constant? Use a diagram in your answer.

4. Suppose the supply and demand schedules for Japanese cars in the United States are as follows:

PRICE (thousands)	QUANTITY DEMANDED (millions per year)	QUANTITY SUPPLIED (millions per year)
$8	2.75	1.25
$10	2.50	1.50
$12	2.25	1.75
$14	2.00	2.00
$16	1.75	2.25
$18	1.50	2.50
$20	1.25	2.75

    a. Graph these curves and show the equilibrium price and quantity.
    b. Now suppose that a rise in anti-Japanese sentiment in the U.S. reduces the quantity demanded at each price by 500,000 (0.5 million) cars per year. What is the new equilibrium price and quantity? Show this solution graphically. Explain why the quantity falls by less than 500,000 cars per year.
    c. Suppose *instead* that anti-American sentiment in Japan induces the Japanese to reduce their shipments to the U.S. by 500,000 cars per year (at each price). Find the new equilibrium price and quantity, and show it graphically. Explain again why quantity falls by less than 500,000.
    d. What are the equilibrium price and quantity if the shifts described in parts (b) and (c) happen at the same time?

5. The table below summarizes information about the market for principles of economics textbooks:

PRICE	QUANTITY DEMANDED (per year)	QUANTITY SUPPLIED (per year)
$20	2000	0
30	1000	200
40	500	500
50	250	900
60	125	1400

a. What is the market equilibrium price and quantity of textbooks?

b. In order to quell outrage over tuition increases, the college places a $30 limit on the price of textbooks. How many textbooks will be sold now?

c. While the price limit is still in effect, automated publishing increases the efficiency of textbook production. Show graphically the likely effect of this innovation on the market price and quantity.

6. Show how the following demand curves are likely to shift in response to the indicated changes:

a. The effect on the demand curve for snow shovels when a heavy snow falls.

b. The effect on the demand curve for nachos when the price of potato chips declines.

c. The effect on the demand curve for butter when bread prices fall.

7. Discuss the likely effects of

a. rent ceilings on the supply of apartments.

b. minimum wages on the employment of unskilled labor.

Use supply–demand diagrams to show what may happen in each case.

8. On page 95, it is asserted that reducing milk surpluses by slaughtering cows would lower the price of meat. Use two diagrams, one for the milk market and one for the meat market, to illustrate this. (Assume that meat is sold in an unregulated market.)

9. On page 96, it is claimed that either price floors or price ceilings reduce the actual quantity exchanged in a market. Use a diagram or diagrams to support this conclusion, and explain the common sense behind it.

10. The same rightward shift of the demand curve may produce a very small or a very large increase in quantity, depending on the slope of the supply curve. Explain with diagrams.

11. In 1981, when regulations were holding the price of natural gas below its free-market level, then-Congressman Jack Kemp of New York said the following in an interview with the *New York Times*: "We need to decontrol natural gas, and get production of natural gas up to a higher level so we can bring down the price."[10] Evaluate the congressman's statement.

12. From 1979 to 1989 in the United States, the number of working men grew 12% while the number of working women grew 29%. During this time, average wages for men fell slightly while average wages for women rose about 7%. Which of the following two explanations seems most consistent with the data?

a. Women decided to work more, raising their relative supply (relative to men).

b. Discrimination against women declined, raising the relative (to men) demand for female workers.

13. The two diagrams below show supply and demand curves for two substitute commodities: tapes and compact disks (CDs).

a. On the left-hand diagram, show what happens when technological progress makes it cheaper to produce CDs.

b. On the right-hand diagram, show what happens to the market for tapes.

14. (More difficult) Consider the market for milk discussed in this chapter (Tables 4–1 through 4–3 and Figures 4–1 through 4–3). Suppose the government decides to fight kidney stones by levying a tax of 30¢ per quart on sales of milk. Follow these steps to analyze the effects of the tax:

---

[10]The *New York Times*, December 23, 1981.

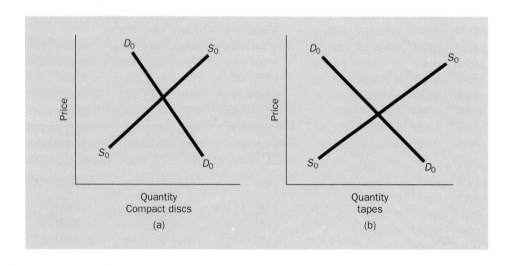

Compact discs

(a)

Quantity
tapes

(b)

a. Construct the new supply curve (to replace Table 4–2) that relates quantity supplied to the price consumers pay. (*Hint*: Before the tax, when consumers paid 70¢, farmers supplied 60 billion quarts. With a 30¢ tax, when consumers pay 70¢ farmers will receive only 40¢. Table 4–2 tells us they will provide only 30 billion quarts at this price. This is one point on the new supply curve. The rest of the curve can be constructed in the same way.)

b. Graph the new supply curve constructed in part (a) on the supply–demand diagram depicted in Figure 4–3. What are the new equilibrium price and quantity?

c. Does the tax succeed in its goal of reducing the consumption of milk?

d. How much does the equilibrium price increase? Is the price rise greater than, equal to, or less than the 30¢ tax?

e. Who actually pays the tax, consumers or producers? (This may be a good question to discuss in class.)

15. (More difficult) The demand and supply curves for hoagies in Collegetown are given by the following two equations:

$$Q = 8,000 - 500P \qquad Q = 2,000 + 1000P,$$

where P is measured in dollars and Q is the number of hoagies per month.

a. Find the equilibrium price and quantity algebraically.

b. If Collegetowners decide they do not really like hoagies that much, which of the following might be the new demand curve?

$$Q = 6,500 - 500P \qquad Q = 9,500 - 500P$$

Find the equilibrium price and quantity after the shift of the demand curve.

c. If, *instead*, two new stores that sell hoagies open up in town, which of the following might be the new supply curve?

$$Q = 1,250 + 1000P \qquad Q = 2,750 + 1000P$$

Find the equilibrium price and quantity after the shift of the supply curve.

PART II

The Macro-

Economy:

Aggregate

Supply and

Demand

Chapter 5

THE REALM OF MACROECONOMICS

Where the telescope ends, the microscope begins. Which of the two has the grander view?

VICTOR HUGO

Economics traditionally has been divided into two fields: **microeconomics** and **macroeconomics**. These inelegant words are derived from the Greek, where "micro" means something small and "macro" means something large. This chapter introduces you to macroeconomics. ¶ We begin the chapter by exploring the dividing line between microeconomics and macroeconomics: How do the two branches of the discipline differ and why? Next, we stress that while the *questions* studied by macroeconomists differ from those addressed by microeconomists, the underlying *tools* each group uses are almost the same. Supply and demand provide the basic organizing framework for constructing macroeconomic models, just as they do for microeconomic models. Third, we define some important macroeconomic concepts, such as recession, inflation, and gross domestic product. Fourth, we look briefly at the broad sweep of American economic history to get some idea of the prevalence and seriousness of the macroeconomic problems of recession and inflation. And, finally, we preview what is to come in subsequent chapters by introducing the notion of government management of the economy.

DRAWING A LINE BETWEEN MACROECONOMICS AND MICROECONOMICS

In microeconomics *we study the behavior of individual decision-making units*. The chicken farmers and other businesses discussed in our book, *Microeconomics*, are all individual decision-making units; so are the consumers who purchase chicken and other commodities. How do they decide what courses of action are in their own best interests? How are these millions of decisions coordinated by the market mechanism, and with what consequences? Questions like these are the substance of microeconomics.

Although Plato and Aristotle might wince at the abuse of their language, microeconomics applies to the decisions of some astonishingly large units. Exxon and the American Telephone and Telegraph Company, for instance, have annual sales that exceed the total production of many nations. Yet someone who studies the pricing policies of AT&T is a microeconomist, whereas someone who studies inflation in Trinidad–Tobago is a macroeconomist. So the micro versus macro distinction in economics is certainly not based solely on size. What, then, is the basis for this time-honored distinction? Whereas microeconomics focuses on the decisions of individual units (no matter how large), *macroeconomics concentrates on the behavior of entire economies* (no matter how small). Rather than looking at the price and output decisions of a single company, macroeconomists study the overall price level, unemployment rate, and other things that we call *economic aggregates*.

AGGREGATION AND MACROECONOMICS

An "economic aggregate" is nothing but an *abstraction* that people find convenient in describing some salient feature of economic life. For example, while we observe the prices of butter, telephone calls, and movie tickets every day, we never observe "the price level." Yet many people (not just economists) find it both meaningful and natural to speak of "the cost of living"—so natural, in fact, that the government's monthly attempts at measuring it are widely publicized by the news media.

Among the most important of these abstract notions is the concept of *domestic product*, which represents the total production of a nation's economy. The process by which real objects like hairpins, baseballs, and theater tickets get combined into an abstraction called total domestic product is called **aggregation**, and it is one of the foundations of macroeconomics. We can illustrate it by a simple example.

AGGREGATION means combining many individual markets into one overall market.

Imagine a nation called Agraria, whose economy is far simpler than the U.S. economy: Business firms in Agraria produce nothing but foodstuffs to sell to consumers. Rather than deal separately with all the markets for pizzas, candy bars, hamburgers, and so on, macroeconomists group them all into a single abstract "market for output." Thus, when macroeconomists in Agraria announce that output in Agraria rose 10 percent this year, are they referring to more potatoes or hot dogs, more soybeans or green peppers? The answer is: They do not care. In the aggregate measures of macroeconomics, output is output, no matter what form it takes.

Amalgamating many markets into one means that distinctions among different products are ignored. Can we really believe that no one cares whether the national output of Agraria consists of $800,000 worth of pickles and $200,000 worth of ravioli rather than $500,000 each of lettuce and tomatoes? Surely this is too much to swallow! Macroeconomists certainly do not believe that no one cares; instead, they rest the case for aggregation on two foundations.

1. While the *composition* of demand and supply in the various markets may be terribly interesting and important for *some* purposes (such as how income is distributed and what kinds of diets the citizens enjoy or endure), it may be of little consequence for the economy-wide issues of inflation and unemployment—the issues that concern macroeconomists.

2. During economic fluctuations, markets tend to move in unison. When demand in the economy rises, there is more demand for potatoes *and* tomatoes, more demand for artichokes *and* pickles, more demand for ravioli *and* hot dogs.

Though there are exceptions to these two principles, both seem serviceable enough as approximations. In fact, if they were not, there would be no discipline called macroeconomics, and this book would be only half as long as it is. Lest this cause you a twinge of regret, bear in mind that many people feel that unemployment and inflation would be far more difficult to control without macroeconomics—which would be even more regrettable.

THE LINE OF DEMARCATION REVISITED

These two principles—that markets normally move together and that the composition of demand and supply may be unimportant for some purposes—enable us to draw a different kind of dividing line between the territories of microeconomics and macroeconomics.

In macroeconomics, we typically assume that most details of resource allocation and income distribution are of secondary importance to the study of the overall rates of inflation and unemployment.

In microeconomics, we typically ignore inflation and unemployment and focus instead on how individual markets allocate resources and distribute income.

To use a well-worn metaphor, the macroeconomist analyzes the determination of the size of the economic "pie," paying scant attention to what is inside it or to how it gets divided among the dinner guests. A microeconomist, on the other hand, assumes that the pie is of the right size and shape, and frets over its ingredients and its division. If you have ever baked or eaten a pie, you will realize that either approach alone is a trifle myopic.

In some chapters of *Macroeconomics* (especially in Parts 2 and 3), macroeconomic issues are discussed as if they could be divorced from questions of resource allocation and income distribution. In *Microeconomics* (especially those in Parts 2 through 5), microeconomic problems are investigated with scarcely a word about overall inflation and unemployment. Only in certain sections of *Macroeconomics* (especially Parts 4 and 5) are the two modes of analysis brought to bear simultaneously on the same social problems. This is done solely for the sake of pedagogical clarity. In reality, the crucial interconnection between macroeconomics and microeconomics is with us all the time. There is, after all, only one economy.

SUPPLY AND DEMAND IN MACROECONOMICS

Some students reading this book will be taking a course that concentrates on macroeconomics while others will be studying microeconomics. The discussion of supply and demand in Chapter 4 serves as an invaluable introduction to both fields because the basic apparatus of supply and demand is just as fundamental to macroeconomics as it is to microeconomics.

Figure 5–1 shows two diagrams that should look familiar from Chapter 4. In Figure 5–1(a), there is a downward-sloping demand curve, labeled *DD*, and an upward-sloping supply curve, labeled *SS*. The axes labeled "Price" and "Quantity" do not specify what commodity they refer to because this is a multipurpose diagram. To start on familiar terrain, first imagine that this is a picture of the market for milk, so the price axis measures the price of milk while the quantity axis measures the quantity of milk demanded and supplied. As we know, if there are no interferences with the operation of a free market, equilibrium will be at point *E* with a price P_0 and a quantity of output Q_0.

Next, suppose something happens to shift the demand curve outward. For example, we learned in Chapter 4 that an increase in consumer incomes might have this effect. Figure 5–1(b) shows this shift as a rightward movement of the demand curve from D_0D_0 to D_1D_1. Equilibrium shifts from *E* to *A*, so both price and output rise.

| Figure | 5-1 | TWO INTERPRETATIONS OF A SHIFT IN THE DEMAND CURVE |

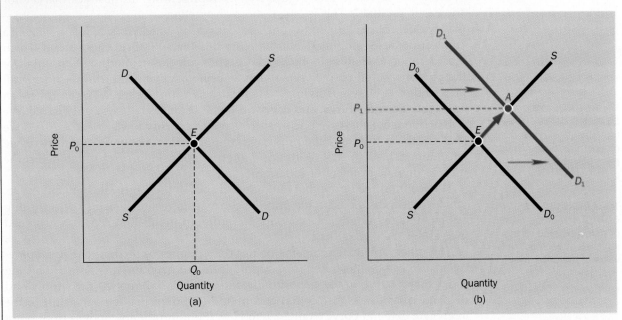

Part (a) shows an equilibrium at point *E*, where demand curve *DD* intersects supply curve *SS*. Part (b) shows how this equilibrium moves from point *E* to point *A* if the demand curve moves outward. If this graph represents the market for milk, as it did in Chapter 4, then it shows an increase in the price of milk. But if the graph represents the aggregate market for "domestic product," then it shows inflation—a rise in the general price level.

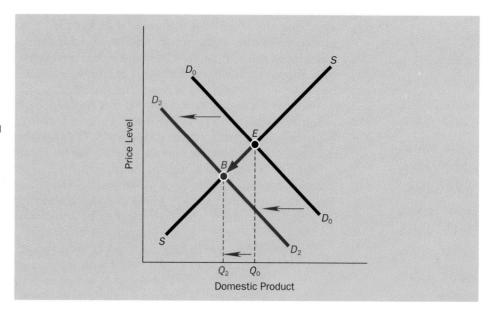

AN ECONOMY SLIPPING INTO A RECESSION

In this aggregate supply–demand diagram, there is an initial equilibrium at point E, where demand curve D_0D_0 intersects supply curve SS. When the demand curve shifts inward from D_0D_0 to D_2D_2, equilibrium moves to point B, and output falls from Q_0 to Q_2.

The **AGGREGATE DEMAND CURVE** shows the quantity of domestic product that is demanded at each possible value of the price level.

The **AGGREGATE SUPPLY CURVE** shows the quantity of **domestic** product that is supplied at each possible value of the price level.

INFLATION refers to a sustained increase in the general price level.

A **RECESSION** is a period of time during which the total output of the economy declines.

Now let us reinterpret Figure 5–1 as representing an abstract market for "domestic product." This is one of those abstractions—an economic aggregate—that we described earlier. No one has ever seen, touched, smelled, or eaten a "unit of domestic product," but these are the kinds of abstractions upon which macroeconomic analysis is built. Consistent with this reinterpretation, think of the price measured on the vertical axis as being another abstraction—the overall price index, or "cost of living."[1] Then curve DD in Figure 5–1(a) is called an **aggregate demand curve**, and curve SS is called an **aggregate supply curve**. We will derive these curves explicitly from economic theory in Chapters 7–10. As we shall see there, they are rather different from the microeconomic counterparts we encountered in Chapter 4. With this reinterpretation, Figure 5–1(b) can depict the macroeconomic problem of **inflation**.

We see from the figure that the outward shift of the aggregate demand curve, whatever its cause, pushes the price level up. If aggregate demand keeps shifting out month after month, the economy will suffer from inflation, that is, a sustained increase in the general price level.

The other principal problems of macroeconomics, recession and unemployment, also can be illustrated on a supply–demand diagram, this time by shifting the demand curve in the opposite direction. Figure 5–2 repeats the supply and demand curves of Figure 5–1(a) and in addition depicts a leftward shift of the aggregate demand curve from D_0D_0 to D_2D_2. Equilibrium now moves from point E to point B so that domestic product (total output) declines. This is what we normally mean by a **recession**.

---

[1]The appendix to Chapter 6 explains how such price indexes are calculated.

GROSS DOMESTIC PRODUCT

GROSS DOMESTIC PRODUCT (GDP) is the sum of the money values of all final goods and services produced in the domestic economy during a specified period of time, usually one year.

The economy's total output, we have just seen, is one of the major variables of concern to macroeconomists. While there are several ways to measure it, the most popular choice undoubtedly is the **gross domestic product**, a term you have probably encountered in the news media. The gross domestic product, or "GDP" for short, is the most comprehensive measure of the output of all the factories, offices, and shops in the U.S. economy. Specifically, it is the sum of the money values of all final goods and services produced *in the domestic economy* within the year.

Several features of this definition need to be underscored.[2] First, you will notice that:

We add up the *money values* of things.

The GDP consists of a bewildering variety of goods and services: mousetraps and computers, tanks and textbooks, ballet performances and rock concerts. How are we to combine all of these into a single number? To an economist, the natural way to do this is first to convert every good and service into *money* terms. If we want to add 10 apples and 20 oranges, we first ask: How much *money* does each cost? If apples cost 20¢ and oranges cost 25¢, then the apples count for $2 and the oranges for $5, so the sum is $7 worth of "output." The market *price* of each good or service is used as an indicator of its *value* to society for a simple reason: *someone* is willing to pay that much money for it.

This decision raises the question of what prices to use in valuing the different outputs. The official data offer two choices. First, we can value each good and service at the price at which it was actually sold during the year. If we do this, the resulting measure is called **nominal GDP**, or *money GDP*, or *GDP in current dollars*. This seems like a perfectly sensible choice. But as a measure of output, it has one serious drawback: nominal GDP rises when prices rise, even if there is no increase in actual production. For example, if hamburgers cost $2.00 this year but cost only $1.50 last year, then 100 hamburgers will contribute $200 to this year's nominal GDP but only $150 to last year's. But 100 hamburgers are still 100 hamburgers—output has not grown.

NOMINAL GDP is calculated by valuing all outputs at current prices.

For this reason, government statisticians have devised an alternative measure that corrects for inflation by valuing all goods and services at some fixed set of prices. (Currently, the prices of 1987 are used.) For example, if the hamburgers were valued at $1.50 each in both years, $150 worth of hamburger output would be included in GDP in each year. When we treat every output in this way, we obtain **real GDP** or *GDP in constant dollars*. The news media often refer to it as "GDP corrected for inflation." Throughout most of this book, and certainly when we are discussing the nation's output, it is real GDP that we shall be concerned with. The distinction between nominal and real GDP leads us to a working definition of a *recession* as a period in which *real* GDP declines. For example, between 1990 and 1991, nominal GDP rose from $5546 billion to $5723 billion; but real GDP *fell* from $4897 billion to $4861 billion.

REAL GDP is calculated by valuing all outputs at the prices that prevailed in some agreed-upon year (currently 1987). Therefore, real GDP is a far better measure of changes in total production.

---

[2]Certain exceptions to the definition are dealt with in Appendix B of Chapter 7, especially on page 172. Some instructors may prefer to take up that material here.

The next important aspect of the definition of GDP is that:

The GDP for a particular year includes only goods and services produced during that year. Sales of items produced in previous years are explicitly excluded.

For example, suppose you buy a perfectly beautiful 1979 Dodge next week and are overjoyed by your purchase. The national income statistician will not share your glee because she already counted your car in the GDP in 1979 when it was first produced and sold; the car will never be counted again. The same holds true of houses. Old houses (unlike old cars) often sell for more than their original purchasers paid; yet the resale values of houses do not count in GDP since they were already counted in the years they were built. For the same reason, exchanges of other existing assets are not included in GDP.

FINAL GOODS AND SERVICES are those that are purchased by their ultimate users.

Third, you will note the use of the phrase **final goods and services** in the definition. The adjective "final" is the key word here. For example, when a supermarket buys milk from a farmer, the transaction is not included in the GDP because the supermarket does not want the milk for itself. It buys milk only for resale to consumers. Only when the milk is sold to consumers is it considered a final product. When the supermarket buys it, economists consider it an **intermediate good**. The GDP does not include sales of intermediate goods or services.[3]

An **INTERMEDIATE GOOD** is a good purchased for resale or for use in producing another good.

Fourth, the adjective "domestic" directs attention to production within the geographic boundaries of the United States. Some Americans work abroad, and many American companies have offices or factories in foreign countries. All these people and businesses produce valuable outputs, but none of this is counted in the GDP of the United States. (It is counted, instead, in the GDPs of the foreign countries.) On the other hand, quite a number of foreigners and foreign companies produce goods and services in the U.S. All this activity does count in our GDP.[4]

Finally, although the definition does not state this explicitly:

For the most part, only goods and services that pass through organized markets count in the GDP.

This, of course, excludes many economic activities. For example, illegal activities are not included in the GDP. Thus, gambling services in Chicago are not in the GDP, but gambling services in Atlantic City are. The definition reflects the statisticians' confession that they could not hope to measure the value of many of the economy's most important activities, such as housework, do-it-yourself repairs, and leisure time. While these are certainly economic activities that result in currently produced goods or services, they all lack that important measuring rod—a market price.

This omission results in certain oddities. For example, suppose that each of two neighboring families hires the other to clean house, generously paying $1000 a week for the services. Each family can easily afford such generosity since it collects an identical salary from its neighbor. Nothing real changes, but GDP goes up by $104,000 a year. This example is not fanciful. The accompanying boxed insert shows that including the value of housework would have a profound effect on the measurement of GDP.

---

[3]Actually, there is another way to add up the GDP by counting a portion of each intermediate transaction. This is explained in Appendix B of Chapter 7, especially pages 176–77.

[4]There is another concept, called gross *national* product, which counts the goods and services produced by all Americans, regardless of where they work. For consistency, the outputs produced by foreigners working in the United States are not included in GNP. In practice, the two measures—GDP and GNP—are very close.

Housework and GDP

How large is a country's economic output? Certainly much bigger than its gross domestic product (GDP), which excludes big chunks of activity . . . [performed] within the home, such as cleaning, caring for children and decorating. This has the bizarre result that, if a man marries his cleaner, turning a paid employee into an unpaid housewife, then GDP falls instantly even though much the same work gets done. A recent study by the OECD confirms what every household drudge has always claimed—working at home is more valuable than it is believed to be by those who spend their time making the wheels of commerce and industry turn.

But how to put a value on it? There are two main methods. The first is to value the time spent doing housework using the person's wage in the formal economy, ie, the opportunity cost of his—or more likely her—time. The snag with this, however, is that it produces the ludicrous result that washing-up done by an investment banker is worth more than washing-up done by a nurse. The second method is to value that time at the wage rate of a maid. Doing this, the [study] concludes that the value of housework would add between one-third to one-half to the GDP of the five large countries which it studied. [See table] . . .

The hours spent doing housework have fallen over the years as more women have taken paid jobs. But the value of housework has not necessarily dropped because productivity has been increased by blenders, dishwashers and the like. When unemployment rises, people spend more time doing up their homes. If governments included this in GDP, there would be fewer recessions.

SOURCE: *The Economist*, July 4, 1992, p. 58.

Percentage Increase in GDP if Unpaid Housework Was Valued at Market Prices

Australia	49%
France	46%
United States	44%
Canada	41%
Germany	32%

SOURCE: Ann Chadeau, "What Is Households' Non-market Production Worth?," OECD Economic Studies No. 18.

LIMITATIONS OF THE GDP: WHAT GDP IS NOT

Having seen in some detail what the GDP *is*, it is worth pausing to expand upon what it *is not*. In particular:

Gross domestic product is not a measure of the nation's economic well-being.

The GDP is not intended to measure economic well-being, and does not do so for several reasons.

1. *Only market activity is included in GDP.* As we have just seen, a great deal of work done in the home contributes to the nation's well-being, but it is not measured in the GDP because it has no price tag. One important implication of this exclusion arises when we try to compare the GDPs of developed and less-developed countries. Americans are always incredulous to learn that the per capita GDP of the poorest African countries is less than $250 a year. Surely, no one could survive in America on $5 a week. How can Africans do it? Part of the answer, of course, is that these people are incredibly

poor. We shall study their plight in Chapter 21. But another part of the answer is that:

International GDP comparisons are vastly misleading when the two countries differ greatly in the fraction of economic activity that each conducts in organized markets.

This fraction is relatively large in the United States and relatively small in the less-developed countries, so when we compare their respective measured GDPs we are not comparing the same economic activities at all. Many things that get counted in the U.S. GDP are not counted in the GDPs of less-developed nations. So it is ludicrous to think that these people, poor as they are, survive on what to Americans would amount to $5 a week.

A second implication is that GDP statistics take no account of the so-called "underground economy." This includes not just criminal activities, but a great deal of legitimate business activity that is conducted in cash (or by barter) to escape the tax collector. Naturally, we have no good data on the size of the underground economy; but some observers think it may amount to 10 percent or more of U.S. GDP. In some foreign countries, it is surely a much bigger share than this.

2. *GDP places no value on leisure.* As a country gets richer, one of the things that happens is that its citizens take more and more leisure time. The steady decrease in the length of the typical workweek in the United States is clear evidence for this. As a result, the gap is steadily widening between official GDP and some truer measure of national well-being that would include the value of leisure time. For this reason, growth in GDP systematically *underestimates* the growth in national well-being. But there are also reasons why the GDP *overstates* how well-off we are. For example:

3. *"Bads" as well as "goods" get counted in GDP.* Suppose there is a natural disaster—such as Hurricane Andrew, which devastated parts of Florida and Louisiana in September 1992. Surely the well-being of the United States was diminished by this catastrophe. Scores of people were killed; many homes and businesses were destroyed. Yet the disaster probably raised U.S. GDP. Consumers spent more to clean up and replace lost homes and possessions. Businesses spent more to rebuild and repair damaged stores and plants. The government spent more for disaster relief and cleanup. Yet no one would think America was better off for its higher GDP.

Wars represent an extreme example. Mobilization for outright war always causes a country's GDP to rise rapidly. But men and women serving in the army could be producing civilian output. Factories assigned to produce armaments could instead be making cars, washing machines, and televisions. A country at war is surely worse off than a country at peace, but this fact will not be reflected in its GDP.

4. *Ecological costs are not netted out of the GDP.* Many of the activities in a modern industrial economy that produce goods and services also have undesirable side effects on the environment. Automobiles provide enjoyment and a means of transportation, but they also despoil the atmosphere. Factories pollute rivers and lakes while manufacturing valuable commodities. Almost everything seems to produce garbage, which creates a serious disposal problem. None of these ecological costs are deducted from the GDP in an effort to give us a truer measure of the *net* increase in economic welfare that our

economy produces. Is this foolishness? Not if we remember the job that national income statisticians are trying to do: they are measuring the economic activity conducted through organized markets, not national welfare.

THE ECONOMY ON A ROLLER COASTER

Having defined several of the basic concepts of macroeconomics, let us breathe some life into them by perusing the economic history of the United States. Figures 5–3 and 5–4 provide a capsule summary of this history since the Civil War.

Figure 5–3 charts the behavior of the growth rate of real GDP. The fact that the growth rate is almost always positive indicates that the main feature has been *economic growth*. In fact, the average annual growth rate over this period has been about 3.3 percent. But the figure also shows that recessions—periods of falling real GDP—have been a persistent feature of America's economic performance. Especially before the Korean War, the graph gives the impression of an economy on a roller coaster. The ups and downs that are apparent in Figure 5–3 are called *economic fluctuations*, or sometimes *business cycles*.

DEFLATION refers to a sustained *decrease* in the general price level.

The history of the inflation rate displayed in Figure 5–4 also shows more positive numbers than negative ones—more inflation than **deflation**. Although the price level rose about 13-fold since 1869, the upward trend is of rather recent

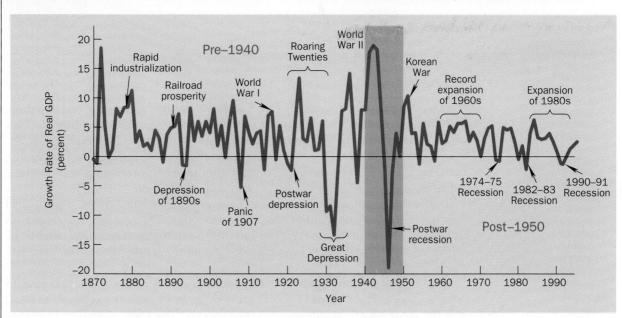

| Figure | **5-3** | **THE GROWTH RATE OF REAL GROSS DOMESTIC PRODUCT OF THE UNITED STATES, 1870–1993** |

This time series chart displays the growth rate of real gross domestic product in the United States from 1870 to 1993. (Here real GDP is measured in 1987 prices.) The Great Depression (1929–1939) stands out vividly. The years during and just after World War II are shaded. Does the growth rate look smoother to the right of this shaded area?

SOURCE: Constructed by the authors from Commerce Department data for 1929–1993. Data for 1869–1928 are based on research by Professor Christina Romer.

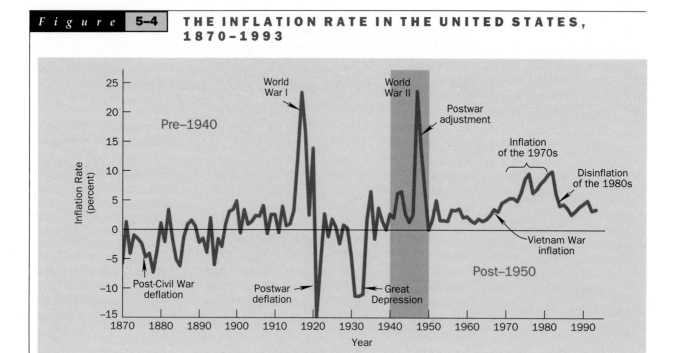

Figure **5-4** THE INFLATION RATE IN THE UNITED STATES, 1870–1993

This time series chart portrays the behavior of the U.S. inflation rate from 1870 to 1993. (The specific price index used is called the GDP deflator, and it is defined as the ratio of nominal GDP divided by real GDP.) The difference between the 1870–1940 period and the 1950–1993 period is pronounced.

SOURCE: Constructed by the authors from Commerce Department data for 1929–1993. Data for 1869–1928 were kindly provided by Professor Christina Romer.

vintage. Prior to World War II, Figure 5–4 shows periods of inflation and deflation, with little or no tendency for one to be more common than the other. Indeed, prices in 1940 were barely higher than at the close of the Civil War. However, this capsule history does show some large gyrations in the inflation rate, including sharp bursts of inflation during and right after the two world wars and dramatic deflations in the 1870s, 1880s, 1921–1922, and 1929–1933.

In sum, although both real GDP and the price level have grown a great deal over the past 123 years, neither has grown smoothly. The ups and downs of both real growth and inflation have been important economic events that need to be explained. Parts 2 and 3 develop a macroeconomic theory designed to do precisely that.

As you look at these graphs, the Great Depression of the 1930s is bound to catch your eye. The decline in economic activity from 1929 to 1933 in Figure 5–3 was the most severe in our nation's history, and the rapid deflation in Figure 5–4 was most unusual. The Depression is but a dim memory now, but those who lived through it will never forget it.

While statistics usually conceal the true drama of economic events, this is not so of the Great Depression—instead they stand as bitter testimony to its severity. The production of goods and services dropped 30 percent, business investment almost ceased entirely, and the unemployment rate rose ominously from about

Life in "Hooverville"

During the worst years of the Great Depression, unemployed workers often congregated in shanty-towns on the outskirts of many major cities. Conditions in these slums were deplorable. With a heavy dose of irony, these communities were known as "Hoovervilles," in honor of the president of the United States who preached rugged individualism. A contemporary observer described a Hooverville in New York City as follows:

It was a fairly popular "development" made up of a hundred or so dwellings, each the size of a dog house or chickencoop, often con-structed with much ingenuity out of wooden boxes, metal cans, strips of cardboard or old tar paper. Here human beings lived on the margin of civilization by foraging for garbage, junk, and waste lumber. I found some splitting or sawing wood with dull tools to make fires; others were picking through heaps of rubbish they had gathered before their doorways or cooking over open fires or battered oilstoves. Still others spent their days improving their rent-free homes, making them sometimes fairly solid and weather-proof. . . . Most of them, according to the police, lived by begging or trading in junk; when all else failed they ate at the soup kitchens or public canteens. They were of all sorts, young and old, some of them rough-looking and suspicious of strangers. They lived in fear of being forcibly re-moved by the authorities, though the neighborhood people in many cases helped them and the police tolerated them for the time being.

SOURCE: Mathew Josephson, *Infidel in the Temple* (New York: Knopf, 1967), pages 82–83.

3 percent in 1929 to 25 percent in 1933. One person in four was jobless. From the data alone, you can conjure up pictures of soup lines, beggars on street corners, closed factories, and homeless families. (See the boxed insert above.)

The Great Depression was a worldwide event. No country was spared its ravages, which literally changed the history of many nations. In Germany, it facilitated the ascendancy of Nazism. In the United States, it enabled Franklin Roosevelt's Democratic party to engineer one of the most dramatic political re-alignments in history and to push through a host of political and economic reforms.

The worldwide depression also caused a much-needed revolution in the think-ing of economists. Up until the 1930s, the prevailing economic theory held that a capitalist economy, while it occasionally misbehaved, had a natural tendency to cure recessions or inflations by itself. The roller coaster bounced around but did not normally run off the tracks.

This optimistic view was not confined to academia. It characterized the views of most politicians (including President Herbert Hoover) and business leaders as well. As the great American humorist Will Rogers remarked with characteristic sarcasm:

> It's almost been worth this depression to find out how little our big men knew. Mayby [sic] this depression is just "normalcy" and we don't know it. It's made a dumb guy as smart as a smart one. . . . Depression used to be a state of mind, Now it's a state of coma, now it's permanent. Last year we said, "Things can't go on like this," and they didn't, they got worse.[5]

---

[5]From *Sanity Is Where You Find It* by Will Rogers, edited by Donald Day; copyright © 1955 by Rogers Company; reprinted by permission of Houghton Mifflin Company; pages 120–21.

The stubbornness of the Great Depression shook almost everyone's faith in the ability of the economy to right itself. In Cambridge, England, this questioning attitude led John Maynard Keynes, one of the world's most respected economists, to write *The General Theory of Employment, Interest, and Money* (1936). Probably the most important book in economics of the twentieth century, it carried a rather revolutionary message. Keynes discarded the notion that the economy always gravitated toward high levels of employment, replacing it with the assertion that—if a pessimistic outlook led business firms and consumers to curtail their spending plans—the economy might be condemned to years of stagnation.

While this doleful prognosis sounded all too realistic at the time, Keynes closed his book on a hopeful note. For he showed how government actions might prod the economy out of its depressed state. The lessons he taught the world then are the lessons we will be learning in Parts 2 and 3. They show how governments can manage their economies so that recessions will not turn into depressions and depressions will not last as long as the Great Depression. While Keynes was working on *The General Theory*, he wrote his friend George Bernard Shaw that, "I believe myself to be writing a book on economic theory which will largely revolutionize . . . the way the world thinks about economic problems." In many ways he was right, though parts of the Keynesian message remain controversial to this day.

FROM WORLD WAR II TO 1973

The Great Depression finally ended when the country mobilized for war in the early 1940s. With government spending at extraordinarily high levels, the economy boomed and the unemployment rate fell as low as 1.2 percent during the war.

Wartime spending of this magnitude usually leads to inflation, but much of the potential inflation during World War II was contained by price controls. With prices held below the levels at which quantity supplied equaled quantity demanded, many goods had to be rationed, and shortages of consumer goods were common. All of this ended with a burst of inflation when controls were lifted after the war.

The period from the end of the war until the early 1960s was marked by several short recessions. Moderate but persistent inflation also became a fact of life. When the economy emerged from recession in 1961, it entered a period of unprecedented—and noninflationary—growth which was credited widely to the success of what came to be called "The New Economics," a term the media created for the economic policies prescribed by Keynes in the 1930s. For a while it looked as if we could avoid both unemployment and inflation. But the optimistic verdicts were premature in both cases.

Inflation came first, beginning about 1966. Its major cause, as it had been so many times in the past, was high levels of wartime spending—this time for the Vietnam War. Unemployment followed when the economy ground to a halt in 1969. Despite a short and mild recession, inflation continued at 5 to 6 percent a year.

Faced with persistent inflation, President Richard Nixon stunned the nation by instituting wage and price controls in 1971, the first time this had ever been done in peacetime. The controls program, which will be discussed in Chapter 16,

Biographical Note

John Maynard Keynes was something of a child prodigy. After an outstanding scholastic career at Eton and Cambridge, Keynes took the civil service examination. Ironically, his second-place score was not good enough to land him the position he wanted—in the Treasury. Some years later, reflecting on the fact that his lowest score on the exam was in the economics section, he suggested with characteristic immodesty that, "The examiners presumably knew less than I did." He was probably right.

During World War I, Keynes was called to the Treasury to assist in planning the financial aspects of the war. There his unique combination of daring and intellect quickly established him as a dominant figure. At the war's end, he represented the British Treasury at the peace conference in Versailles. The conference was a turning point in Keynes's life, though it was one of his few failures. He sought unsuccessfully to persuade the Allies to take a less punitive attitude toward the vanquished Germans, and then stormed out of the conference to write his *Economic Consequences of the Peace* (1919), which created a furor. In it Keynes argued that the Germans could never meet the harsh economic terms of the treaty, and that its

JOHN MAYNARD KEYNES (1883–1946)

viciousness posed the threat of continued instability and perhaps another war in Europe.

No longer welcome in government, Keynes returned to Cambridge and to his circle of literary and artistic friends in London's Bloomsbury district—a remarkable group that included Virginia Woolf, Lytton Strachey, and E. M. Forster. In 1925 he married the beautiful ballerina Lydia Lopokova, who gave up her stage career for him (though she later acted in a theater that Keynes himself established).

Between the wars, Keynes devoted himself to making money, to economic theory, and to political economy. He managed to make both himself and King's College rich by speculating in international currencies and commodities—allegedly by studying the newspapers while still in bed each morning! In 1936, he published his masterpiece, *The General Theory of Employment, Interest, and Money*, on which much of modern macroeconomics is based.

A heart attack in 1937 reduced Keynes's activities, but he returned to the Treasury during World War II to conduct several delicate financial negotiations with the Americans. Then, as the capstone to a truly remarkable career, he represented Great Britain—and by all accounts dominated the proceedings—at the 1944 conference in Bretton Woods, New Hampshire, that established an international financial system that served the Western world for 27 years.

He died at home of a heart attack as Lord Keynes, Baron of Tilton, a man who had achieved almost everything that he sought, and who had only one regret: he wished he had drunk more champagne.

held inflation in check for a while. But inflation worsened dramatically in 1973, mainly because of an explosion in food prices caused by poor harvests around the world.

THE GREAT STAGFLATION, 1973–1980

Then things began to get much worse, not only for the United States, but for all oil-importing nations. A 1973 war between Israel and the Arab nations led to a quadrupling of the price of oil by the Organization of Petroleum Exporting Countries (OPEC). At the same time, continued poor harvests in many parts of the globe pushed world food prices higher. Prices of other raw materials also skyrocketed. Naturally, higher costs of fuel and other materials soon were reflected in the prices of manufactured goods.

By unhappy coincidence, these events coincided with the lifting of wage and price controls. Just as had happened after World War II, the elimination of controls led to a temporary acceleration of inflation as prices that had been held artificially below equilibrium levels were allowed to rise. For all these reasons, the inflation rate in the United States soared to above 12 percent during 1974.

Meanwhile, the U.S. economy was slipping into what was, up to then, its longest and most severe recession since the 1930s. Real GDP fell between late 1973 and early 1975, and the unemployment rate rose to nearly 9 percent. With both inflation and unemployment unusually virulent in 1974 and 1975, a new term—**stagflation**—was coined to refer to the simultaneous occurrence of economic *stag*nation and rapid in*flation*.

> **STAGFLATION** is inflation that occurs while the economy is growing slowly ("stagnating") or having a recession.

Thanks partly to government actions, but mostly to natural economic forces, a sustained recovery from recession began in 1975. Inflation tumbled rapidly as the adjustment to the end of price controls ended and food and energy prices stopped soaring. The severity of the recession also put a brake on inflation, just as it had in the past. In total, the inflation rate tumbled from over 12 percent back down to the 5–7 percent range.

But the price of oil soared again in 1979 following a revolution in Iran, bringing stagflation back. This time, inflation hit the astonishing rate of 16 percent during the first half of 1980 and credit controls were clamped on. Output fell at an extraordinarily rapid pace, but only for a few months. By late 1980, recovery was underway.

REAGANOMICS AND ITS AFTERMATH

When President Ronald Reagan assumed office in January 1981, the economy was showing signs of reviving, but the inflation rate seemed stuck near 10 percent. The new president promised to change things with a package of policies called "supply-side economics."[6]

At first, things did change dramatically—but not in the way President Reagan wanted. While inflation fell remarkably to only about 4 percent in 1982, the lowest rate in a decade, the economy slumped into its worst recession since the Great Depression. When the 1981–1982 recession hit bottom, the unemployment rate was approaching 11 percent, the financial markets were in disarray, and the word "depression" had reentered the American vocabulary.

However, the recovery that began in the winter of 1982–1983 proved to be one of the most vigorous and long-lasting in our history. Unemployment fell more or less steadily for about six years, eventually dropping below 5½ percent. Meanwhile, inflation remained tame. All this provided an ideal economic platform on which President George Bush ran to succeed Reagan—and to continue his policies.

Unfortunately for President Bush, the good times did not continue to roll. Shortly after he took office, the economy began to sputter. Then, in 1990–1991, the U.S. experienced another recession—precipitated, according to some observers, by yet another spike in oil prices before the Persian Gulf War. While the 1990–1991 recession was below average in size, the economy had failed to recover by the

---

[6]Supply-side economics is discussed further in Chapter 11.

time of the 1992 election. In fact, the growth rate during George Bush's presidency was the weakest for any four-year period since World War II. This fact was not lost on candidate Bill Clinton, who hammered away at the lackluster economic performance of 1989–1992. Most observers believe that the weak economy was the main factor behind George Bush's electoral rout.

THE PROBLEM OF MACROECONOMIC STABILIZATION: A SNEAK PREVIEW

This brief look at the historical record shows that our economy has not generally produced steady growth without inflation. Rather, it has been buffeted by periodic bouts of unemployment or inflation, and sometimes has been plagued by both. There was also a hint that government policies may have had something to do with this performance. Let us now expand upon this hint.

STABILIZATION POLICY is the name given to government programs designed to prevent or shorten recessions and to counteract inflation (that is, to *stabilize* prices).

We can provide a preliminary analysis of **stabilization policy**, the name given to government programs designed to prevent or shorten recessions and to counteract inflation, by using the basic tools of aggregate supply and aggregate demand analysis. To facilitate this, we have reproduced as Figures 5–5 and 5–6 two of the diagrams found earlier in this chapter (Figures 5–1[b] and 5–2), but we now give them slightly different interpretations.

Figure 5–5 offers a simplified view of government policy to fight unemployment. Suppose that, in the absence of government intervention, the economy would reach an equilibrium at point E, where demand curve D_0D_0 crosses supply curve SS. Now if the output corresponding to point E is so low that many workers are unemployed, *the government can reduce unemployment by increasing aggregate demand.* Chapter 11 will consider in detail how the government might do this. In

Figure **5-5**   **STABILIZATION POLICY TO FIGHT UNEMPLOYMENT**

This diagram duplicates Figure 5–1(b), but here we assume that Point *E*—the intersection of demand curve D_0D_0 and supply curve *SS*—corresponds to high unemployment. With the kind of policy tools that we will study in later chapters, the government can shift the aggregate demand curve outward to D_1D_1. This would raise output and lower unemployment.

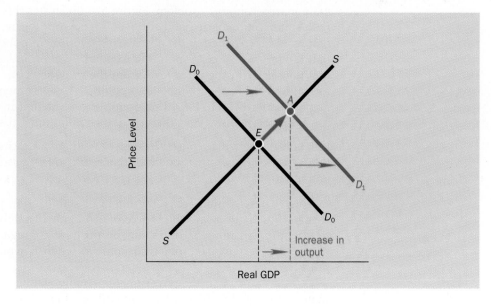

| Figure | 5-6 | STABILIZATION POLICY TO FIGHT INFLATION |

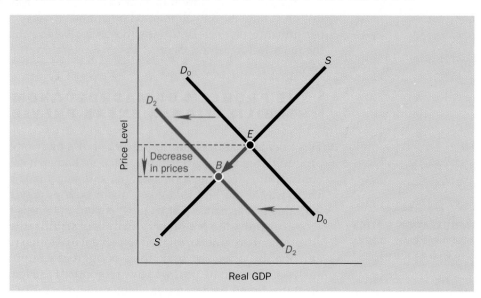

This diagram duplicates Figure 5–2, but here we assume that point *E*—the equilibrium the economy would attain without government intervention—represents high inflation (that is, the price level corresponding to point *E* is far above last year's price level). By using its policy instruments to shift the aggregate demand curve inward to D_2D_2, the government can keep this year's price level lower than it would otherwise have been; in other words, the government can reduce inflation.

the diagram, such an action would shift the demand curve to D_1D_1, causing equilibrium to move to point *A*. In general:

Recessions and unemployment are often caused by insufficient aggregate demand. When this is so, government policies that successfully augment demand—such as increases in government spending—can be an effective way to increase output and reduce unemployment.

The opposite type of demand management is called for when inflation is the main macroeconomic problem. Figure 5–6 illustrates this case. Here again, point *E*, the intersection of demand curve D_0D_0 and supply curve *SS*, is the equilibrium that would be reached in the absence of government policy. But now we suppose that the price level corresponding to point *E* is considered "too high," meaning that the *change* in the price level from the previous period to this one would be too rapid if the economy moved to point *E*. A government program that reduces demand from D_0D_0 to D_2D_2 (for example, a reduction in government spending) can keep prices down and thereby reduce inflation. Thus:

Inflation is frequently caused by aggregate demand racing ahead too fast. When this is the case, government policies that reduce aggregate demand can be effective anti-inflationary devices.

This, in brief, summarizes the intent of stabilization policy. When aggregate demand fluctuations are the source of economic instability, the government can limit both recessions and inflations by pushing aggregate demand ahead when it would otherwise lag, and restraining it when it would otherwise grow too quickly.

Does it work? Can the government actually stabilize the economy? That is a matter of some debate, a debate we will be examining in Part 3. But a look back at Figures 5–3 and 5–4 may be enlightening right now. First, cover the portions of Figures 5–3 and 5–4 that deal with the period beginning in 1941, the portions from the shaded area rightward in each figure. The picture that emerges for the 1870–1940 period is of an economy whose gyrations were frequent and sometimes quite pronounced.

Now do the reverse. Cover the data before 1950 and look only at the postwar period. There is, indeed, a difference. Instances of negative real GDP growth are less common and business fluctuations look less severe. While perfection has not been achieved, things do look much better. When we turn to inflation, however, things look rather worse. Gone are the periods of deflation and price stability that occurred before World War II. Prices now seem only to rise.

This quick tour through the data suggests that something has changed. The U.S. economy behaved differently in 1950–1993 than it did in 1870–1940. Although there is controversy on this point, many economists attribute this shift in the economy's behavior to lessons the government has learned about managing the economy—lessons we will be learning in Part 3.

When you look at the pre-1940 data, you are looking at an unmanaged economy that went through booms and recessions for "natural" economic reasons. The government did little about either. When you examine the post-1950 data, on the other hand, you are looking at an economy that has been increasingly managed by government policy—sometimes successfully and sometimes unsuccessfully. While the recessions are less severe, a cost seems to have been exacted: the economy appears to be more inflation-prone than it was in the more distant past. These two changes in our economy may be connected. But, to understand why, we will have to provide some relevant economic theory.

Summary

1. **Microeconomics** studies the decisions of individuals and firms, how these decisions interact, and how they influence the allocation of society's resources and the distribution of income. **Macroeconomics** looks at the behavior of entire economies and studies the pressing social problems of inflation and unemployment.

2. While their respective subject matters differ greatly, the basic tools of microeconomics and macroeconomics are virtually identical. Both rely on the supply and demand analysis introduced in Chapter 4.

3. Macroeconomic models use abstract concepts like "the price level" and "domestic product" that are derived by amalgamating many different markets into one. This process is known as **aggregation**; it should not be taken literally but should be viewed as a useful approximation.

4. The best specific measure of the abstract concept "domestic product" is **gross domestic product (GDP)**, which is obtained by adding up the money values of all **final goods and services** produced in a given year. These outputs can be evaluated at current market prices (to get **nominal GDP**) or at the prices of some

previous year (to get **real GDP**). Neither **intermediate goods** nor transactions that take place outside organized markets are included in GDP.

5. The GDP is meant to be a measure of the *production* of the economy, not of the increase in its *well-being*. For example, the GDP places no value on housework and other do-it-yourself activities, nor on leisure time. On the other hand, even commodities that might be considered as "bads" rather than "goods" are counted in the GDP (for example, activities that harm the environment).

6. America's economic history is one of growth punctuated by periodic **recessions**; that is, periods in which real GDP declined. While the distant past included some periods of falling prices (**deflation**), more recent history shows only rising prices (**inflation**).

7. The Great Depression of the 1930s was the worst in our country's history. It had profound effects both on our nation and on countries throughout the world and led also to a revolution in economic thinking, thanks to the work of John Maynard Keynes.

8. From World War II to the early 1970s, the American economy exhibited much steadier growth than it had in the past. Many observers attributed this to the implementation of the economic policies that Keynes suggested. At the same time, however, the price level seems only to rise, never to fall, in the modern economy. The economy seems to have become more "inflation prone."

9. Since 1973, the U.S. economy has suffered through several serious recessions. Between 1973 and about 1981, inflation was also unusually virulent. This unhappy combination of economic stagnation with rapid inflation was nicknamed "**stagflation**." Since 1982, however, inflation has been low and mostly steady.

10. One major cause of inflation is that **aggregate demand** may grow more quickly than **aggregate supply**. In such a case, a government policy that reduces aggregate demand may be able to check the inflation.

11. Similarly, recessions often occur because aggregate demand grows too slowly. In this case, a government policy that stimulates demand may be an effective way to fight the recession.

Key Concepts and Terms

Microeconomics	Inflation	Final goods and services
Macroeconomics	Deflation	Intermediate goods
Domestic product	Recession	Stagflation
Aggregation	Gross domestic product (GDP)	Stabilization policy
Aggregate demand and aggregate supply curves	Nominal versus real GDP	

Questions for Review

1. Which of the following problems are likely to be studied by a microeconomist and which by a macroeconomist?

   a. The allocation of a university budget.
   b. Why the economy took so long to recover from the 1990–1991 recession.
   c. Why Japan's economy grows faster than the United States' economy, while Britain's grows slower.
   d. Why "clone" computers have gained market share from IBM.

2. You probably use "aggregates" frequently in everyday discussions. Try to think of some examples. (Here is one: Have you ever said, "The students at this college generally think . . ."? What, precisely, did you mean?)

3. Use an aggregate supply and demand diagram to study what would happen to an economy in which the aggregate demand curve never moved while the aggregate supply curve shifted outward year after year.

4. Try asking a friend who has not studied economics in which year he or she thinks prices were higher: 1870 or 1900? 1920 or 1940? (In both cases, prices were higher in the earlier year.) Most people your age think that prices have always risen. Why do you think they have this opinion?

5. Which of the following transactions are included in gross domestic product, and by how much does each raise GDP?

   a. Smith pays a carpenter $10,000 to build a garage.
   b. Smith purchases $3000 worth of materials and builds himself a garage, which is worth $10,000.
   c. Smith goes to the woods, cuts down a tree, and uses the wood to build himself a garage that is worth $10,000.
   d. The Jones family sells its old house to the Reynolds family for $130,000. The Joneses then buy a newly constructed house from a builder for $175,000.
   e. You purchase a used computer from a friend for $250.
   f. Your university purchases a new mainframe computer from IBM, paying $250,000.
   g. You win $100 in an Atlantic City casino.
   h. You make $100 in the stock market.
   i. You sell a used economics textbook to your college bookstore for $25.
   j. You buy a new economics textbook from your college bookstore for $50.

6. Give some reasons why gross domestic product is not a suitable measure of the well-being of the nation. (Have you noticed newspaper accounts in which journalists seem to use GDP for this purpose?)

UNEMPLOYMENT AND INFLATION: THE TWIN EVILS OF MACROECONOMICS

When men are employed,
they are best contented.

BENJAMIN FRANKLIN

Inflation is repudiation.

CALVIN COOLIDGE

 Among the many trials faced by Odysseus, the hero of Homer's *Odyssey*, one of the most difficult was to steer his fragile boat through a narrow strait. On one side lay the rock of the monster Scylla, which threatened to break his craft into pieces, and on the other was the menacing whirlpool of Charybdis. The makers of national economic policy face a similarly difficult task in trying to chart a middle course between the Scylla of unemployment and the Charybdis of inflation. If they steer the economy far from the rocks of unemployment, they run the risk of being swept up in the swift currents of inflation. But if they maintain a safe distance from inflation, they may smash against the rocks of unemployment. ¶In Parts 2 and 3 we will explain how economic planners attempt to strike a balance between high employment and low inflation, why these goals cannot be attained with machinelike precision, and why improvement on one front generally spells deterioration on the other. A great deal of attention will be paid to the *causes* of inflation and unemployment. ¶ But before getting involved in such weighty issues of theory and policy, we pause in this chapter to take a close look at the twin evils themselves: Why does a rise in unemployment cause such social distress? Why is inflation so loudly deplored? Can we measure the costs of unemployment and inflation? The answers to some of these questions may seem obvious at first. But we will see that there is more to them than meets the eye.

The chapter is divided into two parts. The first deals with unemployment. After discussing the human and economic costs of high unemployment, we explain how government statisticians measure unemployment. Then we consider how the elusive concept of "full employment" can be defined. We conclude by investigating our country's system of unemployment insurance.

The second part of the chapter is devoted to inflation. We begin by exploding some persistent myths about inflation. But the costs of inflation are not all mythical. For example, inflation capriciously redistributes income and wealth from one group of people to another, and certain laws make inflation impose heavy economic costs that could be avoided if the laws were written differently. This last cost stems from failure to understand one of the **12 Ideas for Beyond the Final Exam**: the effect of inflation on interest rates. Finally, we define and analyze the difference between creeping and galloping inflation and explode another myth about inflation: that creeping inflation always leads to galloping inflation.

An appendix explains how inflation is measured.

THE COSTS OF UNEMPLOYMENT

The human costs of unemployment are probably sufficiently obvious. Years ago, loss of a job meant not only enforced idleness and a catastrophic drop in income, it often led to hunger, cold, ill health—even death. This is the way one unemployed worker during the Great Depression described his family's plight in a mournful letter to the governor of Pennsylvania:

> *I have six little children to take care of. I have been out of work for over a year and a half. Am back almost thirteen months and the landlord says if I don't pay up before the 1 of 1932 out I must go, and where am I to go in the cold winter with my children? If you can help me please for God's sake and the children's sakes and like please do what you can and send me some help, will you, I cannot find any work. I am willing to take any kind of work if I could get it now. Thanksgiving dinner was black coffee and bread and was very glad to get it. My wife is in the hospital now. We have no shoes to were [sic]; no clothes hardly. Oh what will I do I sure will thank you.*[1]

Nowadays, unemployment does not have such dire consequences for most families, although it still holds these terrors for some. Part of the sting has been taken out of unemployment by our system of unemployment insurance (discussed below), and there are other social welfare programs to support the incomes of the poor. Yet most families still suffer a painful loss of income when a breadwinner becomes unemployed.

---

[1]From *Brother, Can You Spare a Dime? The Great Depression 1929–1933*, by Milton Meltzer, page 103. Copyright © 1969 by Milton Meltzer. Reprinted by permission of Alfred A. Knopf, Inc.

UNEMPLOYMENT RATES FOR SELECTED GROUPS, 1992

This figure shows that, in 1992, unemployment rates for specific demographic groups varied widely. Similar patterns hold in most years.

SOURCE: Bureau of Labor Statistics

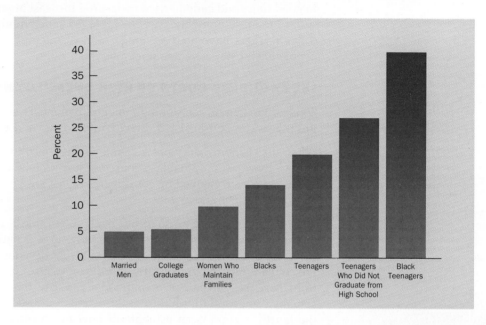

Even families that are well protected by unemployment compensation suffer when joblessness strikes. Ours is a work-oriented society. A man's place has always been in the office or shop, and lately this has become true for many women as well. A worker forced into idleness by a recession endures a psychological cost that is no less real for our inability to measure it. Martin Luther King put it graphically: "In our society, it is murder, psychologically, to deprive a man of a job . . . You are in substance saying to that man that he has no right to exist."[2] High unemployment has been linked to higher incidence of certain types of crimes, psychological disorders, divorces—even suicides.

Nor are the costs only psychological. Accumulated work experience is a valuable asset. When forced into idleness, workers not only cease accumulating experience, but lengthy periods of unemployment may make them "rusty," and thus less productive when they are reemployed. Short periods of unemployment exact different kinds of costs. A record of steady employment is important in applying for a new job. And a worker who has frequently been laid off will lack this record of reliability.

It is important to realize that these costs, whether large or small in total, are distributed most unevenly across the population. In 1992, for example, the **unemployment rate** among all workers averaged 7.5 percent. But, as Figure 6–1 shows, 14.1 percent of black workers were unemployed, as were 9.9 percent of women who maintained families. For teenagers, the situation was worse still, with unemployment at 20 percent, and that of black teenagers about 40 percent.

The **UNEMPLOYMENT RATE** is the number of unemployed people, expressed as a percentage of the **labor force.**

[2]Quoted in Coretta Scott King (ed.), *The Words of Martin Luther King* (New York: Newmarket Press, 1983), page 45.

Married men had the lowest rate—about 5 percent. These relationships among unemployment rates are typical:

In good times and bad, married men suffer the least unemployment and teenagers suffer the most; nonwhites are unemployed much more often than whites; blue-collar workers have above-average rates of unemployment; and well-educated people have below-average unemployment rates.

THE ECONOMIC COSTS OF HIGH UNEMPLOYMENT

Some of the human costs of high unemployment are, as we just noted, intangible. But others can be translated directly into dollars and cents because:

When the economy does not generate enough jobs to employ all those who are willing to work, a valuable resource is lost. Potential goods and services that might have been enjoyed by consumers are lost forever. This is the real economic cost of high unemployment.

And these costs are by no means negligible. Table 6–1 summarizes the idleness of workers and machines, and the resulting loss of national output, for some of the years of lowest economic activity in recent decades. The second column lists the civilian unemployment rate, and thus measures unused labor resources. The third lists the percentage of industrial capacity that U.S. manufacturers were actually using, and thus indicates the extent of unused plant and equipment. And the fourth column is an estimate of how much more output (real GDP) could have been produced if these labor and capital resources had been fully employed. For comparison, the bottom line shows the situation in 1990, a year of approximately full utilization of resources.

While Table 6–1 shows extreme examples, inability to utilize all of the nation's available resources has been a recurrent problem for our economy, especially in the 1980s. The blue line in Figure 6–2 shows actual real GDP in the United States from 1952 to 1992, while the black line shows the real GDP we *could have* produced if "full-employment" had been maintained. This last statement defines a concept called **potential GDP**.

It *is* possible to push employment beyond its normal full employment level. This occurs whenever the unemployment rate dips below the "full-employment

POTENTIAL GROSS DOMESTIC PRODUCT is the real GDP the economy would produce if its labor and other resources were fully employed.

T a b l e **6–1**	THE ECONOMIC COSTS OF HIGH UNEMPLOYMENT		
YEAR	CIVILIAN UNEMPLOYMENT RATE (percent)	CAPACITY UTILIZATION RATE (percent)	PERCENTAGE OF REAL GDP LOST DUE TO IDLE RESOURCES
1958	6.8	75.0	4.4
1961	6.7	77.3	3.3
1975	8.5	72.3	4.6
1982	9.7	70.3	7.4
1992	7.5	78.6	2.3
1990	5.5	83.0	0

SOURCES: Bureau of Labor Statistics; Federal Reserve System; and Robert J. Gordon, *Macroeconomics*, Sixth Edition (Boston: Little, Brown, 1993).

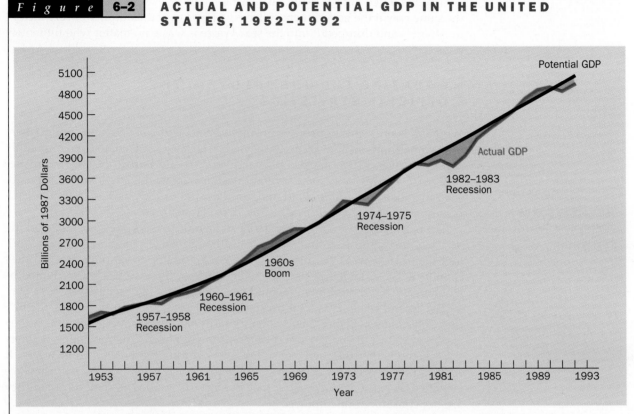

| *Figure* **6-2** | **ACTUAL AND POTENTIAL GDP IN THE UNITED STATES, 1952-1992** |

This chart compares the growth of actual GDP (blue line) with that of potential GDP (black line). There have been two lengthy periods during which real GDP remained below its potential (1957–1963 and 1974–1987), but only one lengthy period during which GDP remained above potential (1965–1970). The large short-fall of GDP from potential in the 1980s stand out.

SOURCES: U.S. Department of Commerce and Robert J. Gordon, *Macroeconomics*, Sixth edition (Boston: Little, Brown, 1993). Professor Gordon's estimates of potential GDP are generally considered quite conservative; other estimates of the GDP gap are therefore higher.

unemployment rate." Consequently, it *is* possible for actual GDP to exceed potential GDP. Figure 6–2 shows several instances where this happened, shaded in blue. But it also shows, quite dramatically, that actual GDP has fallen short of potential GDP often since 1974—sometimes by huge amounts. In fact:

A conservative estimate of the cumulative gap between actual and potential GDP over the years 1974–1992 (all evaluated in 1987 prices) is approximately $1300 billion. At 1993 levels, this loss in output as a result of unemployment would be about 3 months' worth of production. And there is no way to redeem these losses. The labor wasted in 1991 cannot be utilized in 1994.

Those who argue that unemployment is nothing to worry about today because of unemployment insurance, or because unemployment is concentrated among certain kinds of workers (such as teenagers), or because many unemployed workers become reemployed within a few weeks, should ponder Figure 6–2. Is the loss of this much output really no cause for worry? Would these optimists react the same way if the government collected a fraction of the output of every factory in America and dumped it into the sea? Waste is waste no matter who ultimately pays the cost.

COUNTING THE UNEMPLOYED: THE OFFICIAL STATISTICS

We have been using figures on unemployment without yet considering where they come from, or how accurate they are. The basic data come from a monthly survey of over 50,000 households conducted by the Bureau of Labor Statistics (BLS). The census-taker asks several questions about the employment status of each member of the household and, on the basis of the answers, classifies each person as *employed*, *unemployed*, or *not in the* **labor force**.

The **LABOR FORCE** is the number of people holding or seeking jobs.

The first category is simplest to define. It includes everybody currently working at a job, including part-time workers. Although some part-time workers work less than a full week because they choose to, others do so only because they cannot find a suitable full-time job. Nevertheless, these workers are counted as employed, even though many would consider them "underemployed."

The second category is a bit trickier. For those not currently working, the BLS first determines whether they are temporarily laid off from a job to which they expect to return. If so, they are counted as unemployed. The remaining workers are asked whether they actively sought work during the previous four weeks. If they did, they are also counted as unemployed. But if they did not, they are classified as *out of the labor force*; that is, since they failed to look for a job they are not considered unemployed.

A **DISCOURAGED WORKER** is an unemployed person who gives up looking for work and is therefore no longer counted as part of the labor force.

This seems a reasonable way to draw the distinction—after all, we do not want to count college students who work during the summer months as unemployed between September and May. Yet, there is a problem: research has shown that many unemployed workers give up looking for jobs after a time. These so-called **discouraged workers** are victims of poor job prospects, just like the officially unemployed. Ironically, when they give up hope, the official unemployment statistics decline! Some critics have therefore argued that an estimate should be made of the number of discouraged workers and that these people should be added to the roles of the unemployed. In 1992 the BLS estimated that about 1.1 million workers fell into this category.

Involuntary part-time work, loss of overtime or shortened work hours, and discouraged workers are all examples of "hidden" or "disguised" unemployment. Those who are concerned about these phenomena argue that we should include them in the official unemployment rate because, if we do not, the magnitude of the problem will be underestimated. Others, however, argue that measured unemployment overestimates the problem because, to count as unemployed, a person need only *claim* to be looking for a job, even if he or she is not really interested in finding one.

TYPES OF UNEMPLOYMENT

Providing jobs for those willing to work is one principal goal of macroeconomic policy. How are we to define this goal? One clearly *incorrect* answer would be "a zero measured unemployment rate." Ours is a dynamic, highly mobile economy.

FRICTIONAL UNEMPLOYMENT is unemployment that is due to normal turnover in the labor market. It includes people who are temporarily between jobs because they are moving or changing occupations, or for similar reasons.

Households move from one state to another. Individuals quit jobs to seek better positions or retool for more attractive occupations. These and other phenomena produce some minimal amount of unemployment—people who literally are *between* jobs. Economists call this the level of **frictional unemployment**.

The critical distinguishing feature of frictional unemployment is that it is short-lived. A frictionally unemployed person has every reason to expect to find a new job soon. People tend to think of frictional unemployment as irreducible, but that is not true. During World War II, for example, unemployment in this country fell below 2 percent—substantially below the frictional level.

Frictional unemployment is irreducible only in the sense that—under normal circumstances—it is socially undesirable to do so. Geographical and occupational mobility play important roles in our market economy—enabling people to search for better jobs. Similarly, waste is avoided by allowing inefficient firms, or firms producing items no longer in demand, to be replaced by new firms. Inhibition of either of these phenomena must hamper the workings of the market economy. But, if these adjustment mechanisms are allowed to operate, there will always be some temporarily unemployed workers looking for jobs; and there will always be some firms with unfilled positions looking for workers. This is the genesis of frictional unemployment.

STRUCTURAL UNEMPLOYMENT refers to workers who have lost their jobs because they have been displaced by automation, because their skills are no longer in demand, or for similar reasons.

A second type of unemployment is often difficult to distinguish from frictional unemployment, but it has very different implications. **Structural unemployment** arises when jobs are eliminated by changes in the structure of the economy, such as automation or permanent changes in demand. The crucial difference between frictional and structural unemployment is that, unlike frictionally unemployed workers, structurally unemployed workers cannot realistically be considered "between jobs." Instead, they may find their skills and experience unwanted in the changing economy in which they live. They are thus faced with either a prolonged period of unemployment or the necessity of making a major change in their occupation. For older workers, learning a new occupation may be nearly impossible.

CYCLICAL UNEMPLOYMENT is the portion of unemployment that is attributable to a decline in the economy's total production. Cyclical unemployment rises during recessions and falls as prosperity is restored.

The remaining type of unemployment, **cyclical unemployment**, will occupy most of our attention. Cyclical unemployment arises when the level of economic activity declines, that is, in a recession. Thus when economists speak of maintaining "full employment," they do not mean achieving zero measured unemployment, but rather limiting unemployment to its frictional and structural components. A key question, therefore, is: How much measured unemployment is that?

HOW MUCH EMPLOYMENT IS "FULL EMPLOYMENT"?

President John F. Kennedy, in 1961, was the first to commit the federal government to a specific numerical goal. Looking at experience in the prosperous early 1950s, he picked a 4 percent unemployment target. But during the 1970s, the 4 percent goal was rejected as outmoded, and no new numerical target was put in its place. There were two major reasons for rejecting 4 percent.

First, some economists argued that the 4 percent target had to be adjusted upward because the composition of the labor force had changed. In particular, there were many more young workers in the 1970s than in the 1950s, and teenagers always have higher rates of unemployment than adults. Second, they suggested, the increased generosity of unemployment compensation (which is discussed just below) had reduced the incentive to get off the unemployment rolls. Why work, if unemployment benefits and other programs provide an income nearly as large as the salary one could earn on the job?

In the 1980s, there was considerable debate over exactly how much measured unemployment corresponded to **full employment**. Some observers argued that full employment came at a measured unemployment rate above 6 percent. Others pointed out that the main factors that had raised the full-employment unemployment rate in the 1970s were reversed in the 1980s: the teenage labor force dwindled, and unemployment benefits went to a smaller percentage of the unemployed.

As is so often the case, actual events helped settle the argument. Measured unemployment fell below 6 percent late in the 1980s and remained there until the end of 1990. This persuaded many economists that full employment came at an unemployment rate around $5\frac{1}{2}$ percent. But some felt it might be lower, and others thought it was higher. The definition of "full employment" remains controversial.

UNEMPLOYMENT INSURANCE: THE INVALUABLE CUSHION

One surprising feature of the 1980s was the equanimity with which the electorates of the United States and other industrial countries tolerated high unemployment rates. One major reason was **unemployment insurance**.

One of the most valuable pieces of legislation to emerge from the trauma of the Great Depression was the Social Security Act of 1935. Among other things, it established an unemployment insurance system that is now administered by each of the 50 states under federal guidelines. Thanks to this system, many—but not all—American workers can never experience the complete loss of income that devastated so many during the 1930s.

While the precise amounts vary substantially, the average weekly benefit check to unemployed workers in 1992 was about $180. This amounted to about 45 percent of average earnings. Though a 55 percent drop in earnings still poses serious problems, the importance of this 45 percent income cushion can scarcely be exaggerated, especially since it may be supplemented by funds from other welfare programs. Families that are covered by unemployment insurance simply do not have to go hungry when they lose their jobs, and they are only rarely dispossessed from their homes.

Who is eligible to receive these benefits? Precise qualifications vary from state to state, but some stipulations apply quite generally. Only experienced workers qualify; so persons just joining the labor force (such as recent graduates of high schools and colleges) or reentering after a prolonged absence (such as women resuming work after years of child rearing) cannot collect benefits. Neither can those who have quit their jobs, except under unusual circumstances. And benefits end after a stipulated period of time. For all these reasons, less than one-third of the almost 10 million people who were unemployed during 1992 actually received benefits.

The importance of unemployment insurance to the unemployed is obvious. But there are also significant benefits to citizens who never become unemployed. During recession years, many billions of dollars are paid out in unemployment benefits, and since recipients probably spend most of their benefits, unemployment insurance limits the severity of recessions by providing additional purchasing power when and where it is most needed.

The unemployment insurance system is one of several "cushions" that have been built into our economy since 1933 to prevent the possibility of another Great Depression. By giving money to those who become unemployed, the system helps prop up aggregate demand during recessions.

While the U.S. economy is now probably "depression proof," this should not be a cause for too much rejoicing, for the long-lasting recession of the early 1990s amply demonstrated that we are far from "recession proof."

UNEMPLOYMENT INSURANCE AND THE COSTS OF UNEMPLOYMENT

The fact that unemployment insurance and other social welfare programs replace a significant fraction of lost income has led some skeptics to claim that unemployment is no longer a serious problem. But the fact is that:

Unemployment insurance is just what the name says—an *insurance* program. And insurance can never prevent a catastrophe from occurring; it can only *spread the costs* of a catastrophe among many people instead of letting them all fall on the shoulders of those few unfortunate souls whom it affects directly.

Fire insurance is an example. If your family is covered by fire insurance and your house burns down, you will probably suffer only a small financial loss because the insurance company will pay most of the expenses. Where does it get the money? It cannot create it out of thin air. Rather, it must have collected the funds from the many other families who purchased insurance but did not suffer any fire damages. Thus, one family's loss of perhaps $100,000 is covered by the insurance payments of 500 families each paying $200 a year. In this way, the costs of the catastrophe are spread among hundreds of families, and in the process, made much more bearable.

But despite the insurance, the family whose house is destroyed by fire suffers anguish and inconvenience. No insurance policy can eliminate this. Furthermore, society loses a valuable resource—a house. It will take much wood, cement, nails, paint, and labor to replace the burnt-out home. *An insurance policy cannot insure society against losses of real resources.*

The case is precisely the same with insurance against unemployment. All workers and employers pay for the insurance policy by a tax that the government levies on wages and salaries. With the funds so collected, the government compensates the victims of unemployment. Thus, instead of letting the costs of unemployment fall entirely on the minority of workers who lose their jobs:

Our system of payroll taxes and unemployment benefits *spreads* the costs of unemployment over the entire population. But it does not eliminate the basic economic cost.

THE COSTS OF INFLATION

Both the human and economic costs of inflation are less obvious than the costs of unemployment. But this does not necessarily make them any less real, for if one thing is crystal clear about inflation, it is that people do not like it.

Public opinion polls consistently show that inflation ranks high on people's list of major national problems, generally even ahead of unemployment. Surveys also find that inflation, like unemployment, causes a deterioration in consumers' sense of well-being—it makes people unhappy. Finally, studies of elections suggest that voters penalize the party that occupies the White House when inflation is high.

The fact is beyond dispute: People consider inflation to be something bad. The question is: Why?

INFLATION: THE MYTH AND THE REALITY

At first, the question may seem ridiculous. During times of inflation, people keep paying higher prices for the same quantities of goods and services they had before. So more and more income is needed just to maintain the same standard of living. Is it not obvious that this erosion of **purchasing power**—that is, the decline in what money will buy—makes everyone worse off?

The **PURCHASING POWER** of a given sum of money is the volume of goods and services it will buy.

This would indeed be the case were it not for one very significant fact. The wages people earn are also prices—prices for labor services. During a period of inflation, wages also rise and, in fact, the average wage typically rises more or less in step with prices. Thus, contrary to popular myth, workers as a group are not usually victimized by inflation.

The **REAL WAGE RATE** is the wage rate adjusted for inflation. It indicates the volume of goods and services that money wages will buy.

The purchasing power of wages—what is called the **real wage**—is not systematically eroded by inflation. Sometimes wages rise faster than prices, and sometimes prices rise faster than wages. The fact is that in the long run wages tend to outstrip prices as new capital equipment and innovation increase output per worker.

Figure 6–3 illustrates this simple fact. The blue line shows the annual rate of increase of consumer prices in the United States for each year since 1948, while the black line shows the annual rate of wage increase. The difference between the two indicates the rate of growth of *real* wages. Generally, wages rise faster than prices, reflecting the steady advance of technology and of labor productivity; so real wages rise.

The feature of Figure 6–3 that virtually jumps off the page is the way the two lines dance together. Wages normally rise rapidly when prices rise rapidly, and rise slowly when prices rise slowly. But you should not draw any hasty conclusions from this association. We cannot, for example, learn from this figure whether rising prices cause rising wages or whether rising wages cause rising prices. Remember the warnings given in Chapter 1 about trying to infer causation just by looking at data. But analyzing cause and effect is not our purpose right now. We merely want to explode the myth that inflation inevitably erodes real wages.

Why is this myth so widespread? Imagine a world without inflation in which wages are rising 2 percent a year because of the increasing productivity of labor. Now imagine that, all of a sudden, inflation sets in and prices start rising 4 percent a year but that nothing else changes. Figure 6–3 suggests that, with perhaps a small delay, wage increases will accelerate to 2 percent plus 4 percent, or 6 percent a year.

Will workers view this change with equanimity? Probably not. To each worker, the 6 percent wage increase will be seen as something he earned by the sweat of his brow. In his view, he *deserves* every penny of his 6 percent raise. And, in a sense, he is right because "the sweat of his brow" earned him a 2 percent increment

F i g u r e **6-3** **RATES OF CHANGE OF WAGES AND PRICES IN THE UNITED STATES, 1948–1992**

This chart compares the rate of price inflation (blue line) with the rate of growth of nominal wages (black line) in the postwar period. The patterns are clearly quite similar, with wages and prices normally accelerating or decelerating together. Notice that wage increases generally outstrip price increases; that is, *real* wages normally rise from year to year.

SOURCE: Bureau of Labor Statistics.

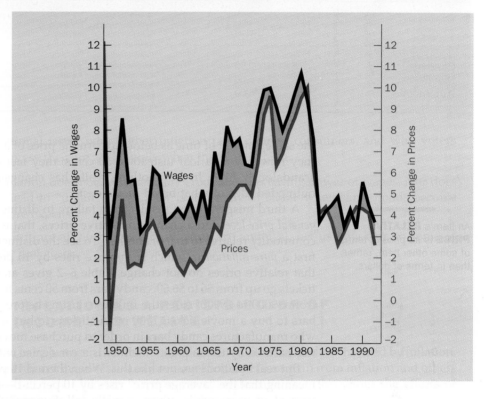

in real wages that, when the inflation rate is 4 percent, can only be achieved by increasing his money wages by a total of 6 percent. An economist would divide the wage increase in the following way:

REASON FOR WAGE INCREASE	AMOUNT
Higher productivity	2%
Compensation for higher prices	4%
Total	6%

But the worker will probably keep score differently. Feeling that he earned the entire 6 percent by his own merits, he will view inflation as having "robbed" him of 4 percent of his just deserts. The higher the rate of inflation, the more of his raise the worker will feel has been stolen from him.

Of course, nothing could be further from the truth. Basically, the economic system is rewarding the worker with *the same 2 percent real wage increment for higher productivity regardless of the rate of inflation.* The "evils of inflation" are often exaggerated because of a failure to understand this mechanism.

A second reason for misunderstanding the effects of inflation is that people are in the habit of thinking in terms of the number of dollars it takes to buy something rather than in terms of the *purchasing power* of these dollars. For example, if inflation doubles both prices and wages, workers will have to labor exactly

"Sure, you're raising my allowance. But am I actually gaining any purchasing power?"

Table 6–4	INFLATION AND THE TAXATION OF INTEREST INCOME							
(1)	**(2)**	**(3)**	**(4)** LOSS OF PURCHASING	**(5)** REAL	**(6)**	**(7)**	**(8)**	**(9)** EFFECTIVE
INFLATION RATE (percent)	NOMINAL INTEREST RATE (percent)	INTEREST INCOME (dollars)	POWER DUE TO INFLATION (dollars)	INTEREST INCOME (dollars)	TAXES PAID (dollars)	REAL INCOME AFTER TAX (dollars)	(as a percentage of $1000 loan)	RATE OF TAXATION (percent)
0	3	30	0	30	10	20	2%	$33\frac{1}{3}$
6	9	90	60	30	30	0	0%	100

Now let's consider the same transaction when the inflation rate is 6 percent and Scrooge and Diamond Jim settle on a 9 percent nominal interest rate. Scrooge collects $90 in interest (column 3). But, with 6 percent inflation, the purchasing power of the $1000 he lends declines by $60 (column 4). Thus his real interest income is again $30 (column 5). However, the tax collector taxes the $90 *nominal* interest income, not the $30 real interest income, so Scrooge must pay $30 (one-third of $90) in taxes (column 6). As we can see in column 7, his after-tax real income on the loan is zero since the tax collector takes all his real income. Thus the effective tax rate on Scrooge's real interest income is 100 percent (column 9), far larger than the $33\frac{1}{3}$ percent rate intended by Congress.

So a tax system that works well at zero inflation misfires at 6 percent inflation because it taxes nominal, rather than real, interest. This little example illustrates a general, and very serious, problem:

Because it fails to recognize the distinction between nominal and real interest rates, our tax system levies high, and presumably unintended, tax rates on interest income when there is high inflation. And similar problems arise in the taxation of capital gains, corporate profits, and other items. Many economists feel that these high tax rates discourage saving, lending, and investing, and that high inflation therefore retards economic growth.

CAPITAL GAIN is the difference between the price at which an asset is sold and the price at which it was bought.

A particularly acute version of this problem arises in the taxation of **capital gains**—the difference between the price at which an investor sells an asset and the price she paid for it. An example will bring out the point. Between 1979 and 1993 the price level doubled, approximately. Consider some stock that was purchased for $5000 in 1979 and sold for $7500 in 1993. The investor actually *lost* purchasing power in the transaction because $7500 in 1993 purchased less than $5000 in 1979. Yet, since the law levies taxes on nominal capital gains, with no correction for inflation, the investor will be taxed on the $2500 nominal capital gain as though there had been a profit rather than a loss.

Many economists have proposed that this, presumably unintended, feature of the law be changed by taxing only capital gains that exceed inflation. But, up to now, Congress has not adopted this suggestion.

USURY LAWS, INTEREST RATE CEILINGS, AND OTHER IMPEDIMENTS

A **USURY LAW** sets down a maximum permissible interest rate for a particular type of loan. Loans at rates above the usury ceiling are illegal.

Another example of laws that malfunction under inflation is **usury laws**, which set *maximum* permissible interest rates on particular types of loans. Usury laws date back to biblical days and command widespread popular support. The problem is that, when they place ceilings on *nominal* interest rates rather than on *real* interest rates, they can have perverse effects in an inflationary environment.

In our previous example of Scrooge and Diamond Jim, suppose that a usury law sets a maximum rate of 8 percent on consumer loans. Diamond Jim is willing to pay a 9 percent nominal interest rate and Scrooge is willing to lend at this rate. But the law intervenes: "Thou shalt not charge usurious interest." The deal cannot be completed, and both Diamond Jim and Scrooge go away disappointed.

The problem is that usury ceilings were set in periods of fairly steady prices, when there was no great difference between nominal and real interest rates. If, for example, the usury law set the legal maximum at an 8 percent *real* rate of interest, it would not prevent Scrooge from lending to Diamond Jim. As it is, however, a loan carrying a 3 percent real interest rate is perfectly legal at zero inflation but illegal at 6 percent inflation!

Usury laws set in nominal terms created so much havoc during the period of double-digit inflation in 1979–1980 that Congress took drastic action to curtail them. Consequently, usury ceilings on interest rates are far less prevalent today than they were a decade ago, and are set at higher levels in states that still have them.

Usury laws and problems with the tax system are just two examples of a general phenomenon:

Many of the laws that govern our financial system become extremely counterproductive in an inflationary environment, causing problems that were never intended by the legislators.

And it is important to note that *these costs of inflation are not purely redistributive.* Society as a whole loses when mutually beneficial transactions are prohibited by obsolete legislation, when saving and investing are discouraged, and when loans are not provided to those who need them.

Why do such laws stay on the books so long? One reason is a general lack of understanding of the difference between real and nominal interest rates. People fail to understand that it is normally the *real* rate of interest that matters in an economic transaction because only that rate reveals how much borrowers pay and lenders receive *in terms of the goods and services that money can buy.* They focus on the high nominal interest rates caused by inflation, even when these rates correspond to low real interest rates. Here are some other examples that may help you appreciate how widespread and important this interest rate illusion is.

REGULATION OF PUBLIC UTILITIES   During 1980, when the rate of inflation rose above 12 percent, there was a public uproar when regulated utilities asked the regulatory agencies to permit them to earn a rate of return closer to 11 percent— a *negative* real rate of return! They frequently found that their requests were considered exorbitant by the commissions and by the general public. The consequence was that many utilities could not afford to borrow the money needed to serve expanding public demand.

RECORD PROFIT RATES   Amazingly, even business managers were subject to the same form of illusion. Often they were taken aback by the notion that their investors actually lost out (earned a negative *real* rate of return) when the company was earning a 10 percent profit. The managers noted that 10 percent was the company's highest earnings rate in recent history. But with inflation at 12 percent, it turned out that in real terms it was in fact the firm's lowest.

H y p e r i n f l a t i o n   a n d   t h e   P i g g y   B a n k

While mild inflations are barely noticeable in everyday life, hyperinflation makes all sorts of normal economic activities more difficult and transforms a society in strange and unexpected ways. This article, excerpted from *The New York Times*, illustrates some of the problems that hyperinflation created for Nicaraguans in 1989.

For generations, Nicaraguans have guarded their savings in piggy banks . . . But no longer. In a country where inflation recently reached 161 percent for a two-week period, a penny saved is a penny spent. "No one wants a bank now," said a potter who has given over his kilns to making beer mugs. "We've given up even making them."

The demise of the piggy bank is only the least of the complications that have vexed the public as inflation and Government efforts to combat it have sent the value of the Nicaraguan córdoba fluctuating wildly.

After inflation became unbearable, the Government replaced all of its currency in February 1988 at a new rate of 10 córdobas to a dollar. But by December, the new money had reached 4,500 to the dollar, and despite months of harsh austerity measures, it has now surged upward again, reaching 26,250 to the dollar.

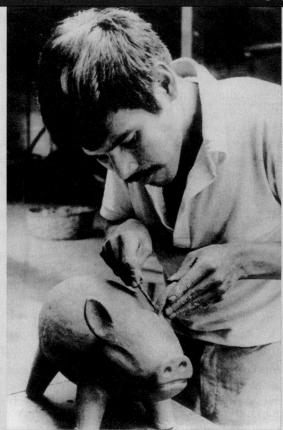

That kind of uncertainty has left the banking system in shambles, despite savings accounts that offer up to 70 percent interest a month. . . . And it has left a legacy of quirks that now extends throughout the country's daily life . . . .

In many parts of the country, enterprising mechanics have converted the nation's once-precious stock of coins into something more valuable: metal washers to fit the nuts and bolts of rapidly deteriorating machinery . . . .

In Managua, it is still necessary to deposit a copper-colored one-córdoba coin to make a pay phone call. But . . . not everybody even remembers what a one-córdoba coin looks like, and fewer still actually own one. That is probably just as well for the phone system, because if anyone bothered to carry the coins, they could make about 26,250 phone calls for a dollar . . . .

Beating the exchange rates is particularly trying for restaurant owners who must have any price increases approved by the Government Institute of Tourism. Since that process consumes precious amounts of time, restaurant owners must aim high with their requests in the anticipation that new inflation will make their prices competitive, but still profitable, at some future date.

When exchange rates are changing, therefore, prices at a given restaurant can shoot far out of sight, emptying it of patrons for days or weeks. Then, as has happened recently, a new devaluation can make the same prices absurdly low in dollar terms. A steak dinner for two at one of Managua's leading restaurants on a recent weekend cost a little over $3, if you could get a table.

SOURCE: Mark A. Uhlig, "Is Nicaraguan Piggy Bank an Endangered Species?" *The New York Times*, June 24, 1989.

THE COSTS OF CREEPING VERSUS GALLOPING INFLATION

If you review the costs of inflation that have been discussed in this chapter, you will see why the distinction beween creeping and galloping inflation is so fundamental. Many economists think we can live very nicely in an environment of creeping inflation. No one believes we can survive very well under galloping inflation.

Under creeping inflation, the rate at which prices rise is relatively easy to predict and to take into account in setting interest rates (as long as the law allows). Under galloping inflation, where prices are rising at ever-increasing rates, this is extremely difficult, and perhaps impossible, to accomplish. The potential redistributions become monumental, and as a result, lending and borrowing may cease entirely.

Any inflation makes it difficult to write long-term contracts. With creeping inflation, the "long term" may be 20 years, or 10 years, or 5. But with galloping inflation, the "long term" may be measured in weeks or even hours. Restaurant prices may change before you finish your dessert. Railroad fares may go up while you are in the middle of your journey. When it is impossible to enter into contracts of any duration longer than a few hours, economic activity becomes paralyzed. We conclude that:

The horrors of galloping inflation either are absent in creeping inflation or are present in such muted forms that they can scarcely be considered horrors.

CREEPING INFLATION DOES NOT NECESSARILY LEAD TO GALLOPING INFLATION

We noted earlier that inflation is surrounded by a mythology that bears precious little relation to reality. It seems appropriate to conclude this chapter by disposing of one particularly persistent myth: that creeping inflation invariably leads to galloping inflation.

There is neither statistical evidence nor theoretical support for the myth that creeping inflation inevitably leads to galloping inflation. To be sure, creeping inflations sometimes accelerate. But at other times they slow down.

While creeping inflations have many causes, galloping inflations have occurred only when the government has printed incredible amounts of money, usually to finance wartime expenditures.

These children in Germany during the hyperinflation of the 1920s are building a pyramid with cash, worth no more than the sand or sticks used by children elsewhere.

In the German inflation of 1923, the government finally found that its printing presses could not produce enough paper money to keep pace with the exploding prices. Not that it did not try. By the end of the inflation, the *daily* output of currency was over 400 quadrillion marks! The Hungarian authorities in 1945–1946 tried even harder. The average growth rate of the money supply was more than 12,000 percent *per month*. Needless to say, these are not the kind of inflation problems that are likely to face the United States in the foreseeable future.

But this should not be interpreted to imply there is nothing wrong with creeping inflation. Much of this chapter has been spent analyzing the very real costs of any inflation, no matter how slow. A case against even moderate inflation can indeed be built, but it does not help this case to shout foolish slogans like "Creeping inflation always leads to galloping inflation." Fortunately, it is simply not true.

Summary

1. Unemployment exacts heavy financial and psychological costs from those who are its victims, costs that are borne quite unevenly by different groups in the population.

2. In recent decades, the U.S. economy often has produced less output than it could have were it operating at full employment. This shortfall between actual and **potential GDP** was particularly large in the 1980s.

3. The **unemployment rate** is measured by a government survey that some critics claim understates the unemployment problem. Others, however, contend that the survey methods overstate the problem.

4. **Frictional unemployment** arises when people are between jobs for normal reasons. Thus, most frictional unemployment is desirable.

5. **Structural unemployment** is due to shifts in the pattern of demand or to technological change that makes certain skills obsolete.

6. **Cyclical unemployment** is the portion of unemployment that rises in recessions and falls when the economy booms.

7. President Kennedy first enunciated the goal of 4 percent unemployment in 1961. But few economists think this is a realistic target for the 1990s. Most now think that **"full employment"** comes at an unemployment rate between 5 and 6 percent.

8. **Unemployment insurance** replaces nearly one-half the lost income of unemployed persons who are insured. But less than one-third of the unemployed collect benefits, and no insurance program can bring back the lost output that could have been produced had these people been working.

9. People have many misconceptions about inflation. For example, many people believe that inflation systematically erodes **real wages**, are appalled by rising prices even when wages are rising just as fast, and blame inflation for any unfavorable changes in **relative prices**. All of these are myths.

10. Other costs of inflation are real, however. For example, inflation often redistributes income from lenders to borrowers.

11. This redistribution can be eliminated by adding the **expected rate of inflation** to the interest rate. But legal limitations sometimes prevent this, and expectations often prove to be inaccurate.

12. The **real rate of interest** is the **nominal rate of interest** minus the expected rate of inflation.

13. Since the real rate of interest indicates the command over real resources that the borrower surrenders to the lender, it is of primary economic importance.

14. Yet public attention often is riveted on nominal rates of interest, and this confusion can lead to costly policy mistakes when high inflation converts high nominal interest rates into very low real interest rates. This is one of the **12 Ideas for Beyond the Final Exam**.

15. Because nominal, not real, interest is taxed, our tax system levies heavy taxes on interest income when inflation is high.

16. **Creeping inflation**, which proceeds at moderate and fairly predictable rates year after year, carries far lower social costs than **galloping inflation**, which proceeds at high and variable rates.

17. The notion that creeping inflation inevitably leads to galloping inflation is a myth with no foundation in economic theory and no basis in historical fact.

Key Concepts and Terms

Unemployment rate	Full employment	Real rate of interest
Potential GDP	Unemployment insurance	Nominal rate of interest
Labor force	Purchasing power	Expected rate of inflation
Discouraged workers	Real wage	Inflation and the tax system
Frictional unemployment	Relative prices	Usury laws
Structural unemployment	Redistribution by inflation	Creeping inflation
Cyclical unemployment		Galloping inflation

Questions for Review

1. Why is it not as terrible to become unemployed nowadays as it was during the Great Depression?

2. "Unemployment is no longer a social problem because unemployed workers receive unemployment benefits and other benefits that make up for most of their lost wages." Comment.

3. Using what you learned about aggregate demand and aggregate supply in Chapter 5, try to explain why the U.S. economy has failed so frequently to produce up to its potential. (You will learn more about this question in later chapters, so don't worry if you find the question difficult now.)

4. Why is it so difficult to define "full employment"? What unemployment rate should the government be shooting for today?

5. Show why each of the following complaints is based on a misunderstanding about inflation:

   a. "Inflation must be stopped because it robs workers of their purchasing power."

   b. "Inflation is a terrible social disease. It leads to unconscionably high prices for basic necessities."

   c. "Inflation makes it impossible for working people to afford many of the things they were hoping to buy."

   d. "Inflation must be stopped today, for if we do not stop it, it will surely accelerate to ruinously high rates and lead to disaster."

6. What is the *real interest rate* paid on a credit-card loan bearing 18 percent nominal interest per year, if the rate of inflation is

   a. zero
   b. 3 percent
   c. 6 percent
   d. 18 percent
   e. 24 percent.

7. Suppose you agree to lend money to your friend on the day you both enter college, at what you both expect to be a zero *real* rate of interest. Payment is to be made at graduation, with interest at a fixed *nominal* rate. If inflation proves to be *lower* during your four years in college than what you both had expected, who will gain and who will lose?

8. You have lived with inflation all your life. Think about the costs that inflation has imposed on you personally. How do these costs relate to the material in this chapter?

9. Add a third line to Table 6–4 showing what would happen if the inflation rate went to 12 percent and the real interest rate remained 3 percent.

Appendix | **HOW STATISTICIANS MEASURE INFLATION**

INDEX NUMBERS FOR INFLATION

Inflation is generally measured by the change in some index of the general price level. For example, between 1973 and 1992, the Consumer Price Index (CPI) rose from 44.4 to 140.3, an increase of 216 percent. The meaning of the *change* is clear enough. But what is the meaning of the 44.4 figure for 1973 and the 140.3 figure for 1992?

These numbers are **index numbers**, each expresses the cost of a market basket of goods *relative to its cost in some "base" period.* Since the CPI currently uses 1982–1984 as its base period, the CPI of 140.3 for 1992 means that it cost $140.30 to purchase the same basket of goods and services that cost $100 in 1982–1984.

Now, the particular basket of consumer goods and services under scrutiny really did not cost $100 in 1982–1984. When constructing index numbers, it is conventional to set the index at 100 in the base period. How is this conventional figure used in obtaining index numbers of other years? Very simply. Suppose the budget needed to buy the roughly 250 items included in the CPI was $2200 per month in 1982–1984 and $3087 per month in 1992. Then the index is defined by the following rule:

$$\frac{\text{CPI in 1992}}{\text{CPI in 1982–1984}} =$$

$$\frac{\text{Cost of the 250-item market basket in 1992}}{\text{Cost of the 250-item market basket in 1982–1984}}.$$

Since the CPI in 1982–1984 is set at 100:

$$\frac{\text{CPI in 1992}}{100} = \frac{\$3087}{\$2200} = 1.403$$

or

$$\text{CPI in 1992} = 140.3.$$

Exactly the same sort of equation enables us to calculate the CPI in any other year. We have the rule:

$$\text{CPI in given year} =$$

$$\frac{\text{Cost of market basket in given year}}{\text{Cost of market basket in base year}} \times 100.$$

Of course, not every combination of consumer goods that cost $2200 in 1982–1984 rose to $3087 by 1992. For example, a color TV set that cost $400 in

1982 might still have cost $400 in 1992, but a $400 hospital bill in 1982 might have ballooned to $1200. Since no two families buy precisely the same bundle of goods and services, no two families suffer precisely the same increase in their cost of living unless all prices rise at the same rate. Economists refer to this phenomenon as the **index number problem**.

When relative prices are changing, there is no such thing as a "perfect price index" that is correct for every consumer. Any statistical index will understate the increase in the cost of living for some families and overstate it for others. At best, the index can represent the situation of an "average" family.

THE CONSUMER PRICE INDEX

The most closely watched price index is surely the **Consumer Price Index**, which is calculated and announced each month by the Bureau of Labor Statistics (BLS). When you read in the newspaper or see on television that the "cost of living rose by 0.3 percent last month," chances are the reporter is referring to the CPI.

The CPI is measured by pricing the items on a list representative of a typical urban household budget. To know what items to include and in what amounts, the BLS conducts an extensive survey of spending habits roughly once every decade (the last one was in 1982–1984). This means that the *same* bundle of goods and services is used as a standard for 10 years or so, whether or not spending habits change.[6] Of course, spending habits do change; and this introduces a small error into the CPI's measurement of inflation.

A simple example will help us understand how the CPI is constructed. Imagine that college students purchase only three items—hamburgers, jeans, and movie tickets—and that we want to devise a cost-of-living index (call it SPI, for "student price index") for them. First we would conduct a survey of spending habits in the base year (suppose it is 1983). Table 6–5 represents the hypothetical results. You will

---

[6]Economists call this a *base-period weight index* because the relative importance it attaches to the price of each item depends on how much money consumers actually chose to spend on the item during the base period.

Table **6–5**	**RESULTS OF STUDENT EXPENDITURE SURVEY, 1983**		
ITEM	**AVERAGE PRICE**	**AVERAGE QUANTITY PURCHASED PER MONTH**	**AVERAGE EXPENDITURE PER MONTH**
Hamburger	$0.80	70	$56
Jeans	$24.00	1	$24
Movie ticket	$5.00	4	$20
			Total $100

note that the frugal students of that day spent only $100 per month: $56 on hamburgers, $24 on jeans, and $20 on movies.

Table 6–6 presents hypothetical prices of these same three items in 1994. Each price has risen by a different amount, ranging from 25 percent for jeans up to 50 percent for hamburgers. By how much has the SPI risen? Pricing the 1983 student budget at 1994 prices, we find that what once cost $100 now costs $142, as the calculation in Table 6–7 shows. Thus the SPI, based on 1983 = 100, is

$$\text{SPI} = \frac{\text{Cost of budget in 1994}}{\text{Cost of budget in 1983}} \times 100$$

$$= \frac{\$142}{\$100} \times 100 = 142.$$

So the SPI in 1994 stands at 142, meaning that students' cost of living has increased 42 percent over the 11 years.

HOW TO USE A PRICE INDEX TO "DEFLATE" MONETARY FIGURES

One of the most common uses of price indexes is in the comparison of monetary figures relating to two different points in time. The problem is that, if

there has been inflation, the dollar is not a good measuring rod because it is worth less now than it was in the past.

Here is a simple example. Suppose that the average student spent $100 per month in 1983 but $130 per month in 1994. If there was an outcry that students had become spendthrifts, how would you answer the charge?

The obvious answer is that a dollar in 1994 does not buy what it did in 1983. Specifically, our SPI shows us that it takes $1.42 in 1994 to purchase what $1 would purchase in 1983. To compare the spending habits of students in the two years, we must divide the 1994 spending figure by 1.42. Specifically, _real_ spending per student in 1994 (where "real" is defined by 1983 dollars) is,

$$\text{Real spending in 1994} = \frac{\text{Nominal spending in 1994}}{\text{Price index of 1994}}.$$

Thus,

$$\text{Real spending in 1994} = \frac{\$130}{1.42} = \$91.55.$$

This calculation shows that, despite appearances to the contrary, the change in nominal spending from

Table **6–6**	**PRICES IN 1994**	
ITEM	**PRICE**	**PERCENTAGE INCREASE OVER 1983**
Hamburger	$1.20	50%
Jeans	$30.00	25%
Movie ticket	$7.00	40%

T a b l e **6-7** **COST OF 1983 STUDENT BUDGET IN 1994 PRICES**	
70 hamburgers at $1.20	$84
1 pair of jeans at $30	30
4 movie tickets at $7	28
	Total $142

$100 to $130 actually represented a *decrease* in real spending.

This calculation procedure is called **deflating by a price index**, and it serves to translate noncomparable monetary figures into more directly comparable real figures.

Deflating is the process of finding the real value of some monetary magnitude by dividing by some appropriate price index.

A good practical illustration is the real wage, a concept we have discussed in this chapter. Average hourly earnings in the U.S. economy were $8.02 in 1983 and $10.59 in 1992. Since the CPI in 1992 was 140.3 (with 1982–1984 as the base period), the real wage in 1992 (expressed in 1982–84 dollars) was:

$$\text{Real wage in 1992} = \frac{\text{money wage in 1992}}{\text{price index of 1992}}$$

$$= \frac{\$10.59}{140.3} \times 100 = \$7.55.$$

Thus, by this measure, the real wage fell 5.9 percent over the nine years.

THE GDP DEFLATOR

In macroeconomics, one of the most important of the monetary magnitudes that we have to deflate is the nominal gross domestic product (GDP). The price index used to do this is called the **GDP deflator**. Our general principle for deflating a nominal magnitude tells us precisely how to go from nominal GDP to real GDP:

$$\text{Real GDP} = \frac{\text{Nominal GDP}}{\text{GDP deflator}} \times 100.$$

As with the CPI, the 100 simply serves to establish the base of the index as 100, rather than 1.00.

Economists often consider the GDP deflator to be a better measure of overall inflation in the economy than the Consumer Price Index. The main reason for this is that the two price indexes are based on different market baskets. As already mentioned, the CPI is based on the budget of a typical urban family. By contrast, the GDP deflator is constructed from a market basket that includes *every* item in the GDP—that is, every final good and service produced by the economy. Thus, in addition to prices of consumer goods, the GDP deflator includes the prices of airplanes, lathes, and other goods purchased by business. It also includes government services. For this reason, the measures of inflation that these two indexes give are rarely the same. Usually their disagreements are minor. But sometimes they can be substantial, as in 1980 when the CPI recorded a 13.5 percent inflation rate over 1979 while the GDP deflator recorded only 9.5 percent.

Summary

1. Inflation is measured by the percentage increase in an **index number** of prices, which shows how the cost of some basket of goods has changed over a period of time.

2. Since relative prices are changing all the time, and since different families purchase different items, no price index can represent precisely the change in the cost of living for every family.

3. The **Consumer Price Index (CPI)** tries to measure the cost of living for an "average" urban household by pricing a "typical" market basket every month.

4. Price indexes like the CPI can be used to **deflate** monetary figures to make them more comparable. This amounts to dividing the monetary magnitude by the appropriate price index.

5. The **GDP deflator** is a better measure of economy-wide inflation than is the CPI because it includes the prices of all goods and services in the economy.

Index number	Consumer Price Index	GDP deflator
Index number problem	Deflating by a price index	

Questions for Review

1. On the next page, you will find the yearly average value of the Dow Jones Industrial Average, the most popular index of stock market prices, for four different years. The Consumer Price Index for each year (on a base of 1982–1984 = 100) can be found on the inside back cover of this book. Use these numbers to deflate all four stock market values. In which year were stocks really worth the most?

YEAR	1964	1972	1987	1992
DOW JONES AVERAGE	834	951	2276	3284

2. Just below you will find nominal GDP and the GDP deflator for 1971, 1981, and 1991.

   a. Compute real GDP for each year.
   b. Compute the percentage change in nominal and real GDP from 1971 to 1981, and from 1981 to 1991.
   c. Compute the percentage change in the GDP deflator over these two periods.

GDP STATISTICS

	1971	1981	1991
Nominal GDP (billions of dollars)	1097	3031	5723
GDP deflator	37.0	78.9	117.7

3. Fill in the blanks in the following table of GDP statistics.

YEAR	1990	1991	1992
Nominal GDP	5546.1		6038.5
Real GDP	4897.3	4861.4	
GDP deflator		117.7	121.1

4. Use the following data to compute the College Price Index for 1994 using the base 1972 = 100.

ITEM	PRICE IN 1972	QUANTITY PER MONTH IN 1972	PRICE IN 1994
Button-down shirts	$10	1	$25
Loafers	25	1	55
Sneakers	10	3	35
Textbooks	12	12	40
Jeans	12	3	30
Restaurant meals	5	11	14

5. Average hourly earnings in the U.S. economy during several past years were as follows:

1961	1971	1981	1991
$2.14	$3.45	$7.25	$10.33

Use the CPI numbers provided on the inside back cover to calculate the real wage (in 1982–1984 dollars) for each of these years. Which decade had the fastest growth of money wages? Which had the fastest growth of real wages?

6. The example in the appendix showed that the Student Price Index (SPI) rose by 42 percent from 1983 to 1994. You can understand the meaning of this better if you:

   a. Use Table 6–5 to compute the fraction of total spending accounted for by each of the three items in 1983. Call these the "expenditure weights."
   b. Compute the weighted average of the percentage increases of the three prices shown in Table 6–6, using the expenditure weights you have just computed.
   c. You should get 42 percent as your answer. This shows that "inflation," as measured by the SPI, is a weighted average of the percentage price increases of all the items that are included in the index.

Chapter 7

INCOME AND SPENDING: THE POWERFUL CONSUMER

Men are disposed, as a rule and on the average, to increase their consumption as their income increases, but not by as much as the increase in their income.

JOHN MAYNARD KEYNES

In Chapter 5 we saw how the strength of aggregate demand influences the performance of the economy. When aggregate demand is growing briskly, the economy is likely to be booming, though it may also be having trouble with inflation. When aggregate demand stagnates, a recession is likely to follow. ¶ This chapter begins our detailed study of the theory of income determination, the tool economists use to analyze issues like these. The theory is based on the concepts of aggregate demand and supply. In this and the next two chapters, we construct a simplified model of aggregate demand and learn why the *aggregate demand curve* of Chapter 5 has a negative slope. Then Chapter 10 completes the model by adding the *aggregate supply curve*. ¶ This first model of the macroeconomy can teach us much about the causes of unemployment and inflation. But it is too simple to deal with policy issues because the government and the financial system are largely ignored. These omissions are remedied in Part 3, where government spending, taxation, and interest rates are given appropriately prominent roles. The influence of the exchange rate between the U.S. dollar and foreign currencies is considered in Part 4.

We build our model in steps, starting with aggregate demand. Since consumer spending accounts for the lion's share of total demand, it is natural to begin the analysis there. First, we need some definitions of alternative concepts of economic activity—distinguishing carefully among total *spending* (aggregate demand), total *output*, and total *income*. Next, we turn to the interactions among these three concepts, using a convenient pictorial device that shows how they are all interrelated. Then we note that government attempts to influence consumer spending have sometimes succeeded and sometimes failed, and we pose the question: Why?

The bulk of the chapter is devoted to answering this question. We describe the important relationship between consumer income and consumer spending, and then use it to show how government policies have worked when they have been successful. Then we discuss some complications that arise from the fact that consumer income, though crucial, is not the only factor governing consumer spending. One of these complications holds the clue to why government policies have sometimes failed to influence consumer spending as expected.

AGGREGATE DEMAND, DOMESTIC PRODUCT, AND NATIONAL INCOME

AGGREGATE DEMAND is the total amount that all consumers, business firms, and government agencies are willing to spend on final goods and services.

We have already introduced the concept of **gross domestic product** as the standard measure of the economy's total output.[1] For the most part, goods are produced in a market economy only if firms think they can sell them. **Aggregate demand**, another concept encountered in Chapter 6, is the total amount that all consumers, business firms, government agencies, and foreigners wish to spend on all U.S. final goods and services.

The downward-sloping aggregate demand curve of Chapter 6 alerted us to the fact that aggregate demand is a *schedule*, not a fixed number. The actual numerical value of aggregate demand will depend on the price level, and several reasons for this dependence will emerge in coming chapters.

CONSUMER EXPENDITURE, symbolized by the letter **C**, is the total amount spent by consumers on newly produced goods and services (excluding purchases of new homes, which are considered investment goods).

But the level of aggregate demand also depends on a variety of other factors like consumer incomes, various government policies, and events in foreign countries. We can understand the nature of aggregate demand best if we break it up into its major components.

Consumer expenditure (*"consumption"* for short) is simply the total demand for all consumer goods and services. This is the focus of the current chapter, and we shall represent it by the letter **C**.

INVESTMENT SPENDING, symbolized by the letter **I**, is the sum of the expenditures of business firms on new plant and equipment and households on new homes. Financial "investments" are not included, nor are resales of existing physical assets.

Investment spending, which we represent by the letter **I**, is the amount that firms spend on factories, machinery, and the like plus the amount that families spend on new houses. Notice that this usage of the word "investment" differs from common parlance. Most people speak of "investing" in the stock market or in a bank account. This kind of "investment" merely swaps one form of financial asset (such as money) for another form (such as a share of stock). When economists speak of "investment," they mean instead the purchase of some *new physical* asset, like a drill press or an oil rig or a house. It is only these kinds of investments that lead directly to additional demand for newly produced goods in the economy and, subsequently, to greater productive capacity.

GOVERNMENT PURCHASES, symbolized by the letter **G**, refers to the goods (such as airplanes and paper clips) and services (such as school teaching and police protection) purchased by all levels of government.

The third major component of aggregate demand is **government purchases** of goods and services; that is, items like paper, typewriters, airplanes, ships, and

NET EXPORTS symbolized by **(X − IM)**, is the difference between U.S. exports and U.S. imports. It indicates the difference between what we sell to foreigners and what we buy from them.

labor that are bought by all levels of government—federal, state, and local. We use the shorthand symbol **G** to denote this variable.

The final component of aggregate demand is **net exports**, which are simply defined as U.S. exports minus U.S. imports. The reasoning here is simple. Part of the demand for American goods and services originates beyond our borders— as when foreigners buy our wheat, our computers, and our banking services. So this must be added to domestic demand. Similarly, some items included in *C* and *I* are not American made—think, for example, of German beer, Japanese cars, and Korean textiles. So these must be subtracted, if we want to measure total spending on U.S. products. The inclusion of exports, which we represent by the symbol **X**, and the subtraction of imports, **IM**, leads us to the following shorthand definition of aggregate demand:

Aggregate demand is the sum $C + I + G + (X - IM)$.

The relative sizes of these four components of aggregate demand are indicated in the bar chart in Figure 7–10 (page 178). Consumer spending, the focus of this chapter, is the biggest by far.

The last concept we need for our vocabulary is a way to measure the total *income* of all the individuals in the economy. There are two versions of this: one for before-tax incomes, called **national income**, and one for after-tax incomes, called **disposable income**.[2] The term "disposable income" is meant to be descriptive: it tells us how many dollars consumers actually have available to spend or to save. Because it plays such a prominent role in this chapter, we shall need an abbreviation for it as well; we call it **DI**.

NATIONAL INCOME is the sum of the incomes of all the individuals in the economy earned in the forms of wages, interest, rents, and profits. It excludes transfer payments and is calculated before any deductions are taken for income taxes.

DISPOSABLE INCOME is the sum of the incomes of all the individuals in the economy after all taxes have been deducted and all transfer payments have been added.

THE CIRCULAR FLOW OF SPENDING, PRODUCTION, AND INCOME

Enough definitions. How do these three concepts—domestic product, total expenditure, and national income—interact in a market economy? We can answer this best with a rather elaborate diagram (Figure 7–1). For obvious reasons, Figure 7–1 is called a **circular flow diagram**. It depicts a large circular tube in which a fluid is circulating in a clockwise direction. There are several breaks in the tube where either some of the fluid leaks out or additional fluid is injected in.

Let us examine this system, beginning on the far left. At point 1 on the circle, we find consumers. Disposable income (*DI*) is flowing into them, and two things are flowing out: consumption (*C*), which stays in the circular flow, and saving (*S*), which "leaks out." This just says that consumers normally spend less than they earn and save the balance. The "leakage" to savings, of course, does not disappear, but flows into the financial system. We postpone consideration of what happens there until Chapter 12.

The upper loop of the circular flow represents expenditures, and as we move clockwise to point 2, we encounter the first "injection" into the flow: investment spending (*I*). The diagram shows this as coming from "investors"—a group that includes both business firms and consumers who buy new homes.[3] As the circular flow moves past point 2, it is bigger than it was before. Total spending has increased from *C* to *C + I*.

---

[2]More detailed information on these and other concepts is provided in Appendix B to this chapter.
[3]You are reminded of the specific definition of investment on page 151.

| Figure | 7-1 | **THE CIRCULAR FLOW OF EXPENDITURE AND INCOME** |

The upper part of this circular flow diagram depicts the flow of expenditures on goods and services that comes from consumers (point 1), investors (point 2), government (point 3), and foreigners (point 4), and goes to the firms that produce the output (point 5). The lower part of the diagram indicates how the income paid out by firms (point 5) flows to consumers (point 1), after some is siphoned off by the government in the form of taxes and part of this is replaced by transfer payments (point 6).

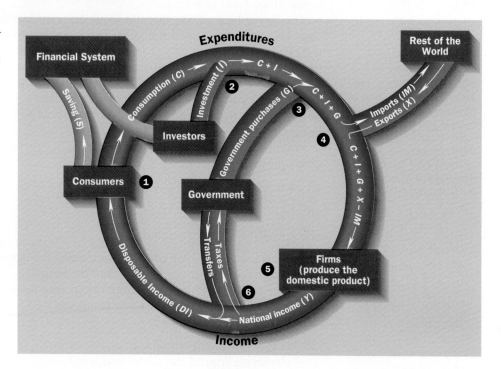

At point 3 there is yet another injection. The government adds its demand for goods and services (G) to those of consumers and investors ($C + I$). Now aggregate demand is up to $C + I + G$.

The final leakage and injection comes at point 4. Here we see export spending entering the circular flow from abroad and import spending leaking out. The net effect of these two forces, net exports, may increase or decrease the circular flow. In either case, by the time we pass point 4 we have accumulated the full amount of aggregate demand, $C + I + G + (X - IM)$.

The circular flow diagram shows this aggregate demand for goods and services arriving at the business firms, which are located at point 5 at the southeast portion of the diagram. Responding to this demand, firms produce the domestic product. As the circular flow emerges from the firms, however, we have renamed it *national income*. Why? The reason is that, except for some complications explained in the appendix:

National income and domestic product must be equal.

Why is this the case? When a firm produces and sells $100 worth of output, it pays most of the proceeds to its workers, to people who have lent it money, and to the landlord who owns the property on which it is located. All of these payments are *income* to some individuals. But what about the rest? Suppose, for example, that the wages, interest, and rent that the firm pays add up to $90, while its output is $100. What happens to the remaining $10? The answer is that the owners of the firm receive it as *profits*. But these owners are also citizens of the country, so their incomes count in national income, too.[4] Thus, when we add up all the wages, interest, rents, *and profits* in the economy to obtain the national *income*, we must arrive at the *value of output*.

The lower loop of the circular flow diagram traces the flow of income by showing national income leaving the firms and heading for consumers. But there is a detour along the way. At point 6, the government does two things. First, it siphons off a portion of the national income in the form of taxes. Second, it adds back government **transfer payments**, like unemployment compensation and social security benefits, which are sums of money that certain individuals receive as outright *grants* from the government rather than as payments for services rendered to employers.

When taxes are subtracted from GDP, and transfer payments are added, we obtain disposable income.[5]

$$DI = GDP - \text{Taxes} + \text{Transfer Payments},$$

or

$$DI = GDP - T,$$

where T is our symbol for taxes net of transfers. Disposable income flows unimpeded to consumers at point 1, and the cycle repeats.

This diagram raises several complicated questions. Although we pose them here, we will not try to answer them at this early stage. The answers will be made clear in subsequent chapters.

1. Is the flow of spending and income growing larger or smaller as we move clockwise around the circle, and why?

2. Is the output that the firms produce at point 5 (the GDP) equal to aggregate demand? If so, what makes these two quantities equal? If not, what happens?

Chapter 8 provides the answers to these two questions.

3. Are the government's accounts in balance, so that what flows in at point 6 (taxes minus transfers) is equal to what flows out at point 3 (government purchases)? What happens if they are not?

This important question is first addressed in Chapter 11 and then recurs many times, especially in Chapter 15, which is devoted to discussing budget deficits.

4. Is our international trade balanced, so that exports equal imports? More generally, what factors determine net exports and what are the consequences of trade deficits or surpluses?

These questions are taken up briefly in Chapters 8 and 9, and then considered fully in Part 5, which is devoted to international economic issues.

However, we cannot discuss any of these issues profitably until we first understand what goes on at point 1, where consumers make decisions, and point 2, where investors make decisions. We turn next, therefore, to the determinants of consumer spending.

TRANSFER PAYMENTS are sums of money that certain individuals receive as outright *grants* from the government rather than as payments for services rendered to employers. Some common examples are social security and unemployment benefits.

---

[4]Some of the income paid out by American companies goes to non-citizens. Similarly, some Americans earn income from foreign firms. This complication is dealt with in Appendix B.

[5]This definition omits a few minor details, which are explained in Appendix B to this chapter.

DEMAND MANAGEMENT AND THE POWERFUL CONSUMER

As we suggested in Chapter 5, the government sometimes wants to shift the aggregate demand curve. There are a number of ways in which it can try to do so. One direct approach is to alter its own spending (G), becoming extravagant when private demand is weak and miserly when private demand is strong. But the government can also take a more indirect route by using taxes and other policy tools to influence *private* spending decisions.

A government desiring to change private spending can concentrate its energies on consumer spending (C), on investment spending (I), or on net exports (X − IM). At various times in our history, the U.S. government has endeavored to change each. Since consumer expenditures constitute about two-thirds of gross national product, C presents the most tempting target.

While there are many things it can do to alter consumer spending, the government's principal weapon is the personal income tax. Many of you already have encountered Form 1040, the unwelcome New Year's greeting that every taxpayer receives from the federal government each January. Many more of you probably have been on a payroll and have seen a share of your wages deducted and sent to the Internal Revenue Service. It should be no mystery, then, how changes in personal taxes affect consumer spending. Any reduction in personal taxes leaves consumers with more disposable income to spend. Any increase in taxes leaves less.

The linkage from taxes to disposable income to consumer spending seems direct and unmistakable, and, in a certain sense, it is. But a look at the history of some major tax changes aimed at altering C is sobering. The varying degrees of success both of the measures themselves and of the predictions of their effects explain why economic research into the relationship between taxes and consumption continues.

CASE 1: THE 1964 TAX REDUCTION

The year 1964 was a good one for economists. For years they had been proclaiming that a cut in personal taxes would be an excellent way to stimulate a stagnating economy. But the plea fell on deaf ears until President John F. Kennedy was persuaded of the basic logic of the argument and his successor, Lyndon Johnson, pushed the legislation through Congress. The 1964 tax cut was designed to spur consumer spending, and it succeeded admirably. Consumers reacted just about as the textbooks of the day predicted, the economy improved rapidly and markedly, and economists smiled knowingly.

CASE 2: THE 1975 TAX REDUCTION

The next major attempt to stimulate the economy by cutting taxes met with much less success. In the spring of 1975, as the economy hit the bottom of a recession, President Gerald Ford and Congress agreed on a temporary tax cut to spur consumer spending: They returned to each taxpayer part of the taxes paid in 1974 and reduced income tax rates for the balance of 1975. However, consumers confounded the wishes of the president and Congress by saving a good deal of their rebates rather than spending them.

CASE 3: THE 1981–1984 TAX CUTS

A series of reductions in personal income tax rates was a major campaign promise of Ronald Reagan, one which was promptly redeemed. Tax rates fell by about 23 percent between 1981 and 1984, and consumer spending increased by more or less the amounts that economists predicted, thereby contributing to the long economic expansion of the 1980s.

Thus tax policy did more or less what it was expected to do in 1964 and 1981–1984 but seemed to be less effective in 1975. Why? This chapter will attempt to provide some answers. We begin by exploring the important relationship between consumer income and consumer spending, more or less retracing the chain of logic that led government economists to the right conclusion in 1964. Once this is accomplished, we turn to some of the complications that made things go awry in 1975.

CONSUMER SPENDING AND INCOME: THE IMPORTANT RELATIONSHIP

An economist interested in predicting how consumer spending will respond to a change in personal income tax payments must first ask how C is related to disposable income; for an increase in taxes is a decrease in after-tax income, and a reduction in taxes is an increase in after-tax income. This section, therefore, will examine what we know about the response of consumer spending to a change in disposable income.

Figure 7–2 depicts the historical paths of C and DI for the United States since 1929. The association is obviously rather close and certainly suggests that consumption will rise whenever disposable income does, and fall whenever income falls. The difference between the two lines is personal saving. Notice how little saving consumers did during the Great Depression of the 1930s, where the two lines are very close together, and how much they did during World War II, when many consumer goods were either unavailable or rationed so there was little on which to spend money.

Of course, knowing that consumer expenditures, C, will move in the same direction as disposable income, DI, is not enough for policy planners. They need to know *how much* one will go up when the other rises a given amount. Figure 7–3 presents the same data as in Figure 7–2, but in a way designed to help answer the "how much" question.

A **SCATTER DIAGRAM** is a graph showing the relationship between two variables (such as consumption and disposable income). Each year is represented by a point in the diagram. The coordinates of each year's point show the value of the two variables in that year.

Economists call such pictures **scatter diagrams**, and they are very useful in predicting how one economic variable (in this case, consumer spending) will change in response to a change in another economic variable (in this case, disposable income). Each dot in the diagram represents the data on C and DI corresponding to a particular year. For example, the point labeled "1976" shows that real consumer expenditures in 1976 were $2207 billion (which we read off the vertical axis), while real disposable incomes amounted to $2441 billion (which we read off the horizontal axis). Similarly, each year from 1929 to 1992 is represented by its own dot in Figure 7–3.

How can such a diagram assist the fiscal policy planner? Imagine that this is 1963 and you must decide whether to recommend to Congress a tax cut of $5 billion, $10 billion, or $15 billion. You have forecasts of what consumer expenditures are expected to be if taxes are not reduced. This, plus other forecasts of

F i g u r e **7–2**	**CONSUMER SPENDING AND DISPOSABLE INCOME IN THE UNITED STATES SINCE 1929**

This time series chart shows the behavior of consumer spending and disposable income in the United States since 1929. Except for the World War II years, the correspondence between the two variables is remarkably close. The distance between the two lines represents consumer saving, which was obviously quite small during the Great Depression of the 1930s and quite large during World War II.

SOURCE: U.S. Department of Commerce.

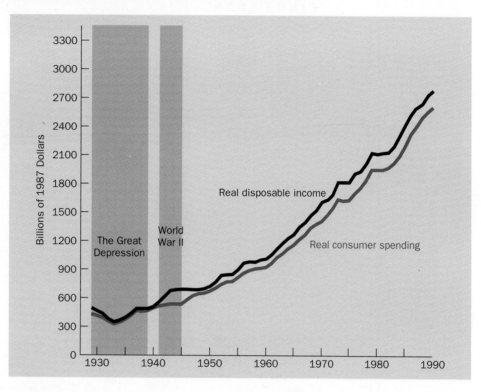

investment, government spending, and net exports has led you to conclude that aggregate demand in 1964 will be insufficient if taxes are not reduced.

To assist your imagination, another scatter diagram is given in Figure 7–4. This one removes the points for 1964 through 1992, which appear in Figure 7–3; after all, these were not known in 1963. Years prior to 1947 have also been removed because both the Great Depression and wartime rationing seriously disturbed the normal relationship between *DI* and *C*. With no more training in economics than you have right now, what would you do?

One rough-and-ready approach is to get a ruler, set it down on Figure 7–4, and sketch a straight line that comes as close as possible to hitting all the points. Try that now. You will not be able to hit each point exactly, but you will find that you can come remarkably close. The line you have just drawn summarizes, in a very rough way, the consumption-income relationship that is the focus of this chapter. We see at once that it confirms something we might have guessed—that a rise in income is associated with a rise in consumer spending. The slope of the line is certainly positive.

The slope of your line is very important.[6] That line has been drawn into Figure 7–5, and we note that its slope is

$$\text{Slope} = \frac{\text{Vertical change}}{\text{Horizontal change}} = \frac{\$90 \text{ billion}}{\$100 \text{ billion}} = 0.90.$$

[6]To review the concept of *slope*, turn back to page 20.

| F i g u r e | 7–3 | SCATTER DIAGRAM OF CONSUMER SPENDING AND DISPOSABLE INCOME IN THE UNITED STATES SINCE 1929 |

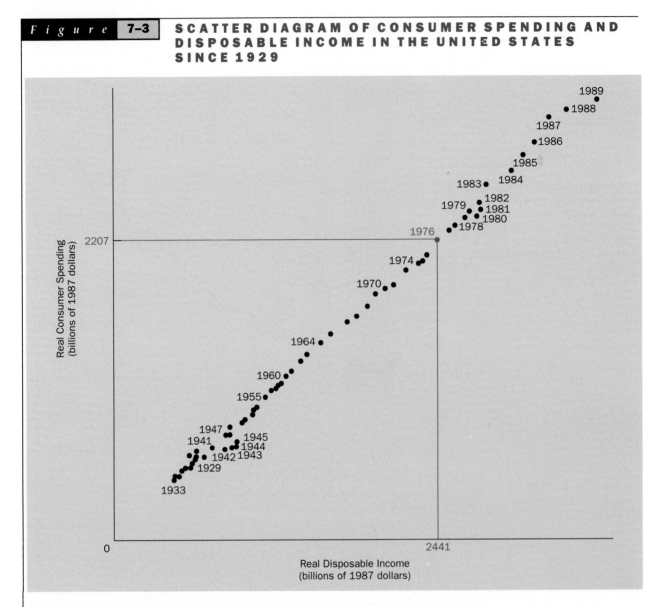

This diagram shows the same data as depicted in Figure 7–2 but in a different manner. Each point on the diagram represents the data for both consumer spending and disposable income during a particular year. For example, the point labeled "1976" indicates that in that year consumer spending was $2207 billion while disposable income was $2441 billion. Diagrams like this one are called "scatter diagrams."

Since the horizontal change involved in the move from *A* to *B* represents a rise in disposable income of $100 billion (from $1000 billion to $1100 billion), and the corresponding vertical change represents the associated $90 billion rise in consumer spending (from $900 to $990 billion), the slope of the line indicates how spending responds to changes in disposable income. In this case, we see that each additional $1 of income leads to 90 cents of additional spending.

Figure	**7-4**

SCATTER DIAGRAM OF CONSUMER SPENDING AND DISPOSABLE INCOME IN THE UNITED STATES, 1947–1963

This scatter diagram omits some of the data found in Figure 7–3 and indicates the information that policy planners might have used in deciding upon the size of the 1964 income tax cut.

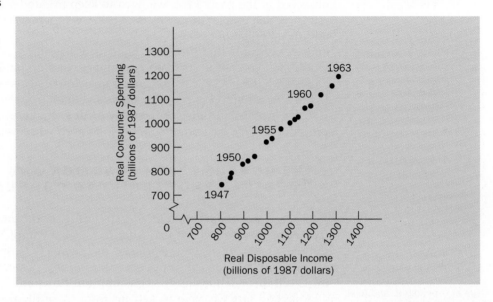

Figure	**7-5**

SCATTER DIAGRAM OF CONSUMER SPENDING AND DISPOSABLE INCOME IN THE UNITED STATES, 1947–1963

This diagram is the same as Figure 7–4 except for the addition of a straight line that comes about as close as possible to fitting all the data points.

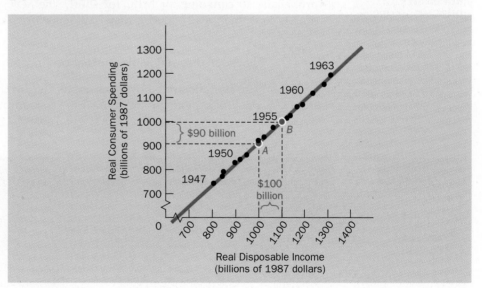

In terms of the policy issue of 1964, this line can therefore help provide an answer to the question, How much more consumer spending will be induced by tax cuts of $5 billion, $10 billion, or $15 billion, if the effects are similar to those observed in the past? First, we need to keep in mind that each dollar of tax cut increases disposable income by $1. Then we apply Figure 7–5's finding that each additional dollar of disposable income increases consumer spending by 90 cents, and we conclude that proposed tax cuts of $5 billion, $10 billion, or $15 billion would be expected to increase consumer spending by $4.5 billion, $9.0 billion, and $13.5 billion, respectively. Similar questions addressed by economists in 1964 led to a decision to cut taxes by about $9 billion.

Later in this and other chapters, we will encounter several reasons why this procedure, while basically valid, must be used with great caution.

THE CONSUMPTION FUNCTION AND THE MARGINAL PROPENSITY TO CONSUME

It has been said that economics is just systematized common sense. Let us, then, try to organize and generalize what has been a completely intuitive discussion thus far. One thing we have learned is that there is a close and apparently reliable relationship between consumer spending, C, and disposable income, DI. Economists call this relationship the **consumption function**.

A second fact we have picked up from these figures is that the *slope* of the consumption function is fairly constant. We infer this from the fact that the straight line in Figure 7–5 comes close to touching every point. If the slope of the consumption function had changed a lot, it would not be possible to do so well with a single straight line. Because of its importance in such applications as the tax-cut example, economists have given a special name to this slope—the **marginal propensity to consume**, or **MPC** for short. The *MPC* tells us how many more dollars consumers will spend if disposable income rises by $1 billion.

$$MPC = \frac{\text{Change in consumption}}{\text{Change in disposable income that produces the change in consumption}}$$

The MPC is best illustrated by an example, and for this purpose we turn away from U.S. data for a moment and look at the consumption and income data of a hypothetical country called Macroland (see Table 7–1). The data for Macroland

The **CONSUMPTION FUNCTION** is the relationship between total consumer expenditure and total disposable income in the economy, holding all other determinants of consumer spending constant.

The **MARGINAL PROPENSITY TO CONSUME** (or MPC for short) is the ratio of the change in consumption to the change in disposable income that produces the change in consumption. On a graph, it appears as the slope of the consumption function.

Table **7–1**	CONSUMPTION AND INCOME IN MACROLAND		
YEAR	**(1)** **CONSUMPTION, C** **(billions of dollars)**	**(2)** **DISPOSABLE INCOME, DI** **(billions of dollars)**	**(3)** **MARGINAL PROPENSITY** **TO CONSUME, MPC**
1989	2700	3200	0.75
1990	3000	3600	0.75
1991	3300	4000	0.75
1992	3600	4400	0.75
1993	3900	4800	0.75
1994	4200	5200	

| *F i g u r e* **7–6** | **THE CONSUMPTION FUNCTION OF MACROLAND** |

This diagram is similar to Figure 7–5, except that it applies to a hypothetical (and blissfully simple!) economy called Macroland. As can be seen, a straight-line consumption function passes through every point exactly. The slope of this line is 0.75, which is the marginal propensity to consume in Macroland.

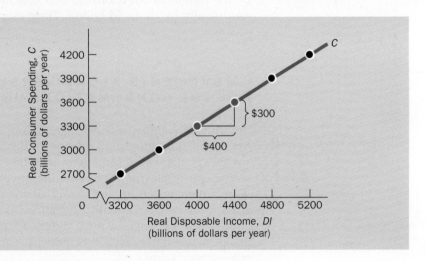

resemble those for the United States, except that in Macroland, C and DI figures happen to be nice round numbers, which facilitates computation.

Columns 1 and 2 of Table 7–1 show annual consumer expenditure and disposable income from 1989 to 1994. These two columns constitute Macroland's consumption function and are plotted in Figure 7–6. Column 3 in the table shows the marginal propensity to consume (MPC), which is the slope of the line in Figure 7–6; it is derived from the first two columns. We can see that between 1991 and 1992, DI rose by $400 billion (from $4000 to $4400) while C rose by $300 billion (from $3300 to $3600). Thus the MPC was

$$\frac{\text{Change in consumption}}{\text{Change in disposable income}} = \frac{\$300}{\$400} = 0.75.$$

As you can easily verify, the MPC between any other pair of years in Macroland is also 0.75. This explains why the slope of the line in Figure 7–5 was so crucial in estimating the effect of a tax cut. This slope, which we found to be 0.90, is nothing but the MPC for the United States. And it is the MPC that tells us how much *additional* spending will be induced by each dollar *change* in disposable income. For each $1 of tax cut, economists expect consumption to rise by $1 times the marginal propensity to consume.

To estimate the *initial* effect of a tax cut on consumer spending, economists must first estimate the MPC and then multiply the amount of the tax cut by the estimated MPC. But since they never know the true MPC with certainty, this prediction is always subject to some margin of error.[7]

The word "initial" in the first sentence is an important one. Later chapters explain why the effects discussed in this chapter are only the beginning of the story.

In 1963, for example, economists multiplied the anticipated $9 billion tax cut by the estimated MPC of 0.90 and concluded that consumer spending would rise initially by about $8 billion. Their estimate seems to have been remarkably accurate.

MOVEMENTS ALONG VERSUS SHIFTS OF THE CONSUMPTION FUNCTION

Unfortunately, this sort of calculation does not always yield such precise results. Among the most important reasons for this is that the consumption function does not always stand still; sometimes it shifts.

You will recall from Chapter 4 the important distinction between a *movement along* a demand curve and a *shift* of the curve. A demand curve depicts the relationship between quantity demanded and only *one* of its many determinants—price. Thus, a change in price causes a *movement along the demand curve*, but a change in any other factor that influences quantity demanded causes a *shift of the entire demand curve*.

Because consumer spending is influenced by factors other than disposable income, a similar distinction is vital to understanding real-world consumption functions. Look back at the definition of the consumption function in the margin of page 160. A change in disposable income leads to a **movement along the consumption function** precisely because the consumption function depicts the relationship between C and DI. (See the red arrow in Figure 7–7.) This is what we have been considering so far. But consumption also has other determinants, and a change in any of these "other determinants" will **shift the entire consumption function**—as indicated by the blue lines in Figure 7–7. These shifts account for many of the errors in forecasting consumption. To summarize:

Any change in disposable income moves us *along* a given consumption function. But a change in any of the other variables that influence consumption *shifts* the entire consumption schedule (see Figure 7–7).

Let us now list some of these "other variables" that can shift the consumption function.

OTHER DETERMINANTS OF CONSUMER SPENDING

WEALTH

One factor affecting consumption is consumers' *wealth*, which is a source of purchasing power in addition to income. Wealth and income are different things. For example, a wealthy person who does not work, but has a healthy bank account, may have little current *income*. Similarly, a high-income individual who spends all she earns will not accumulate wealth. To appreciate the importance of the distinction, consider two consumers, both earning $35,000 this year. One of them has $100,000 in the bank, while the other has no assets at all. Who do you think will spend more this year? Presumably the one with the big bank account.

| F i g u r e | **7-7** | **SHIFTS OF THE CONSUMPTION FUNCTION** |

An increase in disposable income causes a movement along a fixed consumption function, such as the movement from point A to point B on consumption function C_0 (see the red arrow). But a change in any other determinant of consumer spending will cause the whole consumption function to shift upward (consumption function C_1) or downward (consumption function C_2).

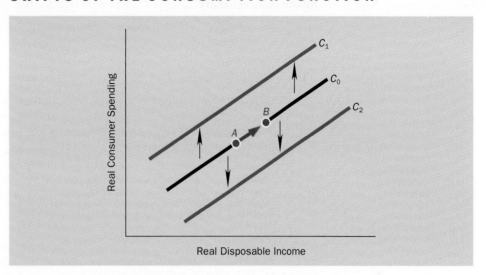

The general point is that current income is not the only source of funds that households have; they can also finance spending by withdrawals from their bank accounts or by cashing in other forms of wealth. A stock market boom may therefore raise the consumption function (see the shift from C_0 to C_1 in Figure 7–7), while a collapse of stock prices may lower it (see the shift from C_0 to C_2).

THE PRICE LEVEL

A good deal of consumer wealth is held in forms whose values are fixed in money terms. Money itself is the most obvious example of this, but government bonds, savings accounts, and corporate bonds are all assets with fixed face values in money terms. The purchasing power of any **money fixed asset** obviously declines whenever the price level rises, which means that the asset can buy less. For example, if the price level rises by 10 percent, a $1000 government bond will buy about 10 percent less than it could when prices were lower. Consequently:

Higher prices decrease the demand for goods and services by eroding the purchasing power of consumer wealth.

A **MONEY FIXED ASSET** is an asset with a face value fixed in terms of dollars, such as money itself, government bonds, and corporate bonds.

This is no trivial matter. It has been estimated that consumers in the United States hold money fixed assets worth over $3 *trillion*, so that each 1 percent rise in the price level reduces the purchasing power of consumer wealth by over $30 billion, a tidy sum. The process, of course, operates equally well in reverse. Since a decline in the price level increases the purchasing power of money fixed assets:

Lower prices increase the demand for goods and services by enhancing the purchasing power of consumer wealth.

For these reasons, a change in the price level will shift the entire consumption function. Specifically:

A higher price level leads to lower real wealth and therefore to less spending *at any given level of real income*. Thus, a higher price level leads to a lower consumption function (such as C_2 in Figure 7–7). Conversely, a lower price level leads to a higher consumption function (such as C_1 in Figure 7–7).

Since students are often confused on this point, it is worth repeating that the depressing effect of the price level on consumer spending works through real *wealth*, not through real *income*. The consumption function is a relationship between *real consumer income* and *real consumer spending*. Thus any decline in real income, regardless of its cause, moves the economy *leftward along a fixed consumption function*; it does not shift the consumption function.[8] By contrast, any decline in *real wealth* will *shift the whole consumption function downward*, meaning that there is less spending at any given level of real income.

THE INFLATION RATE

Prices may be high and rising slowly, or they may be low but rising rapidly. Therefore, the depressing effect of a high *price level* on real consumer spending must be distinguished from any effect on spending of the *rate of inflation* (that is, the rate at which prices are rising).

If there is any effect of inflation on consumer spending, it must be small. Economists are not even sure whether inflation stimulates or depresses spending. It used to be thought that high rates of inflation lead consumers to spend more now to "beat" the higher prices that loom on the horizon. But behavior during the inflationary 1970s belied this idea. Consumers actually spent a *lower* fraction of their disposable incomes in the 1970s than they did in the 1980s.

Because there is no strong evidence that the rate of inflation shifts the consumption function systematically in one direction or the other, we shall assume that the position of the consumption function is influenced by the *price level*, but not by the *inflation rate*.

THE RATE OF INTEREST

A higher rate of interest raises the rewards for saving. For this reason, many people believe it is "obvious" that higher interest rates encourage saving, and therefore discourage spending. Statistical studies of this relationship suggest otherwise, however. With very few exceptions, they show that interest rates have virtually no effect on consumption decisions in the United States. Hence, in developing our model of the economy, we will assume that changes in interest rates do not shift the consumption function.

EXPECTATIONS OF FUTURE INCOMES

It is hardly earth shattering to suggest that consumers' expectations about future income may affect how much they spend today. This final determinant of consumer spending turns out to hold the key to understanding why tax policy succeeded so well in 1964 and the early 1980s, but failed to alter consumer spending much in 1975.

---

[8]This is true even if a rise in the price level lies behind the decline in real income. However, wages and prices normally move together, so there is no reason to expect real wages to fall when the price level rises.

WHY TAX POLICY FAILED IN 1975

To understand how expectations of future incomes affect current consumer expenditures, consider the abbreviated life histories of three consumers given in Table 7–2. The reason for giving our three imaginary individuals such odd names will be apparent shortly.

The consumer named "No Change" earned $100 in each of the four years considered in the table. The consumer named "Temporary Rise" earned $100 in three of the four years, but had a good year in 1975. The consumer named "Permanent Rise" enjoyed a permanent increase in income in 1975 and was clearly the richest.

Now let us use our common sense to figure out how much each of these consumers might have spent in 1975. "Temporary Rise" and "Permanent Rise" had the same income that year. Do you think they spent the same amount? Not if they had some ability to foresee their future income, because "Permanent Rise" was richer in the long run.

Now compare "No Change" and "Temporary Rise." Temporary Rise had 20 percent higher income in 1975 ($120 versus $100) but only 5 percent more over the entire four-year period ($420 versus $400). Do you think his spending in 1975 was closer to 20 percent above No Change's or closer to 5 percent above it? Most people guess the latter.

The point of this example is that it is reasonable for consumers to decide on their *current* consumption spending by looking at their *long-run* income prospects. This should come as no surprise to a college student. Are you spending only what you earn this year? Probably not. But that does not make you a foolish spendthrift. On the contrary, you know that your college education gives you a reasonable expectation of much higher income in the future, and you are spending with that in mind.

Now let us see what all this has to do with the failure of the 1975 income tax rebate. For this purpose, imagine that the three rows in Table 7–2 now represent the entire economy under three different government policies. Recall that 1975 was the year of the rebate. The first row ("No Change") shows the unchanged path of disposable income if no tax cut was enacted. The second ("Temporary Rise") shows an increase in disposable income attributable to a tax cut *for one year only*. The bottom row ("Permanent Rise") shows a policy that increases *DI* in *every future year* by cutting taxes permanently in 1975. Which of the two lower rows do you imagine would have generated more consumer spending in 1975?

Table **7–2**	**INCOMES OF THREE CONSUMERS**				
	INCOMES IN EACH YEAR				
CONSUMER	**1974**	**1975**	**1976**	**1977**	**TOTAL INCOME**
No change	100	100	100	100	400
Temporary Rise	100	120	100	100	420
Permanent Rise	100	120	120	120	460

The bottom row ("Permanent Rise"), of course. What we have concluded, then, is this:

Permanent cuts in income taxes cause greater increases in consumer spending than do temporary cuts of equal magnitude.

The application of this analysis to the case of the 1975 tax cut is immediate. The rebates were clearly one-time increases in income like that experienced by "Temporary Rise" in Table 7–2. No future income was affected, and so consumers did not curtail their spending as much as government officials had hoped. The general lesson is

A permanent increase in income taxes provides a greater deterrent to consumer spending than does a temporary increase of equal magnitude.

We have, then, what appears to be a general principle, backed up both by historical evidence and common sense. Permanent changes in income taxes have a more significant impact on consumer spending than do temporary changes. Though it may now seem obvious, this is not a lesson you would have learned from the introductory textbooks of 20 years ago. It is one that we learned the hard way, through bitter experience.

THE PREDICTABILITY OF CONSUMER BEHAVIOR

We have now learned enough to see why the economist's problem in predicting how consumers will react to an increase or decrease in taxes is not nearly as simple as suggested earlier in this chapter.

The principal problem seems to be anticipating how taxpayers will view any changes in the income tax law. If the government *says* that a tax cut is permanent, will consumers *believe* it and increase their spending accordingly? Perhaps not, if the government has a history of raising taxes after promising to keep them low. Similarly, when (as in 1975) the government explicitly announces that a tax cut is temporary, will consumers always believe this? Or might they greet such an announcement with a hefty dose of skepticism? This is quite possible if there is a long history of "temporary" tax changes that stayed on the books indefinitely.

Thus the effectiveness of any *future* tax policy move may well depend on the government's *past* track record. A government that repeatedly uses a succession of so-called "permanent" tax cuts and tax increases for short-run stabilization purposes may find consumers beginning to ignore the tax changes entirely. The story of the boy who cried wolf should probably be required reading for fiscal policy planners.

Nor is this the only problem. Consumer spending may be influenced by large and rapid accumulations of wealth (as happened immediately after World War II) or of sizable losses of wealth (such as the drastic decline in the stock market in 1987). Poor forecasts of future prices may lead consumption forecasts astray. And there are further hazards that we have not even mentioned here. Economic predictions are inexact, and predictions of consumption illustrate this well.

There is much more that could be said about the determinants of consumption, but it is best to leave the rest to more advanced courses. For we are now ready to apply our knowledge of the consumption function to the construction of the first model of the whole economy. While it is true that income determines consumption, the consumption function in turn helps to determine the level of income. If that sounds like circular reasoning, read the next chapter!

Summary

1. **Aggregate demand** is the total volume of goods and services purchased by consumers, businesses, government units, and foreigners. It can be expressed as the sum $C + I + G + (X - IM)$, where C is **consumer spending**, I is **investment spending**, G is **government purchases**, X is exports, and IM is imports.

2. Aggregate demand is a schedule: the aggregate quantity demanded depends (among other things) on the price level. But, for a given price level, aggregate demand is a number.

3. Economists reserve the term "investment" to refer to purchases of newly produced factories, machinery, and houses.

4. Domestic product is the total volume of final goods and services produced in the country. It is most commonly measured by the gross domestic product.

5. **National income** is the sum of the *before-tax* wages, interest, rents, and profits earned by all individuals in the economy. By necessity, it must be approximately equal to domestic product.

6. **Disposable income** is the sum of the incomes of all individuals in the economy *after taxes and transfers*, and is the chief determinant of consumer expenditure.

7. All of these concepts, and others, can be depicted in a **circular flow diagram** that shows expenditures on all four sources flowing into business firms and national income flowing out.

8. The government often has tried to manipulate aggregate demand by influencing private consumption decisions, usually through the personal income tax. Although this policy seemed to work well in 1964 and 1981, it did not work well in 1975.

9. The close relationship between consumer spending, C, and disposable income, DI, is called the **consumption function**. Its slope, which is used to predict the change in consumption that will be caused by a change in income taxes, is called the **marginal propensity to consume** (MPC).

10. Changes in disposable income move us **along a given consumption function**. Changes in any of the other variables that affect C **shift the entire consumption function**. Among the most important of these other variables are total consumer wealth, the price level, and expected future incomes.

11. Because consumers hold so many **money fixed assets**, they lose out when prices rise, which leads them to reduce their spending.

12. Future income prospects help explain why tax policy did not affect consumption as much as was hoped in 1975. This is because the 1975 tax cut was temporary, and therefore left future incomes unaffected. By contrast, the 1964 and 1981–1984 tax cuts were permanent, and affected future as well as current incomes. It is no surprise, then, that the 1964 and 1981 actions had stronger effects on spending than did the 1975 action.

Key Concepts and Terms

Aggregate demand
Consumer expenditure (C)
Investment spending (I)
Government purchases (G)
Net exports ($X - IM$)
$C + I + G + (X - IM)$

National income
Disposable income (DI)
Circular flow diagram
Transfer payments
Scatter diagram
Consumption function

Marginal propensity to consume (MPC)
Movements along versus shifts of the consumption function
Money fixed assets
Temporary versus permanent tax changes

Questions for Review

1. What are the four components of aggregate demand? Which of these is the largest? Which is the smallest?

2. What is the difference between "investment" as the term is used by most people and "investment" as defined by an economist? Which of the following acts constitute "investment" according to the economist's definition?

   a. IBM opens a new factory to assemble personal computers.

   b. You buy 100 shares of IBM stock.

   c. A small computer company goes bankrupt, and IBM purchases its factory and equipment.

   d. Your family buys a newly constructed home from a developer.

   e. Your family buys an older home from another family. (*Hint*: Are any *new* products demanded by this action?)

3. What would the circular flow diagram (Figure 7–1) look like in an economy with no government? Draw one for yourself.

4. The marginal propensity to consume (MPC) for the nation as a whole is roughly 0.90. Explain in words what this means. What is your personal MPC?

5. Look at the scatter diagram in Figure 7–3. What does it tell you about what was going on in this country in the years 1942–1945?

6. What is a "consumption function," and why is it a useful device for government economists planning a tax cut?

7. On a piece of graph paper, construct the consumption function for Simpleland from the data given below and determine the MPC.

YEAR	CONSUMER SPENDING	DISPOSABLE INCOME
1989	1800	2000
1990	2250	2500
1991	2700	3000
1992	3150	3500
1993	3600	4000

8. In which direction will the consumption function for Simpleland shift if the price level rises? Show this on your graph.

9. Explain why permanent tax cuts are likely to lead to bigger increases in consumer spending than are temporary tax cuts.

10. (More difficult) Between 1990 and 1991, real disposable income (in 1987 dollars) rose only from $3525 billion to $3529 billion, owing to a recession. Use the data on real consumption expenditures given on the inside front cover of this book to compare the change in C to the change in DI. Explain why dividing the two does *not* give a good estimate of the marginal propensity to consume.

11. For several years now, various members of Congress have been recommending the establishment of tax-favored accounts for savers. How would such accounts be expected to shift the consumption function?

Appendix A	**THE SAVING FUNCTION AND THE MARGINAL PROPENSITY TO SAVE**

There is an alternative way of looking at the relationships we have discussed in this chapter. Disposable income that is not spent must be saved. Therefore, we can examine the effect of income on *saving* as well as its effect on consumer *spending*.

To see how saving appears on the consumption function diagram, we have repeated the consumption function of Macroland (see Figure 7–6) in Figure 7–8 and added a 45° line. You will recall that a 45° line marks those points where the distances along the horizontal and vertical axes are equal. (If you wish to review, see page 22.) Since the consumption schedule is below the 45° line, the figure shows that consumer spending is less than income, so some is being *saved*.

To find the amount of saving at each level of income, we need only read the vertical distance from the consumption function up to the 45° line. For example, when income is $4400 billion, saving is the distance *AB*, or $800 billion.

There is also a more direct way to find saving. Table 7–3 repeats the consumption and disposable income data for Macroland from Table 7–1. Then, in column 3, we compute the difference between disposable income and consumption, which gives us **aggregate saving**.

Aggregate saving is the difference between disposable income and consumer expenditure. In symbols, $S = DI - C$.

This subtraction is exactly what we showed graphically in Figure 7–8. Columns 2 and 3 of Table 7–3 constitute what economists call the **saving function**.

The **saving function** is the relationship between total consumer saving and total disposable income in the economy, holding other determinants of saving constant.

The data of Table 7–3 are portrayed in Figure 7–9, which could equally well have been constructed as the difference between the 45° line and the *C* line in Figure 7–8. (Because saving is so much less than consumption, we have stretched the scale of the vertical axis a bit.) Points *A* and *B* correspond to the same points in Figure 7–8. When the consumption function is a straight line, and thus has a constant slope, the same will be true of the saving function. In Figure 7–9, we show this slope as the ratio of distance *EB* to distance *DE* or $200/$800 = 0.25. Economists call this slope the **marginal propensity to save**.

F i g u r e **7-8**	**THE CONSUMPTION FUNCTION OF MACROLAND**

The consumption function of Macroland, which we encountered in Figure 7–6 is repeated here, and a 45° line is added for convenience. Since consumption and saving must always add up to disposable income, the vertical distance between the two lines represents saving. For example, points *A* and *B* indicate that when disposable income is $4400 billion, saving is $800 billion.

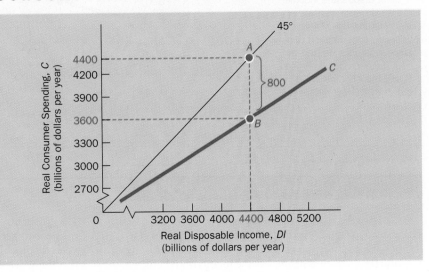

T a b l e **7–3**	**SAVING IN MACROLAND**			

YEAR	CONSUMPTION, C (billions of dollars)	DISPOSABLE INCOME, DI (billions of dollars)	SAVINGS, S (billions of dollars)	MARGINAL PROPENSITY TO SAVE, MPS
1989	2700	3200	500	0.25
1990	3000	3600	600	0.25
1991	3300	4000	700	0.25
1992	3600	4400	800	0.25
1993	3900	4800	900	0.25
1994	4200	5200	1000	0.25

The **marginal propensity to save** (or **MPS**) is the slope of the saving function. It tells us how much more consumers will save if disposable income rises by $1 billion.

You may have noticed that the MPS is 0.25 while the MPC for Macroland is 0.75. They add up to 1, and not by accident. Since the portion of each additional dollar of disposable income that is not spent must be saved, the MPC and the MPS always add up to 1. It is a simple fact of accounting.

The MPC and the MPS always add up to 1, meaning that an additional dollar of income must be divided between consumption and saving. In symbols:

$$MPC + MPS = 1.$$

This enables us to compute either one of them from the other.

F i g u r e **7–9**	**THE SAVING FUNCTION OF MACROLAND**	

The saving function of Macroland, depicted here, can be constructed either from the data in Table 7–3 or from Figure 7–8. This is because when we plot saving against disposable income (as we do here), we are also plotting the difference between consumption and disposable income (the vertical distance between line C and the 45° line in Figure 7–8) against disposable income.

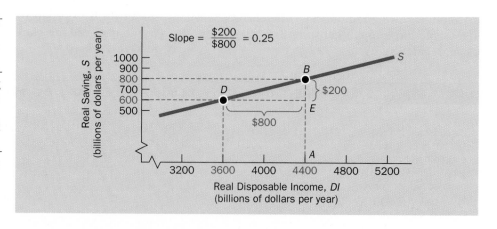

$$Slope = \frac{\$200}{\$800} = 0.25$$

Summary

1. Instead of studying the consumption function, it is possible to study the same data by looking at the **saving function**, which is defined as the relationship between disposable income and consumer saving.

2. Since consumer saving is merely the difference between disposable income and consumer expenditure, everything we have learned about the consumption function applies to the saving function.

3. The amount of additional saving caused by a $1 increase in disposable income is called the **marginal propensity to save**, or MPS.

4. Since each additional $1 of disposable income is either spent or saved, the MPC and the MPS must always add up to 1. Thus, knowledge of one implies knowledge of the other.

Key Concepts and Terms

Aggregate saving   Saving function   Marginal propensity to save

Questions for Review

1. Look at the circular flow diagram in Figure 7–1. (page 153). Where does the saving function enter the picture?

2. If the MPC in the U.S. economy is about 0.90, how large is the MPS?

3. Take the data from Simpleland in Question 7 on page 168 and use them to construct a saving function for Simpleland on a piece of graph paper.

4. (More difficult) If taxes are cut *temporarily* and consumer spending does not increase much, what must happen to consumer saving? Ask your instructor what happened to consumer saving immediately after the 1975 tax cuts.

Appendix B ● **NATIONAL INCOME ACCOUNTING**

The type of macroeconomic analysis presented in this book dates from the publication of John Maynard Keynes's *The General Theory of Employment, Interest, and Money* in 1936. But at that time there was really no way to test Keynes's theories because the necessary data did not exist. It took some years for the theoretical notions used by Keynes to find concrete expression in real-world data. The system of measurement devised for this purpose is called **national income accounting**.

The development of this system of accounts ranks as a great achievement in applied economics, perhaps as important in its own right as Keynes's theoretical work. For without it the practical value of Keynesian analysis would be severely limited. Many men and women spent long hours wrestling with the numerous difficult conceptual questions that arose in translating the theory into numbers, but they had one acknowledged leader: the late Professor Simon Kuznets, who was awarded the Nobel Prize in economics for his contributions to economic measurement techniques. Along the way some more-or-less arbitrary decisions and conventions had to be made. You may not agree with all of them, but the accounting framework that was devised is eminently serviceable, though, inevitably, it has some limitations that must be understood.

DEFINING GDP:
EXCEPTIONS TO THE RULES

We first encountered the concept of **gross domestic product (GDP)** in Chapter 2.

Gross domestic product (GDP) is the sum of the money values of all final goods and services produced during a specified period of time, usually one year.

However, the definition of GDP has certain exceptions we have not yet noted.

First, the treatment of government output involves a minor departure from the principle of using market prices. Outputs of private industries are sold on markets, so their prices are observed. But "outputs" of government offices are not sold; indeed, it is sometimes even difficult to define what those outputs are. Lacking prices for outputs, national income accountants fall back on the only prices they

have: prices for the inputs from which the outputs are produced. Thus:

Government outputs are valued at the cost of the inputs needed to produce them.

This means, for example, that if a clerk at the Department of Motor Vehicles earns $10 an hour and spends one-half hour torturing you with explanations of why you cannot get a driver's license, that particular government "service" is considered as being worth $5, and will increase GDP by that amount.

Second, some goods that are not actually sold on markets during the year are nonetheless counted in that year's GDP. These are the goods that are produced during the year but not sold; that is, goods that firms stockpile as *inventories*. Goods that are added to inventories count in GDP even though they do not pass through markets.

National income statisticians treat inventories as if they were "bought" by the firms that produced them, even though this "purchase" never takes place.

Finally, the treatment of investment goods runs slightly counter to the rule that only final goods are to be counted. In a broad sense, factories, generators, machine tools, and the like might be considered as intermediate goods. After all, their owners want them only for use in producing other goods, not for any innate value that they possess. But this would present a real problem, for factories and machines normally are never sold to consumers. So when would we count them in GDP? National income statisticians avoid this problem by defining investment goods as final products demanded by the firms that buy them.

Now that we have a more complete definition of what the GDP is, let us turn to the problem of actually measuring it. National income accountants have devised three ways to perform this task, and we consider each in turn.

GDP AS THE SUM OF FINAL GOODS
AND SERVICES

The first way to measure GDP seems to be the most natural, since it follows so directly from the circular flow diagram in this chapter. It also turns out to be the most useful definition for macroeconomic analysis. We simply add up the final demands of all consumers, business firms, government, and foreigners. Using the symbols C, I, G, and $(X - IM)$ just as we did in the text, we have:

$$GDP = C + I + G + (X - IM).$$

The I that appears in the actual U.S. national accounts is called **gross private domestic investment**. The word "gross" will be explained presently. "Private" indicates that government investment is considered part of G, and "domestic" just means that machinery sold by American firms to foreign companies is included in exports rather than in I. Gross private domestic investment in the United States has three components: business investment in plant and equipment, residential construction (home building), and inventory investment. We repeat again that *only* these three things are **investment** in national income accounting terminology.

As defined in the national income accounts, **investment** includes only newly produced capital goods, such as machinery, factories, and new homes. It does not include exchanges of existing assets.

In common parlance, all sorts of activities that are not part of the GDP are often called "investment." People are said to "invest" in the stock market when they purchase shares. Or wealthy individuals "invest" in works of art. But since transactions like these merely exchange one type of asset (money) for another (stock or art works), they are not included in the GDP.

The symbol G, for government purchases, represents the *volume of current goods and services purchased by all levels of government*. Thus anything the government pays to its employees is counted in G, as are its purchases of paper, pencils, airplanes, bombs, typewriters, and so forth.

Few citizens realize that *most of what the federal government spends its money on is not for purchases of goods and services*. Instead, it is on **transfer payments**—literally, giving away money—either to individuals or to other levels of government.

The importance of the conceptual distinction lies in the fact that G represents the part of the national product that government uses up for its own purposes—to pay for armies, bureaucrats, paper, and ink—whereas transfer payments merely represent shuffling of purchasing power from one group of citizens to another group. Except for the administrators needed to run the programs, real economic resources are not used up in this process.

In adding up the nation's total output as the sum of $C + I + G + (X - IM)$, we are summing the shares of GDP that are used up by consumers, investors, government, and foreigners, respectively. Since transfer payments merely give someone the capability to spend on C, it is logical to exclude them from our definition of G, including in C only the portion of these transfer payments that is spent. If we included them in G, the same spending would get counted twice: once in G and then again in C.

The final component of GDP is net exports, which are simply exports of goods and services minus imports of goods and services. Notice that both goods *and services* count, though the news media devote most attention to the monthly data on trade in goods ("merchandise trade").

Table 7–4 shows GDP for 1992, in both nominal and real terms, computed as the sum of $C + I + G + (X - IM)$. You will note that the numbers for net exports in the table are actually negative. We will have much to say about America's trade deficit in Part 8.

GDP AS THE SUM OF ALL FACTOR PAYMENTS

There is another way to count up the GDP—by *adding up all the incomes in the economy*. Let's see how this method handles some typical transactions. Suppose General Electric builds a generator and sells it to General Motors for $1 million. The first method of calculating GDP simply counts the $1 million as part of I. The second method asks: What incomes resulted from the production of this generator? The answer might be something like this:

Wages of G.E. employees	$400,000
Interest to bondholders	$ 50,000
Rentals of buildings	$ 50,000
Profits of G.E. stockholders	$100,000

The total is $600,000. The remaining $400,000 is accounted for by inputs that G.E. purchased from other companies: steel, circuitry, tubing, rubber, and so on.

But if we traced this $400,000 back further, we would find that it is accounted for by the wages,

T a b l e **7-4** **GROSS DOMESTIC PRODUCT IN 1992 AS THE SUM OF THE FINAL DEMANDS**		

ITEM	AMOUNT (billions of current dollars)	AMOUNT (billions of 1987 dollars)
Personal consumption expenditures (C)	4139.9	3341.8
Gross private domestic investment (I)	796.5	732.8
Government purchases of goods and services (G)	1131.8	945.2
Net exports (X – IM)	–29.6	–33.6
Exports (X)	640.5	57.0
Imports (IM)	670.1	611.0
Gross domestic product (Y)	6038.5	4986.3

SOURCE U.S. Department of Commerce. Totals do not add up precisely due to rounding.

interest, and rentals paid by these other companies, *plus* their profits, *plus* their purchases from other firms. In fact, for *every* firm in the economy, there is an accounting identity that says:

$$\text{Revenues from sales} = \begin{array}{l}\text{Wages paid} + \\ \text{Interest paid} + \\ \text{Rentals paid} + \\ \text{Profits earned} + \\ \text{Purchases from} \\ \text{other firms.}\end{array}$$

Why must this always be true? Because profits are the balancing item; they are what is *left over* after the firm has made all its other payments. In fact, this accounting identity is really just the definition of profits: sales revenue less all costs of production.

Now apply this accounting identity to *all the firms in the economy*. Total purchases from other firms are precisely what we call *intermediate goods*. What, then, do we get if we subtract these intermediate transactions from both sides of the equation?

$$\begin{array}{l}\text{Revenues from sales} \\ \quad\quad minus \\ \text{Purchases from} \\ \text{other firms}\end{array} = \begin{array}{l}\text{Wages paid} + \\ \text{Interest paid} + \\ \text{Rentals paid} + \\ \text{Profits earned.}\end{array}$$

On the right-hand side, we have the sum of all factor incomes: payments to labor, land, and capital. On the left-hand side, we have total sales minus sales of intermediate goods. This means that we have only sales of *final* goods, which is precisely our definition of GDP. Thus, the accounting identity for the entire economy can be rewritten as:

GDP = Wages + Interest + Rents + Profits,

and this gives national income accountants another way to measure the GDP.

Table 7–5 shows 1992's GDP measured by the sum of all incomes. Once again, a few details have been omitted in our discussion. The sum of wages, interest, rents, and profits actually adds up to only \$4837 billion (whereas GDP is \$6039 billion). We call this sum **national income** because it is the sum of all factor payments. But the actual selling prices of goods include another category of income that we have ignored so far: sales taxes, excise taxes, and the like. National income statisticians call these *indirect business taxes*, and when we add these to national income we obtain the **net national product (NNP)**.

Notice here the use of the adjective "national" rather than "domestic." When we add up all the wages, interest, rents, and profits received by Americans, we will inevitably include some payments derived from production in other countries. Similarly, some of the factor payments made by American businesses go to citizens of other countries. If we subtract the former and add back the latter, we change net national product into net domestic product.

Now we are almost at the GDP. The only difference between GDP and NDP is **depreciation** of the nation's capital stock.

Depreciation is the value of the portion of the nation's capital equipment that is used up within the year. It tells us how much output is needed just to keep the economy's capital stock intact.

The difference between "gross" and "net" simply refers to whether depreciation is included or ex-

Table 7-5	GROSS DOMESTIC PRODUCT IN 1992 AS THE SUM OF INCOMES	
ITEM	**AMOUNT (billions of dollars)**	
Compensation of employees (wages)	3582.0	
plus		
Net interest	442.0	
plus		
Rental income	−8.9	
plus		
Profits	821.5	
Corporate profits		
Proprietors' income		407.2
equals		414.3
National income		
plus	4836.6	
Indirect business taxes and		
miscellaneous items	551.3	
equals		
Net national product	5387.9	
minus		
income received	129.2	
from other countries		
plus		
income paid		
to other countries	121.9	
equals	5380.6	
Net domestic product		
plus	657.9	
Depreciation		
equals		
Gross domestic product	6038.5	

SOURCE: U.S. Department of Commerce. Totals do not add up precisely due to rounding.

cluded. We add depreciation to NDP to get GDP. Thus, GDP is a measure of all final output, taking no account of the capital used up in the process (and therefore in need of replacement). NDP deducts the required replacements to arrive at a *net* production figure.

From a conceptual point of view, most economists feel that NDP is a more meaningful indicator of the economy's output than GDP. After all, the depreciation component of GDP represents the output that is needed just to repair and replace worn out factories and machines; it is not available for anybody to consume.[9] So NDP seems to be a better measure of well-being than GDP. But, alas, GDP is

much easier to measure because depreciation is a particularly tricky item. What fraction of his tractor did Farmer Jones "use up" last year? How much did the Empire State Building depreciate during 1993? If you ask yourself these difficult questions, you will understand why most economists feel that GDP is measured more accurately than is NDP. For this reason, most economic models are based on GDP.

In Table 7–5 you can hardly help noticing the preponderant share of employee compensation in total national income—about 74 percent. Labor is by far the most important factor of production. The return on land is negligible; and interest accounts for about 9 percent. Profits account for the remaining 17 percent, though the size of corporate profits (less than 9 percent of GDP) is much less than the public

---

[9] If the capital stock is used for consumption, it will decline, and the nation will wind up poorer than before.

thinks. If, by some magic stroke, we could eliminate all corporate profits without upsetting the performance of the economy, the average worker would get a raise of about 11 percent!

GDP AS THE SUM OF VALUES ADDED

It may strike you as strange that national income accountants include only *final* goods and services in GDP. Aren't *intermediate* goods part of the nation's product? They are, of course. The problem is that, if all intermediate goods were included in GDP, we would wind up double and triple counting things and therefore get an exaggerated impression of the amount of economic activity that is actually going on.

To explain why, and to show how national income accountants cope with this difficulty, we must introduce a new concept, called **value added.**

The value added by a firm is its revenue from selling a product minus the amount paid for goods and services purchased from other firms.

The intuitive sense of the concept is clear: if a firm buys some inputs from other firms, does something to them, and sells the resulting product for a price higher than it paid for the inputs, we say that the firm has "added value" to the product. If we sum up the values added in this way by all the firms in the economy, we must get the total value of all final products. Thus:

GDP can be measured as the sum of the values added by all firms.

To verify that this is so, look back at the second accounting identity on page 174. The left-hand side of this equation, sales revenue minus purchases from other firms, is precisely the firm's value added. Thus:

$$\text{Value added} = \text{Wages} + \text{Interest} + \text{Rents} + \text{Profits}.$$

Since the second method we gave for measuring GDP is to add up wages, interest, rents, and profits, we see that the value-added approach must also yield the same answer.

The value-added concept is useful in avoiding double counting. Often it is hard to distinguish intermediate goods from final goods. Paint bought by a painter, for example, is an intermediate good. But paint bought by a do-it-yourselfer is a final good. What happens, then, if the professional painter has some paint left over and uses it to refurbish his own garage? The intermediate good becomes a final good. You can see that the line between intermediate goods and final goods is a fuzzy one in practice.

If we measure GDP by the sum of values added, however, it is not necessary to make such subtle distinctions. In this method, *every* purchase of a new good or service counts, but we do not count the entire selling price, only the portion that represents value added.

To illustrate this idea, consider the data in Table 7–6 and how they would affect GDP as the sum of final products. Our example begins when a farmer who grows soybeans sells them to a mill for $3 a bushel. This transaction does *not* count in the GDP, because the miller does not purchase the soybeans for his own use. The miller then grinds up the soybeans and sells the resulting bag of soy meal to a factory that produces soy sauce. The miller receives $4, but GDP still has not increased because the ground beans are also an intermediate product.

T a b l e **7–6**	**AN ILLUSTRATION OF FINAL AND INTERMEDIATE GOODS**		
ITEM	**SELLER**	**BUYER**	**PRICE**
Bushel of soybeans	Farmer	Miller	$ 3
Bag of soy meal	Miller	Factory	4
Gallon of soy sauce	Factory	Restaurant	8
Gallon of soy sauce used as seasoning	Restaurant	Consumers	$10
	Addendum: Contribution to GDP: $10		Total: $25

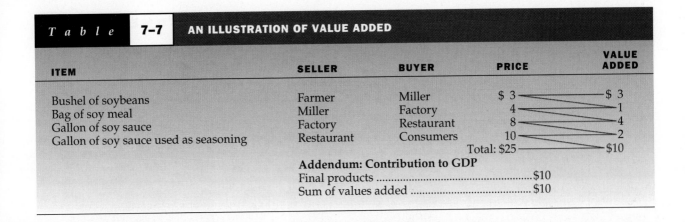

ITEM	SELLER	BUYER	PRICE	VALUE ADDED
Bushel of soybeans	Farmer	Miller	$ 3	$ 3
Bag of soy meal	Miller	Factory	4	1
Gallon of soy sauce	Factory	Restaurant	8	4
Gallon of soy sauce used as seasoning	Restaurant	Consumers	10	2
		Total:	$25	$10

Addendum: Contribution to GDP
Final products $10
Sum of values added $10

Next, the factory turns the beans into soy sauce, which it sells to your favorite Chinese restaurant for $8. Still no effect on GDP.

But then the big moment arrives: The restaurant sells the sauce to you and other customers as a part of your meals, and you eat it. At this point, the $10 worth of soy sauce becomes a final product and is included in the GDP. Notice that if we had also counted the three intermediate transactions (farmer to miller, miller to factory, factory to restaurant), we would have come up with $25—two and one-half times too much.

Why is it too much? The reason is straightforward. Neither the miller nor the factory owner nor the restaurateur value the product we have been considering *for its own sake*. Only the customers who eat the final product (the soy sauce) have had an increase in their material well-being. So only this last transaction counts in the GDP. However, as we shall now see, value-added calculations enable us to come up with the right answer ($10) by counting only *part* of each transaction. The basic idea is to count at each step only the contribution to the value of the ultimate final product that is made at that step, excluding the values of items produced at earlier steps.

Ignoring the minor items (such as fertilizer) that the farmer purchases from others, the entire $3 selling price of the bushel of soybeans is new output produced by the farmer; that is, the whole $3 is value added. The miller then grinds the beans and sells them for $4. He has added $4 − $3 = $1 to the value of the beans. When the factory turns this soy meal into soy sauce and sells it for $8, it has added $8 − $4 = $4 more in value. And finally,

when the restaurant sells it to hungry customers for $10, a further $2 of value is added.

Table 7–7 shows this chain of creation of value added by appending another column to Table 7–6. We see that the total value added by all four firms is $10, exactly the same as the restaurant's selling price. This is as it must be, for only the restaurant sells the soybeans as a final product.

ALTERNATIVE MEASURES OF THE INCOME OF THE NATION

Economists use the term *national income* in two different ways. The most common usage is as a general term indicating the size of the income of the nation as a whole, without being specific about exactly how this income is to be measured. This is the sense in which the term "national income" is used in this book. The second, and much more precise, use of the term refers to a particular concept in national income accounting which we encountered in Table 7–5 on page 175: the sum of wages, interest, rents, and profits.

Aside from this formal definition of national income, what other accounting concept might be used to measure the total income of the nation? The first and most obvious candidate is the GDP itself. GDP, however, is intended to be a measure of *production*, and so has several drawbacks as a measure of *income*.

First, it includes some output that represents income to no one—output that simply replaces worn-out machinery and buildings (depreciation). When we deduct this depreciation, we obtain the net domestic product (NDP), as shown in Figure 7–10.

F i g u r e **7–10** **ALTERNATIVE MEASURES OF THE INCOME OF THE NATION**

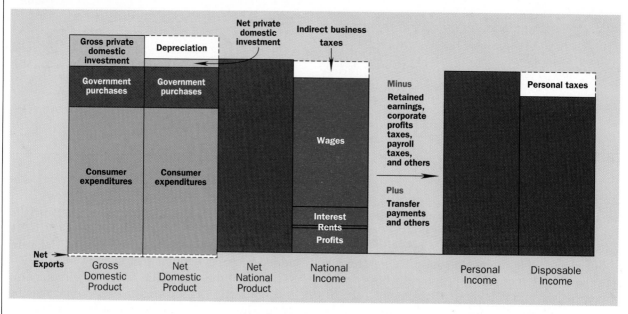

This bar chart indicates the relationships among six alternative measures of the total income of the nation, starting with the largest and most comprehensive measure (GDP) and ranging down to the measure that most closely approximates the spendable income of consumers (disposable income).

Second, we learned earlier that some of the income included in NDP is paid to foreigners, rather than to Americans; and, similarly, some of the income receipts of Americans derive from business activities abroad. Making these two corrections gives us a better measure of American incomes, and turns NDP into net *national* product, NNP—the next bar shown in the figure. As you can see, NNP hardly differs from NDP.

Third, because of sales taxes and related items (indirect business taxes), part of the price paid for each good and service does not represent income to any individual. When we deduct these indirect business taxes from NNP, we arrive again at the formal definition of national income (refer to Figure 7–10).

There are, however, two other measures of income. **Personal income** is meant to be a better measure of the income that actually accrues to individuals. It is obtained from national income by *sub-*

tracting corporate profits taxes, retained earnings, and payroll taxes (because these items are never received by individuals), and then *adding in* transfer payments (because these sources of income are not part of the wages, interest, rents, or profits that constitute the national income). As Figure 7–10 suggests, this adding and subtracting normally results in a number slightly larger than national income. Finally, if we subtract personal income taxes from personal income, we obtain **disposable income**.

Among all the concepts of the nation's income depicted in Figure 7–10, only two are used frequently in the construction of models of the economy: gross domestic product (GDP) and disposable income (*DI*). Since the models presented in this book ignore depreciation and indirect business taxes, GDP is basically identical to national income (see Figure 24–10). Similarly, if we ignore retained earnings, GDP and *DI* differ only by the amounts of taxes and transfers (again, see Figure 7–10).

Summary

1. **Gross domestic product** (GDP) is the sum of the money values of all final goods and services produced during a year and sold on organized markets. There are, however, certain exceptions to this definition.

2. One way to measure the GDP is to add up the final demands of consumers, investors, government, and foreigners: GDP = $C + I + G + (X - IM)$.

3. A second way to measure the GDP is to start with all the factor payments—wages, interest, rents, and profits—that constitute the **national income**, and then add indirect business taxes and **depreciation**.

4. A third way to measure the GDP is to sum up the **values added** by every firm in the economy (and then once again add indirect business taxes and depreciation).

5. Except for possible bookkeeping and statistical errors, all three methods must give the same answer.

Key Concepts and Terms

National income accounting
Gross National Product (GNP)
Gross Domestic Product (GDP)
Gross Private Domestic Investment
Government purchases

Transfer payments
Net exports
National Income
Net Domestic Product (NDP)
Net National Product (NNP)

Depreciation
Value added
Personal Income
Disposable Income (DI)

Questions for Review

1. Which of the following transactions are included in the gross domestic product, and by how much does each raise GDP?

   a. You buy a new car, paying $11,000.
   b. You buy a used car, paying $3000.
   c. Apple builds a $100 million factory to make computers.
   d. Your grandmother receives a government social security check for $1000.
   e. Chrysler manufacturers 2000 automobiles at a cost of $12,000 each. Unable to sell them, it holds them as inventories.
   f. Mr. Black and Mr. Blue, each out for a Sunday drive, have a collision in which their cars are destroyed. Black and Blue each hire a lawyer to sue the other, paying the lawyers $2000 each for services rendered. The judge throws the case out of court.
   g. You sell a poster to your roommate for $20.

2. Explain the difference between final goods and intermediate goods. Why is it sometimes difficult to apply this distinction in practice? In this regard, why is the concept of value added useful?

3. Explain the difference between government spending and government purchases of goods and services (G). Which is larger?

4. Explain why national income and gross domestic product would be essentially equal if there were no depreciation and no indirect business taxes.

5. The following is a complete description of all economic activity in Trivialand for 1993. Draw up versions of Tables 7–4 and 7–5 for Trivialand showing GDP computed in two different ways.

   a. There are thousands of farmers but only two big business firms in Trivialand: Specific Motors (an auto company) and Super Duper (a chain of food markets). There is no government and no depreciation.
   b. Specific Motors produced 1000 small cars, which they sold at $6000 each, and 100 trucks, which they sold at $8000 each. Consumers bought 800 of the

cars, and the remaining 200 cars were exported to the United States. Super Duper bought all the trucks.

c. Sales at Super Duper markets amounted to $14 million, all of it sold to consumers.

d. All the farmers in Trivialand are self-employed and sell all their wares to Super Duper.

e. The costs incurred by all the businesses were as follows:

	SPECIFIC MOTORS	SUPER DUPER	FARMERS
Wages	$3,800,000	$4,500,000	$ 0
Interest	100,000	200,000	700,000
Rent	200,000	1,000,000	2,000,000
Purchases of food	0	7,000,000	0

6. (More difficult) Now complicate Trivialand in the following ways and answer the same questions. In addition, calculate national income, personal income, and disposable income.

a. The government bought 50 cars, leaving only 150 cars for export. In addition, the government spent $800,000 on wages for soldiers and made $1,200,000 in transfer payments.

b. Depreciation for the year amounted to $600,000 for Specific Motors and $200,000 for Super Duper. (The farmers had no depreciation.)

c. The government levied sales taxes amounting to $500,000 on Specific Motors and $200,000 on Super Duper (none on farmers). In addition, the government levied a 10 percent income tax on all wages, interest, and rental income.

d. In addition to the food and cars mentioned in Question 5, consumers in Trivialand imported 500 computers from the United States at $2,000 each.

DEMAND-SIDE EQUILIBRIUM: UNEMPLOYMENT OR INFLATION?

Investment ... is a flighty bird, which needs to be controlled.

J.R. HICKS

We learned in Chapter 5 that the interaction of aggregate demand and aggregate supply determines whether the economy will stagnate or prosper, whether our labor and capital resources will be fully employed or unemployed. And we learned in Chapter 7 that aggregate demand has four components: consumer expenditure (C), investment (I), government purchases (G), and net exports ($X - IM$). It is now time to start building a theory that fits all the pieces together. ¶ Our approach is sequential. Since it is necessary to walk before you can to run, we imagine in this chapter that the price level, the rate of interest, and the international value of the dollar are all constant. None of these assumptions are true, of course, and each will be eliminated later in the book. But these three unrealistic assumptions enable us to construct a simple but useful model of how the state of aggregate demand influences the level of gross domestic product (GDP). In this simple model, only C is variable; the other three components of spending—I, G, and $X - IM$—are all assumed to be fixed. ¶ Subsequent chapters will drop the three unrealistic assumptions in turn. In Chapter 10, we bring in the supply side of the economy, which enables us to treat the price level as variable rather than constant. In Chapter 13, we will see how interest rates—and hence investment—are determined. Finally, Chapters 19–20 bring the exchange rate into the picture and study the determination of net exports.

But first things first. This chapter begins by examining the most volatile component of aggregate demand: investment. What factors determine investment spending, and why is it so variable and hard to predict?[1] Then we add net exports and government purchases to the model. Treating I, G, and $X - IM$ as constants, we next see how equilibrium is established on the demand side of the economy. Finally, we consider a question of great importance to policymakers: Can the economy be expected to achieve full employment of its resources if the government does not intervene?

THE EXTREME VARIABILITY OF INVESTMENT

The first thing to be said about investment spending is that it is extraordinarily variable.

Unlike consumer spending, which follows movements in disposable income with great (though not perfect) reliability, investment spending swings from high to low levels with annoying speed. During recessions, for example, the decline in investment generally constitutes the bulk of the drop in real GDP, even though investment is only a small portion of GDP—about 17 percent in the postwar United States. What accounts for these movements of investment demand?

BUSINESS CONFIDENCE AND EXPECTATIONS ABOUT THE FUTURE

While many factors influence business people's desires to invest, Keynes himself laid great stress on the *state of business confidence*, which in turn depends on *expectations about the future*.

While tricky to measure, it does seem obvious that businesses will build more factories and purchase more new machines when they are optimistic. Conversely, their investment plans will be very cautious if the economic outlook appears bleak. Keynes pointed out that psychological perceptions like these are subject to abrupt shifts, so that fluctuations in investment can be a major cause of instability in aggregate demand. Hence, Hicks's analogy to a "flighty bird" in the chapter's opening quotation.

Unfortunately, neither economists nor, for that matter, psychologists have many good ideas about how to *measure*—much less *control*—business confidence. Therefore, economists usually focus on several more objective determinants of investment—determinants that are easier to quantify and, perhaps even more important, are more easily influenced by government policy.

THE LEVEL AND GROWTH OF DEMAND

Firms have a strong incentive to invest when demand is pushing against capacity. Under these circumstances, business executives are likely to feel that new factories

---

[1]We repeat the warning given in the previous chapter about the meaning of the word *investment*. It *includes* spending by businesses and individuals on *newly produced* factories, machinery, and houses. But it *excludes* sales of used industrial plants, equipment, and homes, and it *also excludes* purely financial transactions, such as the purchase of stocks and bonds.

and machinery can be employed profitably. By contrast, if there is a great deal of unused machinery, empty factories, and the like, managers may not find investment opportunities very attractive.

Because it takes a substantial amount of time to order machinery or to build a factory, investment plans are made with an eye on the future. Even when pressures on current capacity are not particularly severe, a firm that is expecting rapid growth in sales may start investing now in order to have adequate capacity for the future. Furthermore, briskly growing sales are likely to make business people more optimistic. Conversely, slow growth of output will discourage investment. We can summarize this discussion by saying that:

High levels of sales relative to current capacity and expectations of rapid economic growth create an atmosphere favorable to investment. Low levels of sales and slow anticipated growth are likely to discourage investment.

Government stabilization policy thus has a handle on investment spending, for by stimulating aggregate demand it can induce business firms to invest more, though the precise amount may be hard to predict.

TECHNICAL CHANGE AND PRODUCT INNOVATION

Some investments are driven by technology. When a new product like the VCR is invented, or when a technological breakthrough makes an existing product much cheaper or better, as happened with microcomputers, new investment opportunities suddenly appear. In our capitalist market system, entrepreneurs seize these opportunities quickly—building new factories, stores, and offices. These new investments need not be "high tech." The VCR, for example, spawned an entire service industry of video rental shops that now dot the American landscape. Two decades ago, such stores did not even exist.

THE RATE OF INTEREST

The rate of interest is the determinant of investment that will play a pivotal role in later chapters. A good deal of business investment is financed by borrowing, and the interest rate indicates how much firms pay for that privilege. Some investment projects that look profitable at an interest rate of 7 percent will look disastrous if the firm has to pay 12 percent.

The amount that businesses will want to invest depends on the real interest rate they must pay on their borrowings. The lower the real rate of interest, the more investment spending there will be.

In Chapter 13, we will study in some detail how the government can influence the rate of interest. Since interest rates affect investment, policymakers have another handle on aggregate demand—a handle they do not hesitate to use. The point is that, unlike business confidence, expectations, and technology, interest rates are visible and manipulable. Therefore, even if investment responds much more dramatically to changes in confidence than to changes in interest rates, interest rates are nonetheless a more important instrument of government policy. But this is a topic for later in the book.

TAX PROVISIONS

The government has still another important way to influence investment spending—by altering various provisions of the tax law. For example, one of the first things President Clinton proposed after his inauguration was a temporary *investment tax credit*, a subsidy for certain types of capital spending.[2] Under a 10% investment tax credit, for example, a company that spends $100,000 on eligible equipment has its tax bill reduced by $10,000. This obviously reduces the effective cost of investing in machinery. In addition, there is a *tax on corporate profits*, and the government can reduce the statutory tax rate as a way to spur investment—as it did in 1986. There are other, more complicated, tax provisions as well. To summarize:

The tax law gives the government several ways to influence business spending on investment goods. But influence is far from control. Investment remains a "flighty bird."

THE DETERMINANTS OF NET EXPORTS

Another highly variable source of demand for U.S. products is foreign purchases of U.S. goods—our *exports*. However, as we learned in Chapter 7, to obtain the net contribution of foreigners to aggregate demand in the United States we must subtract *imports*, which is the portion of domestic demand that is satisfied by foreign producers.

NATIONAL INCOMES

While both exports and imports depend on many factors, the predominant one is *national income*. Some of the additional consumption and investment spending that American consumers and firms do as their spending rises is on foreign goods. So:

Our imports rise when our GDP rises and fall when our GDP falls.

Similarly, our *exports* are the *imports* of other countries, so it is natural to assume that our exports depend on *their* GDPs, not on our own. Thus:

Our exports are relatively insensitive to our own GDP, but are quite sensitive to the GDPs of other countries.

RELATIVE PRICES OF EXPORTS AND IMPORTS

While GDP levels at home and abroad are important influences on a country's net exports, they are not the only relevant factor. International price differences matter, too. To make things concrete, let us focus on trade between the United States and Japan. Suppose the prices of American goods rise while Japanese prices are constant. This makes U.S. products more expensive *relative to Japanese goods* than was true previously. If American consumers react to the new relative prices by buying more Japanese goods, our *imports rise*. If Japanese consumers react to the same relative price changes by buying fewer American products, our *exports fall*. Both reactions reduce America's net exports.

---

[2]But Congress did not enact the proposal.

Naturally, the effects of a decline in American prices are precisely the opposite: Exports are stimulated and imports are discouraged, so net exports rise. Thus:

A rise in the prices of a country's goods will lead to a reduction in that country's net exports. Analogously, a fall in the prices of a country's goods will raise that country's net exports.

Since trade patterns are governed by the prices of one country's goods *relative to* those of other countries, precisely the same logic applies to changes in Japanese prices. If Japanese prices fall while U.S. prices remain constant, Americans will import more and export less. So $(X - IM)$ will decline. By similar reasoning, rising Japanese prices increase U.S. net exports. Thus:

Price increases abroad raise a country's net exports while price decreases abroad have the opposite effect.

This simple idea holds the key to understanding how rates of exchange among the world's currencies influence exports and imports—a topic we will consider in depth in Chapters 19 and 20. The reason is that exchange rates translate foreign prices into terms customers are familiar with—their own currencies. Consider, for example, Americans interested in buying British sweaters that cost £30. If the British pound is worth $1.50, the sweaters cost potential American buyers $45 each. But, if the pound is worth $2.00, those same sweaters cost Americans $60, and they are likely to buy fewer.

THE MEANING OF EQUILIBRIUM GDP

The fourth component of total spending, government purchases of goods and services (G), is determined in the political arena by our elected representatives. Let us now put the four pieces together and see how they interact, using as our organizing framework the circular flow diagram introduced in the last chapter.

In doing so, we will at first ignore the possibility—raised in Chapter 5—that the government might vary its taxes (T) and spending (G) to steer the economy in some desired direction. Aside from pedagogical simplicity, there is an important reason for doing this. One of the crucial questions surrounding government stabilization policy is whether the economy would *automatically* gravitate toward full employment if the government simply left it alone. John Maynard Keynes, contradicting the teachings of generations of economists before him, claimed that it would not. But Keynes' views remain controversial to this day. We can study this issue best by imagining an economy in which the government never tried to manipulate aggregate demand. This is just what we do in this chapter.

Look now at Figure 8–1, which repeats Figure 7–1 of the last chapter. We can use this circular flow diagram to begin the construction of a simple model of the determination of national income. But first we must understand what we mean by "equilibrium income."

As was explained in the last chapter, total *production* and total *income* must, of necessity, be equal. But the same need not be true of total *spending*. Imagine that, for some reason, the total expenditures, $C + I + G + (X - IM)$, being made after point 4 in the figure are greater than the value of the output being produced by the business firms at point 5.

| Figure 8-1 | THE CIRCULAR FLOW DIAGRAM |

Here we repeat the circular flow of income and expenditures that we introduced in Chapter 7. Equilibrium occurs when $C + I + G + (X - IM)$ is equal to Y.

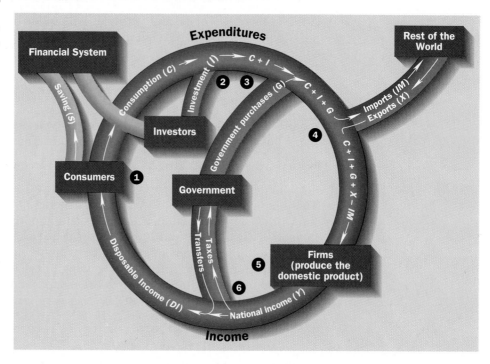

Two things may happen in such a situation. Since consumers, business firms, government, and foreigners together are buying more than firms are producing, businesses are being forced to take goods out of their warehouses to meet customer demands. Thus, inventory stocks must be falling. These inventory reductions are a signal to retailers of a need to increase their orders, and to manufacturers of a need to step up their production. Consequently, production is likely to rise. At some later date, if there is evidence that the high level of spending is not just a temporary aberration, either manufacturers or retailers (or both) may also respond to the buoyant sales performances by raising their prices. Economists therefore say that neither output nor the price level is in **equilibrium** when total spending exceeds the value of current production.

EQUILIBRIUM refers to a situation in which neither consumers nor firms have any incentive to change their behavior. They are content to continue with things as they are.

It is clear from the definition of equilibrium that the economy cannot be in equilibrium when total spending exceeds production, for the falling inventories demonstrate to firms that their production and pricing decisions were not quite appropriate.[3] Thus, since we normally use GDP to measure output:

The equilibrium level of GDP cannot be one at which total spending exceeds the value of output because firms will notice that inventory stocks are being depleted. They may first decide to increase production sufficiently to meet the higher demand. Later they may decide to raise prices as well.

---

[3]All the models in this book assume, strictly for simplicity, that firms want constant inventories. Deliberate changes in inventories are treated in more advanced courses.

Now imagine the other case, in which the flow of spending reaching firms falls short of current production. Some output cannot be sold and winds up as additions to inventories. The inventory pile-up acts as a signal to firms that at least one of their decisions was wrong. Once again, they will probably react first by cutting back on production, causing GDP to fall. If the imbalance persists, they may also lower prices to stimulate sales. But they certainly will not be happy with things as they are. Thus:

The equilibrium level of GDP cannot be one at which total spending is less than the value of output, because firms will not allow inventories to continue to pile up. They may decide to decrease production, or they may decide to cut prices in order to stimulate demand. Normally, firms are reluctant to cut prices until they are certain that the low level of demand is not a temporary phenomenon. So they rely more heavily on reductions in output.

EQUILIBRIUM ON THE DEMAND SIDE OF THE ECONOMY

We have now determined, through a process of elimination, the level of output that is consistent with peoples' desires to spend. We have reasoned that GDP will rise whenever it is below total spending, $C + I + G + (X - IM)$, and that GDP will fall whenever it is above $C + I + G + (X - IM)$. Equilibrium can only occur, then, when there is just enough spending to absorb the current level of production. Under such circumstances, producers conclude that their price and output decisions are correct, and have no incentive to change them. We conclude that:

The **equilibrium level of GDP on the demand side** is the one at which total spending equals production. In such a situation, firms find their inventories remaining at desired levels; so there is no incentive to change output or prices.

Thus the circular flow diagram has helped us to understand the concept of equilibrium GDP on the demand side. It has also shown us how the economy is driven toward this equilibrium. It leaves unanswered, however, three important questions:

1. How large is the equilibrium level of GDP?
2. Will the economy suffer from unemployment, inflation, or both?
3. Is the equilibrium level of GDP on the demand side also consistent with firms' desires to produce? That is, is it also an equilibrium on the *supply* side?

The first two questions will occupy our attention in this chapter; the third question is reserved until Chapter 10.

CONSTRUCTING THE EXPENDITURE SCHEDULE

Our first objective is to determine precisely the equilibrium level of GDP and to see what factors it depends upon. To make the analysis more concrete, we turn to a numerical example. Specifically, we examine the relationship between total spending and GDP in Macroland, the hypothetical economy that was introduced in the last chapter.

Columns 1 and 2 of Table 8–1 repeat the consumption function of Macroland that we first encountered in Table 7–1. They show how consumer spending, C, depends on national income, which we now begin to symbolize by the letter Y. Columns 3–5 provide the other three components of total spending, I, G, and $X - IM$, through the simplifying assumptions that each is just a fixed number regardless of the level of GDP. Specifically, we assume that investment spending is $900 billion, government purchases are $1300 billion, and net exports are $-$100 billion—meaning that in Macroland, as in the United States at present, imports exceed exports.

By adding together columns 2 through 5, we calculate $C + I + G + (X - IM)$, or total expenditure, which is displayed in column 6. Columns 1 and 6 are shaded and show how total expenditure depends on income in Macroland. We call this the **expenditure schedule**.

Figure 8–2 shows the construction of the expenditure schedule graphically. The black line labeled C is the consumption function of Macroland and simply duplicates Figure 7–6 of the last chapter. It plots on a graph the numbers given in columns 1 and 2 of Table 8–1.

The blue line, labeled $C + I$, displays our assumption that investment is fixed at $900 billion, regardless of the level of GDP. It lies a fixed distance (corresponding to $900 billion) above the C line. If investment were not always $900 billion, the two lines would either move closer together (at income levels at which investment was below $900 billion) or grow farther apart (at income levels at which investment was above $900 billion). For example, our list of determinants of investment spending suggested that I might be larger at higher levels of GDP. Because of this added investment—which is called **induced investment**—the resulting $C + I$ schedule would have a steeper slope than the C schedule.

The brown line, labeled $C + I + G$ adds in government purchases. Since they are assumed to be $1300 billion regardless of the size of GDP, the brown line is parallel to the blue line and $1300 billion higher.

Finally, the red line labeled $C + I + G + (X - IM)$ adds in net exports. It is parallel to the brown line and $100 billion below, reflecting our assumption that net exports in Macroland are always $-$100 billion. Once again, if imports depend on GDP, as our previous discussion suggested, the $C + I + G$ and $C + I + G + (X - IM)$ lines would not be parallel.

An **EXPENDITURE SCHEDULE** shows the relationship between national income (GDP) and total spending.

INDUCED INVESTMENT is the part of investment spending that rises when GDP rises and falls when GDP falls.

Table 8–1	TOTAL EXPENDITURE IN MACROLAND (billions of dollars)				
(1) INCOME (Y)	**(2)** CONSUMPTION (C)	**(3)** INVESTMENT (I)	**(4)** GOVERNMENT PURCHASES (G)	**(5)** NET EXPORTS ($X - IM$)	**(6)** TOTAL EXPENDITURE
4800	3000	900	1300	−100	5100
5200	3300	900	1300	−100	5400
5600	3600	900	1300	−100	5700
6000	3900	900	1300	−100	6000
6400	4200	900	1300	−100	6300
6800	4500	900	1300	−100	6600
7200	4800	900	1300	−100	6900

Figure	8–2	CONSTRUCTION OF THE EXPENDITURE SCHEDULE

This figure shows in a diagram what Table 8–1 showed numerically—the construction of a total expenditure schedule from its components. Line *C* is the consumption function that we first encountered in Figure 7–6. Line *C* + *I* adds investment (assumed always to be $900 billion in this example), and line *C* + *I* + *G* adds government purchases (which are $1300 billion). Line *C* + *I* + *G* + (*X* − *IM*) is the expenditure schedule and is obtained by adding net exports to *C* + *I* + *G*. For example, when GDP is $6000, *C* is $3900, *I* is $900, *G* is $1300, and (*X* − *IM*) is −$100, for a total of $6000.

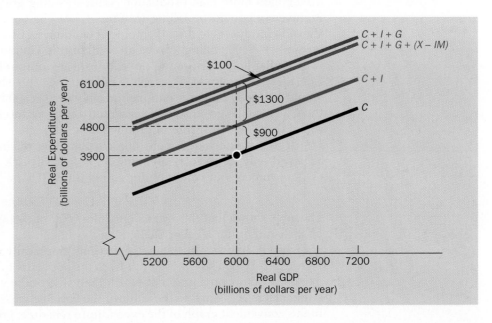

THE MECHANICS OF INCOME DETERMINATION

We are now ready to determine demand-side equilibrium in Macroland. Look first at Table 8–2, which presents the logic of our circular flow argument in tabular form. The first two columns of this table reproduce the expenditure schedule that was constructed in Table 8–1. The other columns explain the process by which equilibrium is approached. Let us see why a GDP of $6000 billion must be the equilibrium level.

Table	8–2	THE DETERMINATION OF EQUILIBRIUM OUTPUT

(1) OUTPUT (*Y*) (billions of dollars)	(2) TOTAL SPENDING (*C* + *I* + *G* + *X* − *IM*) (billions of dollars)	(3) BALANCE OF SPENDING AND OUTPUT	(4) INVENTORIES ARE:	(5) PRODUCERS WILL RESPOND BY:
4800	5100	Spending exceeds output	Falling	Producing more
5200	5400	Spending exceeds output	Falling	Producing more
5600	5700	Spending exceeds output	Falling	Producing more
6000	6000	Spending = output	Constant	Not changing production
6400	6300	Output exceeds spending	Rising	Producing less
6800	6600	Output exceeds spending	Rising	Producing less
7200	6900	Output exceeds spending	Rising	Producing less

Consider first any output level below $6000 billion. For example, at output level $Y = \$5200$ billion, total expenditure is $5400 billion (column 2), which is $200 billion more than production. With spending greater than output (column 3), inventories will be falling (column 4). As the table suggests, this will be a signal to producers to raise their output (column 5). Clearly, then, no output level below $Y = \$6000$ billion can be an equilibrium. Output is too low.

A similar line of reasoning can eliminate any output level above $6000 billion. Consider, for example, $Y = \$6800$ billion. The table shows that total spending would be $6600 billion if national income were $6800 billion. So $200 billion of the GDP would go unsold. This would raise producers' inventory stocks and signal them that their rate of production is too high.

Just as we concluded from our circular flow diagram, equilibrium will be achieved only when total spending, $C + I + G + (X - IM)$, is equal to GDP (Y). In symbols, our condition for equilibrium GDP is:

$$Y = C + I + G + (X - IM).$$

The table shows that this occurs only at a GDP of $6000 billion. This, then, must be the equilibrium level of GDP.

Figure 8–3 shows this same conclusion graphically, by adding a 45° line to Figure 8–2. Why a 45° line? Recall from the appendix to Chapter 1 that a 45° line marks all points on a graph at which the value of the variable measured on the horizontal axis is equal to the value of the variable measured on the vertical axis. In this convenient graph of the expenditure schedule, gross domestic product (Y) is measured on the horizontal axis and total expenditure, $C + I + G + (X - IM)$, is measured on the vertical axis. So the 45° line shows all the points

---

F i g u r e **8–3**   **INCOME-EXPENDITURE DIAGRAM**

This figure adds a 45° line—which marks off points where expenditure and output are equal—to Figure 8–2. Since the condition for equilibrium GDP is that expenditure and output must be equal, this line can be used to determine the equilibrium level of GDP. In this example, equilibrium is at point E, where GDP is $6000 billion—precisely as we found in Table 8–2.

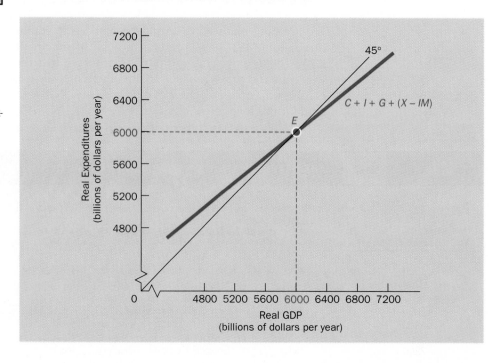

at which output and spending are equal; that is, where $Y = C + I + G + (X - IM)$. The 45° line therefore displays all the points at which the economy *can possibly* be at equilibrium, for if total spending is not equal to production, firms will not be content with current output levels.

Now we must compare these *potential* equilibrium points with the *actual* combinations of spending and output that the economy can attain, given the behavior of consumers and investors. That behavior, as we have seen, is described by the $C + I + G + (X - IM)$ line in Figure 8–3, which shows how total expenditure varies as income changes. Thus, the economy will *always* be on the expenditure line because only points on the $C + I + G + (X - IM)$ line are consistent with the spending plans of consumers and investors. Similarly, *if* the economy is in equilibrium, it *must* be on the 45° line. As Figure 8–3 shows, these two requirements together imply that the only viable equilibrium is at point E, where the $C + I + G + (X - IM)$ line intersects the 45° line. Only this point is consistent both with equilibrium and with the actual desires to consume and invest.

Notice that to the left of the equilibrium point, E, the expenditure line lies above the 45° line. This means that total spending exceeds total output, as we have already noted in words and with numbers. Hence inventories will be falling and firms will conclude that they should increase production. Thus production will rise toward the equilibrium point, E. The opposite is true to the right of point E. Here spending falls short of output, inventories are rising, and firms will cut back production—thereby moving closer to E.

In other words, whenever production is above the equilibrium level, market forces will drive output down. And whenever production is below equilibrium, market forces will drive output up. Thus, in either case, deviations from equilibrium will be eliminated.

Diagrams like this one will recur so frequently in this and the next several chapters that it will be convenient to have a name for them. Let us therefore call them **income-expenditure diagrams** since they show how expenditures vary with income. Sometimes we shall also refer to them simply as **45° line diagrams**.

An **INCOME-EXPENDITURE DIAGRAM,** also called a **45° LINE DIAGRAM**, plots total real expenditure (on the vertical axis) against real income (on the horizontal axis). The 45° line marks off points where income and expenditure are equal.

THE AGGREGATE DEMAND CURVE

Chapter 5 sketched a framework for macroeconomic analysis by introducing aggregate demand and aggregate supply curves which relate aggregate quantities demanded and supplied to the price level. The expenditure schedule graphed in Figure 8–3 is not the aggregate demand curve. How could it be, for we have yet to bring the price level into our discussion? It is now time to remedy this omission and derive the aggregate demand curve, for only then will we be able to analyze inflation.

Fortunately, no further mechanical apparatus is required. The price level can be brought into our income-expenditure analysis by recalling something we learned in the last chapter: At any given level of real income, higher prices lead to lower real consumer spending. The reason, you will recall, is that consumers own many assets whose values are fixed in money terms, and which therefore lose purchasing power when prices rise.[4] With real wealth lower, consumers

---

[4]The money in your bank account is a prime example. If prices rise, it will buy less.

spend less. Therefore total spending in the economy falls *even with no change in real income.*

In terms of our 45° line diagram, then, a rise in the price level will pull down the consumption function depicted in Figure 8–2 and, hence, will pull down the total expenditure schedule as well. Conversely, a fall in the price level will raise both the C and $C + I + G + (X - IM)$ schedules in the diagram. The two parts of Figure 8–4 illustrate both these sorts of shifts.

What, then, do changes in the price level do to the equilibrium level of real GDP on the demand side? Common sense says that, with lower spending, equilibrium GDP should fall. And Figure 8–4 shows that this conclusion is correct. Part (a) shows that a rise in the price level, by shifting the expenditure schedule downward from $C_0 + I + G + (X - IM)$ to $C_1 + I + G + (X - IM)$ leads to a reduction in the equilibrium quantity of real GDP demanded from Y_0 to Y_1. Part (b) shows that a fall in the price level, by shifting the expenditure schedule upward from $C_0 + I + G + (X - IM)$ to $C_2 + I + G + (X - IM)$, leads to a rise in the equilibrium quantity of real GDP demanded from Y_0 to Y_2. In summary:

A rise in the price level leads to a lower equilibrium level of real aggregate quantity demanded. This relationship between the price level and the equilibrium quantity of real GDP demanded is depicted in Figure 25–5 and is precisely what

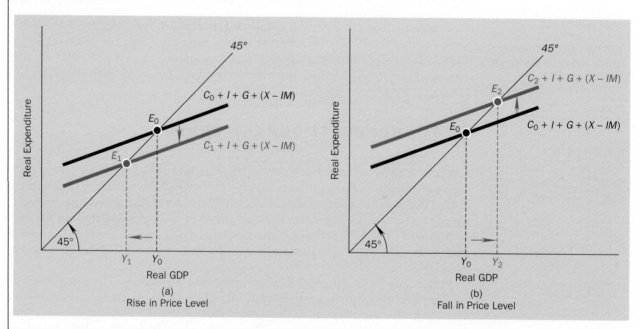

Figure 8–4 THE EFFECT OF THE PRICE LEVEL ON EQUILIBRIUM AGGREGATE QUANTITY DEMANDED

Because a change in the price level causes the expenditure schedule to shift, it changes the equilibrium quantity of real GDP demanded. Part (a) shows what happens when the price level rises, causing the expenditure schedule to shift downward from $C_0 + I + G + (X - IM)$ to $C_1 + I + G + (X - IM)$. Equilibrium quantity demanded falls from Y_0 to Y_1. Part (b) shows what happens when the price level falls, causing the expenditure schedule to shift upward from $C_0 + I + G + (X - IM)$ to $C_2 + I + G + (X - IM)$. Equilibrium quantity demanded rises from Y_0 to Y_2.

F i g u r e **8–5**   **THE AGGREGATE DEMAND CURVE**

The graphic analysis in Figure 8–4 showed that higher prices lead to lower aggregate quantity demanded. This relationship is called the aggregate demand curve and is shown in this figure.

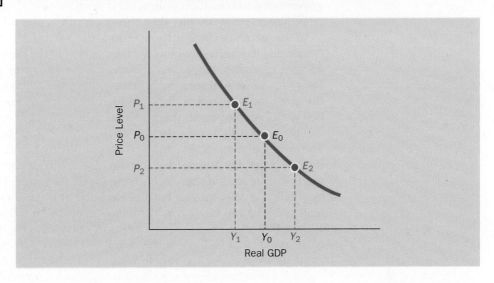

we called the **aggregate demand curve** in earlier chapters. It comes directly from the 45° line diagrams in Figure 8–4. Thus, points E_0, E_1, and E_2 in Figure 8–5 correspond precisely to the points bearing the same labels in Figure 8–4.

The effect of higher prices on consumer wealth is just one of several reasons why the aggregate demand curve relating the price level to real GDP demanded slopes downward. Another reason comes from international trade. In our discussion of the determinants of net exports (see page 184–85), we pointed out that higher U.S. prices will depress exports (X) and stimulate imports (IM), provided that foreign prices are held constant. That means that, other things equal, a higher U.S. price level will reduce the $(X - IM)$ component of total expenditure, thereby shifting the $C + I + G + (X - IM)$ line downward and lowering real GDP as depicted in Figure 8–4(a).

Later in the book, after we have studied interest rates and exchange rates, we will encounter still more reasons for a downward-sloping aggregate demand curve. All of them imply that:

An income-expenditure diagram like Figure 8–3 can be drawn up only for a *specific* price level. At different price levels, the $C + I + G + (X - IM)$ schedule will be different and, hence, the equilibrium quantity of GDP demanded will be different.

As we shall now see, this finding is critical to understanding the genesis of unemployment and inflation.

DEMAND-SIDE EQUILIBRIUM AND FULL EMPLOYMENT

We now turn to the second major question of this chapter: Will the economy achieve an equilibrium at full employment without inflation, or will there be unemployment, inflation, or both? This is one of the crucial questions surrounding government stabilization policy, for if the economy always gravitates toward full employment *automatically*, then the government should simply leave it alone.

In the income-expenditure diagrams used so far, the equilibrium level of GDP demanded has been shown as the intersection of the expenditure schedule and the 45° line, regardless of whatever level of GDP might correspond to full employment. However, as we will see now, when equilibrium GDP falls above full employment, the economy probably will be plagued by inflation. And when equilibrium falls below full employment, there will be unemployment and recession.

This remarkable fact was one of the principal messages of Keynes's *General Theory of Employment, Interest, and Money*. Writing during the Great Depression, it was natural for him to focus on the case in which equilibrium falls short of full employment so that there are unemployed resources. Figure 8–6 illustrates this possibility. A vertical line has been erected at the full-employment level of GDP (called "potential GDP"), which is assumed to be $7000 billion in the example. We see that the $C + I + G + (X - IM)$ curve cuts the 45° line at point E, which corresponds to a GDP ($Y = 6000 billion) below potential GDP. In this case, the expenditure curve is too low to lead to full employment.

Such a situation might arise because either consumers or investors are unwilling to spend at normal rates, because government spending is low, because foreign demand is weak, or because the price level is "too high." Any of these would depress the $C + I + G + (X - IM)$ curve. Unemployment must then occur because not enough output is demanded to keep the entire labor force busy.

The distance between the *equilibrium* level of output demanded and the *full-employment* level of output (that is, potential GDP) is called the **recessionary gap**—

The **RECESSIONARY GAP** is the amount by which the equilibrium level of real GDP falls short of potential GDP.

F i g u r e **8-6**	**A RECESSIONARY GAP**

Sometimes equilibrium GDP may fall below potential GDP, so that some workers are unemployed. This diagram illustrates such a case. The horizontal distance *EB* between equilibrium GDP and potential GDP is called the recessionary gap.

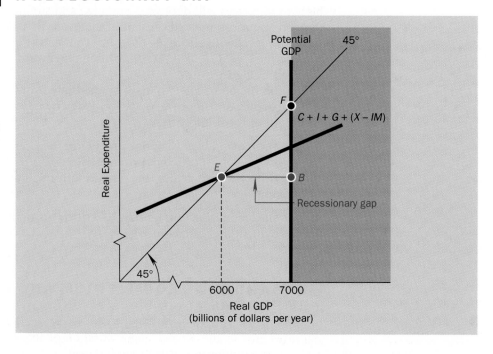

F i g u r e **8-7**   **AN INFLATIONARY GAP**

Sometimes equilibrium GDP may lie above potential GDP, meaning that there are more jobs than required for full employment. This diagram illustrates such a case. The horizontal distance BE between potential GDP and equilibrium GDP is called the inflationary gap. It is gradually eliminated by rising prices, which pull the $C + I + (X - IM)$ schedule down until it passes through point F.

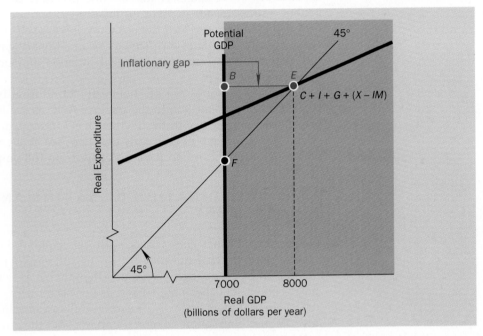

and is shown by the horizontal distance from E to B. While Figure 8–6 is entirely hypothetical, real-world gaps of precisely this sort were shown shaded brown in Figure 6–2 (page 127). They are a pervasive feature of recent U.S. economic history.

It is clear from Figure 8–6 that full employment can be reached only by raising the total spending schedule to eliminate the recessionary gap. Specifically, the $C + I + G + (X - IM)$ schedule must move upward until it cuts the 45° line at point F. Can this happen without government intervention? We know that a sufficiently large drop in the price level can do the job. But is that a realistic prospect? We shall return to this question after we bring the supply side into the picture. But first let us consider the other case, in which equilibrium GDP exceeds full employment.

Figure 8–7 illustrates this possibility. Now the expenditure schedule intersects the 45° line at point E, where GDP is $8000 billion. But this exceeds the full employment level, $Y = 7000 billion. A case like this can arise when consumer or investment spending is unusually buoyant, when foreign demand is unusually strong, when the government spends too much, or when a "low" price level pushes the $C + I + G + (X - IM)$ curve upward.

To reach an equilibrium at full employment, the price level would have to rise enough to drive the expenditure schedule *down* until it passed through point F. The horizontal distance BE—which indicates the amount by which the quantity of GDP demanded exceeds potential GDP—is called the **inflationary gap**. If there is an inflationary gap, a higher price level or some other means of reducing total expenditure is necessary to reach an equilibrium at full employment. Real-world inflationary gaps were shown shaded blue in Figure 8–2.

The **INFLATIONARY GAP** is the amount by which equilibrium real GDP exceeds the full-employment level of GDP.

In sum, only if the price level and spending plans are "just right" will the expenditure curve intersect the 45° line precisely at full employment, so that neither a recessionary gap nor an inflationary gap occurs. Are there reasons to expect this outcome? Does the economy have a self-correcting mechanism that automatically eliminates recessionary or inflationary gaps and propels it toward full employment? And how is it that inflation and unemployment sometimes occur together?

These are questions we are not ready to address because we have not yet brought *aggregate supply* into the picture. And, as we learned in Chapter 5, the price level is determined by the interaction of *both* aggregate demand *and* aggregate supply. However, it is not too early to get an idea about why things can go wrong, why the economy can find itself far away from full employment.

THE COORDINATION OF SAVING AND INVESTMENT

To understand what goes wrong with the economy in a recession, it is useful to pose the following question: Must the full-employment level of GDP be an equilibrium? Decades ago, economists thought the answer was yes. Since Keynes, most economists believe the answer is not necessarily.

To help us understand why, Figure 8–8 offers a simplified version of the circular flow diagram that ignores exports, imports, and the government. In this version,

Figure 8–8   A SIMPLIFIED CIRCULAR FLOW

Here we show a simplified version of the circular flow of income and expenditures shown in Figure 8–1. The simplification amounts to shutting off the pipes leading into and out of the government, and into and out of the rest of the world. Thus, this circular flow represents an economy with no government and no foreign trade.

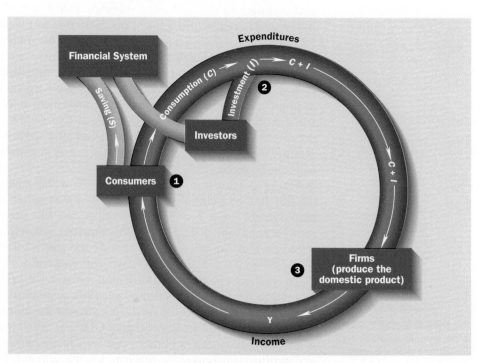

version, there is just one place for income to "leak out" of the circular flow: at point 1, where consumers save some of their income. Similarly, there is just one place for this lost spending to be replaced: at point 2, where investment enters the circular flow.

What happens if firms produce exactly the full-employment level of GDP at point 3 in the diagram? Will this income level be maintained as we move around the circle? Or will it shrink or grow? The answer is that full-employment income will be maintained only if the spending by investors at point 2 exactly balances the saving done by consumers at point 1. In other words:

The economy will reach an equilibrium at full employment only if the amount that consumers wish to save out of full-employment incomes happens to be equal to the amount that investors want to invest. If these two magnitudes are unequal, then full employment will not be an equilibrium for the economy.

Specifically, we can see from the circular flow diagram that if saving exceeds investment at full employment, then the total demand arriving at the firms (point 3) will fall short of total output because the added investment spending is not enough to replace the leakage to saving. With demand inadequate to support production at full employment, we know that the GDP must fall below potential. There will be a recessionary gap. Conversely, if investment exceeds saving when the economy is at full employment, then total demand will exceed potential GDP and production will rise above the full-employment level. There will be an inflationary gap.

Now this discussion does nothing but restate what we already know in different words.[5] But these words hold the key to understanding why the economy can find itself stuck below full employment (or above it, for that matter), for *the people who do the investing are not the same people who do the saving*. In a modern capitalist economy, investing is done by one group of individuals (primarily corporate executives and home buyers) while saving is done by another group.[6] It is easy to imagine that their plans may not be well coordinated. If they are not, we have just seen how either unemployment or inflation can arise.

Notice that these problems would never arise if the acts of saving and investing were not separated in time or space. Imagine a primitive economy of farmers, each of whom invests only in his own farm. There is no borrowing or lending, and no financial system. In this world, any farmer wanting to buy a new plow or tractor (that is, wanting to *invest*) would have to refrain from consuming part of his income (that is, would have to *save*). Therefore, the amount that all farmers together planned to save out of full-employment income would have to be equal to the amount of planned investment. Total spending and production would always have to be equal at full employment.

Almost the same holds true in a centrally planned economy. There the state decides how much will be invested and has a great deal of leverage over how much saving people do. If the planners do their calculations correctly, they can

---

[5] In symbols, our equilibrium condition without government or foreign trade is $Y = C + I$. If we note that Y is also the sum of consumption plus saving, $Y = C + S$, it follows that $C + S = C + I$, or $S = I$, is a restatement of the equilibrium condition. A more complicated version of the saving = investment approach is described in Appendix A.

[6] In a modern economy, it is not only households that save. Businesses save also, in the form of retained earnings. Nonetheless, households are the ultimate source of the saving needed to finance investment.

At The FRONTIER

UNEMPLOYMENT AND INFLATION AS COORDINATION FAILURES

The idea that recessions are times when the market system fails to perform properly is a very old one, predating Keynes. As we have seen in this chapter, Keynes attributed this failure to a *lack of coordination* between the decisions of savers and those of investors. If savers want to save more out of full-employment income than investors want to invest, full employment cannot be an equilibrium for the economy. GDP must be lower and unemployment must be higher.

In recent years, economic theorists have begun to formalize Keynes's common sense notion that coordination failures may be the root cause of recessions and unemployment. Although normally couched in mathematical terms, replete with

symbols and complicated diagrams, the basic idea is elementary and is well illustrated by the parable of the football game.

Picture a crowd watching a football game. Now something exciting happens and the fans

rise from their seats. The people in the front rows begin standing first, and those seated behind them are forced to stand if they want to see the game. Soon everyone in the stadium is on their feet.

But with everyone standing,

force saving to be equal to investment at full employment. Consequently, business fluctuations were not historically major problems for the former Soviet and Chinese economies. (They had plenty of others!) However, as these two countries liberalized their economies, they found that they had to deal with the inflation and unemployment problems that have long plagued the West.

Keynes observed that modern market economies differ from either primitive societies or centrally planned societies in this fundamental way, and that this flaw in the market mechanism leaves them vulnerable to recessions. However, one should not conclude that in order to avoid unemployment and recession the U.S. economy should revert to either a primitive form of capitalism or to rigid central planning. These "remedies" are far worse than the disease. Fortunately, there are policies the government can follow in an advanced capitalist economy to ease the pain of unemployment and recession—policies that we shall be studying in the following chapters.

no one can see any better than when everyone was sitting. And the fans are enduring the further discomfort of being on their feet. (Never mind that stadium seats are uncomfortable!) So everyone in the stadium would be better off if everyone would sit down. But coordinating the decisions of tens of thousands of fans is virtually impossible. So everyone stands.

In the terminology of economics, the football stadium has *two equilibria*—a superior one with everyone sitting, and an inferior one with everyone standing. In practice, we all know what happens. The crowd rises to its feet on every exciting play, sits during lulls in the action, and then rises again at the slightest hint of excitement. Thus it vacillates between the good equilibrium and the bad equilibrium.

Now, what does all this have to do with unemployment? Recall Keynes's idea that unemploy-

ment arises because the decisions of savers and investors are not coordinated. If left to their own devices, individuals acting in their own best interests might choose actions that lead to the inferior equilibrium with high unemployment (analogous to standing at the football game) even though there is a superior equilibrium with low unemployment (like sitting at the game). Although people prefer the equilibrium with low unemployment, they may be unable to coordinate their decisions in order to produce it.

If high unemployment does in fact arise from *coordination failures* like this, the government might be able to do something to cure it. Keynes certainly thought so. However, the football analogy reminds us that a central authority may not find it easy to solve the coordination problem.

The coordination failure idea may also help to explain why it is so hard to stop inflation.

Everyone prefers stable prices to rising prices. But stopping inflation is a bit like watching a football game.

Think of yourself as the seller of a product. If everyone else in the economy would hold their prices steady, you would happily hold yours steady, too. Hence, zero inflation is an equilibrium for the economy, just as sitting at the football game is an equilibrium for the football stadium. But, if you believe that others will continue to raise their prices at, say, 5 percent per year, you may find it dangerous not to increase yours apace. Hence, 5 percent inflation may also be an equilibrium, like standing at a football game. Everyone in society may agree that the equilibrium with no inflation is better than the equilibrium with 5 percent inflation. But society may nonetheless get stuck with 5 percent inflation, just as football fans must frequently stand at ball games.

Summary

1. Investment is the most volatile component of aggregate demand, largely because it is tied so closely to the state of business confidence and to expectations about the future performance of the economy.

2. Government policy cannot influence business confidence in any reliable way, so policies designed to alter investment spending are aimed at more objective, though possibly less important, determinants of investment. Among these are interest rates, the overall state of aggregate demand, and tax incentives.

3. Net exports depend on GDPs and relative prices both here and abroad.

4. The **equilibrium** level of national income on the demand side is the level at which total spending just equals the value of production (GDP). Since total spending is the sum of consumption, investment, government purchases, and net exports, the condition for equilibrium is $Y = C + I + G + (X - IM)$.

5. Income levels below equilibrium are bound to rise because, when spending exceeds output, firms will see their inventory stocks being depleted and will react by stepping up production.

6. Income levels above equilibrium are bound to fall because, when total spending is insufficient to absorb

total output, inventories will pile up and firms will react by curtailing production.

7. The determination of the equilibrium level of GDP on the demand side can be portrayed on a convenient **income-expenditure diagram** as the point at which the **expenditure schedule**—defined as the sum of $C + I + G + (X - IM)$—crosses the 45° line. The 45° line is significant because it marks off points at which spending and output are equal—that is, at which $Y = C + I + G + (X - IM)$—and this is the basic condition for equilibrium.

8. An income-expenditure diagram can only be drawn up for a specific price level, however. Thus the equilibrium GDP so determined depends on the price level.

9. Because higher prices reduce the purchasing power of consumers' wealth and hence reduce their spending, equilibrium real GDP demanded is lower when prices are higher. This downward-sloping relationship is known as the **aggregate demand curve**.

10. Equilibrium GDP can be above or below **potential GDP**, which is defined as the GDP that would be produced if the labor force were fully employed.

11. If equilibrium GDP exceeds potential GDP, the difference is called an **inflationary gap**. If equilibrium GDP falls short of potential GDP, the resulting difference is called a **recessionary gap**.

12. Such gaps can occur because the saving that consumers want to do at full-employment income levels may differ from the investing that investors want to do. This problem is not likely to arise in a planned economy or in a primitive economy.

Key Concepts and Terms

Equilibrium level of GDP
Expenditure schedule
Induced investment
$Y = C + I + G + (X - IM)$

Income-expenditure (or 45° line) diagram
Aggregate demand curve
Full-employment level of GDP (or potential GDP)

Recessionary gap
Inflationary gap
Coordination of saving and investment

Questions for Review

1. For the last several years, imports have exceeded exports in the United States economy. This is often considered a major problem. Does this chapter give you any hints about why? (You may want to discuss this issue with your instructor, and you will certainly learn more about it in later chapters.)

2. Why is not any arbitrary level of GDP an equilibrium for the economy? (Do not give a mechanical answer to this question, but explain the economic mechanism involved.)

3. From the following data, construct an expenditure schedule on a piece of graph paper. Then use the income-expenditure (45° line) diagram to determine the equilibrium level of GDP.

INCOME	CONSUMPTION	INVESTMENT	GOVERNMENT PURCHASES	NET EXPORTS
1800	1610	120	60	20
1850	1655	120	60	20
1900	1700	120	60	20
1950	1745	120	60	20
2000	1790	120	60	20

4. From the following data, construct an expenditure schedule on a piece of graph paper. Then use the income-expenditure (45° line) diagram to determine the equilibrium level of GDP. Compare your answer with your answer to Question 3.

INCOME	CONSUMPTION	INVESTMENT	GOVERNMENT PURCHASES	NET EXPORTS
1800	1640	90	60	20
1850	1670	105	60	20
1900	1700	120	60	20
1950	1730	135	60	20
2000	1760	150	60	20

5. Suppose investment spending was always $250, government purchases were $100, net exports were always −$50, and consumer spending depended on the price level in the following way:

PRICE LEVEL	CONSUMER SPENDING
80	740
90	720
100	700
110	680
120	660

On a piece of graph paper, use these data to construct an aggregate demand curve. Why do you think this example supposes that consumption declines as the price level rises?

6. Does the economy this year seem to have an inflationary gap or a recessionary gap? (If you do not know the answer from reading the newspaper, ask your instructor.)

7. Why were there no recessions in the former Soviet Union?

8. (More difficult)[7] Consider an economy in which the consumption function takes the following simple algebraic form:

---

[7]The answer to this question is provided in Appendix B.

$$C = 300 + 0.75DI$$

and in which investment (I) is always 900 and net exports are always -100. Government purchases are fixed at 1300 and taxes are fixed at 1200. Find the equilibrium level of GDP and compare your answer to Table 8–2 and Figure 8–3. (HINT: Remember that in this case disposable income is GDP minus taxes: $DI = Y - T = Y - 1200$.)

9. (More difficult) An economy has a consumption function:

$$C = 200 + 0.8 \, DI.$$

The government budget is balanced with government purchases and taxes both fixed at 1000. Net exports are 100. Investment is 600. Find equilibrium GDP.

Appendix A   THE "LEAKAGES" AND "INJECTIONS" APPROACH

There is another way of looking at the determination of the equilibrium level of GDP on the demand side. In the text, we studied the condition that total expenditure, $C + I + G + (X - IM)$, is equal to the value of production (Y). As an alternative, we can study the condition that the three "leakages" from the circular flow diagram (Figure 8–1—saving (S), taxes (T), and imports (IM)—just balance the three "injections"—investment (I), government purchases (G), and exports (X)—so that the amount of money going around the circle is maintained; that is:

$$
\begin{aligned}
\text{Leakages} &= \text{Injections} \\
S + T + IM &= I + G + X.
\end{aligned}
$$

It must be emphasized at the outset that this is not a *new* approach. It is merely another way of looking at precisely the same phenomenon. The reason is that income (Y) must be either spent on consumer goods (C), saved (S), or paid to the government in taxes (T). Since $Y = C + S + T$ *always*, and since $Y = C + I + G + (X - IM)$ when Y is at its equilibrium value, we can describe equilibrium by the condition that:

$$C + S + T = C + I + G + (X - IM).$$

After cancelling C on both sides, this equation is equivalent to the previous one.

GRAPHICAL ANALYSIS

This way of looking at equilibrium has a different graphic representation. It does not use the 45° line diagram, but it contains precisely the same information.

Recall that in an appendix to Chapter 7 we constructed the saving schedule, which we repeat here as Figure 8–9. Since the equilibrium condition now under scrutiny is $S + T + IM = I + G + X$, we need to add T and IM to this line. In our numerical example of Macroland, $T = 1200$ and $IM = 750$, so the "leakages schedule" (the sum of $S + T + IM$) shown in Figure 8–10 is parallel to the saving schedule in Figure 8–9, but $1950 billion higher.

To complete the story, we add to Figure 8–10 a horizontal line at a height equal to the sum of investment plus government purchases plus exports, which is $900 + $1300 + $650 = $2850 billion in our example. Call this the "injections schedule." Point E then shows the equilibrium level of GDP, which is at an income level of $6000 billion. As must be the case, this is the same answer we obtained with the 45° line diagram.

You will notice that at income levels below $6000 billion, injections ($I + G + X$) exceed leakages ($S + T + IM$), just as $C + I + G + (X - IM)$ exceeded output in the 45° line diagram. Similarly, at income

---

F i g u r e   **8-9**   **THE SAVING SCHEDULE**

This diagram shows the relationship between saving and income in Macroland and duplicates Figure 7–9 (page 170).

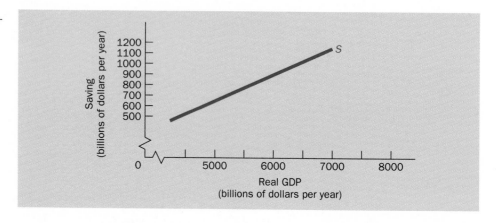

| Figure | 8-10 | **DETERMINATION OF EQUILIBRIUM GDP BY LEAKAGES = INJECTIONS** |

This diagram depicts the equilibrium of the economy at point E, where the sum of saving plus taxes plus imports ($S + T + IM$) equals the sum of investment plus government purchases plus exports ($I + G + X$). The equilibrium is at a real GDP of $6000 billion, which, as must be the case, is the same conclusion that we reached with the aid of the 45° line diagram (Figure 8–3).

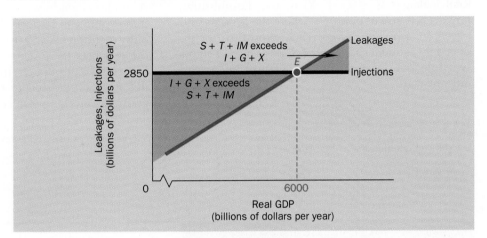

levels above $6000 billion, leakages exceed injections. (In the 45° line diagram, Y exceeded $C + I + G + (X - IM)$ in this range.) This must be the case since the two graphs are alternative depictions of the same phenomena. The economic analyses behind them are precisely the same.

INDUCED INVESTMENT

In the chapter we mentioned the possibility of *induced investment*, that is, that investment rises as GDP rises. But we did not examine this possibility in

our graphs. (However, this case did arise in Review Question 4.) The reason is that what matters in the 45° line diagram is the slope of the *combined* $C + I + G + (X - IM)$ schedule, not the *individual* slopes of the C, I, and $(X - IM)$ schedules. So an upward-sloping investment schedule makes little difference to the analysis.

When using the leakages = injections approach, however, the slope of the investment schedule becomes more apparent, though not really more important. So Figure 8–11 illustrates the case of

| Figure | 8-11 | **INCOME DETERMINATION WITH INDUCED INVESTMENT** |

When investment rises with GDP ("induced investment"), the investment schedule, and hence the $I + G + X$ line, acquires a positive slope. Apart from this, the determination of equilibrium output is precisely as it was before. Point E, where the leakages and injections schedules cross, is the equilibrium.

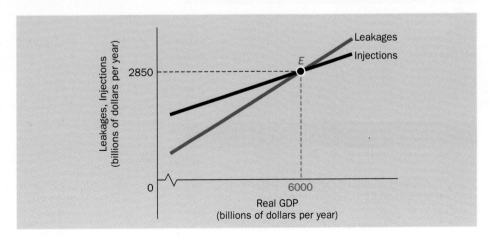

induced investment. In this diagram, the investment schedule is upward sloping, and so the schedule of total leakages ($I + G + X$) is, too. Equilibrium, however, is still at point E—where the leakage and injections schedules cross. Thus allowance for induced investment changes the slope of the injections schedule, but does not alter our analysis in any significant way.[8]

---

[8]Some students may wonder what happens if the slope of the injections schedule exceeds that of the leakages schedule. This is a difficult question that is best reserved for more advanced

VARIABLE IMPORTS

A similar amendment to the analysis must be made if the volume of imports depends on GDP—a possibility mentioned early in the chapter. Consider again the leakages ($S + T + IM$) schedule depicted in Figure 8–11. If imports are increasing as GDP rises, this line will be steeper than indicated in the diagram. But nothing else changes.

---

courses. Suffice it to say here that the simple model of income determination constructed in this chapter will not work in such a case.

Summary

1. The condition for equilibrium GDP—which we gave in the chapter as the equation of total spending with output, $Y = C + I + G + (X - IM)$—can be restated as the requirement that saving plus taxes plus imports be equal to the sum of investment plus government purchases plus exports: $S + T + IM = I + G + X$. In shorthand, total **leakages** equal total **injections**. This does not change anything, but simply says the same thing in different words.

2. These different words lead to a different graphical presentation, in which we look for equilibrium at the point where the upward-sloping leakages schedule crosses the horizontal line depicting injections.

3. **Induced investment**—that is, investment that rises as the GDP rises—would give the injections schedule a positive slope, but require no other change in the analysis.

4. If imports grow with GDP, the slope of the leakages schedule in the diagram increases, but nothing else changes.

Key Concepts and Terms

$S + T + IM = I + G + X$
Saving schedule

Leakages schedule
Injections schedule

Induced investment

Questions for Review

1. Take the data in Review Question 3 at the end of the chapter and add the following information: taxes are fixed at 60, exports are 200, and imports are 180. Construct the leakages schedule that adds up $S + T + IM$ and the injections schedule that adds up $I + G + X$ on a piece of graph paper. (In doing so, remember that any income that is not consumed or paid in taxes must be saved.) Use these constructions to find the equilibrium level of GDP.

2. Do the same thing with the data in Review Question 4 at the end of the chapter.

| *Appendix B* | THE SIMPLE ALGEBRA OF INCOME DETERMINATION |

The model of demand-side equilibrium that the chapter presented graphically and in tabular form can also be handled with some simple algebra.

Written as an equation, the consumption function in our example is:

$$C = 300 + 0.75DI$$
$$= 300 + 0.75(Y - T),$$

since, by definition DI $= Y - T$. This is simply the equation of a straight line with a slope of 0.75 and an intercept of $300 - 0.75T$. Since $T = 1200$ in our example, the intercept is -600 and the equation can be written more simply as:

$$C = -600 + 0.75Y.$$

Investment in the example was assumed to be 900, regardless of the level of income, government purchases were 1300, and net exports were -100. So the sum $C + I + G + (X - IM)$ is:

$$C + I + G + (X - IM)$$
$$= -600 + 0.75Y + 900 + 1300 - 100$$
$$= 1500 + 0.75Y,$$

which describes the expenditure curve in Figure 8–3. Since the equilibrium quantity of GDP demanded is defined by:

$$Y = C + I + G + (X - IM),$$

we can solve for the equilibrium value of Y by substituting $1500 + 0.75Y$ for $C + I + G + (X - IM)$ to get:

$$Y = C + I + G + (X - IM) = 1500 + 0.75Y.$$

To solve this equation for Y, first subtract $0.75Y$ from both sides to get:

$$0.25Y = 1500.$$

Then divide both sides by 0.25 to obtain the answer:

$$Y = 6000.$$

This, of course, is precisely the solution we found by graphical and tabular methods in the chapter.

The method of solution is easily generalized to deal with any set of numbers in our equations. Suppose the consumption function is:

$$C = a + bDI = a + b(Y - T).$$

(In the example, $a = 300$, T $= 1200$, and $b = 0.75$.) Then the equilibrium condition that $Y = C + I + G + (X - IM)$ implies:

$$Y = a + bDI + I + G + (X - IM)$$
$$= a - bT + bY + I + G + (X - IM).$$

Subtracting bY from both sides leads to:

$$(1 - b)Y = a - bT + I + G + (X - IM),$$

and dividing through by $1 - b$ gives:

$$Y = \frac{a - bT + I + G + (X - IM)}{+ 1 - b}.$$

This formula, which is certainly *not* to be memorized, is valid for any numerical values of a, b, T, G, I, and $(X - IM)$ (so long as b is between zero and one.)

Questions for Review

1. Find the equilibrium level of GDP demanded in an economy in which investment is always $300, net exports are always $-$50, the government budget is balanced with purchases and taxes both equal to $400, and the consumption function is described by the following algebraic equation:

$$C = 150 + 0.75DI.$$

Hint: Do not forget that DI $= Y - T$.

2. Do the same for an economy in which investment is $250, net exports are zero, government purchases and taxes are both $400, and the consumption function is:

$$C = 250 + 0.5DI.$$

3. In each of the above cases, how much saving is there in equilibrium? (*Hint*: Income not consumed must be saved.) Is saving equal to investment?

4. Imagine an economy in which consumer expenditure is represented by the following equation:

$$C = 50 + .75DI.$$

Imagine also that investors want to spend 500 at every level of income ($I = 500$), net exports are zero ($X - IM = 0$), government purchases are 300 and taxes are 200.

a. What is the equilibrium level of income?
b. If the full employment level of income is 3000, is there a recessionary or inflationary gap? If so, how much?
c. What will happen to the equilibrium level of income if investors become optimistic about the country's future and raise their investment to 600?

d. Is there a recessionary or inflationary gap now? How much?

5. Ivyland has the following consumption function:

$$C = 100 + .8DI.$$

Firms in Ivyland always invest $700 and net exports are zero, initially. The government budget is balanced with spending and taxes both equal to $500.

a. Find the equilibrium level of GDP.
b. How much is saved? Is saving equal to investment?
c. Now suppose an export-promotion drive succeeds in raising net exports to $100. Answer (a) and (b) under these new circumstances.

CHANGES ON THE DEMAND SIDE: MULTIPLIER ANALYSIS

A definite ratio, to be called the Multiplier, *can be established between income and investment.*

JOHN MAYNARD KEYNES

In the last chapter we derived the economy's *aggregate demand curve*, which shows how the equilibrium quantity of real GDP demanded depends on the price level—holding all other factors constant. But often these "other factors" do not remain constant and, as a consequence, the entire aggregate demand curve shifts. This chapter is the first of several that are devoted to enumerating these "other factors" and explaining how and why they make the aggregate demand curve shift. ¶ The central concept of this short chapter is the *multiplier*—the idea that an increase in spending will bring about an *even larger* increase in equilibrium GDP. We approach this idea from three different perspectives, each of which provides different insights into the multiplier process. First, the multiplier is illustrated graphically using the income-expenditure diagram from Chapter 8. Next, we reach the same conclusion through the use of a numerical example, and finally, we offer an algebraic statement. Each of these is an expression of the remarkable multiplier result. ¶ Near the end of the chapter, we use multiplier analysis to explain how economic developments abroad affect the U.S. economy and why a drive to increase national saving might not succeed.

THE MAGIC OF THE MULTIPLIER

Because it is subject to such abrupt swings, investment spending is often the cause of business fluctuations in the United States and elsewhere. Let us, therefore, ask what would happen to equilibrium income in our fictitious country, Macroland, if firms there suddenly decided to spend more on investment goods. As we shall see, such a decision would have a *multiplied* effect on GDP in Macroland; that is, each $1 of additional investment spending would add more than $1 to GDP. The same would be true in the U.S. economy.

For simplicity, we continue to assume that the price level is fixed—an assumption we will drop in the very next chapter. Refer first to Table 9–1, which looks very much like Table 8–1 (page 188). The only difference is that we assume here that, for some reason, firms in Macroland now want to invest $200 billion more than they previously did—for a total of $1100 billion. The **multiplier** principle says that Macroland's GDP will rise by more than the $200 billion increase in investment. Specifically, the multiplier is defined as the ratio of the change in equilibrium GDP (Y) divided by the original change in spending that causes the change in GDP. In shorthand, when we deal with the multiplier for investment (I), the formula is

$$\text{Multiplier} = \frac{\text{Change in } Y}{\text{Change in } I}.$$

The **MULTIPLIER** is the ratio of the change in equilibrium GDP (Y) divided by the original change in spending that causes the change in GDP.

Let us verify that the multiplier is indeed greater than 1. Table 9–1 shows how to derive a new expenditure schedule by adding up C, I, G, and (X − IM) at each level of Y, just as we did in Chapter 8. If you compare the last column of Table 9–1 with that of Table 8–1, you will see that the new expenditure schedule lies uniformly above the old one by $200 billion.

Figure 9–1 illustrates this diagrammatically. The schedule marked $C + I_0 + G + (X - IM)$ is derived from the last column of Table 8–1, while the higher

Table **9–1**		TOTAL EXPENDITURE AFTER A $200 BILLION RISE IN INVESTMENT SPENDING (billions of dollars)				
(1) INCOME (Y)	**(2)** CONSUMPTION (C)	**(3)** INVESTMENT (I)	**(4)** GOVERNMENT PURCHASES (G)	**(5)** NET EXPORTS (X − IM)	**(6)** TOTAL EXPENDITURE	
4800	3000	1100	1300	− 100	5300	
5200	3300	1100	1300	− 100	5600	
5600	3600	1100	1300	− 100	5900	
6000	3900	1100	1300	− 100	6200	
6400	4200	1100	1300	− 100	6500	
6800	4500	1100	1300	− 100	6800	
7200	4800	1100	1300	− 100	7100	

This table shows the construction of a total expenditure schedule for Macroland after investment has risen to $1100 billion. As indicated by the shaded numbers, only income level Y = $6800 billion is an equilibrium on the demand side of the economy because only at this level is total spending (C + I + G + X − IM) equal to production (Y).

This figure depicts the multiplier effect of a rise in investment spending of $200 billion. The expenditure schedule shifts upward from $C + I_0 + G + (X - IM)$ to $C + I_1 + G + (X - IM)$, thus moving equilibrium from point E_0 to point E_1. The rise in income is $800 billion, so the multiplier is $800/$200 = 4.

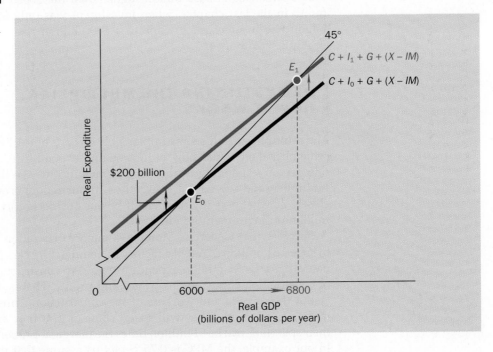

schedule marked $C + I_1 + G + (X - IM)$ is derived from the last column of Table 9–1. The two expenditure lines are parallel and $200 billion apart.

So far no act of magic has occurred—things look just as you might expect. But one more step will bring the multiplier rabbit out of the hat. Let us see what the upward shift of the expenditure line does to equilibrium income. In Figure 9–1, equilibrium moves outward from point E_0 to point E_1; that is, from $6000 billion to $6800 billion. The difference is an increase in national income of $800 billion. All this from a $200 billion stimulus to investment? That is the magic of the multiplier.

Because the change in I is $200 billion and the change in equilibrium Y is $800 billion, by applying our definition, the multiplier is

$$\text{Multiplier} = \frac{\text{Change in } Y}{\text{Change in } I} = \frac{\$800}{\$200} = 4.$$

This tells us that, in our example, every additional dollar of investment demand will add $4 to the equilibrium GDP!

This does indeed seem mysterious. Can something be created from nothing? Let us, therefore, check to be sure that the graph has not deceived us. The first and last columns of Table 9–1 show in numbers what Figure 9–1 shows in a picture. Notice that, at any income level below $6800 billion, spending, $C + I + G + (X - IM)$, exceeds output (Y). As we know, this cannot be an equilibrium situation because inventories would be disappearing. On the other hand, at any income level above $6800 billion inventories would be piling up, since $C + I + G + (X - IM)$ is less than Y.

Only at $Y = \$6800$ billion are spending and production in balance, as Table 9–1 shows. This is $800 billion higher than the $6000 billion equilibrium GDP found in the last chapter, when investment was only $900 billion. Thus a $200 billion rise in investment leads to a $800 billion rise in equilibrium GDP. The multiplier really is 4.

DEMYSTIFYING THE MULTIPLIER: HOW IT WORKS

The multiplier result seems implausible at first, but it loses its mystery once we remember the circular flow of income and expenditure, and the simple fact that one person's spending is another person's income. To illustrate the logic of the multiplier, and see why it is exactly 4 in our model economy, let us look more closely at what actually happens if businesses decide to spend an additional $1 million on investment goods.

Suppose that Generous Motors—a major corporation in Macroland—decides to spend $1 million to retool a factory to manufacture cars powered by compressed natural gas. Its $1 million expenditure goes to construction workers and owners of construction companies as wages and profits. That is, it becomes their *income*.

But the owners and workers of the construction firms will not keep their $1 million in the bank. They will spend some of it. If they are "typical" consumers, their spending will be $1 million times the marginal propensity to consume (MPC). In our example, the MPC is 0.75. So let us assume that they spend $750,000 and save the rest. *This $750,000 expenditure is a net addition to the nation's demand for goods and services exactly as Generous Motors' original $1 million expenditure was.* So, at this stage, the $1 million investment has already pushed GDP up some $1.75 million.

But the process by no means stops here. Shopkeepers receive the $750,000 spent by construction workers, and these shopkeepers in turn also spend 75 percent of their new income. This accounts for $562,500 (75 percent of $750,000) in additional consumer spending in the "third round." Next follows a fourth round in which the recipients of the $562,500, in their turn, spend 75 percent of this amount, or $421,875, and so on. At each stage in the spending chain, people spend 75 percent of the additional income they receive, and the process continues. Consumption grows in each round.

Where does it all end? Does it all end? The answer is that it does, indeed, eventually end—with GDP a total of $4 million higher than it was before Generous Motors spent the original $1 million. The multiplier, is, indeed, 4.

Table 9–2 displays the basis for this conclusion. In the table, "round 1" represents Generous Motors' initial investment, which creates $1 million in income for construction workers; "round 2" represents the construction workers' spending which creates $750,000 in income for shopkeepers. The rest of the table proceeds accordingly. Each entry in column 2 is 75 percent of the previous entry, and column 3 tabulates the running sum of column 2.

We see that after 10 rounds of spending, the initial $1 million investment has mushroomed to $3.77 million, and the sum is still growing. After 20 rounds, the total increase in GDP is over $3.98 million—near its eventual value of $4 million. While it takes quite a few rounds of spending before the multiplier chain is near 4, we see from the table that it hits 3 rather quickly. If each income recipient in

| Table | 9–2 | THE MULTIPLIER SPENDING CHAIN |

(1) ROUND NUMBER	(2) SPENDING IN THIS ROUND	(3) CUMULATIVE TOTAL
1	$1,000,000	$1,000,000
2	750,000	1,750,000
3	562,500	2,312,500
4	421,875	2,734,375
5	316,406	3,050,781
6	237,305	3,288,086
7	177,979	3,466,065
8	133,484	3,599,549
9	100,113	3,699,662
10	75,085	3,774,747
⋮	⋮	⋮
20	4,228	3,987,317
⋮	⋮	⋮
"Infinity"	0	4,000,000

This table shows how the multiplier unfolds through time. Round 1 is Generous Motors' initial spending, which leads to $1 million in additional income to construction workers. Round 2 shows the construction workers spending 75 percent of this amount, since the marginal propensity to consume is 0.75. The other rounds proceed accordingly, with spending in each successive round equal to 75 percent of that in the previous round. Technically, the full multiplier of 4 is reached only after an "infinite" number of rounds. But, as can be seen, we are very close to the full amount after 20 rounds.

the chain waits, say, two months before spending his new income, the multiplier will reach 3 in only about 10 months.

Figure 9–2 provides a graphical presentation of the numbers in the last column of Table 9–2. Notice how the multiplier builds up rapidly at first and then tapers off to approach its ultimate value (4 in this example) gradually.

ALGEBRAIC STATEMENT OF THE MULTIPLIER

Figure 9–2 and Table 9–2 probably make a persuasive case for the fact that the multiplier eventually reaches 4. But for the remaining skeptics we offer a simple algebraic proof.[1] Most of you learned about something called an "infinite geometric progression" in high school. This term refers to an infinite series of numbers, each one of which is a fixed fraction of the previous one. The fraction is called the "common ratio." A geometric progression beginning with 1 and having a common ratio of 0.75 would look like this:

$$1 + 0.75 + (0.75)^2 + (0.75)^3 + \ldots .$$

More generally, a geometric progression beginning with 1 and having a common ratio R would be

$$1 + R + R^2 + R^3 \ldots .$$

---

[1]Students who blanch at the sight of algebra should not be put off. Anyone who can balance a checkbook (even many who cannot!) will be able to follow the argument.

F i g u r e **9–2**	**HOW THE MULTIPLIER BUILDS**

This diagram portrays the numbers from Table 9–2 and shows how the multiplier builds through time. Notice how the effect grows quickly at first and how the full effect is almost reached after 20 rounds.

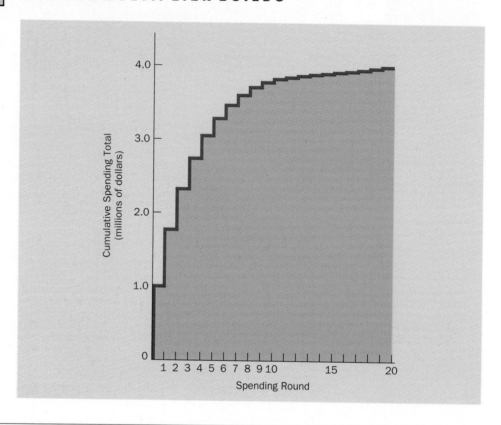

A simple formula enables us to sum such a progression as long as R is less than 1.[2] The formula is[3]

$$\text{Sum of infinite geometric progression} = \frac{1}{1 - R}.$$

Now we can recognize that the multiplier chain in Table 9–2 is just an infinite geometric progression with 0.75 as its common ratio. That is, each \$1 spent by Generous Motors leads to a $(0.75) \times \$1$ expenditure by construction workers, which in turn leads to a $(0.75) \times (0.75 \times \$1) = (0.75)^2 \times \$1$ expenditure by the

---

[2]If R exceeds 1, nobody can possibly sum it—not even with the aid of a modern computer—because the sum is not a finite number.

[3]The proof of the formula is simple. Let the symbol S stand for the (unknown) sum of the series:

$$S = 1 + R + R^2 + R^3 + \ldots.$$

Then, multiplying by R,

$$RS = R + R^2 + R^3 + R^4 + \ldots.$$

By subtracting RS from S, we obtain:

$$S - RS = 1$$

or

$$S = \frac{1}{1 - R}.$$

shopkeepers, and so on. Thus, for each initial dollar of investment spending, the progression is

$$1 + 0.75 + (0.75)^2 + (0.75)^3 + (0.75)^4 + \ldots .$$

Applying the formula for the sum of such a series, we find that:

$$\text{Multiplier} = \frac{1}{1 - 0.75} = \frac{1}{0.25} = 4.$$

Notice how this result can be generalized. If we did not have a specific number for the marginal propensity to consume, but simply called it "MPC," the geometric progression in Table 9–2 would have been

$$1 + \text{MPC} + (\text{MPC})^2 + (\text{MPC})^3 + \ldots ,$$

which has the MPC as its common ratio. Applying the same formula for summing a geometric progression to this more general case gives us the following general result:

OVERSIMPLIFIED FORMULA FOR THE MULTIPLIER

$$\text{Multiplier} = \frac{1}{1 - \text{MPC}}.$$

We call this formula "oversimplified" because it ignores many factors that are important in the real world. One of them is international trade—in particular, the fact that a country's imports depend on its GDP. This complication is dealt with in Appendix B. A second factor is *inflation*, a complication we will address in the next chapter. A third is *income taxation*, a point we will elaborate in Chapter 11. The last important influence arises from the *financial system* and, after we discuss money and banking in Chapters 12 and 13, we will explain it in Chapter 14. As it turns out, each of these factors *reduces* the size of the multiplier.

We can begin to appreciate just how unrealistic the "oversimplified" formula is by considering some real numbers for the U.S. economy. The marginal propensity to consume (MPC) has been estimated many times and is about 0.9. From our oversimplified formula, then, it would seem that the multiplier should be about

$$\text{Multiplier} = \frac{1}{1 - 0.9} = \frac{1}{0.1} = 10.$$

In fact, the actual multiplier for the U.S. economy is believed to be less than 2. This is quite a discrepancy! But it does not mean that anything we have said about the multiplier so far is incorrect. Our story is simply incomplete. As we progress through this and subsequent chapters, you will learn why the multiplier is below 2 even though the MPC is close to 0.9. For now, we simply point out that:

While the multiplier is larger than 1 in the real world, it cannot be calculated with any degree of accuracy from the oversimplified formula. The actual multiplier is *much lower* than the formula suggests.

THE MULTIPLIER EFFECT OF CONSUMER SPENDING

Business firms that invest are not the only ones that can work the magic of the multiplier; so can consumers. To see how the multiplier works when the process

An **INDUCED INCREASE IN CONSUMPTION** is an increase in consumer spending that stems from an increase in consumer incomes. It is represented on a graph as a movement along a fixed consumption function.

An **AUTONOMOUS INCREASE IN CONSUMPTION** is an increase in consumer spending without any increase in incomes. It is represented on a graph as a shift of the entire consumption function.

is initiated by an upsurge in consumer spending, we must distinguish between two types of change in consumer spending.

When C rises because income rises—that is, when consumers move outward *along a fixed consumption function*—we call the increase in C an **induced increase in consumption**. However, if instead C rises because the entire consumption function *shifts up*, we call this an **autonomous increase in consumption**. The name indicates that consumption changes independently of income, and Chapter 7's discussion pointed out that a number of events, such as a change in the price level or in the value of the stock market, can initiate such a shift.

Let us suppose that, for some reason, consumer spending rises autonomously by $200 billion. In this case, our table of aggregate demand would have to be revised to look like Table 7–3. Comparing this to Table 9–1, we note that each entry in column 2 is $200 billion *higher* than the corresponding entry in Table 7–1 (because consumption is higher), and each entry in column 3 is $200 billion *lower* (because investment is lower).

The equilibrium level of income is clearly Y = $6800 billion once again. Indeed, the entire expenditure schedule (column 6) is the same as it was in Table 9–1. The initial rise of $200 billion in spending leads to an ultimate rise of $800 billion in GDP, just as occurred in the case of higher investment spending. In fact, Figure 9–1 applies directly to this case once we note that the upward shift is now caused by an autonomous change in C rather than in I. The multiplier for autonomous changes in consumer spending, then, is also 4 (= $800/$200).

The reason is straightforward. It does not matter who injects an additional dollar of spending into the economy, whether it is business investors or consumers. Wherever it comes from, 75 percent of it will be respent if the MPC is 0.75, and the recipients of this second round will, in turn, spend 75 percent of their additional income, and so on and on. And that is what constitutes the multiplier process.

THE MULTIPLIER EFFECT OF GOVERNMENT PURCHASES

What about the third component of total spending, government purchases (G)? Table 9–4, which can usefully be compared to earlier tables, shows that G has the

T a b l e	9–3	TOTAL EXPENDITURE AFTER CONSUMERS DECIDE TO SPEND $200 BILLION MORE (billions of dollars)				
(1) INCOME (Y)	(2) CONSUMPTION (C)	(3) INVESTMENT (I)	(4) GOVERNMENT PURCHASES (G)	(5) NET EXPORTS (X − IM)	(6) TOTAL EXPENDITURE
4800	3200	900	1300	− 100	5300
5200	3500	900	1300	− 100	5600
5600	3800	900	1300	− 100	5900
6000	4100	900	1300	− 100	6200
6400	4400	900	1300	− 100	6500
6800	4700	900	1300	− 100	6800
7200	5000	900	1300	− 100	7100

This table shows the construction of the total expenditure schedule for Macroland following an autonomous increase of $200 billion in consumption rather than in investment. Notice that columns 2 and 3 differ from the corresponding columns in Table 9–1, but column 6 is the same in both tables. Thus the expenditure schedule in the 45° line diagram is the same as in the earlier example.

Table 9-4	TOTAL EXPENDITURE AFTER THE GOVERNMENT SPENDS $200 BILLION MORE ON GOODS AND SERVICES (billions of dollars)				
(1) INCOME (Y)	(2) CONSUMPTION (C)	(3) INVESTMENT (I)	(4) GOVERNMENT PURCHASES (G)	(5) NET EXPORTS (X − IM)	(6) TOTAL EXPENDITURE
4800	3000	900	1500	− 100	5300
5200	3300	900	1500	− 100	5600
5600	3600	900	1500	− 100	5900
6000	3900	900	1500	− 100	6200
6400	4200	900	1500	− 100	6500
6800	4500	900	1500	− 100	6800
7200	4800	900	1500	− 100	7100

This table shows the total expenditure schedule for Macroland after government purchases have risen to $1500 billion. Once again, only income level Y = $6800 billion is an equilibrium on the demand side of the economy.

very same multiplier as I and C. The consumption, investment, and net export columns in Table 9–4 are the same as in Chapter 8. The only change appears in column 4, where we have raised government purchases from $1300 billion to $1500 billion.

Summing the four components as usual gives us our new total expenditure schedule in columns 1 and 6. Clearly, this is the same total expenditure column as in Tables 9–1 and 9–3. So the equilibrium level of GDP must also be the same: $6800 billion, or $800 billion more than we found in the previous chapter. The multiplier is, once again, 4.

Figure 9–1 can again be used to illustrate the conclusion graphically—just think of the upward shift as being caused by a change in G this time.

The multipliers are identical because the logic behind them is identical. The multiplier spending chain set in motion when Generous Motors spent $1 million to build a factory could equally well have been kicked off by the federal government buying $1 million worth of new cars from Generous Motors. Thereafter, each recipient of additional income would spend 75 percent of it (the assumed marginal propensity to consume), until $4 million in new income had eventually been created.

The idea that changes in G have multiplier effects on GDP will play a central role in the discussion of government stabilization policy that begins in Chapter 11. So it is worth noting here that:

Changes in the volume of government purchases of goods and services will change the equilibrium level of GDP in the same direction, and by a multiplied amount.

THE MULTIPLIER EFFECT OF NET EXPORTS

At this point, it will not surprise you to learn that a change in net exports has precisely the same multiplier effect on equilibrium GDP as a change in any of the other components of spending. Let us quickly verify that this is so by turning to Table 9–5.

Here net exports are assumed to have risen from − $100 billion (their value in Chapter 8) to + $100 billion—an increase of $200 billion. Table 9–5, which looks

T a b l e 9-5	TOTAL EXPENDITURE AFTER NET EXPORTS RISE BY $200 BILLION (billions of dollars)				
(1) INCOME (Y)	(2) CONSUMPTION (C)	(3) INVESTMENT (I)	(4) GOVERNMENT PURCHASES (G)	(5) NET EXPORTS (X − IM)	(6) TOTAL EXPENDITURE
4800	3000	900	1300	100	5300
5200	3300	900	1300	100	5600
5600	3600	900	1300	100	5900
6000	3900	900	1300	100	6200
6400	4200	900	1300	100	6500
6800	4500	900	1300	100	6800
7200	4800	900	1300	100	7100

This table shows the construction of the total expenditure schedule for Macroland following an increase of $200 billion in net exports rather than in consumption or investment. Notice that columns 3 and 5 differ from the corresponding columns in Table 26–1, but column 6 is the same in both tables. Thus the expenditure schedule in the 45° line diagram is the same as in the earlier example.

just like the previous tables, shows us that equilibrium once again occurs at a GDP of $Y = \$6800$ billion.

The reason is hardly mysterious. When foreigners buy U.S. products, they put income into the hands of Americans, just as domestic investment does. As this income is spent and respent, a multiplier process is set in motion, raising GDP. Specifically, in this example an increase of $200 billion in net exports leads to an increase of $800 billion in GDP (from $6000 billion to $6800 billion). So the multiplier is 4. Once again, Figure 9–1 applies.

Although we will have much more to learn about how the U.S. economy is linked to the economies of other countries in Part 4, this simple analysis of the multiplier effect of foreign trade already teaches us an important lesson: *Booms and recessions tend to be transmitted across national borders.*

Why is that? Suppose a boom abroad raises aggregate demand and GDP in foreign countries. With rising incomes, foreigners will buy more American goods—which means that U.S. exports will rise. But a rise in our exports will, via the multiplier, raise GDP in the United States. By this mechanism, rapid economic growth abroad contributes to rapid economic growth here.

Of course, the same mechanism also operates in the downward direction. Suppose some of the countries that trade with us slip into recession. As their GDPs decline, so do their *imports*. But this means that the United States will experience a decline in *exports* which, through the multiplier, will pull down GDP here. Hence a recession abroad can contribute to recessionary conditions in the United States.

Naturally, what foreign countries do to us, we also do to them. Thus rapid economic growth in the United States tends to produce boom conditions in the countries from which we buy, and recessions here tend quickly to spill beyond our borders. In summary:

The GDPs of the major economies are linked by trade. A boom in one country tends to raise its imports and hence push up exports and GDP in other countries. Similarly, a recession in one country tends to pull GDP down in other countries.

THE MULTIPLIER IN REVERSE

A good way to check your understanding of the multiplier process is to run it in reverse: What happens if, for example, consumers autonomously decide to spend less? For example, suppose a wave of thriftiness comes over the people of Macroland so that, no matter what their total income, they now want to spend $200 billion *less* than they did previously rather than the $200 billion *more* assumed in Table 9–1.

A decision to spend $200 billion less out of any given level of income is, by definition, a *downward* shift of the total expenditure schedule by $200 billion. This is shown in Figure 9–3, where the $C + I + G + (X - IM)$ schedule falls from $C_0 + I + G + (X - IM)$ to $C_1 + I + G + (X - IM)$. The horizontal distance between these two parallel lines is the $200 billion drop in spending.

There are two ways of calculating the multiplier. First, our oversimplified multiplier formula tells us that the multiplier is

$$\frac{1}{1 - \text{MPC}} = \frac{1}{1 - 0.75} = \frac{1}{0.25} = 4.$$

So a $200 billion drop in spending will lead to a multiplier effect of $800 billion. Alternatively, we can read this conclusion from Figure 9–3. Here the economy's equilibrium point moves down the 45° line from point E_0 to E_1; income drops from $6000 billion to $5200 billion—a decline of $800 billion.

Figure **9–3** **THE MULTIPLIER IN REVERSE**

This diagram shows the multiplier effect of an autonomous decline in consumer spending of $200 billion. The decline appears as a downward shift of $200 billion in the expenditure schedule, which falls from $C_0 + I + G + (X - IM)$ to $C_1 + I + G + (X - IM)$. Equilibrium, which is always at the intersection of the expenditure schedule and the 45° line, moves from point E_0 to point E_1, and income falls from $6000 billion to $5200 billion.

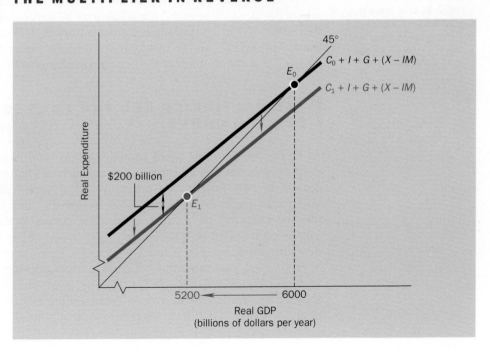

Now compare the analysis of a decline in spending summarized in Figure 9–3 with the previous analysis of an increase in spending shown in Figure 9–1. You will see that everything is simply turned in the opposite direction. The multiplier works in both directions.

THE PARADOX OF THRIFT

This last example of multiplier analysis teaches us an important lesson: it shows that an increase in the desire to save will lead to a cumulative fall in GDP. And, *because saving depends on income*, the resulting decline in national income will pull saving down. In consequence, saving may fail to rise despite an increase in the public's desire to save.

Let us be a bit more specific about this remarkable result. Before the upsurge in saving, consumers were spending $3900 billion out of a total national income of $6000 billion, as we can see in Table 8–1 on page 188. How much was being saved? Since taxes in Macroland are assumed to be fixed at $1200 billion, disposable income was $DI = Y - T = \$6000 - \$1200 = \$4800$. Hence saving was $900 billion ($= \$4800 - \$3900$).

In Figure 9–3, GDP falls to $5200 billion, so disposable income drops to $4000. Since investment, government purchases, and net exports are all unchanged, the entire $800 billion drop in GDP must come out of consumption, which therefore falls by $800 billion (to $3100 billion). Thus DI is down to $4000 billion and C is down to $3100 billion, leaving total saving still $900 billion. The effort to save more has been totally frustrated by the decline in GDP.[4]

The **PARADOX OF THRIFT** is the fact that an effort by a nation to save more may simply reduce national income and fail to raise total saving.

This remarkable result is called the **paradox of thrift**, because it shows that, while saving may pave the road to riches for an individual, if the nation as a whole decides to save more, the result may be a recession and the falling incomes that come with it. The paradox of thrift is important because it is contrary to most people's thinking, and it means that a greater desire to save may be a mixed blessing if it is not accompanied by an equally greater desire to invest.

THE MULTIPLIER AND THE AGGREGATE DEMAND CURVE

At this point, we must recall something that was mentioned at the start of the chapter: income-expenditure diagrams such as Figures 9–1 and 9–3 can be drawn up only for a given price level. A different price level leads to a different total expenditure curve. This means that our oversimplified multiplier formula measures *the increase in real GDP demanded that would occur if the price level were fixed*. That is, it measures the *horizontal shift* of the economy's aggregate demand curve.

Figure 9–4 illustrates this conclusion by supposing that the price level that underlies Figure 9–1 is $P = 100$. The top panel simply repeats Figure 9–1 and shows how an increase in investment spending from $900 to $1100 billion leads to an increase in GDP from $6000 to $6800 billion.

---

[4]It is even possible to devise examples in which total saving goes *down* when people attempt to save more. This will happen, for example, if there is *induced investment*.

| *F i g u r e* **9-4** | **TWO VIEWS OF THE MULTIPLIER** |

The top panel repeats Figure 9–1. The bottom panel shows two aggregate demand curves. Curve D_0D_0, which applies when investment is $900 billion, shows that equilibrium GDP on the demand side comes at $Y = 6000 billion when $P = 100$ (point E_0). Curve D_1D_1, which applies when investment is $1100 billion, shows that equilibrium GDP on the demand side comes at $Y = 6800 billion when $P = 100$ (point E_1). The horizontal distance between points E_0 and E_1 in the bottom panel indicates the oversimplified multiplier effect.

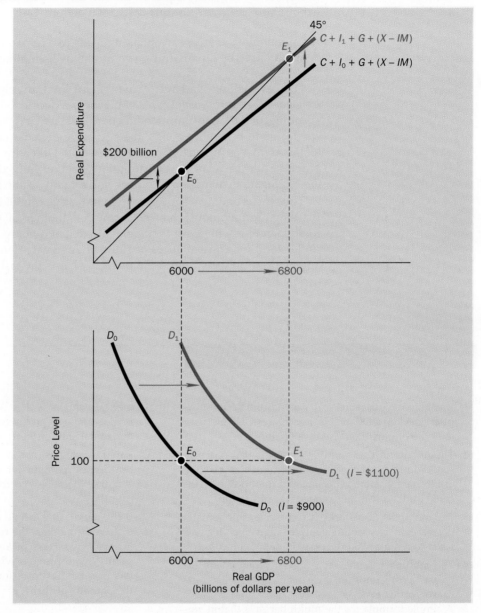

The bottom panel shows two downward-sloping aggregate demand curves. The first, labeled D_0D_0, depicts the situation when investment is $900 billion. Point E_0 on this curve indicates that, at the given price level ($P = 100$), the equilibrium quantity of GDP demanded is $6000 billion. It corresponds exactly to point E_0 in the top panel. The second aggregate demand curve, D_1D_1, depicts the situation after investment has risen to $1100 billion. Point E_1 on this curve indicates that the equilibrium quantity of GDP demanded when $P = 100$ has risen to $6800 billion, which corresponds exactly to point E_1 in the top panel.

As Figure 9–4 shows, the horizontal distance between the two aggregate demand curves is exactly equal to the increase in real GDP shown in the income-expenditure diagram—in this case, $800 billion. Thus:

An autonomous increase in spending leads to a horizontal shift of the aggregate demand curve by an amount given by the oversimplified multiplier formula.

Thus everything we have learned about the multiplier applies to *shifts of the economy's aggregate demand curve*. If businesses decide to increase their investment spending, or if the consumption function shifts up, or if the government or foreigners decide to buy more goods, the aggregate demand curve moves horizontally to the right—as indicated in Figure 9–4. If either investment or government purchases decrease, or the consumption function shifts down, or net exports fall, the aggregate demand curve moves horizontally to the left.

Thus the economy's aggregate demand curve cannot be expected to stand still for long. Autonomous changes in one or another of the four components of total spending will cause the aggregate demand curve to move around. But to understand the consequences of shifts of aggregate demand, we must bring the aggregate supply curve into the picture. That is the task of the next chapter.

Summary

1. Any autonomous increase in expenditure has a **multiplier** effect on GDP; that is, it increases GDP by more than the original increase in spending.

2. The reason for this multiplier effect is that one person's additional expenditure constitutes a new source of income for another person, and this additional income leads to still more spending, and so on.

3. The multiplier also works in reverse: an autonomous decrease in any component of aggregate demand leads to a multiplied decrease in national income.

4. The multiplier is the same for an **autonomous increase in consumption**, investment, government purchases, or net exports.

5. A simple formula for the multiplier says that its nu-

merical value is $1/(1 - MPC)$. This formula, which is too simple to give accurate results, measures the horizontal shift of the aggregate demand curve.

6. Rapid (or sluggish) economic growth in one country contributes to rapid (or sluggish) growth in other countries because one country's imports are other countries' exports.

7. If the nation as a whole decides to save more, that is, to consume less, the resulting decline in national income may serve to make everyone poorer. This possibility that thriftiness, while a virtue for the individual, may be disastrous for an entire nation, is called the **paradox of thrift**.

Key Concepts and Terms

The multiplier	Autonomous increase in	Paradox of thrift
Induced increase in consumption	consumption	

Questions for Review

1. Try to remember where you last spent a dollar. Explain how this dollar will lead to a multiplier chain of increased income and spending. (Who received the dollar? What will he or she do with it?)

2. Use both numerical and graphical methods to find the multiplier effect of the following shift in the consumption function in an economy in which investment is always $110, government purchases are always 50 and net exports are always −20.

INCOME	CONSUMPTION BEFORE SHIFT	CONSUMPTION AFTER SHIFT
540	440	460
570	460	480
600	480	500
630	500	520
660	520	540
690	540	560
720	560	580
750	580	600

(*Hint*: What is the marginal propensity to consume?)

3. Turn back to Review Question 3 in Chapter 8 (page 200). Suppose investment spending rises to $130, and the price level is fixed. By how much will the equilibrium GDP increase? Derive the answer both numerically and graphically.

4. Explain the paradox of thrift. Why do you think it is called a paradox?

5. (More difficult) Suppose the consumption function is as given in Review Question 8 of Chapter 8 (page 201)

$$C = 300 + 0.75DI$$

and investment (I) rises to 1100 while net exports ($X − IM$) remain at − 100, government purchases remain at 1300, and taxes remain at 1200. Use the equilibrium condition $Y = C + I + G + (X − IM)$ to find the equilibrium level of GDP. (In working out the answer, assume the price level is fixed.) Compare your answer to Table 9–1 and Figure 9–1. Now compare your answer to the answer to Review Question 8 of Chapter 8. What do you learn about the multiplier?

6. (More difficult) Look back at Review Question 9 of Chapter 8 (page 201). What is the multiplier for this economy? If G rises by 100, what happens to Y? What happens to Y if both G and T rise by 100 at the same time?

Appendix A   **THE SIMPLE ALGEBRA OF THE MULTIPLIER**

Appendix B to Chapter 8 presented a general expression for the equilibrium level of GDP when the price level is fixed, investment (I), government purchases (G), taxes (T), and net exports ($X - IM$) are all constant, and the consumption function is

$$C = a + b\mathrm{DI} = a + b(Y - T).$$

The answer obtained there (which can be found on page 205) was

$$Y = \frac{a - bT + I + (X - IM)}{1 - b}.$$

From this formula, it is easy to derive the oversimplified multiplier formula algebraically and to show that it applies equally well to a change in investment, autonomous consumer spending, government purchases, or net exports. To do so , suppose that any of the symbols in the numerator of the multiplier formula increases by 1 unit. In any

of these cases, GDP would rise from the previous formula to

$$Y = \frac{a - bT + I + (X - IM) + 1}{1 - b}.$$

By comparing this with the previous expression for Y, we see that a 1 unit change in any component of spending changes equilibrium GDP by

$$\text{change in } Y = \frac{a - bT + I + (X - IM) + 1}{1 - b}$$
$$- \frac{a - bT + I + (X - IM)}{1 - b}$$

or

$$\text{change in } Y = \frac{1}{1 - b}.$$

Recalling that b is the marginal propensity to consume, we see that this is precisely the oversimplified multiplier formula.

| *Appendix B* | **THE MULTIPLIER IN THE PRESENCE OF FOREIGN TRADE** |

In Chapters 8 and 9, we assumed that net exports were a fixed number. But in fact a nation's imports depend on its GDP. The reason is simple: higher GDP leads to higher incomes, some of which is spent on foreign goods. Thus:

Our imports rise as our GDP rises and fall as our GDP falls.

Similarly, our *exports* are the *imports* of other countries, so it is natural to assume that our exports depend on *their* GDPs, not on our own. Thus:

Our exports are relatively insensitive to our own GDP, but are quite sensitive to the GDPs of other countries.

This appendix derives the implications of these rather elementary observations. In particular, it shows that:

International trade lowers the value of the multiplier.

To see why, we begin with Table 9–6, which adapts the concrete example of Macroland from Chapter 8 to allow imports to depend on GDP. Columns 2–4 are the same as in Table 8–1 on page 188; they show C, I, and G at alternative levels of GDP. Columns 5 and 6 record revised assumptions about the behavior of exports and imports. Exports are fixed at $650 billion regardless of (our) GDP. But

imports are assumed to rise by $60 billion for every $400 billion rise in GDP, which is a simple numerical example of the idea that imports depend on GDP. Column 7 subtracts imports from exports to get net exports, $(X - IM)$, and column 8 adds up the four components of total expenditure, $C + I + G + (X - IM)$.

The equilibrium, you can see, occurs at $Y = \$6000$ billion, just as it did in Chapter 8.

Figures 9–5 and 9–6 display the same conclusion graphically. The upper panel of Figure 9–5 shows that exports are fixed at $650 billion regardless of GDP while imports increase as GDP rises, just as in Table 9–6. The difference between exports and imports, or net exports, is positive until GDP reaches around $5300 billion and negative once GDP surpasses that amount. The bottom panel of Figure 9–5 shows the subtraction explicitly and makes it clear that:

Net exports decline as GDP rises.

Figure 9–6 carries this analysis over to the 45° line diagram. We begin with the familiar $C + I + G + (X - IM)$ line of Chapters 8 and 9, in black. There we simply assumed that net exports were fixed at $- \$100$ billion regardless of GDP. Now that we have amended our model to note that net exports decline with GDP, the sum $C + I + G + (X - IM)$ rises more slowly than we previously assumed. This

| *Table* | **9–6** | **EQUILIBRIUM INCOME WITH VARIABLE IMPORTS** |

(1) GROSS DOMESTIC PRODUCT (Y) (billions)	(2) CONSUMER EXPENDITURES (C) (billions)	(3) INVESTMENT (I) (billions)	(4) GOVERNMENT PURCHASES (G) (billions)	(5) EXPORTS (X) (billions)	(6) IMPORTS (IM) (billions)	(7) NET EXPORTS (X − IM) (billions)	(8) TOTAL EXPENDITURE [C + I + G + (X − IM)] (billions)
4800	3000	900	1300	650	570	+ 80	5280
5200	3300	900	1300	650	630	+ 20	5520
5600	3600	900	1300	650	690	− 40	5760
6000	3900	900	1300	650	750	− 100	6000
6400	4200	900	1300	650	810	− 160	6240
6800	4500	900	1300	650	870	− 220	6480
7200	4800	900	1300	650	930	− 280	6720

Figure 9-5

THE DEPENDENCE OF NET EXPORTS ON GDP

This graph displays the data on exports, imports, and net exports found in Table 9–6. Exports, X, are independent of GDP while imports, IM, rise as GDP rises (top panel). As a result, net exports, $(X - IM)$, decline as GDP rises (bottom panel).

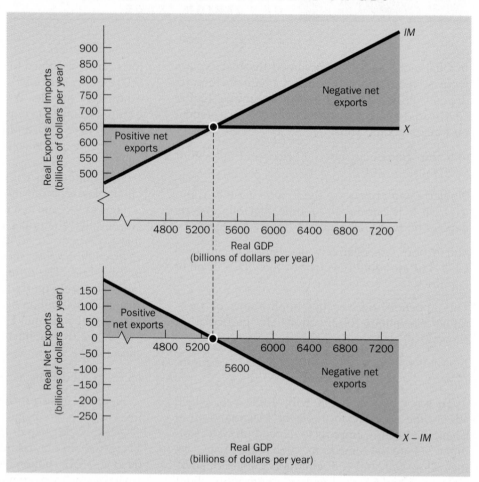

Figure 9-6

EQUILIBRIUM GDP WITH FOREIGN TRADE

In the presence of variable imports, equilibrium GDP occurs where the blue $C + I + G + (X - IM)$ line, rather than the black one, crosses the 45° line. In the graph, equilibrium is at point E, where GDP is $6000 billion. This matches the equilibrium we found in Chapter 8 (Figure 8–1 on page 186) with fixed imports because we have rigged the example to come out that way.

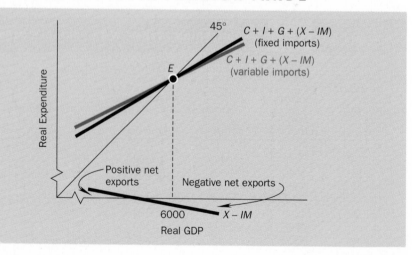

Table 9–7			EQUILIBRIUM INCOME AFTER A $160 BILLION RISE IN EXPORTS				
(1) GROSS DOMESTIC PRODUCT (Y) (billions)	**(2)** CONSUMER EXPENDITURES (C) (billions)	**(3)** INVESTMENT (I) (billions)	**(4)** GOVERNMENT PURCHASES (G) (billions)	**(5)** EXPORTS (X) (billions)	**(6)** IMPORTS (IM) (billions)	**(7)** NET EXPORTS (X − IM) (billions)	**(8)** TOTAL EXPENDITURE [C + I + G + (X − IM)] (billions)
4800	3000	900	1300	810	570	+240	5440
5200	3300	900	1300	810	630	+180	5680
5600	3600	900	1300	810	690	+120	5920
6000	3900	900	1300	810	750	+60	6160
6400	4200	900	1300	810	810	0	6400
6800	4500	900	1300	810	870	−60	6640
7200	4800	900	1300	810	930	−120	6880

is shown by the blue line. Note that it is less steep than the black line.

Let us now consider what happens if exports rise by $160 billion while imports remain as in Table 9–6. Table 9–7 shows us that equilibrium now occurs at a GDP of $Y = \$6400$ billion. Naturally, higher exports have raised domestic GDP. But consider the magnitude. A $160 billion increase in exports (from $650 billion to $810 billion) leads to an increase of $400 billion in GDP (from $6000 billion to $6400 billion). So the multiplier is 2.5 (= $400/$160).[5]

---

[5]EXERCISE: Construct a version of Table 9–6 to show what would happen if imports rose by $160 billion at every level of GDP while exports remained at $650 billion. You should be able to show that the new equilibrium would be $Y = \$5600$.

This same conclusion is shown graphically in Figure 9–7, where the line $C + I + G + (X_0 − IM)$ represents the original expenditure schedule and the line $C + I + G + (X_1 − IM)$ represents the expenditure schedule after the rise in exports. Equilibrium shifts from point E to point A, and GDP rises by $400 billion.

Notice that the multiplier in this example is 2.5, whereas in the chapter, with net exports taken to be a fixed number, it was 4. This simple example illustrates a general result: *international trade lowers the numerical value of the multiplier*. Why is this so? Because, in an open economy, any autonomous increase in spending is partly dissipated in purchases of foreign goods, which creates additional income for foreigners rather than for domestic citizens.

Figure 9–7	THE MULTIPLIER WITH FOREIGN TRADE

This diagram shows a $160 billion increase in exports as a vertical shift of the total expenditure schedule from $C + I + G + (X_0 − IM)$, to $C + I + G + (X_1 − IM)$. As a result, equilibrium shifts from point E to point A, and GDP rises from $6000 billion to $6400 billion. The multiplier is therefore 2.5 (= $400/$160).

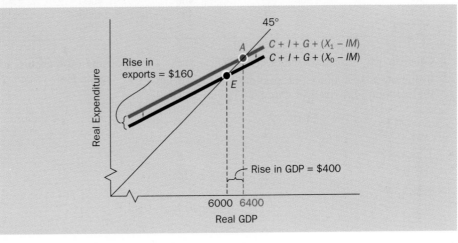

Figure 9–6 shows this same conclusion graphically. Because net exports decline as GDP rises, the total expenditure line is *flatter* in the presence of variable imports [blue $C + I + G + (X - IM)$ line] than it would be with fixed imports (black line). As we know from earlier chapters, the *size* of the multiplier depends on the *slope* of the expenditure schedule—steeper expenditure schedules lead to larger multipliers. Since variable imports flatten the expenditure schedule, they lower the multiplier.[6]

---

[6]For those who like formulas, we can amend the oversimplified multiplier formula to allow for international trade. That formula

Thus international trade gives us the first of what will eventually be several reasons why the oversimplified multiplier formula overstates the true value of the multiplier.

---

was: multiplier $= 1/(1 - b)$ where b is the marginal propensity to consume. If we define the *marginal propensity to import* as the rise in imports per dollar of GDP (the marginal propensity to import is 0.15 in our example) and symbolize it by the letter m, the formula for the multiplier with foreign trade is: multiplier $= 1/(1 - b + m)$. This formula clearly shows that a higher value of m leads to a lower multiplier.

Summary

1. Because imports rise as GDP rises while exports are insensitive to (domestic) GDP, net exports decline as GDP rises.

2. International trade reduces the value of the multiplier.

Questions for Review

1. Suppose exports and imports of a country are given by

GDP	EXPORTS	IMPORTS
$2500	$400	$250
3000	400	300
3500	400	350
4000	400	400
4500	400	450
5000	400	500

Calculate net exports at each level of GDP.

2. If domestic expenditure (the sum of $C + I + G$) in the economy described in Question 1 is as shown

below, construct a 45°-line diagram and locate the equilibrium level of GDP.

GDP	DOMESTIC EXPENDITURES
$2500	$3100
3000	3400
3500	3700
4000	4000
4500	4300
5000	4600

3. Now raise exports to $650 and find the equilibrium again. How large is the multiplier?

Chapter 10

SUPPLY-SIDE EQUILIBRIUM: UNEMPLOYMENT *and* INFLATION?

We might as well reasonably dispute whether it is the upper or the under blade of a pair of scissors that cuts a piece of paper, as whether value is governed by [demand] or [supply].

ALFRED MARSHALL

In Chapter 8 we learned that the level of prices, in conjunction with the economy's total expenditure schedule, governs whether the economy will experience a recessionary or an inflationary gap. If the $C + I + G + (X - IM)$ schedule is "too low," a *recessionary gap* will arise, while a $C + I + G + (X - IM)$ schedule that is "too high" leads to an *inflationary gap*. Which sort of gap actually occurs is of considerable importance because a recessionary gap normally spells unemployment while an inflationary gap leads to inflation. ¶ The tools provided in Chapter 8, however, are not sufficient to determine which sort of gap will arise because, as we know, the position of the expenditure schedule depends on the price level. And the price level is determined by *both aggregate demand and aggregate supply*. Thus, the task of the present chapter is to bring the supply side of the economy into the picture. ¶ We begin by explaining how the *aggregate supply curve* is derived from business costs. Next we consider the interaction of aggregate supply and aggregate demand, and the joint determination of output and the price level. With this apparatus in hand, we return to recessionary and inflationary gaps and study how the economy adjusts to each. Doing this puts us in a position to deal with the crucial question raised in earlier chapters: Does the economy have an efficient self-correcting mechanism? We shall see that the answer is "yes, but." Yes, but it works slowly. Finally, we use aggregate supply-aggregate demand analysis to explain the vexing problem of *stagflation*—the simultaneous occurrence of high unemployment *and* high inflation—that plagued the economy in the 1980s.

TWO SIDES TO THE SUPPLY SIDE

In 1981, President Ronald Reagan brought to Washington a doctrine called "supply-side economics"—a new theory advertised as a replacement for the Keynesian theory we studied in the last three chapters. Reaganite supply-side economics, which was controversial from the start and remains so, emphasized tax incentives that allegedly would increase saving and investment—and thus augment the supply of capital.

Twelve years later, the American voters repudiated Reaganomics and voted in President Bill Clinton who, ironically, also ran on what might be called a "supply-side" platform. Clintonomics, with its emphasis on upgrading the skills of the American workforce through education and training, was starkly different from Reaganomics. But the two programs share one idea in common: that what happens on the supply side of the economy matters a great deal for inflation, unemployment, and economic growth.

It is therefore time for us to consider the origins of the aggregate supply curve and the factors that can make it shift. Only when we have done so will we be ready to analyze the *joint* determination of output *and* the price level—with its consequences for inflationary and recessionary gaps.

THE AGGREGATE SUPPLY CURVE

In earlier chapters we noted that aggregate demand is a schedule, not a fixed number. The quantity of real GDP that will be demanded depends on the price level, as summarized in the economy's *aggregate demand curve*.

Analogously, the concept of *aggregate supply* does not refer to a fixed number, but rather to a schedule (a *supply curve*). The volume of goods and services that will be provided by profit-seeking enterprises depends on the prices they obtain for their outputs, on wages and other production costs, on the state of technology, and on other things. The relationship between the price level and the quantity of real GDP supplied, *holding all other determinants of quantity supplied constant*, is called the economy's **aggregate supply curve**.

The **AGGREGATE SUPPLY CURVE** shows, for each possible price level, the quantity of goods and services that all the nation's businesses are willing to produce during a specified period of time, holding all other determinants of aggregate quantity supplied constant.

A typical aggregate supply curve is drawn in Figure 10–1. It slopes upward, meaning that as prices rise more output is produced, *other things held constant*. It is not difficult to understand why. Producers in the U.S. economy are motivated mainly by profit. The profit made by producing a unit of output is simply the difference between the price at which it is sold and the unit cost of production:

$$\text{profit per unit} = \text{price} - \text{cost per unit}.$$

So the response of output to a rising price level—which is what the slope of the aggregate supply curve shows—depends on the response of costs.

AN AGGREGATE SUPPLY CURVE

This graph shows a typical aggregate supply curve. It has a positive slope (that is, it rises as we move to the right), meaning that the quantity of output supplied rises as the price level rises.

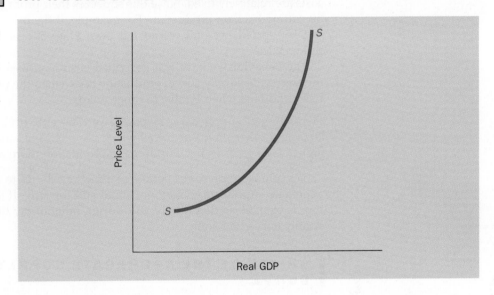

One critical fact affecting this response is that labor and other inputs used by firms normally are available at relatively fixed prices for some period of time—though certainly not forever. There are many reasons for this. Some workers and firms enter into long-term labor contracts that set money wages up to three years in advance. Even where there are no explicit contracts, employees typically have their wages increased only once per year. During the interim period, money wages are fixed. Much the same is true of other factors of production. Many firms get deliveries of raw materials under long-term contracts at prearranged prices. None of these contracts lasts forever, of course, but many of them last long enough to matter.

Why is it significant that firms often purchase inputs at prices that stay fixed for considerable periods? Because firms decide how much to produce by comparing their selling prices with their costs of production; and production costs depend, among other things, on input prices. If the selling prices of the firm's products rise while wages and other factor costs are fixed, production becomes more profitable, and so firms will increase output.

A simple example will illustrate the idea. Suppose a firm uses one hour of labor to manufacture a gadget that sells for $9. If workers earn $8 per hour, and the firm has no other production costs, its profit per unit is

$$\text{profit per unit} = \text{price} - \text{cost per unit}$$
$$= \$9 - \$8 = \$1.$$

Now what happens if the price of a gadget rises to $10, but wage rates remain constant? The firm's profit per unit becomes

$$\text{profit per unit} = \text{price} - \text{cost per unit}$$
$$= \$10 - \$8 = \$2.$$

With production more profitable, it is likely that the firm will supply more gadgets.

The same process operates in reverse. Suppose selling prices fall while input costs are relatively fixed. Since this squeezes their profit margins, firms may react by cutting back on production. For example, if the price of a gadget fell from $9 to $8.50, profit per unit would fall from $1 to 50¢, and firms would probably produce less.

The behavior we have just described is summarized by the upward slope of the aggregate supply curve: production rises when the price level (henceforth, *P*) rises, and falls when *P* falls. In other words:

The aggregate supply curve slopes upward because firms normally can purchase labor and other inputs at prices which are fixed for some period of time. Thus, higher selling prices for output make production more attractive.[1]

The phrase "for some period of time" alerts us to the possibility that the aggregate supply curve may not stand still for long. If wages or prices of other inputs change, as they surely will during inflationary times, then the aggregate supply curve will shift.

SHIFTS OF THE AGGREGATE SUPPLY CURVE

We have concluded so far that, for given levels of wages and other input prices, there will be an upward-sloping aggregate supply curve relating the price level to aggregate quantity supplied. But what factors determine the *position* of this curve? What things can make it shift?

THE MONEY WAGE RATE

Our discussion suggests the most obvious determinant of the position of the aggregate supply curve: the money wage rate. Wages are the major element of cost in the economy, accounting for more than 70 percent of all inputs. Since higher wage rates mean higher costs, they spell lower profits at any given prices.

Let us return to our example and consider what would happen to a gadget producer if the money wage rose to $8.75 per hour while the price of a gadget remained $9. Profit per unit would decline from

$$\$9 - \$8 = \$1$$

to

$$\$9 - \$8.75 = \$0.25.$$

With profits squeezed, the firm would probably cut back on production.

This is the way firms in our economy typically react to a rise in wages. Therefore, a wage increase leads to a decrease in aggregate quantity supplied at current prices. Graphically, the aggregate supply curve shifts to the left (or inward), as shown in Figure 10–2. In this diagram, when wages are low, firms are willing to supply $6000 billion in goods and services at a price level of 100 (point *A*). After wages increase, however, these same firms are willing to supply only $5500 billion

---

[1]There are both differences and similarities between the *aggregate* supply curve and the *microeconomic* supply curves studied in Parts 2–4 of *Microeconomics*. Both are based on the idea that quantity supplied depends on how output prices move relative to input prices. But the aggregate supply curve pertains to the behavior of the overall price level, whereas a microeconomic supply curve pertains to the price of some particular commodity.

Figure **10-2**

This diagram shows what happens to the economy's aggregate supply curve when money wages rise. Higher wages shift the supply curve inward from S_0S_0 to S_1S_1, leading, for example, to an output level of $5500 billion (point B), rather than $6000 (point A), when the price level is 100. The aggregate supply curve will shift inward in the same manner if the price of any other input (such as energy) increases.

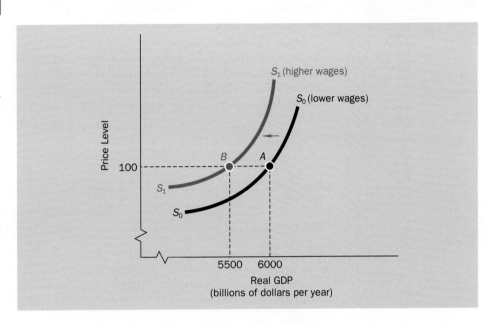

at this price level (point B). By similar reasoning, the aggregate supply curve will shift to the right (or outward) if wages fall. Thus:

A rise in the money wage rate causes the aggregate supply curve to *shift inward*, meaning that the quantity supplied at any price level *declines*. A fall in the money wage rate causes the aggregate supply curve to *shift outward*, meaning that the quantity supplied at any price level *increases*.

PRICES OF OTHER INPUTS

In this regard, there is nothing special about wages. An increase in the price of *any* input that firms buy will shift the aggregate supply curve in the same way. That is

The aggregate supply curve is shifted inward by an increase in the price of any input to the production process, and it is shifted *outward* by any decrease.

While there are many inputs other than labor, the one that has attracted the most attention in recent years is energy. We have much to say about energy in this book, including further discussion in this chapter. But for present purposes the important thing to realize is that increases in the price of energy, such as those that took place in the early 1980s and again during the 1990 Gulf War, push the aggregate supply curve inward more or less as shown in Figure 10–2. By the same token, a rise in the price of *any* input we import from abroad would have the effect shown in the figure.

TECHNOLOGY AND PRODUCTIVITY

Another factor that determines the position of the aggregate supply curve is the state of technology. Suppose, for example, that a technological breakthrough

PRODUCTIVITY is the amount of output produced by a unit of input.

increases the **productivity** of labor, that is, output per hour of work. If wages do not change, such an improvement in productivity will *decrease* business costs and thus improve profitability and encourage more production.

Once again, our gadget company will help us understand how this works. Suppose the price of a gadget stays at $9 and the hourly wage rate stays at $8, but gadget workers become much more productive. Specifically, suppose the labor input required to manufacture a gadget falls from one hour (which costs $8) to three-quarters of an hour (which costs $6). Then profit per unit rises from

$$\$9 - \$8 = \$1$$

to

$$\$9 - \$6 = \$3.$$

The lure of higher profits should induce gadget manufacturers to increase production. In brief, we have concluded that:

Improvements in productivity shift the aggregate supply curve outward.

Figure 10–2 can be viewed as applying to a *decline* in productivity. Since the 1970s, slow growth of productivity has been a persistent problem for the U.S. economy. Many people feel that the productivity slowdown, which we will discuss at length in Chapter 17, contributed to the stagflation of the 1970s.

AVAILABLE SUPPLIES OF LABOR AND CAPITAL

The last determinant of the position of the aggregate supply curve is obvious, but we list it anyway for the sake of completeness. The bigger the economy—as measured by its available supplies of labor and capital—the more it is capable of producing. So:

As the labor force grows or improves in quality, and as the capital stock is increased by investment, the aggregate supply curve shifts *outward* to the right, meaning that more output can be produced at any given price level.

These, then, are the major "other things" that we hold constant when drawing up an aggregate supply curve: wage rates, prices of other inputs (such as energy), technology, labor force, and capital stock. While a change in the price level moves the economy *along a given supply curve*, a change in any of the other determinants of aggregate quantity supplied *shifts the entire supply schedule*.

THE SHAPE OF THE AGGREGATE SUPPLY CURVE

One other feature of the aggregate supply curve depicted in Figure 10–1 merits comment. We have drawn our supply curve with a characteristic curvature: it is relatively flat at low levels of output and gets steeper at high levels of output (as we move to the right). There is a reason for this.

When economic activity is weak, product demand slack, and capacity utilization low, firms are likely to respond to an upsurge in demand by bringing their unused capital and labor resources back into production. They will find, therefore, that costs of production do not rise much as output expands. As a result, they will find it neither necessary nor advisable to raise prices much. Rapidly rising output with relatively unchanged prices means an aggregate supply curve that is relatively flat.

By contrast, if the economy is booming, demand is buoyant, and production is straining capacity, firms will be able to increase output only by hiring more workers, acquiring more capital, or putting workers on overtime. Whatever they do, unit costs of production rise—even with wages and other input prices constant. Price increases will thus be encouraged by cost developments and, incidentally, will not be resisted forcefully on the demand side. So any rise in output will be accompanied by a significant rise in prices. The aggregate supply curve will be steep. Thus:

The slope of the aggregate supply curve, which tells us the price increase that is associated with a unit increase in quantity supplied, generally rises as the degree of resource utilization rises.

EQUILIBRIUM OF AGGREGATE DEMAND AND SUPPLY

In Chapter 8 we learned that the price level is a crucial determinant of whether equilibrium GDP is below full employment (a "recessionary gap"), precisely at full employment, or above full employment (an "inflationary gap"). We are now in a position to analyze which type of gap, if any, will actually occur in any particular case by combining the analysis of aggregate supply just completed with the analysis of aggregate demand from the last two chapters to determine *simultaneously* the equilibrium level of real GDP (Y) and the equilibrium price level (P).

Figure 10–3 displays the mechanics. The aggregate demand curve *DD* and the aggregate supply curve *SS* intersect at point *E*, where real GDP is $6000 billion and the price level is 100. As can be seen in the graph, at any higher price

---

F i g u r e **10–3**   **EQUILIBRIUM OF REAL GDP AND THE PRICE LEVEL**

This diagram shows how the equilibrium levels of real GDP and the price level are simultaneously determined by the intersection of the aggregate demand curve (*DD*) and the aggregate supply curve (*SS*). In this example, equilibrium occurs at point *E*, with a real GDP of $6000 billion and a price level of 100.

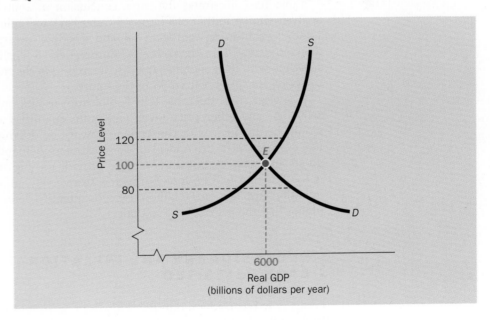

	(1) PRICE LEVEL	(2) AGGREGATE QUANTITY DEMANDED (billions of dollars)	(3) AGGREGATE QUANTITY SUPPLIED (billions of dollars)	(4) BALANCE OF SUPPLY AND DEMAND	(5) PRICES WILL
Table 10–1			**THE DETERMINATION OF THE EQUILIBRIUM PRICE LEVEL**		
	75	6400	5600	Quantity demanded exceeds quantity supplied	Rise
	80	6300	5700	Quantity demanded exceeds quantity supplied	Rise
	100	6000	6000	Quantity demanded equals quantity supplied	Remain the same
	120	5800	6200	Quantity supplied exceeds quantity demanded	Fall
	150	5600	6400	Quantity supplied exceeds quantity demanded	Fall

level, such as 120, aggregate quantity supplied would exceed aggregate quantity demanded. There would be a glut on the market as firms found themselves unable to sell all their output. As inventories piled up, firms would compete more vigorously for the available customers, thereby forcing prices down. The price level would fall, as would production.

At any price level lower than 100, such as 80, quantity demanded would exceed quantity supplied. There would be a shortage of goods on the market. With inventories disappearing and customers knocking on their doors, firms would be encouraged to raise prices. The price level would rise, and so would output.

Only when the price level is 100 are the quantities of real GDP demanded and supplied equal. Hence, only the combination $P = 100$, $Y = \$6000$ is an equilibrium.

Table 10–1 illustrates the same conclusion in another way, using a tabular analysis similar to that of Chapter 8 (refer back to Table 8–2 page 259). Columns 1 and 2 constitute an aggregate demand schedule corresponding to the aggregate demand curve *DD* in Figure 10–3. Columns 1 and 3 constitute an aggregate supply schedule with the general shape discussed in this chapter. It corresponds exactly to aggregate supply curve *SS* in the figure.

It is clear from the table that equilibrium occurs only at $P = 100$ and $Y = \$6000$. At any other price level, aggregate quantities supplied and demanded would be unequal, with consequent upward or downward pressure on prices. For example, at a price level of 80, customers demand $6300 billion worth of goods and services, but firms wish to provide only $5700 billion. The price level is too low and will be forced upward. Conversely, at a price level of, say, 120, quantity supplied ($6200 billion) exceeds quantity demanded ($5800 billion), implying that the price level must fall.

RECESSIONARY AND INFLATIONARY GAPS REVISITED

Let us now reconsider a question we posed, but could not answer, in Chapter 8: Will equilibrium occur at, below, or beyond full employment?

We could not give a complete answer to this question in Chapter 8 because we had no way to determine the equilibrium price level, and therefore no way to tell which type of gap, if any, would arise. The aggregate supply and demand analysis summarized in Figure 10–3 gives us the information we need to determine the price level. But we find that our answer is nonetheless the same as it was in Chapter 8: anything can happen.

The reason is that nothing in Figure 10–3 tells us where full employment is; it could be above the $6000 billion equilibrium level or below it. Depending on the locations of the aggregate demand and aggregate supply curves, then, we can reach equilibrium above full employment (an inflationary gap), at full employment, or below full employment (a recessionary gap). In the short run, with wages and other input costs fixed, that is all there is to it.

All three possibilities are illustrated in Figure 10–4. The three upper panels are familiar from Chapter 8. As we move from left to right, the expenditure schedule rises from $C + I_0 + G + (X - IM)$ to $C + I_1 + G + (X - IM)$ to $C + I_2 + G + (X - IM)$, leading respectively to a recessionary gap, an equilibrium at full employment, and an inflationary gap. In fact, the upper left-hand diagram looks just like Figure 8–6 (page 194), and the upper right-hand diagram duplicates Figure 8–7 (page 195). We stressed in Chapter 8 that any one of the three cases is possible, depending on the price level and the expenditure schedule.

In the three lower panels, the equilibrium price level is determined at point E by the intersection of the aggregate supply curve (SS) and the aggregate demand curve (DD). But the same three possibilities emerge nonetheless.

In the lower left-hand panel, aggregate demand is too small to provide jobs for the entire labor force, so there is a recessionary gap equal to distance EB, or $1000 billion. This corresponds precisely to the situation depicted on the income–expenditure diagram immediately above it.

In the lower right-hand panel, aggregate demand is so high that the economy reaches an equilibrium well beyond full employment. There is an inflationary gap equal to BE, or $1000 billion, just as in the diagram immediately above it.

In the lower middle panel, the aggregate demand curve D_1D_1 is at just the right level to produce an equilibrium at full employment. There is neither an inflationary nor a recessionary gap, as in the diagram just above it.

It may seem, therefore, that we have done nothing but restate our previous conclusions. But, in fact, we have done much more. Because now that we have studied the determination of the equilibrium price level, we are able to examine how the economy adjusts to either a recessionary gap or an inflationary gap. Specifically, since wages are fixed in the short run, any one of the three cases depicted in Figure 10–4 can obtain. But, in the long run, wages will adjust to labor market conditions. It is to that adjustment process that we now turn.

ADJUSTING TO AN INFLATIONARY GAP: INFLATION

Suppose the economy starts with an inflationary gap, as in the lower right-hand panel of Figure 10–4. As we shall see now, the tight labor market produces an inflation that eventually eliminates the gap, though perhaps in a slow and painful way. Let us see how this works.

If equilibrium GDP is above potential, jobs are plentiful and labor is in great demand. Although some workers are unemployed, this minimal unemployment

Figure 10-4   RECESSIONARY AND INFLATIONARY GAPS REVISITED

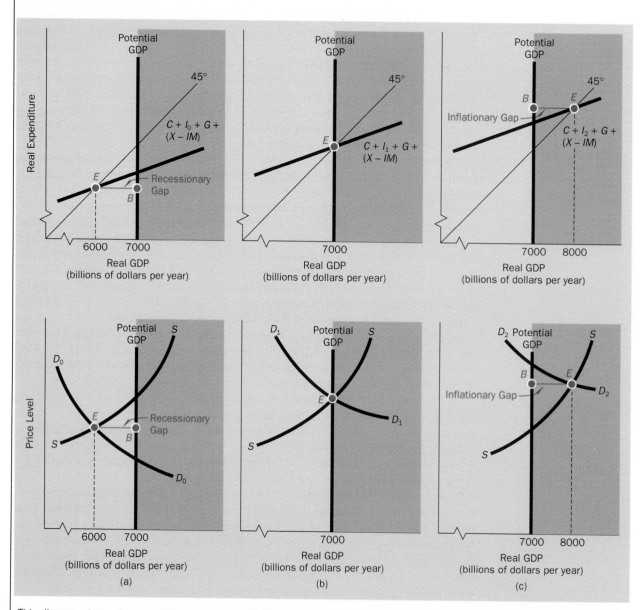

This diagram shows three possible types of equilibrium on two different diagrams. In the top row, income-expenditure diagrams from Chapter 8 are used to depict a recessionary gap, an equilibrium at full employment, and an inflationary gap. In the bottom row, these same three situations are shown on aggregate supply and demand diagrams. In each case, the aggregate supply curve is the same (SS), equilibrium occurs at point E, and full-employment GDP is $7000 billion. In part (a), the aggregate demand curve D_0D_0 is relatively low, so that equilibrium falls below full employment. There is a recessionary gap measured by the distance EB, or $1000 billion. In part (b), the aggregate demand curve D_1D_1 is higher, and equilibrium occurs precisely at full employment. There is no gap of either kind. In part (c), the aggregate demand curve D_2D_2 is so high that equilibrium occurs beyond full employment. There is an inflationary gap measured by the distance BE, or $1000 billion.

is less than the frictional level—that is, less than the number we usually expect to be jobless because of moving, changing occupations, and so on. Many firms, on the other hand, are having trouble finding workers. They may even be having trouble hanging on to their current employees, as other firms try to lure them away with higher wages.

Such a situation is bound to lead to rising money wages, and rising wages add to business costs, thus shifting the aggregate supply curve inward. (Remember, an aggregate supply curve is drawn for a *given* money wage.) But as the aggregate supply curve shifts inward—eventually moving from S_0S_0 to S_1S_1 in Figure 10–5, for example—the size of the inflationary gap steadily declines. This is the process by which inflation erodes the inflationary gap, eventually leading the economy to an equilibrium at full employment (point F in Figure 10–5).

There is a straightforward way of looking at the economics that underlies the self-correcting process. The inflation problem arises because buyers are demanding more output than the economy is capable of producing at normal operating rates. To paraphrase an old cliché, there is too much demand chasing too little supply. Naturally, such an environment encourages price hikes. Rising prices eat away at the purchasing power of consumers' wealth, forcing them to cut back on consumption, as explained in Chapter 7. In addition, exports fall and imports rise, as explained in Chapter 8. Eventually, aggregate quantity demanded is scaled down to the economy's capacity to produce; and, at this point, the self-correcting process stops. That, in essence, is the unhappy process by which the economy cures itself of the problem of excessive aggregate demand.

One caveat should be mentioned. The conclusion that an inflationary gap sows the seeds of its own destruction holds *only in the absence of additional forces propelling the aggregate demand curve outward*. But in Chapter 9 we have already encountered

---

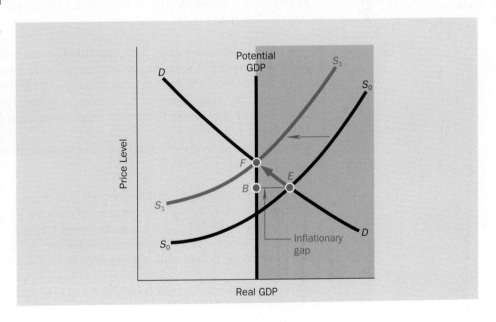

| *F i g u r e* **10–5** | **THE ELIMINATION OF AN INFLATIONARY GAP** |

When the aggregate supply curve is S_0S_0 and the aggregate demand curve is *DD*, the economy will initially reach equilibrium (point *E*) with an inflationary gap. The resulting inflation of wages will push the supply curve inward until it has shifted to the position indicated by curve S_1S_1. Here, with equilibrium at point *F*, the economy is at normal full employment. But, during the adjustment period from *E* to *F*, there will have been inflation.

several forces that might shift the aggregate demand curve outward. As you can see by manipulating the aggregate demand–aggregate supply diagram, if aggregate demand is shifting out at the same time that aggregate supply is shifting in, there will certainly be inflation, but the inflationary gap may not shrink. (Try this as an exercise, to make sure you understand how to use the apparatus.) So not all inflations come to a natural end.

DEMAND INFLATION AND STAGFLATION

Simple as it is, this adjustment model teaches us a number of important lessons about inflation in the real world. First of all, Figure 10–5 reminds us that the real culprit in this particular inflation is excessive aggregate demand—relative to potential GDP. The aggregate demand curve is initially so high that it intersects the aggregate supply curve well beyond full employment. The resulting intense demand for workers pushes wages higher; and higher wages lead to higher prices. While aggregate demand in excess of potential GDP is not the only possible cause of inflation in the real world, it certainly is the cause in our example.

However, business managers and journalists may blame inflation on rising wages. In a superficial sense, of course, they are right, because higher wages do indeed lead firms to raise their prices. But in a deeper sense they are wrong. Both rising wages and rising prices are symptoms of an underlying malady: too much aggregate demand. Blaming labor for inflation in such a case is a bit like blaming high doctor bills for making you ill.

Second, we see that output falls while prices rise as the economy adjusts from point *E* to point *F* in Figure 10–5. This process thus provides our first (but not our last!) explanation of the phenomenon of **stagflation**. We see that:

STAGFLATION is inflation that occurs while the economy is growing slowly or having a recession.

A period of stagflation is part of the normal aftermath of a period of excessive aggregate demand.

It is easy enough to understand why stagflation occurs in this case. When aggregate demand is excessive, the economy will temporarily produce beyond its normal capacity. Labor markets tighten and wages rise. Machinery and raw materials may also become scarce and so start rising in price. Faced by higher costs, the natural reaction of business firms is to produce less and to charge a higher price. That is stagflation.

It may be useful to review what we have learned about inflationary gaps thus far.

If aggregate demand is exceptionally high, the economy may reach a short-run equilibrium above full employment (an inflationary gap). When this occurs, the tight situation in the labor market soon forces wages to rise. Since rising wages raise business costs, prices rise; there is inflation. As higher prices cut into consumer purchasing power and net exports, the inflationary gap begins to close. As the inflationary gap is closing, output falls and prices continue to rise; so the economy experiences stagflation until the gap is eliminated. At this point, a long-run equilibrium is established with a higher price level and with GDP equal to potential GDP.

AN EXAMPLE FROM RECENT HISTORY: 1988 TO 1990

The stagflation that follows a period of excessive aggregate demand is, you will note, a rather benign form of the dreaded disease. After all, while output is falling, it nonetheless remains above potential GDP; and unemployment is low. Some observers think the U.S. economy experienced such a period between 1988 and 1990, when the unemployment rate dropped below many people's estimate of the full-employment rate and, indeed, inflation accelerated.

The long economic expansion that began at the very end of 1982 brought the unemployment rate down to 5.5 percent by mid 1988 and (briefly) to a 15-year low of 5 percent by March 1989. Most economists believe that 5 percent is below the full-employment unemployment rate, that is, that the U.S. economy had an inflationary gap in 1989. As the theory suggests, inflation began to accelerate—from 4.4 percent in 1988 to 4.6 percent in 1989 and 6.1 percent in 1990.

In the meantime, the economy was stagnating. Real GDP growth fell from 3.3 percent during 1988 to 1.6 percent in 1989 and −0.5 percent in 1990. Inflation was eating away at the inflationary gap, which was virtually gone by mid-1990, when the recession started. Yet inflation remained high through the early months of the recession. The U.S. economy was in the stagflation phase. In sum, the economy behaved more or less as our simple model suggests.

ADJUSTING TO A RECESSIONARY GAP: DEFLATION OR UNEMPLOYMENT?

Let us now consider what can happen when the economy finds itself in equilibrium *below* full employment—that is, when there is a *recessionary* gap. This might be caused, for example, by inadequate consumer spending or by anemic investment spending. Figure 10–6 illustrates such a case and gives an impression of the economic situation inherited by President Clinton when he took office in January 1993.

You might expect that we could just run our previous analysis in reverse: High unemployment leads to falling wages; falling wages reduce business costs and shift the aggregate supply curve outward, so firms cut prices; falling wages and prices eliminate the recessionary gap by propping up aggregate quantity demanded; and full employment is restored. The economy moves smoothly from point E to point F in Figure 10–6. Very simple. But somewhat misleading in our modern economy.

Why is it misleading? Our brief review of the historical record in Chapter 5 showed that, while the economy may have operated like this long ago, it certainly does not work this way now. The history of the United States shows several examples of deflation before World War II but none since then. Not even the severe recession of 1981–1982, during which unemployment climbed above 10 percent, was able to force average prices and wages down—though it certainly slowed their rates of increase. Similarly, the recession of the early 1990s reduced inflation, but certainly did not bring deflation.

Exactly why wages and prices rarely fall in our modern economy has been a subject of intense and continuing controversy among economists for years.

Some economists emphasize institutional factors like minimum wage laws, union contracts, and a variety of government regulations that place legal floors

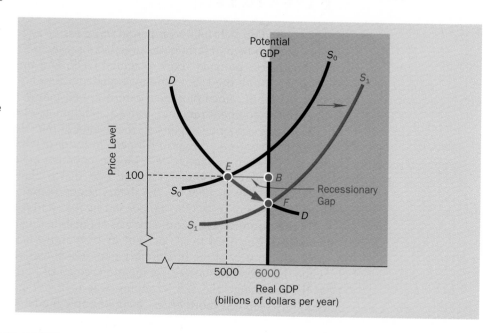

F i g u r e 10-6   THE ELIMINATION OF A RECESSIONARY GAP

At point *E* there is a recessionary gap because the aggregate demand curve *DD* crosses the aggregate supply curve $S_0 S_0$ below the level of potential GDP. If wages fall, the aggregate supply curve gradually shifts outward until it reaches the position indicated by supply curve $S_1 S_1$. Here the economy has attained a full-employment equilibrium at point *F*. But if wages fall very slowly, the economy gets stuck with a recessionary gap and high unemployment for a long time.

under particular wages and prices. Because most of these institutions are of relatively recent vintage, this theory successfully explains why wages and prices fall less frequently now than they did before World War II. However, only a small minority of the U.S. economy is subject to legal restraints on wage and price cutting. So it seems doubtful that legal restrictions can provide a complete explanation.

Other observers subscribe to the theory that workers have a profound psychological resistance to accepting a wage reduction. This theory certainly has the ring of truth. Think how you would react if your boss announced she was cutting your hourly wage rate. You might quit, or you might devote less care and attention to your job. If the boss suspects you will react this way, she may be reluctant to cut your wage. Nowadays, genuine wage reductions are rare enough to be newsworthy.

While no one doubts that wage cuts are bad for morale, the psychological theory has one major drawback. It fails to explain why the psychological resistance to wage cuts apparently started only after World War II. Until a satisfactory answer to this question is provided, many economists will remain skeptical.

A third explanation is based on a fact we emphasized in Chapter 5—that business cycles were less severe in the postwar period than they were in the prewar period. Because workers and firms came to believe that recessions would not turn into depressions, the argument goes, they may have decided to wait out the bad times rather than accept wage or price reductions that they would later regret.

Yet another theory is based on the old adage, "you get what you pay for." The idea is that workers differ in productivity, but that productivities of individual employees are hard to identify. Firms therefore worry that a general wage reduction will result in the loss of their best workers—since these are the ones who have the best opportunities elsewhere in the economy. Rather than take this chance, the argument goes, firms prefer to maintain high wages even in recessions.

There are other theories as well, none of which commands a clear majority of professional opinion. But, regardless of the cause, we may as well accept the fact that, in our modern economy, prices and wages generally fall only sluggishly when demand is weak.

The implications of this rigidity are quite serious, for a recessionary gap cannot cure itself without some deflation. And if wages and prices will not fall, recessionary gaps like EB in Figure 10–6 will linger for a long time. That is:

When aggregate demand is low, the economy may get stuck with a recessionary gap for a long time. If wages and prices fall very slowly, the economy will endure a prolonged period of production below potential GDP.

DOES THE ECONOMY HAVE A SELF-CORRECTING MECHANISM?

Now a situation like this would, presumably, not last forever. As the recession lengthened, and perhaps deepened, more and more workers would be unable to find jobs at the prevailing high wages. Eventually their resistance to wage cuts, whatever the cause, would be worn down by their need to be employed.

Firms, too, would become increasingly willing to cut prices as the period of weak demand lasted longer and managers became convinced that the slump was not merely a temporary aberration. Prices and wages did, in fact, fall during the Great Depression of the 1930s. And they might fall again if a sufficiently drastic depression were allowed to occur. They certainly slowed markedly in the weak markets of the early 1990s.

However, nowadays political leaders of both parties believe it is folly to wait for falling wages and prices to eliminate a recessionary gap. They agree that *some* government action is both necessary and appropriate under recessionary conditions. But there is still vocal—and highly partisan!—debate over how much and what kind of intervention is warranted. One reason for the disagreement is that the **self-correcting mechanism** does operate—if only weakly—to cure recessionary gaps.

Consider recent history as an example. Even the weak, and long-delayed, recovery from the 1990–1991 recession was, after all, a recovery. After peaking at 7.8 percent in June 1992, the unemployment rate began a slow descent which brought it to 6.7 percent by the time this book went to press (September 1993). Meanwhile the inflation rate was falling from 6.1 percent in 1990 to 3.1 percent in 1991, 2.9% in 1992, and 2.8% in the first 8 months of 1993. Qualitatively, this is just the sort of behavior the theoretical model predicts. But it sure took a long time! Hence the practical policy question is: How long can we afford to wait?

Our overall conclusion about the economy's ability to right itself, then, seems to run something like this:

The economy does indeed have a self-correcting mechanism that tends to eliminate either unemployment or inflation. However, this mechanism works slowly and unevenly. In addition, its beneficial effects on either inflation or unemployment are sometimes swamped by strong forces (such as rapid increases or decreases in aggregate demand) pushing in the opposite direction. Thus the self-correcting mechanism cannot always be relied upon.

A t   T h e F R O N T I E R

DOES GDP RETURN TO POTENTIAL?

The theory of aggregate supply and demand described in this chapter treats **potential GDP** as a fixed number at any point in time. Potential GDP may grow over time as the economy acquires more labor and capital. But it is not supposed to be affected by changes in *aggregate demand*. Thus, when a spurt in aggregate demand temporarily drives real GDP above its potential level, we expect actual GDP to gravitate back toward potential, as shown in Figure 10–5. Similarly, when a decline in aggregate demand pulls real GDP below potential, we expect a subsequent period of rapid growth to bring GDP back toward potential (see Figure 10–6).

This is the theory of the **self-correcting mechanism** to which most economists ascribe. However, some controversial recent research has cast doubt not only on this conventional view, but also on the entire concept of potential GDP. Since the debate is basically statistical, considerable technical sophistication is required to understand it. But the central issue is easily explained.

If there really is a self-correcting mechanism, we should see its imprint in actual data for the United States and other countries. Specifically, we should see that real GDP typically grows rapidly when it is below potential and slowly when it is above potential. For many years, this is in fact what economists thought they saw. After all, neither booms nor recessions last forever; they are both just memories in the end.

Or are they? It is precisely this "finding" that new research calls into question. When the statistical details are stripped away, the debate boils down to the following simple question: If real GDP spurts this year, should we raise our forecast of what real GDP is likely to be ten years from now?

The conventional view is that we should not. Because the self-correcting mechanism eventually returns real GDP to its potential level, the best guess we can make about GDP far in the future is always that it will be near potential. Transitory ups and downs in real GDP growth should not change the long-run forecast because they do not change the economy's long-run potential GDP.

The maverick view, which began to appear in scholarly journals in the late 1980s, is that today's growth rate leaves a lasting imprint on output. Proponents argue that a 1 percent rise in this year's real GDP should lead us to raise our forecast of real GDP ten years from now by *more than* 1 percent! For this to be true, a boom must raise potential GDP and a slump must lower it. But, if there is no tendency for the economy to return to any fixed level of potential GDP, the theory of the self-correcting mechanism goes out the window.

Which view is correct? The issue may seem easy to resolve. Just look to see whether real GDP does in fact return to its previous path. Economists are trying to do precisely that, but the statistical problem is harder than it seems. To learn about the consequences of *current* events for events ten years into the future, you need data covering a very long span of time. There are data on U.S. GDP dating back to about the Civil War; but they are much less accurate than modern data. Besides, very old data are relevant to the present only if the economy's self-correcting mechanism has not changed much over time. But no one really believes that is so.

So the controversy continues in the pages of scientific journals and in unpublished papers circulated by mail. However, one thing *has* changed already at the research frontier. Complacent acceptance of the old theory is gone. Research economists are now asking two fundamental questions. Are the new statistical findings correct? And, if they are, what theory will explain them?

STAGFLATION FROM SUPPLY SHIFTS

We have so far encountered one type of stagflation in this chapter—the stagflation that follows in the aftermath of an inflationary boom. However, that is not what happened in the more serious stagflationary episodes of the 1970s and early 1980s. What was going on during those years that caused so much unemployment and inflation at the same time? What were the causes of this more virulent type of stagflation? Several things, but the principal villain was the rising price of energy.

In 1973 the Organization of Petroleum Exporting Countries (OPEC) reached a collusive agreement that quadrupled the price of crude oil. American consumers found the prices of gasoline and home heating fuels increasing sharply. American businesses found that one important input to the production process—energy—rose drastically in price, thus increasing the costs of doing business. OPEC struck again in 1979–1980, this time doubling the price of oil. Then the same thing happened a third time, albeit on a smaller scale, when Iraq invaded Kuwait in 1990.

Higher energy prices, we observed earlier, make the economy's aggregate supply curve shift inward in the manner shown in Figure 10–2. If the aggregate supply curve shifts inward, as it surely did in 1973–1974, 1979–1980, and 1990, production will be reduced. And in order to reduce demand to the available supply, prices will have to rise. The result is the worst of both worlds: falling production and rising prices.

This conclusion is shown graphically in Figure 10–7, which superimposes an aggregate demand curve, *DD*, on the two aggregate supply curves of Figure 10–2.

Figure	10–7	**STAGFLATION FROM AN ADVERSE SHIFT IN AGGREGATE SUPPLY**

This diagram illustrates how stagflation arises if the aggregate supply curve shifts inward to the left (from S_0S_0 to S_1S_1). If the aggregate demand curve does not change, equilibrium moves from point *E* to point *A*. Output falls as prices rise, which is what we mean by stagflation. The diagram indicates roughly what happened in the United States during 1990–1991, when higher energy prices caused stagflation around the time of the Persian Gulf War.

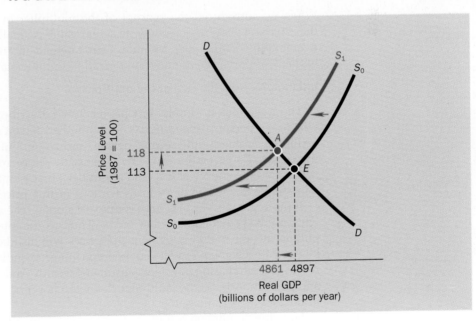

The economy's equilibrium shifts upward to the left, from point E to point A. Thus, output falls while prices rise. In brief:

Stagflation is the typical result of adverse supply shifts.

The numbers used in Figure 10–7 are roughly indicative of what happened in the United States between 1990 (represented by supply curve S_0S_0 and point E) and 1991 (represented by supply curve S_1S_1 and point A). Real GDP, in 1987 prices, fell by $36 billion, while the price level rose about 4 percent.

The stories of the 1973–1975 and 1979–1980 periods were similar, but much more severe. After each "energy shock," inflation soared and the economy weakened. Thus the general lesson to be learned from the U.S. experience with supply shocks is both clear and important:

The typical results of an adverse supply shock are a fall in output and an acceleration in inflation. This is one reason why the world economy was plagued by stagflation in the mid-1970s and early 1980s. And it can happen again if another series of supply-reducing events takes place.

Of course, supply shifts can work in the other direction as well. The world oil market weakened markedly in 1986, and oil prices plummeted. Just after the Persian Gulf War, the price of oil tumbled by about 50 percent. Both of these favorable supply shocks stimulated U.S. economic growth somewhat and curbed inflation. In 1986, the Consumer Price Index actually fell for a few months! The aggregate supply curve was shifting outward.

Favorable supply shocks tend to push output up and reduce inflation.

| INFLATION AND THE MULTIPLIER

When we introduced the concept of the multiplier in Chapter 9, we said that there were several reasons why its actual value is smaller than suggested by the oversimplified multiplier formula. One emerged in an appendix to Chapter 9: variable imports. We are now in a position to understand the second:

Inflation reduces the size of the multiplier.

The basic idea is simple. In Chapter 9, we described a multiplier process in which one person's spending becomes another person's income, which leads to further spending by the second person, and so on. But this story is confined to the demand side of the economy. Let us therefore consider what is likely to happen on the supply side as the multiplier process unfolds. Will the additional demand be taken care of by firms without raising prices?

If the aggregate supply curve is upward sloping, the answer is no; more goods will only be provided at higher prices. Thus, as the multiplier chain progresses, pulling income and employment up, prices will also be rising. And this, as we know from Chapter 7, will dampen consumer spending because rising prices reduce the purchasing power of consumers' wealth. And it will also reduce exports and raise imports. So the multiplier chain will not proceed as far as it would have in the absence of inflation.

How much inflation results from the rise in demand? How much of the multiplier chain is cut off by inflation? The answers depend on the slope of the economy's aggregate supply curve.

For a concrete example of the analysis, let us return to the $200 billion increase in investment spending used in Chapter 9. As we learned there (see especially page 219), $200 billion in additional investment spending eventually leads—through the multiplier process—to *a horizontal shift of $800 billion in the aggregate demand curve*. But to know the actual quantity that will ultimately be produced, and the actual price level, we must bring the aggregate supply curve into the picture.

Figure 10–8 does this. Here we show the $800 billion horizontal shift of the aggregate demand curve, from D_0D_0 to D_1D_1, that is derived from the oversimplified multiplier formula (which ignores rising prices). The aggregate supply curve, SS, then tells us how this expansion of demand is apportioned between higher output and higher prices. We see that as the economy's equilibrium moves from point E_0 to point E_1, real GDP does not rise by $800 billion. Instead, prices rise, which, as we know, tends to cancel out part of the rise in quantity demanded. So output increases only from $6000 billion to $6600 billion—an increase of $600 billion. Thus, in our example, inflation reduces the multiplier from $800/$200 = 4 to $600/$200 = 3. In general:

As long as the aggregate supply curve is upward sloping, any increase in aggregate demand will push up the price level. This, in turn, will drain off some of the higher real demand by eroding the purchasing power of consumer wealth and by reducing net exports. Thus, inflation reduces the value of the multiplier below that suggested by the oversimplified formula.

F i g u r e **10–8**   **INFLATION AND THE MULTIPLIER**

This figure illustrates the complete analysis of the multiplier, including the effect of inflation. The simple multiplier of Chapter 9, which ignored changes in the price level, appears here as a *horizontal* shift of $800 billion in the aggregate demand curve, meaning that the multiplier would be $800/$200 = 4 if prices did not rise. However, when aggregate demand shifts from D_0D_0 to D_1D_1, prices rise. In the diagram, the price level increases from 100 to 120 or by 20 percent. Consequently, equilibrium real income increases from $6000 billion to only $6600 billion—for a rise of $600 billion, or a multiplier of $600/$200 = 3.

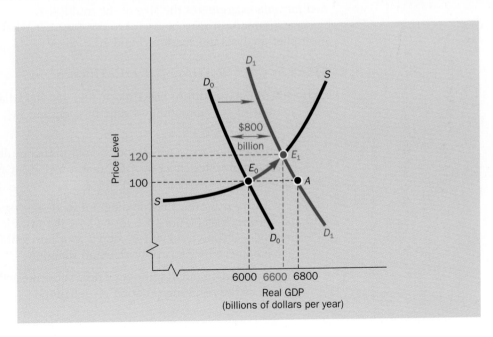

Notice also that the price level in this example has been pushed up (from 100 to 120, or 20 percent) by the rise in investment demand. This, too, is a general result:

As long as the aggregate supply curve is upward sloping, any outward shift of the aggregate demand curve will cause some rise in prices.

The economic behavior behind these results certainly cannot be considered surprising. Firms faced with large increases in quantity demanded at their original prices respond to these changed circumstances in two natural ways: they raise production (so GDP rises), and they raise prices (so the price level rises). But this rise in the price level reduces the purchasing power of the bank accounts and bonds held by consumers, and they too react in the natural way: they cut down on their spending. Such a reaction amounts to a movement *along* aggregate demand curve D_1D_1 in Figure 10–8 from point A to point E_1.

Higher prices thus play their usual dual role in a market economy: they encourage suppliers to produce more, and they encourage demanders to consume less. In this way, equilibrium is reestablished at higher levels of output and higher prices through the process of inflation.

Figure 10–8 also shows us exactly where the oversimplified multiplier formula goes wrong. By ignoring the effects of the higher price level, the oversimplified formula erroneously supposes that the economy moves horizontally from point E_0 to point A. As the diagram clearly shows, output does not actually rise this much. Output *would* rise this much only if the aggregate supply curve were horizontal, meaning that output can rise indefinitely without any increase in price. (Verify this for yourself by penciling in an imaginary horizontal aggregate supply curve through points E_0 and A in Figure 10–8.) That is, the oversimplified multiplier formula tacitly assumes that the aggregate supply curve is horizontal. Normally, this is an unrealistic assumption, which is one reason why the oversimplified formula exaggerates the size of the multiplier.

As a summary, it may be useful to put together what we have learned about multiplier analysis in Chapters 9 and 10.

STEPS IN CALCULATING THE MULTIPLIER

1. Shift the expenditure schedule in the 45° line diagram vertically by the amount of the autonomous shift in spending (as, for example, in Figure 9–1 on page 209).

2. Use the 45° line diagram, or the oversimplified multiplier formula, to calculate the multiplier effect on GDP that *would* occur *if* the price level did not change (again, see Figure 9–1).

3. Now move from the 45° line diagram to an aggregate supply and demand diagram such as Figure 10–8 to see how the price level will react. Enter the multiplier effect calculated in step 2 as a horizontal shift of the aggregate demand curve in the supply–demand diagram.

4. The supply–demand diagram will now show the actual effect on real output as well as the resulting inflation or deflation.[2]

---

[2]The change in the price level reacts back on the 45° diagram. See Review Question 11 at the end of the chapter.

A ROLE FOR STABILIZATION POLICY

Chapter 8 emphasized the volatility of investment spending, and Chapter 9 noted that changes in investment have multiplier effects on aggregate demand. This chapter took the next step by showing how shifts in the aggregate demand curve cause fluctuations in both real GDP growth and inflation—fluctuations that are widely decried as undesirable. It also suggested that the economy's self-correcting mechanism works, but slowly, thereby leaving room for government stabilization policy to improve the workings of the free market. Can the government really do this? If so, how? These are the questions for Part 3.

Summary

1. The economy's **aggregate supply curve** relates the quantity of goods and services that will be supplied to the price level. It normally slopes upward to the right because the costs of labor and other inputs are relatively fixed in the short run, meaning that higher selling prices make input costs relatively "cheaper" and therefore encourage greater production.

2. The position of the aggregate supply curve can be shifted by changes in money wage rates, prices of other inputs, technology, or quantities or qualities of labor and capital.

3. The aggregate supply curve normally gets steeper as output increases. This means that, as output and capacity utilization rise, any given increase in aggregate demand leads to more inflation and less growth of real output.

4. The **equilibrium price level** and the **equilibrium level of real GDP** are jointly determined by the intersection of the economy's aggregate supply and aggregate demand schedules. This intersection may come at full employment, below full employment (a recessionary gap), or above full employment (an inflationary gap).

5. If there is an **inflationary gap**, the economy has a mechanism that erodes the gap through a process of inflation. Specifically, unusually strong job prospects push wages up, which shifts the aggregate supply curve to the left and reduces the inflationary gap.

6. One consequence of this **self-correcting mechanism** is that, if a surge in aggregate demand opens up an inflationary gap, part of the economy's natural adjustment to this event will be a period of stagflation; that is, a period in which prices are rising while output is falling.

7. The economy also has a self-correcting mechanism that erodes a **recessionary gap**. This mechanism works in much the same way as the inflationary-gap mechanism: a weak labor market reduces wages, thereby shifting the aggregate supply curve outward. But this happens only slowly.

8. An inward shift of the aggregate supply curve will cause output to fall while prices rise; that is, it will cause **stagflation**. Among the events that have caused such a shift are abrupt increases in the price of foreign oil.

9. Adverse supply shifts like this plagued our economy when oil prices skyrocketed in 1973–1974, 1979–1980, and again in 1990, leading to stagflation each time.

10. Among the reasons why the oversimplified multiplier formula is wrong is the fact that it ignores any inflation that may be caused by an increase in aggregate demand. Such **inflation decreases the multiplier** by reducing both consumer spending and net exports.

Key Concepts and Terms

Aggregate supply curve
Productivity
Equilibrium of real GDP
  and the price level

Inflationary gap
Self-correcting mechanism
Stagflation

Recessionary gap
Inflation and the multiplier

Questions for Review

1. In an economy with the following aggregate demand and aggregate supply schedules, find the equilibrium levels of real output and the price level. Graph your solution. If full employment comes at $2800 billion, is there an inflationary or a recessionary gap?

AGGREGATE QUANTITY DEMANDED (in billions)	PRICE LEVEL	AGGREGATE QUANTITY SUPPLIED (in billions)
3200	85	2600
3150	90	2650
3000	95	2800
2900	110	2900
2800	130	3000

2. Suppose a worker receives a wage of $15 per hour. Compute the real wage (money wage deflated by the price index) corresponding to each of the following possible price levels: 85, 95, 100, 110, 120. What do you notice about the relationship between the real wage and the price level? Relate this to the slope of the aggregate supply curve.

3. In 1989, capacity utilization averaged 84 percent. In 1992, it averaged 80 percent. In which year do you think the economy found itself on a steeper portion of its aggregate supply curve? Explain why.

4. Explain why a decrease in the price of foreign oil shifts the aggregate supply curve outward to the right. What are the consequences of such a shift?

5. Comment on the following statement: "Inflationary and recessionary gaps are nothing to worry about because the economy has a built-in mechanism that cures either type of gap automatically."

6. Give *two* different explanations of how the economy can suffer from stagflation.

7. Why do you think wages tend to be rigid in the downward direction?

8. Add the following aggregate supply and demand schedules to the example in Question 3 of Chapter 8 (page 200) to see how inflation affects the multiplier.

(1) PRICE LEVEL	(2) AGGREGATE DEMAND (when investment is $120)	(3) AGGREGATE DEMAND (when investment is $130)	(4) AGGREGATE SUPPLY
90	$1930	$2030	$1830
95	1915	2015	1865
100	1900	2000	1900
105	1885	1985	1935
110	1870	1970	1970
115	1855	1955	2005

Draw these schedules on a piece of graph paper. Then:

a. Notice that the difference between columns 2 and 3 (the aggregate demand schedule at two different levels of investment) is always $100. Discuss how this relates to your answer in the previous chapter.
b. Find the equilibrium GDP and the equilibrium price level both before and after the increase in investment. What is the value of the multiplier?

9. Explain in words why rising prices reduce the multiplier effect of an autonomous increase in aggregate demand.

10. Use an aggregate supply and demand diagram to show that multiplier effects are smaller when the aggregate supply curve is steeper. Which case gives rise to more inflation—the steep aggregate supply curve or the flat one? What happens to the multiplier if the aggregate supply curve is vertical?

11. (More difficult) Assume that investment spending rises. Draw a set of graphs illustrating the Steps in Calculating the Multiplier listed on page 246. Your aggregate supply and demand diagram from steps 3 and 4 will show a change in the price level. How would this change in the price level react back on the 45° line diagram you used in step 1? In view of this, use the 45° line diagram to show that inflation reduces the multiplier.

PART III

Fiscal

and

Monetary

Policy

Chapter 11

MANAGING AGGREGATE DEMAND: FISCAL POLICY

Next, let us turn to the problems of our fiscal policy. Here the myths are legion and the truth hard to find.

JOHN F. KENNEDY

In the model of the economy constructed in Part 2, the government played an entirely passive role. It did a fixed amount of spending and collected a fixed amount of taxes, and that was it. We concluded from this analysis that such an economy has a very weak tendency to move toward high employment with low inflation. Furthermore, we hinted in Chapter 5 that well-designed government policies might improve the economy's performance. It is now time to pick up that hint—and to learn about some of the difficulties the government must overcome if it is to conduct a successful stabilization policy. ¶ Traditionally, the government has used its taxing and spending powers to influence the demand side of the economy. So this chapter begins there, in the domain of conventional **fiscal policy**. The next two chapters take up the government's other main tool for managing aggregate demand: *monetary policy.* ¶ We start by allowing taxes to depend on income—as they do in the real world—and then considering the multipliers for tax policy. As we shall see, none of this requires any fundamental change in the way we analyze the determination of GDP and the price level. However, it does reduce the size of the multiplier.

As Presidents Reagan, Bush, and Clinton have all realized, the effects of tax policy are not limited to aggregate *demand*. Taxes also affect aggregate *supply*. So the last parts of the chapter examine both the Reagan-Bush and Clinton versions of "supply-side economics."

ISSUE: SHOULD FISCAL POLICY BE USED TO STIMULATE THE ECONOMY?

It is widely believed that the weak economy cost President George Bush the 1992 election. That very same weakness posed a dilemma for the incoming Clinton administration. Should it try to stimulate economic activity by using the tools of fiscal policy, that is, by raising government spending or cutting taxes? Or should it instead try to reduce the large government budget deficit, which everyone acknowledged to be a problem? The two objectives are in conflict because government policy stimulates the economy by raising spending or cutting taxes but reduces the deficit by raising taxes or cutting spending.

The Clinton administration's answer gave primacy to deficit reduction. This chapter begins by describing the principles that policymakers should—and sometimes do!—use to answer such questions. But we will have much more to say about the budget deficit in Chapter 15.

INCOME TAXES AND THE CONSUMPTION SCHEDULE

Before attempting to address such difficult policy questions, we must think a little harder about how to integrate taxes into our model of income determination. We do this in stages. First, we contrast **fixed taxes**, which are the only kind we have considered so far, with **variable taxes**, which are much more important in practice. Then we will see how each type of tax affects income determination and the multiplier.

Most of the taxes collected by the federal, state, and local governments vary with the level of GDP. In some cases, the reason is obvious: *personal* and *corporate income tax* collections, for example, depend on how much income there is to be taxed. But even *sales tax* receipts depend indirectly on GDP because consumer spending is higher when GDP is higher. On the other hand, there are some taxes—such as property taxes levied by local governments—that do not vary with GDP. Therefore, we will call the first kind of tax *variable taxes* and the second kind *fixed taxes*.

Why is this distinction important? Remember that gross domestic product (GDP) is the difference between disposable income (*DI*) and taxes (*T*):

$$Y = DI - T.$$

Thus when taxes are increased, disposable income falls—and hence so does consumption—*even if GDP is unchanged*. As a result:

An increase in taxes shifts the consumption schedule in our 45° line diagram downward. Similarly, a reduction in taxes shifts the consumption schedule upward.

But precisely how the consumption schedule shifts depends on the nature of the tax change. If a fixed tax is increased, the resulting decrease in disposable income is the *same* regardless of the level of GDP; hence the decline in consumer

---

The government's **FISCAL POLICY** is its plan for spending and taxation. It is designed to steer aggregate demand in some desired direction.

FIXED TAXES are tax taxes that do not vary with the level of GDP.

VARIABLE TAXES are taxes that do vary with the level of GDP.

spending is the same. In a word, the *C* schedule shifts downward in a parallel manner, as shown in Figure 11–1(a).

But more often than not tax policy changes disposable income by amounts that depend on the level of income, normally being larger at high income levels than at low ones. This is true, for example, whenever Congress varies the bracket rates in the personal income tax code, as it did in 1993. Since an increase in tax rates decreases disposable income more when GDP is higher, the downward shift of the *C* schedule is sharper at high income levels than at low ones. Figure 11–1(b) illustrates how this type of tax policy shifts the consumption schedule.

The two parts of Figure 11–1, then, explain the first reason why the distinction between fixed and variable taxes is important. Figure 11–2 illustrates the second. Here we show two consumption lines, C_1 and C_2. C_1 is the consumption schedule used in previous chapters; it is constructed on the assumption that taxes are fixed at $1200 billion regardless of GDP. C_2 depicts a more realistic case in which tax collections are 20% percent of GDP. You will notice that C_2 is flatter than C_1. This is no accident. In fact:

Variable taxes such as the income tax flatten the consumption schedule in a 45° line diagram.

It is easy to understand why, and Table 11–1 helps us do so. It shows in column 1 alternative values of GDP ranging from $4.5 trillion to $7.5 trillion. Column 2 then indicates that taxes are always one-fifth of this amount. Column 3 subtracts column 2 from column 1 to arrive at disposable income (*DI*). Column 4 then gives the amount of consumer spending corresponding to each level of *DI*. The consumption schedule we need for our 45° line is therefore found in columns 1 and 4.

Notice that for each $500 billion increase in GDP (say, from $5500 billion to $6000 billion), consumer spending rises by $300 billion (from $3600 billion to $3900 billion). Thus the slope of line C_2 in Figure 11–2 is $300/$500 = 0.6. But, if you look back at any of the tables in Chapter 9, you will find that consumption

---

F i g u r e **11–1**   **HOW TAX POLICY SHIFTS THE CONSUMPTION SCHEDULE**

Because consumption depends on disposable income, not GDP, any change in taxes will shift the consumption schedule relating consumption to GDP. Part (a) shows how the curve shifts for changes in fixed taxes. Part (b) shows how the *C* curve shifts if the tax cut (or tax increase) is larger at high incomes than at low incomes.

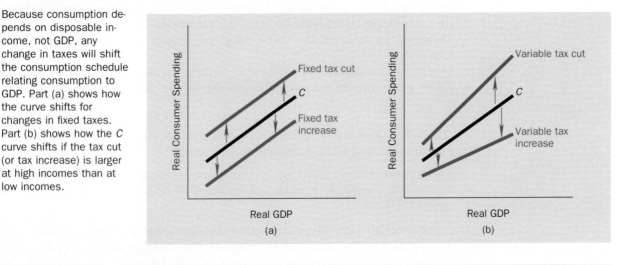

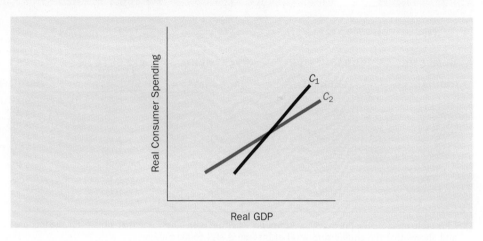

F i g u r e **11-2** **THE CONSUMPTION SCHEDULE WITH FIXED AND VARIABLE TAXES**

Line C_1 is the consumption schedule used in earlier chapters, when taxes were taken to be fixed. If, instead, tax receipts rise with GDP, the consumption schedule is flatter—see line C_2.

there rose by $300 billion each time GDP increased $400 billion—making the slope $300/$400 = 0.75. (See the steeper line C_1 in Figure 11–2.)

All this sounds terribly mechanical, but the economic reasoning behind it is straightforward. When taxes are fixed, as in schedule C_1, each additional dollar of GDP raises disposable income (*DI*) by $1. Consumer spending then rises by $1 times the marginal propensity to consume (MPC), which is 0.75 in our example. Hence each additional dollar of GDP leads to 75¢ more spending. But when taxes vary with income, each additional dollar of GDP raises *DI* by less than $1 because the government takes a share in taxes. In our example, taxes are 20 percent of GDP, so each additional $1 of GDP leads to 80¢ more disposable income. With an MPC of 0.75, that means that spending rises 60¢ (75 percent of 80¢) each time GDP rises by $1. That is why the slope of the line C_2 in Figure 11–2 is only 0.6, instead of 0.75.

T a b l e **11-1** **THE EFFECTS OF AN INCOME TAX ON THE CONSUMPTION SCHEDULE**

(1) GROSS DOMESTIC PRODUCT (billions)	(2) TAXES (billions)	(3) DISPOSABLE INCOME (GDP minus taxes) (billions)	(4) CONSUMPTION (billions)
$4500	$900	$3600	$3000
5000	1000	4000	3300
5500	1100	4400	3600
6000	1200	4800	3900
6500	1300	5200	4200
7000	1400	5600	4500
7500	1500	6000	4800

This table shows how an income tax lowers the slope of the consumption schedule (column 4) in a concrete example. For every $500 billion increase in GDP, consumption rises by $300 billion in this example (compare columns 1 and 4). So the slope of the C_2 line in Figure 11–2 is $300/$500 = 0.6. In earlier chapters, the slope of the consumption schedule (line C_1 in Figure 11–2) was $300/$400 = 0.75.

T a b l e **11–2**	**TOTAL EXPENDITURE SCHEDULE WITH A 20 PERCENT INCOME TAX**				
(1) **GROSS DOMESTIC** **Y** **(billions)**	**(2)** **CONSUMPTION** **C** **(billions)**	**(3)** **INVESTMENT** **I** **(billions)**	**(4)** **NET EXPORTS** **(X − IM)** **(billions)**	**(5)** **GOVERNMENT PURCHASES** **G** **(billions)**	**(6)** **TOTAL EXPENDITURE** **C + I + G + (X − IM)** **(billions)**
$4500	$3000	$900	−$100	$1300	$5100
5000	3300	900	−100	1300	5400
5500	3600	900	−100	1300	5700
6000	3900	900	−100	1300	6000
6500	4200	900	−100	1300	6300
7000	4500	900	−100	1300	6600
7500	4800	900	−100	1300	6900

This table replaces the previous consumption schedule with a new one that adjusts for the income tax (as shown in Table 28–1) and shows that the equilibrium level of income is still $6000 billion.

Table 11–2 and Figure 11–3 take the next step by replacing the old consumption schedule with this new one in both the tabular presentation of income determination and the 45° line diagram. We see immediately that the equilibrium level of GDP is at point *E*. Here, gross domestic product is $6000 billion, consumption is $3900 billion, investment is $900 billion, net exports are −$100 billion, and government purchases are $1300 billion. As we know, full employment may occur above or below *Y* = $6000 billion. If below, there is an inflationary gap. Prices probably will start to rise, pulling the expenditure schedule down and reducing equilibrium GDP. If above, there is a recessionary gap, and history suggests that prices will fall only slowly. In the interim, there will be a period of high unemployment.

In short, once we adjust the expenditure schedule to include the effects of variable taxes, the determination of national income proceeds exactly as before. The effects of government spending and taxation, therefore, are fairly straightforward and can be summarized as follows:

Government purchases of goods and services add to total spending directly through the *G* component of *C* + *I* + *G* + (*X* − *IM*). Taxes indirectly reduce total spending by lowering disposable income and thus reduce the *C* component of *C* + *I* + *G* + (*X* − *IM*). On balance, then, the government's actions may raise or lower the equilibrium level of GDP, depending on how much spending and taxing it does.

However, there is more to the story. As we will see now:

The multiplier is smaller in the presence of an income tax.

Let us see why.

THE MULTIPLIER REVISITED

We learned in Chapter 9 that the multiplier works through a chain of spending and respending, as one person's expenditure becomes another's income. But, when there is an income tax, some of the additional income leaks out of the circular flow at each stage. Specifically, if the income tax rate is 20 percent, when Generous Motors spends $1 million on salaries, workers actually receive only $800,000 in *after-tax* (that is, disposable) income. If workers spend 75 percent of this amount (because the MPC is 0.75), spending in the next round will be only $600,000. Notice that this is only *60 percent* of the original expenditure, not *75 percent* as in our earlier example—just as we observed in the last section.

Thus the multiplier chain for each original dollar of spending shrinks from

$$1 + 0.75 + (0.75)^2 + (0.75)^3 + \ldots = \frac{1}{1 - 0.75} = \frac{1}{0.25} = 4$$

to

$$1 + 0.6 + (0.6)^2 + (0.6)^3 + \ldots = \frac{1}{1 - 0.6} = \frac{1}{0.4} = 2\tfrac{1}{2}.$$

This is clearly a large reduction in the multiplier. We thus have a third reason why the oversimplified multiplier formula of Chapter 9 gives an exaggerated impression of the size of the multiplier:

REASONS WHY THE OVERSIMPLIFIED MULTIPLIER FORMULA IS WRONG

1. It ignores variable imports, which serve to reduce the size of the multiplier.
2. It ignores price-level changes, which also reduce the multiplier.
3. It ignores income taxes, which serve to reduce the size of the multiplier.

The last of these three reasons is very important in practice.

F i g u r e **11-3** **INCOME DETERMINATION WITH A VARIABLE INCOME TAX**

This diagram adds a 20 percent income tax to the model economy portrayed in earlier chapters. Because of this, the $C + I + G + (X - IM)$ schedule is flatter. But otherwise things look just as before. In particular, equilibrium is at point E, where the $C + I + G + (X - IM)$ schedule crosses the 45° line. Thus equilibrium GDP is $6000 billion.

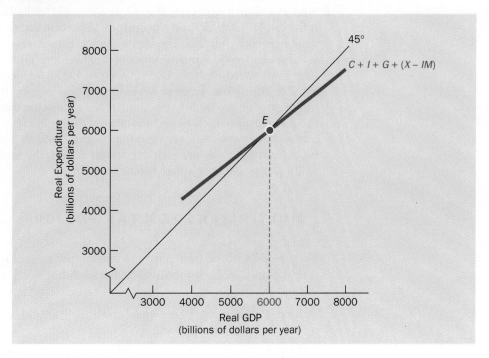

F i g u r e **11–4**

THE MULTIPLIER IN THE PRESENCE OF AN INCOME TAX

This diagram illustrates that an economy with an income tax (in this case a 20 percent income tax) has a lower multiplier than an economy without one. Specifically, the $C + I + G + (X - IM)$ curve is shifted upward by a $400 billion increase in G, and the diagram shows that equilibrium GDP rises by $1000 billion—from $6000 billion to $7000 billion. The multiplier is therefore $1000/$400 = $2\frac{1}{2}$, whereas without an income tax it was 4.

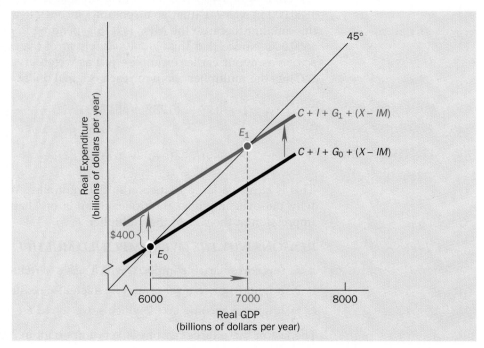

This conclusion about the multiplier is shown graphically in Figure 11–4, where we have drawn our $C + I + G + (X - IM)$ schedules with a slope of 0.6 to reflect an MPC of 0.75 and a tax rate of 20 percent rather than the 0.75 slope that we used in earlier chapters. The figure depicts the effect of an increase in government purchases of goods and services of $400 billion, which shifts the $C + I + G + (X - IM)$ schedule from $C + I + G_0 + (X - IM)$ to $C + I + G_1 + (X - IM)$. Equilibrium moves from point E_0 to point E_1—a growth in GDP from $Y = $6000 billion to $Y = $7000 billion. Thus, if we ignore for the moment any increases in the price level (which would reduce the multiplier shown in Figure 11–4), a $400 billion increment in government spending leads to a $1000 billion increment in GDP. So when taxes are included in our model, the multiplier is only $1000/$400 = $2\frac{1}{2}$, just as we concluded before.

MULTIPLIERS FOR TAX POLICY

Because they work indirectly via consumption, multipliers for tax changes are more complicated than multipliers for spending such as G. They must be worked out in two steps.

Step 1. We must figure out how much any change in the tax law affects consumer spending.

Step 2. We must enter this vertical shift of the consumption schedule in the 45° line diagram and see how it affects output.

A reduction in income taxes provides a convenient example of this two-step procedure because we have already done Step 1 in an earlier chapter. Specifically, in Chapter 7 we studied how consumer spending would respond to a cut in income taxes. We concluded that, if the tax reduction were viewed as permanent, consumers would increase their spending by an amount equal to the tax cut times the marginal propensity to consume. (If you need review, turn back to pages 156–61.)

To create a simple and familiar numerical example, let us suppose that income taxes fall from $0.2Y$ (that is, 20 percent of GDP) to $0.2Y - \$400$ billion—meaning that tax receipts decline by $400 billion at each level of GDP. Step 1 instructs us to multiply the $400 billion tax cut by the marginal propensity to consume (MPC), which is 0.75, to get $300 billion as the vertical shift of the consumption schedule.

Step 2 then amounts to multiplying this $300 billion increase in consumption by the multiplier—which is 2.5 in our example—giving $750 billion as the rise in GDP. Figure 11–5 verifies that this is so by entering a $300 billion vertical shift of the consumption function into the 45° line diagram and noting that GDP does indeed rise by $750 billion as a result.

Notice something interesting here. The $400 billion tax cut raises GDP by $750 billion. Thus the multiplier is $700/$400 = 1.875. But the multiplier for the $400 government purchases that we worked out on page 255 and depicted in Figure 11–4 was 2.5. What's going on here? Apparently:

The multiplier for changes in taxes is smaller than the multiplier for changes in government purchases.

The reason is not mysterious. While G is a direct component of total expenditure, taxes are not. Taxes work indirectly, first by changing disposable income and then by changing C. Since some of the change in disposable income affects *saving* rather than *spending*, a one-dollar tax cut does not pack as much punch as a dollar

---

F i g u r e **11–5**   **THE MULTIPLIER FOR A REDUCTION IN FIXED TAXES**

In this example, the $C + I + G + (X - IM)$ schedule is shifted vertically upward by $300 billion, from $C_0 + I + G + (X - IM)$ to $C_1 + I + G + (X - IM)$, by a $400 billion tax cut. Equilibrium GDP therefore increases from $6000 billion to $6750 billion. So the multiplier is $750/$400 = 1.875.

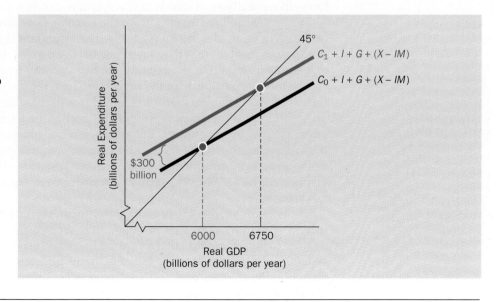

of G. That is why we had to multiply the $400 billion change in taxes by 0.75 to get the $300 billion shift of the C schedule shown in Figure 11–5.

The fact that the multiplier for taxes is smaller than the multiplier for G has a surprising implication:

If government purchases (G) and taxes (T) rise by equal amounts, the government seems to be giving to the public with one hand and taking away an equal amount with the other. But the effects do not cancel out. Instead, the equilibrium level of GDP on the demand side rises. Similarly, if G and T fall by equal amounts, the equilibrium level of GDP on the demand side falls.

For example, we have seen that a $400 billion increase in G raises GDP by $1000, while a $400 billion cut in T lowers GDP by just $750 billion. Thus if *both G and T* were raised by $400 billion, GDP would go up by $250 billion.

The intuitive explanation is that every dollar of government spending adds $1 to total expenditure in the economy while every dollar collected in taxes reduces consumer spending by less than $1. The rest comes out of saving. (In our example, consumers take one quarter of any tax hike out of saving and three-quarters out of spending.)

The moral of the story is that fiscal policies that keep the deficit the same do not necessarily keep aggregate demand the same. A cut in government spending balanced by an equal cut in tax revenues can be expected to reduce Y—a lesson that politicians frequently forget.

GOVERNMENT TRANSFER PAYMENTS

Finally, we should mention the last major tool of fiscal policy: **government transfer payments**. A transfer, you will remember, is a payment by government to an individual that is not compensation for work done or for any other direct contribution to production. How are transfers treated in our models of income determination—like purchases of goods and services (G) or like taxes (T)?

The answer follows readily from the circular flow diagram back on page 186 or the accounting identity on page 154. The important thing to understand about transfer payments is that they intervene between gross domestic product (Y) and disposable income (DI) in precisely the *opposite* way from income taxes.

Specifically, starting with the wages, interest, rents, and profits that constitute the national income, we *subtract* income taxes to calculate disposable income. We do so because these taxes represent the portion of incomes that are *earned* but never *received* by consumers. But then we must *add* transfer payments because they represent sources of income that are *received* although they were not *earned* in the process of production. Thus, *transfer payments are basically negative taxes*; giving a consumer $1 in the form of a transfer payment is equivalent to reducing her taxes by $1.

So, in terms of the 45° line diagram, increases in transfer payments can be treated simply as decreases in taxes. And we see that Figure 11–5, which we devised to illustrate a tax cut, can also be used to illustrate a rise in unemployment benefits, or in social security benefits, or in any other such transfer payment. Similarly, the analysis of a decrease in transfer payments would proceed exactly like the analysis of an increase in taxes.

PLANNING EXPANSIVE FISCAL POLICY

Now, at last, you are ready to pretend that you were in President Clinton's shoes in January 1993, trying to decide whether to use fiscal policy to stimulate the economy—and, if so, by how much. Suppose that the economy would have a GDP of $6000 billion if last year's budget were simply repeated. Suppose further that your goal is to achieve a fully employed labor force and that staff economists tell you this would require a GDP of approximately $7000 billion. Finally, just to keep the calculations manageable, imagine that the price level is fixed. What sort of budget should you recommend to Congress?

This chapter has taught us that the government has three ways to raise GDP by $1000 billion. Congress can raise government purchases, reduce taxes, or increase transfer payments by enough to close the recessionary gap between actual and potential GDP.

Figure 11–6 illustrates the problem, and its cure through higher government spending, on our 45° line diagram. Figure 11–6(a) shows the equilibrium of the economy if no changes are made in the budget. Except for the full-employment line at $Y = \$7000$ and the corresponding recessionary gap, it looks just like Figure 11–3. With an expenditure multiplier of $2\frac{1}{2}$, you can figure out that an additional $400 billion of government spending will be needed to push the GDP up $1000 billion and eliminate this gap ($1000 ÷ $2\frac{1}{2}$ = $400).

So you might vote to raise G from $G_0 = \$1300$ billion to $G_1 = \$1700$ billion, hoping to move the $C + I + G + (X − IM)$ line in Figure 11–6(a) out to the position indicated in Figure 11–6(b), thereby achieving full employment. Of course, you might prefer to achieve this fiscal stimulus by lowering income taxes rather than by increasing expenditures. Or you might prefer to rely on more generous transfer

---

| *F i g u r e* **11–6** | **FISCAL POLICY TO ELIMINATE A RECESSIONARY GAP** |

This diagram shows, with more precision than can actually be achieved in practice, how fiscal policy can eliminate a recessionary gap. Part (a) shows the gap: Equilibrium GDP ($6000 billion) falls short of potential GDP ($7000 billion). Part (b) shows how fiscal policy—by moving the $C + I + G + (X − IM)$ curve up just enough—can wipe out this gap and restore full employment. With a multiplier of $2\frac{1}{2}$, a rise in G of $400 billion or a cut in taxes large enough to shift C up by $400 billion would do the trick.

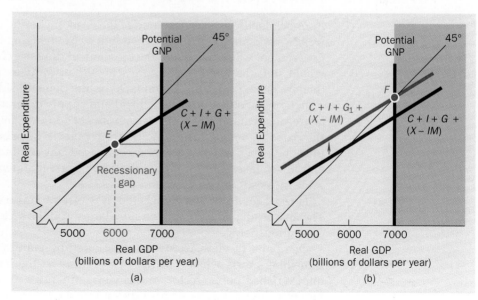

payments. The point is that there are a variety of budgets capable of pushing the economy up to full employment by increasing GDP by $1000 billion. Figure 11–6 applies equally well to any of them.

PLANNING RESTRICTIVE FISCAL POLICY

The preceding example assumed that the basic problem of fiscal policy is to overcome a deficiency of aggregate demand, as was the case at the start of the Clinton administration. Often this is so. But early in the Bush administration in 1989 many people believed that the problem was the opposite: aggregate demand exceeded the economy's capacity to produce and inflation was on the rise. In such a case, fiscal policy should assume a restrictive stance in order to reduce inflation.

It does not take much imagination to run our previous analysis in reverse. If, under a continuation of current budget policies, there would be an inflationary gap, contractionary fiscal policy tools can eliminate it. Either by cutting spending programs out of the budget, or by raising taxes, or by some combination of these policies, the government can pull the $C + I + G + (X - IM)$ schedule down to a noninflationary position and achieve an equilibrium at full employment.

Notice the difference between this way of eliminating an inflationary gap and the natural self-correcting mechanism of the economy that we discussed in Chapter 10. There we observed that, if the economy were left to its own devices, a cumulative but self-limiting process of inflation eventually would eliminate the inflationary gap and return the economy to full employment. Here we see that it is not necessary to put the economy through the inflationary wringer. Instead, a restrictive fiscal policy can limit aggregate demand to the level that the economy can produce at full employment.

THE CHOICE BETWEEN SPENDING POLICY AND TAX POLICY

In principle, fiscal policy can nudge the economy in the desired direction equally well by changing government spending or by changing taxes. For example, if the government wants to expand the economy, it can raise G or lower T. Either policy would shift the total expenditure schedule upward, as depicted in Figure 11–6, thereby raising the equilibrium GDP on the demand side.

In terms of our aggregate demand and supply diagram, either policy shifts the aggregate demand curve outward, from D_0D_0 to D_1D_1 in Figure 11–7. As a result, the economy's equilibrium moves from point E to point A. Both real GDP and the price level rise. As this diagram points out, any combination of higher spending and lower taxes that produces the same aggregate demand curve leads to the same increases in real GDP and prices.

How, then, do we decide whether it is better to raise spending or to cut taxes? The answer depends mainly on how large a public sector we want, and this is a contentious issue.

One point of view, expressed most often by political liberals, is that there is something amiss when a country as wealthy as the United States has such an impoverished public sector. In this view, America's most pressing needs are not for more designer jeans, sports cars, and VCRs, but rather for better schools, more efficient public transportation systems, and cleaner and safer city streets. People

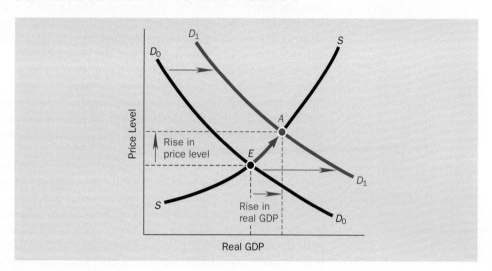

| Figure | 11–7 |

EXPANSIONARY FISCAL POLICY

Any of a variety of expansionary fiscal policies will push the aggregate demand curve outward to the right as depicted by the shift from D_0D_0 to D_1D_1 in this aggregate supply and demand diagram. The economy's equilibrium moves upward to the right along aggregate supply curve SS, from point E to point A. Comparing A with E, we note that output is higher but prices are also higher. The expansionary policy has caused some inflation.

on this side of the debate believe that we should *increase* spending when the economy needs stimulus, and pay for these improved public services by *increasing taxes* when the economy needs to be reined in.

An opposing opinion, advocated forcefully by both Presidents Reagan and Bush, was ascendant in the 1980s. In this view, the government sector is already too large; we are foolish to rely on government to do things that private individuals and businesses could do better on their own; and the growth of government interferes too much in our everyday lives, and in so doing circumscribes our freedom. Those who hold this view argue for *tax cuts* when macroeconomic considerations call for expansionary fiscal policy, and for *reductions in public spending* when restrictive policy is required.

Too often the use of fiscal policy for economic stabilization is erroneously associated with a large and growing public sector—that is, with "big government." This need not be the case. Individuals favoring a smaller public sector can advocate an active fiscal policy just as well as those who favor a larger public sector. Advocates of big government budgets should seek to expand demand (when appropriate) through higher government spending and contract demand (when appropriate) through tax increases. By contrast, advocates of small public budgets should seek to expand demand by cutting taxes and reduce demand by cutting expenditures.

SOME HARSH REALITIES

The mechanics outlined so far in this chapter make the fiscal policy planner's job look rather simple. The elementary diagrams suggest, rather misleadingly, that the authorities can drive GDP to any level they please simply by manipulating spending and tax programs. It seems as though they should be able to hit the full-employment bull's eye every time.

But, in fact, a better analogy is to shooting through dense fog at an erratically moving target with an inaccurate gun. The target is moving because, in the real world, the investment, net exports, and consumption schedules are constantly shifting due to changes in expectations, new technological breakthroughs, events abroad, and so on. This means that the policies decided upon today, which are to take effect at some future date, may no longer be appropriate by the time that future date rolls around. Policy must be based, to some extent, on *forecasting*, and no one has yet discovered a foolproof method of economic forecasting.[1] Since our forecasting ability is so modest, and because fiscal policy decisions sometimes take a long time to be carried out, the government may occasionally find itself fighting the last inflation just when the new recession gets under way.

A second misleading feature of our diagrams is that multipliers are not known with as much precision as our examples suggest. Thus while the "best guess" may be that a $20 billion cut in government purchases will reduce GDP by $40 billion, the actual outcome may be as little as $20 billion or as much as $60 billion. It is therefore impossible to "fine tune" every wobble out of the economy's growth path through fiscal policy; economic science is simply not that precise. The point is even more cogent with respect to tax policy, for here we get involved in trying to guess whether consumers will view tax changes as permanent or temporary.

A third complication is that our target—full-employment GDP—may be only dimly visible, as if through a fog. The present time is a good example of this since economists are now debating what measured unemployment rate corresponds to full employment.

Finally, in trying to decide whether to push the unemployment rate lower, legislators would like to know how large the inflation cost is likely to be. As we know, an expansionary fiscal policy that reduces a recessionary gap by increasing aggregate demand will lower unemployment. But it also tends to be inflationary. This undesirable side effect may make the government hesitant to use fiscal policy to combat recessions.

Is there a way out of this dilemma? Can we carry on the battle against unemployment without aggravating inflation? During the late 1970s, a small but influential minority of economists, journalists, and politicians argued that we could. They called their approach "supply-side economics." The idea helped sweep Ronald Reagan into office in 1980. But by 1992 Bill Clinton won the presidency by running against it. Popular opinion had certainly changed! Just what is supply-side economics?

THE IDEA BEHIND SUPPLY-SIDE TAX CUTS

The central idea of supply-side economics is that certain types of tax cuts can be expected to increase aggregate supply. For example, taxes can be cut in ways that raise the rewards for working, saving, and investing. *If people actually respond to these incentives*, such tax cuts would increase the total supplies of labor and capital in the economy, thereby increasing aggregate supply.

Figure 11–8 illustrates the idea on an aggregate supply and demand diagram. If policy measures can shift the economy's aggregate supply to position S_1S_1, then prices will be lower and output higher than if the aggregate supply curve were

---

[1]Some problems and techniques of economic forecasting are considered in Chapter 14.

Figure **11-8**	**THE IDEA BEHIND SUPPLY-SIDE TAX CUTS**

The basic idea of supply-side tax cuts is that, if they achieve their desired objective, they shift the economy's aggregate supply curve outward to the right. For example the aggregate supply curve might be $S_1 S_1$ under a program of supply-side tax cuts, whereas it would only be $S_0 S_0$ without such tax cuts. If aggregate demand is the same in either case, the supply-side tax cuts would lead to the equilibrium point *B* instead of the equilibrium point *A*. Comparing *B* with *A*, we see that the program reduces prices and raises output.

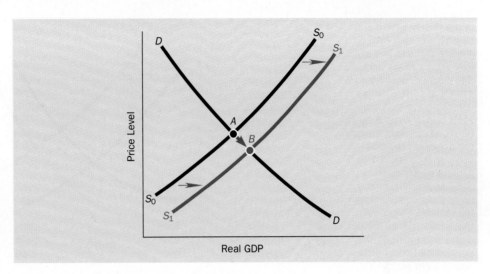

$S_0 S_0$. Policymakers will have succeeded in reducing inflation and raising real output (lowering unemployment) at the same time. The trade-off between inflation and unemployment will have been defeated. This is the goal of supply-side economics.

What sorts of policies do supply siders advocate? Here is a small sample of their long list of recommended tax cuts:

1. *Lower Personal Income Tax Rates*. Sharp cuts in personal taxes were the cornerstone of President Reagan's economic strategy. Tax rates on individuals were reduced in stages between 1981 and 1984 and then again in 1986. By 1987, the richest Americans were in the 28 percent tax bracket, and most taxpayers were in the 15 percent bracket. Such low tax rates, supply siders argued, augment the supplies of both labor and capital.

2. *Reduce Taxes on Income from Savings*. One extreme form of this proposal would simply exempt from taxation all income from interest and dividends. Since income must be either consumed or saved, this would, in effect, change our present personal income tax into a tax on consumer spending.

3. *Reduce the Corporation Income Tax*. By reducing the tax burden on corporations, it is argued, the government can provide both greater investment incentives (by raising the profitability of investment) and more investable funds (by letting companies keep more of their earnings). This advice was followed in 1981 by making depreciation allowances more generous[2] and in 1986 by lowering the corporate tax rate.

---

[2]A company investing in a machine or factory may not deduct the entire cost of that asset as a business expense in the year it is purchased. Instead, it must spread the cost over the lifetime of the asset in a series of tax deductions called *depreciation allowances*. Naturally, firms prefer to get these allowances sooner rather than later, because higher depreciation in the early years of an investment means an immediate cut in tax burdens.

A tax cut specifically aimed at the supply side, if successful, will shift *both* aggregate demand *and* aggregate supply to the right. In this diagram, equilibrium is initially at point *E*, where demand curve D_0D_0 intersects supply curve S_0S_0. After the supply-side tax cut, the aggregate demand curve is D_1D_1 and the aggregate supply curve is S_1S_1, so equilibrium is at point *C*. As compared with the results of a tax cut that works only on the demand side (point *A*), the supply-side tax cut raises output more and prices less.

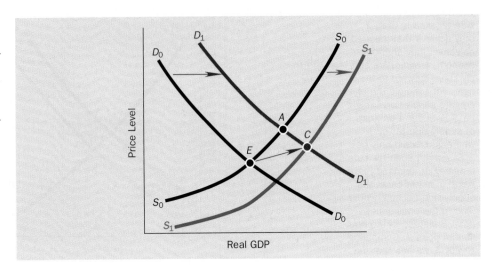

---

4. *Provide Tax Credits for Research and Development.* To encourage companies to spend money on research and development, Congress allows special tax reductions for firms that do so. The hope is obvious: more R & D should lead to improvements in technology.

Let us suppose, for the moment, that a successful supply-side tax cut is enacted to help close a recessionary gap. Since *both* aggregate demand *and* aggregate supply increase simultaneously, the economy may be able to avoid the painful inflationary consequences of an expansionary fiscal policy that were shown in Figure 11–7.

Figure 11–9 illustrates this conclusion. The two aggregate demand curves and the initial aggregate supply curve S_0S_0 are carried over directly from Figure 11–7. But we have introduced an additional supply curve, S_1S_1, to reflect the successful supply-side tax cut depicted in Figure 11–8. The equilibrium of the economy moves from *E* to *C*, whereas with a conventional demand-side tax cut it would have moved from *E* to *A*. As compared with point *A*, output is higher and prices are lower at point *C*.

A good deal, you say! Indeed it is. The supply-side argument is extremely attractive in principle. The question is: Does it work in practice? Can we actually do what is depicted in Figure 11–9? Let us consider some difficulties.

SOME FLIES IN THE OINTMENT

Supply-side economics was, and remains, controversial. Critics rarely question the goals of supply-side economics or the basic idea that lower taxes improve incentives. They argue, instead, that supply siders exaggerate the beneficial effects of tax cuts and ignore some undesirable side effects. Here is a brief rundown of some of the main objections to supply-side tax cuts:

1. *Small Magnitude of Supply-Side Effects*. The first objection is that supply siders are simply too optimistic: we really do not know how to do what Figure 11–8 shows. While it is easy, for example, to design tax cuts that make working more *attractive* financially, people may not actually behave this way. Instead, they may find themselves able to afford the goods and services they want with fewer hours of labor, and react by working *less*. Most of the statistical evidence suggests that we should expect tax reductions to lead to very small increases in either labor supply or household savings. As economist Charles Schultze once quipped: "There's nothing wrong with supply-side economics that division by ten couldn't cure."

2. *Demand-Side Effects*. The second objection is that supply siders underestimate the effects of tax cuts on aggregate demand. If you cut personal taxes, individuals *may possibly* work more, but they *will certainly* spend more. If you reduce business taxes and thereby encourage expansion of industrial capacity, business firms will demand more investment goods.

   The combined implications of these two objections are depicted in Figure 11–10. Here we depict a small outward shift in the aggregate supply curve (which reflects the first objection) and a large outward shift of the aggregate demand curve (which reflects the second). The result is that the economy's equilibrium moves from point A (the intersection of S_0S_0 and D_0D_0) to point E (the intersection of S_1S_1 and D_1D_1). Prices rise as output expands. The outcome differs only a little from the straight "demand-side" fiscal stimulus depicted in Figure 11–7 (page 261).

3. *Problems in Timing*. The most promising types of supply-side tax cuts seek to encourage greater business investment or R&D. But the benefits from

---

F i g u r e **11–10** **A MORE PESSIMISTIC VIEW OF SUPPLY-SIDE TAX CUTS**

If the effect of supply-side tax initatives on the aggregate supply curve is actually much smaller than suggested by Figure 11–8, the anti-inflationary impact will be correspondingly smaller. As you can see in this diagram, it is possible that a large shift in the aggregate demand curve could overwhelm the favorable effects of the tax cuts on the price level.

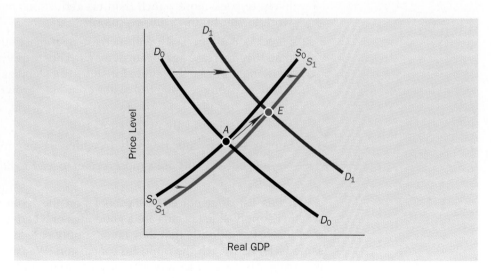

such activities do not arrive overnight. It may, in fact, take years before we see any substantial increases in industrial capacity. Thus it seems certain that the *expenditures* on investment goods come before the *expansion of capacity*. In a word, supply-side tax cuts will have their primary effects on aggregate demand in the short run. Effects on aggregate supply come later.

4. *Effect on the Distribution of Income.* The preceding objections all pertain to the likely effects of supply-side policies on aggregate supply and demand. But there is a different problem that bears mention: most supply-side initiatives increase income inequality. While raising the incomes of the wealthiest members of our society may not be their primary aim, most supply-side cuts cannot help but concentrate their benefits on the rich simply because it is the rich who own most of the capital.

    Indeed, this tilt toward the rich is almost an inescapable corollary of supply-side logic. The basic aim of supply-side economics is to increase the incentives for working and investing, that is, to increase the gap between the rewards of those who succeed in the economic game (by working hard, investing well, or by just plain luck) and those who fail. It can hardly be surprising, therefore, that supply-side policies tend to increase economic inequality.

5. *Losses of Tax Revenue.* You can hardly help noticing that most of the policies suggested by supply siders involve cutting one tax or another. Thus, unless some other tax is raised or spending is cut, supply-side tax cuts are bound to raise the government budget deficit—as they certainly did in the 1980s.

TOWARD ASSESSMENT OF SUPPLY-SIDE ECONOMICS

On balance, most economists have reached the following conclusions about supply-side tax initiatives:

1. The likely effectiveness of supply-side tax cuts depends on what kinds of taxes are cut. Tax reductions aimed at stimulating business investment are likely to pack more punch than tax reductions aimed at getting people to work longer hours or to save more.

2. Such tax cuts probably will increase aggregate supply much more slowly than they increase aggregate demand. Thus supply-side policies should not be thought of as a substitute for short-run stabilization policy, but rather as a way to promote (slightly) faster economic growth in the long run.

3. Demand-side effects of supply-side tax cuts are likely to overwhelm supply-side effects, especially in the short run.

4. Supply-side tax cuts are likely to widen income inequalities.

5. Supply-side tax cuts are almost certain to lead to bigger, not smaller, budget deficits.

But this list does not close the books on the issue. It does not even tell us whether supply-side tax cuts are a good idea or a bad one. Some people will look over this list and decide that they favor supply-side tax cuts; others, perusing the same facts, will reach the opposite conclusion. We cannot say that either group is "wrong" because, like almost every economic policy, supply-side economics has its pros and cons.

Clintonomics: A New Brand of Supply-Side Economics

President Bill Clinton advertised his economic program as a reversal of Reaganomics. In many ways, it is. But there are also similarities in that both Clintonomics and Reaganomics focus on aggregate supply rather than on aggregate demand. The following excerpt from the Clinton administration's first economic report puts the emphasis squarely on investment and on increases in the economy's capacity to produce.

In recent years, our leaders . . . embraced trickle-down policies that benefitted the wealthy at the expense of the middle class and the working poor. We have deluded ourselves that somehow economic growth and fairness are at odds, when in fact they go hand in hand. While the privileged few have prospered, millions of Americans who worked hard and played by the rules have been left behind. . . . Debt has soared as individuals, businesses, and governments have lived beyond their means. Our commitment to invest in the future and to bequeath a promising future to our children has somehow fallen by the wayside.

To reverse the legacy of failure and move toward our vision of the future, drastic changes in Federal policy are needed.

The over-arching theme of the Clinton Administration's economic plan is *increasing public and private investment* in the broadest sense. To ensure more productive, higher-wage jobs and greater economic opportunities for ourselves and our children, we need to devote a larger share of our current resources to modernizing factories and equipment, developing skills, and accelerating the advance of technology. We must increase the share of the Government's budget devoted to investment in future growth and must create incentives for the private sector to shift from consumption to investment. The need to increase investment motivates all three elements of the Clinton economic plan: stimulus, investment, and deficit reduction.

The *stimulus* package* is designed to ensure that recovery from recession is strong and durable.

What we call stimulus in this plan, however, is not a conventional prescription for adding to consumer demand by cutting taxes or creating make-work jobs. Instead, it is a down payment on longer-run investment.

The *investment* package proposes major additions to ongoing activities that expand America's capacity to produce . . . It is designed to help fill the investment deficit by increasing spending for highways and other infrastructure, to enhance the opportunities and skills of future workers, to accelerate the development and use of science and technology, to improve the delivery of health care for underserved groups, and to increase incentives and opportunities for productive employment.

The *deficit reduction* plan makes a vital contribution to increasing investment and raising standards of living by gradually reducing the structural deficit in the Federal budget. Cutting the deficit will reduce the Federal Government's drain on national savings, lower long-term interest rates, and encourage productive private investment.

*The stimulus package was blocked in the Senate by a Republican filibuster and never became law.
SOURCE: *A Vision of Change for America*, White House report, February 17, 1993, pages 1, 21–22.

Why, then, did so many economists and politicians react so negatively to supply-side economics in the early 1980s? The main reason seems to be that the claims made by the most ardent supply siders were clearly excessive. Naturally, these claims were proven wrong. But showing that wild claims are wild does not dispose of the kernel of truth in supply-side economics: reductions in marginal tax rates do improve economic incentives. Any specific supply-side tax cut must be judged on its individual merits.

CLINTONOMICS AS SUPPLY-SIDE ECONOMICS

During the 1992 presidential campaign, Bill Clinton attacked the Reagan-Bush brand of supply-side economics as "trickle-down economics," and argued that it had failed. He emphasized, in particular, the last two items in our assessment: the effects on income inequality and the budget deficit. The voters apparently agreed.

Ironically, however, candidate Clinton also ran on an avowedly supply-side platform—though it was quite different from Reaganomics. President Clinton's emphasis was and is on building up the nation's resources of labor, capital, and technology so that our capacity to produce will be higher in the long run. This, of course, is precisely the goal of supply-side economics: to push the aggregate supply curve outward.

But, unlike Presidents Reagan and Bush, President Clinton did not propose to accomplish this mainly by cutting taxes. While some tax cuts were included in the Clinton plan, especially tax credits for investment and R&D, there were also tax increases. The real emphasis of Clintonomics is on improving the quality of the American workforce through more and better education and training. It is a program plainly focused on the long run. Only time will tell how well it works.

Summary

1. The government's **fiscal policy** is its plan for managing aggregate demand through its spending and taxing programs. It is made jointly by the president and Congress.

2. The net effect of the government on aggregate demand—and hence on equilibrium output and prices—depends on whether the expansionary effects of its spending are greater or smaller than the contractionary effects of its taxes.

3. Since consumer spending (C) depends on disposable income (DI), and DI is GDP minus taxes, any change in taxes will shift the consumption schedule on a 45° line diagram. The nature of this shift depends on whether it is **fixed taxes** or **variable taxes** that are changed.

4. Such shifts in the consumption function caused by tax policy are subject to the same multiplier as autonomous shifts in G, I, or $X - IM$.

5. An income tax reduces the size of this common multiplier.

6. The multiplier for changes in taxes is smaller than the multiplier for changes in government purchases.

7. **Government transfer payments** are treated like negative taxes, not like government purchases of goods and services, because they influence total spending only indirectly through their effect on consumption.

8. If the multipliers were known precisely, it would be possible to plan any of a variety of fiscal policies to eliminate either a recessionary or an inflationary gap. Recessionary gaps can be cured by raising G, cutting taxes, or increasing transfers. Inflationary gaps can be cured by cutting G, raising taxes, or reducing transfers.

9. Active stabilization policy can be carried out either by means that tend to expand the size of government (by raising either G or T when appropriate) or by means that hold back the size of government (by reducing either G or T when appropriate).

10. Expansionary fiscal policy can cure recessions, but it normally exacts a cost in terms of higher inflation. This dilemma has led to a great deal of interest in **"supply-side" tax cuts** designed to stimulate aggregate supply.

11. Supply-side tax cuts aim to push the economy's aggregate supply curve outward to the right. If successful, they can expand the economy and reduce inflation at the same time—a highly desirable outcome.

12. But critics point out at least five serious problems with supply-side tax cuts: they also stimulate aggregate demand; the beneficial effects on aggregate supply may be small; the demand-side effects occur before the supply-side effects; they make the income distribution more unequal; and large tax cuts lead to large budget deficits.

Fiscal policy

Fixed taxes

Variable taxes

Government transfer payments

Effect of income taxes on the multiplier

Supply-side tax cuts

1. America is beginning to reap a "peace dividend" from the end of the Cold War, that is, a reduction in military expenditures. How would GDP in the United States be affected if the peace dividend were

   a. used to reduce the budget deficit, so that government purchases fell?

   b. used for other public purposes, so that government purchases remained the same?

2. Consider an economy in which tax collections are always $400 and in which the four components of aggregate demand are as follows:

GDP	TAXES	DI	C	I	G	(X − IM)
$680	$400	$280	$210	$100	$400	$15
740	400	340	255	100	400	15
800	400	400	300	100	400	15
860	400	460	345	100	400	15
920	400	520	390	100	400	15

Find the equilibrium of this economy graphically. What is the marginal propensity to consume? What is the multiplier? What would happen to equilibrium GDP if government purchases were reduced by $30 and the price level were unchanged?

3. Now consider a related economy in which investment is also $100, government purchases are also $400, net exports are also $15, and the price level is also fixed. But taxes now vary with income, and as a result the consumption schedule looks like the following:

GDP	TAXES	DI	C
$680	$360	$320	$255
740	380	360	285
800	400	400	315
860	420	440	345
920	440	480	375

Find the equilibrium graphically. What is the marginal propensity to consume? What is the tax rate? Use your diagram to show the effect of a decrease of

$30 in government purchases. What is the multiplier? Compare this answer to your answer to Question 2 above. What do you conclude?

4. Explain why G has the same multiplier as I, but taxes have a different multiplier.

5. Return to the hypothetical economy in Question 2 and suppose that *both* taxes and government purchases are increased by $60. Find the new equilibrium under the assumption that consumer spending continues to be exactly three-quarters of disposable income (as it is in Question 2).

6. If the government today decides that aggregate demand is excessive and is causing inflation, what options are open to it? What if it decides that aggregate demand is too weak instead?

7. Suppose that you are in charge of the fiscal policy of the economy in Question 2. There is an inflationary gap and you want to reduce income by $60. What specific actions can you take to achieve this goal?

8. Now put yourself in charge of the economy in Question 3, and suppose that full employment comes at a GDP of $920. How can you push income up to that level?

9. Which of the proposed supply-side tax cuts appeals to you most? Draw up a list of arguments for and against enacting such a cut right now.

10. (more difficult) Advocates of an investment tax credit (see Chapter 8, page 184) argue that it will raise aggregate supply by spurring investment. But, of course, any increase in investment spending will also raise aggregate demand. Compare the effects on aggregate supply and demand of three different types of investment tax credit:

    a. The credit is applied to *all* investments.

    b. The credit is applied only to purchases of certain types of assets, such as industrial equipment.

    c. The credit is applied only once investment exceeds some base level.

Which of the three seems more desirable. Why?

| *Appendix* | ALGEBRAIC TREATMENT OF FISCAL POLICY AND AGGREGATE DEMAND |

In this appendix we explain the simple algebra behind the fiscal policy multipliers discussed in the chapter. In so doing, we deal only with a simplified case in which prices do not change. While it is possible to work out the corresponding algebra for the more realistic aggregate demand-aggregate supply analysis with variable prices, the analysis is rather complicated and is best left to more advanced courses.

We start with the example used in the chapter (especially on pages 254 and 256). The government spends $1300 billion on goods and services ($G = 1300$) and levies an income tax equal to 20 percent of GDP. So, if the symbol T denotes tax receipts:

$$T = .20\,Y.$$

Since the consumption function we have been working with is

$$C = 300 + 0.75\,DI,$$

where DI is disposable income, and since disposable income and GDP are related by the accounting identity

$$DI = Y - T,$$

it follows that the C schedule used in the 45° line diagram is described by the algebraic equation:

$$
\begin{aligned}
C &= 300 + 0.75(Y - T) \\
&= 300 + 0.75(Y - .2Y) \\
&= 300 + 0.75(.8Y) \\
&= 300 + 0.6\,Y.
\end{aligned}
$$

We can now apply the equilibrium condition

$$Y = C + I + G + (X - IM).$$

Since investment in this example is $I = 900$ and net exports are -100, substituting for C, I, G, and $(X - IM)$ into this equation gives

$$
\begin{aligned}
Y &= 300 + 0.6\,Y + 900 + 1300 - 100 \\
0.4Y &= 2400 \\
Y &= 6000.
\end{aligned}
$$

This is all there is to finding equilibrium GDP in an economy with a government.

To find the multiplier for government spending, increase G by 1 and resolve the problem:

$$
\begin{aligned}
Y &= C + I + G + (X - IM) \\
Y &= 300 + 0.6Y + 900 + 1301 - 100 \\
0.4Y &= 2401 \\
Y &= 6002.5
\end{aligned}
$$

So the multiplier is $6002.5 - 6000 = 2.5$, as stated in the text.

To find the multiplier for an increase in fixed taxes, change the tax schedule to

$$T = .2Y + 1.$$

Disposable income is then

$$
\begin{aligned}
DI = Y - T &= Y - (.2Y + 1) \\
&= .8Y - 1,
\end{aligned}
$$

so the consumption function is

$$
\begin{aligned}
C &= 300 + 0.75DI \\
&= 300 + 0.75(.8Y - 1) \\
&= 299.25 + 0.6Y.
\end{aligned}
$$

Solving for equilibrium GDP as usual gives

$$
\begin{aligned}
Y &= C + I + G + (X - IM) \\
Y &= 299.25 + 0.6Y + 900 + 1300 - 100 \\
0.4Y &= 2399.25 \\
Y &= 5998.125
\end{aligned}
$$

So a $1 increase in fixed taxes lowers Y by $1.875. The tax multiplier is -1.875.

Now let us proceed to a more general solution, using symbols rather than specific numbers. The equations of the model are as follows

$$Y = C + I + G + (X - IM) \qquad (1)$$

is the usual equilibrium condition;

$$C = a + bDI \qquad (2)$$

is the same consumption function we have used in the appendixes of Chapters 8 and 9;

$$DI = Y - T \qquad (3)$$

is the accounting identity relating disposable income to GDP;

$$T = T_0 + tY \qquad (4)$$

is the tax function, where T_0 represents fixed taxes (which are zero in our numerical example) and t represents the tax rate (which is 0.2 in the example). Finally, I, G, and $(X - IM)$ are just fixed numbers.

We begin the solution by substituting (3) and (4) into (2) to derive the consumption schedule relating C to Y:

$$C = a + b\,DI$$
$$C = a + b(Y - T)$$
$$C = a + b(Y - T_0 - tY)$$
$$C = a - bT_0 + b(1 - t)Y. \qquad (5)$$

You will notice that a change in fixed taxes (T_0) shifts the *intercept* of the C schedule while a change in the tax rate (t) changes its *slope*, as explained in the text (pages 251–53).

Next substitute (5) into (1) to find equilibrium GDP:

$$Y = C + I + G + (X - IM)$$
$$Y = a - bT_0 + b(1 - t)Y + I + G + (X - IM)$$
$$[1 - b(1 - t)]Y = a - bT_0 + I + G + (X - IM)$$

or

$$Y = \frac{a - bT_0 + I + G + (X - IM)}{1 - b(1 - t)}. \qquad (6)$$

Equation (6) shows us that the multiplier for G, I, a, or $(X - IM)$ is

$$\text{Multiplier} = \frac{1}{1 - b(1 - t)}.$$

To see that this is in fact the multiplier, raise any of G, I, a, or $(X - IM)$ by 1 unit. In each case, equation (6) would be changed to read:

$$Y = \frac{a - bT_0 + I + G + (X - IM) + 1}{1 - b(1 - t)}.$$

Subtracting equation (6) from this expression gives

the change in Y stemming from a one-unit change in G or I or a:

$$\text{Change in } Y = \frac{1}{1 - b(1 - t)}.$$

We noted in Chapter 9 (page 213) that if there were no income tax $(t = 0)$, a realistic value for b (the marginal propensity to consume) would yield a multiplier of 10, which is much bigger than the true multiplier. Now that we have added taxes to the model, our multiplier formula produces much more realistic numbers. Approximate values for the parameters for the U.S. economy are $b = \frac{9}{10}$ and $t = \frac{1}{3}$. The multiplier formula then gives:

$$\text{Multiplier} = \frac{1}{1 - \frac{9}{10}(1 - \frac{1}{3})}$$
$$= \frac{1}{1 - \frac{3}{5}} = \frac{1}{\frac{2}{5}}$$
$$= 2.5$$

which is not far from its actual estimated value, nearly 2.

Finally, we can see from equation (6) that the multiplier for a change in fixed taxes (T_0) is

$$\text{Tax multiplier} = \frac{-b}{1 - b(1 - t)}.$$

For the example considered in the text and earlier in this appendix, $b = 0.75$ and $t = 0.2$, so the formula gives:

$$\frac{-.75}{1 - .75(1 - .2)} = \frac{-.75}{1 - .75(.8)}$$
$$\frac{-.75}{1 - .6} = \frac{-.75}{.4} = -1.875.$$

According to these figures, each $1 *increase* in T_0 *reduces* Y by $1.875.

Questions for Review

1. In an economy described by the following set of equations:

$$C = 20 + .8DI$$
$$I = 220$$
$$G = 380$$
$$(X - IM) = 20$$
$$T = 100 + .25Y,$$

find the equilibrium level of GDP. Then find the multipliers for government purchases and for fixed taxes. If full employment comes at $Y = 1300$, what are some policies that would get GDP there?

2. This is a variant of the previous problem that approaches things the way a fiscal policy planner might. In an economy whose consumption function and tax

function are as given in Question 1, with investment fixed at 220 and net exports fixed at 20, find the value of G that would make GDP equal to 1300.

3. You are given the following information about an economy.

$$C = 10 + .9\,DI$$
$$I = 140$$
$$G = 540$$
$$(X - IM) = -90$$
$$T = (1/3)Y$$

a. Find equilibrium GDP and the budget deficit.

b. Suppose the government, unhappy with the budget deficit, decides to cut government spending by precisely the amount of the deficit you found in (a). What actually happens to GDP and the budget deficit, and why?

4. (More difficult) In the economy considered in Question 3, suppose the government, seeing that it has not wiped out the deficit, keeps cutting G until it succeeds in balancing the budget. What levels of GDP will then prevail?

Chapter 12

MONEY AND THE BANKING SYSTEM

[Money] is a machine for doing quickly and commodiously what would be done, though less quickly and commodiously, without it.

JOHN STUART MILL

The circular flow diagrams that were used in earlier chapters to explain equilibrium GDP had a "financial system" in their upper left-hand corners. Savings flowed into this system and investment flowed out. Something obviously goes on inside the financial system to channel the savings into investment, and it is time we learned just what this something is. ¶ There is another, equally important, reason for studying the financial system. *Fiscal policy* is not the only lever the government has on the economy's aggregate demand curve; it also exercises significant control over aggregate demand by manipulating *monetary policy*. If we are to understand monetary policy (the subject of Chapters 13 and 14), we must first acquire some understanding of the financial system. ¶ The present chapter has three major objectives. It first seeks to explain the nature of money: what it is, what purposes it serves, and how it is measured. Once this is done, we turn our attention to the banking system, explaining its historical origins, the nature of banking as a business, and why this industry is so heavily regulated. Finally, we learn how banks create money—a subject that is of great importance because you cannot hope to understand monetary policy until you first understand how money is created.

At the end of the chapter, we will see why government authorities must exercise control over the supply of money in a modern economy. This leads naturally into next chapter's discussion of *central banking*, that is, the techniques used to implement monetary policy.

POLICY ISSUE: SHOULD WE DEREGULATE OR REREGULATE THE BANKS?

As this is written, bank regulation stands at a crossroads. Some observers think the United States went too far in deregulating its banking and financial system in the 1980s and needs to take a step or two back in the opposite direction. Such people fear that deregulation has made our financial system more fragile and harder to control. The massive wave of bankruptcies in the savings and loan industry in the 1980s and the much smaller outbreak of bank failures in the early 1990s seemed to support those who claimed that deregulation had gone too far. And, indeed, both banks and, especially, S&Ls were subjected to some new regulations.

Others, however, argue that we should push further down the path of deregulation. True, legal limitations on interest rates have been abolished, and financial institutions can now engage in a much wider spectrum of activities than was true a decade ago. But banking across state lines is still heavily restricted, and banks can neither own nor be owned by industrial companies. Furthermore, these people argue, heavy-handed banking regulators made the 1990–1991 recession worse than need be by discouraging lending. More deregulation, it is claimed, would continue to make our financial system more fluid and our economy more efficient.

To make an informed judgment on the relative merits of deregulation and reregulation, we must first ask a more basic question, Why were banks so heavily regulated in the first place?

Banking is certainly not heavily monopolized. While there are financial giants such as Citibank (New York) and Bank of America (California), the industry is populated by literally thousands of small banks located in cities and towns throughout the country. There are more than 12,000 commercial banks and over 3000 savings institutions nationwide. So why did government regulations formerly tell banks, to some degree, how much they could accept in deposits, how much interest they could pay on these deposits, what types of investments they could make, and so on?

A first reason is that the major "output" of the banking industry—the nation's supply of money—is an important determinant of aggregate demand, as we will see in Chapter 13. Bank managers presumably do what is best for their stockholders. That, at any rate, is their job. But as we shall see, what is best for bank stockholders may not be best for the whole economy. For this reason, the government does not allow bankers to determine the level of the nation's money supply by profit considerations alone.

A second reason for the extensive regulation of banks is concern for the safety of depositors. In a free-enterprise system, new businesses are born and die every day; and no one other than those people immediately involved takes much notice of these goings-on. When a firm goes bankrupt, stockholders lose money and employees may lose their jobs. (The latter may not even happen if new management takes over the assets of the bankrupt firm.) But, except for the case of very large firms, that is about it.

But banking is different. If banks were treated like other firms, depositors would lose money whenever one went bankrupt. That is bad enough by itself, but the real danger comes in the case of a **run on a bank**. When depositors get jittery about the security of their money, they may all rush in at once to cash in their accounts. For reasons we will learn in this chapter, most banks could not survive a "run" like this and would be forced into insolvency. Worse yet, this disease is highly contagious. If Mr. Smith hears that his neighbor has just lost her life savings because the Main Street National Bank went broke, he is quite likely to rush to his own bank to make a hefty withdrawal. In fact, that is precisely what happened to a number of savings banks in the 1980s.

Without modern forms of bank regulation, therefore, one bank failure might lead to another. Indeed, bank failures were common throughout most of American history and have become distressingly common again in recent years. (See Figure 12–1.) But recent bank failures generally have not been precipitated by runs because the government has taken steps to ensure that such an infectious disease, if it occurs, will not spread. It has done this in several ways that will be mentioned in this chapter.

BARTER VERSUS MONETARY EXCHANGE

Money is so much a part of our day-to-day existence that we are likely to take it for granted, failing to appreciate all that it accomplishes. But it is important to realize that money is very much a social contrivance. Like the wheel, it had to be invented. The most obvious way to trade commodities is not by using money, but by **barter**—a system in which people exchange one good directly for another. And the best way to appreciate what monetary exchange accomplishes is to imagine a world without it.

Under a system of direct barter, if Farmer Jones grows corn and has a craving for peanuts, he has to find a peanut farmer, say, Farmer Smith, with a taste for corn. If he finds such a person (this was called the *double coincidence of wants* by the classical economists), they make the trade. If this sounds easy, try to imagine how busy Farmer Jones would be if he had to repeat the sequence for every commodity he consumed in a week. For the most part, the desired double coincidences of wants are more likely to turn out to be double wants of coincidence, where Jones gets no peanuts and Smith gets no corn. Worse yet, with so much time spent looking for trading partners, Jones would have far less time to grow corn. Thus:

Money greases the wheels of exchange, and thus makes the whole economy more productive.

Under a monetary system, Farmer Jones gives up his corn for money. He does so not because he wants the money per se, but because of what that money can buy. Money makes his shopping tasks much easier, for it allows him simply to locate a peanut farmer who wants money. And what peanut farmer does not? For these reasons, monetary exchange replaced barter at a very early stage of human civilization, and only extreme circumstances, like massive wars and runaway inflations, have been able to bring barter (temporarily) back.

| Figure | 12-1 | BANK FAILURES IN THE UNITED STATES, 1915–1991 |

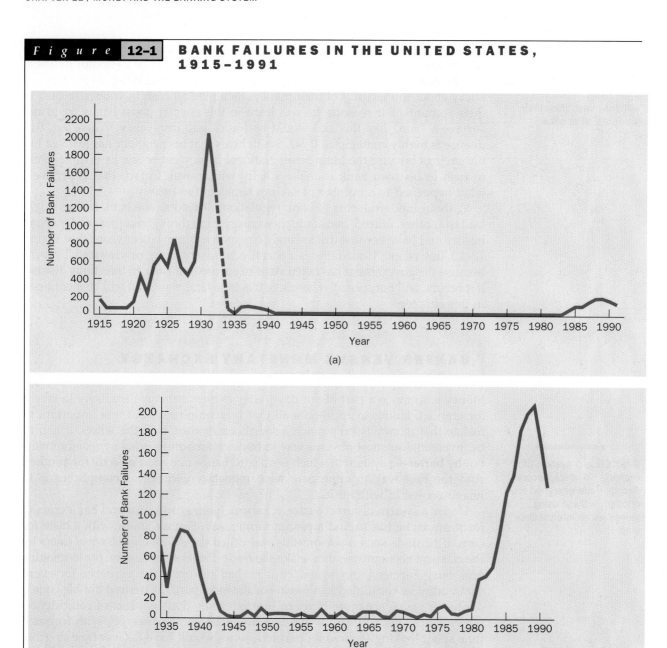

(a)

(b)

This chart shows the number of commercial banks that failed each year from 1915 through 1991. Notice the sharp drop in the number of failures from 1932 to 1934 and the steep rise in recent years. Failures clearly are much less common in the postwar period than they were in earlier years. But they have become much more frequent since the 1980s than they were between World War II and 1980.

SOURCE: Federal Deposit Insurance Corporation.

THE CONCEPTUAL DEFINITION OF MONEY

MONEY is the standard object used in exchanging goods and services. In short, money is the **MEDIUM OF EXCHANGE**.

The **UNIT OF ACCOUNT** is the standard unit for quoting prices.

A **STORE OF VALUE** is an item used to store wealth from one point in time to another.

Monetary exchange is the alternative to barter. In a system of monetary exchange, people trade **money** for goods when they purchase something and trade goods for money when they sell something; but they do not trade goods directly for other goods. This defines money's principal role as the **medium of exchange**. But once it has become accepted as the medium of exchange, whatever object is serving as money is bound to take on other functions as well. For one, it will inevitably become the **unit of account**, that is, the standard unit for quoting prices. Thus, if inhabitants of an idyllic tropical island used coconuts as money, they would be foolish to quote prices in terms of sea shells.

Money may also come to be used as a **store of value**. If Farmer Jones temporarily produces and sells corn of more value than he wants to consume, he may find it convenient to store the difference in the form of money until he wants to use it. This is because he knows that money can be "sold" easily for goods and services at a later date, whereas land, gold, and other stores of value might not be. Of course, if money pays no interest and inflation is substantial, he may decide to forgo the convenience of money and store his wealth in some other form rather than see its purchasing power rapidly eroded. So this role of money is far from inevitable.

Since money may not always serve as a store of value, and since there are many stores of value other than money, it is best not to include the store-of-value function as part of our conceptual definition of money. Instead, we simply label as "money" whatever serves as the medium of exchange.

WHAT SERVES AS MONEY?

Anthropologists and historians will testify that a bewildering variety of things have served as money in different times and places. Cattle, stones, candy bars, cigarettes, woodpecker scalps, porpoise teeth, and giraffe tails are a few of the more colorful examples.

A **COMMODITY MONEY** is an object in use as a medium of exchange, but which also has a substantial value in alternative (nonmonetary) uses.

In primitive or less organized societies, the commodities that served as money generally had value in themselves. If not used as money, cattle could be slaughtered for food, cigarettes could be smoked, and so on. But such **commodity money** generally runs into several severe difficulties. To be useful as a medium of exchange, the commodity must be divisible. This makes cattle a poor choice. It must also be of uniform, or at least readily identifiable, quality so that inferior substitutes are easy to recognize. This may be why woodpecker scalps never achieved great popularity. The medium of exchange must also be storable and durable, which presents a serious problem for candy-bar money. Finally, because commodity money needs to be carried and stored, it is helpful if the item is compact, that is, has high value per unit of volume and weight. (See the boxed insert on page 279).

All of these traits make it sensible that gold and silver have circulated as money since the first coins were struck about 2500 years ago. As they have high value in nonmonetary uses, a lot of purchasing power can be carried without too much weight. Pieces of gold are also storable, divisible (with a little trouble), and of identifiable quality (with a little more trouble).

The same characteristics suggest that paper would make an ideal money. Since we can print any number on it that we please, we can make paper money as divisible as we like and also make it possible to carry a large value in a lightweight and compact form. Paper is easy to store and, with a little cleverness, we can make counterfeiting hard (though never impossible). The Chinese originated paper money in the eleventh century, and Marco Polo brought word of this invention to Europe.

Paper cannot, however, serve as a commodity money because its value per square inch in alternative uses is so small. A paper currency that is repudiated by its issuer can, perhaps, be used as wallpaper or to wrap fish, but these uses will surely represent only a small fraction of the paper's value as money.[1] Contrary to the popular expression, such a currency literally *is* worth the paper it is printed on, which is to say that it is not worth much. Thus paper money is always **fiat money**.

FIAT MONEY is money that is decreed as such by the government. It is of little value as a commodity, but it maintains its value as a medium of exchange because people have faith that the issuer will stand behind the pieces of printed paper and limit their production.

Money in the contemporary United States is almost entirely fiat money. Look at a dollar bill. Next to George Washington's picture it states: "This note is legal tender for all debts public and private." Nowhere on the certificate is there a promise, stated or implied, that the U.S. government will exchange it for anything else. A dollar bill is convertible into 4 quarters, 10 dimes, 20 nickels, or any other similar combination, but not into gold, chocolate, or any other commodity.

Why do people hold these pieces of paper? Only because they know that others are willing to accept them for things of intrinsic value—food, rent, shoes, and so on. If this confidence ever evaporated, these dollar bills would cease serving as a medium of exchange and, given that they make ugly wallpaper, would become virtually worthless.

But don't panic. This is not likely to occur. Our current monetary system has evolved over hundreds of years during which *commodity* money was first replaced by *full-bodied paper money*—paper certificates that were backed by gold or silver of equal value held in the issuer's vaults. Then the full-bodied paper money was replaced by certificates that were only partially backed by gold and silver. Finally,

---

[1]The first paper money issued by the federal government, the Continental dollar, was essentially repudiated. (Actually, the new government of the United States redeemed the Continentals for 1 cent on the dollar in the 1790s.) This gave rise to the derisive expression, "It's not worth a Continental."

Dealing by Wheeling on Yap

Primitive forms of money still exist in some remote places, as this extract from a newspaper article shows.

YAP, Micronesia—On this tiny South Pacific Island . . . the currency is as solid as a rock. In fact, it is rock. Limestone to be precise.

For nearly 2,000 years the Yapese have used large stone wheels to pay for major purchases, such as land, canoes and permission to marry. Yap is a U.S. trust territory, and the dollar is used in grocery stores and gas stations. But reliance on stone money . . . continues.

Buying property with stones is "much easier than buying it with U.S. dollars," says John Chodad, who recently purchased a building lot with a 30-inch stone wheel. "We don't know the value of the U.S.

Stone wheel money from Yap.

dollar."

Stone wheels don't make good pocket money, so for small transactions, Yapese use other forms of currency, such as beer. . . .

Besides stone wheels and beer, the Yapese sometimes spend *gaw*, consisting of necklaces of stone beads strung together around a

whale's tooth. They also can buy things with *yar*, a currency made from large sea shells. But these are small change.

The people of Yap have been using stone money ever since a Yapese warrior named Anagumang first brought the huge stones over-from limestone caverns on neighboring Palau, some 1,500 to 2,000 years ago. Inspired by the moon, he fashioned the stone into large circles. The rest is history . . . .

By custom, the stones are worthless when broken. You never hear people on Yap musing about wanting a piece of the rock. . . .

SOURCE: Adapted from Art Pine, "Hard Assets, or Why a Loan in Yap Is Hard to Roll Over," *The Wall Street Journal*, March 29, 1984, page 1.

we arrived at our present system, in which paper money has no "backing" whatsoever. Like a hesitant swimmer who first dips her toes, then her legs, then her whole body into a cold swimming pool, we have "tested the water" at each step of the way—and found it to our liking. It is unlikely that we will ever take a step back in the other direction.

HOW THE QUANTITY OF MONEY IS MEASURED

Since the amount of money in circulation is of profound importance for the determination of national product and the price level, it is important for the government to know how much money there is, that is, to devise some *measure* of the money supply.

Our conceptual definition of money describes it as the medium of exchange. But this raises difficult questions about just what items to include and exclude when we count up the money supply—questions that have long made the statistical definition of money a subject of dispute. In fact, the U.S. government has several official definitions of the money supply, two of which we will meet in this section.

Some components are obvious. All of our coins and paper money, the small change of our economic system, clearly should count as money. But we cannot stop there if we want to include the main vehicle for making payments in our society, for the lion's share of our nation's payments are made neither in metal nor in paper money, but by check.

Checking deposits are actually no more than bookkeeping entries in bank ledgers. Many people think of checks simply as a convenient way to give coins or dollar bills to someone else. But that is not so. In fact, the volume of money held in the form of checking deposits far exceeds the volume of currency. For example, when you pay the grocer $50 by check, dollar bills rarely change hands. Instead, that check normally travels back to your bank, where $50 is deducted from the bookkeeping entry that records your account and added to the bookkeeping entry for your grocer's account. (If you and the grocer hold accounts at different banks, more books get involved; but still no coins or bills are likely to be moved.)

Since so many transactions are made by check, it seems imperative that checking deposits be included in any useful definition of the money supply. Unfortunately, this is not an easy task nowadays because of the bewildering variety of ways to transfer money by check. Traditional checking accounts in commercial banks are the most familiar. But many people can also write checks on their savings accounts, on their deposits at credit unions, on their mutual funds, their accounts with stockbrokers, and so on.

One popular definition of the money supply draws the line early and includes only coins, paper money, travelers' checks, and certain checkable balances held in banks and savings institutions. In the official U.S. statistics, this narrowly defined concept of money is called **M1**. The left-hand side of Figure 12–2 shows the composition of M1 as of March 1993.

But there are other types of accounts that allow withdrawals by check and which therefore are candidates for inclusion in the money supply. Most notably, *money market deposit accounts* allow only a few checks per month but pay market-determined interest rates. Consumers have found these accounts extremely attractive vehicles for short-term investment, and balances in them now exceed all the checkable deposits included in M1.

In addition, many mutual fund organizations and brokerage houses offer *money market mutual funds*. These funds sell shares and use the proceeds to purchase a variety of short-term securities. But the important point, for our purposes, is that owners of shares in money market mutual funds can withdraw their funds simply by writing a check. So depositors can—and do—use their holdings of fund shares just like checking accounts.

Finally, although you cannot write a check on a *savings account*, many economists feel that modern banking procedures have blurred the distinction between checking balances and savings balances. For example, most banks these days offer convenient electronic transfers of funds from one account to another, either by telephone or by pushing a button on an automated teller. Consequently, savings balances can become checkable almost instantly. For this reason, savings accounts are included—along with money market deposit accounts, money market mutual fund shares, and a few other small items—in the broader definition of the money supply known as **M2**.

The narrowly defined money supply, usually abbreviated **M1**, is the sum of all coins and paper money in circulation, plus certain checkable deposit balances at banks and savings institutions.[2]

The broadly defined money supply, usually abbreviated **M2**, is the sum of all coins and paper money in circulation, plus all types of checking account balances, plus most forms of savings account balances, plus shares in money market mutual funds, and a few other minor items.

[2]This includes travelers' checks and NOW (negotiable order of withdrawal) accounts.

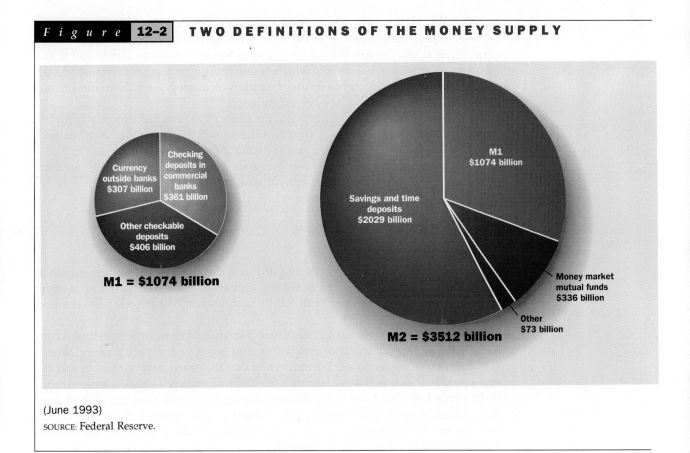

F i g u r e **12–2**   **TWO DEFINITIONS OF THE MONEY SUPPLY**

Currency outside banks $307 billion

Checking deposits in commercial banks $361 billion

Other checkable deposits $406 billion

M1 = $1074 billion

M1 $1074 billion

Savings and time deposits $2029 billion

Money market mutual funds $336 billion

Other $73 billion

M2 = $3512 billion

(June 1993)

SOURCE: Federal Reserve.

The composition of M2 as of March 1993 is shown on the right-hand side of Figure 12–2. You can see that savings deposits predominate, dwarfing everything that is included in M1. Figure 12–2 illustrates two points that are worth remembering. First, our money supply comes not only from banks, but also from savings institutions, brokerage houses, and mutual fund organizations. Second, however, banks still play a predominant role.

Some economists do not want to stop counting at M2; they prefer still broader definitions of money (M3, and so on) which include more types of bank deposits and other closely related assets. The problem with this approach is that there is no obvious place to stop, no clear line of demarcation between those assets that *are* money and those that are merely *close substitutes* for money—so called **near moneys**.

NEAR MONEYS are liquid assets that are close substitutes for money.

An asset's **LIQUIDITY** refers to the ease with which it can be converted into cash.

If we define an asset's **liquidity** as the ease with which it can be converted into cash, there is a range of assets of varying degrees of liquidity. Everything in M1 is completely "liquid"; the money market fund shares and passbook savings accounts included in M2 are a bit less so; and so on, until we encounter such things as short-term government bonds, which, while still quite liquid, would not normally be included in the money supply. Any number of different "Ms" can be defined—and have been—by drawing the line in different places.

And there are still more complexities. For example, credit cards clearly serve as a medium of exchange. So should they be included in the money supply? Yes, you say. But how would we do this? How much money does your credit card represent? Is it the amount you currently owe on the card, which may well be zero? Or is it your entire line of credit, even though you may never use it all? Neither seems a sensible choice, which is one reason why economists have—up to now—ignored credit cards in the definition of money. And there are further definitional issues that we have not mentioned.

But a first course in economics is not the place to get bogged down in complex definitional issues. So we will simply adhere to the convention that *"money" consists only of coins, paper money, and checkable deposits.*

Now that we have defined money and seen how it can be measured, we turn our attention to the principal creators of money—the banks.

HOW BANKING BEGAN

When Adam and Eve left the Garden of Eden, they did not encounter a branch of Citibank. Banking had to be invented, and some time passed before it came to be practiced as it is today. With a little imagination, we can see how the first banks must have begun.

When money was made of gold it was most inconvenient for consumers and merchants to carry it around and weigh and assay it for purity every time a transaction was made. So it is not surprising that the practice developed of leaving one's gold in the care of a goldsmith, who had safe storage facilities, and carrying in its place a receipt from the goldsmith stating that John Doe did indeed own five ounces of gold of a certain purity. When people began trading goods and services for the goldsmiths' receipts, rather than for the gold itself, the receipts became an early form of paper money.

At this stage, paper money was fully backed by gold. But gradually the goldsmiths began to notice that the amount of gold they were actually required to pay out in a day was but a small fraction of the total gold they had stored in their warehouses. Then one day some enterprising goldsmith hit upon a momentous idea that must have made him fabulously wealthy.

His thinking probably ran something like this. "I have 2000 ounces of gold stored away in my vault, for which I collect storage fees from my customers. If I get much more, I'll need an expensive new vault. But in the last year, I was never called upon to pay out more than 100 ounces on a single day. What harm could it do if I lent out, say, half the gold I now have? I'll still have more than enough to pay off any depositors that come in for a withdrawal, so no one will ever know the difference. And I could earn 30 additional ounces of gold each year in interest on the loans I make (at 3 percent interest on 1000 ounces). With this profit, I could lower my service charges to depositors and so attract still more deposits. I think I'll do it."

With this resolution, the modern system of **fractional reserve banking** was born. This system has three important features—features that are crucially important to this chapter.

FRACTIONAL RESERVE BANKING is a system under which bankers keep as reserves only a fraction of the funds they hold on deposit.

1. *Bank profitability.* By getting deposits at zero interest and lending some of them out at positive interest rates, goldsmiths made a profit. The history of banking as a profit-making industry was begun and has continued to this date. *Banks, like other enterprises, are in business to earn profits.*

2. *Bank discretion over the money supply.* When goldsmiths decided that they could get along by keeping only a fraction of their total deposits on reserve in their vaults and lending out the balance, they acquired the ability to *create money.* As long as they kept 100 percent reserves, each gold certificate represented exactly one ounce of gold. So whether people decided to carry their gold or leave it with their goldsmith did not affect the money supply, which was set by the volume of gold.

   With the advent of fractional reserve banking, however, new paper certificates were added whenever goldsmiths lent out some of the gold they held on deposit. The loans, in effect, created new money. In this way, the total amount of money came to depend on the amount of gold that each goldsmith felt compelled to maintain as reserves in his vault. For any given volume of gold on deposit, the lower the reserves the goldsmiths kept, the more loans they could make, and therefore the more money there would be. While we no longer use gold to back our money, this principle remains true today. *Bankers' business decisions influence the supply of money.*

3. *Exposure to runs.* A goldsmith who kept 100 percent reserves never had to worry about a run on his vault. Even if all his depositors showed up at the door at once, he always had enough gold to return their deposits. But as soon as the first goldsmith decided to get by with only fractional reserves, the possibility of a run on the vault became a real concern. If that first goldsmith who lent out half his gold had found 51 percent of his customers at his door one unlucky day, he would have had a lot of explaining to do. Similar problems have worried bankers for centuries. *The danger of a run on the bank has induced bankers to keep prudent reserves and to lend out money carefully.*

PRINCIPLES OF BANK MANAGEMENT: PROFITS VERSUS SAFETY

Bankers have a reputation, probably deserved, for conservatism in politics, dress, and business affairs. From what has been said so far, the economic rationale for this conservatism should be clear. Checking deposits are pure fiat money. Years ago, these deposits were "backed" by nothing more than the bank's promise to convert them into currency on demand. If people lost trust in a bank, the bank was doomed.

Thus, it has always been imperative for bankers to acquire a reputation for prudence. This they did in two principal ways. First, they had to maintain a sufficiently generous level of reserves to minimize their vulnerability to runs. Second, they had to be somewhat cautious in making loans and investments, since any large losses on their loans would undermine the confidence of depositors.

It is important to realize that banking under a system of fractional reserves is an inherently risky business that is rendered relatively safe only by cautious and prudent management. America's continuing history of bank failures bears sober testimony to the fact that many bankers have been neither cautious nor prudent. Why? Because this is not a recipe for high profits. Bank profits are maximized by keeping reserves as low as possible, by making at least some risky investments, and by giving loans to borrowers of questionable credit standing (because these borrowers will pay the highest interest rates).

The art of bank management is to strike the appropriate balance between the lure of profits and the need for safety. When a banker errs by being too stodgy, his bank will earn inadequate profits. When he errs by taking unwarranted risks, his bank may not survive at all. Many banks have perished in the latter way in recent years, especially in the savings and loan industry. (See the boxed insert on the following page.)

BANK REGULATION

DEPOSIT INSURANCE is a system that guarantees that depositors will not lose money even if their bank goes bankrupt.

The public authorities have decided that the balance between profits and safety likely to be preferred by profit-minded bankers often will not be at the place where society wants it struck. So government has thrown up a web of regulations designed to insure the safety of depositors and to control the supply of money.

The principal innovation guaranteeing the safety of bank deposits is **deposit insurance**. Today most bank deposits are insured against loss by the **Federal Deposit Insurance Corporation (FDIC)**—an agency of the U.S. government. If your bank belongs to the FDIC (and most do), your checking account is insured for up to $100,000 regardless of what happens to the bank. Thus, while bank failures may spell disaster for the bank's stockholders, they do not give many depositors cause for concern. Deposit insurance eliminates the motive for customers to rush to their bank just because they hear some bad news about the bank's finances. Many observers give this innovation much of the credit for the pronounced decline in bank failures after 1933, the year in which the FDIC was established. (Refer back to Figure 12–1 on page 276.)

Until 1989, there was a separate government agency that insured the deposits of thrift institutions. However, so many S&Ls and savings banks went bankrupt in the 1980s that the deposit insurance fund was overwhelmed—which is what forced Congress to restructure the industry. (See the accompanying boxed insert.) Unfortunately, the recent rash of bank failures has not been confined to thrift institutions. As Figure 12–1 shows, an alarming number of ordinary commercial banks also failed in the late 1980s and early 1990s. These failures strained the finances of the FDIC, and Congress responded by raising premiums for deposit insurance several times.[3]

In addition to insuring depositors against loss, the government takes steps to see that banks do not get into financial trouble. For one thing, various regulatory authorities conduct periodic *bank examinations and audits* in order to keep tabs on the financial condition and business practices of the banks under their purview. Bank supervision was tightened in 1992 by legislation which permits the authorities to intervene in the affairs of financially troubled banks. There are also laws and regulations that *limit the kinds and quantities of assets in which banks may invest*. For example, most banks are prohibited from purchasing common stock. Both these forms of regulation are clearly aimed at maintaining bank safety.

A final type of regulation also has some bearing on safety but is motivated primarily by the government's desire to control the money supply. We have seen that the amount of money any bank will issue depends on the amount of reserves

---

[3]Banks pay premiums for deposit insurance just as individuals pay premiums for fire, automobile, and life insurance.

After years of procrastination, Congress finally passed legislation in 1989 to clean up the debris left by the collapse of the savings and loan industry. The process is going on right now, and the ultimate bill to the nation's taxpayers may go as high as $150 billion.* How did such a highly regulated industry ever get into such trouble?

The savings and loan business used to be a very simple one: S&Ls accepted saving deposits and lent out money in the form of home mortgages. A web of regulations protected them from competition from commercial banks, so S&L executives led the quiet life. But seeds of disaster were sown when interest rates skyrocketed in the 1970s. S&Ls found themselves losing money because the interest rates they had to pay for new deposits rose far above the rates they were earning on old mortgages. Many thrift institutions were mortally wounded at that time, but staggered on.

Then came financial deregulation in the 1980s. S&Ls were exposed to greater competition and given freedom to expand their lending beyond their traditional domain of home mortgages. Pressure to earn higher rates of return tempted many S&Ls into making risky loans—secured by oil fields, unbuilt shopping centers, and sometimes by nothing at all. The industry began to be populated by financial cowboys instead of stodgy bankers.

Unfortunately, in its zeal to deregulate, the U.S. government forgot that an unregulated savings and loan industry requires more supervision than a regulated one. It was a costly error. Too much imprudent risk-taking and mismanagement was tolerated, and the industry was beset by an outrageous amount of fraud. Then a recession in 1981–1982 and the collapse of oil prices in the mid-1980s piled yet more losses on beleaguered S&Ls—especially in Texas.

Many executives concluded that their only hope was to "bet the bank" on risky investments which, if they paid off, might put them back in the black. Since their banks were going under anyway, they had little to lose if the bets went bad. So gambling S&Ls began to offer above-market interest rates to attract new deposits and wagered the money on speculative ventures, many of which turned sour. Taxpayers were being set up for a crash landing because federal deposit insurance obligated the government to pay off the depositors (up to $100,000 per account) of any thrift institution that went bankrupt. This, many people believed, was the essence of the problem: S&L operators were allowed to gamble with the taxpayers' money.

Although this was well understood by the mid-1980s, Congress and the Reagan administration did nothing about it. Why? Because closing down insolvent S&Ls would entail current expenses that would enlarge the budget deficit. An example will show why. Suppose a bankrupt S&L has $500 million in insured deposits, but its assets are worth only $400 million. If the government takes it over, sells all the assets at market value, and pays off the depositors, it takes in $400 million and pays out $500 million—leaving it $100 million short.

Since neither Congress nor President Reagan wanted to face up to the bill, the problem worsened. The government only got serious about closing down the thrifts early in the Bush administration. But even then the agency created to clean up the mess—the Resolution Trust Corporation (RTC)—was persistently underfunded. So the job dragged on, and on, and on.

Today, the RTC is still in the process of taking over, and eventually trying to sell, hundreds of ailing financial institutions. Tighter regulations, stiffer penalties for fraud, and higher premiums for deposit insurance were also imposed on the industry to make sure the thrift debacle would not be repeated. It has been an expensive lesson for the U.S. government and its taxpayers.

One final point: The cleanup operation is often misleadingly called a "bailout"—a term which suggests that government funds are being used to save ailing firms. Except in a few isolated instances, that is not the case. It is the depositors who are being "bailed out," not the managers and stockholders of the S&Ls, who generally lose their jobs and their investments, respectively.

*In the popular press, cost estimates much higher than $150 billion are sometimes reported. These inflated figures result from misleadingly treating $1 to be paid in the distant future as equivalent to $1 paid today. A dollar payable, say, 10 years in the future is worth considerably less than a dollar payable today.

REQUIRED RESERVES are the minimum amount of reserves (in cash or the equivalent) required by law. Normally, required reserves are proportional to the volume of deposits.

it elects to keep. For this reason, most banks are subject by law to minimum **required reserves**. While banks may (and sometimes do) keep reserves in excess of these legal minimums, they may not keep less. It is this regulation that places an upper limit on the money supply. The rest of this chapter is concerned with the details of this mechanism.

HOW BANKERS KEEP BOOKS

Before we can fully understand the mechanics of modern banking and the process by which money is "created," we must acquire at least a nodding acquaintance with the way in which bankers keep their books. The first thing to know is how to distinguish assets from liabilities.

An **ASSET** of an individual or business firm is an item of value that the individual or firm owns.

An **asset** of a bank is something of value that the bank *owns*. This "thing" may be a physical object, such as the bank building, a computer, or a vault, or it may be just a piece of paper, such as an IOU of a customer to whom the bank has made a loan. A **liability** of a bank is something of value that the bank *owes*. Most bank liabilities take the form of bookkeeping entries. For example, if you have a checking account in the Main Street Bank, your bank balance is a liability of the bank. (It is, of course, an asset to you.)

A **LIABILITY** of an individual or business firm is an item of value that the individual or firm owes. Many liabilities are known as "debts."

There is an easy test to see whether some piece of paper or bookkeeping entry is a bank's *asset* or *liability*. Ask yourself whether, if this paper were converted into cash, the bank would receive the cash (if so, it is an asset) or pay it out (if so, it is a liability). This test makes it clear that loans to customers are bank assets (when loans are repaid, the bank collects), while customers' deposits are bank liabilities (when deposits are cashed in, the bank must pay). Of course, things are just the opposite to the bank's customers: the loans are liabilities and the deposits are assets.

A **BALANCE SHEET** is an accounting statement listing the values of all the assets on the left-hand side and the values of all the liabilities and **net worth** on the right-hand side.

When accountants draw up a complete list of all the bank's assets and liabilities, the resulting document is called the bank's **balance sheet**. Typically, the value of all the bank's assets exceeds the value of all its liabilities. (On the rare occasions when this is not so, the bank is in serious trouble.) In what sense, then, do balance sheets "balance"?

NET WORTH is the value of all assets minus the value of all liabilities.

They balance because accountants have invented the concept of **net worth** to balance the books. Specifically, they define the net worth of a bank to be the difference between the value of all its assets and the value of all its liabilities. Thus, by definition, when accountants add net worth to liabilities, the sum they get must be the same as the value of the bank's assets. In short:

$$\text{Assets} = \text{Liabilities} + \text{Net Worth}.$$

Table 12–1 illustrates this with the balance sheet of a fictitious bank, Bank-a-mythica, whose finances are extremely simple. On December 31, 1993, it had only two kinds of assets (listed on the left-hand side of the balance sheet)—$1 million in cash, which it held as reserves, and $4,500,000 in outstanding loans to its customers, that is, in customers' IOUs. And it had only one type of liability (listed on the right-hand side)—$5 million in checking deposits. The difference between total assets ($5.5 million) and total liabilities ($5 million) was the bank's net worth ($500,000), shown on the right-hand side of the balance sheet.

T a b l e	12–1	BALANCE SHEET OF BANK-A-MYTHICA, DECEMBER 31, 1993

ASSETS		LIABILITIES AND NET WORTH	
Assets		**Liabilities**	
Reserves	$1,000,000	Checking deposits	$5,000,000
Loans outstanding	4,500,000		
Total	$5,500,000	**Net Worth**	
Addendum: Bank Reserves		Stockholders' equity	500,000
Actual reserves	$1,000,000		
Required reserves	1,000,000		
Excess reserves	0		
		Total	$5,500,000

THE LIMITS TO MONEY CREATION BY A SINGLE BANK

Let us now turn to the process of deposit creation. Many bankers will deny that they have any ability to "create" money. The phrase itself has a suspiciously hocus-pocus sound to it. But they are not quite right. For although any individual bank's ability to create money is severely limited in a system with many banks, the banking system as a whole can achieve much more than the sum of its parts. Through the modern alchemy of **deposit creation**, it can turn one dollar into many dollars. But to understand this important process, we had better proceed in steps, beginning with the case of a single bank, our hypothetical Bank-a-mythica.

According to the balance sheet in Table 12–1, Bank-a-mythica is holding cash reserves that are equal to 20 percent of its deposits ($1 million in cash is equal to 20 percent of the $5 million in deposits). Let us assume that this is the minimum reserve ratio prescribed by law and that the bank strives to keep its reserves down to the legal minimum; that is, it strives to keep its **excess reserves** down to zero.

EXCESS RESERVES are any reserves held in excess of the legal minimum.

Now let us suppose that on January 2, 1994, an eccentric widower comes into Bank-a-mythica and deposits $100,000 in cash in his checking account. The bank now has acquired $100,000 more in cash reserves, and $100,000 more in checking deposits. But since deposits are up by $100,000, *required* reserves are up only by 20 percent of this amount, or $20,000, leaving $80,000 in *excess* reserves. Table 12–2 illustrates the effects of this transaction on Bank-a-mythica's balance sheet. It is tables such as this, which show *changes* in balance sheets rather than the balance sheets themselves, that will help us follow the money-creation process.[4]

If Bank-a-mythica does not want to hold excess reserves, it will be unhappy with the situation illustrated in Table 12–2, for it is holding $80,000 in excess reserves on which it earns no interest. So as soon as possible it will lend out the extra $80,000—let us say to Hard-Pressed Construction Company. This loan leads to the balance sheet changes shown in Table 12–3: Bank-a-mythica's loans rise by $80,000 while its holdings of cash reserves fall by $80,000.

[4]Notice that in all such tables, which are called "T accounts," the two sides of the ledger must balance. This is because changes in assets and changes in liabilities must be equal if the balance sheet is to balance both before and after the transaction.

| *T a b l e* **12-2** | **CHANGES IN BANK-A-MYTHICA'S BALANCE SHEET, JANUARY 2, 1994** |

ASSETS		LIABILITIES	
Reserves	+$100,000	Checking deposits	+$100,000
Addendum: Bank Reserve			
Actual reserves	+$100,000		
Required reserves	+ 20,000		
Excess reserves	+ $80,000		

Bank-a-Mythica receives $100,000 cash deposit. It now holds excess reserves of $80,000, since required reserves rise by only $20,000 (20 percent of $100,000).

By combining Tables 12–2 and 12–3, we arrive at Table 12–4, which summarizes all the bank's transactions for the week. Reserves are up $20,000, loans are up $80,000 and, now that the bank has had a chance to adjust to the inflow of deposits, it no longer holds excess reserves.

Looking at Table 12–4 and keeping in mind our specific definition of money, it appears at first that the chairman of Bank-a-mythica is right when he claims not to have engaged in the nefarious practice of "money creation." All that happened was that, in exchange for the $100,000 in cash it received, the bank issued the widower a checking balance of $100,000. This does not change M1; it merely converts one form of money into another.

But wait. What happened to the $100,000 in cash that the eccentric man brought to the bank? The table shows that $20,000 was retained by Bank-a-mythica in its vault. Since this currency is no longer in circulation, it no longer counts in the official money supply. (Notice that Figure 12–2 included only "currency outside banks.") But the other $80,000, which the bank lent out, is still in circulation. It is held by Hard-Pressed Construction, which probably will redeposit it in some other bank. But even before this happens, the original $100,000 in cash has supported a rise in the money supply: there is now $100,000 in checking deposits and $80,000 in cash in circulation, making a total of $180,000. The money-creation process has begun.

| *T a b l e* **12-3** | **CHANGES IN BANK-A-MYTHICA'S BALANCE SHEET, JANUARY 3–6, 1994** |

ASSETS		LIABILITIES
		No change
Loans outstanding	+$80,000	
Reserves	– 80,000	
Addendum: Changes in Reserves		
Actual reserves	–$80,000	
Required reserves	No change	
Excess reserves	–$80,000	

Bank-a-Mythica gets rid of its excess reserves by making a loan of $80,000 to Hard-Pressed Construction Company.

Table	12–4	CHANGES IN BANK-A-MYTHICA'S BALANCE SHEET, JANUARY 2–6, 1994	
ASSETS		**LIABILITIES**	
Reserves	+$20,000	Checking deposits	+$100,000
Loans outstanding	+$80,000		
Addendum: Changes in Reserves			
Actual reserves	+$20,000		
Required reserves	+$20,000		
Excess reserves	No change		

When it receives $100,000 in cash deposits, Bank-A-Mythica keeps only the required $20,000 in reserves and lends out the remaining $80,000 to Hard-Pressed Construction Company. Its excess reserves return to zero.

MULTIPLE MONEY CREATION BY A SERIES OF BANKS

Let us now trace the $80,000 in cash and see how the process of money creation gathers momentum. Suppose that Hard-Pressed Construction Company, which banks across town at the First National Bank, deposits the $80,000 into its bank account. First National's reserves increase by $80,000. But because deposits are up by $80,000, *required* reserves rise by only 20 percent of this amount or $16,000. If the management of First National Bank behaves like that of Bank-a-mythica, the $64,000 of excess reserves will be lent out.

Table 12–5 shows the effects of these events on First National Bank's balance sheet. (The preliminary steps corresponding to Tables 12–2 and 12–3 are not shown separately.) At this stage in the chain, the original $100,000 in cash has led to $180,000 in deposits—$100,000 at Bank-a-mythica and $80,000 at First National Bank—and $64,000 in cash, which is still in circulation (in the hands of the recipient of First National's loan—Al's Auto Shop). Thus, from the original $100,000, a total of $244,000 has been added to the money supply ($180,000 in checking deposits plus $64,000 in cash).

Table	12–5	CHANGES IN FIRST NATIONAL BANK'S BALANCE SHEET	
ASSETS		**LIABILITIES**	
Reserves	+$16,000	Checking deposits	+$80,000
Loans outstanding	+ 64,000		
Addendum: Changes in Reserves			
Actual reserves	+$16,000		
Required reserves	+$16,000		
Excess reserves	No change		

Hard-Pressed deposits its $80,000 in First National Bank, which sets aside the required $16,000 in reserves (20 percent of $80,000) and lends $64,000 to Al's Auto Shop.

numbers in Figure 12–3 are correct. Let us, therefore, think through the logic behind them.

The chain of deposit creation can end only when there are no more *excess* reserves to be loaned out; that is, when the entire $100,000 in cash is tied up in *required* reserves. That explains why the last entry in column 1 must be $100,000. But, with a reserve ratio of 20 percent, excess reserves disappear only when checking deposits expand by $500,000—which is the last entry in column 2. Finally, since balance sheets must balance, the sum of all newly created assets (reserves plus loans) must equal the sum of all newly created liabilities ($500,000 in deposits). That leaves $400,000 for new loans—which is the last entry in column 3.

More generally, if the reserve ratio is some number m (rather than the $\frac{1}{5}$ in our example), each dollar of deposits requires only a fraction m of a dollar in reserves. So R, the common ratio in the above formula, is $1 - m$, and deposits must expand by $1/m$ for each dollar of new reserves that are injected into the system. This suggests the general formula for multiple deposit creation when the required reserve ratio is some number m:

OVERSIMPLIFIED DEPOSIT MULTIPLIER FORMULA

If the required reserve ratio is some fraction, m, each $1 of reserves injected into the banking system can lead to the creation of $1/m$ in new deposits. That is, the so-called "deposit multiplier" is given by:

$$\text{Change in deposits} = (1/m) \times \text{Change in reserves.}$$

Notice that this formula correctly describes what happens in our example. The initial deposit of $100,000 in cash at Bank-a-mythica constitutes $100,000 in new reserves (Table 12–2). Applying a multiplier of $1/m = 1/0.2 = 5$ to this $100,000, we conclude that bank deposits will rise by $500,000—which is just what happens. Remember, however, that the expansion process started when some eccentric widower took $100,000 in cash and deposited it in his bank account. So the public's holdings of *money*—which includes both checking deposits *and cash*—increase by only $400,000 in this case: There is $500,000 *more* in deposits, but $100,000 *less* in cash.

THE PROCESS IN REVERSE: MULTIPLE CONTRACTIONS OF THE MONEY SUPPLY

Let us now briefly consider how this deposit-creation mechanism operates in reverse—as a system of deposit *destruction*. In particular, suppose that our eccentric widower came back to Bank-a-mythica to withdraw $100,000 from his checking account and return it to his mattress, where it rightfully belongs. Bank-a-mythica's *required* reserves would fall by $20,000 as a result of this transaction (20 percent of $100,000), but its *actual* reserves would fall by $100,000. The bank would be $80,000 short, as indicated in Table 12–7(a).

How does it react to this discrepancy? As some of its outstanding loans are routinely paid off, the bank will cease granting new ones until it has accumulated the necessary $80,000 in required reserves. The data for Bank-a-mythica's contraction are shown in Table 12–7(b), assuming that borrowers pay off their loans in cash.[5]

---

[5]In reality, they would probably pay with checks drawn on other banks. Bank-a-mythica would then cash these checks to acquire the reserves.

Table 12–7	CHANGES IN THE BALANCE SHEET OF BANK-A-MYTHICA

(a)		(b)	
ASSETS	LIABILITIES	ASSETS	LIABILITIES
Reserves −$100,000	Checking deposits −$100,000	Reserves +$80,000 Loans outstanding − 80,000	No change
Addendum: Changes in Reserves			
Actual reserves −$100,000		**Addendum: Changes in Reserves**	
Required reserves − 20,000		Actual reserves +$80,000	
Excess reserves − 80,000		Required reserves No change	
		Excess reserves +$80,000	

When Bank-a-Mythica loses a $100,000 deposit, it must reduce its loans by $80,000 to replenish its reserves.

But where did the borrowers get this money? Probably by making withdrawals from other banks. In this case, let us assume it all came from First National Bank, which loses an $80,000 deposit and $80,000 in reserves. It finds itself short some $64,000 in reserves (see Table 12–8[a]) and therefore must reduce its loan commitments by $64,000 (see Table 12–8[b]). This, of course, causes some other bank to suffer a loss of reserves and deposits of $64,000, and the whole process repeats just as it did in the case of deposit expansion.

After the entire banking system had become involved, the picture would be just as shown in Figure 12–3, except that all the numbers would have *minus* signs in front of them. Deposits would shrink by $500,000, loans would fall by $400,000, bank reserves would be reduced by $100,000, and the money supply would fall by $400,000. As suggested by our deposit multiplier formula with $m = 0.2$, the decline in the bank deposits is $1/0.2 = 5$ times as large as the decline in excess reserves.

Table 12–8	CHANGES IN THE BALANCE SHEET OF THE FIRST NATIONAL BANK

(a)		(b)	
ASSETS	LIABILITIES	ASSETS	LIABILITIES
Reserves −$80,000	Checking deposits −$80,000	Reserves +$64,000 Loans outstanding − 64,000	No change
Addendum: Changes in Reserves			
Actual reserves −$80,000		**Addendum: Changes in Reserves**	
Required reserves − 16,000		Actual reserves +$64,000	
Excess reserves − 64,000		Required reserves No change	
		Excess reserves +$64,000	

First National Bank's loss of $80,000 deposit forces it to cut back its loans by $64,000.

One of the authors of this book was a student in Cambridge, Massachusetts, during the height of the radical student movement of the late 1960s. One day a circular appeared urging citizens to withdraw all funds from their checking accounts on a prescribed date, hold them in cash for one week, and then redeposit them. This act, the circular argued, would surely wreak havoc upon the capitalist system. Obviously, some of these radicals were well-schooled in modern money mechanics, for the argument was basically correct. The tremendous multiple contraction of the banking system and consequent multiple expansion that a successful campaign of this sort could have caused might have seriously disrupted the local financial system. But history records that the appeal met with little success. Checking-account withdrawals are not the stuff of which revolutions are made.

WHY THE DEPOSIT CREATION FORMULA IS OVERSIMPLIFIED

So far, our discussion of the process of money creation has made it all seem rather mechanical. If all proceeds according to formula, each $1 in new excess reserves will lead to a $1/m$ increase in new deposits. But in reality things are not this simple. Just as we did in the case of the expenditure multiplier, we must stress that the oversimplified formula for deposit creation is accurate only under very particular circumstances. These circumstances require that:

1. Every recipient of cash must redeposit the cash into another bank rather than hold it.
2. Every bank must hold reserves no larger than the legal minimum.

The "chain" diagram in Figure 12–3 shows clearly what happens if either of these assumptions is violated.

Suppose first that the business firms and individuals who receive bank loans decide to redeposit only a fraction of the proceeds into their bank accounts. Then, for example, the first $80,000 loan would lead to a deposit of less than $80,000—and similarly down the chain. The whole chain of deposit creation would therefore be reduced. Thus:

If individuals and business firms decide to hold more cash, the multiple expansion of bank deposits will be curtailed because fewer dollars of cash will be available to be used as reserves to support new checking deposits. Consequently, the money supply will be smaller.

The basic idea here is simple. Each $1 of cash held by a bank can support several dollars (specifically, $1/m$) of money. But $1 of cash held by an individual is exactly one dollar of money; it supports no bank deposits. Hence, any time cash leaves the banking system, the money supply will decline. And any time cash enters the banking system, the money supply will rise.

Next, suppose that bank managers become more conservative, or that the outlook for loan repayments worsens because of a recession. Then banks might decide to keep more reserves than the legal requirement and lend out less than the amounts assumed in Figure 12–3. If this happens, banks further down the chain receive smaller deposits and, once again, the chain of deposit creation is curtailed. Thus:

If banks wish to keep excess reserves, the multiple expansion of bank deposits will be restricted. A given amount of cash will support a smaller supply of money than would be the case if banks held no excess reserves.

THE NEED FOR MONETARY CONTROL

If we pursue this point a bit further, we will see why government regulation of the money supply is so important for economic stability. We have just suggested that banks will wish to keep excess reserves when they do not foresee profitable and secure opportunities to make loans. This is most likely to happen during the downswing and around the bottom of a business contraction. At such times, the propensity of banks to hold excess reserves will turn the deposit creation process into one of deposit destruction. Thus:

During a recession, profit-oriented banks would be prone to reduce the money supply by increasing their excess reserves—if the monetary authorities did not intervene. As we will learn in subsequent chapters, the money supply is an important influence on aggregate demand, so such a contraction of the money supply would aggravate the recession.

On the other hand, banks will want to squeeze the maximum possible money supply out of any given amount of cash reserves by keeping their reserves at the bare minimum when the demand for bank loans is buoyant, profits are high, and secure investment opportunities abound. This reduced incentive to hold excess reserves in prosperous times means that:

During an economic boom, the behavior of profit-oriented banks is likely to make the money supply expand, adding undesirable momentum to the booming economy and paving the way for a burst of inflation. The authorities must intervene to prevent this.

Regulation of the money supply, then, is necessary because profit-oriented bankers might otherwise provide the economy with a gyrating money supply that dances to the tune of the business cycle. Precisely how the authorities keep the money supply under control is the subject of the next chapter.

Summary

1. It is more efficient to exchange goods and services by using money as a **medium of exchange** than by **bartering** them directly.

2. In addition to being the medium of exchange, whatever serves as money is likely to become the standard **unit of account** and a popular **store of value**.

3. Throughout history, all sorts of things have served as money. **Commodity money** gave way to fullbodied paper money (certificates backed 100 percent by some commodity, like gold), which in turn gave way to partially backed paper money. Nowadays our paper money has no commodity backing whatsoever; it is pure **fiat money**.

4. The most widely used definition of the U.S. money supply is **M1**, which includes coins, paper money, and several types of checking deposits. However, many economists prefer the **M2** definition, which adds to M1 other types of checkable accounts and most savings deposits. Much of M2 is held outside of banks.

5. Under our modern system of **fractional reserve banking**, banks keep cash reserves equal to only a fraction

of their total deposit liabilities. This is the key to their profitability, since the remaining funds can be loaned out at interest. But it also leaves them potentially vulnerable to **runs**.

6. Because of this vulnerability, bank managers are generally conservative in their investment strategy. They also keep a prudent level of reserves. Even so, the government keeps a watchful eye over banking practices.

7. Before 1933, bank failures were common; but they declined sharply when **deposit insurance** was instituted. Nonetheless, recent years have witnessed an upsurge of bank failures and a virtual collapse of the savings and loan industry.

8. Because it holds only fractional reserves, even a single bank can create money. But its ability to do so is

severely limited because the funds it lends out probably will be deposited in another bank.

9. As a whole, the banking system can create several dollars of deposits for each dollar of reserves it receives. Under certain assumptions, the ratio of new deposits to new reserves will be $1/m$, where m is the required reserve ratio.

10. The same process works in reverse, as a system of money destruction, when cash is withdrawn from the banking system.

11. Because banks and individuals may want to hold more cash when the economy is shaky, the money supply would probably contract under such circumstances if the monetary authorities did not intervene. Similarly, the money supply would probably expand rapidly in boom times if it were unregulated.

Key Concepts and Terms

Run on a bank
Barter
Unit of account
Money
Medium of exchange
Store of value
Commodity money
Fiat money

M1 versus M2
Near moneys
Liquidity
Fractional reserve banking
Deposit insurance
Federal Deposit Insurance
    Corporation (FDIC)
Required reserves

Asset
Liability
Balance sheet
Net worth
Deposit creation
Excess reserves

Questions for Review

1. If ours were a barter economy, how would you pay your tuition bill? What if your college did not want the goods or services you offered in payment?

2. How is "money" defined, both conceptually and in practice? Does the U.S. money supply consist of commodity money, full-bodied paper money, or fiat money?

3. What is fractional reserve banking, and why is it the key to bank profits? (*Hint*: What opportunities to make profits would banks have if reserve requirements were 100 percent?) Why does fractional reserve banking give bankers discretion over how large the money supply will be? Why does it make banks potentially vulnerable to runs?

4. Explain why the many bank failures of the 1990s have not led to runs on banks.

5. Suppose that no banks keep excess reserves and no individuals or firms hold on to cash. If someone suddenly discovers $7.5 million in buried treasure, explain what will happen to the money supply if the required reserve ratio is 10 percent.

6. How would your answer to Question 5 differ if the reserve ratio were 25 percent? If the reserve ratio were 100 percent?

7. Each year during Christmas shopping season, consumers and stores wish to increase their holdings of cash. Explain how this could lead to a multiple contraction of the money supply. (As a matter of fact, the authorities prevent this contraction from occurring by methods explained in the next chapter.)

8. Excess reserves make a bank less vulnerable to runs. Why, then, don't bankers like to hold excess reserves?

What circumstances might persuade them that it would be advisable to hold excess reserves?

9. Use tables such as Tables 12–2 and 12–3 to illustrate what happens to bank balance sheets when each of the following transactions occurs:

a. You withdraw $300 from your checking account to buy Christmas presents.

b. Sam finds a $50 bill on the sidewalk and deposits it into his checking account.

c. Mary Q. Contrary withdraws $900 in cash from her account at Hometown Bank, carries it to the city, and deposits it into her account at Big City Bank.

10. For each of the transactions listed in Question 9, what will be the ultimate effect on the money supply if the required reserve ratio is 10 percent? (Assume that the oversimplified deposit multiplier formula applies.)

11. If the government takes over a bankrupt thrift institution with liabilities (mostly deposits) of $2 billion, pays off the depositors, and sells the assets for $1.5 billion, where does the missing $500 million come from? Why?

MONETARY POLICY AND THE NATIONAL ECONOMY

Now that we understand the rudiments of the banking system, we are ready to bring money and interest rates into our model of income determination and the price level. In earlier chapters, we took investment (*I*) to be a fixed number. But this is a poor assumption. Not only is investment highly variable, but it also depends on interest rates. And interest rates are, in turn, heavily influenced by *monetary policy*. The main task of this chapter is to explain how monetary policy affects interest rates and investment and, thereby, aggregate demand. ¶ We begin by learning about the operations of America's *central bank*, the *Federal Reserve System*. The "Fed," as it is often called, is a very special kind of bank. Its customers are banks rather than individuals, and it performs some of the same services for them as your bank performs for you. Although it turns out to be an effective profit maker, its actions are not guided by the profit motive. Instead, the Fed tries to manage the money supply in what it perceives to be the national interest. Just how the Fed does its job, and why its performance has fallen short of perfection, are the first subjects of this chapter.

Next we integrate money into the Keynesian model. The mechanisms through which monetary policy affects aggregate demand are spelled out and analyzed in detail, and we learn an additional reason why the aggregate demand curve slopes downward. By the end of the chapter, we will have constructed a complete macroeconomic model, which we then use in the remaining chapters of Part 3 to investigate a variety of important policy issues.

MONEY AND INCOME: THE IMPORTANT DIFFERENCE

But first we must get some terminology straight. The words "money" and "income" are used almost interchangeably in common parlance. This is a pitfall we must learn to avoid.

Money is a snapshot concept. It is the answer to questions like: "How much money do you have right now?" or "How much money did you have at 3:32 p.m. on Friday, November 5th?" To answer questions like these, you would add up the cash you are (or were) carrying and whatever checking balances you have (or had), and answer something like: "I have $126.33," or "On Friday, November 5th, at 3:32 p.m., I had $31.43."

Income, by contrast, is more like a motion picture; it comes to you only over a period of time. If you are asked "What is your income?" you must respond by saying "$200 *per week*," or "$800 *per month*," or "$10,000 *per year*," or something like that. Notice that there is a unit of time attached to each of these responses. If you just say "My income is $452," without indicating whether it is per week or per month or per year, no one will understand what you mean.

That the two concepts are very different is easy to see. A typical American family has an *income* of perhaps $35,000 per year, but its holdings of *money* at any point in time (using the M1 definition) are more like $2000. Similarly, at the national level, nominal GDP in 1992 was almost $6000 billion, while the money stock (M1) in the middle of the year was only about $950 billion.

While money and income are very different, they are certainly related. This chapter is precisely about that relationship. Specifically, we will look at how the stock of *money* in existence at any moment of time influences the rate at which people will be earning *income*, that is, how money affects the GDP.

THE FEDERAL RESERVE SYSTEM: ORIGINS AND STRUCTURE

A **CENTRAL BANK** is a bank for banks. America's central bank is the **Federal Reserve System**.

When the **Federal Reserve System** was established in 1914, the United States joined the company of most of the other advanced industrial nations. Up until then, the United States, distrustful of centralization of economic power, was almost the only important nation without a **central bank**. Britain's central bank, the Bank of England, for example, dates from 1694.

The impetus for the establishment of a central bank in the United States came not from the power of economic logic but from some painful experiences with economic reality. Four severe banking panics between 1873 and 1907 convinced legislators and bankers alike that a central bank that would regulate credit conditions was not a luxury but a necessity. After the 1907 crisis, the National Monetary Commission was established to find out what was wrong with America's banking system. Its report in 1912 led directly to the establishment of the Federal Reserve System.

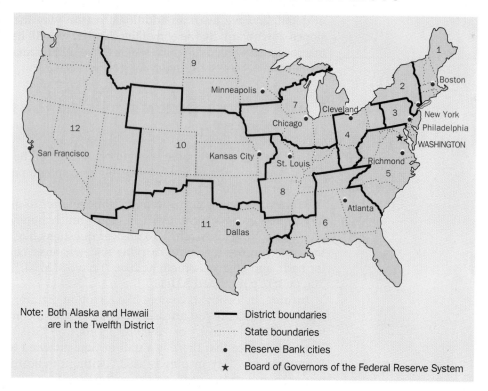

Figure **13–1** **THE TWELVE FEDERAL RESERVE DISTRICTS**

This map shows the boundaries of the 12 Federal Reserve districts and the locations of the 12 Federal Reserve banks. In which Federal Reserve district do you live?

Note: Both Alaska and Hawaii are in the Twelfth District

— District boundaries

········· State boundaries

• Reserve Bank cities

★ Board of Governors of the Federal Reserve System

Although the basic idea of central banking came from Europe, some changes were made when it was imported, making the Federal Reserve System a uniquely American institution. Owing to the vastness of our country, the extraordinarily large number of commercial banks, and our tradition of dual state-federal regulations, it was decided that the United States should have not one central bank but 12. The boundaries of the 12 Federal Reserve districts and the location of each of the 12 district banks are shown in Figure 13–1.

Technically, each of the Federal Reserve banks is a corporation; its stockholders are the banks that belong to it. But your bank, if it is a member of the System, does not enjoy the privileges normally accorded to stockholders: it receives only a token share of the Federal Reserve's immense profits (the bulk is donated to the U.S. Treasury), and it has no say in the decisions of the corporation. The private banks are more like customers of the Fed than like owners.

Who, then, controls the Fed? Most of the power resides in the seven-member Board of Governors of the Federal Reserve System, headquartered in Washington, and especially in its chairman, who is now Alan Greenspan, an economist. Members of the board are appointed by the president of the United States, with the advice and consent of the Senate, for 14-year terms. The president also designates one of the members to serve a four-year term as chairman of the board, and thus to be the most powerful central banker in the world; for the United States differs from many other countries in that the Federal Reserve Board, once appointed by the president, is *independent* of the rest of the government. So long as it stays within the statutory authority delineated by Congress, it alone has responsibility for determining the nation's monetary policy. The power of appointment, however, gives the president considerable long-run influence over Federal Reserve policy.

Closely allied with the Board of Governors is the powerful **Federal Open Market Committee (FOMC)**, which meets periodically in Washington. For reasons to be explained shortly, the decisions of the FOMC largely determine the size of the U.S. money supply. This 12-member committee consists of the seven governors of the Federal Reserve System and the presidents of five of the district banks.

THE INDEPENDENCE OF THE FED

The institutional independence of the Federal Reserve System is looked upon as a source of pride by some and as an antidemocratic embarrassment by others. The proponents of Federal Reserve independence argue that it enables monetary policy decisions to be made on objective, technical criteria and keeps monetary control out of the "political thicket." Without this independence, it is argued, there would be a tendency for politicians to force the Fed to expand the money supply too rapidly, thereby contributing to chronic inflation and undermining faith in America's financial system.

Opponents of this view counter that there is something profoundly undemocratic about having a group of unelected bankers and economists make decisions that affect the well-being of 260 million Americans. Monetary policy, they argue, should be formulated by the elected representatives of the people, just like fiscal policy. Those who argue for executive or congressional control over the Fed can point to historical instances in which monetary and fiscal policy have been at loggerheads—with the Fed undoing or even overwhelming the effects of fiscal policy decisions.

There is plenty of middle ground between the two extremes. One far less drastic proposal would put the Secretary of the Treasury on the Federal Reserve Board and/or shift the term of its chairman to make it coincide with that of the president of the United States. As things stand today, a newly elected president must retain the Fed chairman that his predecessor appointed whether or not he agrees with his policies.

Another suggested reform would require the Fed to announce its ultimate targets for unemployment and inflation and explain how it expects its monetary policy actions to promote these goals. An extreme version of this proposal would force the Fed to adopt the goals of the administration or Congress. But a more moderate version would simply make the Fed announce its own goals and subject them to public scrutiny. A yet weaker proposal in the same vein would force the Fed to announce its policy decisions as soon as they are made. At present, it normally waits about six weeks after each FOMC meeting before announcing its decisions.

How people react to these and other reform proposals that would affect the Fed's independence depends on how they perceive the office. Are governors of the Federal Reserve System akin to judges and therefore, at least in principle, best thought of as nonpartisan and independent technocrats? The 14-year term of office certainly suggests an analogy to the judiciary, but the board's role is most assuredly one that involves policy making, not just "impartial" interpretation of the law. Or are the governors more like members of the Cabinet, that is, policy-making officials who should properly serve only at the pleasure of the president? Since neither analogy fits precisely, the issue is a vexing one.

CONTROLLING THE MONEY SUPPLY: OPEN-MARKET OPERATIONS

Partly for historical reasons, the Fed normally relies on what are called **open-market operations** to manipulate the money supply. Open-market operations have the effect of giving the banks more reserves or taking reserves away from them, thereby triggering a multiple expansion or contraction of the money supply as described in Chapter 12.

How does this work? Suppose the Federal Open Market Committee decides that the money supply is too low. It can issue instructions that the money supply be expanded through operations in the open market. Specifically, this means that the Federal Reserve System *purchases* U.S. government securities (generally short-term securities called "Treasury bills") from any individual or bank that wishes to sell, thus putting more reserves in the hands of the banks.

An example will illustrate the mechanics of open-market operations. Suppose the order is to purchase $100 million worth of securities and that commercial banks are the sellers. *The Fed makes payment by giving the banks $100 million in new reserves.* So, if they held only the required amount of reserves initially, the banks now have $100 million in excess reserves, as shown in Table 13–1.

When the Fed buys $100 million worth of securities from the banks, it adds this amount to the bookkeeping entries that represent the banks' accounts at the Fed (called "bank reserves"). Since deposits have not increased at all, required reserves are unchanged by this transaction. But actual reserves are increased by $100 million, so there are $100 million in excess reserves. This will trigger a multiple expansion of the banking system.

Where does the Fed get the money that it gives to the banks in return for the securities? It could pay in cash, but normally does not. Instead, it manufactures the funds out of thin air or, more literally, by punching the keyboard of a computer terminal. Specifically, the Fed pays the banks for the securities by adding the

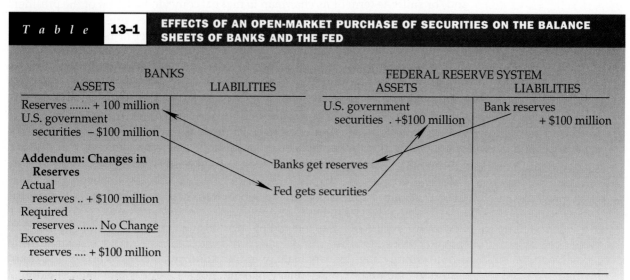

T a b l e **13–1**	EFFECTS OF AN OPEN-MARKET PURCHASE OF SECURITIES ON THE BALANCE SHEETS OF BANKS AND THE FED		
BANKS		**FEDERAL RESERVE SYSTEM**	
ASSETS	LIABILITIES	ASSETS	LIABILITIES
Reserves .... + 100 million		U.S. government	Bank reserves
U.S. government		securities . +$100 million	+ $100 million
securities – $100 million			
Addendum: Changes in Reserves			
Actual	Banks get reserves		
reserves .. + $100 million			
Required	Fed gets securities		
reserves .... <u>No Change</u>			
Excess			
reserves .... + $100 million			

When the Fed buys $100 million worth of securities from the banks, it adds this amount to the bookkeeping entries that represent the banks' accounts at the Fed (called "bank reserves"). Since deposits have not increased at all, required reserves are unchanged by this transaction. But actual reserves are increased by $100 million, so there are $100 million in excess reserves. This will trigger a multiple expansion of the banking system.

appropriate sums to the accounts that the banks maintain at the Fed. Balances held in these accounts constitute bank reserves, just like cash in bank vaults.

While this process of creating bookkeeping entries at the Federal Reserve is commonly referred to as "printing money," the Fed does not literally run the printing presses. Instead, it simply exchanges its IOUs for an existing asset (a government security). But unlike your IOUs, the Fed's IOUs constitute legal bank reserves, and thus can support a multiple expansion of the money supply in the same way that cash does. The banks, not the Fed, actually increase the money supply; but the Fed's actions give the banks the wherewithal to do it.

Once excess reserves are created, multiple expansion of the banking system proceeds in the usual way. It is not hard for the Fed to estimate the ultimate increase in the money supply that will result from its actions. As we saw in the last chapter, each dollar of excess reserves can support $1/m$ dollars of checking deposits, if m is the required reserve ratio. In our example, $m = 0.20$; so $100 million in new reserves can support $100/0.2 = $500 million in new money.

But *estimating* the ultimate monetary expansion is a far cry from *knowing it* with certainty. As we know from Chapter 12, the simple money multiplier formula is predicated on the assumptions that people will want to hold no more cash, and that banks will want to hold no more excess reserves, as the monetary expansion proceeds. In practice, these assumptions are unlikely to be literally true. So, if the Fed is to predict the eventual effect of its action on the money supply correctly, it must estimate both the amount that firms and individuals will want to add to their currency holdings and the amount that banks will want to add to their excess reserves. Neither of these can be estimated with utter precision. In summary:

When the Federal Reserve System wants to increase the money supply, it purchases U.S. government securities in the open market. It pays for these securities by creating new bank reserves, and these additional reserves lead to a multiple expansion of the money supply. However, because of fluctuations in people's desires to hold cash and banks' desires to hold excess reserves, the Fed cannot predict the consequences of these actions with perfect accuracy. Thus, over short periods, control over the money supply must of necessity be imperfect.

The procedures followed when the FOMC wants to *contract* the money supply are just the opposite of those we have just explained. In brief, it orders a *sale* of government securities in the open market. This takes reserves *away* from banks, since banks pay for the securities by drawing down their deposits at the Fed. A multiple *contraction* of the banking system ensues. The principles are exactly the same as when the process operates in reverse—and so are the uncertainties.

OPEN-MARKET OPERATIONS, BOND PRICES, AND INTEREST RATES

When it offers more government bonds for sale on the open market, the Federal Reserve normally depresses the price of bonds. This is illustrated by Figure 13–2, which shows a rightward shift of the (vertical) supply curve of bonds—from S_0S_0 to S_1S_1—with an unchanged demand curve, DD. The price of bonds falls from P_0 to P_1 as equilibrium in the bond market shifts from point A to point B.

Falling bond prices translate directly into rising interest rates. Why is that? Most bonds pay a fixed number of dollars of interest per year. For concreteness,

If the Fed offers bonds for sale in the open market, the supply curve of bonds shifts rightward from S_0S_0 to S_1S_1. In consequence, equilibrium in the bond market shifts from point A to point B. The price of bonds declines from P_0 to P_1. By the same reasoning, an open-market purchase drives bond prices up.

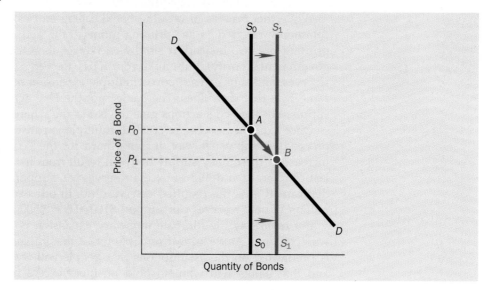

consider a bond that pays $90 each year. If the bond sells for $1000, bondholders earn a 9 percent return on their investment since $90 is 9 percent of $1000. We say that *the interest rate on the bond is 9 percent.* Now suppose the price of the bond falls to $900. The annual interest payment is still $90, so bondholders now earn 10 percent on their money ($90 is 10 percent of $900). *The effective interest rate on the bond has risen to 10 percent.* This relationship between bond prices and interest rates is completely general:

When bond prices fall, interest rates must rise because the purchaser of a bond spends less money than before to earn a given number of dollars of interest per year. Similarly, when bond prices rise, interest rates must fall.

In fact, the relationship amounts to nothing more than two ways of saying the same thing. Higher interest rates *mean* lower bond prices; lower interest rates *mean* higher bond prices.

We thus see that the Fed, through its open-market operations, exercises direct influence over interest rates. Specifically:

An open-market purchase of bonds by the Fed not only raises the money supply but also drives up bond prices and pushes interest rates down. Conversely, an open-market sale of bonds, which reduces the money supply, lowers bond prices and raises interest rates.

CONTROLLING THE MONEY SUPPLY: RESERVE REQUIREMENTS

The Fed also has another way to control the money supply: by varying the minimum required reserve ratio. To see how this works, consider the balance

T a b l e **13–2**	**BALANCE SHEET OF MIDDLE AMERICAN BANK, OCTOBER 25, 1993**

ASSETS		LIABILITIES AND NET WORTH	
Reserves	$ 200,000	Checking deposits	$1,000,000
Loans outstanding	1,000,000	Net worth	200,000
Total assets	$1,200,000	Total liabilities plus net worth	$1,200,000

If the required reserve ratio is 20 percent, Middle American Bank holds exactly its required reserves on October 25, 1993—no more and no less. However, if the reserve ratio falls to 15 percent, its required reserves will fall to only $150,000 (15 percent of $1 million), and it will have $50,000 in excess reserves.

sheet of a hypothetical bank shown in Table 13–2. If the minimum required reserve ratio is 20 percent, and the bank wishes to hold only the legal minimum in reserves, Middle American Bank is in equilibrium on October 25, 1993. Its $1 million in checking deposits mean that its required reserves amount to $200,000, which just matches its actual reserves. Excess reserves are zero.

Now suppose that the Federal Reserve Board decides that the money supply needs to be increased. One action it can take is to lower the required reserve ratio. As an exaggerated example, suppose it reduces reserve requirements to 15 percent of deposits.

Middle American Bank's balance sheet is unaffected by this action, but the bank's managers are sure to react to it. For now required reserves are only $150,000 (15 percent of $1 million), so the bank is holding $50,000 in excess reserves—funds that are earning no interest for the bank. The effect is the same as if a new depositor had brought in cash: the bank now has more money to lend. Once it lends out this $50,000, its balance sheet will be as shown in Table 13–3; it now holds $50,000 less in reserves and $50,000 more in loans.

Although no new deposits are created by this transaction, we know from the previous chapter that the wheels of a multiple expansion of the banking system have been set in motion. For the recipient of the loan will deposit the proceeds in his own bank, giving that bank excess reserves and, therefore, the ability to grant more loans, and so on.

Once again, while the Fed's control over banks' excess reserves may be quite precise, its control over the money supply is a good deal looser. It can and will rely on its past experience to *estimate* the ultimate effect of any change in reserve requirements on the money supply. In normal times, these estimates are quite accurate. That, presumably, is the definition of "normal times." But at other times

T a b l e **13–3**	**BALANCE SHEET OF MIDDLE AMERICAN BANK, OCTOBER 26, 1993**

ASSETS		LIABILITIES	
Reserves	$ 150,000	Checking deposits	$1,000,000
Loans outstanding	1,050,000	Net worth	200,000
Total assets	$1,200,000	Total liabilities plus net worth	$1,200,000

If Middle American Bank does not wish to hold excess reserves, its balance sheet will look like this after it loans out the extra $50,000 in excess reserves. At this point, it once again has no excess reserves.

banks may surprise the Fed by holding larger or smaller excess reserves than anticipated, or businesses and consumers may surprise it by holding more or less currency. In such cases, the Fed will not get the money supply it was shooting for and will have to adjust its policies.

It does not take much imagination to see what the Fed must do to reserve requirements when it wants to engineer a *contraction* of the money supply. If banks are not holding excess reserves, an increase in the required reserve ratio will force them to contract their loans and deposits until their reserve deficiencies are corrected. Of course, if banks do have sufficient excess reserves, they can flout the Fed's wishes. But the Fed normally will be trying to rein in the money supply when the economy is booming, and these are precisely the times when banks will not want to hold more idle reserves than necessary.

In fact, the Fed has not relied much on the reserve ratio as a weapon of monetary control. Current legislation provides for a basic reserve ratio of 12 percent against checking deposits, which changes very infrequently.

CONTROLLING THE MONEY SUPPLY: LENDING TO BANKS

When the Federal Reserve System was first established, its founders did not intend it to pursue an active monetary policy to stabilize the economy. Indeed, the basic ideas of stabilization policy were foreign at the time. Instead, the Fed's founders viewed it as a means of preventing the supplies of money and credit from drying up during economic contractions, as had happened so often in the pre-1914 period.

One of the principal ways in which the Fed was to provide such insurance against financial panics was to act as a "lender of last resort." That is, when risky business prospects made commercial banks hesitant to extend new loans, or when banks were in trouble, the Fed would step in by lending money to the banks, thus inducing the banks to lend more money to their customers. The Fed last performed this role in dramatic fashion in October 1987, when the stock market crash stunned the financial community. Its prompt actions helped avert a financial panic.

When the Fed extends borrowing privileges to a bank in need of reserves, that bank receives a credit in its deposit account at the Fed (see Table 13–4). This addition to bank reserves may lead to an expansion of the money supply; or it may eliminate a reserve deficiency and thereby prevent a multiple contraction of the banking system. In either case, the Fed makes monetary conditions more expansive by making borrowing easier.

The **DISCOUNT RATE** is the interest rate the Fed charges on loans it makes to banks.

Federal Reserve officials can influence the volume of member bank borrowing by setting the *rate of interest charged on these loans.* For historical reasons, this is called the **discount rate** in the United States. In most foreign countries, it is known as the "bank rate." If the Fed wants to give banks more reserves, it can reduce the interest rate that it charges, thereby tempting banks to borrow more. Alternatively, it can soak up reserves by raising its rate and persuading the banks to reduce their borrowings.

While this type of *active* manipulation of the discount rate is practiced widely in foreign countries, where the bank rate is often the centerpiece of monetary policy, it is much less common in the United States, where the Fed usually relies on open market operations in conducting its monetary policy. More often the Fed adjusts the discount rate *passively* to keep it in line with market interest rates.

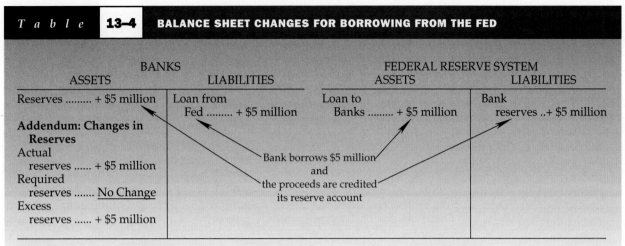

| *T a b l e* **13–4** | **BALANCE SHEET CHANGES FOR BORROWING FROM THE FED** |

When the Fed lends $5 million to a bank, it simply adds this amount to the bookkeeping entry that represents that bank's account at the Fed. Once again, actual reserves increase while required reserves do not change (because bank deposits do not change). Hence this loan would be expected to initiate a multiple expansion of the banking system.

Nonetheless, changes in the discount rate have important psychological effects on financial markets, where they are widely interpreted as signals of the Fed's attitude toward interest rates.

As in the case of changes in reserve requirements and open market operations, the Fed cannot know for sure how banks will react to changes in the discount rate. Sometimes they may respond vigorously to a cut in the rate, borrowing a great deal from the Fed and lending a correspondingly large amount to their customers. At other times they may essentially ignore the Fed's actions. The link between the lending rate and the money supply is a loose one.

Often, though, the Fed tries to tighten this link by using a more direct way of controlling the volume of bank borrowing—**moral suasion**. This phrase refers to some not-so-subtle methods that the Fed has for letting banks know when it thinks they are borrowing too much. Since banks are anxious to maintain the good will of the Fed, they often respond to warnings that they have overused their borrowing privileges—especially when such warnings are accompanied by a veiled threat that these privileges might be suspended if the offending bank does not mend its ways. As the Fed often reminds the banks, borrowing is "a privilege, not a right."

MORAL SUASION refers to informal requests and warnings designed to persuade banks to limit their borrowings from the Fed.

PROPOSALS FOR TIGHTENING MONETARY CONTROL

The fact that each of the Federal Reserve's principal instruments of monetary control is somewhat imperfect has led to a number of suggestions designed to improve the System's ability to regulate the supply of money.

Because banks' discretion over the amount of reserves they hold (subject only to the legal minimums) makes the link between changes in Federal Reserve policy and changes in the money supply rather slippery at times, some economists would like to see a return to a system of 100 percent reserve requirements. Under such a rule, no bank could add to or subtract from its excess reserves because there would never be any excess reserves. Each dollar of bank reserves would support exactly one dollar of deposits, no more and no less; so there would be no such thing as a multiple expansion or contraction of the banking system. The Fed can now control bank reserves with great precision; and under a system of 100 percent reserve requirements, its control over the money supply would be equally precise.

While such a change in banking regulations undoubtedly would make the Fed's job easier, it would also change the face of banking in dramatic and possibly unpredictable ways. It will be recalled from Chapter 13 that banking as we know it today evolved from that first goldsmith's momentous discovery that he could get along with only fractional reserves. This discovery has been the mainspring of bank profits ever since. Abolition of fractional reserve banking should therefore be viewed as a major overhaul of the financial system. This does not necessarily mean that it is a bad idea, only that it should be approached with some caution.

Some observers have suggested that lending to banks, far from aiding the Fed's monetary control, actually undermines it, and therefore the Fed should stop lending except in emergency cases. Their reasoning is as follows: when the Fed tries to force a contraction of the banking system, some banks may resist this desire by borrowing the reserves they need. Similarly, some banks may relinquish reserves to pay back loans just when the Fed wants the money supply to expand.

No doubt this occasionally happens. But there are also times when Federal Reserve lending is a valuable supplement to open market policy. Since it is by no means clear that monetary control would be tighter if lending were abolished, the Fed is understandably reluctant to give up one of its major traditional weapons.

THE MONEY SUPPLY MECHANISM

This completes our discussion of the Fed's methods of controlling the money supply and the limitations of these methods. One point, however, merits further emphasis. We have noted several times that the Fed's control of the money supply is imperfect because banks can and do vary their holdings of excess reserves. Since reserves earn no interest, banks will hold substantial *excess* reserves only when they feel that funds cannot be put to profitable uses. This may happen if shaky business conditions make loans to customers look unusually risky or if interest rates are very low. Conversely, banks will work hard to hold reserves to the legal minimum when loans to customers look safe and when interest rates are high. Thus:

As interest rates rise, banks normally find it more profitable to expand their volume of loans and deposits, thus increasing the supply of money. However, the Fed can shift the relationship between the money supply and interest rates by employing any of its principal weapons of monetary control: open market operations, changes in reserve requirements, or changes in lending policy to banks.

These ideas are depicted graphically in Figure 13–3. Figure 13–3(a) shows a typical money supply schedule labeled *MS*, illustrating the fact that bank behavior makes the money stock rise as interest rates rise.[1] Notice that the sensitivity of the money supply to interest rates is rather weak in the diagram—a large rise in

---

[1]There are many interest rates in the economy. However, they all tend to move up and down together. Hence, for present purposes, we can speak of "the" rate of interest.

F i g u r e **13–3**   **THE SUPPLY SCHEDULE FOR MONEY**

Part (a) shows a typical supply schedule for money. It is rising as we move toward the right, meaning that banks will supply more money when interest rates are higher. Part (b) illustrates what happens to the money supply schedule when the Fed purchases securities in the open market, or lowers required reserves, or provides banks with more loans. The supply schedule shifts outward. Part (c) depicts the effect of using these same policy instruments in the opposite (contractionary) direction. The supply schedule shifts inward.

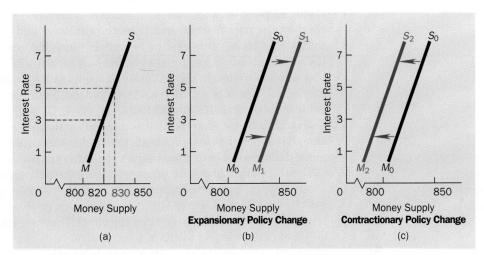

the rate of interest (from 3 percent to 5 percent) induces only a small increase in the supply of money (from \$820 billion to \$830 billion). The drawing is deliberately constructed that way because that is what the statistical evidence shows.

The curve in Figure 13–3(a) shows the money supply schedule corresponding to some specific monetary policy. Figure 13–3(b) portrays how the money supply schedule responds to an *expansionary change in monetary policy*, such as an open market purchase of government bonds, a reduction in reserve requirements, or a drop in the Fed's lending rate. The money supply schedule shifts outward from M_0S_0 to M_1S_1, as indicated by the arrows. After banks have adjusted to the change, there is more money at any given interest rate.

Figure 13–3(c) shows what happens in the reverse case—a *contractionary monetary policy*, such as an open market sale of securities, an increase in reserve requirements, or a rise in the lending rate. The money supply shifts inward from M_0S_0 to M_2S_2.

As we have emphasized, the diagrams make things look rather more precise than they actually are. Since the Fed's control over the money supply schedule is imperfect in the short run, the actual *MS* schedule is obscured by a bit of fog. In what follows, we portray all the graphs as clean straight lines only for pedagogical simplicity. The Fed wishes things were so simple in the real world!

THE DEMAND FOR MONEY

Just as we must know something about both the supply of and the demand for wheat before we can predict how much will be sold and at what price, it is necessary to know something about the **demand for money** if we are to understand the amount of money actually in existence and the prevailing interest rate.

The definition of money given in Chapter 12 suggests the most important reason why people hold money balances: the medium of exchange is needed to carry out purchases and sales of goods and services. More dollars are needed to conduct the nation's business if more purchases and sales are made or if each transaction takes place at a higher price. Since the real gross domestic product (GDP) is normally considered to be the best measure of the total volume of goods and services traded in the economy, it seems safe to assume that the demand for money will rise as real GDP rises. And, indeed, an impressive amount of statistical evidence supports this supposition.

In addition, both common sense and mountains of evidence point to the conclusion that a higher price level leads to a higher demand for money simply because more dollars are needed to conduct the same transactions.

But real output and the price level are not the only factors affecting the demand for money; interest rates matter, too. At first, that may seem surprising because many forms of money pay either no interest or an interest rate which is fixed by law. Why, then, are interest rates relevant? They are relevant because money is only one of a variety of forms in which individuals can hold their wealth. Holders of money *give up* the opportunity to hold one of these other assets, such as government bonds, in order to gain the convenience of money. In so doing, they *give up* the interest that they could have earned on one of these alternative assets.

This is another example of the concept of **opportunity cost**.[2] On the surface, it seems virtually costless to hold money. But, *compared with the next best alternative,* this action is not costless at all. For example, if the best alternative to holding $100 in cash is to put those funds into a government bond that pays 8 percent interest, then the opportunity cost of holding that money is $8 per year (8 percent of $100).

How, then, should the rate of interest influence the quantity of money that people demand? People hold money because it facilitates making transactions. But this benefit comes at a cost: the potential interest that could have been earned by investing the funds in, say, government bonds. It is natural, therefore, to assume that when interest rates are high people make more strenuous efforts to economize on their holdings of money balances than they do when interest rates are low. In a word, rational behavior of consumers and business firms should make the demand to hold money *decline* as the interest rate *rises*. And, once again, careful analysis of the data shows this to be true. To summarize:

People and business firms hold money primarily to finance their transactions. Therefore, the quantity of money demanded increases as real output rises or as prices rise. However, the quantity of money demanded decreases as the rate of interest rises because the rate of interest is the opportunity cost of holding money balances.

It is possible to portray the demand for money by a graphical device, as shown in the three panels of Figure 13–4. In panel (a) we show a downward-sloping demand schedule for money (the curve labeled *MD*)—the quantity of money demanded decreases as the rate of interest rises. But since the quantity of money demanded also depends on real output and the price level, we must hold both real output and the price level constant in drawing up such a curve. Changes in either

---

[2]If you need to review this concept, see Chapter 3.

F i g u r e **13-4** | **THE DEMAND SCHEDULE FOR MONEY**

The downward-sloping line *MD* in part (a) is a typical demand curve for money. It slopes down because money is a less-attractive asset when interest rates on alternative assets are higher. However, such a curve can be drawn up only for particular levels of output and prices. A rise in either real output or the price level will shift the money-demand curve outward, as shown in part (b). Conversely, a fall in either real output or the price level will shift the curve inward, as in part (c).

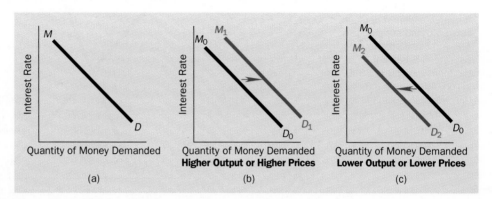

(a)

Higher Output or Higher Prices

(b)

Lower Output or Lower Prices

(c)

of these variables will shift the *MD* curve in the manner indicated in the other two panels because at higher levels of real GDP and higher prices, demand for money is greater; and at lower levels of real GDP and lower prices, demand for money is smaller.

EQUILIBRIUM IN THE MONEY MARKET

As is usual in supply and demand analysis, it is useful to put both sides of the market together on a single graph. Figure 13–5 combines the money supply schedule of Figure 13–3(a) (labeled *MS*) with the money demand schedule of Figure 13–4(a) (labeled *MD*). Point *E* is the equilibrium of the money market. The diagram thus shows that *given* real output and the price level (which locates the *MD* curve) and *given* the Federal Reserve's monetary policy (which locates the *MS* curve), the money market is in equilibrium at an interest rate of 5 percent and a money stock of $830 billion. At any interest rate above 5 percent, the quantity of money supplied would exceed the quantity demanded and the interest rate—which is the price for renting money—would therefore decline. At any interest rate below 5 percent, more money would be demanded than supplied, and so the interest rate would rise. This is familiar ground.

Since the Fed can shift the *MS* curve, it can alter this equilibrium through its **monetary policy**. Expansionary monetary policy actions include purchasing government securities in the open market, reducing reserve requirements, and encouraging banks to borrow. Any of these actions will provide additional excess reserves to the banking system, thus encouraging banks to increase their loans and deposits. As money becomes more plentiful, interest rates drop.

Our supply–demand analysis of the money market shows this in Figure 13–6(a). By shifting the money supply schedule outward from M_0S_0 to M_1S_1, the Fed

MONETARY POLICY refers to actions that the Federal Reserve System takes in order to change the equilibrium of the money market; that is, to alter the money supply, move interest rates, or both.

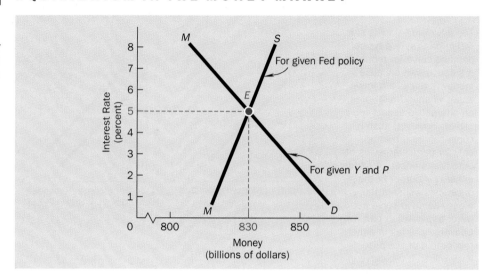

F i g u r e **13-5**   **EQUILIBRIUM IN THE MONEY MARKET**

Equilibrium in the market for money is determined by the intersection of demand curve *MD* and supply curve *MS*. At point *E*, the interest rate is 5 percent, and the money supply is $830 billion. At no other interest rate would the demand for and the supply of money be in balance.

---

moves the market equilibrium from point *E* to point *A*—thus forcing the interest rate down. Contractionary monetary policy actions, such as selling securities in the open market, raising reserve requirements, and discouraging borrowing, have the opposite effect. They push interest rates up, as Figure 13–6(b) shows. Thus:

Monetary policies that expand the money supply normally lower interest rates. Monetary policies that reduce the money supply normally raise interest rates.

INTEREST RATES AND TOTAL EXPENDITURE

We are now ready to see precisely how the Federal Reserve's monetary policy decisions affect unemployment, inflation, and the overall state of the economy. To begin, we go back to the analysis of Chapters 7–11, where we learned that aggregate demand is the sum of consumption spending (*C*), investment spending (*I*), government purchases of goods and services (*G*), and net exports (*X − IM*). We know that *fiscal policy* controls *G* directly and exerts influence over both *C* and *I* through the tax laws. We now want to find out how *monetary policy* affects total spending.

Most economists agree that, of the four components of aggregate demand, investment and net exports are the most sensitive to monetary policy. The effects of monetary and fiscal policy on net exports will be studied in detail in Chapter 20, after we have learned about international exchange rates. The rest of this chapter focuses on investment (*I*).

Business investment in new factories and machinery is sensitive to interest rates for reasons that have been explained in earlier chapters.[3] Since the rate of interest that must be paid on borrowings is one element of the cost of making an invest-

---

[3]See, for example, Chapter 8, page 183.

ment, business executives will find investment prospects less attractive as interest rates rise. Therefore, they will spend less. For similar reasons, *investment in housing* by individuals may also be deterred by high interest rates. Since the interest cost of a home mortgage is the major component of the total cost of owning a home, fewer families will want to buy a new home when interest rates are high than when interest rates are low. We conclude that:

Higher interest rates lead to lower investment spending. But investment (I) is a component of total spending, $C + I + G + (X - IM)$. Therefore, when interest rates rise, total spending falls. In terms of the 45° line diagram of previous chapters, a higher interest rate leads to a lower expenditure schedule. Conversely, a lower interest rate leads to a higher expenditure schedule. (See Figure 13–7.)

MONETARY POLICY AND AGGREGATE DEMAND IN THE KEYNESIAN MODEL

The effect of interest rates on spending provides a mechanism through which monetary policy affects aggregate demand in the Keynesian model. We know from our analysis of the money market that monetary policy can have a profound effect on the rate of interest. Let us, therefore, outline how monetary policy works.

Suppose the Federal Reserve, seeing the economy stuck with unemployment and a recessionary gap, raises the money supply. It would normally do this by purchasing government securities in the open market, but the specific weapon that the Fed uses is not terribly important for present purposes. What matters is that the money supply (M) expands.

With the demand schedule for money (temporarily) fixed, such an increase in the supply of money has the effect that an increase in supply always has in a free market—it lowers the price. (See Figure 13–8.) In this case, the price of renting money is the rate of interest, r; so r falls.

Figure **13-6**

THE EFFECTS OF MONETARY POLICY ON THE MONEY MARKET

The two parts of this figure show the effects of monetary policy on the money supply (M) and the rate of interest (r). In part (a), expansionary monetary policies shift the supply schedule from M_0S_0 to M_1S_1 and push the equilibrium from point E to point A; M rises while r falls. In part (b), contractionary policies pull the supply schedule in from M_0S_0 to M_2S_2 causing equilibrium to move up from point E to point B; M falls as r rises.

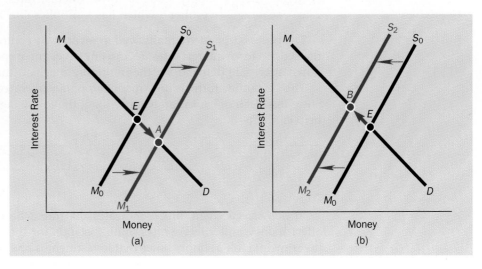

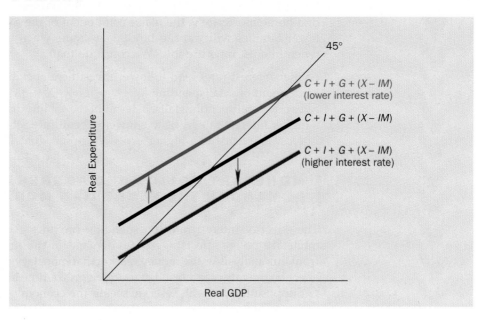

| Figure | 13-7 | THE EFFECT OF INTEREST RATES ON AGGREGATE DEMAND |

Because interest rates are an important determinant of investment spending, *I*, the *C + I + G + (X − IM)* schedule shifts whenever the rate of interest changes. Specifically, as shown here, lower interest rates shift the curve upward and higher interest rates shift it downward.

Next, for reasons we have just outlined, investment spending (*I*) rises in response to the lower interest rates. But, as we learned in Chapter 9, such an autonomous rise in investment kicks off a multiplier chain of increases in output and employment. Thus, finally, we have completed the links from the money supply to the level of aggregate demand. In brief, monetary policy works as follows:

A higher money supply leads to lower interest rates, and these lower interest rates encourage investment, which has multiplier effects on aggregate demand.

The process operates equally well in reverse. By contracting the money supply, the Fed can force interest rates up, causing investment spending to fall and pulling down aggregate demand via the multiplier mechanism.

This, in outline form, is how monetary policy operates in the Keynesian model. Since the chain of causation is fairly long, the following schematic diagram may help clarify it.

$$\boxed{\text{Federal Reserve policy}} \overset{①}{\rightarrow} \boxed{M \text{ and } r} \overset{②}{\rightarrow} \boxed{I} \overset{③}{\rightarrow} \boxed{C + I + G + (X + IM)} \overset{④}{\rightarrow} \boxed{\text{GDP}}$$

In this causal chain, link 1 indicates that the actions of the Federal Reserve affect money and interest rates. Link 2 stands for the effect of interest rates on investment. Link 3 simply notes that investment is one component of total spending. And link 4 is the multiplier, relating an autonomous change in investment to the ultimate change in aggregate demand.

Let us next review what we know about each of these links and fill in some illustrative numbers. In the process, we will see what economists must study if they are to estimate the effects of monetary policy.

Link 1 is the subject of this chapter and of Figure 13–8. Given the initial level of real GDP and prices, the demand schedule for money is shown by curve MD. The Fed's expansionary action shifts the supply schedule out from M_0S_0 to M_1S_1, resulting in an increase in the money stock from $830 billion to $880 billion in this example, and a decline in the interest rate from 5 percent to 3 percent. Thus the first thing an economist must know is how sensitive interest rates are to changes in the supply of money.

Link 2 translates the drop in the interest rate into an increase in investment spending (I), which we take to be $200 billion in this example. To estimate this effect in practice, economists must study the sensitivity of investment to interest rates.

Link 3 instructs us to enter this $200 billion rise in I as an autonomous shift in the $C + I + G + (X - IM)$ schedule of a 45° line diagram. Figure 13–9 carries out this step. The expenditure schedule rises from $C + I_0 + G + (X - IM)$ to $C + I_1 + G + (X - IM)$.

Finally, link 4 applies multiplier analysis to this vertical shift in the expenditure schedule in order to predict the eventual increase in real GDP demanded. In our examples, we have been using a multiplier of 2.5, so multiplying $200 billion by 2.5 gives the final effect on aggregate demand—a rise of $500 billion. This is shown in Figure 13–9 as a shift in equilibrium from E_0 (where GDP is $6000 billion) to E_1 (where GDP is $6500 billion). Of course, the size of the multiplier itself must also be estimated. To summarize:

The effect of monetary policy on aggregate demand depends on the sensitivity of interest rates to the money supply, on the responsiveness of investment spending to the rate of interest, and on the size of the multiplier.

F i g u r e **13–8** **THE EFFECT OF EXPANSIONARY MONETARY POLICY ON THE MONEY SUPPLY AND RATE OF INTEREST**

An expansionary monetary policy pushes the money supply schedule outward from M_0S_0 to M_1S_1, causing equilibrium in the money market to shift from point E_0 to point E_1. The money supply rises from $830 billion to $880 billion, while the interest rate falls from 5 percent to 3 percent.

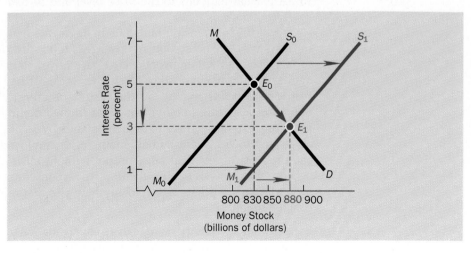

| Figure | 13–9 | THE EFFECT OF EXPANSIONARY MONETARY POLICY ON AGGREGATE DEMAND |

Expansionary monetary policies, which lower the rate of interest, will cause the $C + I + G + (X - IM)$ schedule to shift upward from $C + I_0 + G + (X - IM)$ to $C + I_1 + G + (X - IM)$, as shown here. In this example, since the multiplier is 2.5, a $200 billion rise in investment leads, via the multiplier process, to a $500 billion rise in GDP.

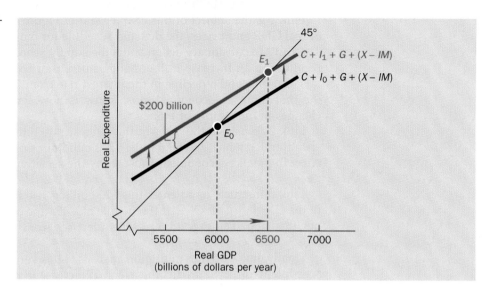

MONEY AND THE PRICE LEVEL IN THE KEYNESIAN MODEL

The analysis up to this point leaves one important question unanswered: What happens to the price level? To find the answer, we must simply remember once again that prices and output are determined jointly by aggregate demand *and* aggregate supply. The analysis of monetary policy that we have completed so far has shown us how an increase in the money supply shifts the aggregate demand curve, that is, increases the *aggregate quantity demanded at any given price level*. But to learn what happens to the price level and to real output, we must consider *aggregate supply* as well.

Specifically, in considering shifts in aggregate demand caused by *fiscal* policy in Chapter 11, we noted that an upsurge in total spending normally induces firms to increase output somewhat *and* to raise prices somewhat. This is just what an aggregate supply curve shows. Whether prices or real output exhibit the greater response depends mainly on the degree of capacity utilization. An economy operating near full employment has a limited ability to increase production; it therefore responds to greater demand mainly by raising prices. On the other hand, an economy with a substantial amount of unemployed labor and unused capital can produce a great deal more output without raising prices.

Since this analysis of output and price responses applies equally well to monetary policy or, for that matter, to anything else that raises aggregate demand, we conclude that:

Expansionary monetary policy causes some inflation under normal circumstances. But how much inflation it causes depends on the state of the economy. If the money supply is expanded when unemployment is high and there is much unused industrial capacity, then the result may be little or no inflation. If, however, increases in the money supply occur when the economy is fully employed, then the main result is likely to be inflation.

The effect of a rise in the money supply on the price level is depicted graphically on an aggregate supply and demand diagram in Figure 13–10. The curved shape of aggregate supply curve SS reflects the assumptions that output rises with little inflation when the economy is depressed, while prices rise with little gain in output when the economy is near full employment.

In the example we have been using, the Fed's actions raise the money supply by $50 billion, and this increases aggregate demand (through the multiplier) by $500 billion. We enter this in Figure 13–10 as a horizontal shift of $500 billion in the aggregate demand curve, from D_0D_0 to D_1D_1. The diagram shows that this expansionary monetary policy raises the economy's equilibrium from point E to point B—the price level therefore rises from 100 to 103, or 3 percent. The diagram also shows that real GDP rises by only $400 billion, which is less than the $500 billion stimulus to aggregate demand. The reason, as we know from earlier chapters, is that rising prices stifle demand.

By taking account of the effect of an increase in the money supply on the price level, we have completed our story about the role of monetary policy in the Keynesian model. We can thus expand our schematic diagram of monetary policy as follows:

$$\boxed{\begin{array}{c}\text{Federal Reserve}\\\text{policy}\end{array}} \overset{①}{\to} \boxed{M \text{ and } r} \overset{②}{\to} \boxed{I} \overset{③}{\to} \boxed{C + I + G + (X + IM)} \overset{④}{\to} \boxed{Y \text{ and } P}$$

F i g u r e **13–10** **THE INFLATIONARY EFFECTS OF EXPANSIONARY MONETARY POLICY**

Raising the money supply normally causes inflation. When expansionary monetary policy causes the aggregate demand curve to shift outward from D_0D_0 to D_1D_1, the economy's equilibrium shifts from point E to point B. Real output expands (in this case by $400 billion), but prices also rise (in this case by 3 percent).

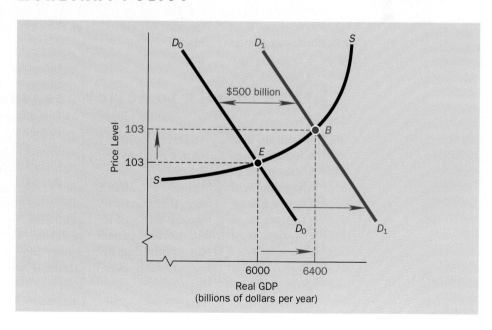

The last link now recognizes that *both* output *and* prices normally are affected by changes in the money supply.

APPLICATION: WHY THE AGGREGATE DEMAND CURVE SLOPES DOWNWARD

This analysis of the effect of money on the price level puts us in a better position to understand why higher prices reduce aggregate quantity demanded; that is, why the aggregate demand curve slopes downward. In earlier chapters, we explained this phenomenon in two ways. First, we observed that rising prices reduce the purchasing power of certain assets held by consumers, especially money and government bonds, and that this in turn retards consumption spending. Second, we noted that higher domestic prices depress exports and stimulate imports.

There is nothing wrong with this analysis. But higher prices have an important effect on aggregate demand through another channel that we are now in a position to understand.

Money is demanded primarily to conduct transactions and, as we have noted in this chapter, a rise in the *average money cost* of each transaction—as a result of a rise in the price level—will increase the quantity of money demanded. This means that when expansionary policy of any kind pushes the price level up, more money will be demanded at any given interest rate.

But, if the supply of money is *not* increased, an increase in the quantity of money demanded at any given interest rate must force the cost of borrowing money—the rate of interest—to rise. As we know, increases in interest rates reduce investment and, hence, reduce aggregate demand. This, then, is the main reason why the economy's aggregate demand curve has a negative slope, meaning that aggregate quantity demanded is lower when prices are higher. In sum:

At higher price levels, the quantity of money demanded is greater. Given a fixed supply schedule, therefore, a higher price level must lead to a higher interest rate. Since high interest rates discourage investment, aggregate quantity demanded is lower when the price level is higher. That is, the aggregate demand curve slopes downward to the right.

FROM MODELS TO POLICY DEBATES

You will no doubt be relieved to hear that we have now provided just about all the technical apparatus we need to analyze stabilization policy. To be sure, you will encounter many graphs in the next few chapters. But most of them are repeats of diagrams with which you are already familiar. Our attention now turns from *building* a theory to *using* that theory to understand important policy issues. The next three chapters take up a trio of important and controversial policy debates that surface regularly in the newspapers: the debate over the efficacy of monetary policy (Chapter 14), the continuing debate over the government budget deficit (Chapter 15), and the controversy over the tradeoff between inflation and unemployment (Chapter 16).

Summary

1. A **central bank** is a bank for banks.

2. The **Federal Reserve System** is America's central bank. There are 12 Federal Reserve banks, but most of the power is held by the Board of Governors in Washington and by the **Federal Open Market Committee.**

3. The Federal Reserve is independent of the rest of the government. There is controversy over whether this **independence** is a good idea, and a number of reforms have been suggested over the years that would make the Fed more accountable to the president or to Congress.

4. The Fed has three major weapons for control of the money supply: **open-market operations, reserve requirements**, and its **lending policy** to the banks.

5. By lowering or raising reserve requirements, the Fed makes it possible for each dollar of reserves to support more or fewer dollars of deposits. Thus, lowering or raising the reserve ratio is one way to increase or decrease the money supply.

6. But the Fed does not do this very often. More typically, it raises the money supply by purchasing government securities in the open market. The Fed's payments to the banks for such purchases provide banks with new reserves and, hence, lead to a larger money supply. Conversely, open market sales of securities take reserves from the banks and lead to a smaller money supply.

7. When the Fed buys bonds, bond prices rise and interest rates fall. When the Fed sells bonds, bond prices fall and interest rates rise.

8. The Fed can also increase the money supply by allowing banks to borrow more reserves, perhaps by reducing the interest rate it charges on such loans. Alternatively, by discouraging borrowing, it can make the money supply contract.

9. None of these weapons, however, gives the Fed perfect control over the money supply in the short run, because it cannot predict perfectly how far the process of deposit creation or destruction will go.

10. The **money supply schedule** shows that more money is supplied at higher interest rates because, as interest rates rise, banks find it more profitable to expand their loans and deposits. This schedule can be shifted by Federal Reserve policy.

11. The **money demand schedule** shows that less money is demanded at higher interest rates because interest is the opportunity cost of holding money. This schedule shifts when output or the price level changes.

12. The **equilibrium** money stock (M) and the equilibrium rate of interest (r) are determined by the intersection of the money supply and money demand schedules.

13. Federal Reserve policy can shift this equilibrium. Expansionary policies cause M to rise and r to fall. Contractionary policies reduce M and increase r.

14. Investment spending (I), including business investment and investment in new homes, is sensitive to interest rates (r). Specifically, I is lower when r is higher.

15. This fact explains how **monetary policy** works in the Keynesian model. Raising the money supply (M) leads to lower r; the lower interest rates stimulate more investment spending; and this investment stimulus, via the multiplier, then raises aggregate demand.

16. However, prices are likely to rise as output rises. The amount of inflation caused by increasing the money supply depends on the levels of unemployment and of capacity utilization. There will be much inflation when the economy is near full employment, but little inflation when there is a great deal of slack.

17. The main reason **why the aggregate demand curve slopes downward** is that higher prices increase the demand to hold money in order to finance transactions. Given the money supply, this pushes interest rates up; and this, in turn, discourages investment.

Key Concepts and Terms

Central bank
Federal Reserve System
Federal Open Market
   Committee (FOMC)
Independence of the Fed
Reserve requirements
Open-market operations

Bond prices and interest rates
Contraction and expansion
   of the money supply
Federal Reserve lending to banks
Moral suasion
Supply of money
Demand for money

Opportunity cost
Equilibrium in the money
   market
Monetary policy
Why the aggregate demand
   curve slopes downward

1. Why does a modern industrial economy need a central bank?

2. A few years ago, Congressman Lee Hamilton proposed legislation that would have reduced much of the secrecy about the Fed's operations, put the secretary of the treasury on the Federal Reserve Board, and made the term of the Fed chairman coincide with that of the president. Which, if any, of these provisions would you favor? Explain your reasons.

3. Suppose there is $100 billion of cash in existence, and that half of it is held in bank vaults as *required* reserves (that is, banks hold no *excess* reserves). How large will the money supply be if the required reserve ratio is $16\frac{2}{3}$ percent? 20 percent? 25 percent?

4. Show the balance sheet changes that would take place if the Federal Reserve Bank of San Francisco purchased an office building from the Bank of America for a price of $100 million. Compare this to the effect of an open-market purchase of securities shown in Table 13–1. What do you conclude?

5. Suppose that the Fed purchases $6 million worth of government bonds from Donald Trump, who banks at Citibank in New York. Show the effects on the balance sheets of the Fed, Citibank, and Donald Trump. (*Hint*: What will Trump do with the $6 million check he receives from the Fed?) Does it make any difference if the Fed buys bonds from a bank or from an individual?

6. Why would the Fed's control over the money supply be tighter under a system of 100 percent reserves?

7. Explain why the quantity of money supplied normally is higher and the quantity of money demanded normally is lower at higher interest rates.

8. Starting sometime in the spring of 1989, the Fed decided that interest rates were too high and took steps to drive them down—a process it continued for more than three years. How could the Fed push interest rates down? Illustrate on a diagram.

9. Explain why both business investments and purchases of new homes are expected to decline when interest rates rise.

10. Explain what a $50 billion increase in the money supply will do to real GDP under the following assumptions:

    a. Each $10 billion increase in the money supply reduces the rate of interest by 0.5 percentage point.
    b. Each 1 percentage point decline in interest rates stimulates $30 billion of new investment spending.
    c. The expenditure multiplier is 2.
    d. There is so much unemployment that prices do not rise noticeably when demand increases.

11. Explain how your answer to Question 10 would differ if each of the assumptions were changed. Specifically, what sorts of changes in the assumptions would make monetary policy very weak?

12. Use graphs like Figures 13–5 and 13–7 to explain why the aggregate demand curve has a negative slope.

13. For years now, the federal government has been trying to lower its budget deficit by reducing spending or raising taxes. If the Federal Reserve wants to maintain the same level of aggregate demand in the face of a deficit reduction, what should it do? What would you expect to happen to interest rates?

14. (More difficult) Consider an economy in which government purchases, taxes, and net exports are all zero, the consumption function is:

$$C = 300 + 0.75\,Y,$$

and investment spending (I) depends on the rate of interest (r) in the following way:

$$I = 1000 - 100\,r.$$

Find the equilibrium GDP if the Fed makes the rate of interest (a) 2 percent ($r = 0.02$), (b) 5 percent, (c) 10 percent.

Chapter 14

THE DEBATE OVER MONETARY POLICY

The love of money is the root of all evil.

THE NEW TESTAMENT

Lack of money is the root of all evil.

GEORGE BERNARD SHAW

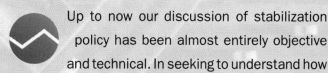 Up to now our discussion of stabilization policy has been almost entirely objective and technical. In seeking to understand how the national economy works and how government policies affect it, we have mostly ignored the intense economic and political controversies that surround the actual conduct of stabilization policy. Chapters 14 through 16 are about precisely these issues. ¶ We begin the chapter by explaining an alternative theory of how money affects the economy, known as *monetarism*. Although the monetarist and Keynesian views seem to contradict one another, we will see that the conflict is more apparent than real. In fact, the disagreement is akin to hearing a Briton say, "Yes," and a Frenchman say, "Oui." The uninitiated hear two different languages, but knowledgeable listeners understand that they mean the same thing. ¶ However, while monetarist and Keynesian *theories* are not very different, there *are* significant differences among economists over the appropriate design and execution of monetary *policy*. These differences occupy the rest of the chapter. We will learn about the continuing debates over the nature of aggregate

supply, over the relative importance of monetary and fiscal policy, and over whether the Federal Reserve should try to control the money stock or interest rates. As we shall see, the resolution of these issues is crucial for the proper conduct of monetary policy and, indeed, to the decision of whether the government should try to conduct any stabilization policy at all. Finally, since economists' abilities to forecast the future are critical for the success or failure of stabilization efforts, some time is devoted to the techniques and accuracy of economic forecasting.

VELOCITY AND THE QUANTITY THEORY OF MONEY

We saw in the last chapter how money influences real output and the price level in the Keynesian model. But there is another way to look at these matters, using a model that is much older than the Keynesian model. This model is known as the **quantity theory of money**, and it is easy to understand once we have introduced one new concept—*velocity*.

We learned in Chapter 12 that because barter is so cumbersome, virtually all economic transactions in advanced economies are conducted by the use of money. This means that if there are, say, $4500 billion worth of transactions in the economy during a particular year, and there is an average money stock of $900 billion during that year, then each dollar of money must get used an average of five times during the year (since 5 × $900 billion = $4500 billion).

VELOCITY indicates the number of times per year that an "average dollar" is spent on goods and services. It is the ratio of nominal GDP to the number of dollars in the money stock. That is:

$$\text{Velocity} = \frac{\text{Nominal GDP}}{\text{Money stock}}$$

The number 5 in this example is called the **velocity of circulation**, or just **velocity** for short, because it indicates the speed at which money circulates. For example, a particular dollar bill might be used to buy a haircut in January; the barber might use it to buy a sweater in March; the storekeeper might then use it to pay for gasoline in May; the gas station owner could pay it out to the painter who paints his house in October; and the painter might spend it on a Christmas present in December. This would mean that the dollar was used five times during the year. If it were used only four times during the year, its velocity would be only 4, and so on. Similarly, a $20 bill circulating with a velocity of 8 would be the monetary instrument used to finance $160 worth of transactions in that year.

No one has data on all the transactions in the economy. To make velocity an operational concept, economists must settle on a precise definition of transactions that they can actually measure. The most popular choice is gross domestic product in current dollars (nominal GDP), even though it ignores many transactions that use money—such as sales of existing assets. If we accept nominal GDP as a measure of the money value of transactions, we are led to a concrete definition of velocity as the ratio of nominal GDP to the number of dollars in the money stock. Since nominal GDP is the product of real GDP times the price level, we can write this definition in symbols as:

$$\text{Velocity} = \frac{\text{Value of transactions}}{\text{Money Stock}} = \frac{\text{Nominal GDP}}{M} = \frac{P \times Y}{M}.$$

The **EQUATION OF EXCHANGE** states that the money value of GDP transactions must be equal to the product of the average stock of money times velocity. That is:

$$M \times V = P \times Y.$$

By multiplying both sides of the equation by M, we arrive at an identity called the **equation of exchange** that relates the money supply and nominal GDP:

$$\text{Money supply} \times \text{Velocity} = \text{Nominal GDP}.$$

Alternatively, stated in symbols, we have:

$$M \times V = P \times Y.$$

Here we have an obvious link between the stock of money, M, and the nominal value of the nation's output. But it is only a matter of arithmetic, not of economics. For example, it does not imply that the Fed can raise nominal GDP by increasing M. Why not? Because V might simultaneously fall by enough to prevent $M \times V$ from rising. In words, if there were more dollar bills in circulation than before, but each bill changed hands more slowly, total spending might not rise. Thus:

The quantity theory of money transforms the equation of exchange from an accounting identity into an economic model by assuming that changes in velocity are so minor that velocity can be taken to be virtually constant.

You can see that if V never changed, the equation of exchange would be a marvelously simple model of the determination of nominal GDP—far simpler than the Keynesian model. To see this, we need only to turn the equation of exchange around to read,

$$P \times Y = V \times M.$$

This equation says, for example, that if the Federal Reserve wants to increase nominal GDP by 12.7 percent, it need only raise the money supply by 12.7 percent. In such a simple world, economists could use the equation of exchange to *predict* nominal GDP simply by predicting the quantity of money. And policymakers could *control* nominal GDP simply by controlling the money supply.

In the real world things are not so simple because velocity is not a fixed number. But this does not necessarily destroy the usefulness of the quantity theory. We explained in Chapter 1 why all economic models make assumptions that are at least mildly unrealistic—without such assumptions they would not be models at all, just tedious descriptions of reality. The question is really whether the assumption of constant velocity is a useful abstraction from annoying detail or a gross distortion of facts.

Figure 14–1 sheds some light on this question by showing the behavior of velocity since 1929. You will note that there are two different measures of velocity, labeled $V1$ and $V2$. Why? Recall from Chapter 12 that there are several ways to measure money, the most popular of which are $M1$ and $M2$. Since velocity (V) is simply nominal GDP divided by the money stock (M), we get a different measure of V for each measure of M. Figure 14–1 shows the velocities of both $M1$ and $M2$.

Several features are apparent. You will undoubtedly notice the difference in the behavior of $V1$ versus $V2$. There is a clear downward trend in $V1$ from 1929 until 1946, a pronounced upward trend until 1981, and quite erratic behavior in recent years. Clearly, *the velocity of M1 is not constant over long periods of time.* However, *the velocity of M2 is much more constant* and shows little if any trend since 1929. Closer examination of monthly or quarterly data on either $V1$ or $V2$ reveals some rather substantial fluctuations of velocity. Such fluctuations have led most economists to conclude that *velocity is not constant in the short run.* And predictions of nominal GDP based on the product of V times M have not fared very well, regardless of how M is measured. It seems, then, that the strict quantity theory of money is not an adequate model of aggregate demand.

THE DETERMINANTS OF VELOCITY

Since it is abundantly clear that velocity is a variable, not a constant, we can use the equation of exchange as a model of GDP determination only by examining

Figure 14-1 **VELOCITY OF CIRCULATION, 1929-1992**

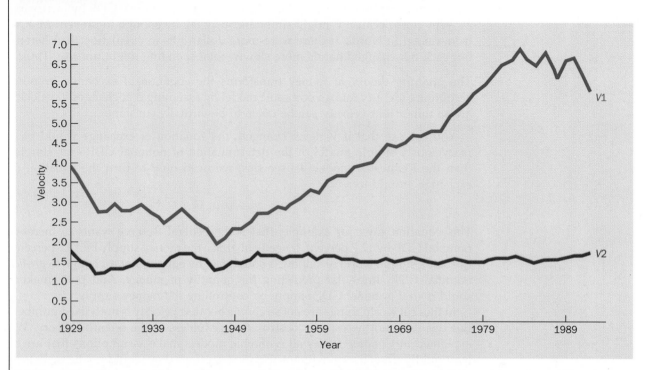

During a period of American history of almost 65 years, the velocity of *M*1 fell from about 3.5 in 1930 to 2 in 1946, and then rose to almost 7 in 1981 before falling again. Clearly, it has not been constant over long periods of time. The velocity of *M*2, however, looks much more stable.

SOURCE: Constructed by the authors; data from Bureau of Economic Analysis, Federal Reserve Board, and Professor Robert Rasche.

the determinants of velocity. What factors decide whether *V*1 or *V*2 will be 4 or 5 or 6; that is, whether a dollar will be used to buy goods and services four or five or six times a year?

Perhaps the principal factor is the *frequency with which paychecks are received.* This can best be explained through a numerical example. Consider a worker who earns $24,000 a year, paid to her in 12 monthly paychecks of $2000 each. Suppose that she spends the whole $2000 over the course of each month and maintains a minimum balance in the checking account of $500. Each payday her bank balance will shoot up to $2500 and then be gradually whittled down as she makes withdrawals to purchase goods and services. Finally, on the day before her next paycheck arrives, her checking balance will be just $500. Over the course of a typical month, then, her average checking account balance will be $1500 (halfway between $2500 and $500).

Now suppose her employer switches to a twice-a-month payroll. Her paychecks come twice as often, but are reduced to $1000 each. There is no reason for her rate of spending to change, but her *cash balances* will change. For now her checking balance will rise only to $1500 on payday (the $500 minimum balance plus the $1000 paycheck), and it will still be drawn down gradually to $500. Her average cash balance will therefore decline to $1000 (halfway between $1500 and $500).

Why is this so? Because, with the next paycheck coming sooner than before, it is not necessary to keep as much cash in the bank in order to carry out a given quantity of transactions.

But what does this have to do with velocity? Notice that when she was on a monthly payroll, this worker's personal velocity was:

$$V = \frac{\text{Annual income}}{\text{Average cash balance}} = \frac{\$24,000}{\$1500} = 16.$$

When she switched to a semimonthly payroll, velocity rose to:

$$V = \frac{\text{Annual income}}{\text{Average cash balance}} = \frac{\$24,000}{\$1000} = 24.$$

The general lesson to be learned is that:

More frequent wage payments mean that people can conduct their transactions with lower average cash balances. Since they will want to hold less cash, money will circulate faster. In other words, velocity will rise.

A second factor influencing velocity is the *efficiency of the payments mechanism*, including how quickly checks clear banks, the use of credit cards, and other methods of transferring funds. It is easy to see how this works.

The example in the previous paragraph assumed that our worker holds her entire paycheck in the form of money until she uses it to make a purchase. But, given that many forms of money pay little or no interest, this method may not be the most rational behavior. If it is possible to convert interest-bearing assets into money on short notice and at low cost, a rational individual might use her paycheck to purchase such assets and then use credit cards for most purchases, making periodic transfers to her checking account as necessary. For the same amount of total transactions, then, she would require lower money balances. This means that money would circulate faster: velocity would rise.

The incentive to limit cash holdings depends on the ease and speed with which it is possible to exchange money for other assets. This is what we mean by the "efficiency of the payments mechanism." As computerization has speeded up the bookkeeping procedures of banks, as financial innovations have made it possible to transfer funds rapidly between checking accounts and other assets, and as credit cards have come to be used instead of cash, the need to hold money balances has declined. By definition, then, velocity has risen.

Fortunately such basic changes in the payments mechanism usually take place only gradually, and thus often are easy to predict. But this is not always so. For example, a host of financial innovations in the 1970s and 1980s—some of which were mentioned in Chapter 12's discussion of the definitions of money—gave analysts fits in predicting velocity and led many to question the usefulness of the concept.

A third determinant of velocity is the *rate of interest*. The basic motive for economizing on money holdings is that most money (at least M1) pays little or no interest, while many alternative stores of value pay higher rates. The higher these alternative rates of interest, the greater the incentive to economize on holding money. Therefore, as interest rates rise, people want to hold less money. So the existing stock of money circulates faster, and velocity rises.

It is this factor that most directly undercuts the usefulness of the quantity theory of money as a guide for monetary policy. For in the last chapter we learned that expansionary monetary policy, which increases M, normally also decreases the interest rate. But if interest rates fall, other things being equal, velocity (V) will also fall. Thus, *when the Fed raises the money supply (M), the product M $\times$ V may go up by a smaller percentage than does M itself.*

One component of the interest rate is worth singling out for special attention: *the expected rate of inflation.* We explained in Chapter 6 why an "inflation premium" equal to the expected inflation rate often gets built into market interest rates.[1] Thus, in many instances, high inflation is the principal cause of high nominal interest rates. High rates of inflation, which erode the purchasing power of money, therefore lead both individuals and businesses to hold as little money as they can get by on—actions that increase velocity. To summarize this discussion of the determinants of velocity:

Velocity is not a strict constant but depends on such things as the frequency of payments, the efficiency of the financial system, the rate of interest, and the rate of inflation. Only by studying these determinants of velocity can we hope to predict the level of nominal GDP from knowledge of the money supply.

MONETARISM: THE QUANTITY THEORY MODERNIZED

The foregoing does not mean, however, that the equation of exchange cannot be a useful framework within which to organize macroeconomic analysis. Under the right circumstances, it can be. And during the past 30 years or so a group of economists called *monetarists* has convincingly demonstrated that this is so.

Monetarists recognize that velocity is not literally constant. But they stress that it is fairly *predictable*—certainly in the long run and probably also in the short run. This leads them to the conclusion that the best way to study economic activity is to start with the *equation of exchange: M $\times$ V = P $\times$ Y.* From here, careful study of the determinants of M (which we provided in the previous two chapters) and of V (which we just completed) can be used to *predict* the behavior of nominal GDP. Similarly, given an understanding of movements in V, control over the money supply gives the Fed *control* over nominal GDP.

These are the central tenets of **monetarism**. When something happens in the economy, monetarists ask two questions:

1. What does this event do to the stock of money?

2. What does this event do to velocity?

From the answers, they assert that they can predict the path of nominal GDP.

By comparing the monetarist approach with the Keynesian approach that we described in the previous chapter, we can put both theories into perspective and understand the limitations of each. As we mentioned earlier, they differ more in style than in substance. Keynesians divide economic knowledge into four neat compartments—marked "C," "I," "G," and "$(X - IM)$"—and unite them all with the equilibrium condition that $Y = C + I + G + (X - IM)$. In Keynesian analysis, money affects the economy by first affecting interest rates.

> **MONETARISM** is a mode of analysis that uses the equation of exchange to organize and analyze macroeconomic data.

---

[1]If you need review, turn back to pages 136–37.

Monetarists, on the other hand, organize their knowledge into two alternative boxes—labeled "*M*" and "*V*"—and then use a simple identity that says $M \times V = P \times Y$ to bring this knowledge to bear in predicting aggregate demand. In the monetarist model, the role of money in the national economy is not necessarily limited to working through interest rates.

The bit of arithmetic that multiplies *M* and *V* to get $P \times Y$ is neither more nor less profound than the one that adds up *C*, *I*, *G* and $(X - IM)$ to get *Y*. And certainly both are correct. The only substantive difference is that the monetarist equation leads to a prediction of *nominal* GDP, that is, the demand for goods and services measured in money terms, while the Keynesian equation leads to a prediction of *real* GDP, that is, the demand for goods and services measured in dollars of constant purchasing power.

Why, then, do we not simply mesh the two theories—using the monetarist approach to study nominal GDP and the Keynesian approach to study real GDP? It seems that by doing so we could use the separate analyses of real and nominal GDP to obtain a prediction of the future behavior of the price level, which, of course, is the ratio of nominal GDP to real GDP.

The reason that this appealing procedure will not work helps point out the major limitation of each theory. *Taken by itself, either theory is incomplete.* Each gives us a picture of the *demand* side of the economy without saying anything about the *supply* side. To try to predict both the price level and real output solely from these demand-oriented models would be like trying to predict the price of peanuts by studying only the behavior of consumers and ignoring that of farmers. It just will not work. In terms of our earlier aggregate supply and demand analysis:

Both the monetarist and Keynesian analyses are ways of studying the aggregate demand curve. In neither case is it possible to learn anything about both output and the price level without also studying the *aggregate supply curve.*

Economists thus are forced to choose between two alternative ways of predicting aggregate demand. Those who choose the monetarist route will use velocity and the money supply to study the demand for *nominal* GDP, that is, they view money as the key determinant of aggregate demand in nominal terms. But then they must turn to the supply side to estimate how any predicted change in nominal demand gets apportioned between changes in production and changes in prices. The schematic diagram on page 317, with its emphasis on interest rates, plays little role in the monetarist analysis of the transmission mechanism for monetary policy.

On the other hand, an economist working with the Keynesian approach will start by using the schematic diagram on page 317 to predict how monetary policy affects the demand for *real* GDP, that is, aggregate demand in real terms. But then he will have to turn to the aggregate supply curve to estimate the inflationary consequences of this real demand.

Which approach works better? There is no generally correct answer for all economies in all periods of time. Therefore, it is not surprising that some economists prefer one approach while others favor the alternative. When velocity behaved predictably in the 1960s and early 1970s, monetarism won many converts—in the United States and around the world. But then velocity behaved erratically and inexplicably here and in other countries during the 1980s, and most economists abandoned monetarism.

FISCAL POLICY, INTEREST RATES, AND VELOCITY

We have now almost reconciled the Keynesian and monetarist views of how the economy operates. Keynesian analysis lends itself naturally to the study of fiscal policy, since G is a part of $C + I + G + (X - IM)$. But we learned in the previous chapter that Keynesian economics also provides a powerful and important role for monetary policy: an increase in the money supply reduces interest rates, which, in turn, stimulates the demand for investment.

Monetarist analysis provides an obvious and direct route by which monetary policy influences both output and prices. But can the monetarist approach also handle fiscal policy? It can, because fiscal policy has an important effect on the rate of interest. And it is not hard to understand how this effect operates.

Let's see what happens to real output and the price level following, say, a rise in government purchases of goods and services. We learned in Chapter 11 that both real GDP (Y) and the price level (P) rise. But Chapter 13's analysis of the demand for money taught us that rising Y and P push the demand curve for money outward to the right. With no change in the supply curve for money, the rate of interest must rise. So *expansionary fiscal policy raises interest rates*.

If the government uses its spending and taxing weapons in the opposite direction, the same process works in reverse. Falling output and (possibly) falling prices shift the demand curve for money inward to the left. With a fixed supply curve for money, equilibrium in the money market leads to a lower interest rate. Thus:

Monetary policy is not the only type of policy that affects interest rates. Fiscal policy also affects interest rates. Specifically, increases in government spending or tax cuts normally push interest rates up, whereas restrictive fiscal policies normally pull interest rates down.

The fact that fiscal policy affects interest rates gives it a role in the monetarist model despite the fact that the equation of exchange, $M \times V = P \times Y$, does not include either government spending or taxation among its variables. Any fiscal policy that a Keynesian would call expansionary—higher spending, lower taxes, and so on—pushes up the rate of interest. And rising interest rates push up velocity because people want to hold less money when the interest they can earn on alternative assets increases. So it is through the V term in $M \times V$ that fiscal policy does its work in the monetarist framework. The equation of exchange, $M \times V = P \times Y$, then implies that nominal GDP must rise when, say, government spending increases—even if M is fixed—because velocity is higher.

Conversely, restrictive fiscal policies like tax increases and expenditure cuts reduce the quantity of money demanded and lower interest rates. The consequent drop in velocity reduces income through the equation of exchange, because the money supply circulates more slowly.

The translation, then, is complete. The Keynesian story about how fiscal policy works can be phrased in the monetarist dialect. And the monetarist tale about monetary policy can be told with a Keynesian accent. Furthermore, both modes of analysis help only to explain the mysteries of aggregate *demand* and must be supplemented by an analysis of aggregate *supply* to be complete. We must conclude, then, that:

The differences between Keynesians and monetarists have been grossly exaggerated by the news media. Indeed, when it comes to matters of basic economic theory, there are hardly any differences at all.

3 2 9

DEBATE: SHOULD STABILIZATION POLICY RELY ON FISCAL OR MONETARY POLICY?

APPLICATION: THE MULTIPLIER FORMULA ONCE AGAIN

The fact that expansionary fiscal policy pushes up interest rates has one other important consequence that we should mention. Recall that higher interest rates deter private investment spending. This means that when the government raises the G component of $C + I + G + (X - IM)$, one of the side effects of its action will be to reduce the I component (by raising interest rates). Consequently, total spending will rise by less than simple multiplier analysis might suggest. The fact that a surge in government demand (G) discourages some private demand (I) provides another reason why the oversimplified multiplier formula, $1/(1 - MPC)$, exaggerates the size of the multiplier:

Because a rise in G (or, for that matter, an autonomous rise in any component of total expenditure) pushes interest rates higher, and hence deters some investment spending, the increase in the sum $C + I + G + (X - IM)$ is smaller than what the oversimplified multiplier formula predicts.

Combining this observation with our previous analysis of the multiplier, we now have the following complete list of:

REASONS WHY THE OVERSIMPLIFIED MULTIPLIER FORMULA IS WRONG

1. It ignores variable imports, which reduce the size of the multiplier.
2. It ignores price-level changes, which reduce the size of the multiplier.
3. It ignores the income tax, which reduces the size of the multiplier.
4. It ignores the rising interest rates that accompany any autonomous increase in spending, which also reduce the size of the multiplier.

Notice that all four of these adjustments point in the same direction—toward a smaller multiplier. No wonder the actual multiplier (estimated to be below 2 for the U.S. economy) is so much less than the oversimplified formula suggests.

DEBATE: SHOULD STABILIZATION POLICY RELY ON FISCAL OR MONETARY POLICY?

We have seen that the Keynesian and monetarist approaches are more like two different languages than two different theories. However, it is well known that language can influence attitudes in many subtle ways. For example, even though English prose can be translated into French, the British and the French do not always see eye-to-eye.

In a similar vein, the Keynesian language biases things subtly toward thinking first about fiscal policy simply because fiscal actions influence aggregate demand so directly. G is, after all, a part of $C + I + G + (X - IM)$. Monetarists, on the other hand, see a more indirect channel that works through interest rates and velocity, and they wonder if something might not go wrong along the way.

The roles are reversed in the analysis of monetary policy. To monetarists, the equation of exchange—$M \times V = P \times Y$—makes the effect of money on aggregate demand clear and direct. While monetary policy also affects aggregate demand in the Keynesian model, the mechanisms are complex, and there is obviously room for a slip-up. Monetary expansion might not affect the interest rate much, or a fall in the interest rate might not induce much additional investment. Thus, some Keynesians have had their doubts when monetarists attributed great powers to monetary policy.

Years ago, Keynesians and monetarists conducted a spirited and well publicized debate in which extreme monetarists claimed that fiscal policy was futile, while extreme Keynesians argued that monetary policy was useless. But accumulating evidence made each extreme view seem less and less tenable, and this is not a major issue today. Instead:

Most economists today agree that both fiscal and monetary policy have significant effects on aggregate demand. Nonetheless, Keynesians tend to look more toward fiscal policy while monetarists tend to rely more on monetary policy.

More important than the issue of which type of policy is more *powerful* is the question of which type of medicine—fiscal or monetary—cures the patient more *quickly*. Up to now, we have ignored questions of timing and pretended that the authorities instantly noticed the need for stabilization policy, decided upon a course of action, and administered the appropriate medicine. In reality, each of these steps takes time.

First, delays in data collection mean that the latest macroeconomic data pertain to the economy of a few months ago. Second, one of the prices of democracy is that the government often takes a distressingly long time to decide what should be done, to muster the necessary political support, and to put its decisions into effect. Finally, our $6 trillion economy is a bit like a sleeping elephant that reacts rather sluggishly to moderate fiscal and monetary prods. As it turns out, these **lags in stabilization policy**, as they are called, play a pivotal role in the choice between fiscal and monetary policy. Here's why.

The main policy tool for manipulating consumer spending (C) is the personal income tax, and Chapter 7 documented why the fiscal policy planner can feel fairly sure that each $1 of tax reduction will lead to about 90 to 95 cents of additional spending *eventually*. But not all of this will happen at once.

First, consumers must learn about the tax change. Then they may need to be convinced that the change is permanent. Finally, there is the simple force of habit: households need time to adjust their spending habits when circumstances change. For all these reasons, consumers may increase their spending by only 30 to 50 cents for each $1 of additional income within the first few months after a tax cut. Only gradually, will they raise their spending up to about 90 to 95 cents for each additional dollar of income.

Lags are much longer for investment (I), which provides the main vehicle by which monetary policy affects aggregate demand. Planning for capacity expansion in a large corporation is a long, drawn-out process. Ideas must be submitted and approved, plans must be drawn up, funding acquired, orders for machinery or contracts for new construction placed. And most of this occurs *before* any appreciable amount of money is spent. Economists have found that much of the response of investment to changes in interest rates or tax provisions is delayed for several *years*.

The fact that C responds more quickly than I has important implications for the choice among alternative stabilization policies. The reason is that the most common varieties of fiscal policy affect aggregate demand either directly—G is a component of $C + I + G + (X - IM)$—or work through consumption with a relatively short lag, while monetary policy has its major effects on investment. Therefore:

Conventional types of fiscal policy actions, such as changes in G or in personal taxes, probably affect aggregate demand much more promptly than do monetary policy actions.

3 3 1

DEBATE: SHOULD THE FED CONTROL THE MONEY SUPPLY OR CONTROL INTEREST RATES?

Notice that the statement says nothing about which instrument is more *powerful*. It simply asserts that the fiscal weapon acts more *quickly*. This important fact has been used to build a case that fiscal policy should bear the major burden of economic stabilization. But before you jump to such a conclusion, you should realize that the lags we have just described are not the only ones affecting the timing of stabilization policy.

Apart from these lags in expenditure, which are beyond the control of policymakers, there are further lags that are due to the behavior of the policymakers themselves! We are referring here to the delays that occur while the policymakers are studying the state of the economy, contemplating what steps they should take, and putting their decisions into effect. And here most observers believe that monetary policy has an important edge; that is:

Policy lags are normally much shorter for monetary policy than for fiscal policy.

The reasons are apparent. The Federal Open Market Committee (FOMC) meets about eight times a year—and more often if necessary. So monetary policy decisions are made frequently. And once the Fed decides on a course of action, it normally can be executed almost instantly by buying or selling bonds on the open market.

In contrast, Federal budgeting procedures operate on an annual budget cycle. Except in rare circumstances, *major* fiscal policy initiatives can occur only at the time of the annual budget. Tax laws can be changed at any time, but the wheels of Congress grind slowly and it may take many months before Congress acts on a tax change. In sum, one has to be very optimistic to suppose that important fiscal policy actions can be taken on short notice. Even President Clinton's first budget, which passed through Congress in record time in 1993, took almost six months from introduction to enactment.

So where does the combined effect of expenditure lags and policy lags leave us? With nothing conclusive, we are afraid. As the late Arthur Okun put it, the debate over whether the nation should rely only on monetary policy or only on fiscal policy is a bit like arguing whether a safe car is one with good headlights or one with good brakes. It is unwise to drive at night unless you have both.

DEBATE: SHOULD THE FED CONTROL THE MONEY SUPPLY OR CONTROL INTEREST RATES?

Once we recognize that monetary policy is an important tool of stabilization policy, other questions arise. In several cases, the answers are the subject of intense dispute.

One major controversy is over how the Federal Reserve should conduct monetary policy. Some economists argue that the Fed should use open-market operations and its other tools to control the rate of interest (r) while others, especially monetarists, insist that the Fed should concentrate on controlling the money supply (M). To understand the nature of this debate, we must first understand why the Fed cannot control both M and r at the same time.

Figure 14–2 will help us see why. It shows an initial equilibrium in the money market at point E, where money demand curve M_0D_0 crosses money supply curve MS. Here the interest rate is $r = 5$ percent and the money stock is $M = \$830$ billion. Let us assume that these are the Fed's targets for M and r; it wants to keep the money supply and interest rates just where they are.

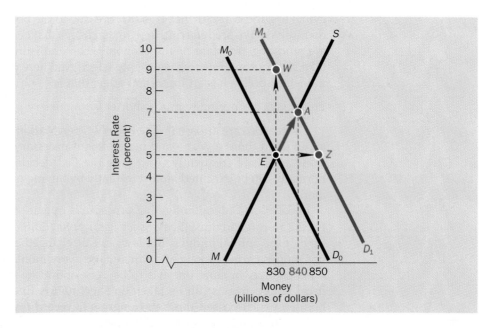

Figure. **14–2**   **THE FEDERAL RESERVE'S POLICY DILEMMA**

This diagram illustrates the dilemma facing the Fed when the demand schedule for money shifts. In this case, we suppose that it increases from M_0D_0 to M_1D_1. If the equilibrium at point E satisfied its goals both for the money supply ($830 billion) and for the rate of interest (5 percent), either one or both of these goals will have to be abandoned after the demand schedule shifts. Points W, A, and Z illustrate three of the many choices. At W, the Fed is keeping the money supply at $830 billion through contractionary policies, but at a cost of skyrocketing interest rates. At Z, the Fed is holding interest rates at 5 percent, but the required expansionary monetary policies raise the money supply to $850 billion. At A, the Fed is not adjusting its policy and is accepting an increase in both the money supply and the rate of interest.

If the demand curve for money holds still, this is possible. But suppose the demand for money is not so obliging. Suppose, instead, that the demand curve shifts outward to the position indicated by M_1D_1 in Figure 14–2. As we learned in the last chapter (see, especially, Figure 13–4 on page 311), this might happen because output increases or because prices rise. Or it might happen simply because people decide to hold more money. Whatever the reason, the Fed can no longer achieve both of its previous targets.

If the Fed takes no action, the outward shift in the demand curve will push up both the quantity of money (M) and the rate of interest (r). Figure 14–2 shows this graphically. If the demand curve for money shifts outward from M_0D_0 to M_1D_1 and there is no change in monetary policy (so that supply schedule MS does not move), equilibrium moves from point E to point A. The money stock rises to $840 billion and the interest rate rises to 7 percent.

However, the supply of money is one of the major determinants of aggregate demand. Consequently, if the economy is already operating near full employment, the Fed might be unwilling to let M rise. In that case, it can use any of its contractionary weapons to prevent M from rising. But, if it does this, it will push

333

DEBATE: SHOULD THE FED CONTROL THE MONEY SUPPLY OR CONTROL INTEREST RATES?

r up even higher because, with no increase in the money supply, an even higher interest rate is necessary to keep quantity supplied and quantity demanded equal.

This is also shown in Figure 14–2. After the demand curve for money shifts, point E is unattainable. The Fed must choose from among the points on M_1D_1, and point W is the point on this curve that keeps the money supply at $830 billion. If the supply curve is pushed inward so that it passes through point W, M will remain at $830 billion. However, the interest rate will skyrocket to 9 percent.

Alternatively, if the economy is operating at low levels of resource utilization, the Fed might decide that a rise in M is permissible, but that a rise in r is to be avoided. Why? Because, as we know, investment spending normally declines when interest rates rise. In this case, the Fed would be forced to engage in expansionary monetary policy to prevent the outward shift of the demand curve for money from pushing up r. In terms of Figure 14–2, the interest rate can be held at 5 percent by shifting the supply curve outward to pass through point Z. But to do this, the Fed will have to push the money supply up to $850 billion. To summarize this discussion:

When the demand curve for money shifts outward, the Fed must tolerate a rise in interest rates, a rise in the money stock, or both. It simply does not have the weapons to control *both* the supply of money *and* the interest rate. If it tries to keep M steady, then r will rise sharply. Conversely, if it tries to stabilize r, then M will shoot up.

This explains why the Fed often finds it impossible to control both the money supply and the rate of interest. A shift in the demand schedule for money supply may make previously selected targets for M and r unattainable.

TWO IMPERFECT ALTERNATIVES

For years, economists have debated what the Fed should do about this dilemma. Should it adhere rigidly to its target growth path for the money supply, regardless of the consequences for interest rates? Should it hold interest rates steady even if that causes wild gyrations in the money stock? Or is some middle ground more appropriate? Let us explore the issues before considering what has actually been done.

The main problem with rigid targets for the *supply* of money is that the *demand* for money does not cooperate by growing smoothly and predictably from month to month; instead it dances about quite a bit in the short run. This confronts the recommendation to control the money supply with two problems:

1. It is almost impossible to achieve. Since the volume of money in existence depends on *both* the demand *and* supply schedules, it would require exceptional dexterity on the part of the Fed to keep M on target in the face of significant fluctuations in demand for money.

2. For reasons that were just explained, rigid adherence to money-stock targets might lead to wide fluctuations in interest rates, which could create an unsettled atmosphere for business decisions.

By the same token, even more powerful objections can be raised against exclusive concentration on interest rate movements. Since increases in nominal GDP shift the demand schedule for money outward (as Figure 14–2 shows), a central bank determined to keep interest rates from rising would have to expand the money supply in response. Conversely, when GDP sagged, it would have to contract the money supply to keep rates from falling. Thus, interest rate *pegging* would make the money supply expand in boom times and contract in recessions— with potentially grave consequences for the stability of the economy. Ironically, this is precisely the sort of monetary behavior the Federal Reserve System was designed to prevent. Hence, if the Fed is to control interest rates, it had better formulate flexible targets, not fixed ones.

WHAT HAS THE FED DONE?

In the early part of the postwar period, the predominant Keynesian view held that the interest rate target was much the more important of the two. The rationale for this view was that gyrating interest rates would cause abrupt and unsettling changes in investment spending, and this in turn would make the whole economy fluctuate. Stabilization of interest rates was believed to be the best way to stabilize GDP. If fluctuations in the money supply were required to keep interest rates on a steady course, that would be nothing to worry about. Consequently, the Fed looked mostly at interest rates.

In the 1960s, this prevailing view came under increasing attack by Professor Milton Friedman and other monetarists. They argued that the Fed's obsession with stabilization of interest rates actually *destabilized* the economy because it led to undue fluctuations in the money supply. The monetarist prescription was simple. The Fed should stop worrying about fluctuations in interest rates and make the money supply grow at a constant rate from month to month and year to year.

Monetarism made important inroads at the Fed during the inflationary 1970s. Early in the decade, the central bank began to keep much closer tabs on the money stock than it previously had. More important, a major change in the conduct of monetary policy was announced by then-Chairman Paul Volcker in October 1979. Henceforth, he asserted, the Fed would stick more closely to its target for money stock growth regardless of the implications for interest rates. Interest rates would go wherever the law of supply and demand took them.

According to our analysis, this change in policy should have led to wider fluctuations in interest rates. And it did. Unfortunately, the Fed ran into some bad luck. The ensuing three years were marked by unusually severe gyrations in the demand for money, so the ups and downs of interest rates were far more extreme than anyone had expected. Figure 14–3 gives an indication of just how volatile interest rates were between late 1979 and late 1982. Naturally, this erratic performance led to some heavy criticism of the Fed.

Then, in October 1982, Chairman Volcker announced that the Fed was temporarily abandoning its attempts to stick to a target growth path for the money supply. Although he did not say so, his announcement presumably meant that the Fed started once again to pay more attention to interest rate targets. As you can see in Figure 14–3, interest rates were much more stable after the change in policy. Most observers think this was no coincidence.

Since late 1982, the Fed has distanced itself more and more from the position that the money supply should grow at a constant rate. In 1993, Chairman Alan Greenspan went so far as to state that the Fed was no longer using the various *M*s to guide policy. He strongly hinted that the Fed was targeting interest rates, especially *real* interest rates. In truth, it had little choice. The demand curve for money behaved so erratically and so unpredictably in the 1980s and early 1990s that stabilizing the money stock was probably impossible and certainly undesirable. Whether this situation will continue is anyone's guess.

F i g u r e **14–3**   **THE BEHAVIOR OF INTEREST RATES, 1979–1985**

This chart traces interest rate movements from 1979 through 1985. Notice the extreme volatility of rates during the period from late 1979 to mid-1982—the period in which the Fed was concentrating more on stabilizing the money supply. After mid-1982, interest rates became much less volatile.

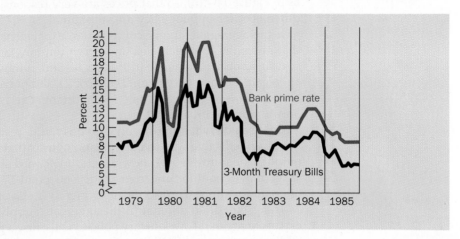

DEBATE: THE SHAPE OF THE AGGREGATE SUPPLY CURVE

Another lively debate over stabilization policy revolves around the shape of the economy's aggregate supply curve. Many economists, including most Keynesians, think of the aggregate supply curve as quite flat in the short run, as in Figure 14–4(a), so that large increases in output can be achieved with little inflation.

F i g u r e **14–4**   **ALTERNATIVE VIEWS OF THE AGGREGATE SUPPLY CURVE**

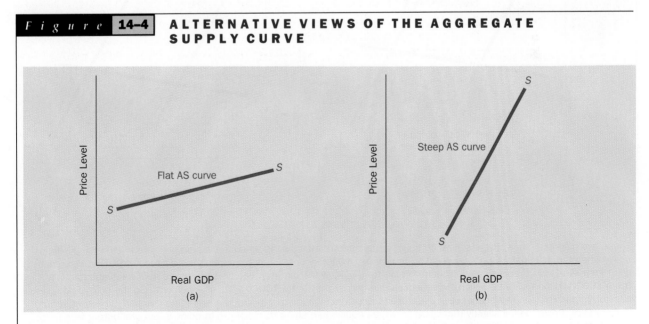

Some economists, especially Keynesians, think of the economy's aggregate supply schedule as very flat, as in part (a). Others, especially monetarists, think of it as quite steep, as in part (b).

Other economists, including most monetarists, envision the supply curve as steep, as in Figure 14–4(b), so that prices are very responsive to changes in output. The differences for public policy are substantial.

If the aggregate supply curve is flat, expansionary fiscal or monetary policy that raises the aggregate demand curve can buy large gains in real GDP at low cost in terms of inflation. In Figure 14–5(a), stimulation of demand raises the aggregate demand curve from D_0D_0 to D_1D_1 and moves the economy's equilibrium from point E to point A. There is a substantial rise in output ($400 billion) with only a pinch of inflation (1 percent).

Conversely, when the supply curve is flat, a restrictive stabilization policy is not a very effective way to cure inflation; instead, it serves mainly to reduce real output, as Figure 14–5(b) shows. Here, a leftward shift of the aggregate demand curve moves equilibrium from point E to point B, lowering real GDP by $400 billion but cutting the price level by merely 1 percent.

Things are quite different if the aggregate supply curve is steep. In that case, expansionary fiscal or monetary policies will cause a good deal of inflation without adding much to real GDP. (See Figure 14–6(a), where expansionary policies shift

Figure **14–5** **STABILIZATION POLICY WITH A FLAT AGGREGATE SUPPLY CURVE**

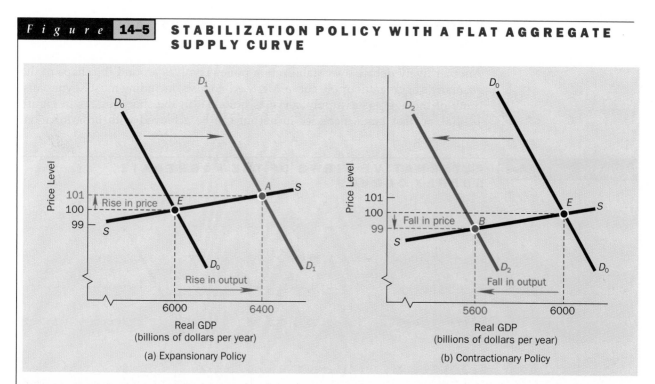

(a) Expansionary Policy

(b) Contractionary Policy

These two diagrams show that stabilization policy is much more effective as an antirecession policy than as an anti-inflation policy when the aggregate supply curve is flat. In part (a), monetary or fiscal policies push the aggregate demand curve outward from D_0D_0 to D_1D_1, causing equilibrium to shift from point E to point A. It can be seen that output rises substantially (from $6000 billion to $6400 billion), while prices rise only slightly (from 100 to 101, or 1 percent). So the policy is quite successful. In part (b), contractionary policies are used to combat inflation by pushing the aggregate demand curve inward from D_0D_0 to D_2D_2. Prices do fall slightly (from 100 to 99) as equilibrium shifts from point E to point B, but real output falls much more dramatically (from $6000 billion to $5600 billion); so the policy has had little success.

Figure **14-6** STABILIZATION POLICY WITH A STEEP AGGREGATE SUPPLY CURVE

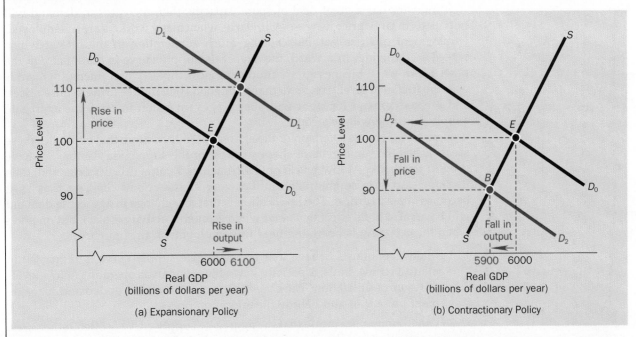

These two diagrams show that stabilization policy is much more effective at fighting inflation than at fighting recession when the aggregate supply curve is steep. In part (a), expansionary policies that push aggregate demand outward from D_0D_0 to D_1D_1 raise output by only $100 billion but push up prices by 10 percent as equilibrium moves from point E to point A. So demand management is not a good way to end a recession. In part (b), contractionary policies that pull aggregate demand inward to D_2D_2 are successful in that they lower prices markedly (from 100 to 90, or about 10 percent) but reduce output only slightly (from $6000 billion to $5900 billion).

equilibrium from *E* to *A*.) Similarly, contractionary policies are effective ways of bringing down the price level without much sacrifice of output, as shown by the shift from *E* to *B* in Figure 14–6(b).

The resolution of this debate is of fundamental importance for the proper conduct of stabilization policy. If the supply curve is flat, stabilization policy is much more effective at combating recession than inflation. If the supply curve is steep, precisely the reverse is true.

But why does the argument persist? Why cannot economists determine the shape of the aggregate supply curve and stop arguing? The answer is that supply conditions in the real world are far more complicated than our simple diagrams suggest. Some industries may have flat supply curves while others have steep ones. For reasons explained in Chapter 10, supply curves shift over time. And, unlike many laboratory scientists, economists cannot perform the controlled experiments that would reveal the shape of the aggregate supply curve directly. Instead, they must use statistical inference to make educated guesses.

Although empirical research is proceeding, our understanding of aggregate supply remains much less settled than our understanding of aggregate demand.

Nevertheless, many economists believe that the dim outline of a consensus view has emerged. This view stresses that the steepness of the aggregate supply schedule depends on the degree of slack in the economy.

If industry has a great deal of spare capacity, then increases in demand will not call forth large price increases. Similarly, when many workers are unemployed, employment can rise without causing much acceleration in the rate at which wages are growing. In a word, the aggregate supply curve is quite flat. On the other hand, when businesses are producing near capacity and unemployment is near the frictional level, greater demand for goods will induce firms to raise prices; and greater demand for labor will push wages up faster. In brief, the aggregate supply schedule will be steep.

Figure 14–7 shows a version of the aggregate supply curve that embodies these ideas. It has the same general shape as most of the supply curves that we have used in this book. At low levels of GDP, such as Y_1, it is nearly horizontal; then its slope starts to rise gradually until at very high levels of GDP, such as Y_2, it becomes almost vertical. The implication is that any change in aggregate demand will have most of its effect on *output* when economic activity is slack but on *prices* when the economy is operating near full employment. In summary:

1. Many economists believe that the aggregate supply curve is rather *flat* in many circumstances, especially when the economy is operating at low levels of resource utilization. They therefore stress the effects of demand management on output and belittle the effects on prices.

2. Other economists argue that the aggregate supply curve is often rather *steep*, especially when the economy has little slack. They therefore emphasize the

---

F i g u r e **14–7** **AN AGGREGATE SUPPLY CURVE WITH BOTH STEEP AND FLAT REGIONS**

The view that the aggregate supply curve is flat is most likely to be accurate when there is much unemployment and unused capacity. The alternative view, that the supply curve is steep, is likely to be more accurate when there is full employment and high capacity utilization.

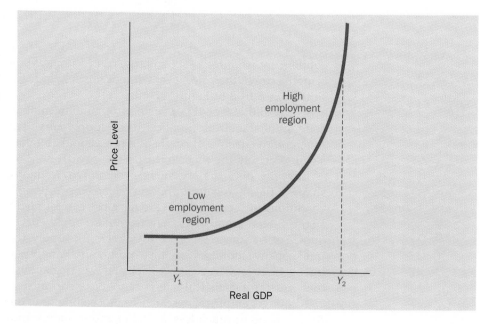

effects of demand management on prices and belittle the effects on real output.

3. A middle-of-the-road view would hold that the aggregate supply curve is probably flat when there is a great deal of unemployment, but steep when the economy is near full employment. Not all economists accept this middle-of-the-road view, but many do.

DEBATE: SHOULD THE GOVERNMENT INTERVENE?

We have yet to consider what may be the most fundamental and controversial issue of all: Is it likely that the government can conduct a successful stabilization policy? Or are its well-intentioned efforts likely to be harmful, so that it would be better to adhere to fixed rules?

This controversy has raged for several decades with no end in sight. It is in part a political or philosophical debate because economists, like other people, come with both liberal and conservative stripes. Liberal economists tend to be more intervention-minded and hence look more favorably on discretionary stabilization policy. Conservative economists are more inclined to keep the government's hands off the economy and hence are more attracted to fixed rules. Such political differences are not surprising. But more than ideology propels the debate. We need to understand the economic issues.

Critics of stabilization policy point to the lags and uncertainties that surround the operation of both fiscal and monetary policies—lags and uncertainties that we have stressed repeatedly in this and earlier chapters. Will the Fed's actions have the desired effects on the money supply? What will these actions do to interest rates and spending? Can fiscal policy actions be taken promptly? How large is the expenditure multiplier? The list could go on and on.

They look at this formidable catalogue of difficulties, add a dash of skepticism about our ability to forecast the future state of the economy (see pages 342–47), and worry that stabilization policy may do more harm than good. These skeptics advise both the fiscal and monetary authorities to pursue a passive policy rather than an active one—adhering to fixed rules that, while incapable of ironing out every bump in the economy's growth path, will at least keep it roughly on track in the long run.

Advocates of activist stabilization policy admit that perfection is unattainable. But they are much *more optimistic* about the prospects for success. And they are much *less optimistic* about how smoothly the economy would function in the absence of demand management. They therefore advocate discretionary increases in government spending (or decreases in taxes) and more rapid growth of the money supply when the economy has a recessionary gap. By this policy mix, they believe, government can keep the economy closer to its full-employment growth path.

Naturally, each side can point to evidence that buttresses its own view. Activists look back with pride at the tax cut of 1964 and the sustained period of economic growth that it helped usher in. They also point to the tax cut of 1975, which was enacted at just about the trough of a severe recession, the Federal Reserve's switch to easy money in 1982, and the Fed's expert steering of the economy in the late 1980s. Advocates of rules remind us of the government's refusal to curb what was obviously a situation of runaway demand during the 1966–1968 Vietnam buildup, its over-expansion of the economy in 1972, the monetary overkill that helped bring on the sharp recession of 1981–1982, and and the absence of antirecession policy in the early 1990s.

The historical record of fiscal and monetary policy is far from glorious. It shows that while there were many instances in which appropriate stabilization policy *could have been* helpful, the authorities instead either took inappropriate steps or did nothing at all. The question of whether the government should adopt passive rules or attempt an activist stabilization policy therefore merits a closer look. As we shall see, the lags in the effects of policy that we discussed earlier in this chapter play a pivotal role in the debate.

LAGS AND THE RULES-VERSUS-DISCRETION DEBATE

The reason that lags lead to a fundamental difficulty for stabilization policy—a difficulty so formidable that it has led many economists to conclude that attempts to stabilize economic activity are likely to do more harm than good—can be explained best by reference to Figure 14–8. Here we chart the behavior of both actual and potential GDP over the course of a business cycle in a hypothetical economy with no stabilization policy. At point *A*, the economy begins to slip into a recession and does not recover to full employment until point *D*. Then, between points *D* and *E*, it overshoots and is in an inflationary boom.

The case for stabilization policy runs like this. The recession is recognized to be a serious problem at point *B*, and appropriate actions are taken. These actions have their major effects around point *C* and therefore curb both the depth and the length of the recession.

But suppose the lags are really much longer than this. Suppose, for example, that delays in taking action postpone policy initiatives until point *C* and that stimulative policies do not have their major effects until after point *D*. Then

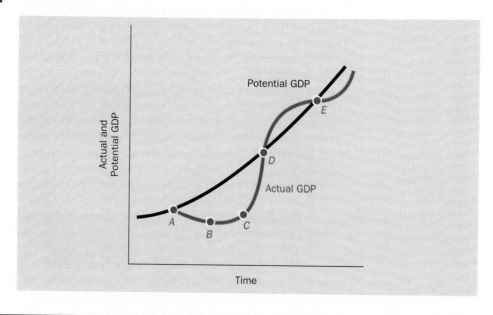

Figure **14-8** | A TYPICAL BUSINESS CYCLE

This is a stylized representation of the relationship between actual and potential GDP during a typical business cycle. The imaginary economy slips into a recession at point *A*, bottoms out around point *B*, and is in a recovery period until point *D*. After point *D*, it enters an inflationary boom that lasts until point *E*.

policy will be of little help during the recession and will actually do harm by overstimulating the economy during the ensuing boom. Thus:

In the presence of long lags, attempts at stabilizing the economy can actually succeed in destabilizing it.

Because of this, some economists argue that we are better off letting the economy alone and relying on its natural self-corrective forces to cure recessions and inflations. Instead of embarking on periodic programs of monetary and fiscal stimulus or restraint, they advise policymakers to stick to fixed rules; that is, to rigid formulas that ignore current economic events.

AUTOMATIC STABILIZERS

The rule generally associated with monetarism has been mentioned already: the Fed should keep the money supply growing at a constant rate. For fiscal policy, proponents of rules often recommend that the government resist temptations to manage aggregate demand actively and rely instead on **automatic stabilizers**—features of the economy that reduce its sensitivity to shocks.

An **AUTOMATIC STABILIZER** is any arrangement that automatically serves to support aggregate demand when it would otherwise sag and to hold down aggregate demand when it would otherwise surge ahead. In this way, an automatic stabilizer reduces the sensitivity of the economy to shifts in demand.

Examples of automatic stabilizers are not hard to find in the federal budget. The personal income tax is the most obvious example. The tax acts as a shock absorber because it makes disposable income, and thus consumer spending, less sensitive to fluctuations in GDP. When GDP rises, disposable income (*DI*) rises also, but by less than the rise in GDP because part of the income is siphoned off by the U.S. Treasury. This helps limit the upward fluctuation in consumption spending. And when GDP falls, *DI* falls less sharply because part of the loss is absorbed by the Treasury rather than by consumers. So consumption does not drop as much as it otherwise might. Thus, as we noted in Chapter 11, income taxes lower the value of the multiplier. In truth, the unloved personal income tax is one of several modern institutions that help ensure us against a repeat performance of the Great Depression.

There are many other automatic stabilizers in our economy. For example, in Chapter 6 we studied the U.S. system of unemployment insurance. This serves as an automatic stabilizer in a similar way. When GDP begins to fall and people lose their jobs, unemployment benefits prevent the disposable incomes of the jobless from falling as much as their earnings. As a result, unemployed workers can maintain their spending, and consumption need not fluctuate as dramatically as employment.

And the list could continue. The basic principle is the same: each of these automatic stabilizers, in one way or another, serves as a shock absorber, thereby lowering the multiplier. And each does so without the need for any decisionmaker to take action. In a word, they work *automatically*.

DEBATE: RULES OR DISCRETION?

Believers in fixed rules assert that we should forget about discretionary policy and put the economy on automatic pilot—relying on automatic stabilizers and the economy's natural, self-correcting mechanisms. Are they right? As usual, the answer depends on many factors.

HOW FAST DOES THE ECONOMY'S SELF-CORRECTING MECHANISM WORK?

We emphasized in Chapter 10 that the economy does have a self-correcting mechanism. If the economy can cure recessions and inflations quickly by itself, then the case for intervention is weak. For if such problems typically last only a short time, then lags in discretionary stabilization policy mean that the medicine will often have its major effects only after the disease is over. (In terms of Figure 14–8, this would be a case where point *D* comes very close to point *A*.)

While extreme advocates of rules argue that this is what indeed happens, most economists agree that the economy's self-correcting mechanism is slow and not terribly reliable, even when supplemented by the automatic stabilizers. On this count, then, a point is scored for discretionary policy.

HOW LONG ARE THE LAGS IN STABILIZATION POLICY?

As we explained earlier, if there are long lags before stabilization measures are adopted or take effect, it is unlikely that policy can do much good. Short lags point in the opposite direction. Thus, advocates of fixed rules emphasize the length of lags while proponents of discretion discount them.

Who is right? It all depends on the circumstances. Sometimes fiscal policy actions are taken promptly, and the economy feels much of the stimulus from expansionary policy within a year after slipping into a recession. While far from an instant cure, such timely actions certainly would be felt soon enough to do some good. But, as we have seen, very slow fiscal responses may actually be destabilizing. Since history offers examples of each type, no general conclusion can be drawn.

HOW ACCURATE ARE ECONOMIC FORECASTS?

One way to cut down the policy-making lag enormously is to have good economic forecasts. If we could see a recession coming a full year ahead of time (which we certainly *cannot* do), even a rather sluggish policy response would still be timely. (In terms of Figure 14–8, this would be a case where the recession is predicted well before point *A*.)

It therefore behooves us to take a look at the techniques that economists in universities, government agencies, and private businesses have developed over the years to assist them in predicting what the economy will do. There are a variety of techniques, none of them foolproof.

TECHNIQUES OF ECONOMIC FORECASTING

THE USE OF ECONOMETRIC MODELS

An **ECONOMETRIC MODEL** is a set of mathematical equations that embody the economist's model of the economy.

Among the most widely publicized forecasts are those generated by the use of **econometric models** of the economy. Put simply, an econometric model is merely a mathematical version of the models of macroeconomic activity that we have described in Parts 2 and 3. The difference is that the basic notions are cast in the form of mathematical equations rather than in diagrams. For example, our consumption function could have been expressed by the formula:

$$C = a + bDI,$$

where *C* is consumer spending and *DI* is disposable income, instead of by a graph.[2]

The builder of an econometric model takes equations like these and uses actual data to estimate the sizes of *a* and *b*. For example, statistical analysis may lead a forecaster to the conclusion that the correct magnitude of *a* in the previous formula is approximately 300 and that the most reasonable value of *b* is 0.75. Then the consumption function formula is:

$$C = 300 + 0.75\ DI.$$

This formula shows us that consumer spending is \$300 (billion) plus 75 percent of disposable income. The economist can complete the model by adding a definition of disposable income as GDP minus tax receipts:

$$DI = Y - T,$$

and appending the fact that GDP is the sum of *C*, *I*, *G* and (*X* − *IM*):

$$Y = C + I + G + (X - IM).$$

In this simple model, then, we have a total of three equations. If we hypothesize that government purchases, tax receipts, net exports, and investment are all unaffected by the relationships in the model, then these three equations are just enough to determine the values of the three remaining variables: *C*, *DI*, and *Y*. These last three variables are called the model's *endogenous variables*, meaning that their values are determined *inside* the model. The remaining variables—*G*, *T*, *I* and (*X* − *IM*)—are called the model's *exogenous variables* because they must be provided from *outside* the model. With this nomenclature, it is easy to describe how the user of an econometric model forecasts the state of the economy:

An econometric forecaster uses a model to transform forecasts of the exogenous variables into corresponding forecasts of the endogenous variables.

Models actually used to forecast the behavior of the U.S. economy have hundreds of variables and equations. Because of their complexity, the only practical way to solve them for forecasts of all the endogenous variables is to use a high-speed computer. But making the forecasts accurate is another thing entirely because of the "garbage in, garbage out" problem: If you feed junk into a computer, that's exactly what comes out at the end. In the forecasting context, this "junk" can be either bad predictions of the exogenous variables or inaccurate equations. This is why model builders are constantly seeking to improve their equations. But they have yet to achieve perfection.

And, even if they did, their forecasts would still not be infallible because there is a certain amount of unavoidable randomness in macroeconomic behavior. After all, we are dealing with the behavior of literally millions of individuals and business firms, and events essentially outside our control can sometimes exert a profound influence on our economy. (Example: The near-collapse of OPEC in 1986 made inflation lower than forecasters expected.) So forecasts of the exogenous variables are bound to be wide of the mark at times. Furthermore, econometric models are basically complicated statistical summaries of the past. No one can really be sure that the future will be like the past. But this is what we assume whenever we use an econometric model for forecasting. (See the accompanying boxed insert.)

---

[2]This is nothing but the formula for a straight line with a slope of *b* and an intercept of *a*.

At The FRONTIER

ARE ECONOMETRIC MODELS USEFUL FOR POLICY ANALYSIS?

Econometric models of the U.S. economy are used routinely in Washington, D.C., and elsewhere to produce numerical estimates of the effects of government policies. Some economists are highly critical of this procedure, however, arguing that the models give misleading answers. Newer and more complicated methods, they maintain, are necessary to evaluate the effects of policy.

One major shortcoming of standard econometric models was first pointed out by Professor Robert E. Lucas, Jr., of the University of Chicago. He argued that changes in economic policy often alter people's behavior, thereby making the future different from the past.* An econometric model is nothing but a complicated summary of the statistical patterns found in historical data. Therefore, when we use such a model to assess the likely effects of policy, we tacitly assume that the future will be like the past. If this proves to be untrue, the conclusions we reach may be quite wrong.

But why should a change in policy upset historical behavior patterns? A noneconomic example may help explain why.** If you watch football, you know that teams almost always punt on fourth down when they have three or more yards to go. Now suppose the rules were changed to allow a team five downs rather than four. Someone who

knew nothing about football, but simply extrapolated past behavior, would continue to expect teams to punt on fourth down. But, in fact, the rule change would probably make punting on fourth down a rare event.

Professor Lucas argued that many government policy changes are like rule changes in football: they may induce people, acting in their own best interests, to alter their behavior. We encountered one example of this in Chapter 24, when we discussed why consumers will react less strongly to a *temporary* drop in income than to a *permanent* one (see pages 604–606). Suppose economists have estimated the marginal propensity to consume, and hence the multiplier. Now suppose stabilization policy improves, making recessions shorter and shallower. Consumers who understand this will assume that any income loss from a recession is now more transitory than it used to be. In consequence, they will cut their spending by less. So the marginal propensity to consume should decline, making our previous econometric estimate (based on past behavior) a bad one.

Virtually all economists concede that Lucas is correct *in principle*. However, they continue to debate how important his criticism is *in practice*. Some ignore the problem and continue to use econometric models for policy analysis. Others are working on complex new methods that use economic theory and statistical analysis to deduce people's *objectives* from their observed *behavior*. The idea is that, even if observed behavior (punting on fourth down) changes when the rules change, underlying objectives (winning football games) do not. Unfortunately, the new methods, which are far too complicated to explain here, are quite difficult to apply. Because of this, no one has yet been able to use them to build a complete model of the economy.

*Robert E. Lucas, Jr., "Econometric Policy Evaluation: A Critique," in K. Brunner and A.H. Meltzer (eds.), *The Phillips Curve and Labor Markets*, Carnegie-Rochester Conference Series, No. 1 (Amsterdam: North-Holland), 1976.
**This example is from Thomas J. Sargent, *Rational Expectations and Inflation* (New York: Harper & Row), 1986, pages 1–2.

LEADING INDICATORS

A second forecasting method, pioneered at the National Bureau of Economic Research, exploits observed historical timing relationships through the use of certain **leading indicators** that have in the past given advance warning of economic events.

For example, the stock market is a leading indicator because stock market downturns normally begin several months before downturns in industrial production. *Why* does this happen? Does the decline in the stock market cause economic downturns by reducing consumer spending? Or are both the stock market and industrial production just reacting to some other influence, with the stock market's reaction coming sooner? Certainly these are fascinating questions. But the answers may not be crucial to a forecaster *if* the stock market continues to be as good a leading indicator of industrial production in the future as it has been in the past. In that event, we will be able to make use of the observed relationship between stock prices and industrial production for forecasting even if we do not entirely understand its origins.

As it turns out, however, excessive reliance on any single leading indicator produces an unimpressive forecasting record. An obvious solution is to look at many indicators. But once we start to do this, we will often receive conflicting signals. If one indicator is rising rapidly while another is falling, what are we to do?

One way to resolve this conflict is to form an average of several leading indicators. For example, every month the news media report the latest reading on the Commerce Department's composite index, which is a weighted average of 11 of their leading indicators. (See the boxed insert on page 347.) Figure 14–9 compares the behavior of this index with movements in real GDP. As you can see, the agreement is usually quite good. The leading indicators occasionally call for a recession that never comes (as in 1966), and occasionally they give clear early warning signals of a downturn (as in 1979). But often movements of the leading indicators are followed so closely by movements in real gross domestic product that the advance warning they provide comes too late to be of much use to policymakers.

SURVEY DATA

A third method of forecasting utilizes periodic surveys of the intentions of business and consumers. The Bureau of Economic Analysis of the Commerce Department and the Securities and Exchange Commission regularly ask firms how much money they plan to invest in factories and machinery over the next 3 to 12 months. These data are published in the financial press and are widely used by economists in industry, government, and academia. The Survey Research Center of the University of Michigan and the Conference Board (a business organization) regularly conduct surveys of how consumers feel about both their personal finances and the general state of the economy. Some economists have found that this information is useful in forecasting consumer spending.

JUDGMENTAL FORECASTS

This term is used to describe the forecasts of those desperate (and probably prudent!) forecasters who refuse to rely on any one method, but look instead at every available scrap of evidence. They study the outputs of the econometric models; they watch the leading indicators; and they scrutinize the findings of

> A **LEADING INDICATOR** is a variable that, experience has shown, normally turns down before recessions start and turns up before expansions begin.

| Figure | 14-9 | REAL GDP AND THE LEADING INDICATORS, 1950–1993 |

This diagram compares the path of the leading indicators (in blue) with that of real GDP (in black). The scales have been adjusted to make the two series comparable. It can be seen that the leading indicators sometimes give advance warning of a turning point in economic activity (for example, in 1979) but often give false signals of turning points that never occur (for example, 1984).

SOURCE: *Business Conditions Digest* and *Survey of Current Business*.

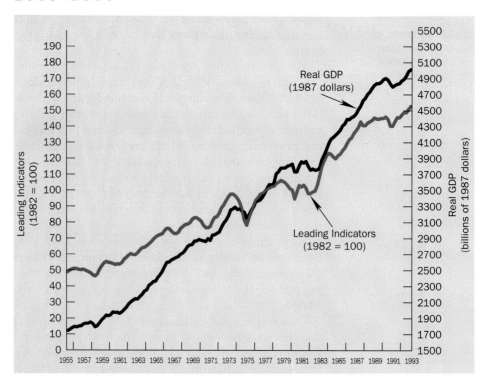

surveys. At times, it seems, they even gaze at the stars. Somehow, judgmental forecasters distill all this information in their heads and arrive at a forecast of GDP and other key variables. How do they go about it? An outside observer can never really tell, since the very nature of judgmental forecasting precludes the existence of a formula that can be written down or precisely described.

THE ACCURACY OF ECONOMIC FORECASTS

Which method wins the prize for the most accurate forecasts? First, no technique is clearly superior all the time. If it were, no one would do it any other way. Second, because econometric forecasters use surveys, lead-lag patterns, and judgment in forming their predictions of exogenous variables, and since judgmental forecasters watch the models closely, a clean comparison is impossible. In recent years, however, it seems that the most accurate forecasts have been derived by judgmental adjustment of forecasts from econometric models.

How accurate are economic forecasts? That depends both on the variable being forecast (consumption, for example, is easier than investment) and on the time period (for example, the tumultuous years 1973–1983 were difficult times for forecasters; the placid 1984–1989 period was much easier).

To give a rough idea of magnitudes, forecasts of the inflation rate for the year ahead typically err by plus or minus 1 to $1\frac{1}{2}$ percentage points. But in a bad year

The Index of Leading Indicators

The Commerce Department's widely publicized index of leading indicators is a weighted average of 11 economic variables that have been shown to be useful in predicting business fluctuations. While the components of the index sometimes change, at the time of this writing they are:

1. Stock market prices.

2. The money supply (M2), expressed in 1987 dollars.

3. An index of consumer expectations.

4. The percentage change in sensitive materials prices.

5. The average work week of production workers in manufacturing.

6. Initial claims for unemployment insurance. (This component enters negatively since rising unemployment is a sign of bad times.)

7. New building permits.

8. New orders for consumer goods and materials, in 1982 dollars.

9. Contracts and orders for investment goods, in 1982 dollars.

10. The change in manufacturers' unfilled orders for durable goods, in 1982 dollars.

11. Vendor performance (an indicator of how easy or difficult it is for firms to get deliveries of inputs).

for forecasters, errors of 3 percentage points or so are common. Forecasts of real GDP for the coming year made during the 1970s and 1980s also typically erred by between 1 and $1\frac{1}{2}$ percent. The biggest errors by far came in recession years such as 1974 and 1982. Apart from these periods, errors of under 1 percent have been typical.[3]

Is this record good enough? That depends on what the forecasts are used for. It is certainly not good enough to support so-called fine tuning, that is, attempts to keep the economy always within a hair's breadth of full employment. But it probably is good enough if our interest in using discretionary stabilization policy is to close persistent and sizable gaps between actual and potential GDP.

OTHER DIMENSIONS OF THE RULES-VERSUS-DISCRETION DEBATE

While lags and forecasting play major roles in the debate between advocates of rules and advocates of discretionary policy, these are not the only battlegrounds.

THE SIZE OF GOVERNMENT

One bogus argument that is nonetheless often heard is that an activist fiscal policy must inevitably lead to a growing public sector. Since proponents of fixed rules tend also to be opponents of big government, they view this as undesirable. Of

---

[3]See, for example, Victor Zarnowitz, "The Record and Improvability of Economic Forecasting," National Bureau of Economic Research, Working Paper No. 2099, December 1986, or Stephen K. McNees, "How Accurate Are Macroeconomic Forecasts?" *New England Economic Review*, July/August 1988, pp. 15–36.

course, others think that a larger public sector is just what society needs. This argument, however, is completely beside the point because, as we pointed out in Chapter 11 (page 261): *One's opinion about the proper size of government should have nothing to do with one's view on stabilization policy.* For example, President Ronald Reagan was as conservative as they come and devoted to *shrinking* the size of the public sector. But his tax-cutting initiatives in the early 1980s constituted an extremely *activist* policy to spur the economy.

UNCERTAINTIES CAUSED BY GOVERNMENT POLICY

Advocates of rules are on stronger ground when they argue that frequent changes in tax laws, government spending programs, or monetary conditions make it difficult for firms and consumers to formulate and carry out rational plans. They argue that the authorities can provide a more stable environment for the private sector by adhering to fixed rules, which are known to businesses and consumers.

While no one disputes that a more stable environment is better for private planning, supporters of discretionary policy point out the difference between stability in the government budget (or in Federal Reserve operations) and stability in the economy. The goal of stabilization policy is to help *prevent* gyrations in the pace of economic activity by *causing* timely gyrations in the government budget (or in monetary policy). Which atmosphere is better for business, they ask, one in which fiscal and monetary rules keep things peaceful on Capitol Hill and at the Federal Reserve System while recessions and inflations rack the economy, or one in which policy instruments are changed abruptly on occasion but the economy grows more steadily? They think that the answer is self-evident.

A POLITICAL BUSINESS CYCLE?

A final argument used by advocates of rules is political rather than economic in nature. Fiscal policy, they note, is decided upon by elected politicians: the president and members of Congress. When elections are on the horizon (and for members of the House of Representatives they *always* are), these men and women may be as concerned with keeping their offices as with doing what is right for the economy. This leaves fiscal policy subject to all sorts of "political manipulations," meaning that inappropriate actions may be taken to attain short-run political goals. A system of purely automatic stabilization, its proponents argue, would eliminate this peril by replacing the rule of men by the rule of law.

It is certainly *possible* that politicians could deliberately *cause* economic instability to help their own reelection. And some observers of these "political business cycles" have claimed that several American presidents have taken full advantage of the opportunity. Furthermore, even if there is no insidious intent, politicians may take the wrong actions for perfectly honorable reasons. Decisions in the political arena are never clear-cut, and it certainly is easy to find examples of grievous errors in the history of U.S. fiscal policy.

So, taken as a whole, the political argument against discretionary policy seems to have a great deal of merit. But what are we to do about it? It is foolhardy to believe that fiscal and monetary decisions could or should be made by a group of objective and nonpartisan technicians. Steering the economy is not like steering a rocket to the moon. Because policy actions that help on the employment front normally do harm on the inflation front, and vice versa, the "correct" policy action is almost always an inherently political matter. In a democracy, if we take such decisions out of the hands of elected officials, in whose hands shall we put them?

This harsh fact may seem worrisome in view of the possibilities for political chicanery. But it should not bother us any more (or any less!) than similar maneuvering in other areas of policy making. After all, the same problem besets international relations, issues of national defense, formulation and enforcement of the law, and so on. Politicians make all these decisions for us, subject only to sporadic accountability at election times. Is there really any reason why economic decisions should be different?

CONCLUSION: WHAT SHOULD BE DONE?

Where do all these considerations leave us? On balance, is it better to conduct the best discretionary policy we can, knowing full well that we will never do it perfectly? Or is it wiser to rely on fixed rules and the automatic stabilizers?

In weighing the pros and cons that we have discussed in this chapter, one's basic view of the economy is central. Some economists believe that the economy, if left unmanaged, would generate a series of ups and downs that are hard to predict, but that it would correct each of them by itself in a relatively short period of time. They conclude that, because of long lags and poor forecasts, our ability to anticipate whether the economy will be heading up or down by the time policy actions have their effects is quite limited. And so they are led to advocate fixed rules.

Other economists liken the economy to a giant glacier with a great deal of inertia. This means that if we observe an inflationary or recessionary gap today, it is likely still to be there a year or two from now because the self-correcting mechanism works so slowly. In such a world, accurate forecasting is not imperative, even if policy lags are long. If we base policy on a forecast of a $200 billion gap between actual and potential GDP a year from now, and the gap turns out to be only $100 billion, then we still will have done the right thing despite the inaccurate forecast. Holders of this view of the economy, then, are likely to advocate the use of discretionary policy.

While there is no consensus on this issue either among economists or among politicians, a prudent view might be that:

The case for active discretionary policy is strong when the economy has a serious deficiency or excess of aggregate demand. However, advocates of fixed rules are right that it is unwise to try to iron out every little wiggle in the growth path of GDP.

But the decision cannot be made solely on economic grounds. Political judgments enter as well. In the end:

The question of whether the government should take an active hand in managing the economy, which is a major debate among economists today, is as much a matter of ideology as of economics. Liberals have always looked to government activism to solve social problems, while conservatives have consistently pointed out that many efforts of government fail despite the best intentions.

Since no one can decide whether liberal or conservative political attitudes are the "correct" ones on purely objective criteria, the rules-versus-discretion debate is likely to go on for quite some time.

Summary

1. Monetarist and Keynesian analyses are two different ways of studying the determination of aggregate demand. Neither is a complete theory of the behavior of the economy until aggregate supply is brought into the picture.

2. **Velocity** (V) is the ratio of nominal GDP to the stock of money (M). It indicates how quickly money circulates, that is, how many times money changes hands in a year.

3. Among the determinants of velocity is the rate of interest (r). At higher interest rates, people find it less attractive to hold money because money pays no or little interest. Thus, when r rises, money circulates faster, and V rises.

4. **Monetarism** is a type of analysis that focuses attention on velocity and the money supply (M). Though monetarists realize that V is not constant, they believe that it is predictable enough to make it a useful tool for policy analysis and forecasting.

5. Because it raises output and prices, and hence increases the demand for money, expansionary fiscal policy pushes interest rates higher. This is how a monetarist explains the effect of fiscal policy. Because higher r leads to higher velocity, it leads to a higher product $M \times V$ even if M is unchanged.

6. Because fiscal policy actions affect aggregate demand either directly through G or indirectly through C, the expenditure lags between fiscal actions and their effects on aggregate demand are probably fairly short. By contrast, monetary policy operates mainly on investment, I, which responds slowly to changes in interest rates.

7. However, the policy-making lag normally is much longer for fiscal policy than for monetary policy. Hence, when the two lags are combined, it is not clear which type of policy acts more quickly.

8. Because it cannot control the demand curve for money, the Federal Reserve cannot control *both* M and r. If the demand for money changes, the Fed must decide whether it wants to hold M steady, hold r steady, or adopt some compromise position.

9. Monetarists emphasize the importance of stabilizing the growth path of the money supply while many Keynesians put more emphasis on keeping interest rates on target.

10. In practice, the Fed has changed its views on this issue several times. For decades, it attached primary importance to interest rates. Between 1979 and 1982, it stressed its commitment to stable growth of the money supply. But since 1982 it has deemphasized money growth.

11. When the aggregate supply curve is very flat, increases in aggregate demand will add much to the nation's real output and add little to the price level. Under those circumstances, stabilization policy has much to recommend it as an antirecession device; but it has little power to combat inflation.

12. When the aggregate supply curve is steep, increases in aggregate demand increase real output rather little and succeed mostly in pushing up prices. In such a case, stabilization policy can do much to fight inflation but is not a very effective way to cure unemployment.

13. The aggregate supply curve is likely to be relatively flat in an economy with much unemployment but relatively steep in an economy producing near capacity levels.

14. When there are long **lags in the operation of fiscal and monetary policy**, it becomes possible that attempts to stabilize economic activity may actually succeed in destabilizing it.

15. The U.S. economy has a number of **automatic stabilizers** which make it less vulnerable to shocks than it would otherwise be. Among these are the personal income tax and unemployment benefits.

16. Economic forecasts are made by **econometric models**, by exploiting **leading indicators**, and by judgment. Each method seems to play a role in arriving at good forecasts. But no method is foolproof, and economic forecasts are not as accurate as we would like.

17. Some economists believe that our imperfect knowledge of the channels through which stabilization policy works, and the long lags involved, make it unlikely that discretionary stabilization policy can succeed.

18. Other economists recognize these difficulties but do not believe they are quite as serious. They also place much less faith in the economy's ability to cure recessions and inflations on its own. They therefore think that **discretionary policy** is not only advisable, but essential.

19. Stabilizing the economy by fiscal policy need *not* imply a tendency toward "big government."

Quantity theory of money
Velocity
Equation of exchange
Effect of interest rate on velocity
Monetarism
Effect of fiscal policy on interest
 rates

Lags in stabilization policy
Shape of the aggregate supply
 curve
Controlling M versus controlling r

Automatic stabilizers
Econometric models
Leading indicators
Judgmental forecasts
Rules versus discretionary policy

Questions for Review

1. How much money (including cash and checking account balances) do you typically have at any particular moment? Divide this into your total income over
the past 12 months to obtain your own personal velocity. Are you typical of the nation as a whole?

2. Just below, you will find data on nominal gross national product and the money supply (M1 definition)
for selected years. Compute velocity in each year. Can
you see any trend?

YEAR	MONEY SUPPLY (M1) (billions of dollars) (end of year)	NOMINAL GNP (billions of dollars)
1972	249	1207
1982	475	3150
1992	1027	6039

3. Use the concept of opportunity cost to explain why
velocity is higher at higher interest rates.

4. How does monetarism differ from the quantity theory
of money? How does it differ from Keynesian
analysis?

5. Given the behavior of velocity shown in Figure 14–
1, does it make more sense for the Federal Reserve
to formulate targets for M1 or M2?

6. Distinguish between the expenditure lag and the policy lag in stabilization policy. Does monetary or fiscal
policy have the shorter expenditure lag? What about
the policy lag?

7. Explain why their contrasting views on the shape of
the aggregate supply curve lead some economists to
argue much more strongly for stabilization policies

to fight unemployment and others to argue much
more strongly for stabilization policies to fight inflation.

8. Use a supply and demand diagram similar to Figure
14–2 (page 332) to show the choices open to the Fed
following an unexpected decline in the demand for
money. If the Fed is following a monetarist policy
rule, what will happen to the rate of interest?

9. Explain why lags make it possible for policy actions
intended to stabilize the economy actually to destabilize it instead.

10. Which of the following events would strengthen the
argument for the use of discretionary policy, and
which would strengthen the argument for rules?

 a. Structural changes make the economy's self-correcting mechanism work more quickly and reliably
than before.

 b. New statistical methods are found that improve
the accuracy of economic forecasts.

 c. A Republican president is elected when there is an
overwhelmingly Democratic Congress. The Congress and the president differ sharply on what
should be done about the national economy.

11. (More difficult) Use the following hypothetical econometric model of the U.S. economy to obtain a forecast
of the GDP in 1996:

$$C = 300 + 0.75DI$$
$$DI = Y - T$$
$$Y = C + I + G + (X - IM)$$

T, I, G, and $(X - IM)$ are the exogenous variables,
and their forecasted values for 1996 are $T = 1200$,
$I = 900$, $G = 1300$, $(X - IM) = -100$.

12. (More difficult) Answer the same question for an economy described by:

$$C = 18 + 0.9DI$$
$$DI = Y - T$$
$$T = 10 + \tfrac{1}{3}Y$$
$$Y = C + I + G + (X - IM)$$

with forecasts $I = 200$, $G = 880$, $(X - IM) = 0$.

13. Some observers think that from 1987 to 1990 the Federal Reserve under Alan Greenspan succeeded in using deft applications of monetary policy to "fine tune" the U.S. economy into the full-employment zone without worsening inflation. Use the data on money supply, interest rates, real GDP, unemployment, and the price level given on the inside rear cover of this book to evaluate this claim. What happened after 1990? Is our discussion of lags in monetary policy relevant here?

Chapter 15

BUDGET DEFICITS AND THE NATIONAL DEBT: FACT AND FICTION

Blessed are the young,
for they shall inherit
the national debt.

HERBERT HOOVER

There is a belief that runs deep in the American character that there is something inherently wrong with government budget deficits. Opinion polls consistently show that the public wants smaller deficits. Yet for more than a decade our political process failed to produce them. Somehow, President Clinton seemed to change all that with his February 1993 State of the Union address, and deficit reduction became Washington's latest political fad. What is the economic substance in this debate? What kinds of problems do large deficits pose for the economy, both now and in the future? Should we strive to balance the budget? And if so, by what means? These are the questions for this chapter. ¶ We begin by explaining why the principles of stabilization policy that we have been learning in Part 3 do not imply that the budget should always be balanced. (Neither, however, do they lead to the conclusion that it should always have a massive deficit!) Next we look at the facts: we discuss the size of the national debt, how it grew so large, and why some economists claim that the federal budget deficit is mismeasured.

With the facts established, we examine the alleged ill effects of deficits. We shall see that many popular arguments against deficits are based on faulty reasoning. But not all are. In particular, we devote special attention to two potentially severe costs of deficit spending: it can be inflationary, and it can "crowd out" private investment spending.

THE PARTISAN POLITICAL DEBATE OVER THE BUDGET DEFICIT

President Clinton's economic plan pushed deficit reduction to the top of the national agenda. Whatever else you think of the president's economic policies, it is clear that they focussed attention on the deficit in a way that had not been done in a long time. The political battle that ensued from the winter to the summer of 1993 showed just how contentious these issues are. After all, deficit reduction is about raising taxes and cutting spending—neither of which holds much appeal to politicians who must face the voters.

"The 'Twilight Zone' will not be seen tonight, so that we may bring you the following special on the federal budget."

Critics of President Clinton complained that he relied too heavily on tax increases and did not cut civilian spending enough. The proposed energy tax was a particular target of the critics because some of it fell on the middle class; and, ultimately, it was replaced by a small increase in the gasoline tax. The president's supporters replied that it was unrealistic to expect substantial deficit reduction without higher taxes. They noted that the president's tax plan placed most of the burden on upper income groups, and that the overall plan was well balanced between higher taxes and lower spending.

When the partisan political dust settled, Congress and the president had agreed on a five-year plan that is estimated to reduce the federal budget deficit in fiscal year 1998 by $146 billion (compared to what it otherwise would have been). Over the five year period 1994–1998, the new budget cuts $255 billion from spending and raises $250 billion in higher taxes. If all goes according to plan—which, of course, it never does—the federal budget deficit will fall from $285 billion in fiscal 1993 to around $180 billion in fiscal 1998. That is a big improvement. But $180 billion is still a long way from zero.

SHOULD THE BUDGET BE BALANCED?

It is commonly believed that the government budget should be balanced. Indeed, most of the 50 states *require* their governments to have balanced budgets. Is a zero deficit an appropriate target for fiscal policy?

The basic principles that we discussed in Chapter 11 certainly do not lead to this conclusion. Instead, they point to the desirability of budget *deficits* when private demand, $C + I + (X - IM)$, is too weak and budget *surpluses* when private demand is too strong. The budget should be balanced, according to these principles, only when $C + I + G + (X - IM)$ under a balanced-budget policy approximately equals full-employment levels of output. This may sometimes occur, but it will not necessarily be the norm.

In brief, according to this approach, the focus of fiscal policy should be on *balancing aggregate supply and aggregate demand*, not on balancing the budget. But why do these two criteria differ? The reason should be clear from our earlier discussion of stabilization policy.

Consider the fiscal policy that would be followed under a balanced-budget policy. If private spending sagged for some reason, the multiplier would pull

GDP down. Since personal and corporate tax receipts fall sharply when GDP declines, the budget would swing into the red. That would require either lower spending or higher taxes—exactly the opposite of the appropriate policy response. Thus:

Attempts to balance the budget—as done, say, by President Herbert Hoover during the Great Depression—will prolong and deepen recessions.

Budget balancing can also lead to inappropriate fiscal policy under boom conditions. If rising tax receipts induce a budget-balancing government to spend more or cut taxes, fiscal policy will "boom the boom"—with disastrous inflationary consequences. Fortunately, believers in budget balancing usually are not alarmed by surpluses.

Actually, the issue is even more complicated than we have indicated so far. As we learned in Chapter 13, fiscal policy is not the only way the government affects aggregate demand. The government also influences aggregate demand through its monetary policy. For this reason:

The appropriate fiscal policy depends, among other things, on the stance of monetary policy. While a balanced budget may be appropriate under one monetary policy, a deficit or a surplus may be appropriate under another monetary policy.

An example will illustrate the point. Suppose Congress and the president believe that the aggregate supply and demand curves will intersect approximately at full employment if the budget is balanced. Then a balanced budget would seem to be the appropriate fiscal policy.

But suppose now that monetary policy turns contractionary, pulling the aggregate demand curve inward to the left as shown in Figure 15–1 and creating a recessionary gap. If the fiscal authorities wish to restore real GDP to its original level, they must shift the aggregate demand curve back to its original position, D_0D_0. To do this, they must either raise spending or cut taxes, thereby opening up a budget deficit. Thus the change in monetary policy changes the appropriate fiscal policy from a balanced budget to a deficit.

By the same token, a given target for aggregate demand implies that any change in fiscal policy will alter the appropriate monetary policy. For example, suppose Figure 15–1 indicates the effects of reducing the budget deficit by cutting government spending. If the authorities do not want real GDP to fall, monetary policy must become sufficiently more expansionary to restore the aggregate demand curve to D_0D_0. Indeed, it was precisely this mix of policy changes—a smaller budget deficit balanced by easier money—that the Clinton administration sought in 1993.

So a balanced budget should not be expected to be the norm. How, then, can we tell whether any particular deficit is too large or too small? That is a good question, but a complicated one. Before attempting an answer, we should get some facts straight.

DEFICITS AND DEBT: SOME TERMINOLOGY

First some critical terminology. The title of this chapter contains two terms that seem similar but mean different things: *budget deficits* and the *national debt*. We must learn to distinguish between the two.

| Figure 15-1 | THE INTERACTION OF MONETARY AND FISCAL POLICY |

Both monetary and fiscal policy affect the aggregate demand curve. If monetary policy turns contractionary, the aggregate demand curve shifts inward from D_0D_0 to D_1D_1 thereby lowering real GDP from Y_0 to Y_1. If Y_0 represented full employment with a balanced budget, then Y_1 represents an economy with a recessionary gap. Expansionary fiscal policy can push the aggregate demand curve back to D_0D_0, but only by opening up a deficit in the government budget.

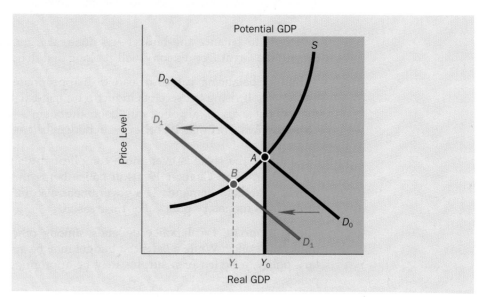

The **BUDGET DEFICIT** is the amount by which the government's expenditures exceed its receipts during a specified period of time, usually one year.

The **NATIONAL DEBT** is the federal government's total indebtedness at a moment in time. It is the result of previous deficits.

The **budget deficit** is the amount by which the government's expenditures exceed its receipts during some specified period of time, usually one year. For example, during fiscal year 1993, the government raised about $1140 billion in taxes but spent almost $1425 billion, leaving a deficit of about $285 billion.[1]

The **national debt**, also called the public debt, is the total value of the government's indebtedness at a moment in time. Thus, for example, the national debt at the end of fiscal year 1993 was about $4.4 trillion.

These two concepts—debt and deficits—are closely related because the government accumulates *debt* by running *deficits* or reduces its debt by running surpluses. The relationship between the debt and the deficit can be explained by a simple analogy. As you run water into a bathtub ("run a deficit"), the accumulated volume of water in the tub ("the debt") rises. Alternatively, if you let water out of the tub ("run a surplus"), the level of the water ("the debt") falls. Analogously, budget deficits raise the national debt while budget surpluses lower it.

Having made this distinction, let us look first at the size and nature of the accumulated public debt, and then at the annual budget deficit.

SOME FACTS ABOUT THE NATIONAL DEBT

How large a public debt do we have? How did we get it? Who owns it? Is it really growing rapidly?

---

[1]*Reminder:* The fiscal year of the U.S. government ends on September 30. Thus, fiscal year 1993 ran from October 1, 1992, to September 30, 1993.

To begin with the simplest question, the public debt is enormous. At the end of 1993 it amounted to over $4.4 trillion, about $17,000 for every man, woman, and child in America. But over 30 percent of this outstanding debt was owned by agencies of the U.S. government—in other words, one branch of the government owed it to another. If we deduct this portion, the net national debt was just about $3 trillion, or around $11,600 per person.

Furthermore, when we compare the debt with the gross domestic product— the volume of goods and services our economy produces in a year—it does not seem so large after all. With a GDP of about $6.5 trillion in late 1993, the net debt was under one-half of the nation's yearly income. By contrast, many families who own homes owe *several years'* worth of income to the bank that granted them a mortgage. Many U.S. corporations also owe their bondholders much more than one-half of a year's sales.

But before these analogies make you feel too comfortable, we should point out that simple analogies between public and private debt are almost always misleading. A family with a large mortgage debt also owns a home with a value that presumably exceeds the mortgage. A solvent business firm has assets (factories, machinery, inventories, and so forth) that far exceed its outstanding bonds in value.

Is the same thing true of the U.S. government? No one knows for sure. How much is the White House worth? Or the national parks? And what about military bases, both here and abroad? Simply because these government assets are *not* sold on markets, no one knows for sure whether or not the federal government's assets exceed its debt. However, one heroic attempt to measure the value of the government's assets concluded that they fell slightly below the national debt by 1984.[2] And since then the government has accumulated debt much faster than it has accumulated assets.

Figure 15–2 charts the irregular increase in the national debt from 1915 to 1992. Until the 1980s, most of the debt was acquired either during wars, especially World War II, or during recessions. When economic activity falls, tax receipts of the federal government fall because of the heavy reliance on income taxes. As we shall see later, the *cause* of the debt is quite germane to the question of whether or not the debt is a burden. So it is important to remember that:

Until about 1983, almost all of the U.S. national debt stemmed from financing wars and from losses of tax revenues that accompany recessions.

The growth of the debt looks enormous in Figure 15–2. But we must remember that everything grows in a growing economy. Private debt and business debt have grown rapidly since 1915; it would be surprising indeed if the public debt had not grown also. The fact is that federal debt grew *less* rapidly than private debt for most of the period from World War II until about 1980.

In addition, the debt is measured in dollars and, in an inflationary environment, the amount of purchasing power that each dollar represents declines each year. A good way to put the numbers into perspective is to express each year's national debt as a fraction of that year's nominal GDP. This is done in Figure 15–3. Here, in contrast to Figure 15–2, we see an unmistakable downward trend from the dizzying heights of World War II until the recession of 1974–1975. In 1945, the national debt was the equivalent of 13 months' national income. By 1974, this

---

[2]Robert Eisner, *How Real Is the Federal Deficit?* (New York: Free Press, 1986), page 29.

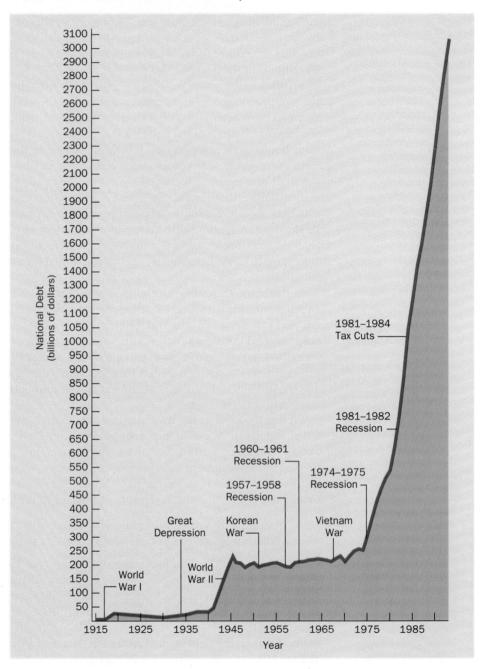

Figure 15-2 **THE U.S. NATIONAL DEBT, 1915–1993**

This graph charts the behavior of the public debt in the United States, after subtracting out the portion of the debt that is held by government agencies. It is clear that, prior to the 1980s, just about all the increases could be accounted for by wars and recessions. Few people realize that the public debt was about the same in 1972 as it was in 1945. But since 1975, it has grown rapidly.

SOURCE: Constructed by the authors from data in *Historical Statistics of the United States* and *Economic Report of the President.*

figure had been whittled down to two months. If we use this as a crude indicator of the nation's ability to "pay off" its debt, then the burden of the debt was certainly far smaller in 1974 than it was in 1945.

This last graph also calls attention to a disturbing fact: the national debt grew faster than GDP during the 1980s and early 1990s, reversing the pattern that had

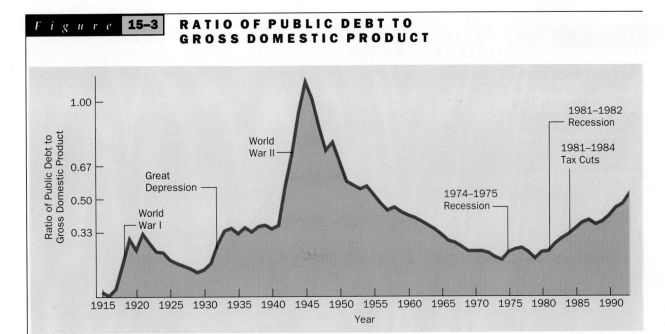

Figure **15-3**

RATIO OF PUBLIC DEBT TO GROSS DOMESTIC PRODUCT

This graph takes the data from Figure 15–2 and divides each year's debt by the gross domestic product of that year. We can see that the debt grew relative to GDP during the two world wars, during the Great Depression, during the 1974–1975 recession, and since 1981. Other than that, the debt generally has fallen relative to GDP.

prevailed since 1945. By 1993, the debt exceeded five months' GDP—nearly triple its value in 1974. This is one reason why many economists are alarmed by continued large budget deficits.

INTERPRETING THE BUDGET DEFICIT

We have observed that the federal government's annual budget deficits have been extremely large under the Reagan administration. As Figure 15–4 shows, the budget deficit ballooned from $79 billion in fiscal year 1981 to $208 billion by fiscal year 1983—setting a record which has subsequently been eclipsed several times. The budget for fiscal year 1993, which ended just as this edition went to press, is expected to show a deficit of $285 billion. These are enormous, even mind-boggling, numbers. But what do they mean? How are they to be interpreted?

THE STRUCTURAL DEFICIT

First, it is important to understand that the same fiscal program can lead to a large or small deficit, depending on the state of the economy. Failure to appreciate this point has led many people to assume that a larger deficit always signifies a more expansionary fiscal policy. But that is not always true.

Think, for example, about what happens to the budget when the economy experiences a recession and GDP falls. The government's most important sources

| *Figure* | **15–4** | **OFFICIAL BUDGET DEFICITS SINCE 1981 (FISCAL YEARS)** |

The budget deficit almost tripled between fiscal year 1981 and fiscal year 1983 and did not change much between then and fiscal 1986. After dipping for a few years, it then soared from fiscal 1989 through fiscal 1993.

SOURCE: *Economic Report of the President.*

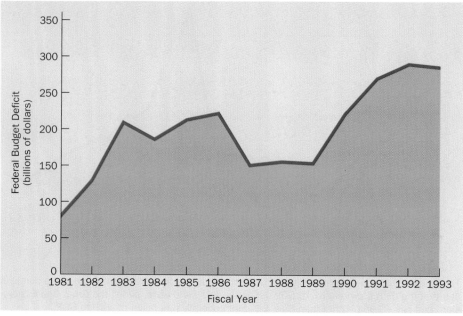

of tax revenue—income taxes, corporate taxes, and payroll taxes—all shrink because firms and people pay lower taxes when they earn less. Similarly, some types of government spending, notably transfer payments like unemployment benefits, rise when GDP falls because more people are out of work.

Remember that the deficit is the difference between government expenditures, which are either purchases or transfer payments, and tax receipts:

$$\text{Deficit} = G + \text{Transfers} - \text{Taxes.}$$

Since a falling GDP means higher expenditures and lower tax receipts:

The deficit rises in a recession and falls in a boom, even with no change in fiscal policy.

Figure 15–5 depicts the relationship between GDP and the budget deficit. The government's fiscal program is summarized by the blue and black lines. The horizontal black line labeled G indicates that federal purchases of goods and services are approximately unaffected by GDP. The rising blue line labeled "Taxes minus Transfers" indicates that taxes rise and transfer payments fall as GDP rises. Notice that the same fiscal policy (that is, the same two lines) can lead to a large deficit if GDP is Y_1, a small deficit if GDP is Y_2, a balanced budget if GDP is Y_3, or even a surplus if GDP is as high as Y_4. Clearly, the deficit itself cannot be a good measure of the government's fiscal policy.

For this reason, many economists pay less attention to the *actual* deficit or surplus and more attention to what is called the **structural deficit or surplus**. This is a hypothetical construct that replaces both the spending and taxes in the *actual* budget by estimates of how much the government *would be* spending and

The **STRUCTURAL BUDGET DEFICIT** is the hypothetical deficit we *would have* under current fiscal policies if the economy were operating near full employment.

| F i g u r e | **15–5** | **THE EFFECT OF THE ECONOMY ON THE BUDGET** |

Since government purchases (*G*) do not depend on GDP, but taxes and transfer payments do, the deficit shrinks as GDP rises—even for a fixed fiscal policy. In this figure, the deficit is *AB* if GDP is Y_1, but only *CD* if GDP is Y_2. At still higher levels of GDP, the same policies could produce a balanced budget (at Y_3) or even a surplus (at Y_4).

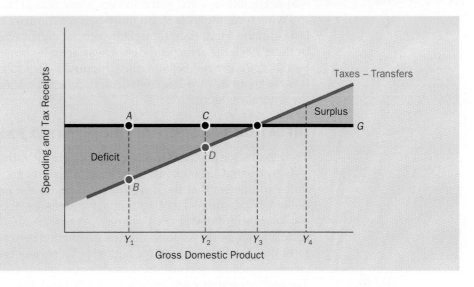

receiving, given current tax rates and expenditure rules, if the economy were operating at some fixed high-employment level. For example, if the high-employment benchmark in Figure 15–5 was Y_2, while actual GDP was only Y_1, the actual deficit would be *AB* while the structural deficit would be only *CD*.

Because it is based on the spending and taxing the government would be doing at some fixed level of GDP, rather than on actual expenditures and receipts, the structural deficit is insensitive to the state of the economy. It changes only when policy changes. That is why most economists view it as a better measure of the thrust of fiscal policy than the actual deficit.

This new concept helps us understand the changing nature of the large budget deficits of the 1980s. Table 15–1 displays both the actual deficit and the structural deficit every other year since 1981. Because of recessions in 1983 and 1991, the

---

| T a b l e | **15-1** | **UNEMPLOYMENT AND THE DEFICIT** |

FISCAL YEAR	OFFICIAL DEFICIT (billions of dollars)	+	ADJUSTMENT TO HIGH EMPLOYMENT (billions of dollars)	=	STRUCTURAL DEFICIT (billions of dollars)
1981	−79		+42		−37
1983	−208		+103		−105
1985	−212		+35		−177
1987	−150		+31		−119
1989	−153		+7		−146
1991	−270		+90		−180
1993	−285		+79		−206

SOURCE: Congressional Budget Office, except for fiscal 1993, which is an estimate from the Office of Management and Budget.

difference between the two budgets was particularly large in those years. But it was negligible in 1989, when the economy was at full employment.

Two interesting facts stand out when we compare the numbers in the first and last columns. First, even though the official deficit was smaller in fiscal 1989 than in fiscal 1983, the structural deficit was actually larger in 1989—despite years of budget "stringency." Second, the structural deficit rose steadily from 1989 to 1993. It is the trend toward larger structural deficits that most alarms keen students of the federal budget.

INFLATION ACCOUNTING FOR INTEREST PAYMENTS[3]

The next major problem is one of measurement rather than interpretation.

Government accountants treat interest payments in the obvious way: every dollar of interest that the government pays on the national debt is counted as a dollar of spending—just like military purchases, social security payments, and the salaries of members of Congress. At first blush, this seems the natural thing to do. But it ignores the fundamental distinction between real and nominal interest rates that we emphasized in Chapter 6. To review the analysis:

The real interest rate tells us the amount of purchasing power the borrower turns over to the lender for the privilege of borrowing. To this we must add an *inflation premium*, equal to the expected rate of inflation, to get the **nominal interest rate**. The inflation premium compensates the lender for the expected erosion of the purchasing power of her money and is best thought of as repayment of principal.[4]

The last sentence has important implications for the government budget—implications that few people understand.

From an economic point of view, the portion of the government's interest payments that merely compensates lenders for inflation should be counted as *repayment of principal*, not as *interest expense*, because it simply returns to lenders the purchasing power of their original loans. Only the *real* interest that the government pays should be treated as an expenditure item in the budget. Breaking up interest payments in this way is called **inflation accounting**. Since so few people understand inflation accounting, it is worth taking the time to illustrate the idea with an analogy and a simple example.

INFLATION ACCOUNTING means adjusting standard accounting procedures for the fact that inflation lowers the purchasing power of money.

Imagine that you lend a roommate, who is enrolled in a chemistry course, a bar of radium that you happen to own. Your roommate uses the radioactive bar (carefully!) in experiments for a year, and then returns it to you. Has your loan been repaid in full? Certainly not. Because of the natural process of radioactive decay, the bar you get back is smaller than the bar you originally loaned. To pay you back in full, your roommate would have to give you enough additional radium to replace the portion that eroded during the year.

The analogy to interest rates on loans is straightforward: inflation erodes the purchasing power of money just as radioactive decay erodes radium. So, in figuring out how many dollars constitutes repayment of principal, we must take inflation into account. Let's illustrate this by a concrete example: comparing a loan made at zero inflation (no decay) with a loan made at 10 percent inflation (rapid decay).

---

[3]This section contains difficult material which may be skipped in shorter courses.

[4]If you need review, see pages 136–37.

First, suppose the government borrows $1000 for a year when the inflation rate is zero, paying 2 percent interest. At the end of the year it must pay back $1000 in principal and $20 in interest, for a total of $1020. Of this, only $20—the interest payment—is an expenditure item in the budget. The repayment of principal does not appear in the budget since it is not spending. The loan transaction is summarized simply in column 1 of Table 15–2.

Now let us see how inflation (radioactive decay of money) complicates the accountant's job. Suppose the same transaction takes place when the rate of inflation is 10 percent. If the real rate of interest is still 2 percent, the nominal rate of interest must be about 12 percent.

More precisely, to compensate the lender for 10 percent inflation, and nothing more, the government must return $1.10 for each dollar originally borrowed. A real interest rate of 2 percent means that the government must return 2 percent more than this, or $1.02 \times \$1.10 = \$1.122$ per dollar borrowed. Since each dollar of lending earns 12.2 cents in interest, the nominal interest rate is 12.2 percent.

At a nominal interest rate of 12.2 percent, a government that borrows $1000 at the start of the year will have to repay $1,122 at year's end. Conventional accounting procedures will treat $1000 of this as repayment of principal (and hence not as an expenditure) and $122 as interest (which *is* an expenditure). This conventional accounting treatment is indicated in column 2 of Table 15–2.

But these numbers are misleading since $1000 at the end of the year is not full repayment of principal because inflation has eroded the real value of money. The correct inflation accounting treatment recognizes that it takes $1100 at the end of the year to buy what $1000 bought at the beginning of the year. So $1100 is treated as repayment of principal, leaving only $22 ($1122 − $1100) to be treated as interest. The correct inflation accounting treatment of the loan is shown in column 3 of Table 15–2.

To recapitulate, the proper economic treatment of a loan in an inflationary environment must recognize that more dollars (in our example, $1100) must be returned to the lender in order to give back the purchasing power of the original loan ($1000). Only the excess of the nominal interest payment ($122) over the compensation for inflation ($100) should be counted as interest.

T a b l e **15-2**	**ACCOUNTING FOR A $1000 LOAN AT A 2 PERCENT REAL INTEREST RATE**		
		AT 10% INFLATION	
	(1)	**(2)**	**(3)**
ITEM	**AT ZERO INFLATION**	**CONVENTIONAL ACCOUNTING**	**INFLATION ACCOUNTING**
Interest (included in budget)	$ 20	$ 122	$ 22
plus			
Principal (excluded from budget)	1,000	1,000	1,100
equals			
Total payment	$1,020	$1,122	$1,122
Addendum:			
Purchasing power of principal repayment	$ 1000	$ 909	$1,000

This example holds the following lesson for interpreting budget deficit figures:

Inflation distorts the government budget under conventional accounting procedures by exaggerating interest expenses.

The example also suggests how this error can be corrected:

To correct the deficit for inflation, we must subtract the inflation premium from the interest paid on the national debt, thereby counting only *real* interest payments.

This treatment, by the way, corresponds exactly to the way inflation accounting is done by major corporations.

As Table 15–3 shows, making the inflation adjustment to interest payments would have reduced reported deficits by $80–90 billion in recent years, a sizable adjustment.

OTHER MEASUREMENT ISSUES

There are other complicated issues in measuring and interpreting the federal budget deficit. We conclude this section by mentioning just two.

1. *State and local budget surpluses*. Part of the reason for the federal deficit is that the federal government gives a good deal of money (over $150 billion in recent years) to state and local governments in the form of *grants-in-aid* each year. These funds have helped state and local governments run small annual surpluses in recent years. Thus, the *combined* deficits of governments at *all* levels has been smaller than the *federal* deficit.

2. *Capital expenditures*. Some federal spending goes to purchase capital of various sorts—government buildings, military equipment, and so on. There is nothing unusual about borrowing to purchase assets. Private businesses and individuals do it all the time. For this reason, many people have suggested that the federal government compile a separate capital budget, just as most state and local governments now do.

CONCLUSION: WHAT HAPPENED SINCE 1981?

Table 15–4 puts our two major adjustments—for inflation accounting and for unemployment—together and compares the official deficits recorded since 1981

T a b l e **15–3**	INFLATION ACCOUNTING AND THE DEFICIT				
FISCAL YEAR	**OFFICIAL DEFICIT (billions of dollars)**	+	**INFLATION ADJUSTMENT FOR INTEREST PAID (billions of dollars)**	=	**INFLATION ADJUSTED DEFICIT (billions of dollars)**
1981	−79		+62		−17
1983	−208		+32		−176
1985	−212		+43		−169
1987	−150		+50		−100
1989	−153		+80		−73
1991	−270		+90		−180
1993	−285		+83		−202

SOURCE: Congressional Budget Office, Office of Management and Budget, and authors' estimates.

Table 15-4 ACTUAL AND ADJUSTED BUDGET DEFICITS				
FISCAL YEAR	(1) OFFICIAL DEFICIT (billions of dollars)	+ (2) ADJUSTMENT FOR INFLATION (billions of dollars)	+ (3) ADJUSTMENT TO HIGH EMPLOYMENT (billions of dollars)	= (4) ADJUSTED DEFICIT (−) OR SURPLUS (+) (billions of dollars)
1981	−79	+62	+42	+25
1983	−208	+32	+103	−73
1985	−212	+43	+35	−134
1987	−150	+50	+31	−69
1989	−153	+80	+7	−66
1991	−270	+90	+90	−90
1993	−285	+83	+79	−123

SOURCE: Congressional Budget Office, Office of Management and Budget, and authors' calculations.

(column 1) with the corresponding figures for the structural, inflation-corrected deficit (column 4). The difference between the two columns is startling in some years. For example, the apparently substantial budget deficit of 1981 was actually a surplus on a structural, inflation-corrected basis. But since fiscal year 1983 even the structural, inflation-corrected budget has been in substantial deficit. And this concept of the deficit has grown alarmingly in recent years.

But what does this all mean? It certainly does *not* mean that in 1991, for example, only $90 billion in additional tax revenue (column 4) would have balanced the budget. What the numbers *do* mean is this. Of the $270 billion deficit in 1991 (column 1), about $90 billion was an artifact of poor accounting procedures and another $90 billion was attributable to the fact that the unemployment rate was well above full employment. This does not make the deficit disappear, but it does put it into some perspective.

BOGUS ARGUMENTS ABOUT THE BURDEN OF THE DEBT

Having gained some perspective on the facts, let us now turn to some of the arguments advanced by those who claim that budget deficits place an intolerable burden on future generations.

Argument 1: Our children and grandchildren will be burdened by heavy interest payments. Higher taxes will be necessary to make these payments.

Answer: It is certainly true that a higher debt will necessitate higher interest payments and, other things being equal, this will force our children and grandchildren to pay higher taxes. But think who will receive the higher interest payments as income: our children and grandchildren! Thus one group of future Americans will be making interest payments to another group of future Americans. While some people will gain and others will lose, the future generation as a whole will come out even. We conclude that:

As long as the national debt is owned by domestic citizens, as the bulk of the U.S. debt is, future interest payments will merely shuffle money from one group of Americans to another. These transfers may or may not be desirable, but they hardly constitute a burden to the nation as a whole.

However, this argument *is* valid—and worrisome—for the 18 percent of our debt that is held by foreigners. Paying interest on this portion of the debt will burden future Americans in a concrete way: in the 21st century, a portion of America's GDP will have to be sent abroad to pay interest on the debts we incurred in the 1980s. For this reason, many thoughtful observers are more concerned about the amount America is borrowing from abroad than they are about the total budget deficit.[5]

Argument 2: It will ruin the nation when we repay the enormous debt.

Answer: A first answer to this merely rephrases the answer to the previous argument: only the part owned by foreigners involves any burden; the rest is paid by one group of Americans to another. But there is an even more fundamental point. *Unlike a private family, the nation need never pay off its debt.* Instead, each time the principal is due, the U.S. Treasury can simply "roll it over" by floating more debt. Indeed, this is precisely what the Treasury does.

Is this a bit of chicanery? How can the U.S. government get away with making loans that it never intends to pay back? The answer lies in the fallacy of comparing the U.S. government to a family or an individual. People cannot be extended credit in perpetuity because they will not live that long. Sensible lenders will not extend long-term credit to very old people because their heirs cannot be forced to pay up. But the U.S. government will never "die"; at least, we hope not! So this problem does not arise. In this respect, the government is in much the same position as a large corporation. The American Telephone and Telegraph Company never worries about paying off its debt. It too rolls it over by floating new debt all the time.

Argument 3: Like any family or any business firm, a nation has a limited capacity to borrow. If it exceeds this limit, it is in danger of being unable to pay its creditors. It may go bankrupt with calamitous consequences for everyone.

Answer: This is another example of a false analogy. What is claimed about private debtors is certainly true. But the U.S. government need never fear defaulting on its debt. Why? First, because it has enormous power to raise revenues by taxation. If you had such power, you would never have to fear bankruptcy either.

But there is a more fundamental point—one that distinguishes the U.S. debt from that of most other nations. *The American national debt is an obligation to pay U.S. dollars:* each debt certificate obligates the Treasury to pay the holder so many U.S. dollars on a prescribed date. But the U.S. government is the source of these dollars. It prints them! *No nation need ever fear defaulting on debts that call for repayment in its own currency.* At the very worst, it can always print whatever money it needs to pay off its creditors. This is not an option open to countries like Mexico, Brazil, and Argentina, whose debts generally call for payment in U.S. dollars.

---

[5]We will discuss the linkages between the federal budget deficit and foreign borrowing in greater detail in Chapter 20.

It does not follow, however, that acquiring more foreign debt through budget deficits is necessarily a good idea for the U.S. government. Sometimes it is clearly a bad idea. As we know, printing money to pay the debt will expand aggregate demand and cause inflation. In addition, as we will learn in Chapter 19, printing more dollars will make the international value of the dollar fall. We may not relish either of these outcomes. The point is not that budget deficits are either good or bad; they can be either under the appropriate circumstances. Rather, the point is that worrying about a possible default on the national debt is unnecessary and even foolish.

Having cleared the air of these fallacious arguments, we are now in a position to explore some genuine problems that may arise when the government spends more than it takes in through taxation.

BUDGET DEFICITS AND INFLATION

One indictment of deficit spending that certainly *does* have validity under most circumstances is the charge that it is inflationary. Why? Because when government policy pushes up aggregate demand, firms may find themselves unwilling or unable to produce the higher quantities that are being demanded at the going prices. Prices will therefore have to rise.

Figure 15–6 is an aggregate supply and demand diagram that shows this analysis graphically. Initially, equilibrium is at point E_0—where demand curve D_0D_0 and supply curve SS intersect. Output is $6000 billion, and the price index is at 100. The diagram indicates that the economy is operating below full employment; there is a recessionary gap. If the government does nothing to reduce the

---

F i g u r e **15–6** | **THE INFLATIONARY EFFECTS OF DEFICIT SPENDING**

In this diagram, expansionary fiscal policy pushes the aggregate demand curve out from D_0D_0 to D_1D_1, causing equilibrium to move from E_0 (where there is unemployment) to E_1 (where there is full employment). But because aggregate supply curve SS slopes upward, the price level is pushed up from 100 to 106; that is, there is a 6 percent inflation.

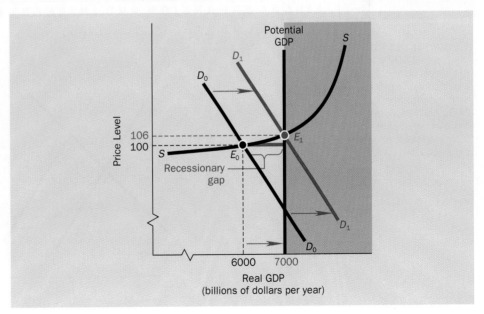

resulting unemployment, we know from Chapter 10 that this recessionary gap will linger for a long time. The economy will suffer through a prolonged period of unemployment.

Rather than permit such a long recession, we know the government can raise its spending or cut its taxes enough to shift the aggregate demand schedule upward from D_0D_0 to D_1D_1. Such a policy can wipe out the recessionary gap and the associated unemployment—but not without an inflationary cost. The diagram shows the new equilibrium price level at 106, or 6 percent higher than before the government acted.

Thus the cries that budget deficits are "inflationary" have the ring of truth. How much truth, of course, depends on the slope of the aggregate supply curve. Deficit spending will not cause much inflation if the economy has lots of slack and the aggregate supply curve consequently is flat. But deficit spending will be highly inflationary in a fully-employed economy with a steep aggregate supply curve.

THE MONETIZATION ISSUE

Some people worry about the inflationary consequences of deficits for a rather different reason. They fear that the Federal Reserve may have to "monetize" part of the deficit, by which they mean that the Fed may feel compelled to purchase some of the newly issued government debt. Let us explain, first, why the Fed might make such purchases, and second, why these purchases are called **monetizing the deficit**.

The central bank is said to **MONETIZE THE DEFICIT** when it purchases the bonds that the government issues.

Deficit spending, we have just noted, normally drives up both real GDP and the price level. As we have emphasized before, such an economic expansion shifts the demand curve for money outward to the right—as depicted in Figure 15–7. The figure shows that, if the Federal Reserve takes no actions to shift the money supply curve, interest rates will rise.

F i g u r e 15–7 FISCAL EXPANSION AND INTEREST RATES

If expansionary fiscal policy pushes real GDP and the price level higher, the demand curve for money will shift outward from M_0D_0 to M_1D_1. Equilibrium in the money market shifts from point A to point B, so interest rates rise.

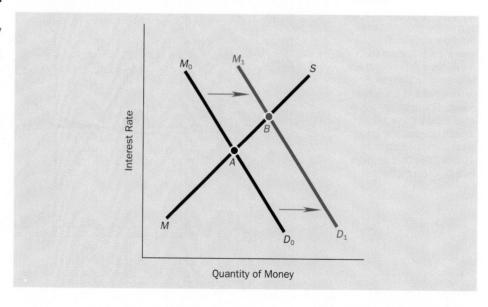

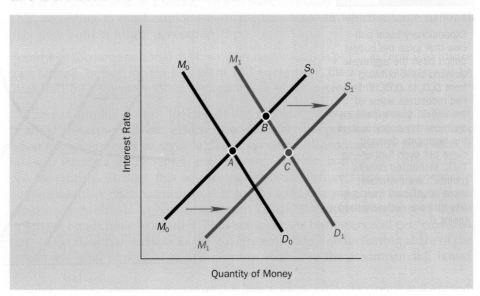

F i g u r e **15-8** **MONETIZATION AND INTEREST RATES**

If the Federal Reserve does not want a fiscal expansion to raise interest rates, it must increase the money supply. In this diagram, the fiscal expansion shifts the demand curve for money from M_0D_0 to M_1D_1, precisely as it did in Figure 15–7. To keep the rate of interest constant, the Fed will have to shift the money supply curve outward from M_0S_0 to M_1S_1. Points *A* and *C* correspond to the same rate of interest.

Suppose now that the Fed does not want interest rates to rise. What can it do? To prevent the incipient rise in *r*, it must engage in *expansionary monetary policies* that shift the supply curve for money outward to the right—as indicated in Figure 15–8. As noted in Chapter 13, expansionary monetary policies normally take the form of open-market purchases of government bonds. So deficit spending might induce the Federal Reserve to increase its purchases of government bonds, that is, to buy up some of the newly issued debt.

But why is this called *monetizing* the deficit? The reason is simple. As we learned in Chapter 13, open-market purchases of bonds by the Fed give banks more reserves, which leads, eventually, to an increase in the money supply. This is also shown in Figure 15–8: The outward shift of the money supply schedule from M_0S_0 to M_1S_1 leads to an increase in the money supply. By this indirect route, then, larger budget deficits may lead to an expansion of the money supply. To summarize:

If the Federal Reserve takes no countervailing actions, an expansionary fiscal policy that increases the budget deficit will raise real GDP and prices, thereby shifting the demand curve for money outward and driving up interest rates. If the Fed does not want interest rates to rise, it can engage in expansionary open-market operations, that is, purchase more government debt. If the Fed does this, the money supply will increase. In this case, we say that part of the deficit is *monetized*.

Monetized deficits are more inflationary than nonmonetized deficits for the simple reason that expansionary monetary and fiscal policy *together* are more inflationary than expansionary fiscal policy *alone*. Figure 15–9 illustrates this simple conclusion. The aggregate supply curve and aggregate demand curves D_0D_0 and D_1D_1 are carried over without change from Figure 15–6. The shift from D_0D_0 to D_1D_1 represents the effect of expansionary fiscal policy (raising the budget

At The FRONTIER

THE THEORY OF DEBT NEUTRALITY

Most economists, politicians, and business people worry that continuing large deficits will lead to high interest rates, weak investment, and perhaps higher inflation. But a vocal minority of economists subscribes to the new theory of **debt neutrality**, which implies that deficits do nothing at all. Why? Because rational citizens save more whenever the government deficit increases.

The argument is straightforward. When the government runs a deficit, it issues bonds. Each bond is a pledge to make specified interest and principal payments in the future. But it is also a promise to raise enough future tax revenue to meet those obligations. Advocates of debt neutrality insist that these two aspects of government bonds must cancel out precisely. Deficits are therefore mere bookkeeping operations that cut taxes now and raise them in the future. If the government cuts John Q. Citizen's 1993 tax bill by $1000, he can simply save the $1000, let it accumulate at compound interest, and use the proceeds to pay his future taxes.

Some economists question this conclusion on the grounds that people are less farsighted and rational than the theory supposes. If your friend Joe lends you $50 from Monday to Friday, this five-day loan may not change your plans significantly. But government bonds last much longer than five days. If you receive $50 now rather than five *years* from now, it may well change your behavior. Farsighted individuals should also know that they will not live long enough to pay back the government's debt. Since some of the future tax burden falls on their children, a tax cut financed by issuing bonds makes the currently living generations richer.

Or does it? A part of the theory proposed by Professor Robert Barro of Harvard argues that the same analysis applies when taxes are shifted from one generation to the next.* People care about their children. So, if the government cuts their taxes and raises their children's taxes, private citizens can easily undo the fiscal operation. They need only save the tax cut, let it accumulate at compound interest, and leave the money in their wills.

The model works in theory. Does it work in practice? Most economists think not. But no one is sure because we have no person-by-person data on how bequests relate to taxes. Instead, economists must deduce what the theory implies for *macroeconomic* behavior and compare that to what actually happens. Here serious problems arise because there are no controlled experiments in economics. When many things are changing at once, it is difficult to isolate the economic effects of the deficit. For example, as the text points out (page 376), a recession *raises* the deficit but *lowers* interest rates. But that does not mean that larger deficits cause lower interest rates.

Because budget deficits, private saving, and interest rates are subject to a variety of influences, research on the theory of debt neutrality continues at the frontier. The Reagan tax cuts of 1981–1984 may have provided something close to a controlled experiment. If debt is neutral, Americans should have saved their tax cuts. Most studies of the episode, however, conclude that consumers spent most of their tax cuts, just as the mainstream view predicts. But proponents of debt neutrality are not convinced that this is conclusive evidence.

*Robert J. Barro, "Are Government Bonds Net Wealth?," *Journal of Political Economy*, 1974, pages 1095–1117.

different sets of circumstances, one or the other force may prove to be the stronger. Near the bottom of a recession, for example, a surge in G will probably produce a considerable rise in real output because the economy will be in the flat region of the aggregate supply curve (see Region I in Figure 15–10). Then crowding in will be strong. On the other hand, when resources are more fully employed, the economy will be operating in the steep portion of its aggregate supply curve

| Figure 15-10 | A TYPICAL AGGREGATE SUPPLY CURVE |

The aggregate supply curve depicted here has three regions. In Region I, output can increase with almost no change in prices because there is a great deal of unused labor and spare industrial capacity. Thus the supply curve is virtually horizontal. In Region III, resources are more or less fully employed, so even rather small increases in output necessitate substantial price increases; the supply curve is very steep. Region II is intermediate between these two extremes.

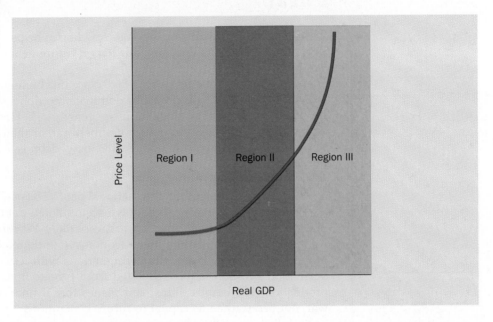

(Region III in Figure 15–10). Then a rise in aggregate demand will mainly push up the price level, raise the demand for cash balances, and crowd out private borrowers.[6]

Let us summarize what we have learned about the crowding-out controversy.

SUMMARY

1. The basic argument of the crowding-out hypothesis is sound: *unless there is enough additional saving*, more government borrowing will force out some private borrowers who are discouraged by the high interest rates. This will reduce investment spending and cancel out some of the expansionary effects of higher government spending.

2. This force is rarely strong enough to cancel out the *entire* expansionary thrust of government spending, however. Some net stimulus to the economy remains.

3. If the deficit spending induces substantial growth in GDP, then there will be more saving. There might even be so much more that private industry could borrow *more* than before, despite the increase in government borrowing.

4. The crowding-out effect is likely to dominate when the economy is operating near full employment. The crowding-in effect is likely to dominate when there is a great deal of slack.

[6]EXERCISE: Show that any given horizontal shift in the aggregate demand curve has a smaller effect on real GDP in Region III than it does in Region I.

THE TRUE BURDEN OF THE NATIONAL DEBT

This analysis of crowding out versus crowding in helps us to understand whether or not budget deficits impose a burden on future generations:

When government budget deficits take place in a high-employment economy, the crowding-out effect will probably dominate. So deficits will exact a burden by leaving a smaller capital stock to future generations. However, deficits in a slack economy may well lead to *more* investment rather than *less*. In this case, where the crowding-in effect dominates, the new debt is a blessing rather than a burden.

"Would you mind explaining again how high interest rates and the national deficit affect my allowance?"

Which case applies to the U.S. national debt? To answer this, let us go back to the historical facts and recall how we accumulated debt prior to the 1980s. The first cause was the financing of wars, especially World War II. Since this debt was contracted in a fully-employed economy, it undoubtedly constituted a burden in the formal sense. It left future generations with less capital because some of our nation's resources were diverted from private investment into government production. The bombs, ships, and planes that it financed were used up in the war, not bequeathed as capital to future generations.

Yet what were the alternatives? We could have financed the entire war by taxation and thus placed the burden on consumption rather than on investment. But that would truly have been ruinous, and probably impossible, given the colossal wartime expenditures. Or we could have printed money. But that would have unleashed an inflation that nobody wanted. Or we could have done much less government spending and perhaps not have won the war. So, in retrospect, the generations alive today and in the future may not feel unduly burdened by the decisions of the people in power in the 1940s. One need only imagine the sort of burden we would have inherited had the United States not won the war.

A second major contributor to the national debt was a series of recessions. But these are precisely the circumstances under which increasing the debt might prove to be a blessing rather than a burden. So, if we look for the classic type of deficit to which the valid burden-of-the-debt argument applies— deficits acquired in a fully-employed peacetime economy—we do not find many in the U.S. record.

It is in this context that the budget deficits of the past decade or so are a sharp departure from the past. The tax cuts of 1981–1984 blew a large hole in the government budget. And the recession of 1981–1982 ballooned the deficit even further. By the late 1980s, the U.S. economy had recovered to full-employment, but a structural deficit of around $150 billion per year remained. This was something that had never happened before. Then, in the early 1990s, the structural deficit racheted up again—to above $200 billion per year. Such large structural deficits pose a real threat of crowding out and a serious potential burden on future generations.

Let us now summarize our evaluation of the burden of the national debt and thereby clarify one of the **12 Ideas for Beyond the Final Exam** introduced in Chapter 1.

THE BURDEN OF THE NATIONAL DEBT

First, the arguments that a large national debt may lead the nation into bankruptcy, or unduly burden future generations who have to make onerous payments of interest and principal, are mostly bogus. ¶ Second, the national debt *will* be a burden if it is sold to foreigners or contracted in a fully-employed peacetime economy. In the latter case, it will reduce the nation's capital stock. ¶ Third, there are circumstances in which budget deficits are appropriate for stabilization reasons. ¶ Fourth, until the 1980s, the actual public debt of the U.S. government was mostly contracted as a result of wars and recessions—precisely the circumstances under which the valid burden-of-the-debt argument does not apply. However, the large deficits of recent years cannot all be attributed to recessions, and are therefore worrisome.

THE ECONOMIC EFFECTS OF BUDGET DEFICITS: CAUSATION VERSUS CORRELATION

Anyone who has followed the debate over budget deficits in the press is bound to have been confused by the contradictory claims and counter-claims. Do deficits lead to high interest rates? Some say yes, others say no. Are deficits inflationary? Some say yes, others say no. Are large deficits a roadblock to economic expansion? Some say yes, others say no. Some even claim that deficit reduction is the key to growth. And somehow each participant in the debate finds data to support his or her view.

Who is right? Let us use what we have learned about the economic effects of budget deficits to make some sense of this confusion. We can do so by contrasting two imaginary case studies which, however, bear a certain resemblance to events in the United States in the 1980s and early 1990s.

CASE 1: A TAX CUT

Suppose the government opens up a budget deficit by reducing taxes. What should happen? According to the theory we have developed, aggregate demand should increase. And that, in turn, should raise both real GDP (Y) and the price level (P), as Figure 15–6 (page 367) shows. The rise in Y and P should shift the demand curve for money outward, thereby raising the rate of interest (r)—as in Figure 15–7 (page 368)—and subsequently lowering investment. Thus, in response to the large deficit, the economy should experience rapid GDP growth, high inflation, and high interest rates. The general conclusion is:

If the government deliberately undertakes expansionary fiscal policies, like cutting taxes or raising spending, the deficit should rise and:

1. Real GDP should grow faster;

2. Interest rates should rise (which harms investment);

3. Inflation should rise.

This conclusion is recorded for future reference in the first column of Table 15–5.

T a b l e **15–5**	DEFICITS AND THE ECONOMY: A SUMMARY	
EXPECTED EFFECT ON:	**CASE 1** **FISCAL POLICY ACTIONS** **RAISE THE DEFICIT**	**CASE 2** **A RECESSION** **RAISES THE DEFICIT**
Real GDP growth	Up	Down
Interest rate	Up	Down
Inflation rate	Up	Down

CASE 2: A RECESSION

Now suppose the budget deficit increases for an entirely different reason. For example, suppose consumer spending declines sharply. What will happen? The decline in aggregate demand will lower both real GDP and prices. With both Y and P falling, the quantity of money demanded will decline. And the decrease in the demand for money will pull down interest rates, which will stimulate investment. Finally, as we have noted in this chapter, when GDP falls so do tax receipts; so the deficit will widen.[7] Thus, in this case, we expect larger deficits to be accompanied by weaker GDP growth, slower inflation, and lower interest rates. The general conclusion is:

If the economy experiences a recession for reasons unconnected with fiscal policy, the deficit should rise and:

1. Real GDP should fall;

2. Interest rates should fall;

3. Inflation should fall.

This conclusion is recorded in the second column of Table 15–5.

Table 15–5 shows just how different the two cases are. The deficit rises in both cases. But in the first case Y, P, and r all rise, while in the second case they all fall.[8] In the real world, of course, deficits are sometimes caused by fiscal policy actions (as in Case 1) and sometimes caused by other factors (as in Case 2). And that is why different people, looking at the same facts, can reach different conclusions about deficits.

The point is that "looking at the facts" is not enough. Simple correlations between the budget deficit and some other economic variable are not terribly informative. You must be able to distinguish between *cause* and *effect*. In Case 1, changes in fiscal policy were the driving force; in a very real sense, a higher deficit *caused* Y, P, and r to rise. But in Case 2, there was no change in fiscal policy; a higher deficit was an *effect* of a recession.

The U.S. in recent years has displayed examples of both cases. In 1981–1984, President Reagan's tax cuts increased the deficit substantially and helped propel the economy forward—as in Case 1. In 1981–1982, and then again in 1990–1991, the U.S. economy suffered through recessions which raised the deficit while the

---

[7]EXERCISE: Test your understanding by working out the diagrams for this example.

[8]EXERCISE: To test your understanding, construct a version of Table 15–5 that applies to *falling* deficits caused by (a) a tax increase or (b) an autonomous increase in consumer spending. Be sure you can explain each entry in the table.

economy sagged—as in Case 2. No wonder the charges and countercharges were so confused, and the evidence so confusing. (See Question 10 at the end of the chapter.)

CONCLUSION: THE ECONOMICS AND POLITICS OF THE BUDGET DEFICIT

Given what we have learned about the theory and facts of budget deficits, we are now in a position to address some of the issues that have been debated in the political arena for a decade or more.

1. *How did we get such a large deficit?* Triple-digit deficits began in 1982. At first, the most important cause was the steep recession, not President Reagan's budget policies. As we saw in Table 15–1 (page 361), the structural deficit was far smaller than the actual deficit in, say, 1983.

   But by the mid-1980s, with the economy improved and the tax cuts fully effective, the structural deficit was tremendous. By the late 1980s, deliberate fiscal policy actions (and inactions) accounted for virtually all of the deficit. Whether the blame for failing to address the deficit problem rests with the two Republican presidents or the Democratic Congress is a matter of politics, not economics. But the fact is that little was done to mitigate the problem.

2. *Is the deficit really a problem?* Once again, the answer to the question was different in 1981–1983 from what it has been since. In 1981–1982, the economy went through a deep recession. And in 1983, the first year of the recovery, unemployment was still far above full employment. Under these circumstances, crowding out would not be expected to be a serious problem and actions to close the deficit would have threatened the recovery. According to the basic principles of fiscal policy, a large deficit was probably appropriate.

   But things were much different by the late 1980s. Crowding out became a more serious issue as the economy neared full employment. So budget deficits should have fallen. But the actual deficit did not fall and the structural deficit actually rose. Since the mid-1980s, we have had persistently large structural deficits regardless of whether the economy was strong or weak. So worries about the burden of the national debt, once mostly myths, have become all too realistic.

3. *What can be done about the deficit?* There is no magic in the Clinton approach to deficit reduction. It is a matter of simple arithmetic that you close a budget deficit by raising taxes and/or by reducing spending, and President Clinton proposed (and Congress enacted) some of each. (See the accompanying boxed insert.) Either of these routes is a contractionary fiscal policy that reduces aggregate demand.

Is that a problem? Not necessarily, if fiscal and monetary policies are well coordinated. If fiscal policy turns contractionary to reduce the deficit, monetary policy can turn expansionary to counteract the effects on aggregate demand. In this way, we can hope to shrink the deficit without shrinking the economy. Such a change in the policy "mix" should also bring down interest rates, since both tighter budgets and easier money tend to push interest rates down. This, indeed, was the central hope of Clintonomics. And, at least initially, it appeared to be working. Interest rates fell dramatically while the plan was announced, debated, and enacted and, as of the time of this writing, have remained low.

The Politics and Economics of Deficit Reduction: The Clinton Program

The structural budget deficit ballooned during the presidency of George Bush (see Table 15–1 on page 361). But neither President Bush nor challenger Bill Clinton ran on a platform of heavy deficit reduction in 1992. (Third-party candidate Ross Perot did.) After all, the political wisdom of the day was that deficit reduction—which means raising people's taxes or cutting government programs—was political death. Much of the nation was therefore surprised when President Clinton proposed a tough deficit-reduction program in February 1993.

The White House document *A Vision of Change for America* and the new president's first State of the Union address altered the terms of the deficit debate fundamentally—and somewhat incredibly. What was once political suicide was somehow transformed into political elixir. Deficit reduction became all the rage. Within weeks, Congress was vying with the President over who could cut the deficit more! In fact, the anti-deficit momentum grew so strong so quickly that it threatened other parts of the president's program. It is said that the American Congress and body politic can only concentrate on one thing at a time. For most of 1993, that one thing was deficit reduction.

President Clinton's original economic plan had three components:*

1. a small stimulus package—about $15 billion a year for two years—designed to spur the sluggish economy. This was killed by a Republican filibuster in the Senate, partly because it would have increased the deficit. Senators apparently forgot that you get fiscal stimulus only by raising the deficit.

2. a five-year program of new public investment initiatives, which was scheduled to grow to $55 billion annually by the fourth year. This program was scaled back during the Congressional appropriations process. Here, again, the president's requests to replace old spending with new spending ran head-on into the deficit-reduction tide. "How can you propose new spending when we need to cut the deficit?"

3. a large, multi-year deficit reduction program that would have pared the annual deficit by about $140 billion by fiscal year 1997.** To the amazement of many, the president's deficit-reduction program not only sailed through but was actually enlarged by Congress. When it became law in August 1993, the deficit reduction program was slightly larger than President Clinton's proposal and composed slightly more of spending cuts and slightly less of tax increases. But, on the whole, it closely resembled what the president had asked for in February.

Had the economics of deficit reduction changed between 1992 and 1993? Hardly. It was the politics of the issue that was somehow transformed, as political taboo turned into political virtue. Indeed, some economists worried that a Congress that had once been allergic to deficit reduction was taking a good thing too far.

*One of the authors of this book participated in the design of the Clinton plan.
**Reducing the deficit by $140 billion while adding $55 billion in new spending required a total of $195 billion in proposed spending cuts and tax increases.

Summary

1. Rigid adherence to budget balancing would make the economy less stable by reducing aggregate demand (via tax increases and reductions in government spending) when private spending is low, and raising aggregate demand when private spending is high.

2. Since both monetary and fiscal policy influence aggregate demand, the appropriate **budget deficit** or surplus depends on monetary policy. Similarly, the appropriate monetary policy depends on budget policy.

3. The **national debt** has grown dramatically relative to GDP since the early 1980s, reversing the previous postwar trend.

4. One major reason for the large budget deficits of the early 1980s and early 1990s was the fact that the economy operated well below full employment. The **structural deficit**, which uses estimates of what the government's receipts and outlays would be at full employment, was much smaller than the official deficit.

5. Inflation exaggerates the deficit because all **nominal interest payments** are counted as expenditures. Under **inflation accounting**, only **real interest payments** would count as expenditures, and the deficit would be seen to be much smaller.

6. If we correct the official deficit for inflation and adjust it to high levels of employment, we find that deficits in the structural, inflation-corrected budget began only around 1983. Before that, there were balanced budgets or surpluses.

7. Arguments that the public debt will burden future generations, who will have to make huge payments of interest and principal, are based on false analogies. In fact, most of these payments are simply transfers from some Americans to other Americans. However, there is a legitimate worry about the portion of the national debt that is owned by foreigners.

8. The bogus argument that a large national debt can bankrupt a country like the United States ignores the fact that our national debt consists of obligations to pay U.S. dollars—a currency the government can raise by taxation or create by printing money.

9. Under normal circumstances, budget deficits are somewhat inflationary because they expand aggregate demand. They are even more inflationary if they are **monetized**, that is, if the Federal Reserve buys some of the newly issued government debt in the open market.

10. Unless the deficit is substantially monetized, deficit spending forces interest rates higher and discourages private investment spending. This is called the **crowding-out effect**. If there is a great deal of crowding out, then deficits really do impose a **burden on future generations** by leaving them a smaller capital stock to work with.

11. But there is also a **crowding-in effect** from higher government spending (G). If expansionary fiscal policy succeeds in raising real output (Y), more investment will be induced by the higher Y.

12. Whether crowding out or crowding in dominates depends mainly on the state of the economy. When unemployment is high, crowding in is probably the stronger force, so higher G does not cause lower investment. But when the economy is near full employment, the proponents of the crowding-out hypothesis are probably right: high government spending mainly displaces private investment.

13. Whether or not deficits are a burden therefore depends on how and why the government ran these deficits in the first place. If deficits are contracted to fight recessions, it is possible that more investment is crowded in by the increases in income that these deficits make possible than is crowded out by the increases in interest rates. Deficits contracted to carry on wars certainly impair the future capital stock, though they may not be considered a burden for noneconomic reasons. Since these two cases account for most of the debt the U.S. government contracted until the mid-1980s, that debt cannot reasonably be considered a serious burden. However, recent deficits are more worrisome on this score. This is one of the **12 Ideas for Beyond the Final Exam**.

14. If deficits arise from deliberate fiscal policy actions, then larger deficits should lead to more rapid growth of real output, higher prices, and higher interest rates.

15. But if deficits arise from a recession, we should find larger deficits accompanied by declining GDP, lower inflation, and lower interest rates.

Key Concepts and Terms

Budget deficit
National debt
Real versus nominal interest
   rates

Inflation accounting
Structural deficit or surplus
Monetization of deficits
Crowding out

Crowding in
Burden of the national debt
Mix of monetary and fiscal
   policy

Questions for Review

1. Explain the difference between the budget deficit and the national debt. If we reduce the deficit, will the debt stop growing?

2. Explain how the U.S. government has managed to accumulate a debt of over $4 trillion. To whom does it owe this debt? Can the debt be considered a burden on future generations?

3. Comment on the following: "Deficit spending paves the road to ruination. If we keep it up, the whole nation will go bankrupt. Even if things do not go this far, what right have we to burden our children and grandchildren with these debts while we live high on the hog?"

4. Calculate the budget deficit and the inflation-corrected deficit for an economy with the following data:

   Government expenditures other than interest = 180
   Tax receipts = 200
   Interest payments = 60
   Interest rate = 6 percent
   Inflation rate = 3 percent
   National debt at start of year = 1000
   (*Note:* 6 percent interest on a $1000 debt is $60.)

5. Explain in words why the structural budget might show a surplus while the actual budget is in deficit. Illustrate this with a diagram like Figure 15–5.

6. If the Federal Reserve begins to increase the money supply more slowly than before, what will happen to the government budget deficit? (*Hint:* What will happen to tax receipts and interest expenses?) If the

government wants to offset the effects of the Fed's actions on aggregate demand, what might it do? How will this affect the deficit?

7. Newspaper reports have suggested that the Clinton administration has pressured the Fed to expand the money supply faster. (The administration has denied it.) In view of your answer to Question 6, why do you think that might be?

8. Given the current state of the economy, do you think the Fed should monetize more of the deficit? (*Note:* There is no one correct answer to this question. It is a good question to discuss in class.)

9. Explain the difference between crowding out and crowding in. Given the current state of the economy, which effect would you expect to be dominant right now?

10. Evaluate each of the following statements. (*Note:* The facts in each case are correct; concentrate on the conclusion that is reached.)

   a. "In 1993, the deficit was larger than in 1991. But interest rates were lower. Therefore, larger deficits do not cause higher interest rates."

   b. "In 1991, we had a huge deficit and a recession. In 1988 and 1989, we had smaller deficits and a stronger economy. Therefore, deficit spending does not stimulate the economy."

   c. "If we compare 1980–1981 with 1991–1992, we find much larger deficits but much lower inflation in the last two years than in the first two. Therefore, it is clear that deficit spending is not inflationary."

THE TRADE-OFF BETWEEN INFLATION AND UNEMPLOYMENT

*We must seek to reduce
inflation at a lower
cost in lost output and
unemployment.*

JIMMY CARTER

 Inflation is now extremely low throughout the industrialized world: about 3 percent in the United States, about 2 percent in France, and about 1 percent in Japan, for example. The early 1990s were also characterized by extremely weak economic performance in most of the advanced economies: the U.S stubbornly refused to snap back from the 1990–1991 recession, Japan suffered its worst slowdown in decades, and Western Europe was mired in a steep slump. ¶ Most economists believe that this conjunction of events is no coincidence. Rather, they insist, the period of slow growth and high unemployment was the price we paid to reduce the rate of inflation. Although some optimists claim that it is possible to reduce inflation without suffering from unemployment, the world clearly paid a heavy price for the disinflation of the early 1990s. Was this price inevitable, or could we have avoided it? That is the question for this chapter. ¶ You may recall from Chapter 1 that the existence of an agonizing trade-off between inflation and unemployment is one of the **12 Ideas For Beyond the Final Exam**. The importance of this trade-off can hardly be overestimated. It is probably the one area of macroeconomics where confusion is most widespread. And because this confusion can have disastrous consequences for the conduct of stabilization policy, the trade-off merits the comprehensive examination that we give it in this chapter.

We begin the chapter by reviewing briefly what we have already learned about inflation. Then we contrast the differing empirical implications of inflation that emanates from rapid growth of aggregate demand versus from slow growth in aggregate supply. We next examine how people's expectations about inflation affect the nature of the trade-off, and consider the special things that can happen if these expectations are "rational"—a term that will be defined precisely. Finally, we discuss some of the political and economic aspects of the trade-off between inflation and unemployment and look into some suggested remedies.

DEMAND-SIDE INFLATION VERSUS SUPPLY-SIDE INFLATION: A REVIEW

Since this chapter is the capstone of Part 3, we should begin by reviewing some of what we learned about inflation in earlier chapters.

One major cause of inflation, though certainly not the only one, is *excessive growth of aggregate demand.* We know, first of all, that any autonomous increase in spending—whether by consumers, investors, the government, or foreigners—will have a multiplier effect on aggregate demand. So each additional $1 of C or I or G or (X − IM) will lead to more than $1 of additional demand. Second, we know that firms normally find it profitable to supply the additional output only at higher prices. Hence, such a stimulus to aggregate demand will normally pull up *both* real output *and* prices.

| Figure 16-1 | INFLATION FROM THE DEMAND SIDE |

An increase in aggregate demand, whether it comes from consumers, investors, foreigners, or the government, shifts the aggregate demand curve outward from D_0D_0 to D_1D_1. The economy's equilibrium moves from point A to point B. Since point B corresponds to a higher price level than does point A, there is inflation (that is, a rising price level) as the economy moves from A to B.

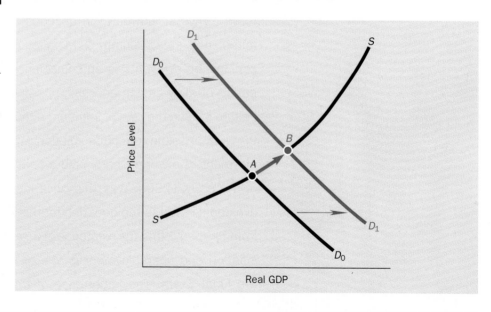

F i g u r e **16–2**   **INFLATION FROM THE SUPPLY SIDE**

A decrease in aggregate supply—which can be caused by such factors as an autonomous increase in wages, or by an increase in the price of foreign oil—can cause inflation. When the aggregate supply curve shifts to the left, from S_0S_0 to S_1S_1, the equilibrium point moves from A to B. Comparing B with A, we see that the price level is higher, which means there must have been *inflation* (rising prices) in the interim. Notice also that adverse supply shifts make real output decline while prices are rising; that is, they produce *stagflation*.

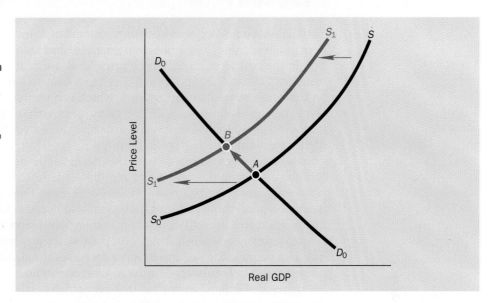

Figure 16–1, which is familiar from earlier chapters, reviews this conclusion. Initially, the economy is at point A, where aggregate demand curve D_0D_0 intersects aggregate supply curve SS. Then something happens to increase demand, and the aggregate demand curve shifts horizontally to D_1D_1. The new equilibrium is at point B, where both prices and output are higher than they were at A.

The slope of the aggregate supply curve measures the amount of inflation that accompanies any specified rise in output and therefore embodies the trade-off between unemployment and inflation. We concluded in the last chapter that this trade-off will be favorable when the economy is operating with underutilized resources of capital and labor. Under such circumstances, firms can expand their operations substantially without running into higher costs. On the other hand, if the stimulus to demand occurs in a fully employed economy, firms will find it difficult to raise output and so will respond mostly by raising prices. Thus, the tradeoff is unfavorable when unemployment is low.

But we have learned in this book (especially in Chapter 10) that inflation need not always emanate from the demand side. Restrictions in the growth of aggregate supply—caused, for example, by an increase in the price of foreign oil—can shift the economy's aggregate supply curve inward. This is illustrated in Figure 16–2, where the aggregate supply curve shifts from S_0S_0 to S_1S_1, and the economy's equilibrium consequently moves from point A to point B. Prices rise as output falls. We have *stagflation*.

Thus, while inflation can be initiated from either the *demand* side or the *supply* side of the economy, there is a crucial difference. Demand-side inflation is normally accompanied by rising real GDP (see Figure 16–1), while supply-side inflation may well be accompanied by falling GDP (see Figure 16–2). This is a crucial distinction, as we shall see in this chapter.

APPLYING THE MODEL TO A GROWING ECONOMY

You may have noticed that our simple model of aggregate supply and aggregate demand determines an equilibrium *price level* and an equilibrium *level of real GDP*. But, in the real world, neither the price level nor real GDP remains constant for very long. Instead, both normally rise from year to year.

This is illustrated in Figure 16–3, which is a scatter diagram of the U.S. price level and the level of real GDP for every year from 1970 to 1992. The points are labeled to show the clear upward march of the economy through time—toward higher prices and higher levels of output.

It is certainly no mystery why this occurs. The normal state of affairs is for *both* the aggregate demand curve *and* the aggregate supply curve to shift to the right each year. Aggregate supply grows because there are more workers, more machinery, and more factories each year, and because technology improves. Aggregate demand grows because a growing population means more demand for both consumer and investment goods, because the government increases its spending, and because the Federal Reserve increases the money supply. We can think of each point in Figure 16–3 as the intersection of an aggregate supply curve and an aggregate demand curve for that particular year. To help you visualize this, the curves for 1980 are sketched in the diagram.

| *Figure* 16–3 | THE PRICE LEVEL AND REAL OUTPUT IN THE UNITED STATES, 1970–1992 |

This scatter diagram shows, for each year from 1970 to 1992, the price level (GDP deflator) and real GDP for the United States. Clearly the normal state of affairs is for both variables to rise from one year to the next.

SOURCE: U.S. Department of Commerce, Bureau of Economic Analysis.

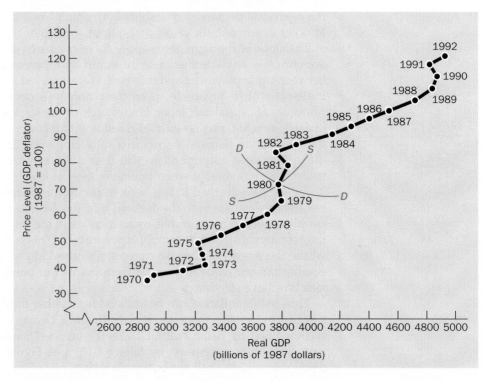

| Figure | 16-4 | AGGREGATE SUPPLY AND DEMAND ANALYSIS OF A GROWING ECONOMY |

This diagram illustrates how the aggregate supply and demand analysis of earlier chapters can be applied to a real-world economy, in which both the supply curve and the demand curve normally shift outward from one year to the next. In this example, demand curve D_0D_0 and supply curve S_0S_0 represent the U.S. economy in 1991. Equilibrium was at point A, with a price level of 118 and real GDP of $4860 billion. Demand curve D_1D_1 and supply curve S_1S_1 represent 1992. During the year, the price index rose by 3 points (about 2.5 percent) and output increased by $130 billion (or 2.7 percent).

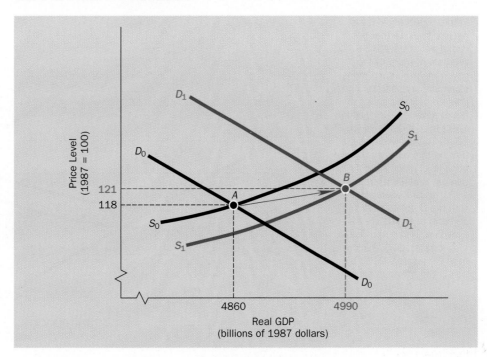

Figure 16–4 illustrates how our theoretical model of aggregate supply and aggregate demand applies to a growing economy. The numbers are chosen so that curves D_0D_0 and S_0S_0 roughly represent the year 1991, and the curves D_1D_1 and S_1S_1 roughly represent 1992, except that nice round numbers are used. Thus the equilibrium in 1991 was at point A, with a real GDP of $4860 billion (in 1987 dollars) and a price level of 118, while the equilibrium a year later was at point B, with real GDP at $4990 billion and the price level at 121, or 2.5 percent higher. The blue arrow in the diagram shows how equilibrium moved from 1991 to 1992. It points upward and to the right, meaning that both prices and output increased.

DEMAND-SIDE INFLATION AND THE PHILLIPS CURVE

Let us now use our theoretical model to rerun history. Suppose that between 1991 and 1992 the aggregate demand curve grew *faster* than it actually did. What difference would this have made for the performance of the national economy? Figure 16–5 provides the answers. Here the demand curve D_0D_0 and both supply curves are exactly as they were in the previous diagram, but the demand curve D_2D_2 is farther to the right than the demand curve D_1D_1 in Figure 16–4. Equilibrium is at point A in 1991 and point C in 1992. Comparing point C in Figure 16–5 with point B in Figure 16–4, we see that output would have increased more over the year ($260 billion versus $130 billion) and prices would also have increased more

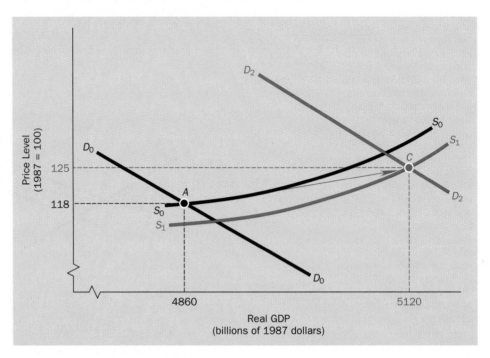

Figure **16-5** THE EFFECTS OF FASTER GROWTH OF AGGREGATE DEMAND

In this hypothetical example, we imagine that because either private citizens spent more or the government pursued more expansionary policies, aggregate demand grew faster between 1991 and 1992 than it did in Figure 16–4. The consequence is that, in this diagram, the price level rises 7 points (almost 6 percent) from 1991 to 1992 compared with the 3 points (or 2.5 percent) in Figure 16–4. Growth of real output is also greater: $260 billion here versus only $130 billion in the previous figure.

(to 125 instead of 121); that is, there would have been more *inflation*. This is generally what happens when the growth rate of aggregate demand speeds up.

For any given rate of growth of the aggregate supply curve, a faster rate of growth of the aggregate demand curve will lead to more inflation and faster growth of real output.

Figure 16–6 illustrates the opposite case. Here we imagine that the aggregate demand curve shifted out *less* than in Figure 16–4. That is, demand curve D_3D_3 in Figure 16–6 is to the left of demand curve D_1D_1 in Figure 16–4. The consequence, we see, is that the shift of the economy's equilibrium from 1991 to 1992 (from point *A* to point *E*) would have entailed *less inflation* and *slower growth of real output* than actually took place. This again is generally the case.

For any given rate of growth of the aggregate supply curve, a slower rate of growth of the aggregate demand curve will lead to less inflation and slower growth of real output.

If we put these two findings together, we have a clear prediction from our theory:

If fluctuations in the economy's real growth rate from year to year are caused primarily by variations in the rate at which aggregate demand increases, then the data should show the most rapid inflation occurring when output expands most rapidly and the slowest inflation occurring when output expands most slowly.

Does the theory fit the facts? We will put it to the test in a moment, but first let us translate it into a prediction about the relationship between inflation and unemployment. Faster growth of real output naturally means faster growth in the number of jobs and, hence, *lower unemployment*. Conversely, slower growth of real output means slower growth in the number of jobs and, hence, *higher unemployment*. So we conclude that, if business fluctuations emanate from the demand side, unemployment should be low when inflation is high and inflation should be low when unemployment is high.

Figure 16–7 illustrates this idea. The actual unemployment rate in the United States in 1992 averaged 7.3 percent, and the inflation rate from 1991 to 1992 was about 2.5 percent. This is point *b* in Figure 16–7, which corresponds to equilibrium point *B* in Figure 16–4. The faster growth rate of demand depicted by point *C* in Figure 16–5 would have led to higher inflation and lower unemployment. For the sake of a concrete example, we suppose that unemployment would have been 6.3 percent and inflation would have been 5.9 percent; this is point *c* in Figure 16–7. Point *E* in Figure 16–6 summarized the results of slower growth of aggregate demand: unemployment would have been higher and inflation lower. In Figure 16–7, this is represented by point *e*, with an unemployment rate of 8.3 percent and an inflation rate of 1.3 percent. This figure shows graphically the principal empirical implication of our theoretical model:

If fluctuations in economic activity are primarily caused by variations in the rate at which the aggregate demand curve shifts outward from year to year, then the data should show an inverse relationship between unemployment and inflation, as in Figure 16–7.

F i g u r e **16–6**   **THE EFFECTS OF SLOWER GROWTH OF AGGREGATE DEMAND**

Here, the aggregate demand curve is assumed to shift outward less than it did in Figure 16–4. Consequently, the movement from equilibrium point *A* to equilibrium point *E* from 1991 to 1992 entails a smaller rise in the price level and a smaller increase in real output than actually occurred.

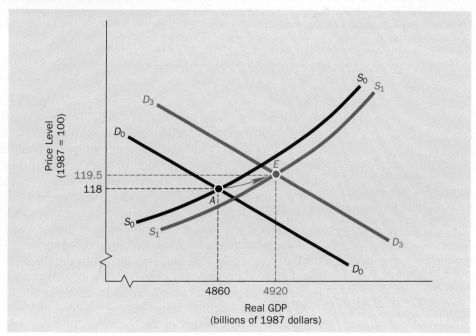

F i g u r e **16–7**   **ORIGINS OF THE PHILLIPS CURVE**

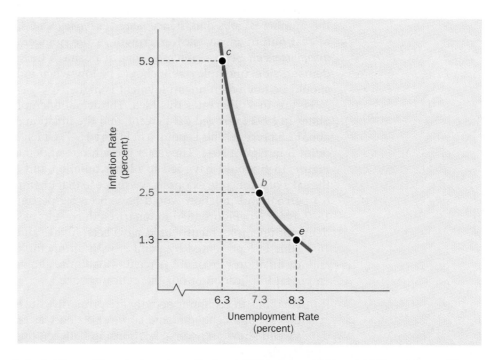

The three previous diagrams indicated three different rates of growth of real GDP between 1991 and 1992 and three different inflation rates. Since each different real growth rate corresponds to a different rate of unemployment, we can put the information contained in the three preceding diagrams together in a scatter diagram to show the relationship between inflation and unemployment. Points *b*, *c*, and *e* in this figure correspond to points *B*, *C*, and *E* in Figures 16–4, 16–5, and 16–6, respectively. The inflation numbers are read directly from the previous three graphs. The unemployment numbers are indicative of the fact that faster growth (Figure 16–5) is associated with lower unemployment (point *c*), while slower growth (Figure 16–6) is associated with higher unemployment (point *e*). Scatter diagrams like this one are called "Phillips curves," after their inventor, A.W. Phillips.

A **PHILLIPS CURVE** is a graph depicting the rate of unemployment on the horizontal axis and either the rate of inflation or the rate of change of money wages on the vertical axis. Phillips curves are normally downward sloping, indicating that higher inflation rates are associated with lower unemployment rates.

Now we are ready to look at real data. Do we actually observe such an inverse relationship between inflation and unemployment? More than 30 years ago, economist A. W. Phillips plotted data on unemployment and the rate of change of *wages* (not prices) for several extended periods of British history on a series of scatter diagrams, one of which is reproduced as Figure 16–8. He then sketched in a curve that seemed to "fit" the data well. This type of curve, which is now called a **Phillips curve**, shows that wage inflation normally is high when unemployment is low and is low when unemployment is high. So far, so good.

Phillips curves have also been constructed for *price* inflation, and one of these for the postwar United States is shown in Figure 16–9. The curve appears to fit the data well, though not perfectly. As viewed through the eyes of our theory, these facts suggest that economic fluctuations in Great Britain between 1861 and 1913 and in the United States between 1954 and 1969 probably were accounted for primarily by changes in the growth of aggregate demand. The simple model of demand-side inflation really does seem to describe what happened.

Figure 16-8 THE ORIGINAL PHILLIPS CURVE

This scatter diagram, reproduced from the original article by A.W. Phillips, shows the rate of change of money wages and the rate of unemployment in Great Britain between 1861 and 1913. Each year is represented by a point in the diagram.

SOURCE: A.W. Phillips, "The Relation Between Unemployment and the Rate of Change of Money Wages in the United Kingdom, 1861–1957." *Economica*, New Series, vol. 25, November 1958.

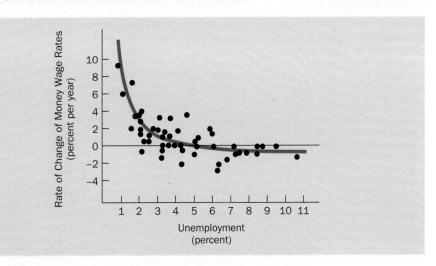

During the 1960s and early 1970s, economists often thought of the Phillips curve as a "menu" of the choices available to policymakers. In this view, policymakers could opt for low unemployment and high inflation—as in 1969. Or they might prefer higher unemployment coupled with lower inflation—as, for example, in 1961. The Phillips curve, it was thought, described the *quantitative* trade-off between inflation and unemployment. And, for a number of years, it worked rather well.

Figure 16-9 A PHILLIPS CURVE FOR THE UNITED STATES

This Phillips curve relates *price* inflation (rather than wage inflation) to the unemployment rate in the United States for the years 1954–1969. Though it misses badly in a few instances (for example, 1958), it generally "fits" the data well.

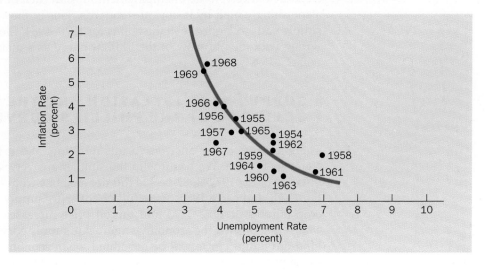

Figure **16-10** **A PHILLIPS CURVE FOR THE UNITED STATES?**

This scatter diagram adds the points for 1970–1984 to the scatter diagram shown in Figure 16–9. It is clear that inflation in each of those years was higher than the Phillips curve would have led us to predict.

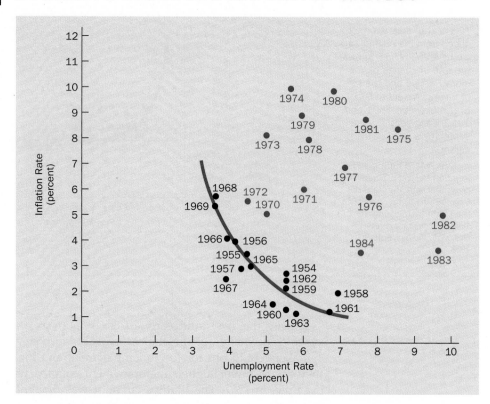

Then something happened. The economy in the 1970s and early 1980s behaved far worse than the Phillips curve shown in Figure 16–9 led economists to expect. In particular, given the unemployment rates in each of those years, inflation was astonishingly high by historical standards. This is shown in Figure 16–10, which simply adds to Figure 16–9 the points for 1970–1984. Clearly something had gone wrong with the old view of the Phillips curve as a menu for policy choices. But what?

SUPPLY-SIDE INFLATION AND THE COLLAPSE OF THE PHILLIPS CURVE

There are two major answers to this question, and a full explanation contains elements of each. We begin with the simpler answer, which is that much of the inflation of the 1972–1982 period did not emanate from the demand side. Instead, the 1970s and early 1980s were full of adverse "supply shocks"—events like the crop failures of 1972–1973 and the oil price increases of 1973–1974 and 1979–1980—that pushed the economy's aggregate supply curve inward to the left. What kind of Phillips curve will be generated when economic fluctuations come from the supply side?

To find out, let us take the events of 1979 and 1980 as an example. In Figure 16–11, aggregate demand curve D_0D_0 and aggregate supply curve S_0S_0 represent the economic situation in 1979. Equilibrium was at point *A*, with a price level of 66 and real output of $3797 billion. By 1980, the aggregate demand curve had shifted out to the position indicated by D_1D_1, and, under normal conditions, the aggregate supply curve would have shifted out as well. But 1979–1980 was anything but normal. The Iranian revolution led to a shutdown of Iran's oilfields for months and a doubling of the price of oil.

Thus, instead of shifting *outward* as it normally does from one year to the next, the aggregate supply curve shifted *inward* from 1979 to 1980, to S_1S_1. The equilibrium for 1980 (point *B* in the figure) therefore wound up to the left of the equilibrium point for 1979. Real output declined slightly and prices—led by energy costs—rose rapidly.

Now, in a growing population with more people looking for jobs each year, a stagnant economy that is not generating new jobs suffers a rise in the unemployment rate. This is precisely what happened in the United States; the unemployment rate averaged 5.8 percent in 1979 and 7.1 percent in 1980. Thus, inflation and unemployment increased at the same time: the Phillips curve basically shifted upward. A general conclusion is that:

If fluctuations in economic activity emanate from the supply side, higher rates of inflation will be associated with higher rates of unemployment, and lower rates of inflation will be associated with lower rates of unemployment.

The instances of major supply shocks during the 1970s stand out clearly in Figure 16–10. (Remember these are *real* data, not textbook examples.) Food prices boomed in 1972–1974 and again in 1978. Energy prices soared in 1973–1974 and again in 1979–1980. Clearly, the inflation and unemployment data generated by the U.S. economy in 1972–1974, and again in 1978–1980, are consistent with our model of supply-side inflation. It was supply shocks, many economists believe, that made the Phillips curve shift.

F i g u r e **16–11** **STAGFLATION FROM A SUPPLY SHOCK**

Instead of shifting outward as it normally does, the aggregate supply curve shifted inward—from S_0S_0 to S_1S_1—between 1979 and 1980. Coupled with fairly slow growth of the aggregate demand curve—from D_0D_0 in 1979 to D_1D_1 in 1980—equilibrium moved from point *A* to point *B*. There was a slight decline of real output, and prices rose rapidly.

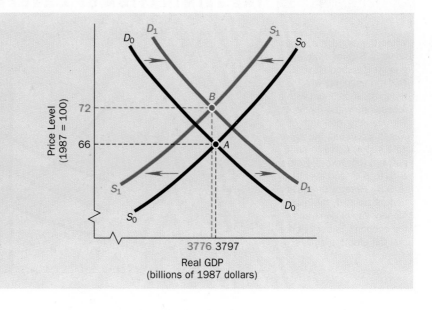

WHAT THE PHILLIPS CURVE IS NOT

But there is another view of what went wrong in the 1970s. This one holds that policymakers misinterpreted the Phillips curve and tried to pick unsustainable combinations of inflation and unemployment.

Specifically, the Phillips curve is a *statistical relationship* between inflation and unemployment that we expect to emerge *if changes in the growth of aggregate demand are the predominant factor accounting for economic fluctuations*. But the curve was widely misinterpreted as depicting a number of *alternative equilibrium points* that the economy could achieve and from which policymakers could choose.

We can understand the flaw in this reasoning by quickly reviewing an earlier lesson. We know from Chapter 10 that the economy has a **self-correcting mechanism** that will cure both inflations and recessions *eventually* even if the government does nothing. Why is this relevant here? Because it tells us that many combinations of output and prices cannot be maintained indefinitely. Some will "self-destruct." For example, if the economy finds itself far away from the normal full-employment level of unemployment, forces will be set in motion that tend to erode the inflationary or recessionary gap.

Figure 16–12 depicts the case of a recessionary gap where aggregate supply curve S_0S_0 intersects aggregate demand curve DD at point A. With equilibrium output well below potential GDP, there is unused industrial capacity and unsold output. So firms will not raise prices much. At the same time, the availability of unemployed workers eager for jobs limits the rate at which labor can push up wage rates. But wages are the main component of business costs, so when wages decline (relative to what they would have been without a recession) so do costs. And lower costs stimulate greater production. This idea is shown in Figure 16–12 as an outward shift of the aggregate supply curve—from S_0S_0 to S_1S_1.

F i g u r e **16–12**   **THE ELIMINATION OF A RECESSIONARY GAP**

When the aggregate supply curve is S_0S_0 and the aggregate demand curve is DD, the economy will reach an equilibrium with a recessionary gap (point A). The resulting deflation of wages will cause the aggregate supply curve to shift outward (downward) from S_0S_0 to S_1S_1 and eventually to S_2S_2. Here, with equilibrium at point C, the recessionary gap is gone and the economy is back at normal full employment.

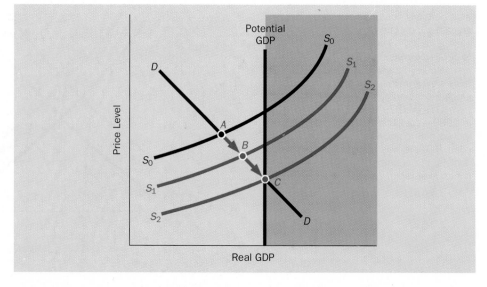

F i g u r e **16-13** **THE VERTICAL LONG-RUN PHILLIPS CURVE**

In the long run, points like *a*, where unemployment is above the normal "full-employment" unemployment rate, are unsustainable. The economy's natural self-correcting mechanism (which was described in Figure 16–12) will erode the recessionary gap by reducing both inflation and unemployment. In the diagram, this will force the economy toward a point like *c*. The long-run choices, therefore, are among points like *c* and *f*, which constitute what is called the vertical (long-run) Phillips curve, not among points like *d* and *a* on the downward-sloping (short-run) Phillips curve.

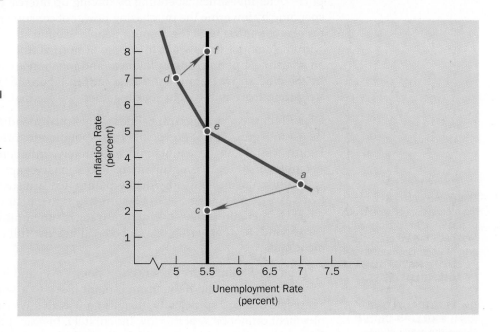

As can be seen in the figure, the outward shift of the aggregate supply curve brought on by the recession pushes equilibrium output up as the economy moves from point *A* to point *B*. Thus the size of the recessionary gap begins to shrink. This process continues until the aggregate supply curve reaches the position indicated by S_2S_2 in Figure 16–12. Here wages have fallen enough to eliminate the recessionary gap, and the economy has reached a full-employment equilibrium at point *C*.[1]

We can relate this to our discussion of the origins of the Phillips curve with the help of Figure 16–13, which is a hypothetical Phillips curve. Point *a* in Figure 16–13 corresponds to point *A* in Figure 16–12: it shows the initial recessionary gap with unemployment (assumed to be 7 percent) above full employment, which we assume to occur at 5.5 percent.

But we have just seen that point *A* in Figure 16–12—and therefore also point *a* in Figure 16–13—is not sustainable. The economy tends to rid itself of the recessionary gap through the disinflation process we have just described. The adjustment path from *A* to *C* depicted in Figure 16–12 would appear on our Phillips curve diagram as a movement toward less inflation and less unemployment—something like the blue arrow from point *a* to point *c* in Figure 16–13.

Similarly, points representing inflationary gaps—such as point *d* in Figure 16–13—are not sustainable. They are also gradually eliminated by the self-correcting mechanism that we studied in Chapter 10. Wages are forced up by the

---

[1]This simple analysis assumes that the aggregate demand curve does not move during the adjustment period. If it is shifting to the right, the recessionary gap will disappear even faster, but inflation will not slow down as much. EXERCISE: Construct the diagram for this case by adding a shift in the aggregate demand curve to Figure 16–12.

abnormally low unemployment, and this in turn pushes prices higher. Higher prices deter investment spending by forcing up interest rates and deter consumer spending by lowering the purchasing power of consumer wealth. The inflationary process continues until the amount people want to spend is brought into balance with the amount firms want to supply at normal full employment. During such an adjustment period, unemployment and inflation are both rising—as indicated by the blue arrow from point *d* to point *f* in Figure 16–13.

Putting these two conclusions together, we see that:

On a Phillips curve diagram, neither points corresponding to an inflationary gap (like *d* in Figure 33–13) nor points corresponding to a recessionary gap (like *a* in Figure 33–13) can be maintained indefinitely. Inflationary gaps lead to rising unemployment and rising inflation. Recessionary gaps lead to falling inflation and falling unemployment. All the points that are sustainable in the long run (such as *c, e,* and *f* in Figure 33–13) correspond to the same rate of unemployment, which is therefore called the **natural rate of unemployment**. The natural rate corresponds to what we have so far been calling the "full-employment" unemployment rate.

> The economy's self-correct-ing mechanism always tends to push the unemployment rate back toward a specific rate of unemployment that we call the **NATURAL RATE OF UNEMPLOYMENT**.

> The **VERTICAL (LONG-RUN) PHILLIPS CURVE** shows the menu of infla-tion/unemployment choices available to society in the long run. It is a vertical straight line at the natural rate of unemployment.

Thus the Phillips curve connecting points *d, e,* and *a* is not a menu of policy choices. While we can move from a point like *e* to a point like *d* by stimulating aggregate demand sufficiently, there is no way that we can stay at point *d*. Unemployment cannot be kept this low indefinitely. Instead, policymakers must choose from among points like *c, e,* and *f,* all of which are vertically above one another at the natural rate of unemployment. For rather obvious reasons, the line connect-ing these points has been dubbed the **vertical (long-run) Phillips curve**. It is this vertical Phillips curve, connecting points like *e* and *f,* that represents the true long-run menu of policy choices. We thus conclude:

THE TRADE-OFF BETWEEN INFLATION AND UNEMPLOYMENT

In the short-run, it is possible to "ride up the Phillips curve" toward lower levels of un-employment by stimulating aggregate demand. Conversely, by restricting the growth of demand, it is possible to "ride down the Phillips curve" toward lower rates of inflation (see, for example, point *a* in Figure 16–13). Thus there is a *trade-off between unem-ployment and inflation* in the short run. Stimulating demand will improve the unemploy-ment picture but worsen inflation; restricting demand will lower inflation but aggravate the unemployment problem. ¶ However, *there is no such trade-off in the long run*. The economy's self-correcting mechanism ensures that unemployment eventually returns to the "natural rate," no matter what happens to aggregate demand. In the long run, faster growth of demand leads only to higher inflation, not to lower unemployment; and slower growth of demand leads only to lower inflation, not to higher unemployment.

FIGHTING UNEMPLOYMENT WITH FISCAL AND MONETARY POLICY

Now let us apply this analysis to a concrete policy problem, one that has troubled many presidents including Ronald Reagan in 1981 and Bill Clinton in 1993. How, if at all, should the government's ability to manage aggregate demand through fiscal and monetary policy be used to combat unemployment?

To create an example that comes close to the one inherited by President Clinton in early 1993, imagine that a new president takes office when the inflation rate is about 3 percent and the unemployment rate is about 7 percent—point *a* in Figure 16–13. Suppose he views 7 percent unemployment as intolerably high. Should he adopt a policy of boosting the growth of aggregate demand by expansionary fiscal and monetary policies? Let us consider the costs and benefits.

Suppose first that nothing is done. The economy's self-correcting mechanism will start into motion and gradually erode the recessionary gap that point *a* represents. Both unemployment and inflation will decline gradually as the economy moves along the blue arrow from point *a* to point *c* in Figure 16–13. Eventually, the diagram shows, the economy will return to the natural rate of unemployment (5.5 percent) and inflation will fall from 3 percent to 2 percent.

The eventual outcome is quite satisfactory—lower unemployment and lower inflation. But it may take an agonizingly long time to get there. Suppose now that the president is impatient and wants to see unemployment decline faster. Some combination of expansionary fiscal and monetary policy can push the economy up the short-run Phillips curve from point *a* toward point *e* in Figure 16–13. Faster economic growth will push unemployment down to 5.5 percent more rapidly, which will make the president (and the voters) happy. But it will also short-circuit the disinflation process that would otherwise take place. So inflation will remain near 3 percent.

This, then, is the choice: Wait patiently while the economy's self-correcting mechanism pulls unemployment down to the natural rate—leading to a long-run equilibrium like point *c* in Figure 16–13. Or rush the process along with expansionary stabilization policy—and wind up with the same unemployment rate but higher inflation. In what sense, then, do policymakers face a *trade-off* between inflation and unemployment? The answer is that:

The cost of reducing unemployment more rapidly by expansionary fiscal and monetary policies is a permanently higher inflation rate.

Figures 16–14 and 16–15 are intended to give the flavor of what the real menu of choices looks like to a president considering whether or not to fight unemployment aggressively. Figure 16–14 contrasts the behavior of the unemployment rate over time under a "passive policy," which simply relies on the economy's self-correcting mechanism, with the behavior under an extremely "activist policy," which makes the unemployment rate jump down to 5.5 percent immediately.

If nothing is done, unemployment will gradually decline from 7 percent to 5.5 percent, as shown by the black "passive policy" path in Figure 16–14. This corresponds to the case where the economy moves from point *a* to point *c* in Figure 16–13.

On the other hand, if a super-activist stabilization policy raises aggregate demand so much that unemployment drops to the natural rate immediately, the economy will follow the blue "activist policy" path in Figure 16–14.[2]

The shaded area in the figure summarizes the difference between these two paths and therefore depicts the payoff to anti-unemployment policy. But there are also costs.

[2]This option is unrealistic. More realistic options would lie between the two paths shown in Figure 16–14.

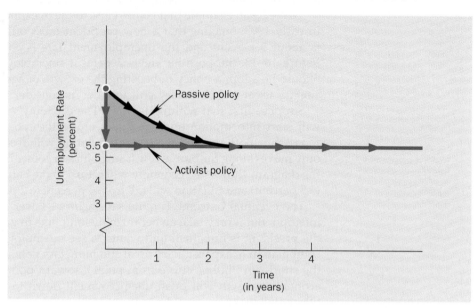

THE PAYOFF TO ANTI-UNEMPLOYMENT POLICY

If expansionary fiscal and monetary policy are used to speed up economic growth ("activist policy" path), the unemployment rate will fall more quickly than if we just rely on the economy's self-correcting mechanism ("passive policy" path). In this example, both paths wind up at 5.5 percent unemployment, the presumed natural rate, but the blue "activist policy" path gets there sooner. The shaded area indicates the gains that the policy has reaped on the unemployment front.

Figure 16–15 gives a rough impression of how the inflation rate might behave under the two alternative policies. The "passive policy" shows inflation drifting down because the unemployment rate remains above 5.5 percent, which is the natural rate, for a long time. The activist policy pushes the unemployment rate down to 5.5 percent immediately, so inflation does not decline. The shaded area therefore measures the inflationary costs of getting unemployment down faster.

Notice the differences in timing between the shaded areas of Figures 16–14 and 16–15. The gains on the unemployment front are transitory—though that does not necessarily make them unimportant, for it may mean that millions of people find work sooner. But the inflationary costs are permanent.

WHAT SHOULD BE DONE?

Should the government pay the inflationary costs of fighting unemployment? When the benefits depicted in Figure 16–14 are balanced against the costs shown in Figure 16–15, have we made a good bargain? The Clinton administration apparently did not think so. Perhaps because the budget deficit it inherited was already so high, it decided not to use fiscal policy to expand demand.

How do policymakers make such decisions? Our analysis highlights three critical issues on which the answer depends.

THE COSTS OF INFLATION AND UNEMPLOYMENT

We spent an entire chapter (Chapter 6) examining the social costs of inflation and unemployment. Most of the costs of the extra unemployment depicted in Figure 16–14, we concluded, are easily translated into dollars and cents. Basically, we need only estimate the real GDP that is lost each year. However, the costs of the

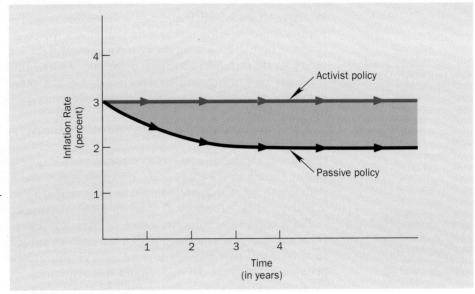

Figure **16–15** THE COST OF ANTI-UNEMPLOYMENT POLICY

The unemployment gains depicted in the preceding figure do not come to us without cost. The expansionary policy prevents inflation from falling (blue "activist policy" path) as it would under the "passive policy" of relying on the self-correcting mechanism. The shaded area indicates the legacy of extra inflation that we inherit as a side-effect of bringing unemployment down sooner.

higher inflation shown in Figure 16–15 are harder to measure. Thus there is considerable controversy over the costs and benefits of using demand management to fight unemployment.

Some economists and public figures, including Federal Reserve Chairman Alan Greenspan, believe that inflation is extremely costly. They may therefore deem it unwise to accept the trade-off embodied in Figures 16–14 and 16–15 in order to get the unemployment rate down faster. As just noted, the Clinton administration apparently agreed in 1993.[3] But politicians tend to have different attitudes when elections are near.

THE POSITION OF THE ECONOMY

We have stated several times in this book that the shape of the economy's aggregate supply curve, and hence the shape of the short-run Phillips curve, depends on the degree of resource utilization. If resources are virtually fully employed, the aggregate supply curve (and thus the Phillips curve) will be steep, which means that the inflationary costs of expansionary policy will be substantial and the unemployment gains minimal. On the other hand, if there is a great deal of unemployed labor and unutilized industrial capacity, the aggregate supply curve (and hence the short-run Phillips curve) may be nearly horizontal. In that case, unemployment can be reduced a great deal with little cost in terms of higher inflation. The Phillips curves we have drawn in this chapter have this characteristic shape.

Because the Phillips curve is shaped this way, the trade-off for unemployment-fighters looks more favorable when markets are slack and less favorable when they are tight.

---

[3]In fact, the large budget deficit undoubtedly played a bigger role in the Clinton administration's decision not to use expansionary fiscal policy.

THE EFFICIENCY OF THE ECONOMY'S SELF-CORRECTING MECHANISM

We have emphasized that, once a recession is underway, it is the economy's natural self-correcting mechanism that closes the recessionary gap. The obvious question here is: How long do we have to wait? If the self-correcting mechanism—which works through reductions in the rate of wage inflation—is slow and halting, the costs of waiting will be enormous. On the other hand, if wage inflation responds promptly, the unemployment necessary to bring down inflation may not be great.

This is another issue that is surrounded by controversy. Most economists believe that the weight of the evidence points to extremely sluggish wage behavior. The rate of wage inflation appears to respond only slowly to economic slack. In terms of our Figure 16–13 (page 393), this means that the economy will traverse the path from *a* to *c* at an agonizingly slow pace, so that a long period of weak economic activity will be necessary if there is to be any appreciable effect on inflation.

But a significant minority opinion finds this assessment far too pessimistic. Economists in this group argue that the costs of reducing inflation are not nearly so severe and that the key to a successful anti-inflation policy is its effects on people's *expectations*. To understand this argument, we must first examine why expectations are relevant to the Phillips-curve trade-off.

INFLATIONARY EXPECTATIONS AND THE PHILLIPS CURVE

Recall from Chapter 10 that the main reason why the economy's aggregate supply curve slopes upward—that is, why output increases as the price level rises—is that businesses typically purchase labor and other inputs under long-term contracts that fix the cost of the input in *money* terms. (The money wage rate is the clearest example.) If such contracts are in force when prices of goods go up, then *real* wages fall. Labor therefore becomes cheaper in real terms, which persuades businesses to expand employment and output. Buying cheaply and selling dearly is, after all, the route to higher profits.

Table 16–1 illustrates how this works in a concrete example. We suppose that workers and firms agree today that the money wage to be paid a year from now

Table **16–1**	**MONEY AND REAL WAGES UNDER UNEXPECTED INFLATION**		
INFLATION RATE (percent)	**PRICE LEVEL ONE YEAR FROM NOW**	**MONEY WAGE ONE YEAR FROM NOW (dollars per hour)**	**REAL WAGE ONE YEAR FROM NOW (dollars per hour)**
0	100	10.00	10.00
2	102	10.00	9.80
4	104	10.00	9.62
6	106	10.00	9.43

NOTE: Each real wage figure is obtained by dividing the $10 nominal wage by the corresponding price level a year later and multiplying by 100. Thus, for example, when the inflation rate is 4 percent, the real wage at the end of the year is ($10/104) × 100 = $9.62.

Table 16-2	MONEY AND REAL WAGES UNDER EXPECTED INFLATION		
EXPECTED INFLATION RATE (percent)	EXPECTED PRICE LEVEL ONE YEAR FROM NOW	MONEY WAGE ONE YEAR FROM NOW (dollars per hour)	EXPECTED REAL WAGE ONE YEAR FROM NOW (dollars per hour)
0	100	10.00	10.00
4	104	10.40	10.00
8	108	10.80	10.00
12	112	11.20	10.00

will be $10 per hour. The table then shows the real wage corresponding to each alternative rate of inflation. Clearly, the higher the inflation rate, the higher the price level at the end of the year and the lower the real wage.

Lower real wages provide an incentive for the firm to increase output, as we have just noted. But lower real wages also impose losses of purchasing power on workers. Thus, there is a sense in which workers are "cheated" by inflation if they sign a contract specifying a fixed money wage in an inflationary environment.

Many economists doubt that workers will sign such contracts *if they can see inflation coming.* Would it not be wiser, these economists ask, to insist on being compensated for inflation in advance? After all, firms should be willing to offer higher money wages if they expect inflation, because they realize that higher money wages need not imply higher *real* wages. Table 16–2 illustrates how this can be done. For example, if 4 percent inflation is expected, the contract could stipulate that the wage rate be increased to $10.40 (which is 4 percent more than $10) at the end of the year. That would keep the real wage at $10, the same as it would be under zero inflation. The other money wage figures in Table 16–2 are derived similarly.

If workers and firms behave this way, and forecast inflation accurately, then the real wage will not decline as the price level rises. Instead, prices and wages will go up together, leaving the real wage unchanged. Workers will not lose from inflation, and firms will not gain. (In the table, the expected future real wage is $10 per hour regardless of the expected rate of inflation.) But then there would be no reason for firms to raise production when the price level rises. In a word, the aggregate supply curve would become *vertical.* In general:

If workers can see inflation coming, and if they receive compensation for it in advance so that inflation does not erode *real* wages, then the economy's aggregate supply curve will not slope upward. It will be a vertical line at the level of output corresponding to potential GDP.

Such a curve is shown in part (a) of Figure 16–16. Since we derived the Phillips curve from the aggregate supply curve earlier in the chapter, it follows that even the *short-run* Phillips curve would be vertical under these circumstances (see part [b] of Figure 16–16).[4]

If this analysis is correct, it has profound implications for the costs and benefits of inflation fighting. To see this, refer back to Figure 16–13 on page 393, and use the graph to depict the strategy of fighting inflation by causing a recession. In order

---

[4]See Discussion Question 7 at the end of the chapter.

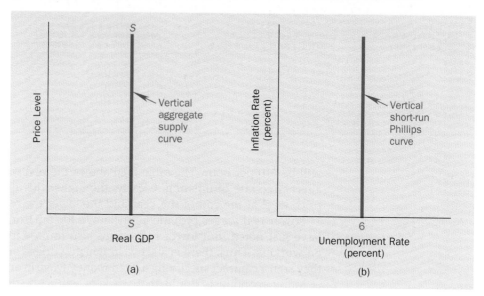

| *F i g u r e* **16–16** | A VERTICAL AGGREGATE SUPPLY CURVE AND THE CORRESPONDING VERTICAL PHILLIPS CURVE |

If workers foresee inflation, and if they also receive full compensation for it in advance, then inflation will no longer erode real wages. In that case, firms will have no incentive to raise production as prices rise, and the aggregate supply curve will be vertical as in part (a). Since we derived the short-run Phillips curve from the aggregate supply curve, the short-run Phillips curve will also become vertical (part [b]).

to move from point *e* (representing 5 percent inflation) to point *c* (representing 2 percent inflation), the economy must take a long and unpleasant detour through point *a*. Specifically, contractionary policies must push the economy down the Phillips curve toward point *a* before the self-correcting mechanism takes over and moves the economy from *a* to *c*. In other words, we must endure a recession to reduce inflation.

But what if even the *short-run* Phillips curve were *vertical* rather than downward sloping? Then this unpleasant recessionary detour would not be necessary. It would be possible for inflation to fall without unemployment rising. The economy could jump directly from point *e* to point *c*.

Is this analysis correct? Can we really slay the inflationary dragon so painlessly? Not necessarily, for our discussion of expectations so far has made at least one unrealistic assumption: that inflation can be predicted accurately. Under this assumption, as Table 16–2 shows, real wages are unaffected by inflation—leaving the aggregate supply curve vertical, even in the short run.

But forecasts of inflation are often inaccurate. Suppose workers underestimate inflation. For example, suppose they expect 4 percent inflation but actually get 6 percent. Then real wages will decline by 2 percent. More generally, real wages will fall if workers underestimate inflation *at all*. The effect of inflation on real wages will be somewhere in between that shown in Tables 16–1 and 16–2.[5] So firms will retain some incentive to raise production as the price level rises. The aggregate supply curve will remain upward sloping. We thus conclude that:

---

[5]To make sure you understand why, construct a version of Table 16–2 based on the assumption that workers expect 4 percent inflation (and hence set next year's wage at $10.40 per hour), regardless of what the actual rate of inflation is. If you do this correctly, your table will show that higher inflation leads to lower real wages, as in Table 16–1.

The short-run aggregate supply curve is *vertical* when inflation is predicted accurately, but *upward sloping* when inflation is underestimated. Thus, only an *unexpectedly* high inflation will raise output, because only unexpected inflation reduces real wages. (To see this, compare Tables 16–1 and 16–2.) Similarly, only an *unexpected* decline in inflation will lead to a recession.

Since people often fail to anticipate changes in inflation correctly, this seems to leave our earlier analysis of the Phillips curve almost intact. And, indeed, most economists nowadays believe that the Phillips curve is downward sloping in the short run but vertical in the long run.

THE THEORY OF RATIONAL EXPECTATIONS

However, a vocal minority of economists disagrees. This group, believers in the hypothesis of *rational expectations*, insists that the Phillips curve is vertical even in the short run. To explain their point of view, we must first explain what rational expectations are. Then we will be in a position to understand why rational expectations have such radical implications for the trade-off between inflation and unemployment.

WHAT ARE *RATIONAL* EXPECTATIONS?

In many economic contexts, people must formulate expectations about what the future will bring. For example, those who invest in the stock market need to forecast the future prices of the stocks they buy and sell. And we have just discussed why workers and businesses may want to forecast future prices before agreeing on a money wage. **Rational expectations** is a controversial hypothesis about how such forecasts are made.

As used by economists, a forecast (an "expectation") of a future variable is considered rational if the forecaster makes *optimal* use of all relevant information that is *available*. Let us elaborate on the italicized words in this definition, using as an example a hypothetical stock market investor who has rational expectations.

First, proponents of rational expectations recognize that *information is limited.* An investor interested in buying General Motors stock would like to know how much profit the company will make in the coming years. Armed with such information, she could predict the future price of GM stock more accurately. But that information is simply not available. Her forecast of the future price of GM stock is not "irrational" just because she does not know GM's future profits. On the other hand, if GM stock normally goes down on Fridays and up on Mondays, she should be aware of this fact.

Next we have the word *optimal.* As used by economists, this means using proper statistical inference to process all the relevant information that is available before making a forecast. In a word, to have rational expectations, your forecasts do not have to be correct; but they cannot have systematic errors that could be avoided by applying better statistical methods. This requirement, while exacting, is not quite as outlandish as it may seem. A good billiards player makes expert use of the laws of physics even without understanding the theory. Similarly, an experienced stock market investor may make good use of information even without formal training in statistics.

RATIONAL EXPECTATIONS are forecasts which, while not necessarily correct, are the best that can be made given the available data. Rational expectations, therefore, cannot err systematically. If expectations are rational, forecasting errors are pure random numbers.

RATIONAL EXPECTATIONS AND THE TRADE-OFF

Let us now see how the hypothesis of rational expectations has been used to deny that there exists any trade-off between inflation and unemployment—even in the short run.

Although they recognize that inflation cannot always be predicted accurately, rational expectationists insist that workers will not make *systematic* errors. The preceding argument about expectations tacitly assumed that workers normally *underestimate* inflation when it is rising. Advocates of rational expectations deny that this is possible. Workers, they argue, will always make the best possible forecast of inflation, using all the latest data and the best available economic models. Such forecasts will sometimes be too high and sometimes be too low; but they will not err systematically in one direction or the other—regardless of whether inflation is rising or falling. Consequently:

If expectations are rational, the difference between the *actual* rate of inflation and the *expected* rate of inflation (the forecasting error) must be a pure random number.

Now recall that the argument in the previous section concluded that employment is affected by inflation only to the extent that inflation *differs* from what was expected. But, under rational expectations, no *predictable* change in inflation can make the *expected* rate of inflation deviate from the *actual* rate of inflation. Hence, according to the rational expectations hypothesis, unemployment will always remain at the natural rate—except for random, and therefore totally unpredictable, gyrations due to forecasting errors. Thus:

If expectations are rational, the inflation rate can be reduced without the need for a period of high unemployment because the short-run Phillips curve is vertical.

According to the rational expectations view, the government's ability to manipulate aggregate demand gives it no ability to control real output and unemployment because the aggregate supply curve is vertical—even in the short run. (To see why, experiment by moving an aggregate demand curve when the aggregate supply curve is vertical, as in Figure 16–16[a].) Any *predictable* change in aggregate demand will lead to a change in the expected rate of inflation, and hence will leave real wages unaffected.

The government therefore can influence output only by making *unexpected* changes in aggregate demand. But, according to the rational expectations hypothesis, this is not easy to do because people understand what policymakers are up to. If the monetary and fiscal authorities typically react to high inflation by reducing aggregate demand, people will soon come to anticipate this reaction. And anticipated reductions in aggregate demand do not cause *unexpected* changes in inflation.

AN EVALUATION

Since proponents of rational expectations believe that inflation can be reduced without losses of output, they tend to be hawks in the war against inflation. Though the theory has attracted many adherents, most economists still believe there is a short-run trade-off between inflation and unemployment. There are several reasons for this.

1. Many contracts for labor and other raw materials cover such long periods of time that the expectations on which they were based, while rational at the time, may appear quite irrational from today's point of view. For example, when three-year labor contracts were drawn up late in 1980, inflation

was above 10 percent. It might therefore have been rational to expect the 1984 price level to be 30 percent above the 1981 price level and to have set 1984 wages accordingly. By late 1982, such an expectation would have been plainly irrational. But it might already have been written into contracts. If so, real wages wound up much higher than intended, giving firms a powerful incentive to reduce employment—even though no one behaved irrationally.

2. Many people believe that inflationary expectations do not adapt as quickly to changes in the economic environment as the rational expectations hypothesis assumes. If, for example, the government embarks on an anti-inflation policy, workers may continue to expect high inflation for quite a while. Thus they may continue to insist on rapid money wage increases. Then, if inflation actually slows down, real wages will end up rising faster than anyone expected, and unemployment will result. Such behavior may not be strictly *rational*. But, to many observers, it seems realistic.

3. The facts have not been kind to the rational expectations point of view. The theory suggests that unemployment should hover around the natural rate most of the time, with random gyrations in one direction or the other. Yet this does not seem to be the case. The theory also predicts that preannounced (and thus expected) anti-inflation programs should be relatively painless. Yet, in practice, inflation fighting looks to be very costly. Finally, many direct tests of the rationality of expectations have cast doubt on the hypothesis. For example, survey data on peoples' expectations rarely meet the exacting requirements of rationality.

As a piece of pure logic, then, the rational expectations argument is impeccable. But there is controversy over how best to apply the idea in practice. The issues are far from settled and research continues. But the evidence to date leads most economists to reject the extreme rational expectationist position for short-run analysis. In the long run, however, the rational expectations viewpoint should be more or less appropriate since people will not hold incorrect expectations indefinitely. As Abraham Lincoln said, you cannot fool all of the people all of the time.

WHY ECONOMISTS (AND POLITICIANS) DISAGREE

This chapter has now taught us some of the reasons why economists often disagree about the proper conduct of national economic policy. And it also helps us understand some of the related political debates.

Should the government take stern actions to reduce inflation? You will say *yes* if you believe that (1) inflation is more costly than unemployment, (2) the short-run Phillips curve is steep, (3) expectations react quickly, and (4) the economy's self-correcting mechanism works smoothly and rapidly. These views on the economy tend to be held by monetarists and rational expectationists and by the (generally conservative) politicians who listen to them.

But you will say *no* if you believe that (1) unemployment is more costly than inflation, (2) the short-run Phillips curve is flat, (3) expectations react sluggishly, and (4) the self-correcting mechanism is slow and unreliable. These views are held by many Keynesian economists, so it is not surprising that the (generally liberal) politicians who follow their advice often oppose the use of recession to fight inflation.

The tables turn, however, when the question is whether to use demand management to bring a recession to a rapid end. The Keynesian view of the world—that unemployment is costly, that the short-run Phillips curve is flat, that expectations adjust slowly, and that the self-correcting mechanism is unreliable—leads to the conclusion that the benefits of fighting unemployment are high while the costs are low. And so Keynesians are eager to fight recessions. The monetarist and rational expectationist positions on these four issues are precisely the reverse, and so are the policy conclusions.

THE DILEMMA OF DEMAND MANAGEMENT

So we have seen that the makers of monetary and fiscal policy face an agonizing trade-off. If they stimulate aggregate demand to reduce unemployment, they will aggravate inflation. If they restrict aggregate demand to fight inflation, they will cause higher unemployment.

But wait. Early in the chapter we learned that when inflation comes from the supply side, inflation and unemployment are *positively* associated: we suffer from more of both or enjoy less of each. Does this mean that monetary and fiscal policymakers can escape the trade-off between inflation and unemployment? Certainly not.

THE TRADE-OFF BETWEEN INFLATION AND UNEMPLOYMENT

Adverse shifts in the aggregate supply curve can cause both inflation and unemployment to rise together, and thus can destroy the statistical Phillips curve relationship. Nevertheless, anything that monetary and fiscal policy can do will make unemployment and inflation move in opposite directions because monetary and fiscal policy give the government control only over the *aggregate demand* curve, not over the *aggregate supply* curve. ¶ Thus, no matter what the source of inflation, and no matter what happens to the Phillips curve, the makers of monetary and fiscal policy must still face up to the disagreeable trade-off between inflation and unemployment. This is a principle that many policymakers have failed to recognize, and one of the **12 Ideas** that we hope you will remember well **Beyond the Final Exam.**

Naturally, the unpleasant nature of this trade-off has led to a vigorous search for a way out of the dilemma. Both economists and public officials have sought a policy that might offer improvements on both fronts simultaneously, or that might ease the pain of either unemployment or inflation. The rest of this chapter considers some of these ideas.

ATTEMPTS TO IMPROVE THE TRADE-OFF DIRECTLY

One class of policies aims to reduce the natural rate of unemployment. For example, vocational training and retraining programs, if successful, help unemployed workers with obsolete skills acquire abilities that are currently in demand. By so doing, they help alleviate upward pressures on wage rates in jobs where qualified workers are in short supply.

For example, if an unemployed steelworker is taught to assemble computers, then progress is made against both inflation and unemployment, since one former steelworker leaves the ranks of the unemployed while one new worker helps alleviate the shortage of skilled labor in the computer industry. A similar role is played by the United States Employment Service and similar agencies at the state and local levels—which try to improve the match of workers to jobs by funneling information from prospective employers to prospective employees.

The idea sounds appealing and has many adherents; indeed, the Clinton administration has pledged to expand retraining programs for displaced workers. But, up to now, training and placement programs have achieved only modest successes. Too often, people are trained for jobs that do not exist by the time they finish their training—if indeed they ever existed. Even when they work, these programs are expensive, which restricts the number of workers that can be accommodated.

Over the last two decades, many government regulations over prices and provision of service were reduced or made more flexible in such industries as airlines, trucking, railroads, telecommunications, and energy. Presidents Ford, Carter, and Reagan all vigorously promoted deregulation, often citing the anti-inflationary impact as a reason.[6] Prices have generally fallen in the deregulated industries. However, even though most economists applaud deregulation on microeconomic grounds, they doubt that it has had a large effect on the economy-wide inflation rate.

WAGE-PRICE CONTROLS

WAGE-PRICE CONTROLS are legal restrictions on the ability of industry and labor to raise wages and prices.

To many people, the most natural way to control inflation is to impose mandatory **wage-price controls**. After all, if we do not like something, why not just outlaw it? Wage-price controls have rarely been used in the United States, but some foreign countries have experimented with them much more.

Economists generally oppose controls for reasons we learned back in Chapter 4. When price ceilings are effective, they force the price below the equilibrium price, so that quantity demanded exceeds quantity supplied. This is shown in Figure 16–17, where the equilibrium price of hamburgers is assumed to be $1.50. If controls do not allow the price of hamburgers to rise above $1, quantity demanded will exceed quantity supplied by one million hamburgers per year.

With price no longer serving as the rationing device, some other method of rationing is necessary. One possibility is long lines of eager eaters waiting their turn for burgers. Scenes like this used to be typical in the former Soviet bloc and were seen in America when gasoline was rationed in the 1970s.

Another is government ration coupons, giving the owner the right to buy a hamburger—a device used successfully for many goods during World War II. Neither of these measures is likely to be popular with·the electorate in peacetime. And both are likely to spawn black markets, which erode respect for law and order at the same time they abrogate the effects of controls. As critics are fond of pointing out, controls give perfectly law-abiding citizens incentives to break the law in an effort to circumvent the controls.

---

[6]For a full discussion of regulation and deregulation, see *Microeconomics* Chapter 18.

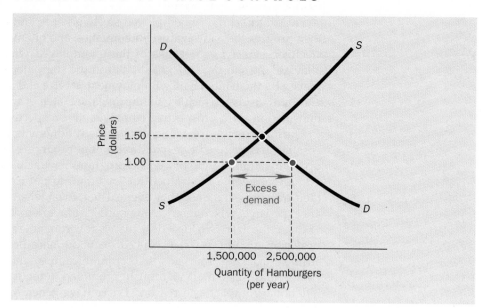

Figure **16-17**   THE EFFECTS OF PRICE CONTROLS

This diagram portrays the market for hamburgers under an effective price control system. Since the equilibrium price is $1.50 per hamburger, a regulation that holds the price at $1 makes the quantity of hamburgers demanded (2,500,000 per year) exceed the quantity supplied (1,500,000 per year). There is a shortage of one million hamburgers per year, and some sort of rationing scheme probably is necessary.

And the problems spawned by price controls go deeper than this. Among the principal factors determining the equilibrium price of hamburgers are the prices of raw agricultural commodities such as beef. But prices of raw agricultural commodities cannot be controlled by the government because they depend on the weather and other acts of nature. If price controls hold the price of hamburgers at $1 while the price of beef skyrockets, it may become unprofitable to sell hamburgers. If so, hamburgers will start disappearing from restaurant menus.

With hamburgers unavailable, consumers will turn to other goods, thereby putting upward pressure on the prices of items such as fish and soybeans. Thus, price controls on hamburgers will cause the hamburger industry to contract and necessitate additional price controls on fish and soybeans. And so it goes. Each extension of price controls to a new commodity requires additional controls to support it, in an ever-expanding chain. Thus, for price controls to be effective, they must be nearly universal—which is next to impossible. This, of course, is precisely the lesson the formerly socialist nations learned so painfully.

Nonetheless, there is an intellectually defensible case for wage–price controls under the right circumstances. Inflation gathers a substantial momentum once workers, consumers, and business managers begin to expect that it will continue. These **inflationary expectations** encourage workers to demand higher wage increases. Firms, in turn, are willing to grant the workers' demands because they believe they will be able to pass the cost increases on to consumers in a general inflationary environment. Thus, to a great extent, *inflation occurs because people expect it to occur.* Phrased in terms of our Phillips curve analysis, *inflationary expectations shift the Phillips curve upward*, so that any given rate of unemployment corresponds to a higher rate of inflation.

A tough and thorough program of wage and price controls, it is argued, can break the vicious cycle of inflationary expectations. By announcing controls, the government serves notice on workers that they do not need anticipatory wage increases to preserve their purchasing power. And firms are warned that they may not be able to pass on higher costs to consumers. By breaking inflationary expectations, supporters argue, a controls program can shift the Phillips curve down and reduce the rate of inflation.

Under the right conditions, this argument may be correct. Some economists, for example, believe that controls helped such countries as Argentina and Israel reduce galloping inflations in the 1980s. But these were extreme circumstances, and there was much more to the anti-inflation programs than merely controls. America's 1971–1974 experiment with wage–price controls under President Nixon, however, is generally considered to have failed. Most studies of the period conclude that the controls *lowered* inflation while they were in effect, but then *raised* it when they were lifted.

INDEXING

INDEXING refers to provisions in a law or a contract whereby monetary payments are automatically adjusted whenever a specified price index changes. Wage rates, pensions, interest payments on bonds, income taxes, and many other things can be indexed in this way, and have been. Sometimes such contractual provisions are called *escalator clauses*.

Indexing—which refers to provisions in a law or contract whereby monetary payments are automatically adjusted whenever a specific price index changes—presents a very different approach to the inflation–unemployment dilemma. Whereas the other proposals discussed in this chapter are all designed *to lower the inflation rate*, the primary purpose of indexing is *to reduce the social costs of inflation*.

The mechanics of indexing are best explained by an example, and the most familiar example in the United States is an *escalator clause* in a wage agreement. An escalator clause provides for an automatic increase in money wages—without the need for new contract negotiations—any time the price level rises by more than a specified amount.

Suppose that with the Consumer Price Index (CPI) sitting at 150, a union and a firm agree on a three-year contract setting wages at $10 per hour this year, $11 next year, and $12 in the third year. They might then add an escalator clause stating that wages will be increased above these stipulated amounts by 5 cents per hour for each point by which the CPI exceeds 150 in any future year of the contract. Then, if the CPI reaches 160 in the third year of the contract, workers will receive an additional 50 cents per hour (5 cents for each point by which 160 exceeds 150), for a total wage of $12.50 per hour. In this way, workers are partly protected from inflation. Nowadays, less than half of all workers employed by large unionized firms in the United States are covered by some sort of escalator clause. And very few nonunion workers or employees of small firms enjoy such protection.

Interest payments on bonds or savings accounts can also be indexed, although this is not currently done in the United States.[7] The most extensive indexing to be found in the United States today is in government transfer payments. Social Security benefits, for instance, are indexed so that retirees are not victimized by inflation. Several other government income maintenance and social insurance programs also pay benefits that are tied directly to prices.

---

[7]Some other countries, with much higher inflation than ours, do extensive indexing of interest rates. Brazil and Israel are notable examples.

INDEXING AND THE SOCIAL COSTS OF INFLATION

Some economists believe that the United States should follow the example of several foreign countries and adopt a much more widespread system of indexing. Why? Because, they argue, it would take most of the sting out of inflation. To see how indexing would accomplish this, let us review some of the social costs of inflation that we enumerated in Chapter 6.

One important cost is the capricious redistribution of income caused by unexpected inflation. We saw that borrowers and lenders normally incorporate an *inflation premium* equal to the *expected rate of inflation* into the nominal interest rate. Then, if inflation turns out to be higher than expected, the borrower has to pay to the lender only the agreed-upon nominal interest rate, including the premium for *expected* inflation; he does not have to compensate the lender for the (higher) *actual* inflation. Thus the borrower enjoys a windfall gain and the lender loses out. The opposite happens if inflation turns out to be lower than was expected. But if interest rates on loans were indexed, none of this would occur. Borrowers and lenders would agree on a fixed *real* rate of interest, and then the borrower would compensate the lender for whatever *actual inflation* occurred. No one would have to guess what the inflation rate would be.[8]

A second social cost we mentioned in Chapter 6 stems from the fact that our tax system levies taxes on nominal interest and nominal capital gains. As we learned, this flaw in the tax system leads to extremely high effective tax rates in an inflationary environment. But indexing could fix this problem easily. We need only rewrite the tax code so that only *real* interest payments and *real* capital gains are taxed.

A final problem noted in Chapter 6 is that uncertainty over future price levels makes it difficult to enter into long-term contracts—rental agreements, construction agreements, and so on. One way out of this problem is to write indexed contracts, which specify all future payments in real terms.

In the face of all these benefits, and others we have not mentioned here, why do many economists oppose indexing? Probably the major reason is the fear that indexing will lead to an acceleration of inflation. With the costs of inflation reduced so markedly, they argue, what will persuade governments to pay the price of fighting inflation? What will stop them from inflating more and more? They fear that the answer to these questions is, Nothing. Voters who stand to lose nothing from inflation are unlikely to pressure their legislators into stopping it. Opponents of indexing worry that a mild inflationary disease could turn into a ravaging epidemic in a highly indexed economy.

---

[8]For example, an indexed loan with a 2 percent real interest rate would require a 5 percent nominal interest payment if inflation were 3 percent, a 7 percent nominal interest payment if inflation were 5 percent, and so on.

Summary

1. Inflation can be caused either by rapid growth of aggregate demand or by sluggish growth of aggregate supply.

2. When fluctuations in economic activity emanate from the demand side, prices will rise rapidly when real output grows rapidly. Since rapid growth means more jobs, unemployment and inflation will be inversely related.

3. This inverse relationship between unemployment and inflation is called the **Phillips curve**. U.S. data for the

1950s and 1960s display a Phillips curve relation, but data for the 1970s do not.

4. The Phillips curve is not a menu of *long-run* policy choices for the economy because the **self-correcting mechanism** guarantees that neither an inflationary gap nor a recessionary gap can last indefinitely.

5. Because of the self-correcting mechanism, the economy's true long-run choices lie along a **vertical Phillips curve**, which shows that the so-called **natural rate of unemployment** is the only unemployment rate that can persist indefinitely.

6. In the short run, the economy can move up or down its short-run Phillips curve. *Temporary* reductions in unemployment can be achieved at the cost of higher inflation. Similarly, *temporary* increases in unemployment can be used to fight inflation.

7. Whether it is advisable to use unemployment to fight inflation depends on four principal factors: the relative social costs of inflation versus unemployment, the efficiency of the economy's self-correcting mechanism, the current position of the economy, and how quickly inflationary expectations adjust.

8. If workers expect inflation to occur, and if they demand (and receive) compensation for inflation, output will be independent of the price level. Both the aggregate supply curve and the short-run Phillips curve are vertical in this case.

9. However, errors in predicting inflation will still change real wages and hence will still change the quantity of output that firms wish to supply. Thus, *unpredicted* movements in the price level will lead to a normal, upward-sloping aggregate supply curve.

10. According to the hypothesis of **rational expectations**, errors in predicting inflation are purely random. This means that, except for some random (and uncontrollable) gyrations, the aggregate supply curve is vertical even in the short run.

11. Many economists reject the rational expectations view of the world. Some deny that expectations are "rational" and believe instead that people tend, for example, to underpredict inflation when it is rising. Others point out that contracts signed years ago cannot possibly embody expectations that are "rational" in terms of what we know today.

12. When fluctuations in economic activity are caused by shifts of the aggregate supply curve, output will grow slowly (causing unemployment to rise) when inflation speeds up. Hence, the rates of unemployment and inflation will be positively related. Many observers feel that this sort of **stagflation** is why the Phillips curve collapsed in the 1970s.

13. Even if inflation is initiated by supply-side problems, so that inflation and unemployment occur together, the monetary and fiscal authorities still face this trade-off: anything they do to improve unemployment is likely to worsen inflation, and anything they do to reduce inflation is likely to aggravate unemployment. The reason is that monetary and fiscal policy mainly influence the aggregate demand curve, not the aggregate supply curve. This is one of our **12 Ideas for Beyond the Final Exam**.

14. Policies that improve the functioning of the labor market—including retraining programs and employment services—can lower the natural rate of unemployment. To date, however, the U.S. government has had only modest success with these measures.

15. Some small amount of progress against inflation may also be made by eliminating government regulations that keep prices high. Indeed, much of this has already been done.

16. One argument in favor of short-term **wage–price controls** is that they can reduce **inflationary expectations** and thereby rob inflation of some of its momentum.

17. However, legal limits on wage and price increases seriously interfere with the workings of a market economy.

18. **Indexing** is another way to approach the trade-off problem. Instead of trying to improve the trade-off, it concentrates on reducing the social costs of inflation—perhaps eliminating them, altogether. Opponents of indexing worry, however, that the economy's resistance to inflation may be lowered by indexing.

Key Concepts and Terms

Demand-side inflation
Supply-side inflation
Phillips curve
Stagflation caused by supply shocks
Self-correcting mechanism

Natural rate of unemployment
Vertical (long-run) Phillips curve
Trade-off between unemployment and inflation in the short run and in the long run
Inflationary expectations

Rational expectations
Wage–price controls
Indexing (escalator clauses)
Real versus nominal interest rates

Questions for Review

1. Some observers in the 1970s denied that policymakers faced a trade-off between inflation and unemployment. What made them say this? Were they correct?

2. "There is no sense in trying to shorten recessions through fiscal and monetary policy because the effects of these policies on the unemployment rate are sure to be temporary." Comment on both the truth of this statement and its relevance for policy formulation.

3. Why is it said that decisions on fiscal and monetary policy are, at least in part, political decisions that cannot be made on "objective" economic criteria?

4. What is a "Phillips curve"? Why did it seem to work so much better in the 1954–1969 period than it did in the 1970s?

5. Explain why expectations about inflation affect the wages that result from labor–management bargaining.

6. What is meant by "rational" expectations? Why does the hypothesis of rational expectations have such stunning implications for economic policy? Would believers in rational expectations want to shorten a recession by expanding aggregate demand? Would they want to fight inflation by reducing aggregate demand?

7. Show that, if the economy's aggregate supply curve is vertical, fluctuations in the growth of aggregate demand produce only fluctuations in inflation with no effect on output. Relate this to your answer to the previous question.

8. Suppose that a program of wage–price controls is under consideration by the government. What are the possible benefits to the nation from such a program? What are the possible costs? How would you balance the benefits against the costs?

9. Long-term government bonds now pay approximately 6 percent *nominal* interest. Would you prefer to trade yours in for an indexed bond that paid a 3 percent *real* rate of interest? What if the real interest rate offered were 2 percent? What if it were 1 percent? What do your answers to these questions reveal about your personal attitudes toward inflation?

10. In the late 1980s, the unemployment rate in the United States hovered in the 5–5.5 percent range and the inflation rate rose slightly. What do these facts suggest about the numerical value of the natural rate of unemployment?

11. It is said that the Federal Reserve Board typically cares more about inflation and less about unemployment than the administration. If this is true, why might President Clinton have been worried about what Fed Chairman Alan Greenspan would do in early 1993, when inflation increased for a few months?

12. The year 1993 opened with the unemployment rate around 7 percent, real GDP growing slowly, inflation about 3 percent, and the federal budget deficit over $300 billion.

    a. Make an argument for engaging in contractionary monetary or fiscal policies under these circumstances.
    b. Make an argument for engaging in expansionary monetary or fiscal policies under these circumstances.
    c. Which argument do you find more persuasive?

PART IV

The United
States in
the World
Economy

PRODUCTIVITY AND GROWTH IN THE WEALTH OF NATIONS

The enormous wealth of Britain is attributable [primarily] to . . . the wonderful skill of her entrepreneurs . . . and the superiority of her workmen in rapid and masterly execution. . . . The English laborer . . . gives his work more care, attention and diligence, than the workmen of most other nations.

JEAN BAPTISTE SAY, 1819

Japan commercially, I regret to say, does not bear the best reputation for executing business. Inferior goods, irregularity and indifferent shipments have caused no end of worry . . . you are a very satisfied easy-going race . . . the habits of national heritage.

FROM A REPORT OF AN AUSTRALIAN EXPERT FOR THE JAPANESE GOVERNMENT, 1915

This chapter introduces a major new topic, one of rapidly growing importance for all Americans: the place of the United States in the world economy. Exports and imports account for an ever-rising share of the country's output and consumption. We are conscious as never before of the effective competition the United States faces from other industrial economies. Our prosperity depends increasingly on that of other countries, and theirs, in turn, depends vitally on ours. ¶ This chapter takes a long-run view of such developments. It compares for a number of countries the growth in living standards and *productivity* (output per hour of work) over many decades; it seeks to provide some explanation for those growth patterns; and it indicates the directions in which the trends suggest we are going. ¶ Human history in the last two centuries has been unlike anything ever experienced before. In the world's industrial countries, the quantity and quality of food, clothing, and comforts have reached levels that were never dreamed possible by earlier generations. The change has been so revolutionary that it is difficult to grasp its magnitude. This chapter helps us envision how great the accomplishment has been. It also suggests that the transformation was made possible by productivity growth: the fact that a person in the United States today can produce in an hour perhaps 20 times as much as was possible in 1800. Just two figures will suggest the magnitude of the achievement. In 1800 about 90 percent of America's labor force had to work on farms, but all that farm labor barely managed to produce enough food to feed the country adequately. Today only about 3 percent of U.S. workers earn their living on farms. Yet those few farm workers provide an outpouring of surpluses which the U.S. government constantly struggles to contain.

LIFE IN THE "GOOD OLD DAYS"

The United States, and the thirteen colonies before it, has always been a privileged land with relatively high levels of nutrition. In the eighteenth century, an average white, native-born male who reached the age of 10 could expect to live to somewhere between age 50 and 55. By contrast, an English *nobleman* at that time could expect to live only to something between age 39 and 46.

In the mid-nineteenth century, low incomes, local weather conditions, crop cycles, an almost complete lack of refrigeration, and limited transport of goods bound a large part of even the U.S. population to a minimal and nutritionally inferior variety of foods. Such uninspiring staples as potatoes, lard, cornmeal, and salt pork were the mainstays of diets, particularly outside the population centers. Most travelers' accounts of meals in nineteenth-century America mentioned the ubiquity of some kind of one-pot stew which constituted the main meal of the day for the family. According to one study, "There were, of course, a few people who knew what it was to . . . eat a meal that consisted of more than one course; but there were very, very few such people, and they were all very rich."[1]

Nevertheless, most Americans were right to feel that they lived in a land of unprecedented abundance, for that one-pot stew was quite sure to be there every day. For many centuries most Europeans had devoted nearly half their food budgets to breadstuffs (for example, in 1790 in France, "The price of bread [for a family of five], even in normal times . . . was half . . . the daily wage of common labor."[2] Often the bread took the form of gruel—a sort of cooked breakfast cereal—served in a single bowl with a single spoon, both passed around the table to the entire family.

In bad years, even gruel was unavailable. Famine continued to threaten Europe until the beginning of the nineteenth century, and earlier it had constituted a normal fact of existence. One historian writes,

> . . . two consecutive bad harvests spelt disaster . . . . France, by any standards a privileged country, is reckoned to have experienced 10 general famines during the tenth century; 26 in the eleventh; 2 in the twelfth; 4 in the fourteenth; 7 in the fifteenth; 13 in the sixteenth; 11 in the seventeenth and 16 in the eighteenth.
>
> The same could be said of any country in Europe. In Germany, famine was a persistent visitor to the towns and the flatlands . . .

[1]Ruth Schwartz Cowan, *More Work for Mother: The Ironies of Household Technology from the Open Hearth to the Microwave* (New York: Basic Books, 1983), page 38.

[2]Robert Palmer, *The Age of Democratic Revolution*, Vol. 2, Princeton: Princeton University Press, 1964, page 49.

Late nineteenth century sod house in the Dakotas.

SOURCE: *New York Times Magazine*, March 18, 1990, page 34, which cites Bettman Archive.

. . . the countryside sometimes experienced far greater suffering. The peasants . . . had no solution in case of famine except to turn to the town where they crowded together, begging in the streets and often dying in public squares, as in Venice and Amiens in the sixteenth century.

The towns soon had to protect themselves against these regular invasions . . . . Beggars from distant provinces appeared in the fields and streets of the town(s) . . . starving, clothed in rags and covered with fleas and vermin.[3]

Food shortages were not the only manifestation of unimaginably poor living conditions:

It is difficult for anyone alive now to comprehend how appalling, as recently as a century ago, were the conditions of daily life in all the cities of the Western world, even in the wealthiest parts of town. The stupefying level of filth accepted as normal from the Middle Ages through the Enlightenment were augmented horribly by the Industrial Revolution.[4]

Even in the United States, living conditions in the nineteenth century were far from ideal. Most of the homes that travelers saw in rural America were tiny and crudely built, with no glass windows, no lighting except the fireplace, no indoor plumbing, and scanty homemade furniture. Every winter it was expected that ink would freeze in the inkwells. Urban housing was not much better. In New York City in the 1860s, it was typical for six people to live in a ten-by-twelve room. In 1890 Jacob Riis wrote of the lower Manhattan tenements,

It is said that nowhere in the world are so many people crowded together on a square mile as here. In [one seven-story tenement building] there were 58 babies and 38 children that were over five years of age . . . . In Essex Street two small rooms in a six-story tenement were made to hold a "family" of father and mother, twelve children, and six boarders . . . .[5]

The worst evils of these overcrowded slums were insufficient light and air—narrow airshafts conveyed foul air and disease and served as inflammatory flues when fire broke out. There were no private toilets or washing facilities in these buildings, and cellars and courtyards were foul.

---

[3]Fernand Braudel, *The Structures of Everyday Life: The Limits of the Possible*, Vol. 1, *Civilization and Capitalism, 15th-18th Century* (New York: Harper and Row, 1979), pages 73–75 (footnotes omitted, Braudel's emphasis).

[4]William L. Rathje, "Rubbish!," *The Atlantic Monthly*, Vol. 264, No. 6, December 1989, page 100.

[5]Jacob Riis, *How the Other Half Lives* (New York: Hill and Wang, Inc., 1957), page 77. Originally published by Charles Scribner's Sons, New York, 1890.

Like the common man, the rich have also gained much in terms of health and personal comfort in the course of two or three centuries. By the early 1900s, life expectancy at birth for a member of the British nobility had reached 65 years. But in the mid-sixteenth century, that figure was less than 40 years. More remarkable yet is the fact that longevity of the nobility in these centuries was no better than that of the population as a whole, despite the miserable living conditions of the bulk of the nation.

The dramatic improvement in the comforts enjoyed by the rich is illustrated by the development of home heating technology. The role of the draft in fireplace construction was not discovered until early in the eighteenth century. Until then, the huge fireplaces in the homes of the nobles, though beautiful, were extremely ineffective; they roasted nearby persons on one side and froze them on the other. Winter was a serious threat to rich and poor alike. "Cold weather . . . could be a public disaster, freezing rivers, halting mills [with little or no flour having been stored because preservation methods were largely unknown], bringing packs of dangerous wolves out into the countryside, multiplying epidemics."[6] Not even the highest nobility were spared. The Princess Palatine, the German sister-in-law of Louis XIV, reported that in February 1695 "in the Hall of Mirrors at Versailles at the King's table the wine and water froze in the glasses."[7]

Even the housing of relatively well-off nineteenth-century Americans was still primitive by modern standards. Baths, for example, were rare even in the cities. No homes had electricity and few had gas. Fewer still had hot running water, and not even 2 percent had indoor toilets and cold running water. Boston, with a population of nearly 200,000 in 1860, had only 31,000 sinks, 4,000 baths, and 10,000 water closets—about half of which were extremely primitive affairs. Albany, with a population in 1860 of 62,000, had only 19 private baths and 160 water closets. Outdoor privies were the norm and baths, for the great majority, a luxury.[8]

Though living conditions were vastly improved from earlier centuries, by today's standards, life in the United States just 100 years ago was hard and primitive.

THE MAGNITUDE OF PRODUCTIVITY GROWTH

Today, of course, things are vastly different. By 1985 less than 2 percent of American housing units lacked complete plumbing—defined as hot and cold piped water, a flush toilet, and a bathtub or shower for the exclusive use of that housing unit. Less than 5 percent was occupied by more than one person per room. Of the new, privately owned, one-family houses built in 1991, nearly 60 percent had three bedrooms, 44 percent had two and a half or more bathrooms, and 75 percent had central air conditioning. Statistics for 1987 show that 93 percent of all households had a color television, virtually 100 percent were equipped with electric refrigerators, 75 percent had electric washing machines, 61 percent owned a microwave oven, and 54 percent had two or more vehicles.[9]

---

[6]Braudel, page 299.
[7]*Ibid.*
[8]Edgar W. Martin, *The Standard of Living in 1860* (Chicago: University of Chicago Press, 1942).
[9]U.S. Bureau of the Census, *Statistical Abstract of the United States, 1992* (112th edition) (Washington, D.C.: U.S. Government Printing Office, 1992).

By means such as technical improvement and heavier spending for the purpose, society has also been able to improve living standards in terms of *safety*—a subject usually ignored in discussions of economic progress. Figure 17–1 shows that in six decades the United States was able to cut the number of accidental deaths by more than half—despite the rise in miles traveled per person.

This revolution in manner of living was made possible by an unprecedented rate of growth in human efficiency in producing output. Before reporting the facts, it is necessary to describe the two basic concepts, *labor productivity* and *output per capita*, usually employed to measure first, the productive efficiency of the working population, and second, the resulting average level of economic well-being.

Labor productivity refers to the amount of output turned out by a *given* amount of labor (**gross domestic product [GDP] per labor hour**). Obviously, an increase in productivity means that a human being has become a more effective instrument of production. This can be the result of harder work, better training, more or better equipment, innovative technology, or a variety of other causes.

The **standard of living**, on the other hand, is more naturally measured by **GDP per capita**, that is, by total output (GDP) divided by the number of persons among whom it will be distributed. The more output there is for each person, the better off in economic terms the average person must be.

The fantastic magnitude of the increases in both labor productivity and output per capita since, say, 1800 is best appreciated by contrasting it with the dismal average record of many previous centuries. In Europe, after a long decline, living standards had been increasing intermittently since the eleventh century—the century in which William the Conqueror acquired England. Still, it is estimated

LABOR PRODUCTIVITY refers to the amount of output a worker turns out in an hour (or a week or a year) of labor. It can be measured as total national output (GDP) in a given year divided by the total number of hours of work performed for pay in the country during that year. That is, labor productivity is defined as GDP per hour of labor.

F i g u r e **17–1** **DEATHS FROM ACCIDENTS IN THE UNITED STATES, 1930–1990**

This graph reports the rate per 100,000 population of deaths from accidents in the United States. The graph shows that safety has increased dramatically, and that the number of deaths was reduced by more than half in six decades.

SOURCES: 1930–1960: U.S. Department of Commerce, Bureau of the Census, *Historical Statistics of the United States*, Washington, D.C.: U.S. Government Printing Office, 1975, page 58; 1970–1990: U.S. Department of Commerce, Bureau of the Census, *Statistical Abstract of the United States, 1992*, Washington, D.C.: U.S. Government Printing Office, 1992, page 82.

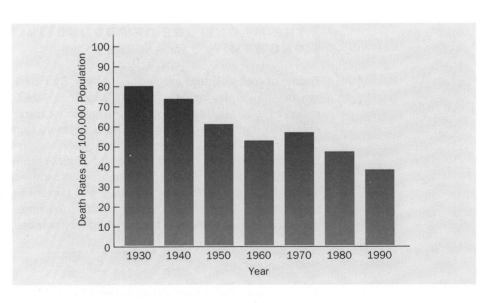

Figure **17-2**

LABOR PRODUCTIVITY, 1870–1989

The productivity growth shown here for five industrial countries is typical of today's leading industrial economies. The explosive pattern of increase is unprecedented in previous history.

SOURCE: Angus Maddison, *Dynamic Forces in Capitalist Development* (New York: Oxford University Press, 1991).

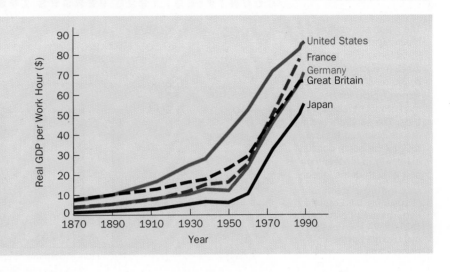

that even by the time of the American Civil War neither labor productivity nor GDP per capita had yet reattained the levels that had been achieved in ancient Rome—about 16 centuries earlier! Thus, on the average, productivity and GDP per capita did not grow at all over 1600 years. Even for those wealthy enough to buy them, the number of important new consumer goods introduced in those 16 centuries was remarkably small. Firearms, glass windowpanes, eyeglasses, mechanical clocks, tobacco, and printed books constitute almost the entire list of major new consumer products invented between the fall of the Roman Empire and the beginning of the nineteenth century. Indeed, some significant amenities, notably elaborate bathing facilities and efficient home heating devices, had disappeared since the fall of Rome.

In contrast, the period since, say, the 1830s has been characterized by an endless explosion of innovations. The railroad and the steamship revolutionized transportation. Steel-making technology changed drastically. The chemical and electronics industries were born and produced hundreds of new consumer products. The range of personal and household goods that we now take for granted—TV sets, dishwashers, cameras, automobiles, personal computers, and many, many others—appeared in an accelerating stream and became commonplace. This has reached a point where today our one unchanging expectation for the future is that it will be characterized by constant change.

Figure 17–2 shows, for five countries, the impressive growth of labor productivity over the past century.[10] For example, it indicates that in this period Japanese

---

[10]Throughout the chapter, as we compare output per capita or output per work hour (productivity) in different countries, we run into a problem. U.S. output is measured in dollars, and Japanese output in yen. It is *not* legitimate to compare them by looking up the number of yen that your bank will give you for a dollar, because that exchange rate changes from day to day, but relative productivity levels do not. Instead we try to measure the outputs of different countries in money (usually dollars) of constant purchasing power. That is, we ask how many yen does it cost to buy in Japan the same bundle of goods that one can buy for (say) $100 in the United States. This figure is referred to as a *purchasing power parity* exchange rate. Such numbers are used in all the international comparisons in this chapter.

F i g u r e **17–3**

IMPROVEMENT IN LIVING STANDARDS, SIX COUNTRIES, 1820 VERSUS 1989

The graph shows how much higher GDP per capita is today than it was in 1820 in each of the six countries shown. The pattern is typical for free-market industrialized countries. The numbers are in dollars adjusted to have roughly the same purchasing power in all countries and at both dates listed.

SOURCE: Angus Maddison, "Explaining the Economic Performance of Nations, 1820–1989," unpublished manuscript, Spring 1992, pages 2 and 3.

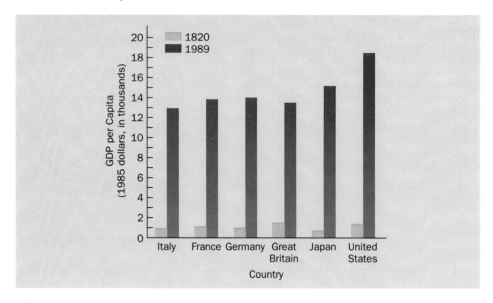

productivity has risen about 2500 percent, French and German productivity levels each went up about 1500 percent, productivity in the United States increased about 1100 percent, and even British productivity jumped by an astonishing 600 percent.

To see the implications of this dramatic rise in productivity for living standards (as measured by output per capita) we must first note what has happened to labor time spent by the typical worker. In the industrialized free-market countries, the number of hours worked per year has fallen significantly—by about 40 percent on the average. This is partly the result of a fall in work hours per day—typically from about 12 hours in 1900 down to some $7\frac{1}{2}$ hours per day by 1979—and partly the result of a decline from six working days to five. But most surprising is the almost total absence of any vacations for most of the population before the twentieth century. The two- or four-week vacation is another luxury made possible by the rise in productivity.

Increases in output per person (or, average income per head) have also been spectacular. Over the 169-year period 1820–1989, output per capita went up almost 2500 percent in Japan, about 1400 percent in Germany and the United States, more than 1200 percent in Italy and France, and close to 900 percent in Great Britain.[11] In the United States, for example, average income measured in dollars

---

[11]It is important to notice that all of these numbers have been corrected to eliminate the effects of inflation. Thus, it is true, of course, that because of the subsequent inflation, a dollar in the mid-1800s could purchase much more bread or many more shoes than it can today, so that a $12 weekly salary then is not as low, in purchasing power, as it may seem. But the statistics reported here have been corrected to eliminate this source of confusion, using the standard statistical method employed for the purpose. That is, since the statistics indicate that U.S. consumer prices have risen by about 6 times since the mid-1800s, a $12 wage then is counted as 6 × $12 = $72 in dollars of today's purchasing power (for more details on the method for correction for inflation, see pages 147–48 in the appendix to Chapter 6).

of constant purchasing power was only about one-fifteenth as large in 1820 as it is today. To imagine what it is like to live on an income so small, one must think of *Egypt, Bolivia, or the Philippines,* whose per capita income today has been calculated to be on a par with that of an average American in the 19th century! Figure 17–3 translates the productivity growth since the beginning of the twentieth century into the resulting and very remarkable rise in living standards—in national output per capita. Obviously, the rise in economic well-being of an average American, and of an average resident of the other countries in Figures 17–2 and 17–3, has been substantial. Indeed, it represents a rise to a standard of living a person in an earlier century can hardly have imagined.

After some 1600 years of zero average growth in productivity and living standards, growth in both of these areas exploded in the world's industrial countries in the nineteenth and twentieth centuries, reaching levels previously unimaginable.

SIGNIFICANCE OF THE GROWTH OF PRODUCTIVITY

THE OVER-WHELMING IMPORTANCE OF PRODUCTIVITY GROWTH IN THE LONG RUN

As we pointed out in our list of **12 Ideas for Beyond the Final Exam**, it is hardly an exaggeration to say that, in the long run, almost nothing counts for the determination of a nation's standard of living but its rate of productivity growth—for only rising productivity can raise standards of living in the long run.

Over long periods of time, small differences in rates of productivity growth compound like interest in a bank account and can make an enormous difference to a society's prosperity. Nothing contributes more to reduction of poverty, to increases in leisure, and to the country's ability to finance education, public health, environmental improvement, and the arts.

Since 1800, productivity in the United States has increased at an average annual rate slightly less than 2 percent. An apparently small change in this figure would have enormous consequences over a long period. Had productivity grown at an average rate of only 1 percent per year instead, an average American today would command about 6.6 times as large a quantity of goods and services as his forebears did in 1800. Actually, though it is hard to believe, real per capita income has risen about 30-fold in this period. And if productivity had grown over the entire interval at an annual rate of 3 percent, average living standards would be an incredible 275 times as high as they were in 1800.

Productivity growth can make an enormous difference in a nation's standing in the hierarchy of the world's economies. It has been remarked that the success of the United States in keeping its annual productivity growth about 1 percent ahead of Great Britain for about a century transformed America from a minor, developing country into a superpower and transformed Great Britain from the world's preeminent power into a second-rate economy. It is Japan's 3-percent average annual productivity growth rate since 1870 that transformed it from one of the world's poorest countries into a nation with one of the highest GDP figures in the world.

THE SECOND MAJOR DEVELOPMENT: CONVERGENCE

Not only has each of the industrial countries grown in productivity and income per capita, but these countries have also become more similar to one another both in terms of labor productivity and GDP per capita. In other words, among the industrial countries, those which were furthest behind in 1870 have been catching up with those that were ahead. For example, in 1870 the productivity level of the leading country (Australia) was about seven times as high as that of the least productive country (Japan). By 1989 that ratio had declined to about 1.5. That is, about three-quarters of the difference between the most productive and the least productive country were eliminated during the 119-year period.

Such a dramatic narrowing of productivity gaps among the industrial countries means that everyone else must be catching up with the leader, and that leader, ever since World War I, has been the United States. This is illustrated in Figure 17–4, which shows what happened to the *relative* labor productivity levels of four leading industrialized countries over the period 1950–1990. Specifically, it shows GDP per worker in each of those countries *as a percentage of the U.S. level.* (The U.S. figure is, therefore, always 100 percent). It indicates that, in 1950, per capita GDP for the average of the countries shown was about 35 percent of that of the United States. By 1990 the average was about 80 percent of the U.S. level. Figure 17–4 also shows that productivity in *each* of these countries has been moving closer to the United States in this 40-year period.[12]

These and other data indicate that levels of labor productivity are converging among the leading industrialized countries.[13]

Figure 17–4 also indicates that, as productivity levels in the other countries have come closer to those in the United States, the speed at which they have approached it has slowed. Note also that, despite the impression given in the press, Japan is still the lowest in this group, and that Germany is falling behind France (and several other countries).

WHY INTERNATIONAL EQUALIZATION?

Why are all these countries growing more alike in productivity and average standards of living? No one has the entire answer, but a good part of the story is probably the speedup of the international spread of new technology. Better communications permit innovative techniques to move from one country to another far more quickly than in the past. Better and more widespread education permits countries to learn technical details from one another and to train their labor forces rapidly to make use of them. At the beginning of the eighteenth century when the Newcomen steam engine (the predecessor of Watt's steam

---

[12]To interpret the graph, remember that if the curve representing some country were to reach precisely the curve for the United States it would mean that this country's productivity per worker is equal to that of the United States.

[13]The reader should be warned that this conclusion has been challenged, at least for the years before World War II, on the grounds that the sample of countries studied happens to include those that have been converging toward the United States because they are the success stories for which statistics are available. Thus, the critics point out, Argentina is omitted from the sample of countries, even though in 1870 many observers would have predicted a brilliant economic future for that country.

| Figure | 17-4 | **LABOR PRODUCTIVITY LEVELS IN FIVE COUNTRIES AS A PERCENT OF U.S. LEVEL, 1950–1990** |

The graph shows that real GDP per worker in each of the countries is approaching the (growing) U.S. level. However, as productivity in those countries gets closer to our own, the catch-up process seems to have slowed. You may also be surprised to see that Japan still is at the bottom of the group and that France is ahead of Germany.

SOURCE: U.S. Department of Labor, Bureau of Labor Statistics, unpublished data.

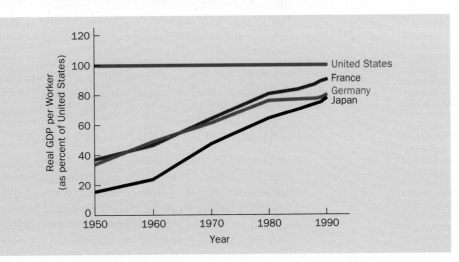

engine) was invented in England, it took half a century for the engine to spread to Western European countries and to the American colonies. In contrast, the innovations in transistor and semiconductor technology since World War II have, on average, taken about two and one-half years to spread among countries.

All industrial countries benefit from the process of shared information; each learns from the innovations that occur in all the others. The British, the French, and the Germans benefit from American computer technology while the United States and others benefit from Japanese advances in robotics.

But there is one crucial asymmetry. Countries that are behind have a great deal to learn from countries that are ahead, but the leaders have less to learn from those that have lagged behind. This is generally believed to be a prime explanation of the convergence in living standards. Meanwhile, the growing speed and efficiency of communications speeds up the entire process.

Lagging countries have more to learn from leaders than leaders can learn from laggards. This fact, and the growing speed with which innovations are spread, help explain why the world's industrial economies are growing more equal.

ARE ALL COUNTRIES PARTICIPATING IN EQUALIZATION?

So far we have seen that a considerable number of countries are growing increasingly similar to one another in terms of productivity and living standards. But we have yet to consider the world's poorest nations—usually referred to as "less developed countries," or LDCs. (See Chapter 21.) Have most of those countries also benefited from the spread of innovation and closed the gap between themselves and the world's economic leaders?

Unfortunately, among the LDCs, where equalization is most desperately needed, the picture is very mixed. Some economies, such as those of Taiwan and

South Korea, have achieved spectacular successes. But, as a group, the LDCs have grown less equal among themselves and have fallen further behind the United States. On average, GDP per capita grew about 3 percent per year in the industrialized countries in the period after World War II. But in the LDCs it rose only about $1\frac{1}{2}$ percent a year on average. A number of LDCs have fallen further behind the United States.

While the leading economies in the world are becoming more equal in terms of productivity and living standards, a number of the poorest countries are falling further behind and are holding back the average performance of the LDCs.

WHY SOME LDCS ARE FALLING BEHIND

In Chapter 21 we will discuss in detail the handicaps that have been blamed by specialist observers for the poor performance of many LDCs. Here we will only note briefly why the forces of equalization just described for the more developed countries do not work for a number of the LDCs.

Two influences are pertinent. First, the poor educational levels in the LDCs and the resulting scarcity of qualified engineers and technicians is a serious impediment to imitation and effective use of the complex technological advances of the industrialized countries. So they do not benefit by learning from others to nearly the extent that the wealthier countries do.

Second, the absence of products to which sophisticated production techniques can readily be applied makes it hard to participate in the growth gains from learning and imitation. A country that depends on products such as bananas, peanuts, and sugar for most of its income has little use for new robot designs or automated manufacturing processes, though it can and often does benefit from agricultural innovations, some of substantial importance. As a result, while the LDCs can and do learn to some degree from the technology of the industrialized economies, they suffer from serious handicaps in this process, handicaps from which the industrial countries are largely immune.

THE U.S. PRODUCTIVITY SLOWDOWN: IS AMERICAN ECONOMIC LEADERSHIP DOOMED?

Since the mid-1960s there has been a sharp decline in the rate of growth of productivity in the United States. From 1950 to 1973, productivity per worker grew at an average rate that has been estimated to be between 2 and $2\frac{1}{2}$ percent per year, which is probably somewhat faster than it had ever grown before over so long a period. Then, between 1973 and 1990 productivity growth fell sharply from its earlier postwar rate, back to between half a percent and one percent per year.

Some observers have concluded that the U.S. economy, and particularly its manufacturing sector, is in terrible trouble, and that the United States seems about to lose its leadership in both productivity and living standards. But these fears are, at the very least, exaggerated, for several reasons.

First, it should be noted carefully that throughout most of this period the *level* of U.S. productivity continued to improve. In almost every year it was higher than the last. It was the *rate of improvement* that slowed from a gallop to a walk, and finally to a crawl. Second, the United States is still by far the world's largest economy in terms of total production, wealth, and factors such as spending on research and development.

423

THE U.S. PRODUCTIVITY SLOWDOWN: IS AMERICAN ECONOMIC LEADERSHIP DOOMED?

F i g u r e **17–5**	**FALL IN PRODUCTIVITY GROWTH RATES, 1950–1973 VERSUS 1973–1990**

This graph confirms that productivity growth *did* decline in the period widely publicized as the "U.S. productivity slowdown." However, at the same time, it also fell throughout the industrial world and not just in the United States. The growth rates continued to be low throughout the 1980s.

SOURCE: U.S. Department of Labor, Bureau of Labor Statistics, unpublished data.

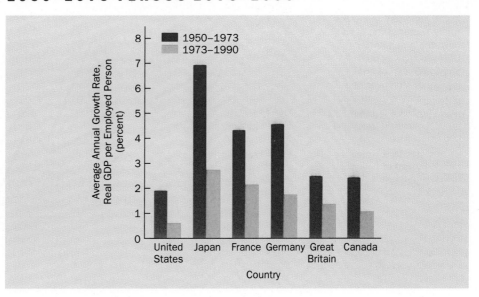

Third, some analysts question whether the U.S. productivity slowdown is as serious as it appears. They argue, first of all, that the United States is not alone in suffering a slowdown in productivity growth. The problem has affected virtually every industrial country. Figure 17–5 compares productivity growth rates for six industrial countries during 1950–1973 with those from 1973–1990—the years when the slowdown occurred. We find that the U.S. growth rate fell 65 percent, while Japan's declined 61 percent, Great Britain's rate fell 46 percent, France's declined 51 percent, Germany's fell 62 percent, and Canada's went down 58 percent. Compared with the others, the U.S. decline does not seem so far out of line.

In addition, very long-run data on U.S. productivity growth exhibit no downward long-term trend. The growth rate of productivity by decade in the United States was virtually constant at about 2 percent per year between about 1870 and 1930. Then, during the Great Depression of the 1930s, productivity growth plunged. With the advent of World War II and the postwar rebuilding of the devastated countries, U.S. productivity growth leaped upward. After this catch-up period, during which a great backlog of ideas for inventions and investment funds that accumulated during the war was gradually depleted, the growth rate fell from its postwar high. On this view of the matter, then, the deceleration of the 1970s, rather than being entirely a drop below its historical norms, was partly a return toward normalcy from a period of extraordinary growth which (in retrospect!) seems to have been predictably temporary.

Much more disturbing, however, is the fact that recently productivity growth in the United States has fallen well below its historical average and has so far shown only limited improvement: growth in American labor productivity fell from its average in the postwar period 1950–1973 to a figure estimated at between 0.6 and 1.1 percent per year in the period 1973–1990. No one has any idea how long this problem, which has beset much of the industrial world, is likely to last.

F i g u r e **17-6**   **ANNUAL GROWTH RATES, MANUFACTURING PRODUCTIVITY, THREE COUNTRIES, 1950–1990**

In the important manufacturing sector of the economy, the graph shows that U.S. productivity has shown no sign of a declining trend. Moreover, the growth rates in other leading economies are now coming closer to the American level.

SOURCE: U.S. Department of Labor, Bureau of Labor Statistics, unpublished data.

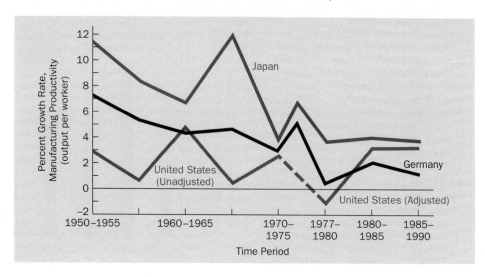

There is one other interesting aspect of the recent decline in the growth rate of *overall* U.S. productivity. Some sectors—such as construction, mining, and services—have had poor recent records. However, the main focus of public concern has been *manufacturing*; Americans seem to believe that this sector of our economy is most vulnerable to foreign competition because of its poor productivity performance. Yet the record shows something quite different: *U.S. manufacturing has experienced no trend toward a declining growth rate.* This is shown in Figure 17–6 which reports the growth rate of labor productivity in American manufacturing over the entire period since World War II. No downward trend is apparent. Moreover, we see that the growth rates of manufacturing productivity in Japan and Germany are no longer far out of line with those of the United States. Indeed, Germany has lately been the laggard of the group.

THE U.S. PRODUCTIVITY GROWTH LAG BEHIND OTHER INDUSTRIAL COUNTRIES

What about the second disturbing fact about U.S. productivity growth—that it has recently been so much lower than that of other industrial countries? As a matter of fact that, too, is an old story. The growth rate of U.S. productivity has been just middling for the better part of a century. Between 1899 and 1913, the U.S. growth rate was already lower than that of Sweden, France, Germany, Italy, and Japan. Our growth rate was also below theirs (except for France) in 1924–1937. U.S. labor productivity grew rapidly relative to other nations only during both world wars, when many other countries were held back by the demands of their military activities.

There is a simple and plausible explanation for the comparatively slow growth of U.S. productivity. It is the equalization of productivity in the world's industrial countries—the convergence phenomenon we have already studied in this chapter.

If the forces making for equalization did in fact dominate the growth paths of those countries, it is necessarily true that productivity in the lagging countries *had* to grow more quickly than in the countries at the head of the line. Otherwise, they could never have grown more equal. The statistical evidence is consistent with the conjecture that the relative productivity growth rates of the various industrialized countries are largely explained by their distance behind the leader.

Viewed in this way, there is little to be alarmed about in the relatively slow growth rate of U.S. productivity compared with that of other countries. Indeed, if the higher growth rates of other countries is attributable in good part to their having much to copy from the United States as a productivity leader, we should not be surprised if the rapid growth rates of those countries were to slow as they approach the high American levels. There are, as a matter of fact, signs that this is beginning to happen. One sign of this is the fact that the high Japanese savings rates that seem to have contributed so much to that nation's productivity growth have fallen sharply in the past decade, perhaps by eight percent. And Japan's and Germany's productivity growth rates have continued on a mostly downward path, while the U.S. rate has recently been mostly rising, so that the gap has narrowed dramatically (see Figure 17–7).

Viewed in long-term perspective, the recent slowdown in U.S. productivity growth and its lag behind other industrial countries seems somewhat less serious than it appears from an examination of the decline from the mid-1960s.

PRODUCTIVITY AND THE DEINDUSTRIALIZATION THESIS

Let us now turn to the popular notion that lagging productivity growth is turning the United States into a service economy, the "deindustrialization thesis." The trends are said to portend a future in which the United States suffers chronic

Figure **17–7** **GROWTH RATES OF LABOR PRODUCTIVITY, FOUR COUNTRIES, 1950–1990**

Note the narrowing of the lead, in terms of greater rapidity of productivity growth in Germany and Japan relative to that of the United States.

SOURCE: U.S. Department of Labor, Bureau of Labor Statistics, unpublished data.

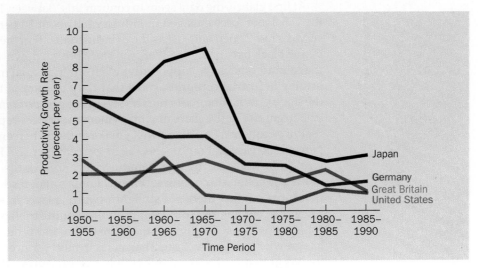

F i g u r e **17–8**   **GROWTH IN THE SHARE OF SERVICE SECTOR JOBS**

The black bars indicate the percentage growth of the share of employment in the service sector of nine industrial countries. It demonstrates that the United States is hardly the only country in which the proportion of labor employed in the services has been rising. Indeed many other countries have done so far more rapidly.

SOURCE: Organization for Economic Cooperation and Development, *Labour Force Statistics, 1970–1990,* and *Quarterly Labour Force Statistics,* No. 3, 1992.

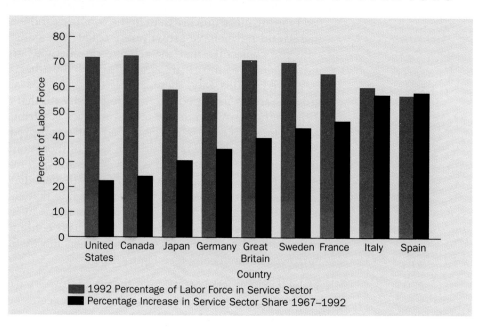

1992 Percentage of Labor Force in Service Sector
Percentage Increase in Service Sector Share 1967–1992

and apparently incurable problems in its trade with other countries because its manufactured products are not competitive with those of foreign countries. As a result, it is argued, the United States will either be forced to bear heavy unemployment or to see its labor force driven into service-sector jobs at low pay, thus transforming the nation into a "service economy" in which people earn their living by flipping hamburgers and washing dishes. The "deindustrialization" story, oversimplified, asserts that slow productivity growth in manufacturing allows other countries to steal our industrial markets away.

At first glance, the data seem to confirm this. Between 1967 and 1992 the share of the U.S. labor force engaged in industry fell about 30 percent, whereas that in the services *rose* 22 percent, just as the deindustrialization thesis asserts. But, as shown by the black bars in Figure 17–8, the story breaks down when we seek to identify the countries that have supposedly stolen our industrial markets. The data, for nine leading industrial countries, show that *every* country in the sample has increased the share of its labor force in the services *by a greater percentage than ours.* If America's 22 percent rise in the share of employment in services represents a move toward a "service economy," what are we to make of the 35 percent rise in Germany, the 46 percent increase in France, and the 31 percent increase in Japan? Which country was "industrialized" by the "deindustrialization" of the United States? Or are all industrial nations becoming service economies and, if so, why?

It turns out that there is a straightforward answer in which productivity plays a key role; but it is very different from the deindustrialization parable. The simple explanation is that throughout the industrial world productivity in manufacturing has grown considerably faster than it has in most services. For example, productivity has grown far faster in automobile manufacturing than in selling real estate. This means that, though manufacturing outputs have grown, less and less of each nation's labor force has been needed to produce them, just as had happened previously in agriculture. So a declining share of each nation's jobs has been provided in the manufacturing sector.

Moreover, after correction for inflation, the ratio of the *outputs* of the manufacturing and service sectors of the industrial economies has remained roughly unchanged over the years, while national unemployment rates have shown no long-term tendency to rise. With manufacturing taking a declining share of the labor force and unemployment not rising, the share of employment in services naturally had to grow.

A hypothetical example makes the point clear. If, over a period of time when productivity in automobile manufacturing doubled, automobile sales rose only 50 percent, there must have been a 25 percent reduction in the number of workers employed in that industry. But if at the same time, productivity in the real estate industry stayed still, while sales volume rose 50 percent, this industry would need 50 percent more workers than before. Thus, with both industries expanding their outputs in exactly the same proportion, some labor must shift out of the auto industry with its high productivity growth, into the real estate industry, with its stagnant productivity. This is the true sense in which *all* the industrial nations are becoming service economies. The share of their outputs constituted by manufactures has generally not fallen, but the share of employment in the service sector has risen universally.

Thus, the growing share of service workers in U.S. employment is not attributable to lack of competitiveness of U.S. manufactures. On the contrary, between 1962 and 1990, years for which data are available, the U.S. share of the total industrial employment of the world's 25 most industrialized economies actually *increased* about 17 percent. (See Figure 17–9, which shows the near parallel growth

---

Figure **17–9**   **SHARES OF WORLD INDUSTRIAL EMPLOYMENT OF FOUR INDUSTRIAL COUNTRIES, 1962–1990***

The graph shows that over the 28 years for which the data are available, Japan has steadily gained a larger share of the world's industrial jobs. But the U.S. share has risen significantly, at the expense of France and Germany.

SOURCE: Organization for Economic Cooperation and Development, *Indicators of Industrial Activity*, various issues, and *Labour Force Statistics*, various issues.

*World manufacturing here encompasses the 25 member-countries of the OECD, which includes the bulk of the free-market industrial economies of the world.

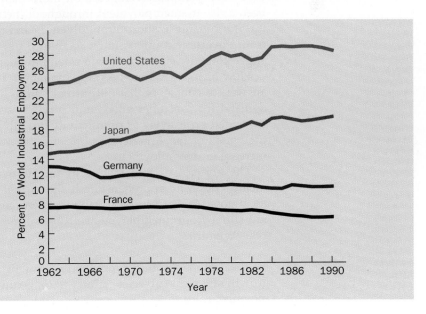

of U.S. and Japanese share of world industrial jobs.) That is hardly a picture of faltering competitiveness in our manufacturing sector.

UNEMPLOYMENT AND PRODUCTIVITY GROWTH

Popular discussions of productivity growth often warn that rapid increases in labor productivity are not as beneficial as they are cracked up to be. We are told that each productivity increase reduces the demand for labor because it means that fewer work hours are needed to produce a given output. As a result, according to this view, productivity growth allegedly creates unemployment. Second, and perhaps somewhat inconsistently, it is argued that if an economy's productivity growth lags behind that of other countries, it will lose jobs to foreign workers, its industry will suffer, and its exports will fall. However, the data do not support either of these conclusions, at least for the long run.

If the spectre of growing long-run unemployment were a reality, we would expect that the 1100-percent increase in output per labor hour in the United States, its 600-percent increase in Great Britain, and its 1500-percent rise in Germany since 1870 would have had devastating effects on the demand for labor in these countries. After all, with productivity rising twelvefold during the last century, output per capita in the United States could have been kept about constant if employment were cut to one-twelfth its initial share of U.S. population. Even with a 50 percent fall in the number of hours an average person works per year, we might expect unemployment of perhaps five-sixths of the U.S. labor force by now.

In fact, nothing of the sort has happened. Unemployment rates for Great Britain, the United States, and Germany going back to the 1870s indicate that over this long period there was no upsurge in unemployment. Before 1914, unemployment in the three countries averaged about 4 percent of the labor force, while in the 1952–1973 period it averaged a bit more than 3 percent. Even though there has been a rise in unemployment throughout the industrial world recently, much of it is attributable to short-term influences and reorientation of public policy away from government intervention to reduce unemployment. There is no evidence suggesting any *long-term* rise in unemployment.

How have we maintained employment in the face of rising productivity? The answer, of course, is that output per capita has hardly remained constant. The demand for consumer goods and services, schools, hospitals, and factories has expanded explosively as productivity growth increased the purchasing power in the hands of the American public. That has sufficed to prevent any long-term increase in unemployment.

The absence of any long-term unemployment trend also undermines the (nearly) opposite apprehension. It shows that Great Britain, which has been the most noted laggard in productivity growth among industrialized countries, did not suffer from unemployment problems markedly more serious than those of other countries.

Neither rapid absolute productivity growth nor a slow relative productivity growth rate need subject a country to long-run and persistent increases in unemployment rates.

Before offering an explanation of this behavior of employment, we turn to the widely held view that a persistent lag in a nation's productivity growth will place it at an increasing competitive disadvantage in international trade, and that it will thereby be excluded increasingly from its export markets, with devastating effects upon its industries.

Here again we use Great Britain, with its relatively poor productivity record, to examine these claims. It is true that the British *share* of exports declined from over 40 percent of world trade in 1870 to less than 10 percent a century later. But that is only because other countries' foreign sales rose even more rapidly than Britain's. The fact is that the total exports of Great Britain have risen spectacularly. In about 100 years, the volume of British exports of goods and services increased about 900 percent.

THE REAL COSTS OF LAGGING PRODUCTIVITY: LAGGING WAGES AND LIVING STANDARDS

From what has just been said, it may seem that it is not too bad to be a productivity laggard. After all, with no trend toward rising unemployment, with exports increasing, with the share of employment in manufacturing pretty well keeping up with other countries, what is so terrible about Great Britain's fate? Indeed, these observations may make one wonder how Britain was able to score these apparent successes despite its comparatively poor productivity performance.

The secret, which also shows the true price the British had to pay, is to be found in that country's lagging real wages. In the nineteenth century, British workers were the best paid in Europe. According to one estimate, which admittedly is not very reliable, in about 1860 an English worker's wages permitted the purchase of about $2\frac{1}{2}$ times the quantity of goods and services as a German worker's. Yet by the end of the 1980s, the purchasing power of a German worker's wages was almost twice as great as that of a British worker. In other words, in a little more than a century the relative position of workers in the two countries had almost been reversed.

How are lagging British wages related to its productivity lag? The answer is straightforward. If Britain cannot compete on world markets by virtue of growing efficiency (productivity), it still can sell its products by providing cheap British labor. Of course, Britain does not volunteer to adopt low real wages; rather, market forces make it happen automatically, because inefficiently produced goods cannot be sold on the international marketplace unless those goods are produced by cheaper inputs. Hence, the invisible hand forces British wages to lag behind. Labor simply cannot extract higher wages from an economy that has little to give.

A country with lagging productivity is likely to be condemned to become an exporter of cheap labor. That is the only way it can keep its industry viable, maintain its exports, and preserve domestic jobs. This is the real danger that the United States faces if its productivity performance is unsatisfactory for any substantial period of time.

More generally, despite everything that has been said in this chapter, there remain good reasons for concern about future U.S. productivity prospects. There certainly is no guarantee that productivity growth in the United States will return to its old historical pace of nearly 2 percent per year. To do so, the economy will require a continued flow of new and improving technology, new factories, new equipment, and the unslackening effort of engineers, scientists, technicians, management, and labor. None of this is easy or cheap, and none of it is guaranteed.

The costs of failure in this arena are very high. Above all, lagging productivity growth must slow or bring to an end the rising living standards and rising real wages which have so long been a prime accomplishment of the U.S. economy. If there is no rise in output per worker, then it will be impossible to keep increasing the quantity of goods and services provided to each consumer. Indeed, something of the sort has already happened. Since about the beginning of the 1970s, the purchasing power of an average American worker's hourly wage has not increased at all.

Though we do not know whether long-run U.S. productivity growth has declined, for the past few years it has fallen below its historical level. Failure to recoup threatens to hold back the growth in U.S. living standards.

CONCLUDING COMMENT

Productivity growth is indeed the stuff of which prosperity is made. The persistent record of U.S. productivity growth is the source of its high standard of living, which is extraordinary both in terms of previous history and in comparison with that of most nations in the world. In the long run, nothing is more important than productivity growth for the economic welfare of the country and for the world. In Chapter 21 we will examine some of the things that can help stimulate this vital ingredient of long-run well-being, which in two centuries transformed the focus of popular and political concerns in many industrial countries from the threat of starvation to the fear of overabundance of products.

Summary

1. Productivity growth over the past century has made a tremendous contribution to **standards of living**. Real U.S. per capita income is more than 8 times as large as it was in 1870. Never in previous history have economic conditions improved so much.

2. For the first time in history, famine is no longer a constant threat in the world's industrialized countries. That is because productivity in agriculture has increased greatly. In 1800 about 90 percent of the U.S. labor force was needed to feed the nation poorly. Today, only about 3 percent of the labor force works on farms and yet produces great abundance.

3. Because of compounding, over longer periods a small increase in rate of productivity growth can make an enormous difference in the economic well-being of a nation. This is one of the **12 Ideas for Beyond the Final Exam**.

4. There is evidence suggesting that at least a small set of the world's leading economies are converging toward similar living standards and similar productivity levels.

5. All nations learn about new technological developments from one another. The international spread of inventions means that research in one country also benefits inhabitants in much of the rest of the world.

6. Since the 1960s, there has been a substantial slowdown in productivity growth in most industrial countries.

7. Lagging productivity holds back real wages and per capita incomes in a country. However, in the long run it will generally not cause unemployment or inability to export enough to pay for the nation's imports.

8. The growth of productivity in U.S. manufacturing shows no sign of a long-term slowdown.

9. The growth rate of U.S. productivity has for many decades been slower than that of a number of other industrial countries. However, at least in part, that reflects the fact that the United States is still the world's productivity leader; so that while we have much to learn from others, they have even more to learn from us.

10. The share of the U.S. labor force employed in the services has increased substantially. But so has that of every industrial free-market economy. A major cause is probably the rapid rise of manufacturing productivity, which means that fewer workers are needed in that economic sector.

11. No one is sure whether or not the current slowdown in overall U.S. productivity is a temporary matter. If it persists, it can threaten relative U.S. living standards in the future.

Key Concepts and Terms

Labor productivity
Standard of living

Gross Domestic Product (GDP)
GDP per labor hour

GDP per capita
Deindustrialization

Questions for Review

1. Try to describe what family budgets were like 120 years ago when U.S. income per person (GDP per capita) was about one-eighth as high as it is today.

2. List some of the inventions that have increased agricultural output in the past century.

3. List some of the inventions that have increased manufacturing output in the last century.

4. List some of the new consumer products of the past century. Which of them became generally available only since World War II?

5. List some foreign inventions widely used in the United States.

6. List some American inventions widely used abroad.

7. If growing productivity has vastly reduced the amount of labor needed to produce a given output, why has it not caused massively growing unemployment?

8. If output per capita in a country doubles every 25 years, how much will it grow in a century?

9. Which do you think are more similar?
   a. Production methods in a U.S. and a German factory today.
   b. Production methods in a U.S. factory today and the methods used in that same U.S. factory 25 years ago.

10. Since the political upheavals in the communist bloc countries in Eastern Europe in 1989, it has been clear that one of their most urgent needs is productivity growth. What are they doing about it?

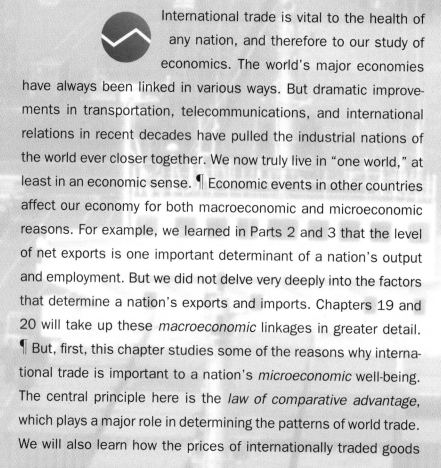

Chapter 18

INTERNATIONAL TRADE AND COMPARATIVE ADVANTAGE

No nation was ever ruined by trade.

BENJAMIN FRANKLIN

International trade is vital to the health of any nation, and therefore to our study of economics. The world's major economies have always been linked in various ways. But dramatic improvements in transportation, telecommunications, and international relations in recent decades have pulled the industrial nations of the world ever closer together. We now truly live in "one world," at least in an economic sense. ¶ Economic events in other countries affect our economy for both macroeconomic and microeconomic reasons. For example, we learned in Parts 2 and 3 that the level of net exports is one important determinant of a nation's output and employment. But we did not delve very deeply into the factors that determine a nation's exports and imports. Chapters 19 and 20 will take up these *macroeconomic* linkages in greater detail. ¶ But, first, this chapter studies some of the reasons why international trade is important to a nation's *microeconomic* well-being. The central principle here is the *law of comparative advantage*, which plays a major role in determining the patterns of world trade. We will also learn how the prices of internationally traded goods are determined by supply and demand in a free world market. Finally, we will examine the effects of government interferences with foreign trade through quotas, tariffs, and other devices designed to protect domestic industries from foreign competition.

ISSUE: THE COMPETITION OF "CHEAP FOREIGN LABOR"

Why do Americans (like the citizens of other nations) often want their government to limit or prevent import competition? One major reason is the common belief that imports take bread out of the mouths of American workers and depress standards of living in this country. According to this view, "cheap foreign labor" steals jobs from Americans and puts pressure on U.S. businesses to lower wages. Moreover, imports allegedly encourage foreign sweatshop operators, who can compete only on the basis of low wages.

Unfortunately, the facts are not consistent with this story. For one thing, wages in industrial countries that export to the United States rose spectacularly during the 1970s and 1980s. Table 18–1 shows that wages in seven leading industrial countries rose from an average of only 46 percent of American wages in 1970 to 122 percent by 1992. By 1992, labor costs in Sweden, the Netherlands, West Germany, and Italy far exceeded our own, and costs in Japan were about equal. Yet American imports of Toyotas from Japan, Volkswagens from Germany, and Volvos from Sweden grew as wages in those countries rose relative to American wages.

By comparison, European and Japanese wages were far below those in the United States in the 1950s, and yet American industry had no trouble marketing our products abroad. In fact, the main problem then was to bring our imports up to the level at which they roughly balanced our bountiful exports. Ironically, our position in the international marketplace deteriorated as wage levels in Europe and Japan began to rise closer to our own.

Clearly, then, cheap foreign labor need not serve as a crucial obstacle to U.S. sales abroad—as a "common sense" view of the matter suggests. In this chapter we will see what is wrong with that view.

WHY TRADE?

The earth's resources are not equally distributed across the planet. While the United States can satisfy its own requirements for such goods as coal and wheat,

T a b l e 18-1	LABOR COSTS IN INDUSTRIALIZED COUNTRIES	
	1970	**1992**
	(percentage of U.S. labor costs)	
France	41	104
United Kingdom	35	91
Italy	42	120
Japan	24	100
Netherlands	51	128
Sweden	70	150
(West) Germany	56	160

Data are compensation estimates per hour and relate to production workers in the manufacturing sector.

SOURCE: U.S. Bureau of Labor Statistics.

it is almost *entirely* dependent on the rest of the world for other products, such as rubber and coffee. Similarly, Saudi Arabia has little land that is suitable for farming, but sits atop a huge pool of oil. Because of the seemingly whimsical distribution of vital resources, every nation must trade with others to acquire what it lacks.

Even if countries had all the resources they needed, other differences in natural endowments—such as climate, terrain, and so on—would lead them to engage in trade. Americans *could*, with great difficulty, grow their own banana trees and coffee shrubs in hothouses. But these crops are much more efficiently grown in Honduras and Brazil, where the climate is appropriate. On the other hand, corn grows well in the United States while mountainous Switzerland is not a good place to grow either bananas or corn.

The skills of a nation's labor force also play a role. If New Zealand has a large group of efficient farmers and few workers with industrial experience while the opposite is true in Japan, it makes sense for New Zealand to specialize in agriculture and let Japan concentrate on manufacturing.

Finally, a small country that tried to produce every product would end up with many industries too small to utilize mass-production techniques, specialized training facilities, and other methods that confer cost advantages on large-scale operations. For example, some countries operate their own international airlines or steel mills for reasons that can only be political, not economic. Inevitably, small nations that insist on competing in industries that are economical only when their scale of operation is large find that these enterprises can survive only with the aid of large government subsidies.

SPECIALIZATION means that a country devotes its energies and resources to only a small proportion of the world's productive activities.

To summarize, the main reason why nations trade with one another is to exploit the many advantages of **specialization**.

International trade is essential for the prosperity of the trading nations because:

1. every country lacks some vital resources that it can get only by trading with others;

2. each country's climate, labor force, and other endowments make it a relatively efficient producer of some goods and an inefficient producer of other goods; and

3. specialization permits larger outputs and can therefore offer economies of large-scale production.

MUTUAL GAINS FROM TRADE

Many people believe that a nation can gain from trade only at the expense of another. Centuries ago, the early writers on international trade pointed out that nothing is produced by the act of trading; the total collection of goods in the hands of the two parties at the end of an exchange is the same as it was before. Therefore, they incorrectly argued, if one country gains from a swap, the other country must necessarily lose.

One of the consequences of this mistaken view was and is a policy prescription calling for each country to do its best to act to the disadvantage of its trading partners—in Adam Smith's terms, to "beggar its neighbors." The idea that one nation's gain must be another's loss means that a country can promote its own welfare only by harming others.

Yet, as Adam Smith and others after him emphasized, in any *voluntary exchange*, both parties *must* expect to gain something from the transaction unless there is misunderstanding or misrepresentation of the facts. Otherwise why would they agree to trade?

But how can mere exchange, with no increase in production, leave *both* parties better off? The answer is that while trade does not increase the physical quantities of the goods available, it does allow each party to acquire items better suited to their needs and tastes. Suppose Scott has four cookies and nothing to drink, while William has two glasses of milk and nothing to eat. A trade of two of Scott's cookies for one of William's glasses of milk does not increase the total supply of either milk or cookies, but it almost certainly improves the welfare of both boys.

By exactly the same logic, both the United States and Mexico must be better off if Mexico voluntarily ships tomatoes to the United States in return for chemicals.

MUTUAL GAINS FROM VOLUNTARY EXCHANGE

Both parties must expect to gain from any *voluntary exchange*. Trade brings about mutual gains by redistributing products in such a way that both parties end up holding a combination of goods that they prefer to the one they held before. This principle, which is one of our **12 Ideas for Beyond the Final Exam**, applies to nations just as it does to individuals.

INTERNATIONAL VERSUS INTRANATIONAL TRADE

The 50 states of the United States may be the most eloquent testimony to the gains from specialization and free trade. Florida specializes in growing oranges, Iowa in growing corn, Pennsylvania makes steel, and Michigan builds cars. All these states trade freely with one another and enjoy great material prosperity. Try to imagine how much lower your standard of living would be if you could only consume items produced in your own state.

The logic of international trade is essentially no different from that underlying trade among different states; the basic reasons for trade are equally applicable *within* a country or *among* countries. Why, then, do we study international trade as a special subject? There are at least three reasons.

POLITICAL FACTORS IN INTERNATIONAL TRADE

First, domestic trade takes place under a single national government, while foreign trade always involves at least two governments. At least in theory, a nation's government is concerned with the welfare of all its citizens. But governments are usually much less deeply concerned with the welfare of citizens of other countries. For example, the Constitution of the United States prohibits overt tariffs and other impediments to trade among states but does not prohibit the United States from imposing tariffs on imports from abroad. A major issue in the economic analysis of international trade, and therefore of this chapter, is the use and misuse of impediments to free international trade.

THE MANY CURRENCIES INVOLVED IN INTERNATIONAL TRADE

Second, all trade within the borders of the United States is carried out in U.S. dollars. But trade across national borders must involve at least two currencies. Rates of exchange between different currencies can and do change. In 1985, it took about 250 Japanese yen to buy a dollar; now it takes only about 110. Variability in exchange rates brings with it a host of complications and policy problems that are discussed in Chapters 19 and 20.

IMPEDIMENTS TO MOBILITY OF LABOR AND CAPITAL

Third, it is much easier for labor and capital to move about within a country than to move from one country to another. If there are jobs in Michigan but none in West Virginia, workers can move freely to follow the job opportunities. Of course, there are personal costs, including the financial cost of moving and the psychological cost of leaving friends and familiar surroundings. But such relocations are not inhibited by immigration quotas, by laws restricting the employment of foreigners, nor by the need to learn a new language.

There are also greater impediments to the transfer of capital across national boundaries than to its movement within a country. For example, many countries have rules limiting the share of foreign ownership in a company. Foreign investment is also subject to special political risks, such as the danger of outright expropriation after a change in government. But even if nothing so extreme occurs, capital invested abroad faces significant risks from variations in exchange rates. An investment valued at 250 million yen will be worth $1 million to American investors if the dollar is worth 250 yen, but $2 million if the dollar is worth just 125 yen.

While labor, capital, and other factors of production do move from country to country when offered an opportunity to increase their earnings abroad, they are less likely to do so than to move from one region of a country to another to gain similar increases.

| THE LAW OF COMPARATIVE ADVANTAGE

The gains from international specialization and trade are clear when one country is better at producing one item while its trading partner is better at producing another. For example, no one finds it surprising that Brazil sells coffee to the United States while America exports aircraft to Brazil. We know that coffee can be produced using less labor and other inputs in Brazil than in the United States. And America can produce passenger aircraft at a lower resource cost than can Brazil.

We say that in such a situation Brazil has an **absolute advantage** in coffee production, and the United States has an absolute advantage in aircraft production. And, in such cases, it is obvious that both countries can gain by producing the item in which they have an absolute advantage, and then trading with one another.

What is much less obvious is the fact that two countries can generally gain from trade *even if one of them is more efficient than the other in producing everything.* A simple parable will help explain why.

Some lawyers are better typists than their secretaries. Should such a lawyer fire her secretary and do her own typing? Not likely. Even though the lawyer

One country is said to have an **ABSOLUTE ADVANTAGE** over another in the production of a particular good if it can produce that good using smaller quantities of resources than can the other country.

may be better than the secretary at both typing and arguing cases, good judgment tells her to concentrate her energies on the practice of law and leave the typing to a lower-paid secretary. Why? Because the *opportunity cost* of an hour devoted to typing is one hour less spent on her legal practice, which is a far more lucrative activity.

This is an example of the principle of **comparative advantage** at work. The lawyer specializes in arguing cases despite her absolute advantage in typing because she has a still greater absolute advantage as an attorney. She suffers some direct loss by not doing her own typing. But that loss is more than compensated for by the earnings she makes selling her legal services to clients.

Precisely the same principle applies to nations, and it underlies the economic analysis of patterns of international trade. The principle, called the *law of comparative advantage*, was discovered by David Ricardo, one of the giants in the history of economic analysis (see the Biographical Note box on page 438); and it is one of our **12 Ideas for Beyond the Final Exam.**

One country is said to have a **COMPARATIVE ADVANTAGE** over another in the production of a particular good relative to other goods if it produces that good least inefficiently as compared with the other country.

THE LAW OF COMPARATIVE ADVANTAGE

Even if one country is at an absolute disadvantage relative to another country in the production of *every* good, it is said to have a *comparative advantage* in making the good at which it is *least inefficient* (compared with the other country). ¶ Ricardo discovered that two countries can still gain by trading even if one country is more efficient than another in the production of *every* commodity—that is, has an absolute advantage in every commodity. ¶ In determining the most efficient patterns of production, it is *comparative* advantage, not *absolute* advantage, that matters. Thus a country can gain by importing a good even if that good can be produced at home more efficiently than it can be produced abroad. Such imports make sense because they enable the country to specialize in producing goods at which it is even more efficient.

THE ARITHMETIC OF COMPARATIVE ADVANTAGE

Let's see precisely how this works using a hypothetical example that gives a somewhat exaggerated impression of the trading positions of the United States and Japan a few years ago. We imagine that labor is the only input used to produce microcomputers and television sets in the two countries. Suppose further that the U.S. has an absolute advantage in both goods, as indicated in Table 18–2. In this example, a year's worth of labor can produce either 50 computers or 50 TV sets in the U.S., but only 10 computers or 40 televisions in Japan. So

T a b l e **18–2**	**ALTERNATIVE OUTPUTS FROM ONE YEAR OF LABOR INPUT**	
	IN THE UNITED STATES	**IN JAPAN**
Computers	50	10
Televisions	50	40

B i o g r a p h i c a l

N o t e

**DAVID RICARDO
(1772–1823)**

David Ricardo was born four years before publication of Adam Smith's *Wealth of Nations*. Descended from a wealthy Jewish family of Portuguese origins, he had about twenty brothers and sisters. Ricardo's formal education ended at the age of 13, and so he was largely self-educated. He began his career by working in his father's stock brokerage firm. At age 21, Ricardo married a Quaker woman and decided to become a Unitarian, a sect then considered "little better than atheist." By Jewish custom, Ricardo's father broke with him, though apparently they remained friendly.

Ricardo then decided to go into the brokerage business on his own and was enormously successful. During the Napoleonic Wars he regularly scored business coups over leading British and foreign financiers, including the Rothschilds. After gaining a huge profit on government securities that he had bought just before the Battle of Waterloo, Ricardo decided to retire from business when he was just over 40 years old.

He purchased a country estate, Gatcomb (now owned by the royal family), where a brilliant group of intellectuals met regularly. Particularly remarkable for the period was the number of women included in the circle, among them Maria Edgeworth, the novelist (who wrote extravagant praise of Ricardo's mind), and Jane Marcet, an author of textbooks, one of which was probably the first textbook in economics. Ricardo's close friends included the economists T. R. Malthus and James Mill, father of John Stuart Mill, the noted philosopher-economist. Malthus remained a close friend of Ricardo even though they disagreed on many subjects and continued their arguments in personal correspondence and in their published works.

James Mill persuaded Ricardo to go into Parliament. As was then customary, Ricardo purchased his seat by buying a piece of land that entitled its owner to a seat in Parliament. There he proved to be a noteworthy advocate of many causes that were against his personal interests.

James Mill also helped persuade Ricardo to write his masterpiece, *The Principles of Political Economy and Taxation*, which may have been the first book of pure economic theory. It was noteworthy that Ricardo, the most practical of practical men, had little patience with empirical economics and preferred instead to rest his analysis explicitly and exclusively on theory. His book made considerable contributions to the analysis of pricing, wage determination, and the effects of various types of taxes, among many other subjects. It also gave us the law of comparative advantage.

Ricardo died in 1823 at the age of 51. He seems to have been a wholly admirable person—honest, charming, witty, conscientious, brilliant—altogether too good to be true.

America is the more efficient producer of both goods. Nonetheless, as our lawyer-secretary example suggests, it pays for the U.S. to specialize and trade with Japan.

We demonstrate this in two steps. First, we note that the U.S. has a comparative advantage in computers while Japan has a comparative advantage in TVs. Then we show that both countries can gain if the United States specializes in producing computers, Japan specializes in producing TVs, and the two countries trade.

The numbers in Table 18–2 show that the United States can produce 50 televisions with a year's labor while Japan can produce only 40; thus the U.S. is 25 percent more efficient than Japan in producing TV sets. However, the U.S. is five times as efficient as Japan in producing computers: it can produce 50 per year of labor rather than 10. Thus America's competitive edge is far greater in computers

Table **18–3**	**EXAMPLE OF THE GAINS FROM TRADE**		
	THE UNITED STATES	**JAPAN**	**TOTAL**
Computers (thousands)	+ 25	– 10	+ 15
Televisions (thousands)	– 25	+ 40	+ 15

than in televisions—which is precisely what we mean by saying that the U.S. has a *comparative advantage* in computers.

Looked at from the Japanese perspective, these same numbers indicate that Japan is only slightly less efficient than America in TV production but drastically less efficient in computer production. So Japan's comparative advantage is in the television industry. According to Ricardo's law of comparative advantage, then, the two countries can benefit if Japan makes TVs, America makes computers, and the two countries trade. Let us check that this is true.

Suppose Japan transfers 1000 years of labor out of the computer industry and into TV manufacturing. According to the figures in Table 18–2, its computer output falls by 10,000 units while its TV output rises by 40,000 units. (See Table 18–3.) Suppose, at the same time, the U.S. transfers 500 years of labor out of television manufacturing (thereby losing 25,000 TVs) and into computer making (thereby gaining 25,000 computers). Table 18–3 shows us that these transfers of resources in the two countries increase the world's production of both outputs! Together, the two countries now have 15,000 additional TVs and 15,000 additional computers—surely a nice outcome.

Was there some sleight of hand here? All that has taken place is an exchange. Yet, somehow the U.S. and Japan gain both computers and TVs. How can such gains in physical output be possible? The explanation is that the process we have just described involves more than just a swap of a fixed bundle of commodities. It is also a *change in the production arrangements*, with some of Japan's inefficient computer production taken over by more efficient American makers, and with some of America's TV production taken over by Japanese television companies who are *less* inefficient at making TVs than Japanese computer manufacturers are at making computers.

When every country does what it can do best, all countries can benefit because more of every commodity can be produced without increasing the amounts of labor used.

If this result still seems a bit mysterious, the concept of opportunity cost will help remove the remaining mystery. If the two countries do not trade, Table 18–2 shows that the United States can acquire a computer on its own by giving up a TV. Thus the opportunity cost of a computer in the U.S. is one television set. But in Japan the opportunity cost of a computer is four TVs (see, again, Table 18–2). Thus, in terms of real resources foregone, it is cheaper—for *either* country— to acquire computers in the United States. By a similar line of reasoning, the opportunity cost of TVs is higher in the U.S. than in Japan, so it makes sense for both countries to acquire their televisions in Japan.[1]

---

[1]As an exercise, provide this line of reasoning.

Figure **18-1**

ABSOLUTE AND COMPARATIVE ADVANTAGE SHOWN BY TWO COUNTRIES' PRODUCTION POSSIBILITIES FRONTIERS

The U.S.'s absolute advantage is shown by its ability to produce more of every commodity using the same quantity of labor as does Japan. Therefore, America's per-capita production possibilities frontier, *US*, is higher than Japan's, *JN*. But the U.S. has a comparative advantage in computer production, in which it is five times as productive as Japan. (It can produce 50 million computers, point *S*, compared with Japan's 10 million, point *N*.) On the other hand, the U.S. is only 25 percent more productive in TV production (point *U*) than Japan (point *J*). Thus, Japan is less inefficient in producing televisions, where it consequently has a comparative advantage.

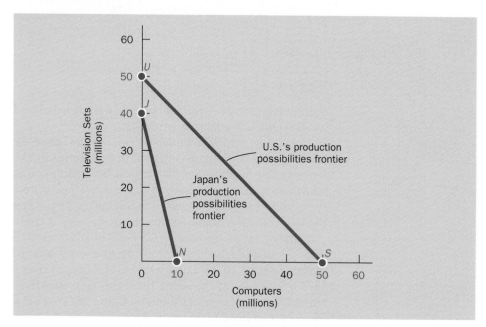

THE GRAPHICS OF COMPARATIVE ADVANTAGE

The gains from trade can also be displayed graphically, and doing so helps us understand how these gains arise.

The lines *US* and *JN* in Figure 18–1 are closely related to the production possibilities frontiers of the two countries, but differ in that they pretend that each country has the same amount of labor available—in this case, a million person-years.[2] For example, Table 18–2 tells us that, for each million person-years of labor, the United States can produce 50 million TVs and no computers (point *U*), 50 million computers and no TVs (point *S*), or any combination between (the line *US*). Similar reasoning can be used to derive line *JN* for Japan.

America's actual production possibilities frontier would be even higher, relative to Japan's, than shown in Figure 18–1 because the U.S. population is larger. But Figure 18–1 is more useful to us because it highlights the differences in efficiency that determine both absolute and comparative advantage. Let us see how.

The fact than line *US* lies *above* line JN means that, with the same amount of labor, the U.S. can obtain more televisions and more computers than Japan. This reflects our assumption that America is the more efficient producer of *both* commodities; that is, that America has an *absolute* advantage in both TVs and computers.

[2]To review the concept of the production possibilities frontier, see Chapter 3.

America's comparative advantage in computer production and Japan's comparative advantage in TV production are shown in a different way—by the relative *slopes* of the two lines. America's frontier is not only higher than Japan's, it is also less steep. What does that mean economically? One way of looking at the difference is to remember that while America can produce five times as many computers per capita as Japan (compare points S and N), it can produce only 25 percent more TVs (compare points U and J). The U.S. is, relatively speaking, much better at computer production than at TV production. That is what we mean when we say it has a *comparative* advantage in computers.

We may express this difference more directly in terms of the slopes of the two lines. The slope of Japan's production possibilities frontier is $OJ/ON = 40/10 = 4$. This means that if Japan reduces its computer output by one unit, it will obtain four television sets. Thus, the *opportunity cost* of a computer in Japan is four TVs, as we observed earlier.

In the case of the U.S., the slope of the production possibilities frontier is $OU/OS = 50/50 = 1$. That is, if the U.S. reduces its computer output by one unit, it gets one additional television. So in the U.S., the *opportunity cost* of a computer is one TV.

A country's absolute advantage in production over another country is shown by its having a higher per-capita production possibilities frontier. The difference in the comparative advantages of the two countries is shown by the difference in the slopes of their frontiers.

Because opportunity costs differ in the two countries, gains from trade are possible. How these gains are divided between the two countries depends on the prices for televisions and computers that emerge from world trade, which is the subject of the next section. But we already know enough to see that world trade must leave a computer costing more than one TV and less than four. Why? Because, if a computer brought less than one TV (its opportunity cost in the U.S.) on the world market, America would produce its own TVs rather than buying them from Japan. Similarly, if a computer cost more than four TVs (its opportunity cost in Japan), Japan would prefer to produce its own computers rather than buy them from the U.S.

We conclude, therefore, that if both countries are to trade, the rate of exchange between TVs and computers must be somewhere between 4 to 1 and 1 to 1. To illustrate the gains from trade in a concrete example, suppose the world price ratio settles at 2 to 1; that is, one computer costs the same as two televisions. How much, precisely, do the U.S. and Japan gain from world trade?

Figure 18–2 is designed to help us see the answer. Production possibilities frontiers *US* in part (b) and *JN* in part (a) are the same as in Figure 18–1. But the U.S. can do better than line *US*. Specifically, with a world price ratio of 2 to 1, the U.S. can buy a TV by giving up only one-half of a computer, rather than one (which is the opportunity cost of TVs in the U.S.). Hence, if the U.S. produces only computers (point *S* in Figure 18–2[b]) and buys its TVs from Japan, America's *consumption possibilities* will be as indicated by the brown line that begins at point *S* and has a slope of 2—indicating that each computer it sells brings the U.S. two television sets. Since trade allows the U.S. to choose a point on *AS* rather than on *US*, trade opens up consumption possibilities that were simply not available before.

The story is similar for Japan. If the Japanese produce only televisions (point *J* in Figure 18–2[a]), they can acquire a computer from the U.S. for every two TVs

F i g u r e **18–2**   **THE GAINS FROM TRADE**

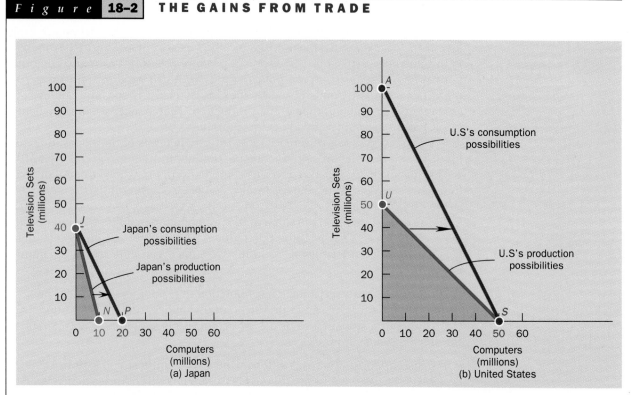

In this diagram, we suppose that trade opens up between the U.S. and Japan and that the world price of computers is twice the world price of TVs. Now the U.S.'s consumption possibilities are all the points on line *AS* (which starts at *S* and has a slope of 2), rather than just the points on its own production possibilities frontier, *US*. Similarly, Japan can choose any point on line *JP* (which begins at *J* and has a slope of 2), rather than just points on *JN*. Thus both nations gain from trade.

they give up as they move along the brown line *JP* (whose slope is 2). This is better than they can do on their own, since a sacrifice of two TVs in Japan yields only one-half of a computer. Hence world trade enlarges Japan's consumption possibilities from *JN* to *JP*.

Figure 18–2 shows graphically that gains from trade arise to the extent that world prices (2 to 1 in our example) differ from domestic opportunity costs (4 to 1 and 1 to 1 in our example). So it is a matter of some importance to understand how prices in international trade are established. This we shall do shortly.

COMPARATIVE ADVANTAGE AND COMPETITION OF "CHEAP FOREIGN LABOR"

But first let us observe that the principle of comparative advantage takes us a good part of the way toward an explanation of the fallacy in the "cheap foreign labor" argument described earlier in the chapter. Given the assumed productive efficiency of American labor and the inefficiency of Japanese labor, we would expect wages to be much higher in the U.S. than in Japan. And, indeed, they were until recent years.

In these circumstances, one might expect American workers to be apprehensive about an agreement to permit open trade between the two countries—"How can we hope to meet the unfair competition of those underpaid Japanese workers?" And Japanese laborers might also be concerned—"How can we hope to meet the competition of those Americans, who are so efficient in producing everything?"

The principle of comparative advantage shows us that both fears are unjustified. As we have just seen, when trade is opened up between Japan and the United States, *workers in both countries will be able to earn higher real wages than before* because of the increased productivity that comes about through specialization.

Figure 18–2 shows this fact directly. We have seen from our illustration that, with trade, Japan can end up with more TVs and more computers than it had before. So the living standards of its workers can rise even though they have been left vulnerable to the competition of the superefficient Americans. The U.S. also can end up with more TVs and with more computers; so the living standards of its workers can rise even though they have been exposed to the competition of cheap Japanese labor. These higher standards of living are, of course, a reflection of the higher real wages earned by workers in both countries.

The lesson to be learned here is elementary: nothing helps raise standards of living more than does a greater abundance of goods.

SUPPLY–DEMAND EQUILIBRIUM AND PRICING IN WORLD TRADE

How the gains from trade are shared depends on the prices that emerge from world trade. As usual, price determination in a free market depends on supply and demand.

When applied to international trade, the supply–demand model runs into several new complications. First, it involves at least two demand curves: that of the exporting country and that of the importing country. Second, it may also involve two supply curves, since the importing country may produce some part of its own consumption. Third, equilibrium does not take place at the intersection point of *either* pair of supply–demand curves. Why? Because if there is any trade, the exporting country's quantity supplied must be *greater* than its quantity demanded, while the quantity supplied by the importing country must be *less* than its quantity demanded.

These complications are illustrated in Figure 18–3, where we show the supply and demand curves of a country that exports wheat, in part (a), and those of one that imports wheat, in part (b). For simplicity, we assume that these countries do not deal in wheat with anyone else.

Where will the two-country wheat market reach equilibrium? The equilibrium price in a free market must satisfy two requirements:

1. The price of wheat must be the same in both countries.
2. The quantity of wheat exported must equal the quantity of wheat imported.

In Figure 18–3, this happens at a price of $2.50 per bushel. At that price, the distance AB between what the exporting country produces (point B) and what it consumes (point A) equals the distance CD between the quantity demanded of the importing country (point D) and its quantity supplied (point C). Thus, at a

Figure 18-3
SUPPLY–DEMAND EQUILIBRIUM IN THE INTERNATIONAL WHEAT TRADE

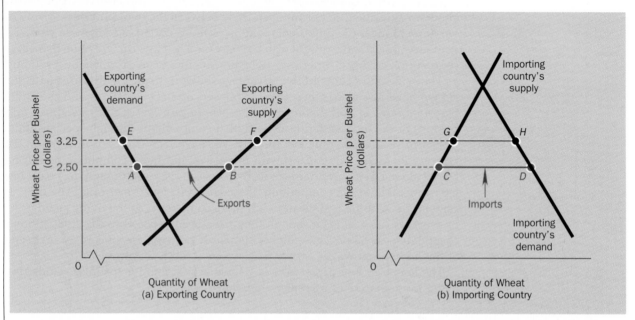

Equilibrium requires that exports, *AB* (which is the exporting nation's quantity supplied, *B*, minus the exporter's quantity demanded, *A*), exactly balance imports, *CD*, by the importing country. At $2.50 per bushel of wheat, there is equilibrium. But at a higher price, say $3.25, there is disequilibrium because export supply, *EF*, exceeds import demand, *GH*.

price of $2.50 per bushel, the amount the exporting country wants to sell is exactly equal to the amount the importing country wants to buy.

At any price above $2.50, producers in both countries will want to sell more and consumers in both countries will want to buy less. For example, if the price rises to $3.25 per bushel, the exporter's quantity supplied will rise from *B* to *F*, and the exporter's quantity demanded will fall from *A* to *E*, as shown in Figure 18–3(a). As a result, there will be more available for export—*EF* rather than *AB*. For exactly the same reason, the price increase will cause higher production and lower sales in the importing country, leading to a reduction in imports from *CD* to *GH* in part (b).

This means that the higher price, $3.25 per bushel, cannot be sustained if the international market is free and competitive. With export supply *EF* far greater than import demand *GH*, there must be downward pressure on price and a move back toward the $2.50 equilibrium price. Similar reasoning shows that prices below $2.50 also cannot be sustained.

We can now see the straightforward role of supply–demand equilibrium in international trade:

In international trade, the equilibrium price is the one that makes the exporting country want to export exactly the amount that the importing country wants to import. Equilibrium will thus occur at a price at which the horizontal distance *AB* in Figure 35–3(a) (the excess of the exporter's quantity supplied over its quantity demanded) is equal to the horizontal distance *CD* in Figure 35–3(b) (the excess of the importer's quantity demanded over its quantity supplied). At this price, the *world's* quantity demanded is equal to the *world's* quantity supplied.

TARIFFS, QUOTAS, AND OTHER INTERFERENCES WITH TRADE

Despite the mutual gains from international trade, the countries of the world often interfere with the operation of free international markets. In fact, until the rise of the free-trade movement about 200 years ago (with such economists as Adam Smith and David Ricardo as its vanguard), it was taken for granted that one of the essential tasks of government was to impede trade—presumably in the national interest.

There were many who argued then (and some who still argue today) that a nation's wealth consists of the amount of gold or other monies at its command. According to this view, the proper aim of government policy was to promote exports and discourage imports, for that would increase the amount foreigners owed the nation.

Obviously, there are limits to which this policy can be pursued. A country *must* import vital foodstuffs or critical raw materials that it cannot supply for itself; for if it does not, it must suffer a severe fall in living standards as well as a deterioration in its military strength. Moreover, it is mathematically impossible for *every* country to sell more than it buys—one country's exports *must* be some other country's imports. If everyone competes in this game and cuts imports to the bone, then obviously exports must go the same way. The result will be that everyone is deprived of the mutual gains that trade can provide.

After the 1930s, the United States moved away from policies designed to reduce competition from foreign imports and gradually assumed a leading role in attempts to promote free trade. Over the course of several decades, tariffs and other trade barriers were reduced. However, a combination of high unemployment rates and a deterioration in America's competitive position since the 1980s have led to continuous political pressure to move back in the other direction. The decade of the 1980s, for example, witnessed new restrictions on U.S. trade in automobiles, lumber, semiconductors, and a variety of other products.

Three main devices are used by modern governments seeking to control trade: tariffs, quotas, and export subsidies.

A **tariff** is simply a tax on imports. An importer of wheat, for example, may be charged $1 for each bushel he or she brings into the country. The United States is generally a low-tariff country, although there are a few notable exceptions. For example, a major controversy arose during 1993 over whether to raise the tariff on imported minivans from 2.5 percent to 25 percent. However, many other countries rely on heavy tariffs to protect their industries. Tariff rates of 100 percent or more are not unheard of.

A **quota** is a legal limit on the amount of a good that may be imported. For example, the government might allow no more than 25 million bushels of wheat to be imported in a year. In some cases, governments ban the importation of certain goods outright—a quota of zero. (See the accompanying boxed insert for

A **TARIFF** is a tax on imports.

A **QUOTA** specifies the maximum amount of a good that is permitted into the country from abroad per unit of time.

Yes, Greeks Had No Bananas

Import quotas are sometimes taken to extremes, producing strange results. Until recently, for example, they made bananas almost impossible to find in Greece—as the following newspaper story attests.

ATHENS—Are there no bananas in Olympia? Yes. Are there no bananas in Thebes? Yes. In Corinth? Yes. In Sparta, Marathon, Delphi? Yes, yes, yes.

Are there no bananas on Crete?

That depends on your definition of banana. Little green pods do grow on that Greek island, on scorched, drooping plants that look as though they want to be banana trees. They are called bananas, but they don't taste much like bananas—or, at least, that's what people say. A foreigner can't easily get a taste of a ripe Cretan banana. They are all sold secretly, on the black market. To buy a banana anywhere in Greece, you need a connection. All over the world, people take bananas for granted. A bunch of bananas off the boat from Panama isn't exactly what dreams are made of, right? Well, in this country, dreams *are* made of bananas. Alien bananas are contraband in

Greece. For Greeks, a sweet, yellow, pulpy Panamanian banana is the forbidden fruit.

"Greece no banana," says the taxi driver at the Athens airport, ecstatically accepting an exotic beauty as a tip. A traveler has just slipped through customs with a bunch in a brown paper bag, defying a five-pound limit. The driver tenderly places his in the glove compartment. "I show it to my grandson," he says.

It has been 12 years now since the last banana boat sailed away from Piraeus. There are children in Greece today who don't even know what a banana is. Greece was a dictatorship in 1971, and dictatorships sometimes do strange things. The one in Greece outlawed the traffic in foreign bananas.

The head of internal security, Col. Stelios Pattakos, gave the

order. He was born on Crete, a bone-dry island, and was friendly toward some farmers there who had it in their heads to try growing a fruit native to equatorial jungles. The colonel got rid of the competition. Still, the Cretan crop was so puny it couldn't satisfy a 50th of the Greek passion for bananas. The price went up. The government imposed controls. And then the banana peddlers went underground.

When the dictatorship collapsed in 1974, Col. Pattakos was sentenced to life imprisonment for nonbanana-related offenses. Democracy returned—but bananas didn't. Bureaucrats do strange things, too.

A banana avalanche, they determined, would hurt the Greek apple business. Everybody would suddenly stop eating apples and start eating bananas. It didn't do any good to argue that comparing apples and bananas was like comparing apples and oranges. So Col. Pattakos got life, and the Greek people got life without bananas.

SOURCE: *The Wall Street Journal*, July 28, 1983, page 1.

An **EXPORT SUBSIDY** is a payment by the government to exporters to permit them to reduce the selling price of their goods so they can compete more effectively in foreign markets.

an example.) The United States now imposes quotas on a smattering of goods, including textiles, sugar, and meat. But most imports are free of quotas.

An **export subsidy** is a payment by the government to an exporter. By reducing the exporter's costs, such subsidies permit exporters to lower their selling prices and to compete more effectively in world trade. While export subsidies are minor in the United States, they are used extensively by some foreign governments to assist their industries—a practice that provokes bitter complaints from American manufacturers about "unfair competition." For example, years of heavy government subsidies helped the European Airbus consortium take a sizable share of the world market for commercial aircraft away from American manufacturers.

HOW TARIFFS AND QUOTAS WORK

Both tariffs and quotas restrict supplies coming from abroad and drive up prices. A tariff works by raising prices and hence cutting the demand for imports, while the sequence associated with a quota is just the reverse—a restriction in supply forces prices up.

Let us use our international trade diagrams to see what a quota does. The supply and demand curves in Figure 18–4 are like those of Figure 18–3. Just as in Figure 18–3, equilibrium in a free international market occurs at a price of $2.50 per bushel (in both countries). At this price, the exporting country produces 125 million bushels (point *B* in part [a]) and consumes 80 million (point *A*); so its exports are 45 million bushels—the distance *AB*. Similarly, the importing country consumes 95 million bushels (point *D* in part [b]) and produces only 50 million (point *C*), so that its imports are also 45 million bushels—the distance *CD*.

Now suppose the government of the importing nation imposes an import quota of (no more than) 30 million bushels. The free-trade equilibrium is no longer possible. Instead, the market must equilibrate at a point where both exports and

---

F i g u r e **18–4**   **QUOTAS AND TARIFFS IN INTERNATIONAL TRADE**

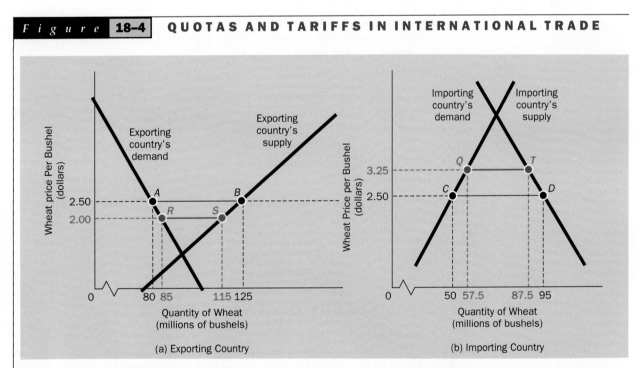

(a) Exporting Country   (b) Importing Country

Under free trade, the equilibrium price of wheat is $2.50 per bushel. The exporting country, in part (a), sends *AB*, or 45 million bushels, to the importing country (distance *CD*). If a quota of 30 million bushels is imposed by the importing country, these two distances must shrink to 30 million bushels. The solution is shown by distance *RS* for exports and distance *QT* for imports. Exports and imports are equal, as must be the case, but the quota forces prices to be unequal in the two countries. Wheat sells for $3.25 per bushel in the importing country but only $2 per bushel in the exporting country. A tariff achieves the same result differently. It *requires* that the prices in the two countries be $1.25 apart. And this, as the graph shows, dictates that exports (= imports) will be equal at 30 million bushels.

imports are 30 million bushels. As Figure 18–4 indicates, this requires different prices in the two countries.

Imports in part (b) will be 30 million—the distance QT—only when the price of wheat in the importing nation is $3.25 per bushel, because only at this price will quantity demanded exceed domestic quantity supplied by 30 million bushels. Similarly, exports in part (a) will be 30 million bushels—the distance RS—only when the price in the exporting country is $2 per bushel. At this price, quantity supplied exceeds domestic quantity demanded by 30 million bushels in the exporting country. Thus the quota *raises* the price in the importing country to $3.25 and *lowers* the price in the exporting country to $2. In general:

An import quota on a product normally will reduce the volume of that product traded, raise the price in the importing country, and reduce the price in the exporting country.

The same restriction of trade can be accomplished through a tariff. In the example we have just completed, a quota of 30 million bushels resulted in a price that was $1.25 higher in the importing country than in the exporting country ($3.25 versus $2). Suppose that, instead of a quota, the importing nation posts a $1.25 per bushel tariff. International trade equilibrium then must satisfy the following two requirements:

1. The price that consumers in the importing country pay for wheat must exceed the price that suppliers in the exporting country receive by $1.25 (the amount of the tariff).

2. The quantity of wheat exported must equal the quantity of wheat imported.

By consulting the graphs in Figure 18–4, you can see exactly where these two requirements are satisfied. If the exporter produces at S and consumes at R, while the importer produces at Q and consumes at T, then exports and imports are equal (at 30 million bushels), and the two domestic prices differ by exactly $1.25. (They are $3.25 and $2.) What we have just discovered is a general result of international trade theory:

Any restriction of imports that is accomplished by a quota normally can also be accomplished by a tariff.

In this case, the tariff corresponding to an import quota of 30 million bushels is $1.25 per bushel.

TARIFFS VERSUS QUOTAS

But while tariffs and quotas can accomplish the same reduction in international trade and lead to the same domestic prices in the two countries, there *are* some important differences between the two types of restrictions.

First, under a quota, profits from the price increases in the importing country usually go into the pockets of the foreign and domestic sellers of the product. Because supplies are limited by quotas, customers in the importing country must pay more for the product. So the suppliers, whether foreign or domestic, receive more for every unit they sell. For example, it has been estimated that U.S. import quotas on Japanese cars in the early 1980s raised the profits of both American and Japanese automakers by billions of dollars per year.

On the other hand, when trade is restricted by a tariff, some of the profits go instead as tax revenues to the *government* of the importing country. In effect, the government increases its tax revenues partly at the expense of its citizens and partly at the expense of foreign exporters, who must accept a reduced price because of the resulting decrease in quantity demanded in the importing country. (Domestic producers again benefit, because they are exempt from the tariff.) In this respect, a tariff is certainly a better proposition than a quota from the viewpoint of the country that enacts it.

Another important distinction between the two measures is the difference in their implications for productive efficiency and prices in the long run. A tariff handicaps all foreign suppliers equally. It still awards sales to the firms and nations who are most efficient and can therefore supply the goods most cheaply.

A quota, on the other hand, necessarily awards its import licenses more or less capriciously—perhaps on a first-come, first-served basis or in proportion to past sales or even on political criteria. There is not the slightest reason to expect the most efficient and least costly suppliers to get the import permits. In the long run, the population of the importing country is likely to end up with significantly higher prices, poorer products, or both.

The U.S. quota on Japanese cars in the 1980s illustrates all of these effects. Japanese automakers responded to the limit on the number of cars by shipping bigger models equipped with more "optional" equipment. The "stripped down" Japanese car became a thing of the past. And the newer, smaller Japanese automakers—like Subaru and Mitsubishi—found it difficult at first to compete in the U.S. market because their quotas were so much smaller than those of Toyota, Nissan, and Honda.

If a country must inhibit imports, there are two important reasons for it to give preference to tariffs over quotas: (1) some of the resulting financial gains from tariffs go to the government of the importing country rather than to foreign and domestic producers; and (2) unlike quotas, tariffs offer no special benefits to inefficient exporters.

WHY INHIBIT TRADE?

To state that tariffs are a better way to inhibit international trade than quotas leaves open a far more basic question, Why limit trade in the first place? There are two primary reasons for adopting measures that restrict trade: first, they may help the importing country get more advantageous prices for its goods, and second, they protect particular industries from foreign competition.

SHIFTING PRICES IN YOUR FAVOR

How can a tariff make prices more advantageous for the importing country if it raises consumer prices there? The answer is that it forces foreign exporters to sell more cheaply by restricting their market. If they do not cut their prices, they will be left with unsold goods. Suppose, as in Figure 18–4(b), that a $1.25 tariff on wheat raises the price of a bushel in the importing country from $2.50 to $3.25 per bushel. This rise in price drives down imports from an amount represented by the length of the black line *CD* to the smaller amount represented by the blue line *QT*. And to the exporting country, this means an equal reduction in exports (see the change from *AB* to *RS* in Figure 18–4[a]).

An Eye for an Eye . . . and a Book for a Shingle?

Trade wars have a way of gathering momentum and moving in unpredictable directions, as the following excerpt shows.

As the authorities in the United States prepare to announce a decision on whether to impose a duty on imports of softwood lumber from Canada, the Canadian Government is threatening retaliation.

The lumber dispute is by far the biggest trade battle between Canada and the United States, the world's largest trading partners. A tariff of the magnitude requested by the American lumber industry would add more than $1 billion to the $3.5 billion price of softwood lumber imported from Canada each year.

"I think you can expect a strong response, but I'm not going to tell you what it is," Pat Carney, Canada's Minister for International Trade, said in an interview today.

She called the American lumber producers' request for a duty "total harassment."

After Washington imposed a tariff on Canadian cedar shingles last May, Ottawa imposed duties on a number of imports from the United States ranging from books to Christmas trees. But trade experts say it is unclear what retaliatory steps the Canadians could take now.

SOURCE: *The New York Times*, October 9, 1986.

As a result, the price at which the exporting country can sell its wheat is driven down (from $2.50 to $2 in the example) while producers in the importing country—being exempt from the tariff—can charge $3.25 per bushel. In effect, such a tariff amounts to government intervention to rig prices in favor of domestic producers and to exploit foreign sellers by forcing them to sell more cheaply than they otherwise would.

However, this technique works only as long as foreigners accept tariff exploitation passively. And, as the boxed insert above suggests, they rarely do. Instead, they retaliate, usually by imposing tariffs or quotas of their own on their imports from the country that first began the tariff game. This can easily lead to a trade war in which no one gains in terms of more favorable prices and everyone loses in terms of the resulting reductions in overall trade. Something like this happened to the world economy in the 1930s and helped prolong the worldwide depression. At present, it is threatening to happen again.

Tariffs or quotas can benefit particular domestic industries in a country that is able to impose them without fear of retaliation. But when every country uses them, everyone is likely to lose in the long run.

PROTECTING PARTICULAR INDUSTRIES

The second, and probably more frequent, reason why countries restrict trade is to protect particular industries from foreign competition. If foreigners can produce steel or watches or shoes more cheaply, domestic businesses and unions in these industries are quick to demand protection; and their governments are often reluctant to deny it to them. It is here that the cheap foreign labor argument is most likely to be invoked.

Protective tariffs and quotas are explicitly designed to rescue firms whose relative inefficiency does not permit them to compete with foreign exporters in an open world market. But it is precisely the harsh competition from abroad that gives consumers the benefits of international specialization. In our numerical example of comparative advantage, one can well imagine the complaints from Japanese computer makers as the opening of trade led to increased importation of U.S. computers. At the same time, American TV manufacturers would probably express equal concern over the flood of imported TVs from Japan. Yet it is Japanese specialization in televisions and U.S. specialization in computers that enables citizens of both countries to enjoy higher standards of living. If governments interfere with this process, consumers in both countries will lose out.

Often, industries threatened by foreign competition argue that some form of protection against imports is needed to prevent loss of jobs. We know from Part 3 that there are better ways to stimulate employment. But a program that limits foreign competition will do a better job of preserving employment *in the particular protected industry*. It will work, but often at a considerable cost to consumers in the form of higher prices and to the economy in the form of inefficient use of resources. Table 18–4 gives some estimates of the costs to American consumers of using tariffs and quotas to save jobs in selected industries. In every case, the costs far exceed the wages of the workers in the protected industries—ranging as high as a colossal $750,000 per job for quotas on steel products.

Nevertheless, complaints over proposals to reduce a tariff or a quota are justified unless something is done to ease the cost to individual workers of switching to the lines of production that trade makes profitable.

The argument for free trade between countries cannot be considered compelling if there is no adequate program to assist the minority of citizens in each country who will be harmed whenever patterns of production change drastically—as would happen, for example, if tariff and quota barriers were suddenly brought down.

Owners of television factories in the United States and of computer factories in Japan may see heavy investments suddenly rendered unprofitable. So would workers whose investments in acquiring special skills and training are no longer marketable. Nor are the costs to displaced workers only monetary. They may have to move to new locations as well as to new industries, uprooting

T a b l e **18–4**	**ESTIMATED COSTS OF PROTECTIONISM**
INDUSTRY	**COST PER JOB SAVED**
Automobiles	$105,000
Book manufacturing	100,000
Dairy products	220,000
Steel	750,000
Sugar	60,000
Textiles	42,000

SOURCE: Gary C. Hufbauer, Diane T. Berliner, and Kimberly Ann Elliott, *Trade Protection in the United States: 31 Case Studies* (Washington: Institute for International Economic Studies), 1986, Table 1.2.

their families, losing old friends and neighbors, and so on. That the *majority* of citizens undoubtedly gain from free trade is no consolation to those who are its victims.

To help alleviate this problem, the United States (and other countries) has set up programs to assist workers who lose jobs because of changing patterns of world trade. In the United States such **trade adjustment assistance** is provided to firms or workers who suffer idle facilities, unprofitability, and unemployment because of sharp increases in imports.

Firms may be eligible for technical assistance designed to improve their efficiency, financial assistance in the form of government loans or government guarantees of private loans, and permission to delay tax payments. Workers are eligible for retraining programs, lengthened periods of eligibility for unemployment compensation, and allowances to help pay for the cost of moving to other jobs. Each form of assistance is designed to ease the burden on the victims of free trade so that the rest of us can enjoy its considerable benefits.

Trade adjustment assistance in the United States began in 1962, and benefits to displaced workers had grown to be extremely generous by the 1970s. However, the Reagan administration—objecting that the program put too much emphasis on *assistance* and not enough on *adjustment*—cut benefits drastically in 1981. One of the things President Clinton has proposed to do is to restore adjustment assistance to its former prominence, though not in the same forms it had taken in the past.

| **TRADE ADJUSTMENT ASSISTANCE** provides special unemployment benefits, loans, retraining programs, and other aid to workers and firms that are harmed by foreign competition.

OTHER ARGUMENTS FOR PROTECTION

NATIONAL DEFENSE AND OTHER NONECONOMIC CONSIDERATIONS

There are times when a tariff or some other measure to interfere with trade may be justified on noneconomic grounds. If a country considers itself vulnerable to military attack, it may be perfectly rational to keep alive industries whose outputs can be obtained more cheaply abroad but whose supplies might be cut off in an emergency. For example, it has been argued that the United States must keep alive its semiconductor industry for precisely these reasons.

The argument has validity. The danger, however, is that industries with the most peripheral relationship to defense are likely to invoke this argument on their behalf. For instance, the U.S. watchmaking industry claimed protection for itself for many years on the grounds that its skilled craftsmen would be invaluable in wartime. Perhaps so, but a technicians' training program probably could have done the job more cheaply and even more effectively by teaching exactly the skills needed for military purposes.

Similarly, the United States has occasionally banned either exports to or imports from nations such as Cuba, Libya, and Afghanistan on political grounds. Such actions often have important economic effects, creating either bonanzas or disasters for particular American industries. But they are justified by politics, not by economics. Noneconomic reasons also explain quotas on importation of whaling products and on the furs of other endangered species.

THE INFANT-INDUSTRY ARGUMENT

Another common argument for protectionism is the so-called **infant-industry argument**. Promising new industries, it is alleged, often need breathing room to flourish and grow. If we expose these infants to the rigors of international competition too soon, the argument goes, they may never develop to the point where they can survive on their own in the international marketplace.

The argument, while valid in certain instances, is less defensible than it seems. It only makes sense to protect an infant industry if the prospective future gains are sufficient to repay the social losses incurred while it is being protected. But if the industry is likely to be so profitable in the future, why doesn't private capital rush in to take advantage of the prospective net profits? The annals of business are full of cases in which a new product or a new firm lost money at first but profited handsomely later. The infant-industry argument for protection stands up to scrutiny only where funds are not available to a particular industry for some reason, despite its glowing profit prospects. And even then it may make more sense to provide a government loan than to provide trade protection.

It is hard to think of examples where the infant-industry argument applies. But even if such a case were found, one would have to be careful that the industry not remain in diapers forever. There are too many cases in which new industries were awarded protection when they were being established and, somehow, the time to withdraw that protection never arrived. One must beware of infant industries that never grow up.

STRATEGIC TRADE POLICY

A stronger argument for (temporary) protection is beginning to have substantial influence on U.S. trade policy. Advocates of this argument, including some top officials in the Clinton administration, agree that free trade for all is the best system. But they point out that we live in an imperfect world in which many nations refuse to play by the rules of the free-trade game. And they fear that a nation that pursues free trade in a protectionist world is likely to lose out. It therefore makes sense, they argue, to *threaten* to protect your markets unless other nations agree to open theirs. (See the accompanying article by columnist William Safire.) And this is exactly what we have done in recent years to such countries as Japan, Korea, and Brazil.

The strategic argument for protection is a hard one for economists to deal with. While it accepts the superiority of free trade, it argues that threatening protectionism is the best way to establish free trade. Such a strategy might work, but it clearly involves great risks. If threats that America will turn protectionist induce other countries to scrap existing protectionist policies, then the gamble will have succeeded. But, if the gamble fails, the world ends up with even more protection than it started with.

The analogy to arms negotiations is pretty obvious. We used to periodically threaten to install new missiles unless the Russians agreed to dismantle some of theirs. When they did, both sides saved money and the world became a safer place. So everyone was better off. But, when they did not, the arms race accelerated and everyone was worse off. Was the threat to build new missiles therefore a wise or a foolish policy? There was never any agreement on this question, and so we should not expect agreement on the advisability of using protectionist measures in a strategic way.

Can Protectionism Save Free Trade?

In this 1983 column, William Safire shook off his longstanding attachment to free trade and argued eloquently for retaliation against protectionist nations.

WASHINGTON—Free trade is economic motherhood. Protectionism is economic evil incarnate. . . Never should government interfere in the efficiency of international competition.

Since childhood, these have been the tenets of my faith. If it meant that certain businesses in this country went belly-up, so be it. . . If it meant that Americans would be thrown out of work by overseas companies paying coolie wages, that was tough. . .

The thing to keep in mind, I was taught, was the Big Picture and the Long Run. America, the great exporter, had far more to gain than to lose from free trade; attempts to protect inefficient industries here would ultimately cost more American jobs.

While playing with my David Ricardo doll and learning nursery rhymes about comparative advantage, I was listening to another laissez-fairy tale: Government's role in the world of business should be limited to keeping business honest and competitive. In God we anti-trusted. Let businesses operate in the free marketplace.

Now American businesses are no longer competing with foreign companies. They are competing with foreign governments who help their local businesses. That means the world arena no longer offers a free marketplace; instead, most other governments are pushing a policy that can be called *helpfulism*.

Helpfulism works like this: A government like Japan decides to get behind its baseball-bat industry. It pumps in capital, knocks off marginal operators, finds subtle ways to discourage imports of Louisville Sluggers, and selects target areas for export blitzes. Pretty soon, the favored Japanese companies are driving foreign competitors batty.

How do we compete with helpfulism? One way is to complain that it is unfair; that draws a horse-laugh. Another way is to demand a "Reagan Round" of trade negotiations under GATT, the Gentlemen's Agreement To Talk, which is equally laughable. Yet another way is to join the helpfuls by subsidizing our exports and permitting our companies to try monopolistic tricks abroad not permitted at home. But all that makes us feel guilty, with good reason.

The other way to deal with helpfulism is through—here comes the dreadful word—*protection*. Or, if you prefer a euphemism, *retaliation*. Or if that is still too severe, *reciprocity*. Whatever its name, it is a way of saying to the cutthroat cartelists we sweetly call our trading partners: "You have bent the rules out of shape. Change your practices to conform to the agreed-upon rules, or we will export a taste of your own medicine."

A little balance, then, from the free trade theorists. The demand for what the Pentagon used to call "protective reaction" is not demagoguery, not shortsighted, not self-defeating. On the contrary, the overseas pirates of protectionism and exemplars of helpfulism need to be taught the basic lesson in trade, which is: tit for tat.

SOURCE: William Safire, "Smoot-Hawley Lives," *The New York Times*, March 17, 1983. Copyright © 1983 by The New York Times Company. Reprinted by permission.

WHAT IMPORT PRICES MOST BENEFIT A COUNTRY?

DUMPING means selling goods in a foreign market at lower prices than those charged in the home market.

One of the most curious features of the protectionist position is the fear of low prices charged by foreign sellers. Countries that subsidize exports are accused of **dumping**—of getting rid of their goods at unconscionably low prices. For example, Japan and Korea have frequently been accused of dumping a variety of goods on the U.S. market.

A moment's thought should indicate why this fear must be considered curious. As a nation of consumers, we should be indignant when foreigners charge us *high* prices, not *low* ones. That is the common-sense rule that guides every consumer, and the consumers of imported commodities should be no exception. Only from the topsy-turvy viewpoint of an industry seeking protection from competition are high prices seen as being in the public interest.

Ultimately, it must be in the best interest of a country to get its imports as cheaply as possible. It would be ideal for the United States if the rest of the world were willing to provide its exports to us free or virtually so. We could then live in luxury at the expense of the rest of the world.

But, of course, what benefits the United States as a whole does not necessarily benefit every single American. If quotas on, say, sugar imports were dropped, American consumers and industries that purchase sugar would gain from lower prices. But owners of and workers in sugar fields would suffer serious losses in the form of lower profits, lower wages, and lost jobs—losses they will fight hard to prevent. For this reason, politics often leads to the adoption of protectionist measures that would likely be rejected on strictly economic criteria.

The notion that low import prices are bad for a country is a fitting companion to the idea—so often heard—that it is good for a country to export much more than it imports. True, this means that foreigners will end up owing us a good deal of money. But it also means that we will have given them large quantities of our products and have gotten relatively little in foreign products in return. That surely is not an ideal way for a country to reap gains from international trade.

Our gains from trade do not consist of accumulations of gold or of heavy debts owed us by foreigners. Rather, our gains are composed of goods and services that others provide minus goods and services we must provide in return.

CONCLUSION: A LAST LOOK AT THE "CHEAP FOREIGN LABOR" ARGUMENT

The preceding discussion should indicate the fundamental fallacy in the argument that American workers have to fear cheap foreign labor. If workers in other countries are willing to supply their products to us with little compensation, this must ultimately *raise* the standard of living of the average American worker. As long as the government's monetary and fiscal policies succeed in maintaining high levels of employment at home, how can we possibly lose by getting the products of the world at bargain prices?

There are, however, some important qualifications. First, our employment policy may not be effective. If workers who are displaced by foreign competition cannot find jobs in other industries, then American workers will indeed suffer from international trade. But that is a shortcoming of the government's employment program, not of its international trade policies.

Second, we have noted that an abrupt stiffening of foreign competition *can* hurt U.S. workers by not giving them an adequate chance to adapt gradually to the new conditions. The more rapid the change, the more painful it will be. If it occurs fairly gradually, workers can retrain and move on to the industries that now require their services. If the change is even more gradual, no one may have to move. People who retire or leave the threatened industry for other reasons simply need not be replaced. But competition that inflicts its damage overnight

Unfair Foreign Competition

Satire and ridicule are often more persuasive than logic and statistics. Exasperated by the spread of protectionism under the prevailing Mercantilist philosophy, French economist Frédéric Bastiat decided to take the protectionist argument to its illogical conclusion. The fictitious petition of the French candlemakers to the Chamber of Deputies, written in 1845 and excerpted below, has become a classic in the battle for free trade.

We are subject to the intolerable competition of a foreign rival, who enjoys, it would seem, such superior facilities for the production of light, that he is enabled to inundate our national market at so exceedingly reduced a price, that, the moment he makes his appearance, he draws off all custom for us; and thus an important branch of French industry, with all its innumerable ramifications, is suddenly reduced to a state of complete stagnation.

This rival is no other than the sun.

Our petition is, that it would please your honorable body to pass a law whereby shall be directed the shutting up of all windows, dormers, skylights, shutters, curtains, in a word, all openings, holes, chinks, and fissures through which the light of the sun is used to penetrate our dwellings, to the prejudice of the profitable manufactures which we flatter ourselves we have been enabled to bestow upon the country. . .

We foresee your objections, gentlemen; but there is not one that

you can oppose to us . . . which is not equally opposed to your own practice and the principle which guides your policy. . .

Labor and nature concur in different proportions, according to country and climate, in every article of production. . . . If a Lisbon orange can be sold at half the price of a Parisian one, it is because a natural and gratuitous heat does for the one what the other only obtains from an artificial and consequently expensive one. . .

Does it not argue the greatest inconsistency to check as you do the importation of coal, iron, cheese, and goods of foreign manufacture, merely because and even in proportion as their price approaches *zero*, while at the same time you freely admit, and without limitation, the light of the sun, whose price is during the whole day at *zero*?

SOURCE: F. Bastiat, *Economic Sophisms* (New York: G. P. Putnam's Sons, 1922).

is certain to impose real costs upon the affected workers, costs that are no less painful for being temporary. That is why our trade laws make provisions for people and industries damaged by import surges. It is also why President Clinton has insisted that a side-agreement on import surges be made part of the North American Free Trade Agreement (NAFTA).

But these are, after all, only qualifications to an overwhelming argument. They call for intelligent monetary and fiscal policies and for transitional assistance to unemployed workers, not for abandonment of free trade. In general, the nation as a whole need not fear competition from cheap foreign labor.

In the long run, labor will be "cheap" only where it is not very productive. Wages will tend to be highest in countries in which high labor productivity keeps costs down and permits exporters to compete effectively despite high wages. It is thus misleading to say that the United States held its own in the international marketplace until recently *despite* the high wages of its workers. Rather it is much more illuminating to point out that the high wages of American workers were a result of high worker productivity, which gave the United States a heavy competitive edge.

We note that in this matter it is *absolute* advantage, not *comparative* advantage, that counts. The country that is most efficient in every output can pay its workers more in every industry.

Summary

1. Countries trade because differences in their natural resources and other inputs create discrepancies in the efficiency with which they can produce different goods, and because **specialization** may offer them greater economies of large-scale production.

2. Voluntary trade will generally be advantageous to both parties in an exchange. This is one of our **12 Ideas for Beyond the Final Exam.**

3. International trade is more complicated than trade within a nation because of political factors, different national currencies, and impediments to the movement of labor and capital across national borders.

4. Both countries will gain from trade with one another if each exports goods in which it has a **comparative advantage**. That is, even a country that is generally inefficient will benefit by exporting the goods in whose production it is *least inefficient*. This is another of the **12 Ideas for Beyond the Final Exam.**

5. When countries specialize and trade, each can enjoy consumption possibilities that exceed its production possibilities.

6. The prices of goods traded between countries are determined by supply and demand, but one must consider explicitly the demand curve and the supply curve of *each* country involved. Thus, in international trade, the equilibrium price must be where the excess of the exporter's quantity supplied over its domestic quantity demanded is equal to the excess of the importer's quantity demanded over its quantity supplied.

7. The **"cheap foreign labor" argument** ignores the principle of comparative advantage, which shows that real wages can rise in both the importing and exporting countries as a result of specialization.

8. **Tariffs** and **quotas** are designed to protect a country's industries from foreign competition. Such protection may sometimes be advantageous to that country, but not if foreign countries adopt tariffs and quotas of their own as a means of retaliation.

9. While the same restriction of trade can be accomplished by either a tariff or a quota, tariffs offer at least two advantages to the country that imposes them: (1) some of the gains go to the government rather than to foreign producers; and (2) there is greater incentive for efficient production.

10. When a nation shifts from protection to free trade, some industries and their workers will lose out. Equity then demands that these people and firms be compensated in some way. The U.S. government offers various forms of **trade adjustment assistance** to do this.

11. Several arguments for protectionism can, under the right circumstances, have validity. These include the national defense argument, the **infant-industry argument**, and the use of trade restrictions for **strategic** purposes. But each of these arguments is frequently abused.

12. **Dumping** will hurt certain domestic producers; but it always benefits domestic consumers.

Key Concepts and Terms

Imports	Comparative advantage	Trade adjustment assistance
Exports	"Cheap foreign labor" argument	Infant-industry argument
Specialization	Tariff	Strategic trade protection
Mutual gains from trade	Quota	Dumping
Absolute advantage	Export subsidy	

Questions for Review

1. You have a dozen eggs worth $1 and your neighbor has a pound of bacon worth about the same. You decide to swap six eggs for a half pound of bacon. In financial terms, neither of you gains anything. Explain why you are nevertheless both likely to be better off.

2. In the eighteenth century, some writers argued that one person in a trade could be made better off only by gaining at the expense of the other. Explain the fallacy in the argument.

3. Country A has mild weather with plenty of rain, plentiful land, but an unskilled labor force. What sorts of products do you think it is likely to produce? What are the characteristics of the countries with which you would expect it to trade?

4. Upon removal of a quota on semiconductors, a U.S. manufacturer of semiconductors goes bankrupt. Discuss the pros and cons of the tariff removal in the short and long runs.

5. Country A's government believes that it is best always to export more (in money terms) than the value of its imports. As a consequence, it exports more to country B every year than it imports from country B. After 100 years of this arrangement, both countries are destroyed in an earthquake. What were the advantages and disadvantages of the surplus to country A? To country B?

6. The table below describes the number of yards of cloth and barrels of wine that can be produced with a week's worth of labor in England and Portugal. Assume that no other inputs are needed.

	IN ENGLAND	IN PORTUGAL
Cloth (yards)	10	12
Wine (barrels)	1	6

a. If there is no trade, what is the price of wine in terms of cloth in England?
b. If there is no trade, what is the price of wine relative to cloth in Portugal?
c. Suppose each country has 1 million weeks of labor available per year. Draw the production possibilities frontier for each country.
d. Which country has an absolute advantage in the production of which good(s)? Which country has a comparative advantage in the production of which good(s)?
e. If the countries start trading with each other, which country will specialize and export which good?
f. What can be said about the price at which trade will take place?

7. Suppose that the United States and Mexico are the only two countries in the world, and that labor is the only productive input. In the United States, a worker can produce 12 bushels of wheat *or* 1 barrel of oil in a day. In Mexico, a worker can produce 2 bushels of wheat *or* 2 barrels of oil per day.

a. What will be the price ratio between the two commodities (that is, the price of oil in terms of wheat) in each country if there is no trade?
b. If free trade is allowed and there are no transportation costs, what commodity would the United States import? What about Mexico?
c. In what range will the price ratio have to fall under free trade? Why?
d. Picking one possible post-trade price ratio, show clearly how it is possible for both countries to benefit from free trade.

8. The table below presents the demand and supply curves for microcomputers in Japan and the United States.

PRICE PER COMPUTER (thousands of dollars)	QUANTITY DEMANDED IN U.S. (thousands)	QUANTITY SUPPLIED IN U.S. (thousands)	QUANTITY DEMANDED IN JAPAN (thousands)	QUANTITY SUPPLIED IN JAPAN (thousands)
0	100	0	100	0
1	90	10	90	25
2	80	20	80	50
3	70	30	70	70
4	60	40	60	80
5	50	50	50	90
6	40	60	40	100
7	30	70	30	110
8	20	80	20	120
9	10	90	10	130
10	0	100	0	140

a. Draw the demand and supply curves for the United States on one diagram and those for Japan on another one.
b. If there is no trade between the United States and Japan, what are the equilibrium price and quantity in the computer market in the United States? In Japan?
c. Now suppose trade is opened up between the two countries. What will be the equilibrium price in the world market for computers? What has happened to the price of computers in the United States? In Japan?
d. Which country will export computers? How many?
e. When trade opens, what happens to the quantity of computers produced, and therefore employ-

ment, in the computer industry in the United States? In Japan? Who benefits and who loses *initially* from free trade?

9. Under current trade law, the president of the United States must report periodically to Congress on countries engaging in unfair trade practices that inhibit U.S. exports. How would you define an "unfair" trade practice? Suppose Country X exports much more to the United States than it imports, year after year. Does that constitute evidence that Country X's trade practices are unfair? What would constitute such evidence?

10. Suppose the United States finds Country X guilty of unfair trade practices and penalizes it with import quotas. So U.S. imports from Country X fall. Suppose, further, that Country X does not alter its trade practices in any way. Is the United States better or worse off? What about Country X?

Chapter 19

THE INTERNATIONAL MONETARY SYSTEM: ORDER OR DISORDER?

*Cecily, you will read
your Political
Economy in my
absence. The chapter
on the Fall of the
Rupee you may omit.
It is somewhat too
sensational.*

**MISS PRISM IN THE IMPORTANCE
OF BEING EARNEST**

The last chapter discussed the reasons for international trade and the benefits that accrue to all nations when countries specialize in producing goods in which they have a comparative advantage. But when goods move across national borders, *money* must generally move in the opposite direction. When the United States buys coffee from Brazil, we must send money to the Brazilians. When Japan purchases petroleum from Saudi Arabia, it must send money to the Saudis, and so on. This chapter is about the system that has been set up to handle these international movements of money—the **international monetary system**. ¶ We begin by investigating a system in which rates of exchange among national currencies are determined in free markets by the laws of supply and demand. We shall see that the main macroeconomic variables studied in Parts 2 and 3—output, the price level, and the rate of interest—each play a role in the determination of a country's exchange rate. This discussion sets the stage for Chapter 20, where we will learn how movements of the exchange rate, in turn, affect the national economy.

Next, we turn to the opposite polar form—an international monetary system in which exchange rates are fixed by government authority, rather than by the market. We do not now live in such a world. Yet studying it will help us understand the current international monetary system, which is a curious hybrid of fixed and floating exchange rates. And it will also help us understand why some people believe that the world should move toward a system with greater fixity in exchange rates.

WHAT ARE EXCHANGE RATES?

The **EXCHANGE RATE** states the price, in terms of one currency, at which another currency can be bought.

We noted in the previous chapter that international trade is more complicated than domestic trade. There are no national borders to be crossed when, say, California lettuce is shipped to Massachusetts. The consumer in Boston pays with *dollars*, just the currency that the farmer in Salinas wants. But if that same farmer ships his lettuce to Japan, consumers there will have only Japanese *yen* with which to pay, rather than the dollars the farmer in California wants. Thus if international trade is to take place, there must be a way to transform one currency into another. The rates at which such transformations are made are called **exchange rates**.

There is an exchange rate between every pair of currencies. For example, $1 is currently the equivalent of about 5.5 French francs. The exchange rate between the franc and the dollar, then, may be expressed as roughly "5.5 francs to the dollar" (meaning that it costs 5.5 francs to buy a dollar) or about "18 cents to the franc" (meaning that it costs 18 cents to buy a franc).

Although exchange rates change all the time, Table 19–1 gives an indication of exchange rates prevailing in July 1980, February 1985, and July 1993, showing how many dollars or cents it cost at each of those times to buy each unit of foreign currency. You will note some dramatic changes in the international value of the dollar over time. In a nutshell, the dollar soared in the period from mid-1980 to early 1985, fell against most major currencies from early 1985 until early 1988,

Table 19–1	EXCHANGE RATES WITH THE U.S. DOLLAR (dollars per unit of foreign currency)				
COUNTRY	**CURRENCY UNIT**	**SYMBOL**	**JULY 1980**	**COST IN DOLLARS FEBRUARY 1985**	**JULY 1993**
Australia	dollar	$	$1.16	$0.74	$.67
Canada	dollar	$	0.87	0.74	0.78
France	franc	FF	0.25	0.10	0.17
Germany	mark	DM	0.57	0.30	0.59
Italy	lira	L	0.0012	0.00049	0.00065
Japan	yen	¥	0.0045	0.0038	0.0092
Mexico	peso	$	0.044	0.0050	0.32*
Sweden	krona	Kr	0.24	0.11	0.13
Switzerland	franc	S. Fr.	0.62	0.36	0.66
United Kingdom	pound	£	2.37	1.10	1.50

*On January 1, 1993, the peso was redefined so that 1000 old pesos were equal to one new peso. Hence the 0.32 listed for July 1993 would be 0.00032 on the old basis.

SOURCE: International Financial Statistics and *The Wall Street Journal*.

and has generally fluctuated without any pronounced trend since. This chapter seeks to explain such currency movements.

Under our present system, currency rates change frequently. When other currencies become more expensive in terms of dollars, we say that they have **appreciated** relative to the dollar. Alternatively, we can look at this same event as the dollar buying less foreign currency, meaning that the dollar has **depreciated** relative to another currency.

What is a depreciation to one country must be an appreciation to the other.

For example, if the dollar cost of a German mark rises from 50 cents to 60 cents, the cost of a U.S. dollar in terms of marks simultaneously falls from 2 marks to 1.67 marks. The Germans have had a currency *appreciation* while we have had a currency *depreciation*.

Notice also that, when many currencies are changing in value, the dollar may be appreciating with respect to one currency but depreciating with respect to another.

Table 19–1 shows that, between February 1985 and July 1993, the dollar *depreciated* sharply relative to the Japanese yen and most European currencies. For example, the British pound rose from $1.10 to $1.50. Yet during that same period the dollar *appreciated* dramatically relative to the Mexican peso; it bought about 200 pesos in 1985 but over 3000 in 1993.[1]

While this is the terminology used to describe movements of exchange rates in free markets, another set of terms is used to describe decreases and increases in currency values when those values are set by government decree. When an officially set exchange rate is altered so that a unit of a nation's currency can buy *fewer* units of foreign currency, we say there has been a **devaluation** of that currency. When the exchange rate is altered so that the currency can buy *more* units of foreign currency, we say there has been a **revaluation.**

EXCHANGE RATE DETERMINATION IN A FREE MARKET

Why is it that a German mark now costs about 60 cents and not 50 cents or 70 cents? In a world of **floating exchange rates**, with no government interferences, the answer would be straightforward. Exchange rates would be determined by the forces of supply and demand, just like the prices of apples, typewriters, and haircuts.

In a leap of abstraction, imagine that the United States and Germany were the only countries on earth, so there was only one exchange rate to be determined. Figure 19–1 depicts the determination of this exchange rate at the point (denoted *E* in the figure) where demand curve *DD* crosses supply curve *SS*. At this price (60 cents per mark), the number of marks demanded is equal to the number of marks supplied.

In a free market, exchange rates are determined by the law of supply and demand. If the rate were below the equilibrium level, the quantity of marks demanded would exceed the quantity of marks supplied, and the price of a mark would be bid up. If the rate were above the equilibrium level, quantity supplied would

A nation's currency is said to **APPRECIATE** when exchange rates change so that a unit of its own currency can buy more units of foreign currency.

The currency is said to **DEPRECIATE** when exchange rates change so that a unit of its currency can buy fewer units of foreign currency.

A **DEVALUATION** is a reduction in the official value of a currency.

A **REVALUATION** is an increase in the official value of a currency.

FLOATING EXCHANGE RATES are rates determined in free markets by the law of supply and demand.

---

[1] In fact, the dollar bought just over 3 pesos in 1993, but that is because the old peso was replaced by a new peso in January 1993, which moved the decimal point three places.

| Figure | **19-1** | **DETERMINATION OF EXCHANGE RATES IN A FREE MARKET** |

Like any price, an exchange rate will be determined by the intersection of the demand and supply curves in a free market. Point *E* depicts this point for the exchange rate between the U.S. dollar and the German mark, which settles at 60 cents per mark in this example.

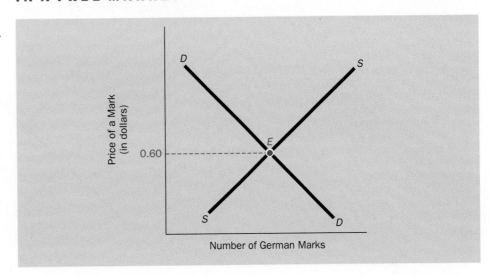

exceed quantity demanded, and the price of a mark would fall. Only at the equilibrium exchange rate is there no tendency for the rate to change.

As usual, supply and demand determine price. What we must ask in this case is: Where do the supply and demand come from? Why does anyone demand a German mark? The answer comes in three parts:

1. *International trade in goods and services.* This was the subject of the last chapter. If, for example, Jane Doe, an American, wants to buy a German automobile, she will first have to buy marks with which to pay the dealer in Munich.[2] So Jane's demand for a German *car* leads to a demand for German *marks*. In general, *demand for a country's exports leads to a demand for its currency.*[3]

2. *International trade in financial instruments like stocks and bonds.* For example, if American investors want to purchase German stocks, they will first have to acquire the marks that the sellers will insist upon. In this way, demand for German financial assets leads to demand for German marks. Thus, *demand for a country's financial assets leads to a demand for its currency.*

3. *Purchases of physical assets like factories and machinery overseas.* If IBM wants to buy out a small German computer manufacturer, the owners will no doubt want to receive marks. So IBM will first have to acquire German currency. In general, *direct foreign investment leads to a demand for a country's currency.*

Now, where does the supply come from? To answer this, just turn all of these transactions around. Germans wanting to buy U.S. goods and services, or invest

---

[2]Actually, she will not do this because banks generally handle foreign exchange transactions for consumers. An American bank probably will buy the marks for her. But the effect is exactly the same as if Jane had done it herself.

[3]See Review Question 2 at the end of the chapter (page 483).

| *F i g u r e* | **19–2** | **THE EFFECT OF AN ECONOMIC BOOM ON THE EXCHANGE RATE** |

If the U.S. economy suddenly booms, Americans will spend more on imports from Germany. Thus the demand curve for German marks will rise from D_1D_1 to D_2D_2 as Americans seek to acquire the marks they need. The diagram shows that this will cause the mark to appreciate, from 60 cents to 65 cents, as equilibrium shifts from point E to point A. Looked at from the U.S. perspective, the dollar will depreciate.

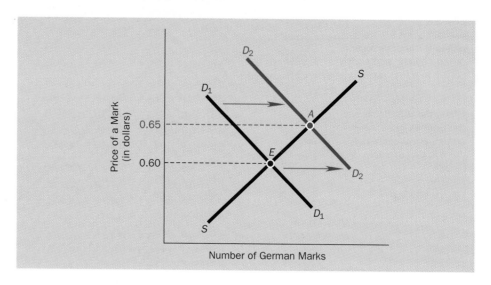

in U.S. financial markets, or make direct investments in America will have to offer their marks for sale in the foreign-exchange market (which is similar to the stock market) to acquire the needed dollars. To summarize:

The demand for a country's currency is derived from the demands of foreigners for its export goods and services and for its assets—including financial assets, like stocks and bonds, and real assets, like factories and machinery. The *supply* of a country's foreign currency arises from its imports, and from foreign investment by its own citizens.

To appreciate the usefulness of even this simple supply and demand analysis, let us consider how the exchange rate between the dollar and the mark would change if there were an economic boom in the United States. One important effect of such a boom would be to stimulate American demand for German products, such as automobiles, cameras, and wines. In terms of the supply–demand diagram shown in Figure 19–2, the increased desires of Americans for German goods would shift the demand curve for German marks out from D_1D_1 (the black line in the figure) to D_2D_2 (the blue line). Equilibrium would shift from point E to point A, and the exchange rate would rise from 60 cents per mark to 65 cents per mark. In a word, the increased demand for marks by U.S. citizens causes the mark to *appreciate* relative to the dollar.

EXERCISE

Test your understanding of the supply and demand analysis of exchange rates by showing why each of the following events would lead to an appreciation of the mark (a depreciation of the dollar) in a free market:

1. A recession in Germany cuts German purchases of American goods.

2. American investors are attracted by prospects for profit on the German stock market.

3. Interest rates on government bonds rise in Germany but are stable in the United States. (*Hint:* Which country's citizens will be attracted by high interest rates in the other country?)

To say that supply and demand determine exchange rates in a free market is at once to say everything and to say nothing. If we are to understand the reasons why some currencies appreciate while others depreciate, we must look into the factors that move the supply and demand curves. Economists believe that the principal determinants of exchange rate movements are rather different in the long, medium, and short runs. So we turn in the next three sections to the analysis of exchange rate movements over these three "runs," beginning with the long run.

THE PURCHASING-POWER PARITY THEORY: THE LONG RUN

As long as there is free trade across national borders, exchange rates should eventually adjust so that the same product costs the same whether measured in dollars in the United States, marks in Germany, yen in Japan, and so on—except for differences in transportation costs and the like. This simple statement forms the basis of the major theory of exchange rate determination in the long run.

The **purchasing-power parity theory of exchange rate determination** holds that the exchange rate between any two national currencies adjusts to reflect differences in the price levels in the two countries.

An example will bring out the basic truth in this theory and also suggest some of its limitations. Suppose that German and American steel are identical and that these two nations are the only producers of steel for the world market. Suppose further that steel is the only tradable good that either country produces.

Question: If American steel costs $180 per ton and German steel costs 300 marks per ton, what must be the exchange rate between the dollar and the mark?

Answer: Since 300 marks or $180 each buys a ton of steel, they must be of equal value. Hence, each mark must be worth 60 cents. Why? Any higher price for a mark, like 75 cents, would mean that steel would cost $225 per ton (300 marks at 75 cents each) in Germany but only $180 per ton in the United States. In that case, all foreign customers would shop for their steel in the United States. Similarly, any exchange rate below 60 cents per mark would send all the steel business to Germany.

EXERCISE

Show why an exchange rate of 50 cents per mark is too low.

The purchasing-power parity theory is used to make long-run predictions about the effects of inflation on exchange rates. To continue our example, suppose that over a five-year period, prices in the United States rise by 25 percent while prices in Germany rise by 50 percent. The purchasing-power parity theory predicts that the mark will depreciate relative to the dollar. It also predicts the amount of the depreciation. After the inflation, American steel costs $225 per ton (one-fourth

Purchasing-Power Parity and the Big Mac

Since 1986, *The Economist* magazine has been using a well-known international commodity—the Big Mac—to assess the purchasing-power parity theory of exchange rates, or as the magazine puts it, "to make exchange-rate theory more digestible." That famous hamburger is now sold in 66 countries, and *The Economist* included 25 of them in its latest survey.*

Here's how it works. In 1993, the average price of a Big Mac in the U.S.A. was $2.28, including sales tax. In Japan, that same commodity sold for ¥391. For those two amounts to be equal, a dollar would have had to have been worth about 391/2.28 = ¥171. In fact, however, the dollar was worth only ¥113 at the time of the survey. This large discrepancy means that, according to the Big Mac standard, the yen was 51 percent overvalued relative to the dollar.

Similar calculations at the time led to the conclusion that the British pound was 23 percent overvalued against the dollar. Since a Big Mac cost £1.79, the implied purchasing-power parity of the pound was 2.28/1.79 = $1.27, versus a market value of $1.56. The cheapest Big Macs in the world at the time were found in Russia, where the burger cost just $1.14 (780 roubles). That implied that the dollar was *under*valued by a whopping 50 percent against the rouble.

Such calculations, based as they are on a single commodity, are not known for their accuracy. Nonetheless, *The Economist* noted, more sophisticated estimates of the purchasing-power parity of the yen at the time were in the $1 = ¥140–180 range, and for the pound in the $1.30–$1.40 range. Not bad for a hamburger.

*"Big MacCurrencies," *The Economist*, April 17, 1993, page 79.

more than $180), while German steel costs 450 marks per ton (50 percent more than 300 marks). For these two prices to be equivalent, 450 marks must be worth $225, or one mark must be worth 50 cents. The mark, therefore, must have fallen from 60 cents to 50 cents.

According to the purchasing-power parity theory, differences in domestic inflation rates are a major cause of adjustments in exchange rates. If one country has higher inflation than another, then its exchange rate should be depreciating.

For many years, the theory seemed to work tolerably well. While precise numerical predictions based on purchasing-power parity calculations were never very accurate (see the accompanying boxed insert), nations with higher inflation did at least experience depreciating currencies. But in the 1980s, this broke down. For example, while the U.S. inflation rate was higher than both Germany's and Japan's throughout the 1980s, the dollar nonetheless rose sharply relative to both the mark and the yen from 1980 to 1985 and again in 1988–1989. Clearly, the theory was missing something. What?

First, changes in any of the interferences with free trade, such as tariffs and quotas, can upset simple calculations based on purchasing-power parity. For example, if German prices rise faster than American prices but, at the same time, foreign countries erect tariff barriers to keep American (but not German) steel out, then the mark might not have to depreciate.

Second, some goods and services cannot be traded across national frontiers. Land and buildings are only the most obvious examples; most services can be traded only to a limited extent (as when tourists from one country rent hotel rooms in another). Inflation rates for goods and services that are *not tradable* have little bearing on exchange rates.

Third, few of the goods that different nations produce and trade are as uniform as the German and American steel in our example. A BMW and a Cadillac, for example, are not identical products. So the price of a BMW *in U.S. dollars* can rise faster than the price of a Cadillac without driving BMWs out of the market entirely. On balance:

Most economists believe that other factors are much more important than relative price levels for exchange rate determination in the short run. But in the long run, purchasing-power parity plays an important role.

ECONOMIC ACTIVITY AND EXCHANGE RATES: THE MEDIUM RUN

Since consumer spending increases when income expands and decreases when income contracts, the same is likely to happen to spending on imported goods. For this reason:

A country's imports will rise quickly when its economy is booming and slowly when its economy is stagnating.

We have already illustrated this point with Figure 19–2. There we saw that a boom in the United States would shift the demand curve for marks outward as Americans bought more German goods. And that, in turn, would lead to an appreciation of the mark (depreciation of the dollar) as Americans sold dollars to buy marks. However, if Germany were booming at the same time, German citizens would be buying more American exports, which would shift the supply curve of marks outward. On balance, the value of the dollar might or might not fall. What matters is whether exports are growing faster than imports. The general lesson is that:

Holding other things equal, a country whose aggregate demand grows faster than the rest of the world's normally finds its currency depreciating because its imports grow faster than its exports. Thus its demand curve for foreign currency shifts outward more rapidly than its supply curve.

This is one reason why it is unwise to interpret a "strong currency" as an indication of a "strong economy." A nation that grows more rapidly than its trading partners may find itself with a depreciating currency.

INTEREST RATES AND EXCHANGE RATES: THE SHORT RUN

While economic activity is important for exchange rate determination in the medium run, "other things" often are not equal in the short run. Specifically, one factor that often seems to call the tune in determining exchange rate movements in the short run is *interest rate differentials*. There is an enormous fund of so-called hot money—owned by banks, multinational corporations, and wealthy individuals of all nations, and amounting to several trillion dollars—that travels around the globe in search of the highest interest rates.

Thus suppose that British government bonds are paying a 6 percent rate of interest when yields on equally safe American government securities rise to 8 percent. British investors will be attracted by the high interest rates in the United

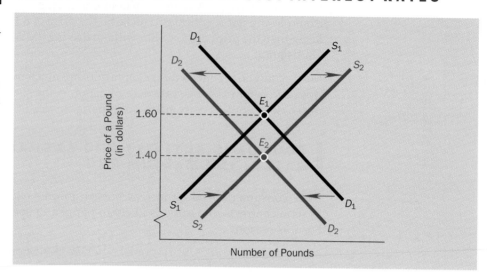

F i g u r e 19–3 THE EFFECT OF A RISE IN U.S. INTEREST RATES

When the U.S. raises its interest rates, more English investors will want to buy American bonds, and so the supply curve of pounds will shift outward from S_1S_1 to S_2S_2. At the same time, fewer Americans will seek to buy British bonds, so the demand curve for pounds will shift inward from D_1D_1 to D_2D_2. The combined effect of these two shifts is to move the market equilibrium from point E_1 to point E_2. The British pound depreciates, and the dollar appreciates.

States and will offer pounds for sale in order to buy dollars, planning to use those dollars to buy American securities. At the same time, American investors will find investing in the United States more attractive than ever, so fewer pounds will be demanded by Americans.

When the demand schedule falls and the supply curve rises, the effect on price is predictable: the pound will depreciate, as Figure 19–3 shows. In the figure, the supply curve of pounds shifts outward from S_1S_1 to S_2S_2 when British investors seek to sell pounds in order to purchase U.S. securities. At the same time, American investors wish to buy fewer pounds because they no longer wish to invest in British securities. Thus the demand curve shifts inward from D_1D_1 to D_2D_2. The result, in our example, is a depreciation of the pound from $1.60 to $1.40. In general:

Holding other things equal, countries with high interest rates are able to attract more capital than are countries with low interest rates. Thus a rise in interest rates often will lead to an appreciation of the currency, and a drop in interest rates will lead to a depreciation.

Most experts in international finance agree that this factor is the major determinant of exchange rates in the short run. It certainly played a predominant role in the stunning movements of the U.S. dollar during the 1980s. Early in the decade, American interest rates rose well above comparable interest rates abroad. In consequence, foreign capital was attracted here, American capital stayed at home, and the dollar soared. Then, in the mid-1980s, the gap between U.S. and foreign interest rates narrowed and the dollar fell.

MARKET DETERMINATION OF EXCHANGE RATES: SUMMARY

We can summarize this discussion of exchange rate determination in free markets as follows:

1. Currency values generally will be *appreciating* in countries whose inflation rates are lower than the rest of the world's because buyers in foreign countries will demand their goods, and thus drive up the currency.

2. Exchange rates would also be expected to rise in countries where aggregate demand is growing more slowly than average, because these countries will be importing rather little.

3. We expect to find appreciating currencies in countries whose interest rates are high because these countries will attract capital from all over the world.

Reversing each of these, we expect that currencies will be *depreciating* in countries with relatively high inflation rates, or rapid demand growth, or low interest rates.

FIXED EXCHANGE RATES AND THE DEFINITION OF THE BALANCE OF PAYMENTS

Some exchange rates today are truly floating, determined by the forces of supply and demand without government interference. But many are not. Furthermore, some people claim that exchange-rate fluctuations are so troublesome that the world would be better off with fixed exchange rates. For these reasons, we turn our attention next to a system of **fixed exchange rates**, or rates that are set by government. Naturally, under such a system the exchange rate, being fixed, is not closely watched. Instead, international financial specialists focus on a country's *balance of payments*—a term we must now define.

To understand what the balance of payments is, look at Figure 19–4, which depicts a situation that might represent, say, the United States just before the dollar fell in value in 1971—an *overvalued* currency. While the supply and demand

FIXED EXCHANGE RATES are rates set by government decisions and maintained by government actions.

| *Figure* | **19-4** | **A BALANCE OF PAYMENTS DEFICIT** |

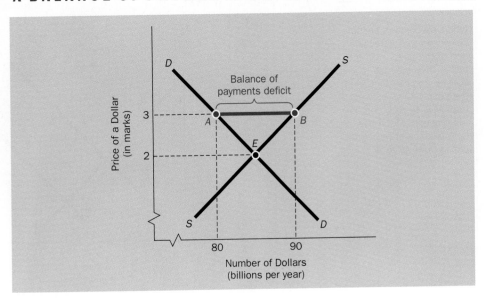

At a fixed exchange rate of 3 marks per dollar, which is well above the equilibrium level of 2 marks per dollar, America's currency is overvalued in this example. As a consequence, more dollars will be supplied (point *B*) than are demanded (point *A*). The difference—distance *AB*, or $10 billion per year—represents the U.S. balance of payments deficit.

curves for dollars indicate an equilibrium exchange rate of 2 marks to the dollar (point *E*), the U.S. government is keeping the rate at 3 marks. Notice that, at 3 marks to the dollar, more people are supplying dollars than are demanding them. In the example, suppliers are selling $90 billion per year, but demanders are purchasing only $80 billion.

This gap between the $90 billion that some people sell and the $80 billion that other people buy is what we mean by America's **balance of payments deficit**— $10 billion per year in this case. It is shown by the horizontal distance between points *A* and *B* in Figure 19–4.

How can market forces be flouted in this way? Since sales and purchases on any market must be equal, as a simple piece of arithmetic, the excess of quantity supplied over quantity demanded of U.S. currency ($10 billion per year in this example) must be bought by the U.S. government. In buying these dollars, it must give up some of the gold and foreign currencies that it keeps as *reserves*. Thus the Federal Reserve would be losing $10 billion in reserves per year as the cost of keeping the dollar at 3 marks.

Naturally, this cannot go on forever; the reserves eventually will run out. And this was the fatal flaw in the system of fixed exchange rates. Once speculators became convinced that the exchange rate could be held for only a short while longer, they would sell dollars in massive amounts rather than hold on to a currency whose value they expected to fall. The supply curve of dollars would shift outward drastically, as shown in Figure 19–5, causing a sharp rise in the balance of payments deficit (from $10 billion to $20 billion in the example). Lacking sufficient reserves, the central bank would have to permit the exchange rate to fall to its equilibrium level, and this might amount to an even larger devaluation than would have been required before the speculative "run" on the dollar began. It was precisely the fear of such a run that induced the United States to end the system of fixed exchange rates in 1971.

The **BALANCE OF PAYMENTS DEFICIT** is the amount by which the quantity supplied of a country's currency (per year) exceeds the quantity demanded. Balance of payments deficits arise whenever the exchange rate is pegged at an artificially high level.

F i g u r e **19–5**   **A SPECULATIVE RUN ON THE DOLLAR**

When speculators become convinced that a devaluation of the dollar is in the offing, they will rush to sell dollars. Their actions shift the supply curve outward from S_1S_1 to S_2S_2 and, in the process, widen the U.S. balance of payments deficit from *AB* to *AC*.

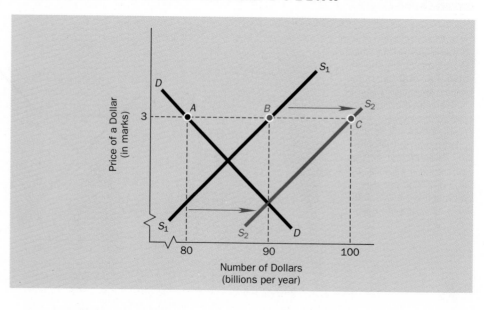

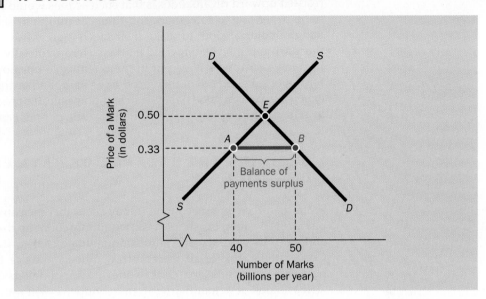

F i g u r e **19–6**   **A BALANCE OF PAYMENTS SURPLUS**

In this example, Germany's currency is undervalued at 33 cents per mark since the equilibrium exchange rate is 50 cents per mark. Consequently, more marks are being demanded (point *B*) than are being supplied (point *A*). The gap between quantity demanded and quantity supplied—distance *AB*, or 10 billion marks per year—measures Germany's balance of payments surplus.

The **BALANCE OF PAYMENTS SURPLUS** is the amount by which the quantity demanded of a country's currency (per year) exceeds the quantity supplied. Balance of payments surpluses arise whenever the exchange rate is pegged at an artificially low level.

For an example of the reverse case, a severely *undervalued* currency, let us consider West Germany in 1973. Figure 19–6 depicts demand and supply curves for marks that intersect at an equilibrium price of 50 cents per mark (point *E* in the diagram). Yet, in the example, we suppose that the German authorities are holding the rate at 33 cents. At this rate, the quantity of marks demanded (50 billion) greatly exceeds the quantity supplied (40 billion). The difference is Germany's **balance of payments surplus,** and is shown by the horizontal distance *AB*.

Germany can keep the rate at 33 cents only by providing the marks that foreigners want to buy: 10 billion marks per year in this example. In return, it receives U.S. dollars, British pounds, French francs, gold, and so on. All of this serves to increase Germany's reserves of foreign currencies. But notice the important difference between this case and the overvalued U.S. dollar.

The accumulation of reserves rarely will *force* a central bank to revalue in the way that depletion of reserves can force a devaluation.

This was another weakness of the system of fixed exchange rates that prevailed between 1944 and 1971. In principle, imbalances in exchange rates could be cured either by a *devaluation* by the country with a balance of payments deficit or by an upward *revaluation* by the country with a balance of payments surplus. In practice, though, it was almost always the deficit countries that were forced to act.

Why did the surplus countries refuse to revalue? One reason was a stubborn refusal to recognize some basic economic realities. They viewed the disequilibrium as the problem of the deficit countries and believed that the deficit countries, therefore, should take the corrective steps. This, of course, is nonsense. Some currencies are overvalued *because* some other currencies are undervalued. In fact, the two statements mean exactly the same thing.

The other reason why exporters in Germany, Japan, and other surplus countries resisted upward revaluations is that such actions would have made their products more expensive to foreigners and thus cut into their sales. And these exporters had the political clout to make their views stick. Meanwhile, since the values of the mark and the yen on world markets were artificially held down, German and Japanese consumers were put in the unenviable position of having to pay more for imported goods than they need have paid. Rather than buy these excessively expensive foreign goods, they watched domestically produced goods go overseas in return for pieces of paper (dollars, francs, pounds, and so on).

DEFINING THE BALANCE OF PAYMENTS IN PRACTICE

From the preceding discussion it may seem that measuring a nation's balance of payments position is a simple task: we simply count up the private demand for and supply of its currency and subtract quantity supplied from quantity demanded. Conceptually, this is all there is to it. But in practice the difficulties are great because we never observe directly the number of dollars demanded and supplied.

If we look at actual market transactions, we will see that the number of U.S. dollars actually *purchased* and the number of U.S. dollars actually *sold* are identical. Unless someone has made a bookkeeping error, this must always be so. How, then, can we recognize a balance of payments surplus or deficit? Easy, you say. Just look at the transactions of the central bank, whose purchases or sales must make up the difference between private demand and private supply. If the Federal Reserve is buying dollars, its purchases measure our balance of payments deficit. If it is selling, its sales represent our balance of payments surplus.

Thus the suggestion is to measure the balance of payments by *excluding official transactions among governments*. This is roughly how the balance of payments surplus or deficit is defined today, though, for a variety of complicated reasons, the U.S. government decided long ago to stop publishing any official statistic called "the balance of payments deficit." Instead, all foreign transactions are listed, and readers are invited to define the balance of payments in any way they wish. Let us now see just what data are published in these official accounts.

THE U.S. BALANCE OF PAYMENTS ACCOUNTS

Using 1992 as an example, Table 19–2 shows the official U.S. balance of payments accounts. There is nothing that purports to measure America's overall balance of payments surplus or deficit. The top section of the table summarizes America's trade in currently produced goods and services—the so-called *current account*. The positive or negative sign attached to each entry indicates whether the transaction represented a *gain* (+) or a *loss* (−) of foreign currency.

Looking first at the top of the table, we see that in merchandise transactions, Americans imported about $96 billion more than they exported, leading to a whopping deficit in what is called the *balance of trade* (see lines 1–3). Because it is available on a monthly basis, this is the number reported most frequently by the news media. In the mid-1980s, America's trade deficits were the largest ever run by any nation. They have fallen substantially since then but are still a source

Table 19–2	U.S. BALANCE OF PAYMENTS ACCOUNTS, 1992 (billions of dollars)		

Current Account			
(1) Balance of trade		−$96.2	
(2) Merchandise exports			+440.1
(3) Merchandise imports			−536.3
(4) Net military transactions		−2.8	
(5) Travel and transportation (net)		+19.7	
(6) Net income from investments and other services		+45.8	
(7) Balance on goods and services		−33.5	
(8) Unilateral transfers (net)		−32.9	
(9) Private			
(10) U.S. Government (nonmilitary)			−14.5
(11) Balance on current account		−66.4	−18.4
Capital Account			
(12) Net private capital flows		+35.6	
(13) Change in the U.S. assets abroad			−53.3
(14) Change in foreign assets in the U.S.			+88.9
(15) Net government capital flows		+43.0	
(16) Change in U.S. government assets			+2.3
(17) Change in foreign official assets in the U.S.			+40.7
(18) Balance on capital account		+78.6	
Addendum			
(19) Sum of lines (11) and (18)		+12.2	
(20) Statistical discrepancy		−12.2	

SOURCE: *Survey of Current Business,* June 1993. Organization of table changed by authors.

of some concern and considerable political controversy. For example, the trade deficit has been a major factor behind the drive for more protectionism that we discussed in Chapter 18.

The entry in line 4 indicates the net effect of a large number of dollars spent by U.S. military installations abroad (transactions that cost us foreign currency) and a large amount of foreign currency earned by selling armaments. On balance, these cost the United States about $2.8 billion in foreign currency. Line 5 shows that in 1992 American tourists and shippers spent $19.7 billion less on foreign services than foreign tourists and shippers spent here.

Line 6 displays a major source of foreign currency earnings for the United States: net income from our investments overseas and from selling other services. In 1992, America earned a net surplus of over $45 billion on this composite of services.

Line 7 gives the net result of all trading in goods and services—*the balance on goods and services.* The entry in line 7 means that the United States spent $33.5 billion more than it received during 1992. Lines 8–10 indicate the so-called unilateral transfers, including both private gifts to foreigners and official foreign aid. Together these cost us almost $33 billion in foreign currency. When these unilateral transfers are subtracted from the deficit on goods and services, we find (in line 11) a large deficit of $66.4 billion in America's *current account.* Many economists take the balance on current account to be the most basic measure of a nation's international transactions.

But this hardly represents our "balance of payments," as it leaves out all purchases and sales of assets. This group of transactions is shown in the *capital account* (lines 12–18) which, in recent years, is where our large foreign borrowing shows up. Line 12 shows that, on balance, foreign individuals and businesses bought about $36 billion more in assets here than private American investors bought from foreigners. The net entry is *plus* $35.6 billion because $53.3 billion dollars flowed *out of* the United States to buy foreign assets (line 13), while $88.9 billion in foreign money flowed into the United States to buy American assets (line 14).

This large surplus in private capital flows, coupled with a larger deficit in the current account, left the United States with a balance of payments deficit in 1992. How are such deficits financed? Mostly, by government capital flows in the opposite direction (such as when foreign governments buy U.S. government bonds). Foreign governments bought $40.7 billion worth of U.S. assets (line 17), while our government sold an additional $2.3 billion in foreign assets (line 16), leaving a surplus in governmental capital flows of $43 billion (line 15).

Thus the accounts do not balance. When we add up the current account (line 11) plus the overall (private plus government) capital account (line 18), we get a $12 billion surplus (line 19). But, of course, this is impossible. Since it is a simple matter of arithmetic that the two accounts together must balance (dollars purchased = dollars sold), the difference is considered a *statistical discrepancy* (line 20).

While part of this huge discrepancy simply comes from errors in data collection and computation, the lion's share reflects the U.S. government's inability to monitor all the flows of money, goods, and services across its borders. When we fail to record the cargo of a truck hauling U.S. goods to Canada, we overstate our current account deficit. When we fail to record foreign capital movements into the United States, we understate our capital account surplus. Such errors and omissions often leave big statistical discrepancies in the balance of payments accounts of the United States and other nations.

A BIT OF HISTORY: THE GOLD STANDARD

It is hard to find examples of strictly fixed exchange rates in the historical record. About the only time exchange rates were truly fixed was under the old **gold standard**, at least when it was practiced in its ideal form.[4]

Under the gold standard, fixed exchange rates were maintained by an automatic equilibrating mechanism that went something like this: all currencies were defined in terms of gold; indeed, some were actually made of gold. When a nation had a deficit in its balance of payments, this meant, essentially, that more gold was flowing *out* than was flowing *in*. Since the domestic money supply was based on gold, losing gold to foreigners meant that the quantity of money fell *automatically*. This raised interest rates and attracted foreign capital. At the same time, the restrictive "monetary policy" pulled down output and prices, thus discouraging

---

[4]As a matter of fact, while the gold standard lasted (on and off) for hundreds of years, it was rarely practiced in its ideal form. Except for a brief period of fixed exchange rates in the late nineteenth and early twentieth centuries, there were periodic adjustments of exchange rates even under the gold standard.

imports and encouraging exports. The balance of payments problem quickly rectified itself. This meant, however, that:

Under the gold standard, no nation had control of its domestic monetary policy, and therefore no nation could control its domestic economy very well.

At least in principle, the effects on surplus countries were perfectly symmetrical under the gold standard. A balance of payments surplus led, via gold inflows, to an increase in the domestic money supply, whether the surplus country liked the idea or not. This raised prices and output, thereby increasing imports and decreasing exports. And it also lowered interest rates, thereby encouraging out-flows of capital. Because of these automatic adjustments, nations rarely reached the point at which devaluations or revaluations were necessary. Exchange rates were fixed as long as countries abided by the rules of the gold standard game.

In addition to the loss of control over domestic monetary conditions, the gold standard posed one other serious difficulty.

A fundamental problem with the gold standard was that the world's commerce was at the mercy of gold discoveries.

Discoveries of gold meant higher prices in the long run and higher real economic activity in the short run, through the standard monetary-policy mechanisms that we studied in Part 3. And when the supply of gold did not keep pace with growth of the world economy, prices had to fall in the long run and employment had to fall in the short run.

THE BRETTON WOODS SYSTEM AND THE INTERNATIONAL MONETARY FUND

The gold standard faltered many times and finally collapsed amid the financial chaos of the Great Depression of the 1930s and World War II. Without it, the world struggled through a serious breakdown in international trade.

Then, as World War II drew to a close, with much of Europe in ruins and with the United States holding the lion's share of the free world's reserves, officials of the industrial nations met at Bretton Woods, New Hampshire, in 1944. Their goal was to establish a stable monetary environment that would facilitate world trade. Since the dollar was the only "strong" currency at that time, it was natural for them to turn to the dollar as the basis of the new international economic order. And that is just what they did.

The Bretton Woods agreements reestablished a system of fixed exchange rates based not on the old gold standard but on the free convertibility of the U.S. dollar into gold. The United States agreed to buy or sell gold to maintain the $35 per ounce price that had been established by President Franklin Roosevelt in 1933. The other signatory nations, which had almost no gold in any case, agreed to buy and sell *dollars* to maintain their exchange rates at agreed-upon levels. Thus all currencies were indirectly on a modified "gold standard." A holder of French francs, for example, could exchange these for dollars at (roughly) 5 francs per dollar and then exchange these into gold at $35 per ounce. In this way, the value of the franc was fixed at 175 francs per ounce of gold (5 francs per dollar times 35 dollars per ounce). The new system was dubbed the **gold-exchange system**, and it was often referred to as the **Bretton Woods system**.

The **International Monetary Fund (IMF)** was set up to police and manage this new system. Using funds that had been contributed by member countries, the

IMF was empowered to make loans to countries that were running low on reserves. A change in exchange rates was to be permitted only in the case of a "fundamental disequilibrium" in a nation's balance of payments—for it was believed that only relatively fixed exchange rates could provide the stable climate needed to restore world trade.

Of course, the Bretton Woods conferees did not define clearly what a "fundamental disequilibrium" was, nor could they have. As the system evolved, it came to mean a chronic *deficit* in the balance of payments of sizable proportions. Such nations would then *devalue* their currencies relative to the dollar. So the system was not really one of fixed exchange rates but rather one where rates were "fixed until further notice."

Several flaws in the Bretton Woods system have already been mentioned in our discussion of the pure system of fixed exchange rates. First, since devaluations were permitted only after a long run of balance of payments deficits, these devaluations (a) could be clearly foreseen and (b) normally had to be large. Speculators then saw opportunities for profit and would "attack" weak currencies with a wave of selling.

This problem led many economists to question whether the system of fixed exchange rates was really providing the stable climate for world trade that had been intended. Was a system where rates were constant for long periods and then altered by large amounts really more conducive to international trade than one where overvalued currencies would gradually depreciate, as they would under a system of floating rates?

The second problem arose from the custom that deficit nations were expected to devalue when forced to, while surplus nations (at that time, mainly West Germany and Japan) could resist upward revaluations. Since the U.S. dollar defined the monetary value of gold (at $35 per ounce), America was the one nation in the world that had no way to devalue its currency relative to gold, no matter how "fundamental" the disequilibrium became. The only way exchange rates between the dollar and foreign currencies could change was if the surplus nations revalued their currencies upward relative to the dollar. They did not do this frequently enough, so the United States, with its chronically overvalued currency, ran persistent balance of payments deficits in the 1960s.

ADJUSTMENT MECHANISMS UNDER THE BRETTON WOODS SYSTEM

Under the Bretton Woods system, devaluation was viewed as a last resort, to be used only after other methods of adjusting to payments imbalances had failed. What were these other methods?

We have already encountered most of them in our discussion of exchange rate determination in free markets (see pages 462–69). Any factor that increases the demand for, say, U.S. dollars or that reduces the supply will push the value of the dollar upward if it is free to adjust. If, however, the exchange rate is pegged, it is the balance of payments deficit rather than the exchange rate that will adjust when supply of or demand for a nation's money changes. Specifically, the U.S. balance of payments deficit will shrink if either the demand for dollars increases or the supply decreases.

The two panels of Figure 19–7 illustrate this adjustment. In each case, the U.S. has a payments deficit, since the official exchange rate (3 marks) exceeds the equilibrium rate (2 marks). The deficit starts at *AB* in each diagram. Then either

F i g u r e   **19-7**   **ADJUSTING TO BALANCE OF PAYMENTS DEFICITS**

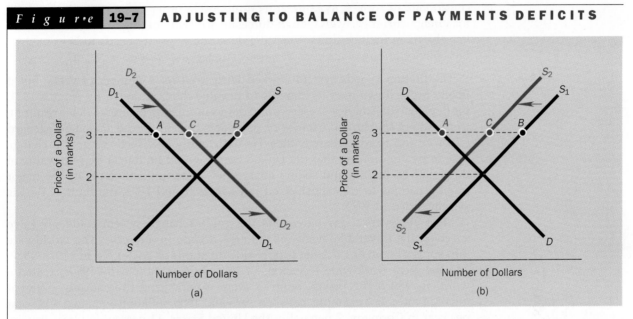

The two parts of this diagram illustrate alternative ways to cut America's balance of payments deficit while maintaining the exchange rate at 3 marks per dollar. Part (a) might represent a reduction in our inflation rate, which would increase world demand for U.S. export products. Or it could represent a rise in American interest rates, which would attract foreign capital. Part (b) might represent a reduction in domestic incomes, which would diminish American appetites for foreign goods. In either case, whether demand rises or supply falls, the balance of payments deficit is reduced: from *AB* to *CB* in part (a) and from *AB* to *AC* in part (b).

the demand curve moves outward as in part (a), or the supply curve moves inward as in part (b). With the exchange rate held at 3 marks to the dollar, the balance of payments deficit shrinks—to *CB* in part (a) or to *AC* in part (b).

Referring back to our earlier discussions of the factors that underlie the demand and supply curves, then, we see that one way a deficit nation can improve its balance of payments is to *reduce its aggregate demand*, thus discouraging imports and cutting down its demand for foreign currency. Another is to *slow its rate of inflation*, thus encouraging exports and discouraging imports. Finally, it can *raise its interest rates* in order to attract more foreign capital.

In a word, deficit nations were expected to follow restrictive monetary and fiscal policies *voluntarily* just as they would have done *automatically* under the old gold standard. However, just as under the gold standard, this medicine was often unpalatable—as it was to the United States in the 1960s.

Surplus nations could, of course, have taken the opposite measures: pursuing expansive monetary and fiscal policies to increase economic growth and lower interest rates. By increasing the supply of the country's currency and reducing the demand for it, such actions would have reduced the balance of payments surplus. But often the countries did not relish the inflation that accompanies expansionary policies; and so, once again, they left the burden of adjustment to the deficit nations. The general point about fixed exchange rates is that:

Under a system of fixed exchange rates, the government of a country loses some control over its domestic economy. There may be times when balance of payments considerations force it to contract its economy in order to cut down its demand for foreign currency, even though domestic needs are calling for expansion. Conversely, there may be times when the domestic economy needs to be reined in, but balance of payments considerations suggest expansion.

The Bretton Woods system worked fairly well for a number of years, but it finally broke down over its inability to devalue the U.S. dollar. By August 1971, the depletion of America's reserves and the accumulation of foreign debts resulting from America's chronic balance of payments deficits forced President Richard Nixon to end fixed exchange rates. He unilaterally abolished the gold exchange system by announcing that the United States would no longer peg the value of the dollar by buying and selling gold. After some futile attempts by the major trading nations to reestablish fixed rates in 1971 and 1972, the Bretton Woods system ended in 1973.

Most observers today agree that the gold-exchange system could not have survived the incredible events of the next decade in any case. The worldwide inflationary boom of 1972, the supply-side inflations of 1972–1974 and 1979–1980, and the great worldwide recessions of 1974–1976 and the early 1980s created a world in which the major countries were experiencing dramatically different inflation rates. For example, between 1975 and 1985, inflation averaged 4 percent per year in Germany, 7 percent in the United States, 11 percent in Great Britain, and 15 percent in Italy. As the purchasing-power theory reminds us, large differences in inflation rates call for *major* changes in currency values. The Bretton Woods system was ill-suited to handle such major changes.

WHY TRY TO FIX EXCHANGE RATES?

In view of these and other severe problems with the Bretton Woods system, why did the international financial community work so hard to maintain fixed rates for so many years? And why do some people today want to return to fixed exchange rates? The answer is that floating exchange rates, determined in free markets by supply and demand, also pose problems.

Chief among these is the possibility that freely floating rates might prove to be highly variable rates, which add an unwanted element of risk to foreign trade. For example, if the exchange rate is 16 cents to the French franc, then a 2000-franc Parisian dress will cost $320. But should the franc appreciate to 20 cents, that same dress would cost $400. An American department store thinking of buying the dress may need to place its order far in advance and will want to know the cost *in dollars*. It may be worried about the possibility that the value of the franc will rise, so that the dress will cost more than $320. And such worries might inhibit trade.

There are two answers to this concern. First, we might hope that freely floating rates would prove to be fairly stable. Prices of most ordinary goods and services, for example, are determined by supply and demand in free markets and yet do not fluctuate unduly. Unfortunately, experience since 1973 has dashed this hope. Exchange rates have been extremely volatile—much more volatile than advocates of floating rates anticipated. This volatility is a major reason why some observers want to move back toward fixed exchange rates.

A second possibility is that speculators might relieve business firms of exchange rate risks—for a fee, of course. Consider the department store example. If French

"Then it's agreed. Until the dollar firms up, we let the clamshell float."

Drawing by Ed Fisher
© 1971, The New Yorker Magazine, Inc.

francs cost 16 cents today, the department store manager can assure herself of paying exactly $320 for the dress several months from now by arranging for a speculator to deliver francs to her at 16 cents on the day she needs them. If the franc appreciates in the interim, it is the speculator, not the department store, that will take the financial beating. And, of course, if the franc depreciates, the speculator will pocket the profits. Thus speculators play an important role in a system of floating exchange rates.

The widespread fears that speculative activity in free markets will lead to wild gyrations in prices, while occasionally valid, are often unfounded. The reason is simple. To make profits, international currency speculators must buy a currency when its value is low (thus helping to support the currency by pushing up its demand curve) and sell it when its value is high (thus holding down the price by adding to the supply curve).

This means that, to be successful, speculators must come into the market as *buyers* when demand is weak (or when supply is strong), and come in as *sellers* when demand is strong (or supply is scant). In doing so, they will help limit price fluctuations. Looked at the other way around, speculators can destabilize prices only if they are systematically willing to lose money.[5]

Notice the stark contrast to the system of fixed exchange rates in which speculation often led to wild "runs" on currencies that were on the verge of devaluation. Speculative activity, which may well be destabilizing under fixed rates, is likely to be stabilizing under floating rates.

We do not mean to imply that speculation makes floating exchange rates trouble-free. At the very least, speculators will demand a fee for their services— a fee that adds to the costs of trading across national borders. In addition, not all exchange-rate risks can be eliminated through speculation. For example, few contracts on foreign currencies nowadays last more than, say, six months or a year. Thus no business can protect itself from exchange-rate changes over periods measured in years. Yet, despite this risk, international trade has flourished under floating exchange rates. Apparently, exchange-rate risk is not as burdensome as some people feared.

THE CURRENT MIXED SYSTEM

Our current international financial system—where some currencies are still pegged in the old Bretton Woods manner, many are floating freely, and others are floating subject to government interferences—has evolved gradually since the United States severed the dollar's link to gold. Though it continues to change and adapt, at least three features have been evident.

The first is the decline in the notion that exchange rates should be fixed for long periods of time. The demand by many countries in the early 1970s that the world quickly return to fixed exchange rates had largely subsided by the mid-1970s. Even where rates are still pegged, devaluations and revaluations are now much more frequent—and smaller—than they were in the Bretton Woods era. Most free-world currency rates change slightly on a day-to-day basis, and market forces generally determine the basic trends, up or down. Even advocates of greater

---

[5]See Review Question 11 at the end of the chapter.

fixity in exchange rates generally propose that governments keep rates within certain *ranges*, rather than literally fix them.

Second, however, some central banks do not hesitate to intervene to moderate exchange movements whenever they feel that such actions are appropriate. Typically, these interventions are aimed at ironing out what are deemed to be transitory fluctuations. But there are times in which central banks oppose basic trends in exchange rates. For example, the Federal Reserve and other central banks sold dollars aggressively in 1985 to push the dollar down, and both the Fed and the Bank of Japan tried to arrest the rise of the yen in 1993. While we certainly no longer have many fixed exchange rates, most of the major currencies are floating less than freely. The terms **"dirty float"** or **"managed float"** have been coined to describe this mongrel system.

The third unmistakable feature of the present international monetary system is the virtual elimination of any role for gold. The trend away from gold actually began before 1971, and by now gold plays essentially no role in the world's financial system. Instead, there is a *free market* in gold in which dentists, jewelers, industrial users, speculators, and ordinary citizens who think of gold as a good store of value can buy or sell as they wish. The price of gold is determined each day by the law of supply and demand and has proved to be quite volatile.

RECENT DEVELOPMENTS IN INTERNATIONAL FINANCIAL MARKETS

THE DANCING DOLLAR

We mentioned earlier that floating exchange rates have not been stable exchange rates. No currency illustrates this better than the U.S. dollar. (See Figure 19–8.)

In 1977 and 1978, the international value of the dollar plummeted until a concerted effort by central banks to buy dollars stopped the fall. The dollar then stabilized for almost two years before starting to rise like a rocket for a period of almost five years. As Table 19–1 (page 461) shows, in 1980 a U.S. dollar bought less than 2 German marks, about 4 French francs, and about 830 Italian lira. By the time it peaked in February 1985, the mighty dollar could buy more than 3 German marks, about 10 French francs, and over 2000 Italian lira. Such major currency changes had dramatic effects on world trade.

The rising dollar was a blessing to Americans who traveled abroad or who bought foreign goods because foreign prices, when translated to dollars by the exchange rate, looked cheap to Americans.[6] But the arithmetic worked just the other way for U.S. firms seeking to sell their goods abroad; foreign buyers found everything American very expensive.[7] It was no surprise, therefore, that as the dollar climbed our exports fell, our imports rose, and our current account registered all-time record deficits. An expensive currency, Americans came to learn, is a mixed blessing.

From early 1985 until early 1988, the value of the dollar fell even faster than it had risen. The cheaper dollar curbed American appetites for imports and alleviated the plight of our export industries, many of which boomed. However, rising

---

[6]EXAMPLE: How much does a 600-franc hotel room in Paris cost in dollars when the franc is worth 20 cents? 16 cents? 10 cents?

[7]EXAMPLE: How much does a $55 American camera cost a German consumer when the mark is worth 55 cents? 44 cents? 33.33 cents?

| F i g u r e | 19-8 | THE UPS AND DOWNS OF THE DOLLAR, 1974–1993 |

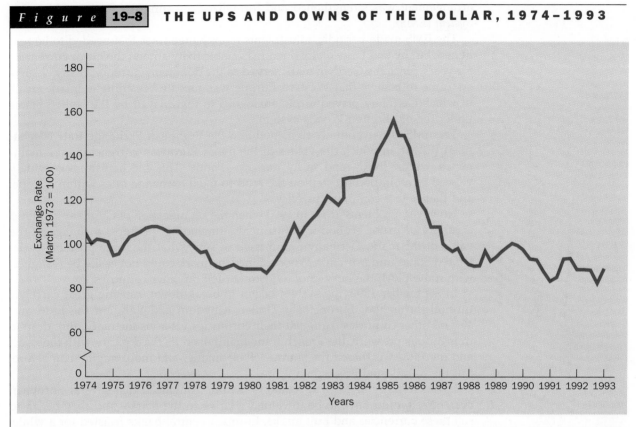

This graph charts the behavior of the international value of the dollar relative to a basket of ten major foreign currencies since 1974. (The index is based on March 1973 = 100.) The net change in the value of the dollar over the entire period is small, but the ups and downs have been pronounced. The stunning climb of the dollar from its 1980 low to its 1985 high stands out on the graph, as does the even more pronounced decline from 1985 to 1988.

SOURCE: Federal Reserve System.

prices for imported goods and foreign vacations were a source of consternation to many American consumers.

Then, in 1988 and 1989, the dollar rose sharply against most major currencies, renewing worries about America's ability to export. Since then, the overall value of the dollar has been relatively stable, but there have been notable movements against particular currencies. In particular, the yen appreciated sharply in 1993.

THE EUROPEAN EXCHANGE RATE MECHANISM

As noted earlier, floating exchange rates are no magical cure-all. One particular problem beset the members of the European Economic Community (EC). These Common Market countries have pledged to create a unified market like the United States. As part of that pledge, they need eventually to establish a single currency for all member countries. Floating rates would make this goal unattainable. So in 1973 some of the member countries entered into an agreement whereby exchange rates among their currencies would remain relatively *fixed* while EC currencies as a group would rise or fall *relative to the rest of the world*. In 1979 this arrangement was strengthened and formalized, creating the *European Monetary System (EMS)*.

The EMS made periodic adjustments to exchange rates that needed to be realigned, but by and large maintained reasonable fixity among the major currencies for years. Since the German mark served as the dominant currency, many observers came to believe that Western Europe was rapidly becoming a "mark area," in which Germany played a role analogous to that played by the United States under the old Bretton Woods system.

The EMS was eventually tightened into the **European Exchange Rate Mechanism (ERM)**, in which the values of the major European currencies were maintained within fixed—and fairly narrow—bands. This mechanism was widely viewed as an important step on the road to fixed exchange rates within Europe, and thence to a common currency.

However, problems arose in 1990 when the reunification of Germany required a variety of major economic adjustments—including, perhaps, a change in the value of the mark. Germany found itself in somewhat the same position as the United States under Bretton Woods: Since the mark could not easily be realigned within the ERM, the burden of adjustment fell on other countries.

In September 1992, the system began to break down, causing great currency turmoil throughout Europe. The United Kingdom and Italy left the ERM and several other countries realigned their currencies vis-a-vis the mark. But, despite tremendous pressure, the French franc maintained its fixed parity with the mark and the ERM weathered the storm—albeit smaller and more fragile than before. But the calm lasted less than a year.

In the summer of 1993, speculators became convinced that several European currencies would have to be devalued relative to the mark—and they began to sell these currencies and buy marks. Europe's central banks resisted for a while, but eventually succumbed to market forces. Currency bands were made so wide that the EC went on a *de facto* floating system even though the ERM remained intact in name. As of this writing, no one knows what might happen to the European Exchange Rate Mechanism next.

Summary

1. **Exchange rates** state the value of one currency in terms of another and thus influence the patterns of world trade in important ways.

2. If governments do not interfere by buying or selling their currencies, exchange rates will be determined in free markets by the usual laws of supply and demand. Such a system is called **floating exchange rates**.

3. Demand for a nation's currency is derived from foreigners' desires to purchase that country's goods and services or to invest in its assets. Any change that increases the demand for a nation's currency will cause its exchange rate to **appreciate** under floating rates.

4. Supply of a nation's currency is derived from the desire of that country's citizens to purchase foreign goods and services or to invest in foreign assets. Any change that increases the supply of a nation's currency will cause its exchange rate to **depreciate** under floating rates.

5. In the long run, purchasing-power parity plays a major role in exchange rate movements. The **purchasing-power parity theory** states that relative price levels in any two countries determine the exchange rate between their currencies. Therefore, countries with relatively low inflation rates normally will have appreciating currencies.

6. Over shorter periods, purchasing-power parity has little influence over exchange-rate movements. The pace of economic activity and the level of interest rates exert greater influence. In particular, interest rate

movements are typically the dominant factor in the short run.

7. Exchange rates can be fixed at nonequilibrium levels by governments that are willing and able to mop up any excess of quantity supplied over quantity demanded, or provide any excess of quantity demanded over quantity supplied. In the first case, the country is suffering from a **balance of payments deficit** because of its overvalued currency. In the second, an undervalued currency has given it a **balance of payments surplus**.

8. In the early part of this century, the world was on a particular system of **fixed exchange rates** called the **gold standard**, in which the value of every nation's currency was fixed in terms of gold. But this created problems because nations could not control their own money supplies and because the world could not control its total supply of gold.

9. After World War II, the gold standard was replaced by the **gold-exchange (or Bretton Woods) system** where rates were again fixed, or rather, fixed until further notice. In this system, the U.S. dollar was the basis of international currency values.

10. The gold-exchange system served the world well and helped restore world trade, but it ran into trouble when the dollar became chronically overvalued since the system provided no way to remedy this situation.

11. Since 1971, the world has moved toward a system of relatively free exchange rates, though there are plenty of exceptions. We now have a thoroughly mixed system of **"dirty" or "managed" floating** which continues to evolve and adapt.

12. Floating rates are not without their problems. For example, importers and exporters justifiably worry about fluctuations in exchange rates. Though these problems seem manageable, some people think that a return to fixed exchange rates is desirable.

13. Under floating exchange rates, investors who speculate on international currency values provide a valuable service by assuming the risks of those who do not wish to speculate. Normally, speculators stabilize rather than destabilize exchange rates, because that is how they make profits.

14. The U.S. dollar rose dramatically in value from 1980 to 1985, making our imports cheaper and our exports more expensive. Then, from 1985 to 1988, the dollar tumbled, which had precisely the reverse effects.

Key Concepts and Terms

International monetary system	Floating exchange rates	Gold standard
Exchange rate	Purchasing-power parity theory	Gold-exchange system
Appreciation	Fixed exchange rates	(Bretton Woods system)
Depreciation	Balance of payments deficit and	International Monetary Fund (IMF)
Devaluation	surplus	"Dirty" or "managed" floating
Revaluation	Current account	The European Exchange Rate
Supply of and demand for foreign	Capital account	Mechanism (ERM)
exchange	Balance of trade	

Questions for Review

1. What items do you own or routinely consume that are produced abroad? From what countries do these come? Suppose you decided to buy more of these things? How would that affect the exchange rates between the dollar and these currencies?

2. If the dollar depreciates relative to the Japanese yen, will the Sony Discman you have wanted become more or less expensive? What effect do you imagine this will have on American demands for Discmen? Does the American demand curve for yen, therefore, slope upward or downward? Explain.

3. During the first half of the 1980s, inflation in (West) Germany was consistently lower than in the United States. What, then, does the purchasing-power parity theory predict should have happened to the exchange rate between the mark and the dollar between 1980 and 1985? (Look at Table 19–1 to see what actually happened.)

4. Use supply and demand diagrams to analyze the effect on the exchange rate between the dollar and the British pound if:
   a. Britain's flow of North Sea oil increases.
   b. British dockworkers refuse to unload ships that arrive with cargo from America but continue to load ships that sail from Britain.
   c. The Federal Reserve raises interest rates in America.
   d. The U.S. government, to help settle the problems of the Middle East, gives huge amounts of foreign aid to Israel and her Arab neighbors.
   e. Both Britain and the United States recover from recessions, but the British recovery is more rapid.
   f. Polls suggest that Britain's conservative government will be replaced by radicals, who vow to nationalize all foreign-owned assets.

5. How are the problems of a country faced with a balance of payments deficit similar to those posed by a government regulation that holds the price of milk above the equilibrium level? (*Hint:* Think of each in terms of a supply-demand diagram.)

6. Look at the U.S. balance of payments accounts table in the text (Table 19–2 on page 473). Figure out where each of the following actions you could have taken in 1992 would have been recorded in these accounts:
   a. You spent the summer traveling in Europe.
   b. Your uncle in Canada sent you $20 as a birthday present.
   c. You bought a new Honda.
   d. You sold some stock you own on the Tokyo Stock Exchange.
   e. You came home from a trip to Canada carrying two cases of Canadian beer, which you sold to a friend. (*Hint*: Would your sale have been recorded anywhere?)

7. For each of the transactions listed in Question 6, indicate how it would affect:
   a. the U.S. balance of payments, if exchange rates were fixed;
   b. the international value of the dollar, if exchange rates were floating.

8. Under the old gold standard, what do you think happened to world prices when there was a huge gold strike in California in 1849? What do you think happened when the world went without any important new gold strikes for 20 years or so?

9. Explain why the members of the Bretton Woods conference in 1944 wanted to establish a system of fixed exchange rates. What was the flaw that led to the ultimate breakdown of the system in 1971?

10. Suppose you want to reserve a hotel room in London for the coming summer but are worried that the value of the pound may rise between now and then, making the rooms too expensive for your budget. Explain how a speculator could relieve you of this worry. (Don't actually try it. Speculators deal only in very large sums!)

11. On page 479, it is pointed out that successful speculators buy a currency when demand is weak and sell it when demand is strong. Use supply and demand diagrams for two different periods (one with weak demand, the other with strong demand) to show why this will limit price fluctuations.

12. Use the following statistics to produce a balance of payments table for the United States, identifying separately the current and capital accounts. (Assume no statistical discrepancy.)

U.S. income on foreign investments (net)	100
U.S. government grants to foreigners	25
Merchandise exports	750
U.S. tourist expenditures abroad	50
U.S. private direct investment abroad	80
Foreign direct investment in the United States	60
Merchandise imports	850

   a. Does the balance of payments show a surplus or a deficit?
   b. What would happen to the exchange rate under flexible exchange rates?

13. In 1993, market forces were pushing up the international value of the Japanese yen. What could the Bank of Japan (Japan's central bank) have done to try to prevent this appreciation? Why might it have failed? Could the Federal Reserve have done the job instead?

Chapter 20

MACROECONOMICS IN A WORLD ECONOMY

No man is an island,

entire of itself.

JOHN DONNE

An **OPEN ECONOMY** is one that trades with other nations in goods and services, and perhaps also in financial assets.

America is not an isolated economy immune from foreign influences. Today, more than ever before, the nations of the world are locked together in an uneasy economic union. Fluctuations in foreign GDP growth, foreign inflation, and foreign interest rates profoundly affect the U.S. economy. Similarly, economic events that originate in our country reverberate around the globe. Without a deeper understanding of these international linkages, we cannot hope to understand many of the most important economic developments of our time. ¶ What we learned in earlier chapters about the macroeconomics of international trade in goods and services was correct, but limited. In particular, it paid no attention to such crucial influences as exchange rates and international financial movements. Changes in exchange rates alter the prices of one country's goods in terms of the currency of another. In Chapter 19, we learned how major macroeconomic variables such as GDP, prices, and interest rates affect exchange rates. In this chapter, we complete the circle by studying how changes in the exchange rate affect the domestic economy. Then we bring international capital flows into the picture and learn how monetary and fiscal policy work in an **open economy**.

POLICY ISSUE: THE U.S. TRADE DEFICIT

Everybody knows that the United States has been importing much more than it has been exporting in recent years. In 1992, for example, our real imports of Japanese automobiles, Korean textiles, French wine, and other products amounted to $615 billion (in 1987 dollars) while our real exports of wheat, computers, banking services, and the like were just $573 billion—leaving a trade deficit of $42 billion. (See Figure 20–1.)

Naturally, deficits of this magnitude have attracted a great deal of attention not only from economists, but also from politicians, the business community, and the news media. Indeed, during the 1980s America's gaping trade deficit rivalled the federal budget deficit as *the* major economic news story. Some critics argue that the trade deficit illustrates the basic weakness of our national economy—though other observers argue that it actually shows our underlying strength! Many economists worry that, by continually buying more than we sell, America is piling up debts that we will live to regret.

| *F i g u r e* **20–1** | **U.S. NET EXPORTS AND THE VALUE OF THE DOLLAR, 1981–1992** |

Real exports exceeded real imports in the United States in the early 1980s. Since then, however, our imports have exceeded our exports. The largest trade deficits occurred in 1985–1987; since 1986, our trade deficit has mostly been declining. The international value of the dollar rose a great deal in the first half of the 1980s, mostly fell in the second half, and has moved around with little trend so far in the 1990s.

SOURCE: U.S. Bureau of Economic Analysis and Federal Reserve System.

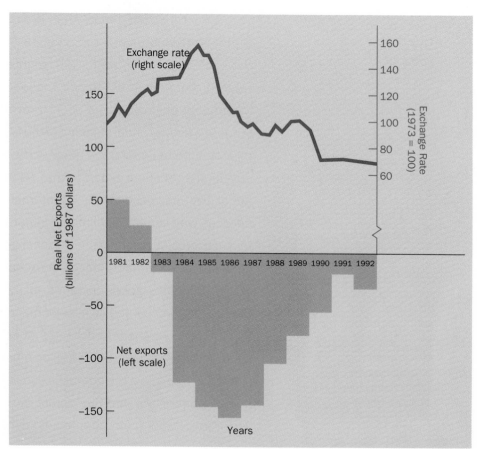

| Figure | 20-2 | THE EFFECTS OF HIGHER NET EXPORTS |

If real exports rise or real imports fall, the economy's aggregate demand curve shifts outward, from D_0D_0 to D_1D_1. Real GDP and the price level both rise as the equilibrium moves from point A to point B.

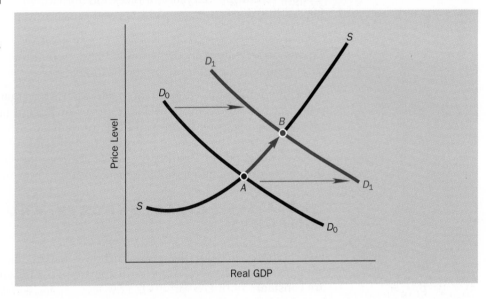

But few people realize that American foreign trade was roughly in balance as recently as a decade ago, as Figure 20–1 shows. And fewer still understand how we came to acquire a chronic trade deficit in so short a time. Lack of knowledge, however, has not prevented these same people from prescribing—and in some cases seeking to legislate—"cures" for our trade problems. By the end of this chapter, you will have a better understanding of the origins and implications of America's trade deficit, and you will be able to make up your own mind about how it can best be cured.

INTERNATIONAL TRADE AND AGGREGATE DEMAND: A QUICK REVIEW

As we know from Part 2 (especially Chapters 8 and 9), a country's net exports, $(X - IM)$, are one component of its aggregate demand, $C + I + G + (X - IM)$. That implies, for example, that an autonomous increase in exports or decrease in imports has a multiplier effect on the economy, just like an increase in consumption, investment, or government purchases.[1] Figure 20–2 depicts this conclusion on an aggregate demand and supply diagram. A rise in net exports shifts the aggregate demand curve outward to the right, thereby raising both GDP and the price level.

But what can make net exports rise? One factor we mentioned in Chapter 8 was a rise in foreign incomes. If foreigners become richer, they are likely to spend more on a wide variety of products, some of which will be American. So America's

---

[1]An appendix to Chapter 9 showed that international trade lowers the numerical value of the multiplier. Nonetheless, autonomous changes in C, I, G, or $(X - IM)$ all have the same multiplier.

exports will rise. Thus Figure 20–2 illustrates the effect on the U.S. economy of a boom in Europe. Similarly, a recession abroad would reduce U.S. exports and hence shift the U.S. aggregate demand curve inward. Thus, as we learned in Chapter 9:

Booms or recessions in one country tend to be transmitted to other countries through international trade in goods and services.

One other important determinant of net exports was mentioned in Chapter 8, but not discussed in depth: the relative prices of foreign and domestic goods. The idea is a simple application of the law of demand: if the prices of the goods of Country X rise, then people everywhere will tend to buy fewer of them—and more of the goods of Country Y. As we shall see shortly, this simple idea holds the key to understanding how exchange rates affect international trade.

RELATIVE PRICES, EXPORTS, AND IMPORTS

First assume—just for this short section—that exchange rates are *fixed*. What happens if the prices of American export goods fall while, say, Japanese prices are constant? With U.S. products now less expensive *relative to Japanese products*, both Japanese and American consumers will probably buy more American goods and fewer Japanese goods. So America's net exports will *rise*, adding to aggregate demand in this country—as shown in Figure 20–2. Conversely, a rise in American prices (relative to Japanese prices) will *decrease* our net exports and aggregate demand. Thus:

For given foreign prices, a fall in the prices of a country's exports will lead to an increase in that country's net exports, and hence to a rise in its real GDP. Analogously, a rise in the prices of a country's exports will decrease that country's net exports and GDP.

Precisely the same logic applies to changes in Japanese prices. If Japanese prices rise, Americans will export more and import less. So $(X - IM)$ will rise, boosting GDP in the United States. Figure 20–2 applies to this case without change. By similar reasoning, falling Japanese prices decrease U.S. net exports and depress our economy. Thus:

Price increases abroad raise a country's net exports and hence its GDP. Price decreases abroad have the opposite effects.

THE EFFECTS OF CHANGES IN EXCHANGE RATES

From here it is a simple matter to figure out how changes in *exchange rates* affect a country's net exports, for currency appreciations or depreciations change international relative prices.

Recall that the basic role of an exchange rate is to convert one country's prices into the currency of another. Table 20–1 uses two examples of U.S.–Japanese trade to remind us of this role. Suppose the dollar depreciates from 150 yen to 120 yen. Then, from the viewpoint of American consumers, a television set that costs ¥60,000 in Japan goes up in price from $400 (that is, 60,000/150) to $500. To Americans, it is just as if TV prices in Japan had risen by 25 percent. Naturally,

	60,000 YEN JAPANESE TV SET		$2000 U.S. HOME COMPUTER	
EXCHANGE RATE	**PRICE IN JAPAN**	**PRICE IN U.S.**	**PRICE IN U.S.**	**PRICE IN JAPAN**
$1 = 150 yen	¥60,000	$400	$2,000	¥300,000
$1 = 120 yen	¥60,000	$500	$2,000	¥240,000

Table 20-1   EXCHANGE RATES AND HOME-CURRENCY PRICES

Americans react by purchasing fewer Japanese products. So American imports go down.

Now consider the implications for Japanese consumers interested in buying American microcomputers that cost $2000. When the dollar falls from 150 yen to 120 yen, they see the price of these computers falling from ¥300,000 (that is, 2,000 × 150) to ¥240,000. To them, it is just as if American producers had offered a 20 percent markdown. Under such circumstances, we expect U.S. sales to the Japanese to rise. So U.S. exports should increase. Putting these two findings together, we conclude that:

A currency depreciation should raise net exports and therefore increase aggregate demand. Conversely, a currency appreciation should reduce net exports and therefore decrease aggregate demand.

For later reference, this conclusion is recorded on an aggregate supply and demand diagram in Figure 20–3. If the currency depreciates, net exports rise and

Figure 20-3   THE EFFECTS OF EXCHANGE RATE CHANGES ON AGGREGATE DEMAND

A depreciation of the exchange rate raises net exports and hence shifts the aggregate demand curve outward to the right, from D_0D_0 to D_1D_1 in the diagram. An appreciation of the currency shifts the aggregate demand curve inward to the left, to D_2D_2. Thus depreciations are expansionary and appreciations are contractionary.

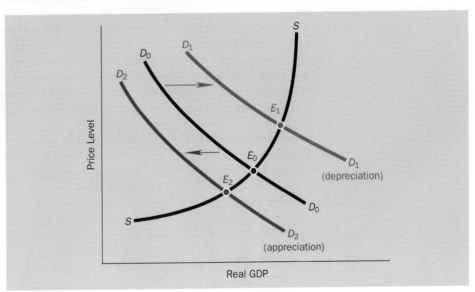

the aggregate demand curve shifts outward from D_0D_0 to D_1D_1. Both prices and output rise as the economy's equilibrium moves from E_0 to E_1. If the currency appreciates, everything operates in reverse: net exports fall, the aggregate demand curve shifts inward to D_2D_2, and both prices and output decline.

Now we are in a position to understand one of the main reasons why the U.S. trade deficit grew so large in the 1980s. Figure 20–1 reminds us that the international value of the dollar soared in the first half of the 1980s. According to the analysis we have just completed, such a stunning appreciation of the dollar should have encouraged U.S. imports, damaged U.S. exports, and been a drag on aggregate demand. That is precisely what happened. In real 1987 dollars, American imports soared by 59 percent between 1981 and 1986, while American exports rose a scant 1 percent. The result is that a $22 billion net export *surplus* in 1981 turned into a $155 billion *deficit* by 1986.

| LAGS IN INTERNATIONAL TRADE AND THE J CURVE [2]

You may have noticed in Figure 20–1 that the highest exchange rate preceded the worst trade deficit. Specifically, the international value of the dollar hit its peak in early 1985; but our trade deficit continued to climb through most of 1986. Something seems wrong here. Since the dollar was falling during most of 1985 and 1986, our analysis predicts that America's net export position should have been improving. Instead, it continued to deteriorate. Why?

Actually, there is nothing wrong with our analysis. It is simply incomplete, for we have failed to note that international trade patterns take time to respond to changes in exchange rates. These lags in international trade give rise to a phenomenon known as the **J curve**. (See Figure 20–4.) The J curve indicates that, following a devaluation or depreciation, a country's trade deficit actually deteriorates for a while (from *A* to *B* in Figure 20–4) before improving (beyond point *B*). Thus a considerable period of time may elapse before any improvement in net exports is apparent. In the U.S. case, net exports first began to turn around late in 1986.

The **J CURVE** shows the typical pattern of response of net exports to a change in currency values. Following a depreciation or a devaluation, net exports usually decline at first and then rise.

To explain the logic of the J curve, let us continue the example of an appreciating yen (depreciating dollar). In the first days and weeks after the yen rises in value, sales of, say, Sony television sets in American stores will be about the same as they were before. But when American stores order more Japanese TV sets to replenish their inventories, they will have to pay more U.S. dollars for each set. Hence our bill for Japanese imports, *when measured in U.S. dollars*, will actually rise.

Similarly, sales of IBM PCs in Japan will initially be about the same; so our exports to Japan will not rise. With imports (measured in dollars) rising and exports unchanged, the balance of trade deteriorates. This is the falling portion of the J curve, from *A* to *B* in Figure 20–4.

Pretty soon, however, American consumers will start reacting to the fact that Sony televisions now cost $500 instead of $400. Their purchases will fall. After some further delay, U.S. retail establishments will reduce their orders from Sony and begin ordering more American TVs instead. At this point, U.S. imports from Japan start to fall. On the other side of the Pacific, Japanese consumers will begin

---

[2]This section can be deleted in shorter courses.

F i g u r e **20–4** **THE J CURVE**

The response of a country's net exports to a decline in the value of its currency tends to follow a J-shaped pattern. In the period immediately following the depreciation or devaluation, everyone imports and exports about the same volume of goods as they did before. But imports cost more in terms of home currency, so net exports decline. This is the descending portion of the J curve, from point *A* to point *B*. After a while, however, imports decline and exports rise, so net exports improve. This is the rising portion of the curve, beyond point *B*.

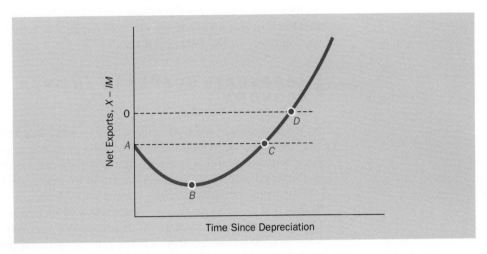

reacting to the fact that $2000 IBM computers now cost fewer yen. So U.S. exports to Japan start to rise. We are now on the rising portion of the J curve. But it takes some time (until point *C* in Figure 20–4) before trade patterns change enough to improve America's trade position with Japan.[3]

Some illustrative numbers will clarify the arithmetic behind the J curve. Suppose that, when the dollar was worth 150 yen, the United States was importing 1 million TV sets at $400 each and exporting 150,000 computers at $2000 each. Then the dollar value of our imports was $400 million and the dollar value of our exports was $300 million, leading to a trade deficit with Japan of $100 million.

Now the dollar depreciates to 120 yen and the dollar price of Japanese TVs rises to $500 (see Table 20–1). At first, purchases are unchanged; so our import bill for the 1 million Japanese TVs increases to $500 million. With exports remaining at $300 million, our trade deficit balloons to $200 million. We are on the downward portion of the J, between *A* and *B* in Figure 20–4.

After some time, however, Americans curtail their purchase of Japanese TVs and the Japanese buy more American computers. For the sake of concreteness, suppose that we now import 800,000 TVs and export 200,000 computers. At a price of $500 each, our TV imports cost $400 million. At a price of $2000 each, our computer exports earn us $400 million. Thus our trade with Japan is now balanced. In terms of Figure 20–4, we have reached point *D*.

Applying the J-curve analysis to U.S. experience in the 1980s is no easy matter. For one thing, the dollar did not decline all at once, but rather in stages beginning

[3]Actually, improvement occurs only if consumers in the two countries are sufficiently responsive to price changes. The changes in export and import volumes must be large enough to offset the fact that Japanese goods now cost more dollars.

in early 1985. Each depreciation set in motion its own little J curve, forming a complex pattern. For another, American firms seemed reluctant to cut their yen prices when the dollar fell, preferring to bolster their profit margins. And Japanese firms seemed even more reluctant to raise their dollar prices, preferring to maintain their market shares despite falling profit margins. Nonetheless, there is no doubt that the J curve goes a long way toward explaining why U.S. net exports responded so sluggishly to the falling dollar.

AGGREGATE SUPPLY IN AN OPEN ECONOMY

So we have concluded that, after some (possibly long) delay, a currency depreciation increases aggregate demand while a currency appreciation decreases it. To complete our model of macroeconomics in an open economy, we must now turn to the implications of international trade for *aggregate supply*.

Part of the story is familiar. As we know from previous chapters, the United States, like all economies, purchases some of its productive inputs from abroad. Oil is only the most prominent example. We also rely on foreign suppliers for various metals (like titanium), many raw agricultural products (like coffee beans), and thousands of other items that are used by American industry. When the dollar depreciates, these imported inputs become more costly in terms of U.S. dollars—just as if foreign prices had risen.

The consequence is clear: with imported inputs more expensive, American firms will be forced to charge higher prices at any given level of output. Graphically, this means that *the aggregate supply curve will shift inward* (to the left).

When the dollar depreciates and the prices of foreign goods rise, the U.S. aggregate supply curve will shift inward, pushing up the prices of American-made goods and services. By exactly analogous reasoning, an appreciation of the dollar will make imported goods cheaper and shift the U.S. aggregate supply curve *outward*, thus pushing American prices down. (See Figure 37–5.)

Beyond this, a depreciating dollar has further inflationary effects that do not show up on the aggregate demand and supply diagram. Most obviously, prices of imported goods are included in American price indexes like the Consumer Price Index (CPI). So when dollar prices of Japanese cars, French wine, and Swiss watches increase, the CPI goes up even if no American price rises. For this and other reasons, the inflationary impact of a dollar depreciation is even greater than that indicated by Figure 20–5.[4]

THE MACROECONOMIC EFFECTS OF EXCHANGE RATES

Let us now put aggregate demand and aggregate supply together and study the macroeconomic effects of changes in exchange rates.

First suppose that the international value of the dollar falls. Referring back to Figures 20–3 and 20–5, we see that this will shift the aggregate demand curve *outward* and the aggregate supply curve *inward*. The result, as Figure 20–6 shows,

---

[4]The diagram should be interpreted as showing the effects of currency depreciations and appreciations on the prices of *domestically-produced* goods.

THE EFFECTS OF EXCHANGE RATE CHANGES ON AGGREGATE SUPPLY

A depreciation of the currency pushes the aggregate supply curve inward, from S_0S_0 to S_1S_1 in the diagram, and is therefore inflationary. A currency appreciation has a deflationary effect because it pushes the aggregate supply curve outward, from S_0S_0 to S_2S_2.

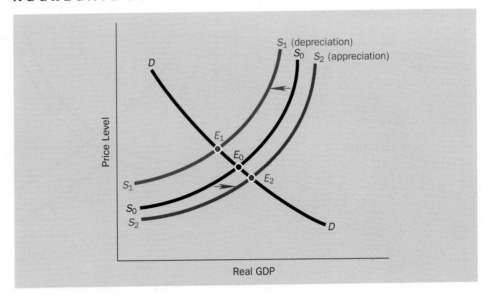

is that the U.S. price level certainly rises. Whether real GDP rises or falls depends on whether the supply or demand shift is the dominant influence. The evidence strongly suggests that aggregate *demand* shifts are usually more important, so we expect GDP to rise. Hence:

A currency depreciation is inflationary and probably also expansionary.

THE EFFECTS OF A CURRENCY DEPRECIATION

If the currency depreciates, aggregate demand increases because net exports are stimulated and aggregate supply decreases because imported inputs become more expensive. Prices rise as equilibrium moves from point *E* to point *A*. If the demand shift is the more important influence, output increases, too.

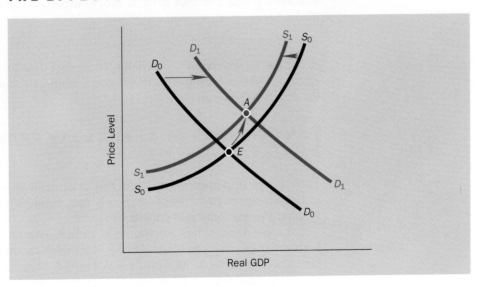

Figure 20-7 **THE EFFECTS OF A CURRENCY APPRECIATION**

If the currency appreciates, aggregate demand declines because net exports fall and aggregate supply increases because imported inputs become cheaper. Prices fall as equilibrium moves from point *E* to point *B*. If the demand shift is the more important influence, output also falls.

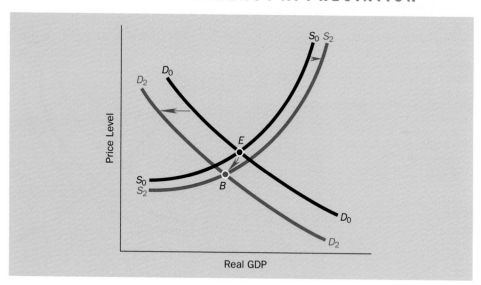

What is the intuitive explanation for this result? When the dollar falls, foreign goods become more expensive to Americans. That is directly inflationary. At the same time, aggregate demand in the United States is stimulated by rising net exports. As long as the expansion of demand outweighs the adverse shift of the aggregate supply curve brought on by the depreciation, real GDP should rise.

Now let's reverse things. Suppose the dollar *appreciates*. In this case, net exports *fall* so the aggregate demand curve shifts *inward*. At the same time, foreign goods become cheaper, so the aggregate supply curve shifts *outward*. (See Figure 20–7.) Once again, we can be sure of the movement of the price level: it falls. Output also falls if the demand shift is more important than the supply shift, as is likely. Thus:

A currency appreciation is certainly disinflationary and is probably contractionary.

In the rest of the chapter, we shall assume that the effect of the exchange rate on aggregate *demand* dominates its effect on aggregate *supply*, because that is what the evidence suggests.

THE EFFECTS OF CHANGES IN EXCHANGE RATES

There is one important piece left in our international economic puzzle. We have analyzed international trade in goods and services rather fully, but we have ignored international movements of *capital*.

For some nations, this omission is of little consequence because they are rarely involved in international capital flows. But things are quite different for the United States, whose dollar is the world's major international currency. The vast majority of international financial flows involve either the buying or selling of assets whose values are stated in dollars. Fortunately, given what we have just learned about the effects of exchange rates, it is easy to add international capital flows to our analysis.

Recall from Chapter 19 that interest-rate differentials and capital flows are typically the most important determinants of exchange rate movements in the short run. Specifically, suppose interest rates in the United States rise while foreign interest rates remain unchanged. We learned in Chapter 19 that this will attract capital to the United States and cause the dollar to appreciate. This chapter has taught us that an appreciating dollar, in turn, will reduce net exports, prices, and output in the U.S.—as indicated in Figure 20–7. Thus:

A rise in interest rates tends to contract the economy by appreciating the currency and reducing net exports.

Notice that this conclusion has a familiar ring. In Chapter 13, while studying how monetary policy works, we observed that higher interest rates deter investment spending and hence reduce the I component of $C + I + G + (X - IM)$. Now, in studying an open economy with international capital flows, we see that higher interest rates also reduce the $(X - IM)$ component. Thus *international capital flows strengthen the negative effects of interest rates on aggregate demand.*

If interest rates in the United States fall, or if those abroad rise, everything we have just said is turned in the opposite direction. There is no need to repeat the analysis. The conclusion is:[5]

A decline in interest rates tends to expand the economy by depreciating the exchange rate and raising net exports.

FISCAL POLICY IN AN OPEN ECONOMY

Now we are ready to use our model to study how fiscal and monetary policy work when the exchange rate is floating and capital is internationally mobile. Doing so will teach us how international economic relations modify the effects of stabilization policies. Fortunately, no new theoretical apparatus is necessary; we only need remember what we have learned in the chapter up to this point. Specifically:

- A rise in the domestic interest rate leads to capital inflows and makes the exchange rate appreciate. A fall in the domestic interest rate leads to capital outflows and makes the exchange rate depreciate.

- A currency appreciation reduces aggregate demand and raises aggregate supply (see Figure 20–7). A currency depreciation raises aggregate demand and reduces aggregate supply (see Figure 20–6).

With this in mind, suppose the government cuts taxes or raises spending. Aggregate demand increases, which pushes up both real GDP and the price level in the usual manner. This is shown as the shift from D_0D_0 to blue line D_1D_1 in Figure 20–8. In a **closed economy**, that is the end of the story. But in an *open* economy with international capital flows, we must add in the macroeconomic effects of an increase in the exchange rate. We do this in two steps.

A **CLOSED ECONOMY** is one that does not trade with other nations in either goods or assets.

---

[5]EXERCISE: Provide the reasoning behind this conclusion.

| Figure | **20-8** | **A FISCAL EXPANSION IN AN OPEN ECONOMY** |

A fiscal expansion pushes the aggregate demand outward, from D_0D_0 to D_1D_1 in the diagram. But it also raises interest rates, which attracts international capital and appreciates the currency. The currency appreciation, in turn, reduces aggregate demand and raises aggregate supply— as shown by the brown curves S_2S_2 and D_2D_2. The result is that equilibrium occurs at point C rather than at point B. Output and prices both rise less than they would in a closed economy.

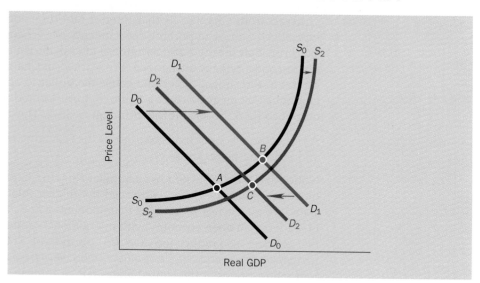

First, why will the exchange rate rise? We know from earlier chapters that a fiscal expansion pushes up interest rates—a fact that is sure to be noticed in international financial markets. At higher interest rates, American securities become more attractive to foreign investors, who go to the foreign exchange market to buy dollars for use in purchasing American securities. This buying pressure drives up the value of the dollar.

Second, what are the effects of a higher dollar? As we know, when the dollar rises in value, American goods become more expensive abroad and foreign goods become cheaper here. So exports fall and imports rise. The $(X - IM)$ component of aggregate demand therefore falls. The fiscal expansion thus winds up increasing both America's *capital account surplus* (by attracting foreign capital) and *current account deficit* (by reducing net exports). In fact, the two must rise by equal amounts because, under floating exchange rates, it is always true that:[6]

current account surplus + capital account surplus = 0.

Since a fiscal expansion leads in this way to a trade deficit, many economists believe that the U.S. trade deficit of the 1980s was a side-effect of the large tax cuts made early in the decade. We will come back to that issue shortly.

But first note that the induced rise in the dollar will shift the aggregate supply curve *outward* and the aggregate demand curve *inward*, as we saw in Figure 20–7. Figure 20–8 adds these two shifts (in brown) to the effect of the original fiscal expansion (in blue). The final equilibrium in an open economy is point C, whereas in a closed economy it would be point B. By comparing points B and C, we can see how international linkages change the picture of fiscal policy that we painted in Part 3.

---

[6]If you need review, turn back to Chapter 19, pages 472–74.

There are two main differences. First, a rising exchange rate offsets part of the inflationary effect of a fiscal expansion by making imports cheaper. Second, a rising exchange rate reduces the expansionary effect on real GDP by reducing $(X - IM)$. Here we have a new kind of "crowding out," different from the one we studied in Chapter 15. There we learned that an increase in G, by raising interest rates, will crowd out some private investment spending. Here a rise in G, by raising interest rates and the exchange rate, crowds out *net exports*. But the effect is the same: the fiscal multiplier is reduced. Thus, we conclude that:

International capital flows reduce the power of fiscal policy.

Table 20–2 suggests that this new international variety of crowding out was much more important than the traditional type of crowding out in the early 1980s. Between 1981 and 1986, the share of investment in GDP actually *increased* slightly (from 16.4 percent to 16.7 percent) despite the rise in the shares of both consumer spending and government purchases. Only the share of net exports, $(X - IM)$, fell—from 0.6 percent to −3.5 percent.

This was an important lesson that American economists learned in the 1980s. In 1980, many economists worried that large government budget deficits would crowd out private investment. By the end of the decade, most were more concerned that deficits were crowding out net exports. Similarly, when the Clinton administration announced its five-year deficit reduction program in February 1993, the expected benefits were split between higher investment and a smaller trade deficit.

MONETARY POLICY IN AN OPEN ECONOMY

Now let us consider how monetary policy works in an open economy with floating exchange rates and international capital mobility. To remain consistent with the history of the 1980s, we consider a tightening, rather than a loosening, of monetary policy.

As we know from earlier chapters, contractionary monetary policy reduces aggregate demand, which lowers both Y and P. This is shown in Figure 20–9 by the shift from D_0D_0 to blue line D_1D_1, and it looks like the exact opposite of a fiscal expansion. Without international capital flows, that would be the end of the story.

But, in the presence of internationally mobile capital, we must think through the consequences for interest rates and exchange rates. We know from previous chapters that a monetary contraction raises interest rates, just like a fiscal expansion. Hence tighter money attracts foreign capital into the United States in search of

T a b l e **20–2**	PERCENTAGE SHARES OF REAL GDP IN THE UNITED STATES: 1981 AND 1986			
YEAR	**C**	**I**	**G**	**X − IM**
1981	64.5%	16.4%	18.5%	0.6%
1986	67.4%	16.7%	19.4%	−3.5%
Change	+2.9	+0.3	+0.9	−4.1

| *F i g u r e* **20-9** | **A MONETARY CONTRACTION IN AN OPEN ECONOMY** |

A monetary contraction pulls the aggregate demand inward, from D_0D_0 to D_1D_1, just like a fiscal contraction. But it raises, rather than lowers, interest rates, which leads to international capital inflows and a currency appreciation. The appreciation decreases net exports and therefore reduces aggregate demand— which shifts inward from D_1D_1 to D_2D_2. But it also reduces foreign prices and raises aggregate supply—as indicated by the shift from S_0S_0 to S_2S_2. The result is that output and prices both fall more in an open economy (point *C*) than they would in a closed economy (point *B*).

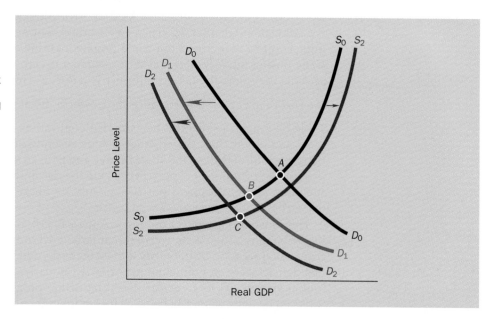

higher rates of return. The exchange rate rises. The appreciating dollar encourages imports and discourages exports; so $(X - IM)$ falls. America therefore winds up with capital flowing in (a surplus on capital account) and an increase in its trade deficit. This time, as you will notice from Figure 20–9:

International capital flows increase the power of monetary policy.

Why do capital flows *strengthen* monetary policy but *weaken* fiscal policy? The answer lies in their effects on interest rates. The main international repercussion of either a fiscal *expansion* or a monetary *contraction* is to raise interest rates and the exchange rate, thereby crowding out net exports. But that means that the initial effects of a fiscal expansion on aggregate demand are *weakened* while the initial effects of a monetary contraction are *strengthened*.

INTERNATIONAL ASPECTS OF REAGANOMICS

This completes our theoretical analysis of the macroeconomics of open economies. Now let us put the theory through its paces by applying it to the changes in U.S. macroeconomic policy in the early 1980s. In the process, we will see that Reaganomics had important international implications that we did not mention in Part 3.

In broadest outline, the early years of the Reagan administration witnessed a dramatic change in the policy mix toward tighter money and much easier fiscal policy. The Federal Reserve's tight monetary policy was already in place when President Reagan was elected; the new administration simply encouraged the Fed to persevere. The expansionary fiscal policy was mainly the result of the tax cuts of 1981–1984, which led to large and persistent federal budget deficits.

Table 20–3 indicates what the theory predicts should have happened under such circumstances. Look first at column 1. We have just concluded that a fiscal expansion should raise real interest rates, make the dollar appreciate, raise real GDP, and be less inflationary than normal because of the rising dollar. This information is recorded by entering + signs for increases and − signs for decreases.

Similarly, our analysis of a monetary contraction says that the tight money component of Reaganomics should have raised real interest rates, made the dollar appreciate, reduced real GDP, and been more disinflationary than usual because of the rising dollar. All this is recorded in column 2.

Column 3 puts the two pieces together. We conclude that the policy mix of fiscal expansion and monetary contraction should have raised interest rates strongly, pushed the value of the dollar up dramatically, and devastated our foreign trade. But its effects on output and inflation are uncertain; the balance depends on whether fiscal expansion overwhelmed monetary contraction or vice-versa.

How well do these predictions square with the facts? Let us take them one at a time. We know from Figure 20–1 that the international value of the dollar soared—rising about 80 percent from its low in mid-1980 to its high in early 1985—and that American foreign trade was clobbered. Real net exports fell from about +$22 billion in 1981 to about −$155 billion in 1986—a swing of $177 billion in just five years. These two facts are just what the theory predicts.

What about interest rates? Figure 20–10 shows an estimate of the real interest rate on long-term U.S. government bonds from 1978 to 1990. (The historic norm for this rate is between 2 and 3 percent.) The real rate of interest rose dramatically between the time of the 1980 election campaign and the time the Reagan economic program was enacted into law (September 1981). It then fell during the 1982 recession, but rose again to very high levels in mid-1984. Again, this is in accord with the theory: except for a brief recessionary interlude, the policy changes raised real interest rates.

What about real GDP? The U.S. economy suffered through a severe recession in 1981–1982. However, it then rebounded strongly and grew steadily for the remainder of the decade. To appraise the effects of Reaganomics on real output, we must consider a longer time frame. If we take the full eight-year period from 1981 to 1989, the average annual growth rate of real GDP was 2.9 percent. Since

T a b l e **20–3**	**EXPECTED EFFECTS OF POLICY**		
VARIABLE	**(1)** **FISCAL EXPANSION**	**(2)** **MONETARY CONTRACTION**	**(3)** **REAGONOMICS**
Real interest rate	+	+	+
Exchange rate	+	+	+
Net exports	−	−	−
Real GDP	+	−	?
Inflation	+	−	?

F i g u r e **20-10** **REAL INTEREST RATES IN THE UNITED STATES, 1978–1990**

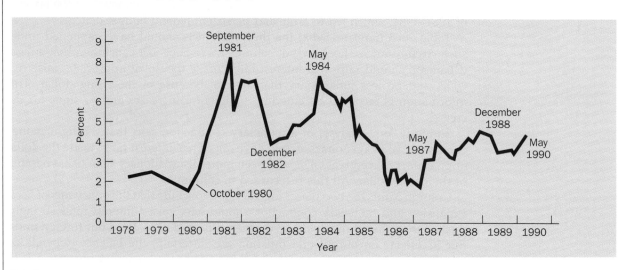

This figure charts the behavior of the real interest rate on ten-year U.S. government bonds on the basis of a survey of inflationary expectations. It rises steeply in 1980–1981.

SOURCE: Richard B. Hoey.

this is just a bit below the average growth rate achieved during the preceding 20 years, the conclusion seems to be that the monetary contraction and fiscal expansion combined had little net effect on the growth rate of aggregate demand.

If this is so, that would leave only the supply shifts caused by the appreciating dollar. Figures 20–8 and 20–9 show that both fiscal expansions and monetary contractions *increase* aggregate supply by appreciating the currency. The rising dollar certainly helped slow inflation in the early 1980s by holding down the prices of imported inputs. In addition, the fact that the deep recession came early in President Reagan's term of office meant that the economy had a recessionary gap throughout the 1981–1986 period. Finally, as we saw in earlier chapters, energy prices were falling rapidly. Each of these factors played a role in the rapid disinflation.

THE LINK BETWEEN THE BUDGET DEFICIT AND THE TRADE DEFICIT

If the good news of the 1980s was the rapid decline in inflation, the bad news was the alarming deterioration of America's foreign trade position. We have already suggested that changes in the monetary–fiscal policy mix were largely responsible for the U.S. trade deficit. But to see the connection between the budget deficit and the trade deficit most clearly, we need to recall two simple pieces of arithmetic.

The first begins with the familiar equilibrium condition for GDP in an open economy:

$$Y = C + I + G + (X - IM).$$

Since GDP can either be spent, saved, or taxed away:

$$Y = C + S + T.^{7}$$

Equating these two expressions for Y gives:

$$C + I + G + (X - IM) = C + S + T.$$

Finally, subtracting C from both sides, and bringing terms involving the government to the lefthand side and terms involving the private sector to the right leads to an accounting relationship between the budget deficit and the trade deficit:

$$G - T = (S - I) - (X - IM).$$

In words, the government budget deficit, $G - T$, must be equal to the surplus of savings over investment plus the trade deficit, $- (X - IM)$.

This result may seem mechanical and not particularly interesting, but our second piece of arithmetic will bring out both the common sense behind this equation and its importance for understanding recent events.

As we have noted repeatedly, under floating exchange rates any deficit or surplus in the current account must be balanced by an equal and opposite surplus or deficit in the capital account. Thus, the current account *deficit*, which is $-(X - IM)$ in the previous equation, can be replaced by the capital account *surplus* to get:

$$G - T = (S - I) + \text{Net capital inflows.}$$

This last equation makes an obvious point. If the U.S. government runs a budget deficit $(G - T)$, that deficit must be financed either by an excess of saving over investment by American businesses and individuals $(S - I)$, or by borrowing from foreigners.

But what is the economic mechanism that makes the trade deficit follow the government budget deficit? There is no mystery. To attract the foreign capital that we must borrow, America must offer interest rates higher than those available abroad. As capital flows into the United States, the value of the dollar rises. And the more costly dollar leads to a larger trade deficit. Thus the adjustments of interest rates and exchange rates that we have been discussing are precisely the way a budget deficit leads to a trade deficit.

Our equation suggests a tight connection between the two deficits. Let us see how things worked out in the case of Reaganomics. Since the Reagan tax cuts led to a large budget deficit, the United States could have avoided a large trade deficit only by saving much more or investing much less. The latter is not a very appealing option and, in any case, generous business tax cuts shielded investment spending from the ravages of high real interest rates. As we saw in Table 20–2, the investment share of GDP hardly changed.

---

[7] If you do not see why, recall that GDP equals disposable income (DI) plus taxes (T), $Y = DI + T$, and that disposable income can either be consumed or saved, $DI = C + S$. These two definitions together imply that $Y = C + S + T$.

That leaves saving. Supply-siders did indeed promise that the tax cuts would raise savings by extraordinary amounts. Had their promises been redeemed, the budget deficit need not have caused a trade deficit. But they were not. With S not rising and I not falling, our fundamental equation leaves only one possibility: a rise in $G - T$ must be reflected in a fall in $(X - IM)$. The government budget deficit thus led to a massive trade deficit.

IS THE TRADE DEFICIT A PROBLEM?

The preceding explanation suggests that America's large trade deficit is a symptom of a deeper trouble: the nation as a whole—including our government—has been spending more than it is producing and has been forced to borrow the difference from foreigners. The trade deficit is just the mirror image of the required capital inflows. Why do we worry about this? Because these capital inflows create debts on which interest and principal payments will have to be made in the future. Thus, on this view, Americans since the 1980s have been mortgaging their future to finance higher consumer spending.

But there is another, quite different, interpretation of the trade deficit. Suppose foreign investors in the 1980s began to see the United States as a much more attractive place to invest their capital. Then capital would have flowed in not because America needed to borrow it, but because foreigners were eager to lend it. In that case, the trade deficit would still be the mirror image of the capital inflows. But it would now signify America's economic strength, not its weakness.

The policy implications of these two views differ dramatically. The first view suggests that we should strive to reduce the trade deficit and, thereby, our need for foreign borrowing. The second view suggests that we should welcome the capital inflows and, therefore, not worry about the trade deficit. Which view is right?

The answer is in dispute. However, most economists ascribe to the first view—that the trade deficit is a problem, not a prize. At least two pieces of evidence persuade them. First, real interest rates in the 1980s were generally high, not low. This suggests that America was forced to pay high interest rates to attract the capital it needed, not that foreigners suddenly decided that America was the place to invest. Second, as we saw in Table 20–2, it was the *consumption* share of GDP, not the *investment* share, that rose between 1981 and 1986. This suggests that America was borrowing to finance a consumption binge, not an investment boom.

ON CURING THE TRADE DEFICIT

We now understand how the United States acquired its massive twin deficits and became the world's most indebted nation. And we have explained why many economists think the trade deficit is a problem. Next comes the hard question that we raised at the beginning of the chapter: What can be done about it? How can we cure our foreign trade problem and end our addiction to foreign borrowing?

The answer, of course, is highly controversial—and the controversies predate the presidency of Bill Clinton. Both economists and politicians disagree over the appropriate course of action. The best we can do here is outline some alternatives.

1. *Change the Mix of Fiscal and Monetary Policy:* The fundamental equation:

$$G - T = (S - I) - (X - IM)$$

suggests a *reduction in the budget deficit* as one good way to reduce the trade deficit. According to the analysis in this chapter, a reduction in G or an increase in T would lead to lower real interest rates in the United States, a depreciating dollar and, eventually, to a shrinking trade deficit.

This is the route that American economists have been urging for years. And, as a matter of fact, the dollar has come down considerably since the mid-1980s, and so has our trade deficit. However, partisan political bickering over how best to reduce the budget deficit made progress on this front agonizingly slow until President Clinton pushed through a comprehensive deficit-reduction plan in 1993.

When the government curtails its spending or raises taxes to reduce its budget deficit, aggregate demand falls. If we do not want deficit reduction to cause an economic contraction in the United States, we must therefore compensate for it by monetary stimulus. Like contractionary fiscal policy, expansionary monetary policy lowers interest rates, depreciates the dollar, and should therefore help reduce the trade deficit.

American policymakers have been pursuing this policy for years. Interest rates have generally been falling since mid-1984 (see Figure 20–10). In the late 1980s, however, the Fed became concerned about the possible inflationary consequences of easy money (and of the falling dollar) and grew more cautious. But when recession began in 1990, the Fed eased up again and interest rates fell.

Notice that these two remedies, in combination, amount to undoing the Reaganomics policy mix of tight money and loose budgets. Between 1980 and 1984, the United States experienced a monetary contraction followed by a fiscal expansion. What we have needed ever since to cure the trade deficit, according to many economists, is precisely the reverse: a monetary expansion coupled with a fiscal contraction. To some extent, this is the policy mix inherent in Clintonomics.

2. *More Rapid Economic Growth Abroad:* If foreign economies grew faster, residents of these countries would buy more American goods. That would raise American exports and reduce our trade deficit. Since the mid-1980s, the United States has been urging our major trading partners to stimulate their economies and to open their markets more to American goods—but with modest success. At first, foreign countries rightly asked why they should tailor their economic policies to America's needs. But more recently, with the European and Japanese economies slumping, domestic needs in those countries have also called for more expansionary policies.

3. *Raise Domestic Savings or Reduce Domestic Investment:* Our fundamental equation calls attention to two other routes to a smaller trade deficit: higher savings or lower investment.

U.S. personal saving rates have been near all-time lows in recent years. If Americans would save more, we could finance more of our government budget deficit at home and therefore would not need to borrow so much abroad. This, too, would lead to a cheaper dollar and a smaller trade deficit. The only trouble is that no one has yet found a reliable way to induce

Saving Patterns and Trade Deficits: The Arithmetic of U.S.–Japanese Economic Relations

The huge U.S. trade deficit with Japan is a significant source of friction between the two countries and has led to frequent calls for protectionist measures here. Our fundamental equation,

$$G - T = (S - I) - (X - IM),$$

teaches us that part of the problem traces to different saving habits in the two countries. The Japanese people are among the biggest savers in the world. So $S - I$ is a large positive number in Japan. Furthermore, unlike the U.S. government, the Japanese government has a budget surplus. It therefore follows that, in order to balance the international books, Japan must generate a large trade *surplus*.

The contrast between the United States and Japan in this regard is marked. While the Japanese people and government together are big net *savers*, the American people and government together are big net *borrowers*. In an integrated world financial system, it is therefore natural that the Japanese should be lending to us. In short, Japan should have capital *outflows* and we should have capital *inflows*—which is just what has

been happening in recent years. Remembering that:

current account surplus +
    capital account surplus = 0

the implication is that Japan should have a current account *surplus*, and we should have a current account *deficit*.

Once again this is only natural. In fact, the United States has had a trade deficit with Japan for a long time—even when our overall trade position and Japan's were nearly balanced. Being an island nation almost devoid of natural resources, Japan must run huge trade deficits in primary products. Much of this trade is with developing countries. To offset this trade deficit in primary products, Japan needs a surplus in trade in manufactured goods. And who are likely to be the leading customers for these goods? The biggest consumers on earth, of course—the Americans.

So it is natural for the United States to run a bilateral deficit in trading goods with Japan. However, that does not imply that an annual deficit of $50 billion or more is appropriate, nor that the Japanese are blameless. In fact, Japan has long been among the most

protectionist of all the advanced industrial nations. Some of this protectionism takes the form of high tariffs and stiff quotas. But most is more subtle, coming instead through a variety of bureaucratic regulations that make importing difficult. So one possible solution to the U.S.–Japan trade problem is to persuade Japan to open its markets more. And the Clinton administration, like the Bush and Reagan administrations before it, is engaging the Japanese in talks on this subject. But no one really thinks that, even in a completely free market, we could sell in Japan nearly as much as they sell here.

Macroeconomic policy might be a more effective tool. Look once again at the fundamental equation:

$$G - T = (S - I) - (X - IM).$$

If Japan stimulated its economy by more expansionary fiscal policy, $G - T$ would rise and $(X - IM)$ would fall. If, at the same time, the United States reduced its budget deficit, $G - T$ would fall here and $(X - IM)$ would rise. In all likelihood, our bilateral trade deficit with Japan would narrow. That is precisely the "deal" that the two countries are trying to work out now.

Americans to save more. A variety of tax incentives for saving has been tried, and more are suggested every year. But there is not much evidence that these incentives have worked. We seem to be a nation of consumers.

If the other cures for our trade deficit fail to work in time, the trade deficit may cure itself in a particularly unpleasant way: by dramatically reducing U.S. domestic investment. Let us see how this might work. As our trade deficits and foreign borrowing persist, foreigners wind up holding more and more U.S. dollar assets. At some point, their willingness to acquire yet more dollar assets will begin to wear thin, and they will start charging us much higher interest rates. At best, higher interest rates lead to lower investment in the United States. At worst, foreigners cease lending to the United States, interest rates skyrocket, and we experience a severe recession. A recession, of course, would reduce our trade deficit substantially by curbing our appetite for imports. But it is a painful cure.

4. *Protectionism:* We have saved the worst remedy for last. One seemingly obvious way to cure our trade deficit is to limit imports by imposing stiff tariffs, strict quotas, and other protectionist devices. We discussed protectionism, and the reasons why almost all economists oppose it, in Chapter 18. Despite the economic arguments against it, protectionism has an undeniable political allure. It seems, superficially, to "save American jobs." And it conveniently shifts the blame for our trade problems onto foreigners.

In addition to depriving us and other countries of the benefits of comparative advantage, there are reasons why protectionism might not even succeed in reducing our trade deficit. One is that other nations might retaliate. If we erect trade barriers to reduce our imports, IM will fall. But if foreign countries erect corresponding barriers to our exports, X will fall, too. On balance, our *net* exports, $(X - IM)$, may or may not improve. However, world trade will surely suffer. This is a game that may have no winners, only losers.

Even if other nations do not retaliate, tariffs and quotas may not improve our trade deficit much. Why? If they succeed in reducing American spending on imports, tariffs and quotas will thereby reduce the supply of dollars on the world market. That would push the value of the dollar up. A rising dollar, of course, would hurt U.S. exports and encourage more imports. The fundamental equation,

$$G - T = (S - I) - (X - IM),$$

reminds us that protectionism can raise $(X - IM)$ only if it reduces the budget deficit, raises saving, or reduces investment.[8]

CONCLUSION: WE ARE NOT ALONE

We do indeed live in a world economy. The major trading nations of the world are linked by exports and imports, by capital flows, and by exchange rates. What happens to national income, prices, and interest rates in one country affects other nations.

Thus policymakers in Europe, Asia, and South America keep a watchful eye on developments in the U.S. economy. If the U.S. economy expands, these other countries have better markets for their exports. If we pursue policies that make the dollar depreciate, they find their currencies appreciating. If interest rates rise in the United States, they see capital flowing out of their countries into ours. Some observers think that, as the "big guy on the block," America bears a special responsibility for the health of the world economy.

---

[8]Here tariffs, which raise revenue for the government, have a clear advantage over quotas, which do not.

But we are not the *only* big guys on the block. Japan is also a giant economy with profound effects on the rest of the world. And, once fully unified, the European Economic Community will make Western Europe the biggest economy of all. What happens in Europe, Japan, and elsewhere often has important effects on the U.S. economy.

That the major economies of the world are linked suggests the need for greater policy coordination among nations. But since the national interests of particular countries often differ, countries are understandably reluctant to surrender any of their sovereignty. Hence international policy coordination remains an elusive goal. Economically speaking, we all live in one world. Politically, however, we live in a world of separate nation-states.

Summary

1. The nations of the world are linked together economically because national income, prices, and interest rates in one country affect those in another. They are thus **open economies**.

2. Because one country's **imports** are another country's **exports**, rapid (or sluggish) economic growth in one country contributes to rapid (or sluggish) growth in other countries.

3. A country's **net exports** depend on whether its prices are high or low relative to those of other countries. Since exchange rates translate one country's prices into the currencies of other countries, the **exchange rate** is a key determinant of net exports.

4. If the currency depreciates, net exports rise and aggregate demand increases, thereby raising both real GDP and the price level. A depreciating currency also reduces aggregate supply by making imported inputs more costly.

5. If the currency appreciates, net exports fall and aggregate demand, real GDP, and the price level all decrease. But an appreciating currency also increases aggregate supply by making imported inputs cheaper.

6. Because there are lags in international trade, net exports follow a **J-curve** pattern after a currency depreciation; that is, the **trade deficit** gets worse before it gets better.

7. **International capital flows** respond strongly to interest rate differentials among countries. Hence higher domestic interest rates lead to currency **appreciations**, and lower interest rates lead to **depreciations**.

8. Contractionary monetary policies raise interest rates and therefore make the currency appreciate. Both the higher interest rates and the dearer currency reduce aggregate demand. Hence international capital flows make monetary policy more powerful than it would be in a **closed economy**.

9. Expansionary fiscal policies also raise interest rates and make the currency appreciate. But, in this case, the international repercussions cancel out part of the demand-expanding effects of the policies. Hence international capital flows make fiscal policy less powerful than it would be in a closed economy.

10. Since Reaganomics in the early 1980s combined tight money with highly expansionary fiscal policy, it raised interest rates, pushed the dollar up, and caused a large trade deficit in the United States.

11. **Budget deficits and trade deficits** are linked by the fundamental equation $G - T = (S - I) - (X - IM)$. This also implies that the budget deficit equals the sum of $S - I$ + capital inflows.

12. It follows from this equation that the U.S. trade deficit must be cured by some combination of lower budget deficits, higher savings, and lower investment.

13. A change in the policy mix toward easier monetary policy and smaller budget deficits is one way to reduce the U.S. trade deficit without contracting the U.S. economy.

14. Protectionist policies might not cure the U.S. trade deficit because (a) they will cause the dollar to appreciate and (b) they may provoke foreign retaliation.

15. International coordination of economic policies is important. But it is also elusive in a world of sovereign nations.

Key Concepts and Terms

Exports
Imports
Net exports
Closed economy
Open economy

Exchange rate
Appreciation
Depreciation
Trade deficit

J curve
International capital flows
Budget deficits and trade deficits
$G - T = (S - I) - (X - IM)$

Questions for Review

1. For years, the U.S. government has been trying to get Japan to expand its economy faster. Explain how more rapid growth in Japan would affect the U.S. economy.

2. If inflation is higher in Germany than in France, and the exchange rate between the two countries is fixed, what is likely to happen to the balance of trade between the two countries?

3. Explain why a currency depreciation leads to an improvement in a country's trade balance. If there is a "J curve," what happens in the short run? Why?

4. Explain why American fiscal policy is less powerful and American monetary policy is more powerful than indicated in the closed-economy model of Part 3.

5. Use an aggregate supply–demand diagram to analyze the effects of a currency appreciation.

6. Explain why $G - T = (S - I) - (X - IM)$.

7. Given what you now know, do you think it was a good idea for the United States to adopt a policy mix of tight money and large government budget deficits in the early 1980s? Why or why not?

8. What, in your view, is the best way for America to reduce its trade deficit?

9. During 1993, the international value of the yen rose sharply. This development worried the Japanese authorities. Why?

10. (More difficult) Suppose consumption and investment are described by:

$C = 100 + .75DI$ (DI = disposable income)
$I = 500 + .2Y - 40r$ (Y = GDP)

Here r, the interest rate, is measured in percentage points (for example, a 9 percent interest rate is $r = 9$). Exports and imports are as follows:

$$X = 150$$
$$IM = -100 + .2Y$$

Government purchases are $G = 750$, and taxes are 20 percent of income.

The price level is fixed and the central bank (called the "Fed") uses its monetary policy to peg the interest rate at $r = 10$.

a. Find equilibrium GDP, the budget deficit or surplus, and the trade deficit or surplus.

b. Suppose the currency depreciates and, as a result, exports and imports change to:

$$X = 200$$
$$IM = -150 + .2Y.$$

Now find equilibrium GDP, the budget deficit or surplus, and the trade deficit or surplus.

PART V

Alternative

Economic

Systems

Chapter 21

GROWTH IN DEVELOPED AND DEVELOPING COUNTRIES

The three great causes most favorable to [growth in] production are, accumulation of capital, fertility of soil, and inventions to save labour.

T.R. MALTHUS

The evidence indicates that a century ago an American could not afford to buy much more than a resident of the Philippines or Egypt consumes today. A few other countries have experienced comparable progress— spectacular growth in the productive powers of their economies. This chapter discusses what determines the rate at which an economy grows, and it examines the pros and cons of rapid growth. Then we turn to the special problems of the less developed countries (LDCs) and look at the measures that have been proposed to increase their rates of growth.

SOME BASIC PRINCIPLES OF GROWTH ANALYSIS

HOW TO MEASURE GROWTH: TOTAL OUTPUT OR OUTPUT PER CAPITA?

Adam Smith, like many of his successors, took it for granted that expansion of productive capacity is inherently desirable. But he also took it for granted, apparently without examining the matter very closely, that growth in the size of population is to be wished for. His reason was that a larger population provides a larger work force, and a larger work force makes a larger national output possible. Few economists since Smith's time have argued in this way. Nowadays we usually measure a nation's prosperity not in terms of its total output but in terms of its output *per person*. India has a GDP about six times as large as Sweden's. But with a population more than 100 times as large as Sweden's, India remains a poor country while Sweden is highly prosperous. The point is that:

If the objective of growth is the material welfare of the *individuals* who make up a country, then the proper measure of the success of a program of economic development is how much it adds to output per person. The relevant index is not total output. It is total output *divided by total population*—that is, **output per capita**.

From this point of view, the appropriate objective of growth is not, as the old cliché puts it, "the greatest good for the *greatest number*"—it is the greatest good *per person* in the economy. Per capita figures tell this story well. To make the appropriate comparison of well-being in Sweden and India, we note that per capita GDP in Sweden is nearly $18,000 a year, whereas in India, even after a generous adjustment to correct for lower prices in that country, the figure is about $1200 a year.[1]

Only where the objective of the government is grandeur or military strength may the number of inhabitants alone seem an appropriate part of its goal. A small country like Finland, for instance, cannot hope to overwhelm a giant neighbor like Russia, even if Finland has a much higher per capita GDP than Russia.[2] But where the goal of the government is not national power but the elimination of poverty, illiteracy, and inadequate medical care, sheer increase in population becomes a questionable pursuit.

---

[1] These per-capita GDP figures, expressed in U.S. dollars, were converted from the national currencies using purchasing-power-parity exchange rates. The source is the International Comparison Program, which is coordinated by the United Nations and supported by the World Bank and the Organization for Economic Cooperation and Development, and published by the World Bank as part of its *World Development Report 1993*, World Development Indicators, New York: Oxford University Press, 1993, p. 296. For an explanation of purchasing-power-parity exchange rates, see Chapter 17, footnote 10.

[2] Even where military power is the primary objective, a large but impoverished population may not be a very effective means to that end. China has long had an enormous population, but in the modern era its military presence is certainly quite recent.

ON GROWTH IN POPULATION: IS LESS REALLY MORE?

In 1798, the Reverend Thomas R. Malthus (who was to become England's first professor of political economy) published *An Essay on the Principle of Population.* This book was to have a profound effect on people's attitudes toward population growth. Malthus argued that sexual drives and other influences induce people to reproduce themselves as rapidly as their means permit. Unfortunately, he said, when the number of humans increases, the production of food and other consumption goods generally cannot keep up.

The problem is the noted *law of diminishing returns* to additional labor used with a fixed supply of land, a relationship we encountered before (in *Microeconomics* Chapter 6). This states that if we use more and more labor to cultivate a fixed stock of land, we will eventually reach a point at which each additional laborer will contribute less additional output than the previous laborer. Ultimately, as the labor force increases, output per worker will decline.

Malthus and his followers concluded that the tendency of humankind to reproduce itself must constantly exert pressure on the economy to keep living standards from rising. Wages will gravitate toward some minimal subsistence level—the lowest income on which people are willing to marry and raise a family. If wages are above subsistence, the population can and will grow. Thus, a wage that is above subsistence will set forces into motion that will drive wages down toward subsistence because of diminishing returns.

Sometimes, according to Malthus, the population will grow beyond the capability of the economy to support it. Then the number of people will be brought back into line by means that are far more unpleasant than a decrease in wages—by starvation and disease or by wars that produce the required number of casualties.

Later in the nineteenth century and during the first half of the twentieth century, the gloomy Malthusian vision seemed to lose credibility. New technology and improved agricultural practices generally enabled the output of food and other agricultural products to increase faster than the population (at least in the wealthier, industrialized nations). In addition, it turned out that as living standards rose, people became less anxious to reproduce, and so the expansion of population slowed substantially. Figure 21–1 illustrates this trend in the United States for more than a century and a half. All in all, it began to look as though population growth constituted no significant threat—it was something with which human technological skills and ingenuity could cope.

More recently, however, there has been renewed concern over population. With improvements in medicine—notably, improved hygiene in hospitals, the use of such public health measures as swamp drainage, and the discovery of antibiotics—death rates have plunged in the developing countries, especially for infants. At the same time, birth control programs in most of these countries have, at least until quite recently, not been very successful. As a result, the populations of developing countries have continued to expand dramatically, eating up a good proportion of any output increases obtained through their governments' economic development programs.

It has been widely concluded that significant improvement in living standards in the developing areas is impossible without a substantial reduction in their population growth. But the "neo-Malthusians" go further than this, arguing that a rapid approach to birthrates so low that populations cease expanding—that is,

| *Figure* **21–1** | **AMERICAN BIRTHRATES, 1820–1990** |

This chart shows that birthrates in the United States have generally been declining since 1820.

SOURCE: U.S. Bureau of the Census, *Historical Statistics of the United States, Colonial Times to 1970, Part I*, Washington, D.C.: U.S. Government Printing Office, 1975; and U.S. Bureau of the Census, *Statistical Abstract of the United States*, Washington, D.C.: U.S. Government Printing Office, various issues.

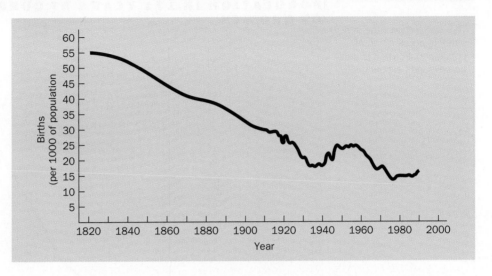

to *zero population growth*—is virtually a matter of life and death even for the most prosperous nations. It is illuminating to consider the logic of their argument.

THE CROWDED PLANET: EXPONENTIAL POPULATION GROWTH

Malthus used an argument that has caught many imaginations ever since:

> *Population, when unchecked, increases in a geometrical ratio. Subsistence increases only in an arithmetical ratio. A slight acquaintance with numbers will shew the immensity of the first power in comparison of the second.*[3]

EXPONENTIAL GROWTH is growth at a constant percentage rate.

In modern discussions, such a "geometric" growth pattern is referred to as **exponential growth**, or "compounded growth" or "snowballing." Exponential growth is growth at a constant *percentage rate*. For example, at a 10 percent growth rate, a population of 100 persons will increase by 10 persons a year; but a population of a million persons will increase by 100,000 persons a year. Thus, although the *rate* of growth is the same for large and small populations, the *numbers* are dramatically different. The bigger the population, the more it will add annually. And each year's growth implies still faster growth in the following year. It is like a snowball rolling downhill, accumulating more snow the bigger it gets, thus expanding faster and faster all the time.

If the population doubles (grows 100 percent) in 35 years, it will quadruple (grow another 100 percent) in 70 years, increase 8-fold in 105 years, 16-fold in 140 years, and so on indefinitely. The doubling sequence 2, 4, 8, 16, 32, 64, and so on, is the basic pattern of exponential growth. Figure 21–2 shows how astronomical such a growth sequence is. Projecting the world's population 175 years into the future on the assumption that population will grow exponentially at about

---

[3]Thomas R. Malthus, *An Essay on the Principle of Population*, (London, 1798), page 20.

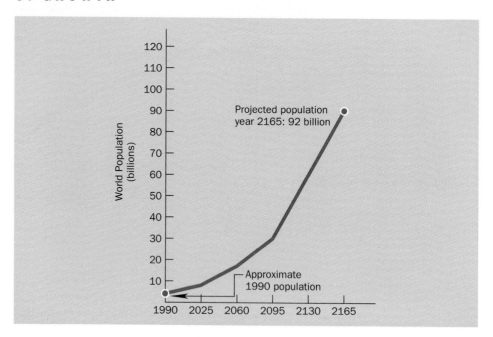

F i g u r e **21-2**

PROJECTED GROWTH OF THE WORLD'S POPULATION IN 171 YEARS AT CURRENT RATE OF GROWTH

This figure shows the sensational acceleration of population growth *if* population expands exponentially.

its current rate, the graph shows that by the year 2165 the population will exceed 90 billion—about 20 times as many people as there are today.

It turns out that in describing the consequences of exponential growth, Malthus was conservative. He did not begin to spell out the wonders and the horrors that his premise implied. Consider some calculations by one leading authority on population (who derived his conclusions simply by carrying through the arithmetic of exponential growth rates):

■ *If population were to grow at today's rates for another 600–700 years, every square foot of the surface of the earth would contain a human being;*

■ *If it were to expand at the same rate for 1200 years, the combined weight of the human population would exceed that of the earth itself;*

■ *If that growth rate were to go on for 6000 years (a very short period of time in terms of biological history), the globe would constitute a sphere whose diameter was growing with the speed of light.*[4]

And none of this is conjecture. It is *sure* to come about *if* the present (exponential) rate of growth of the earth's population continues unabated.

Of course, none of this can really happen. Our finite earth just does not have room for that sort of expansion. The fate of humanity is not determined by the

[4]Ansley J. Coale, "Man and His Environment," *Science*, Vol. 179 (October 9, 1970), pages 132–36. Copyright 1970 by the American Association for the Advancement of Science.

rules of arithmetic—it depends on the course of nature and on the behavior of the human race. It is true that if the number of humans continues to swell until it presses upon the earth's capacity, the process will ultimately be brought to a halt in a Malthusian apocalypse. Disease, famine, and war must finally put a stop to the expansion process.

But there is a better alternative. People can choose to stop raising large families. There is no inevitability about the family of six or ten children. As we have just noted, there has in fact been a long-term decline in the rate of expansion in the wealthier societies such as the United States (see Figure 21–3). Even in the developing nations, as we will see later in this chapter, the birthrate has recently been declining.

A more balanced view of the matter recognizes the serious difficulties that rapid population growth can lead to, and suggests that its encouragement will not serve the interests of society. Yet, it does *not* imply that a great catastrophe is at hand or that the appropriate reaction is panic.

REQUIREMENTS FOR INCREASED GROWTH

What can be done to increase the growth rate of production in an economy? Unfortunately, no one has a handy list of sure-fire recipes.

Growth can be attributed to a number of factors that no one knows how to explain: (1) *inventiveness*, which produces the new technology and other innovations that have contributed so much to economic expansion; (2) *entrepreneurship*, the leadership that recognizes no obstacles and undertakes the daring industrial ventures needed to move the economy ahead; and (3) *the work ethic* that leads a work force to high levels of productivity. No one really knows what features of

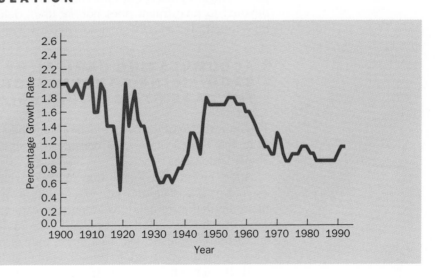

F i g u r e **21–3** ANNUAL PERCENTAGE GROWTH RATE OF THE U.S. POPULATION

After falling rapidly during the first half of the 1980s, the population growth rate turned back up again after 1986. The U.S. Census Bureau projects that this trend will continue well into the next century. The recent growth rates are still far below the rates of the baby-boom years of the 1950s and early 1960s.

SOURCE: U.S. Bureau of the Census, *Current Population Reports*, Series P-25.

economic organization and social psychology actually lead a community to adopt these goals, as Great Britain is said to have done at the beginning of the nineteenth century, as the United States is reputed to have done in the first half of the twentieth century, and as Japan is apparently doing today. We do know, however, that:

Growth requires two things that people can influence directly:

1. A large expenditure on *capital equipment*: factories, machinery, transportation, and telecommunications equipment.
2. The devotion of considerable effort to research and development from which innovations are derived.

Both these types of expenditures help to increase the economy's ability to *supply* goods, which brings us back to the analysis of Parts 2–3. There we stressed that the level (and, consequently, the growth) of national income is determined by the interaction of *aggregate supply and aggregate demand*. It is the need for capital equipment in any growth process that provides a vital link between aggregate demand and aggregate supply, for an economy acquires a larger capital stock by investing. Recall that aggregate demand is the sum of consumption, investment, government spending, and net exports $Y = C + I + G + (X - IM)$. But I is the only part of Y that creates more capital for the future. Such investment can be carried out either by the private sector of the economy or by government. In free market economies government investment is, of course, a much smaller share of the total than it was in centrally directed economies.

The *composition* of aggregate demand is a major determinant of the rate of economic growth. If a larger fraction of total spending goes toward investment rather than toward consumption, government purchases, or net exports, the capital stock will grow faster and the aggregate supply schedule will shift more quickly to the right.

Figure 21–4 shows, for a set of 20 countries on four continents, how investment in one period (in this case, 1973) is related to subsequent growth (1973–1987) in per capita output. The graph confirms that the share of an economy's output devoted to investment does not, *by itself*, determine future growth. But higher investment rates clearly *are* associated with subsequently more-rapid growth.

ACCUMULATING CAPITAL BY SACRIFICING CONSUMPTION: THE CASE OF SOVIET RUSSIA

The importance of the *composition* of demand stands out sharply if we turn away from the United States and consider a *centrally planned* economy, such as the Soviet Union was.

After the Russian Revolution in 1917, when the Soviet Union undertook to expand its industrial output very rapidly, it was clear from the earliest stage of planning that a tremendous amount of capital equipment would be required to carry out the expansion. Not only did the Soviets have to build modern factories and acquire sophisticated machinery, they also needed a **social infrastructure**— a transportation network to bring raw materials to the factories and take finished products to the markets, an efficient telecommunications system, and schools in which to train the population sufficiently to be an effective labor force. All this

| *F i g u r e* **21–4** | **GROWTH AND INVESTMENT, 20 COUNTRIES** |

The graph shows, for twenty countries, how investment in 1973 is related to subsequent growth in per-capita GDP (1973–1987). It is clear that investment alone does not determine future economic growth, but higher investment rates are associated with more rapid growth rates.

SOURCE: Angus Maddison, *The World Economy in the 20th Century*, Paris: Organization for Economic Cooperation and Development, 1989.

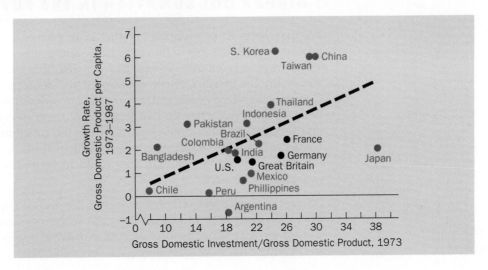

and much more was needed, and all of it required labor, raw material, and fuel for its construction.

Obviously, such a use of resources has its *opportunity cost*. Fuel and steel that are employed to build a train become unavailable for the production of refrigerators and washing machines. The real price of accumulating plant, equipment, and infrastructure is paid in the form of consumer goods that must be given up in order to build that capital equipment. In other words:

Through saving, the public gives up some consumption, which is the price it must pay for the accumulation of plant, equipment, and infrastructure. Without this sacrifice, growth generally cannot occur.

This is the hard lesson that the inhabitants of the Soviet Union lived with for over seventy years. The Soviet leadership was determined to promote rapid economic growth and had imposed on the general public whatever sacrifices of current consumption were deemed necessary for the purpose. Only in the most recent decades was an increase in the supply of consumer goods assigned any priority. Yet, even shortly before its collapse, investment in the U.S.S.R. was still nearly one-third of GDP, while in the United States the figure is about half that amount. As a result, Soviet living standards rose very slowly, particularly because the demands of the military forces joined those of the growth planners in competing for the resources that might otherwise have gone into consumption. That is undoubtedly one of the main reasons for the demise of communism in the U.S.S.R. and the other countries of Eastern Europe.

The reason for this harsh trade-off is clear enough. If the economy is producing at its full potential, then real output Y cannot be increased further. Since $Y = C + I + G + (X - IM)$, a decision to devote more resources to the production of heavy machinery (which is in I) or armaments (which are in G) is simultaneously a decision to forgo some consumption or to import more. Where resources are already fully employed, it is simply not possible to have both more guns *and* more butter.

THE PAYOFF TO GROWTH: HIGHER CONSUMPTION IN THE FUTURE

We may seem to be painting a rather grim picture of growth, and indeed, the process was often harsh in the old U.S.S.R. and in other nations that have enforced a high rate of economic growth. But it is also true that if the growth process is successful, the sacrifice of consumption that it requires is only a temporary loss. Consumers give up goods and services now in order to make possible the construction of productive capacity that will permit them to consume even more goods and services at a later date. After all, from the consumers' point of view, that is what growth is all about. It is not an end in itself, but a means to an end—a standard of living higher than they could have attained without the process of economic expansion.

At least in a consumer-oriented economy, the decision to save in order to promote economic growth is simply an *exchange between present and future consumption.* Consumers sacrifice consumption now in order to be able to increase consumption in the future by more than they gave up in the past.

Of course, the payoff may never come if something goes wrong. An earthquake may destroy factories and roads, or a government with military ambitions may divert the increased productive capacity into the manufacture of armaments. So there is a risk in the decision to give up consumption now for increased consumption later. The growth process is a gamble—it means trading in a relatively sure thing (present consumption) for a risky future return (increased future consumption).

But betting on the future is not necessarily foolhardy. Economies would remain stagnant if people were unwilling to take the required chances. And some of the risk of investment plans can be reduced if decision makers understand fully the terms of the trade-off.

GROWTH WITHOUT SACRIFICING CONSUMPTION: SOMETHING FOR NOTHING?

Some growth can be achieved without much sacrifice of present consumption. For at least one of the main engines of growth can be powered with relatively small increases in the nation's stock of factories, equipment, and infrastructure. Research and development can teach society new and more efficient ways of using the nation's productive resources. Thus, *innovation*—the process of putting inventions into operation—can permit an economy to get more output from the same input quantities, rather than by *expansion* of capital stock.

Everyone knows that this has in fact occurred. From the invention of the steam engine to that of the modern computer, our economy has benefited from a stream of inventions—some sensational, some more routine—which together have increased enormously the productivity of the nation's resources. Estimates of the relative contributions of innovation and accumulation to the growth process differ. A number of analysts attribute considerably more than half of the economic growth of the United States to research and invention. But whatever the correct figure, it is certainly large.

Another way of describing this conclusion is to say that while a substantial proportion of growth is **embodied** in increased quantities of plant, equipment, and infrastructure, a very large proportion of the economy's growth is **disembodied**. That is, it is attributable to better ideas—to improved methods of finding and using the same quantities of resources.

Embodied growth has two serious costs that disembodied growth avoids. First, embodied growth necessarily speeds up the use of society's depletable resources: its iron ore, its petroleum supplies, and its stocks of other minerals and fuels. Second, the resources that are used up in a process of embodied growth must ultimately end up on society's garbage heap. The physical laws of conservation of matter and energy tell us that no raw material can ever disappear. It can be transformed into smoke or solid waste, but unless it is recycled *entirely* (something that is both beyond the capability of our technology and impractical for other reasons), the greater the quantity of resources used in the productive process, the greater the quantity of wastes that must ultimately result.

Economist Kenneth Boulding has likened our planet to a spaceship hurtling through the solar system but constrained by terrestrial littering laws to keep its garbage on board. In spaceship Earth, we can transform waste materials into other forms—as by melting old bottles for reuse or converting them into energy, or by burning combustible garbage for heat—but we cannot simply toss them overboard.

So far, we have enjoyed substantial success in our efforts to achieve growth in output without commensurate increases in our use of resources. One statistical analysis, for example, attributes only about half of the growth in the United States to increased use of physical inputs. The remainder must be ascribed to improvements in technology as well as to increased education and skill of the labor force.[5]

One final remark on disembodied growth is in order. Economists are fond of pointing out that there is no such thing as a free lunch. Except in rare instances, improvements in technology are not "manna from heaven." They result, instead, from the work of scientists and technicians in government and industrial laboratories, from the labor of inventors in their basements or garages, and from the effort of management specialists studying the organization of factories and assembly lines. This means that labor (along with other resources) is diverted from other activities into the production of knowledge. *In a fully employed economy, the opportunity costs of investing in the discovery of new knowledge are the forgone consumption and physical investment of goods that would otherwise have been produced.* So even here, we cannot get something for nothing.

IS MORE GROWTH REALLY BETTER?

A number of writers have raised questions about the desirability of faster economic growth as an end in itself, at least in the wealthier industrialized countries. Yet faster growth does mean more wealth, and to most people the desirability of wealth is beyond question. "I've been rich and I've been poor—and I can tell you, rich is better," a noted stage personality is said to have told an interviewer, and most people seem to have the same attitude about the economy as a whole. To those who hold this belief, a healthy economy is one that is capable of turning

---

[5]Edward F. Denison, *Accounting for United States Economic Growth 1929–1969* (Washington, D.C.: The Brookings Institution, 1974).

The Poverty of Affluence

Does affluence make us better off? Psychologist Paul Wachtel argues that:

. . . the growth economy . . . creates more needs than it satisfies and leaves us feeling more deprived than when we had "less". . . . It is ironic that the very kind of thinking which produces all our riches also renders them unable to satisfy us. Our restless desire for more and more has been a major dynamic for economic growth, but it has made the achievement of that growth largely a hollow victory. Our sense of contentment and satisfaction . . . depends upon our frame of reference, on how what we attain compares to what we expected. If we get farther than we expected we tend to feel good. If we expected to go farther than we have then even a rather high level of success can be experienced as disappointing.

In America, we keep upping the ante. Our expectations keep accommodating to what we have attained. "Enough" is always just over the horizon, and like the horizon it recedes as we approach it. . . . The sense of economic distress and disappointment currently sweeping America has [little] to do with real deprivation and much [to do] with assumptions and expectations.

Paul L. Wachtel, *The Poverty of Affluence, A Psychological Portrait of the American Way of Life*, New York: The Free Press, 1983, pages 16–17.

out vast quantities of shoes, food, cars, and TV sets. An economy whose capacity to provide all these things is not expanding is said to have succumbed to the disease of *stagnation*.

Economists from Adam Smith to Karl Marx saw great virtue in economic growth. Marx argued that capitalism, at least in its earlier historical stages, was a vital form of economic organization by which society got out of the rut in which the medieval stage of history had trapped it. Marx believed that "the development of the productive powers of society . . . alone can form the real basis of a higher form of society. . . ." Marx went on to tell us that only where such great productive powers have been unleashed can one have "a society in which the full and free development of every individual forms the ruling principle."[6] In other words, only a wealthy economy can afford to give all individuals the opportunity for full personal satisfaction through the use of their special abilities in their jobs and through increased leisure activities.

Yet the desirability of further economic growth for a society that is already wealthy has been questioned on grounds that undoubtedly have a good deal of validity. It is pointed out that the sheer increase in quantity of products has imposed an enormous cost on society in the form of pollution, crowding, and proliferation of wastes that need disposal; some economists claim it has had unfortunate psychological and social effects. It is said that industry has transformed the satisfying and creative tasks of the artisan into the mechanical and dehumanizing routine of the assembly line. It has dotted our roadsides with

---

[6]Karl Marx, *Capital*, Vol. I (Chicago: Charles H. Kerr Publishing Co., 1906), page 649.

junkyards, filled our air with smoke, and poisoned our food with dangerous chemicals. The question is whether the outpouring of frozen foods, talking dolls, CD players, and headache remedies is worth its high cost to society. As one well-known economist put it:

> The continued pursuit of economic growth by Western societies is more likely on balance to reduce rather than increase social welfare . . . . Technological innovations may offer to add to men's material opportunities. But by increasing the risks of their obsolescence it adds also to their anxiety. Swifter means of communications have the paradoxical effect of isolating people; increased mobility has led to more hours commuting; increased automobilization to increased separation; more television to less communication. In consequence, people know less of their neighbors than ever before in history.[7]

Virtually every economist agrees that these concerns are valid, though many question whether economic growth is their major cause. Nevertheless, they all emphasize that pollution of air and water, noise and congestion, and the mechanization of the work process are very real and very serious problems. There is every reason for society to undertake programs that grapple with them. *Microeconomics* Chapter 21, which dealt with problems of the environment, examined these issues more closely and described some policies to deal with them.

Despite the costs of growth in terms of human and environmental damage, there is strong evidence that if the economy's total output were kept at its present level, the community would pay a high price over and above the loss of additional goods and services.

First, it is not easy to carry out a decision to prevent further economic growth. Mandatory controls are abhorrent to most Americans. We cannot *order* people to stop inventing means to expand productivity. Nor does it make any sense to order every firm and industry to freeze its output level, since changing tastes and needs require some industries to expand their outputs at the same time that others are contracting. But who is to decide which should grow and which should contract, and how shall such decisions be made? *The achievement of zero economic growth may very well require government intervention on a scale that becomes expensive and even repressive.*

Second, without continued growth it will be no easy matter to finance effective programs to improve the quality of life—programs such as environmental protection. To improve the purity of our air and water and to clean up urban neighborhoods, tens of billions of dollars must be made available every year. Continued growth would enable the required resources to be provided without any reduction in the availability of consumer goods. But without such growth, we may actually be forced to cut back on our programs to protect the environment. Society could thus end up with less goods and a worse environment.

Finally, zero economic growth may seriously hamper efforts to eliminate poverty both within our economy and throughout the world. Much of the earth's population today lives in a state of extreme want. And though wealthier nations have been reluctant to provide more than token amounts of help to the **less developed countries (LDCs)**, less wealth means there would be even less to share. So perhaps the only hope for improved living standards in the impoverished countries of Africa, Asia, and Latin America lies in continued increases in output.

---

[7]E. J. Mishan, *The Costs of Economic Growth* (New York: Frederick A. Praeger Publishers, 1967), pages 171, 175.

PROBLEMS OF THE LESS DEVELOPED COUNTRIES

| LIVING IN THE LDCs

A substantial proportion of the world's population lives in areas whose average per capita GDP is $2,000 or less per year, evaluated (as well as it is possible to do) in terms of today's prices in the United States. Table 21–1 shows that there are countries in which annual per capita GDP is less than $600. Even after adjustment for differences in measurement of GDP in the United States and the poorer countries, this probably comes to an annual GDP figure under $1000.

To us, residents of an economy that offers an average GDP more than 20 times as high as this, such a figure is not only likely to seem incredible, it is all but incomprehensible. Few of us can *really* imagine what life would be like if our family income were reduced to $1000 per year. It is even hard to envision survival on such amounts. It must be emphasized that these figures do *not* represent the living standards of a small group of outcasts from their own societies. Rather, they are *typical* of many people who live in Asia, Africa, and Latin America.

What can life be like in such circumstances? No brief description can really bridge the gulf between our range of experience and theirs. Yet it can offer us a glimpse into a way of life that few of us will want to share.

Inhabitants of many of the less developed countries live with their large families in one-room shanties or apartments; their water supplies are scanty, polluted, and often miles from home; their only source of energy is that of human and beast; and their sparse harvests are wrung from miserable soil in good years,

T a b l e **21–1**	**PER CAPITA GDP IN DEVELOPED AND LESS DEVELOPED COUNTRIES, 1991***
	(measured in U.S. dollars)*
Developed Countries	
United States	$22,130
United Kingdom	16,340
Sweden	17,490
Less Developed Countries	
Bolivia	2,170
China	1,680
Egypt	3,600
Ethiopia	370
Haiti	1,220
India	1,150
Tanzania	570

SOURCE: The World Bank, *World Development Report* 1993, page 296.

*Using purchasing-power-parity exchange rates. See Chapter 34, footnote 10, for an explanation.

Starvation in Africa: A Recurring Tragedy

Reporters assigned to cover events in Africa often find that one of their biggest journalistic challenges is to overcome the numbness and overfamiliarity engendered by the all too predictable cycles of drought, famine and human catastrophe in many parts of that continent. Less than a decade after the famine in Ethiopia in the mid-1980s, when a million people starved to death, newspapers of the world are once again filled with heart-rending photographs of skeletal, near-death Africans. And, once again, these nightmarish pictures are coming from the Horn of Africa.

Severe drought plays an important part in the latest food crisis. But totalitarian government, civil warfare, and economic collapse are bigger villains. The Economist magazine reports that, "The Horn is a catalogue of the malfeasance that drives millions to the brink. There, three countries embroiled in fighting (Ethiopia, Sudan and Somalia) contain more than half of Africa's hungry. Add in the victims of other civil wars (in Angola, Mozambique and Liberia) and the proportion rises to two-thirds."* The economies of these countries have suffered devastating effects from internal strife; according to the *1991 World Bank Annual Report*, GDP in Sudan fell by 5.8 percent in 1990, and output in Ethiopia dropped by about 2.5 percent. In Somalia, the economic situation continues to deteriorate.**

The end of the cold war may presage an end to the cycle of devastation. With the collapse of the Soviet Union, African conflicts are no longer the locus of superpower rivalry. The ex-Soviet Union is now virtually a nonpresence in African affairs, and the United States has adopted new attitudes toward aid in Africa, with amounts and timing starting to be contingent, for the first time, upon progress toward democracy. Experience in Botswana and Kenya, where universal suffrage has forced governments to protect the most at-risk and poor citizens during droughts, has shown that democracy may be the answer.

* "The Horn Is Empty," *The Economist*, May 11, 1991, pages 37–38.
**SOURCE: *The World Bank Annual Report 1991*, Washington, D.C.: The World Bank, 1991, page 113.

with starvation threatened perhaps every five years when the rains do not come and the crops fail. With no surplus in production, no food can be put into reserves, and the old, the infirm, and the very young are likely to perish. The box above describes the most recent manifestation of the recurring cycle of drought and famine in Africa.

The life of a man in an LDC is hard enough, with its low nutritional level, its lack of equipment to help him in his work, and its frequency of debilitating diseases. But his life is luxurious compared with that of a woman. She is usually married by the age of 14, bears 8 or 10 children with minimal medical assistance, and by 35 is often beset by chronic disease and aged far beyond her years. If (as is true of some 80 percent of the population) she inhabits a rural area, she may have to walk miles every day to fetch water for the family. She sews the family's clothes by hand and cooks its meals. There is not enough money for pre-ground flour, so part of a woman's daily work is to pound the grain by hand for food for the family—perhaps an additional two hours of hard labor. She also tends the gardens that produce food for the family, although, except in Moslem countries where women are sequestered, she is also expected to put in a full day in the fields during the six months of the agricultural season.

Another duty of the woman in an LDC is to bring produce, wood, or whatever she has to trade to market a couple of times a week, and she must often walk as

Table 21-2	INFANT MORTALITY AND LIFE EXPECTANCY IN DEVELOPED AND LESS DEVELOPED COUNTRIES, 1992	
	INFANT MORTALITY (deaths per 1000 live births)	LIFE EXPECTANCY AT BIRTH (years) (male/female)
Developed Countries		
United States	9.0	72/79
Germany	7.5	72/78
Sweden	6.0	75/80
Less Developed Countries		
Bolivia	89	58/64
China	34	68/71
Egypt	73	58/61
Ethiopia	139	46/48
Haiti	106	53/56
India	91	58/59
Tanzania	105	49/54

SOURCE: Population Reference Bureau, Inc., *1992 World Population Data Sheet.*

many as 10 miles each way with bundles as heavy as she can carry on her back or on her head. She has no respite in the raising of her children, since they are likely not to have a school to attend when they are well or a hospital to go to when they are sick. It is no wonder that she ages so much faster than a woman in our society.

Table 21–2 gives the percentage of infant deaths for each 1000 live births and the average life expectancy of a newborn child in some countries ranging from the most underdeveloped to the most affluent. The contrasts are dramatic. In Bolivia, 89 babies die of every 1000 that are born, while the comparable figure in Sweden is six. In many countries people survive only until their 40s or 50s, while in Sweden the average life expectancy for men is 75 years and for women is 80 years. There is little question about the quality of life in less developed lands.

Most of the inhabitants of many LDCs are shockingly poor. Malnutrition and disease are widespread. The sheer process of living and surviving taxes the people to the utmost and makes them old before their time.

RECENT TRENDS

Despite population increases, some LDCs, particularly in the Far East, have succeeded in breaking out of the stagnation trap. In those successful economies, if growth were to continue as it was in the 1970s, an average family could look forward to a doubling of its living standards in less than 30 years. Or put another way, in earlier decades standards of living were increasing faster than they did in the United States in the nineteenth century!

While in the 1970s such good news applied to a number of LDCs in several parts of the world, the 1980s were not so favorable. Aside from their debt problems, which will be discussed a bit later, there are several developments that can be considered either as merely unfortunate or as thoroughly ominous for the LDCs.

While the percentage rates of growth of per capita incomes in the LDCs have been impressive, the industrialized countries, with their initially high incomes, have not exactly been standing still. Indeed, largely because their population growth has been slower, the percentage growth rate in per capita incomes has been higher in the developed countries. But even if the *percentage* increases in their per capita incomes had been very similar, *absolute* incomes would have continued to rise more quickly in the richer lands. For example, where per capita income is $100 a year, a $2\frac{1}{2}$ percent growth rate translates into a $2.50 annual improvement; however, where per capita income is $5000 a year, the same $2\frac{1}{2}$ percent rate of growth adds $125 a year to the income of the average person.

A few numbers will indicate how discouraging the relative performance of the LDCs as a group has been. A study of some 70 countries by a group of noted economists[8] calculated a standard index of degree of inequality (called the "Gini index") for three subsets of these countries: the industrialized countries, the middle-income countries, and the LDCs. The study covered the 30-year period 1950–1980, which included the decade of the 1970s, usually considered an era of extraordinary progress for the LDCs. For the industrialized countries, the index of inequality fell by almost 60 percent over the 30-year period, meaning that the poorer of the industrial countries had done a very effective job of catching up with the richer ones. The countries of the middle-income group also came closer to one another, but only to a modest degree, with their inequality index falling 4 percent in 3 decades. But for the LDCs the index actually rose 9 percent, meaning that these poorest of countries were increasingly diverging among themselves into relatively richer and relatively poorer groups.

Even more important, the disparity between the LDCs and the other two groups has been increasing. The average annual growth rates of real GDP were 3.1 percent (compounded) for the industrial countries, 3.0 percent for the middle-income countries, and only 1.5 percent for the LDCs. With average growth rates half as big as those for the more-affluent economies, the LDCs as a group fell further behind the rest of the world for much of the period since World War II.

Figure 21–5 illustrates, for the case of Latin America, the poor growth performance of some of the LDCs in the 1980s. Of the nine countries whose records are reported, 7 actually experienced a *decline* in per capita GDP, with 4 of those falling substantially.

The purchasing power of the average family in an LDC is falling further behind that of a typical family in a wealthy economy.

Many critics, notably those on the left, emphasize that growth has been accompanied by a worsening distribution of income within some of the LDCs. The rise in population has worsened the living standards of people on marginal lands with inadequate rain (about 40 percent of Indian farmers and a large proportion of Africans). Add the massive explosion of urban unemployment, and one gets several hundred million people who are no better off and possibly worse off than ever before.

Another continuing problem within the LDCs is the relatively high growth rate of their populations.

[8]Robert Summers, Irving B. Kravis, and Alan Heston, "Changes in World Income Distribution," *Journal of Policy Modelling*, Vol. 6, May 1986, pages 237–69.

F i g u r e **21-5** **FALLING PER CAPITA OUTPUTS IN LATIN AMERICA, 1981–1990**

Experience since the Industrial Revolution has led us to consider growth in per capita income to be the normal state of affairs for a country. However, this was true only for two of the nine countries in the graph. Four of them, Argentina, Peru, Venezuela, and Bolivia, actually experienced sharp drops in GDP per capita.

SOURCE: Inter-American Development Bank, *Economic and Social Progress in Latin America, 1991*, Special Section: Social Security in Latin America, Washington, D.C.: Johns Hopkins University Press, October 1991, page 273.

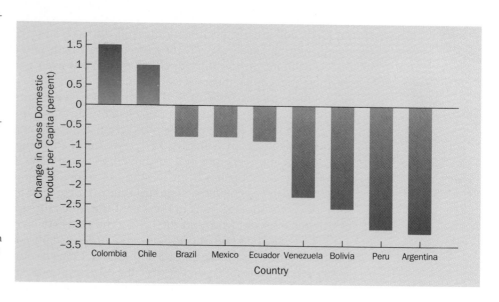

While net population growth has fallen almost to zero in the United States and some countries of Western Europe, the population explosion continues in some of the LDCs, particularly in Africa.

Table 21–3 tells the story. For the sample of LDCs shown, the annual growth rate of population continues about ten times as high as it is in the industrialized countries. Clearly, the more closely the growth in population approximates the growth in national income, the more slowly standards of living will rise, since there will be that many more persons among whom the additional product must be divided.

Finally, the LDCs have shown themselves highly vulnerable to such events as the oil crisis in 1979 and the high real interest rates of the 1980s. Much as the fall in Iranian oil exports and rise in oil prices affected the industrialized economies, it undoubtedly damaged the LDCs even more, leading to enormous deficits and foreign debts for the countries least able to afford them.

IMPEDIMENTS TO DEVELOPMENT IN THE LDCs

No one has produced a definitive list of causes of the poverty of the LDCs, just as no one can pretend to have produced a foolproof prescription for its cure. Yet there is general agreement on the main conditions contributing to the economic problems of LDCs. These include lack of physical capital, rapid growth of populations, lack of education, unemployment, and social and political impediments to business activity. Let us consider each of these.

SCARCITY OF PHYSICAL CAPITAL

The LDCs are obviously handicapped by their lack of modern factories and machinery. In addition, they lack infrastructure—good roads, railroads, port facilities, and so on. But capital is not easy to acquire. If it is to be provided by the populations of the LDCs themselves, they must save the required resources— that is, as we saw earlier in this chapter, they must give up consumption in order to free the resources needed to build plants, equipment, and roads. That is comparatively easy in a rich community, where substantial saving still leaves the public well off in terms of current consumption. But in an LDC, where malnutrition is a constant threat, the bulk of the inhabitants cannot save except at enormous sacrifice to their families. Moreover, in many of the LDCs, tradition imputes little virtue to investment in business, so that even the wealthy are not terribly anxious to put their savings into productive equipment. Thus:

Because of poverty, which makes saving difficult, if not impossible, and because of traditions that do not encourage investment, the LDCs' growth rates of domestically financed capital are lower than those in the developed countries.

One way to help matters is to obtain the funds for investment from abroad. There is a long tradition of foreign investment in developing countries. For example, throughout the first half of the nineteenth century the United States almost constantly drew capital from abroad, though the amounts involved were only a small proportion of U.S. GDP. In recent decades a considerable share of the resources going to the LDCs from abroad has come from foreign governments as part of their aid programs. While some of the resources provided in this way have been used wastefully, informed observers generally agree that the waste incurred under these programs has not been spectacularly great, and they conclude that these capital transfers from the rich countries to the poor have at least worked in the right direction.

Capital can also be transferred to an LDC when a private firm chooses to invest money in such a country to build a factory or to explore for oil in order to increase

T a b l e **21–3**	NATURAL INCREASE IN POPULATION (BIRTHRATE MINUS DEATH RATE) IN DEVELOPED AND LESS DEVELOPED COUNTRIES, 1992
	(births minus deaths as percent of population)
Developed Countries	
United States	0.8
Germany	−0.1
Sweden	0.3
Less Developed Countries	
Bolivia	2.7
China	1.3
Egypt	2.4
Ethiopia	2.8
Haiti	2.9
India	2.0
Tanzania	3.5

SOURCE: Population Reference Bureau, Inc., *1992 World Population Data Sheet.*

its own profits. This too seems to have been helpful to the LDCs. In earlier days, it sometimes gave an unacceptable degree of political influence to the foreign firms, particularly when the LDC was a colony of an industrial country. In recent years this difficulty may have become rarer. Nowadays, it is more often the outside firm that is afraid of the government of the LDC rather than vice versa, with foreign proprietors frequently fearful of rigid control by the government of the LDC in which it invests. Sometimes it even fears outright expropriation—that the government will simply take over its property in the LDC with, or even without, compensation because of the hostile attitudes that residents of many LDCs hold toward large foreign companies.

It is difficult for a resident of an industrialized country like the United States to realize how much hatred and resentment is felt in less developed countries toward the "northern imperialist powers." This resentment is focused in particular on **multinational corporations**—companies such as IBM, Royal Dutch Shell, Volkswagen, and Unilever—which have their headquarters in an industrialized country and their operations in a variety of less developed countries. Multinationals may first process their own raw materials in one country, ship them to another to make them into parts, and assemble them in still a third. Some of these corporations, among them the oil companies, specialize in the extraction and/or marketing of raw materials, while others, such as IBM and Volkswagen, specialize in manufacturing. Many LDCs regard these and other giant foreign corporations as instruments of imperialist exploitation, not as firms that happen to carry on their activities wherever the dictates of efficiency require, contributing benefits to each of the countries in which they operate.

It is true that foreign firms hope to make more money out of an LDC than they put into it, but that is only natural, since otherwise their investment would not have been expected to be profitable, and the funds would therefore not have been invested in the first place. But there are usually *mutual* gains from trade. Investment will be useful to the LDCs if, in the process of earning these profits, foreign firms build factories, infrastructure, and provide jobs that leave the community wealthier than it would otherwise have been. The evidence is that this is in fact what foreign private investment has typically accomplished in recent decades.

A problem with foreign business investment that is more serious is the danger that foreign firms will fail to train indigenous personnel in the skills necessary to run the factories built by those companies. Often the firms bring with them their own managers, engineers, and technicians, and the work force from the LDCs is kept in menial jobs in which on-the-job training is minimal. In recent years the LDCs have begun to deal with this problem by restricting immigration of foreign personnel, giving them work permits only for limited periods and requiring at least some minimum employment of indigenous personnel in key positions.

Another danger posed by foreign investment is that it may prevent future financial independence. Profits are a major source of the funds used for investment. If foreign investment takes over the LDCs' most profitable industries, then newly formed capital—new plants and equipment—will also be owned predominantly by foreigners.

POPULATION GROWTH

Population growth is often described as the primary villain in the LDCs. We have already noted that their populations grow far more rapidly than those in the wealthier countries. And although the growth rate has recently been declining in many of the less developed countries, overall, the population of the LDCs is expanding at a rate that will double in less than 30 years, requiring a doubling of housing, schools, hospitals, and so on—a heavy real cost for an LDC.

The growth in population has been stimulated by improvements in medical care, which have reduced death rates spectacularly. Today, in some areas, death rates (ratio of deaths to population) are only one-quarter or one-fifth as high as birthrates. While formerly it was not unusual for half a nation's children to die before the age of 20, today in many countries this is true of only some 4 percent of those populations. This dramatic decline can be attributed primarily to inexpensive public health measures: reduction in intestinal diseases through purer water supplies; reduction in the incidence of malaria by the draining of swamps; insecticide spraying of the breeding grounds of disease-carrying mosquitoes; eradication of smallpox by vaccination; and so forth. The more expensive treatment of illness, using modern medical techniques and miracle drugs, seems to have contributed far less.

But not all LDCs suffer from serious population problems. India, Indonesia, and Egypt are frequently cited examples of population pressures. On the other hand, many African countries and parts of Latin America still have populations so small that they are denied economies of larger scale communication and transportation. The economy of a sparsely settled country whose electric power and telecommunication lines must traverse great unpopulated areas is under a costly handicap.

Governments in a number of LDCs have been struggling to find workable ways to cut population growth. Programs set up to distribute contraceptives and propaganda against large families have achieved modest success; but in some countries with particularly severe population problems the governments have been dissatisfied with the results of these voluntary efforts. In India, a program making use of compulsory sterilization aroused the anger of the public and finally led to the downfall of the government.

Ironically enough, it was communist China which, along with Singapore, decided to employ strong financial incentives for population control. In China, government support is provided for a first child. For a second, the support is withdrawn and some financial penalties imposed; and for a third child, the penalties are really prohibitive for most people. There is much more to the program, however, than such rather benign financial incentives. For example, in urban areas (where most of the citizens work in state-operated enterprises and are monitored more closely than rural residents), each factory is assigned a person or committee to keep track of birth control. Women workers are required to maintain a record of their menstrual cycles and submit the records to the monitor; a woman who misses a menstrual period is forced to have an abortion. According to a recent issue of *The Economist* magazine, "The *Ningxia Legal Daily* reports that ten couples in the south-western province of Sichuan refused to abort pregnancies which, if brought to term, would have violated the government's one-child family policy. To make them see sense, the men were caned on their bare buttocks, one stroke for each day of the pregnancy, and one of the women was threatened with caning, until all the couples agreed to abortions. 'A complete victory against the diehard elements,' noted the *Legal Daily* with satisfaction" (March 9, 1991, page 33).

Such coercive measures have, indeed, been successful in reducing average birthrates to a bit over one child per couple in the cities and a bit over two children per couple in rural areas (where five or six children used to be the norm). One population expert has warned, however, that the one-child program may prove disastrous for China's economy, because family enterprises have always played an important role, and because twenty years hence it can leave the support of a tremendous aging population to be borne by a depleted labor force.

EDUCATIONAL AND TECHNICAL TRAINING

Everyone knows that educational levels in the LDCs are much lower than they are in the wealthier countries. There are fewer graduates of elementary schools, far fewer graduates of high schools, and enormously fewer college graduates. The percentage of the population that is literate is much lower than in industrialized nations. The issue is how much of a handicap this constitutes for economic growth.

If, by "education," we refer to general learning rather than technical (trade) schooling, the evidence is that it makes considerably less difference for economic growth than is often believed. For example, the number of jobs that clearly require secondary (high school) education rarely seems to exceed 10 percent of the labor force. Various studies that have investigated whether there is a statistical relationship between the economic growth of an economy and its typical educational level have found only weak correlations between the two. Other suggestive evidence can easily be cited. For example, in 1840 when Great Britain ruled the markets of the world, only 59 percent of the British adult population was literate, while in the United States, Scandinavia, and Germany, then all relatively undeveloped countries, the figure was about 80 percent.

All of this is not meant to imply that education is worthless. On the contrary, it obviously offers many benefits in and of itself, which need not be discussed here. But it does suggest that if a government invests in education *purely as a means to stimulate economic growth*, only a very limited outlay on *general* education beyond the achievement of literacy is justifiable on these grounds.

Matters are quite different when we turn to technical training. There is apparently a high payoff to the training of electricians, machinists, draftsmen, construction workers, and the like. While the number of persons involved need not be very high in proportion to the population, the role played by such specialists is crucial. However, the LDCs would find it a very heavy drain upon their scarce foreign currency to send young people abroad to learn these skills in the numbers called for by the needs of the economy. One of the main inhibitions to adequate training in these areas is that in many countries such skills are held in low esteem and considered inferior to training in the liberal arts. Consequently, technical education is often handicapped by low budgets, low teacher salaries—which discourage good people from entering the field—and the prejudice of potential students against such fields.

Training in improved farming methods also has a great deal to contribute. In many of the LDCs, agricultural methods produce yields far lower than the best of the known techniques can offer. As one leading observer, the late Nobel Prize-winner Sir W. Arthur Lewis, remarked:

> *If this gap could be closed, the economies of these countries would be unrecognizable. Indeed . . . no impact can be made on mass living standards without revolutionizing agricultural performance.*[9]

---

[9]W. A. Lewis, *Development Economics: An Outline* (Morristown, N.J.: General Learning Press, 1974), page 25.

There seem to be no easy ways to provide the necessary education to the farmers who cannot spare the time to attend schools, and training their children also involves a number of critical obstacles. Religious beliefs often lead parents to object to schooling of their children, particularly of girls; in areas where literacy is low (where the problem is generally most serious), truly literate and knowledgeable teachers are almost impossible to find in any substantial numbers; and children who do complete schooling have a tendency to leave the farms and move to the cities.

Programs to provide help to the peasants on their own farms have had only limited success. Indeed, lack of training is only part of the problem. Many other things are needed to make modern farming methods possible—farms larger than the five acres that are typical in a number of countries are required to permit the use of modern machinery where it is appropriate. Roads and storage facilities must be built. Credit must be made available to farmers. Financial arrangements must be changed so farmers need no longer give up half their crops to landlords and tax collectors whom farmers can surely regard as little more than parasites and who undermine incentives for improved productivity.

UNEMPLOYMENT

One of the most noteworthy features of the growth of the LDCs has been an increase in unemployment as population shifted out of agriculture into the cities. Increased schooling has stimulated the migration out of the rural areas, as has unionization, which has often produced a huge gap between urban and rural wages. Government investment policies have also favored construction of schools, hospitals, and other facilities in the cities, and as a result, large numbers of migrants have entered the cities to swell the ranks of the unemployed. The unemployment rate among young urban workers has been particularly high; indeed, rates as high as 50 percent are not unheard of.

These figures are compounded by the phenomenon of **disguised unemployment**. For example, ten persons may do a job for which only six are needed. The statistics would show no unemployment among the ten workers, even though four of them really contribute nothing to output. Some observers believe that this is such a widespread problem in rural areas that even a substantial reverse migration of the urban unemployed back to the farms would add very little to production, at least in some of the LDCs.

An important consequence of all this is that in many LDCs unemployment may not be accompanied by any substantial reduction in output, in contrast to the situation in industrialized economies. But this does not mean that unemployment in the LDCs is not a serious problem. What it does mean is that it may sometimes be desirable for those economies to avoid the use of labor-saving equipment, partly because it will result in better use of an abundant resource and partly because it will contribute to the solution of a serious social problem. Thus, increased jobs are desirable perhaps primarily because they absorb unemployed labor. This is in contrast to the usual situation in the developed countries in which increased employment is desirable perhaps primarily because it increases income and output.

SOCIAL IMPEDIMENTS TO ENTREPRENEURSHIP

As was noted earlier in this chapter, one of the magic ingredients of economic growth is **entrepreneurship**. It is clear that the LDCs need entrepreneurs if their economies are to grow rapidly. But in many of these economies there are serious inhibitions to entrepreneurship. Traditional social values often accord relatively low status to business activity. Indeed, those traditional values even prevent businesses from seeking ways to attract and please their customers and their work force. In addition, high positions in business in many LDCs are often determined by family connections and inheritance, not by ability.

In the LDCs, growth will be inhibited until customs can be modified to increase the social status of economic activity, to make it respectable for private business people and managers of public enterprises to do their best to attract business and increase productivity, and to assign responsibility on the basis of ability rather than family connections.

GOVERNMENT INHIBITION OF BUSINESS ACTIVITY

In addition to social impediments to business, the political situation in the LDCs often is detrimental to business success. Business is not helped by unstable governments or by the uncertainty that accompanies such an environment, especially if there is a high likelihood of revolution. Foreign investment will be discouraged where there is fear of expropriation or of unstable currencies that may fall in value and wipe out hard-earned profits. And indigenous business people may live in fear of nationalization or even imprisonment—possibilities that are not likely to encourage investment.

In the normal course of events, governments in the LDCs are often inclined to interfere with business activity in a variety of ways that seem relatively innocuous—but whose effects can be deadly. Price controls are often imposed at levels that make the controlled activity totally unprofitable and cause it to wither. Licenses and other direct controls are frequently administered by incompetent bureaucrats, who tie up business activity in red tape. As a matter of prestige of the currency, exchange rates are often set so high that exports from the LDC cannot compete on the world market. The governments sometimes expropriate and seek to operate foreign firms before they have trained indigenous personnel to run them. In short:

Poorly conceived economic policies can impede business activity and hence economic growth in the LDCs. But, then, it must be admitted that the LDCs have no monopoly on foolish economic policies!

HELP FROM INDUSTRIALIZED ECONOMIES

We have just seen that the two primary needs of the LDCs are technical skills and capital resources. Happily, these are precisely the things that the more prosperous nations are in a position to offer. We have the trained teachers, classrooms, laboratories, and equipment necessary to provide an education of the highest quality to students from the LDCs. However, there is a danger here that has received a great deal of attention, the so-called **brain drain**. This refers to the temptation for students from LDCs to try to stay in the countries where they have studied and enjoy the higher living standard, rather than to return home where their abilities are needed so badly.

There are several ways to deal with this. For example, one can require students to return to their homelands for at least some given number of years after completion of the educational program, or offer higher wages for trained persons in the

LDCs to make returning more attractive. Yet the problem is there, and the large number of doctors, teachers, and other skilled personnel from LDCs who are seeking jobs in the developed countries suggests that it is not negligible.

A second major contribution that the wealthier countries can make to the LDCs is to offer them trained technicians and technical advice from the wealthier countries' own populations. Such counseling and personnel can be very helpful as a temporary measure, but in the long run they can prove detrimental if provision for the training of local personnel for the ultimate replacement of the foreign technicians and advisers is not built into the program.

Third, the world can help the LDCs through research. One of the hardest problems for the developing world is what to do in the rural areas that suffer from inadequate rainfall, where several hundred million people live in both Asia and Africa. These people are badly in need of new dry-farming techniques. Until some are discovered, their poverty will increase as their numbers grow. An international research organization devoted to food production in problem areas in the LDCs would have much to contribute.

Fourth, the developed countries can help by encouraging freedom of trade and investment. This will help those LDCs whose exports are now being held back by barriers to trade. Exports of sugar, meat, cotton, and other agricultural products are inhibited by industrialized countries' tariffs and other restrictions. LDCs would also benefit substantially from a lifting of tariffs and quotas upon the import by industrial countries of processed or manufactured goods. Such restrictive measures make it difficult for LDCs to export anything but raw materials and impedes their industrialization and modernization. All in all, increased freedom of trade is a matter of highest priority for the LDCs. It will probably also prove beneficial to the wealthier countries, as improved incomes in the LDCs make the latter better customers for the exports of the former.[10]

A last, and very important, type of assistance from the developed to the less developed countries takes the form of money or physical resources provided either as loans made on favorable terms or as outright grants (gifts).

LOANS AND GRANTS BY THE UNITED STATES AND OTHERS

Since World War II a number of countries have provided capital to the LDCs. An international organization, the International Bank for Reconstruction and Development (the **World Bank**), was created largely for this purpose. It has 155 member countries, each providing an amount of capital related to its wealth; for instance, the United States has contributed about 21 percent of the total, while Japan and West Germany have supplied 15 percent and 11 percent, respectively. The Bank makes loans that finance its bonds and has acted as guarantor of repayment to encourage some private lending. Since its inception the Bank has approved loans totalling $203.1 billion to 142 countries, mostly for infrastructure,

---

[10]Not everyone agrees with this conclusion. There are those who have argued that participation of LDCs in international trade is bad for them because it weakens their capacity to develop as self-reliant, mature economies. It is believed that new manufacturing industries in the LDCs will not take off without protection from foreign competition; that development of raw material exports creates a politically powerful vested interest that inhibits manufacturing; and that foreign participation in trade and production of exports inhibits domestic investment and the development of local entrepreneurship.

In this view, LDCs are therefore held back by international trade and they would do better to integrate regionally and develop their own home markets without foreigners, who also bring unsuitable habits, tastes, and technology, and impart a crippling inferiority complex to the LDCs.

dams, communications, and transportation. In addition, it provided technical assistance and planning advice.[11]

United States' loans and grants have exceeded the total given by all other countries and international agencies, with U.S. interest and repayment terms generally far more generous than those of other governments. However, the bulk of the assistance provided by the United States has gone to a small number of countries, such as India, Pakistan, South Korea, and Turkey.

During the 1960s, our expenditures on aid ran to more than $3 billion per year. In the past decade, expenditures on foreign aid have become less popular politically, and the amounts provided consequently have gone down sharply and steadily from about half a percent of U.S. GDP in 1965 to about 0.2 percent of GDP in 1990.[12]

France, Great Britain, West Germany, and other industrialized countries now provide about $70 billion per year, which is about one percent of their combined GDPs. Japan, too, has recently begun to make substantial contributions; in 1989 it appropriated about $24.1 billion, or 1.3 percent of its GDP.[13] The Soviet Union also used to be a major source of assistance to the LDCs, providing, along with its associated countries, more than $3 billion per year, or about 0.25 percent of their GDP. The recent economic troubles and political upheavals in the former Soviet bloc make it hard to foresee what will happen to contributions from this source.

Many economists have advocated greater generosity in our assistance to LDCs. It is argued that an effective aid program that really helps the growth of LDCs will also serve our own interests. By making those countries more stable economically and politically, we can contribute to our own economic tranquility. By increasing the LDCs' power to buy and sell, we contribute to the prosperity of the entire world.

CAN LDCs BREAK AWAY FROM POVERTY?

It is easy to jump to the conclusion that the economic problems of the LDCs are staggering and that the prospects of their ever catching up with the industrialized countries are negligible. Yet a number of LDCs and former LDCs have made enormous progress. In Africa, Nigeria, Senegal, and Ghana increased their GDPs during the late 1980s at a rate of about 5 to 6 percent a year, which is considerably faster than their population growth.[14] In the Americas, Costa Rica's performance has been comparable. Even more striking is the expansion of output in a number of places in the Far East—particularly Hong Kong, Taiwan, South Korea, and Singapore, where prosperity is unprecedented and economic activity is expanding at an astonishing rate. Here, per capita GDPs have been growing at a rate of 6.5 percent a year and more. These economies have progressed to a point that makes it inappropriate to continue to classify them as LDCs.

---

[11]World Bank, *The World Bank Annual Report 1991*, Washington, D.C.: 1991.

[12]U.S. Bureau of the Census, *Statistical Abstract of the United States, 1992*, Washington, D.C.: U.S. Government Printing Office, 1992 and *Economic Report of the President, January 1993*, Washington, D.C.: U.S. Government Printing Office, 1993.

[13]*Ibid.*

[14]World Bank, *The World Bank Annual Report*, Washington, D.C.: various years

But the most impressive case is that of Japan. Many of your professors will remember clearly when U.S. business feared the flood of goods produced by cheap Japanese labor, and when the label "made in Japan" suggested inexpensive and shoddy merchandise. From one of the world's impoverished countries, Japan has risen to one of the world's richest. Its goods are now feared by American manufacturers not because they are produced and sold so cheaply, but because their quality is so high. Japanese cars and sophisticated electronic equipment find a ready market in the United States. And as a result, per capita income in Japan has surpassed that in Great Britain.

Clearly, a less developed country need not lag behind forever.

Summary

1. If growth is evaluated in terms of its effect upon the well-being of individuals, a country's economic growth should be measured in terms of *per capita* income, not in terms of GDP or some other index of total output of the economy.

2. A rapidly rising population poses a threat to growth of per capita incomes.

3. On our finite planet, **exponential growth** (growth at a constant percentage rate) is, in general, impossible except for relatively brief periods.

4. Increases in growth depend heavily on entrepreneurship, accumulation of capital equipment, and research and development.

5. Saving is necessary for the accumulation of resources with which to produce factories, machinery, and other capital equipment. Thus, saving is a critical requisite for growth, particularly in less developed countries.

6. Many observers argue that even if continued growth does not lead to catastrophically rapid depletion of resources (as some have predicted), its desirability is nevertheless questionable because it produces pollution, overcrowding, and many other undesirable consequences.

7. Those who favor growth argue that without it there is no chance of ridding the world of poverty.

8. Standards of living in many **LDCs** are extremely low; per capita incomes that are equivalent to $1500 a year

are not uncommon. Life expectancy is low and daily living is very difficult, particularly for women.

9. GDP and per capita incomes in the LDCs grew considerably in the 1970s, though in many cases they slowed in the 1980s.

10. Nevertheless, the gap between family incomes in the less developed and the industrialized countries has continued to widen.

11. In many LDCs, population continues to grow much faster than that in the industrialized countries.

12. Growth in the LDCs is impeded by shortages of capital caused by poverty, traditions that do not encourage investment, rapid population growth, poor education, unemployment, lack of **entrepreneurship**, and government impediments to business.

13. Industrialized countries can help the LDCs by providing capital through loans and grants, by offering training and education to people from those lands, and by encouraging freedom of trade with the LDCs.

14. In the period after World War II many countries, including the United States and the Soviet Union, provided large amounts of money to the LDCs in the form of loans and grants.

15. Several international organizations, most notably the **World Bank**, have been organized to provide economic assistance to the LDCs.

Key Concepts and Terms

Output per capita
Exponential growth
Social infrastructure
Exchange between present and future consumption

Embodied growth
Disembodied growth
Less developed countries (LDCs)
Growth rate in GDP vs. per capita income

Multinational corporations
Disguised unemployment
Entrepreneurship
Brain drain
World Bank

Questions for Review

1. Which do you think has the higher total GDP, Pakistan or Luxembourg? Which has the higher per capita GDP? In which do you think people are better off economically?

2. Suppose population grows at a constant exponential rate and doubles every 12 years. How many times will it have grown in 36 years? How many years does it require to expand to 32 times its initial level?

3. Can you think of any innovations that permit growth without proportionate increases in use of inputs?

4. Name as many undesirable consequences of growth as you can think of.

5. Are the undesirable consequences of growth more likely to be considered serious in a less developed country or in an industrialized country? Why?

6. To many families living in less developed countries, an income equivalent to $2000 per year is considered a high standard of living. Can you make up a budget for a U.S. family of four earning $2000 a year?

7. Explain how it is possible for the per capita income of an LDC to grow at a faster rate than that in the United States and yet for the dollar difference between the incomes of average families in both countries to increase. Can you give a numerical example showing how this happens?

8. Discuss the advantages and disadvantages to an LDC of a U.S. manufacturing company investing in that country.

9. If you were economic adviser to the president of an LDC, what might you suggest that he or she do to encourage increases in saving and investment?

10. No one knows what encourages or discourages the supply of entrepreneurs. Do you have any ideas about policies that may be capable of stimulating entrepreneurship?

11. Name some countries in which entrepreneurship seems to be abundant these days and some countries in which it seems to be scarce. What is your impression about what is happening to the supply of entrepreneurs in the United States?

12. It has been noted that crime overlords who organize drug empires and the managements of law firms that specialize in stimulation of litigation are often, in fact, successful entrepreneurs. Discuss whether these persons contribute to the growth of their economies.

13. What have you read in the newspapers and heard from other sources about the Japanese "growth miracle?" What does it portend for the future of the Japanese economy? For that of the United States?

14. Puerto Rico is reported to have the highest per capita income of any Latin American economy. What does this suggest about possible consequences of statehood for the island? How do you reconcile that statistic with the low economic status of many Puerto Ricans living in the continental United States?

15. Puerto Rico has a per-capita income far lower than that of any other state in the United States. What do you conclude by comparing this fact with those in the previous question?

GLOSSARY

One country is said to have an **ABSOLUTE ADVANTAGE** over another in the production of a particular good if it can produce that good using smaller quantities of resources than can the other country. (436)

ABSTRACTION means ignoring many details in order to focus on the most important elements of a problem. (11)

AGGREGATE DEMAND is the total amount that all consumers, business firms, and government agencies are willing to spend on final goods and services. (151)

The **AGGREGATE DEMAND CURVE** shows the quantity of domestic product that is demanded at each possible value of the price level. (108)

The **AGGREGATE SUPPLY CURVE** shows, for each possible price level, the quantity of goods and services that all the nation's businesses are willing to produce during a specified period of time, holding all other determinants of aggregate quantity supplied constant. (108, 228)

AGGREGATION means combining many individual markets into one overall market. (105)

The **ALLOCATION OF RESOURCES** refers to the decision on how to divide up the economy's scarce input resources among the different outputs produced in the economy and among the different firms or other organizations that produce those outputs. (59)

A nation's currency is said to **APPRECIATE** when exchange rates change so that a unit of its own currency can buy more units of foreign currency. (462)

An **ASSET** of an individual or business firm is an item of value that the individual or firm owns. (286)

An **AUTOMATIC STABILIZER** is any arrangement that automatically serves to support aggregate demand when it would otherwise sag and to hold down aggregate demand when it would otherwise surge ahead. In this way, an automatic stabilizer reduces the sensitivity of the economy to shifts in demand. (341)

An **AUTONOMOUS INCREASE IN CONSUMPTION** is an increase in consumer spending without any increase in incomes. It is represented on a graph as a shift of the entire consumption function. (214)

The **BALANCE OF PAYMENTS DEFICIT** is the amount by which the quantity supplied of a country's currency (per year) exceeds the quantity demanded. Balance of payments deficits arise whenever the exchange rate is pegged at an artificially high level. (470)

The **BALANCE OF PAYMENTS SURPLUS** is the amount by which the quantity demanded of a country's currency (per year) exceeds the quantity supplied. Balance of payments surpluses arise whenever the exchange rate is pegged at an artificially low level. (471)

A **BALANCE SHEET** is an accounting statement listing the values of all the assets on the left-hand side and the values of all the liabilities and **net worth** on the right-hand side. (286)

BARTER is a system of exchange in which people directly trade one good for another, without using money as an intermediate step. (275)

The **BUDGET DEFICIT** is the amount by which the government's expenditures exceed its receipts during a specified period of time, usually one year. (356)

A **CAPITAL GAIN** is the difference between the price at which an asset is sold and the price at which it was bought. (138)

A **CAPITAL GOOD** is an item that is used to produce other goods and services in the future, rather than being consumed today. Factories and machines are examples. (65)

A **CENTRAL BANK** is a bank for banks. America's central bank is the **Federal Reserve System**. (299)

A **CLOSED ECONOMY** is one that does not trade with other nations in either goods or assets. (495)

A **COMMODITY MONEY** is an object in use as a medium of exchange, but which also has a substantial value in alternative (nonmonetary) uses. (278)

One country is said to have a **COMPARATIVE ADVANTAGE** over another in the production of a particular good relative to other goods if it produces that good least inefficiently as compared with the other country. (437)

The **CONCENTRATION RATIO** is the percentage of an industry's output produced by its *four* largest firms. It is intended to measure the degree to which the industry is dominated by a few large firms. (41)

CONSUMER EXPENDITURE, symbolized by the letter **C**, is the total amount spent by consumers on newly produced goods and services (excluding purchases of new homes, which are considered investment goods). (151)

The **CONSUMPTION FUNCTION** is the relationship between total consumer expenditure and total disposable income in the economy, holding all other determinants of consumer spending constant. (160)

A **CONSUMPTION GOOD** is an item that is available for immediate use by households, and that satisfies wants of members of households without contributing directly to future production by the economy. (65)

A **CORPORATION** is a firm that has the legal status of a fictional individual. This fictional individual is owned by a number of persons, called its stockholders, and is run by a set of elected officers (usually headed by a president) and a board of directors. (38)

Two variables are said to be **CORRELATED** if they tend to go up or down together. But correlation need not imply causation. (14)

CREEPING INFLATION refers to an inflation that proceeds for a long time at a moderate and fairly steady pace. (141)

CROWDING IN occurs when government spending, by raising real GDP, induces increases in private investment spending. (371)

CROWDING OUT occurs when deficit spending by the government forces private investment spending to contract. (371)

CYCLICAL UNEMPLOYMENT is the portion of unemployment that is attributable to a decline in the economy's total production. Cyclical unemployment rises during recessions and falls as prosperity is restored. (129)

DEFLATION refers to a sustained *decrease* in the general price level. (113)

A **DEMAND CURVE** is a graphical depiction of a demand schedule. It shows how the quantity demanded of some product during a specified period of time will change as the price of that product changes, holding all other determinants of quantity demanded constant. (78)

A **DEMAND SCHEDULE** is a table showing how the quantity demanded of some product during a specified period of time changes as the price of that product changes, holding all other determinants of quantity demanded constant. (77)

DEPOSIT INSURANCE is a system that guarantees that depositors will not lose money even if their bank goes bankrupt. (284)

The currency is said to **DEPRECIATE** when exchange rates change so that a unit of its currency can buy fewer units of foreign currency. (462)

A **DEVALUATION** is a reduction in the official value of a currency. (462)

The **DISCOUNT RATE** is the interest rate the Fed charges on loans it makes to banks. (306)

A **DISCOURAGED WORKER** is an unemployed person who gives up looking for work and is therefore no longer counted as part of the labor force. (128)

DISPOSABLE INCOME is the sum of the incomes of all the individuals in the economy after all taxes have been deducted and all transfer payments have been added. (152)

DIVISION OF LABOR means breaking up a task into a number of smaller, more specialized tasks so that each worker can become more adept at a particular job. (68)

DUMPING means selling goods in a foreign market at lower prices than those charged in the home market. (454)

An **ECONOMETRIC MODEL** is a set of mathematical equations that embody the economist's model of the economy. (342)

ECONOMIC GROWTH occurs when an economy is able to produce more goods and services for each consumer. (65)

An **ECONOMIC MODEL** is a simplified, small-scale version of some aspect of the economy. Economic models are often expressed in equations, by graphs, or in words. (15)

An **ECONOMY** is a collection of markets in a defined geographical area. (28)

The **EQUATION OF EXCHANGE** states that the money value of GDP transactions must be equal to the product of the average stock of money times velocity. That is:

$$M \times V = P \times Y. \qquad (322)$$

An **EQUILIBRIUM** is a situation in which there are no inherent forces that produce change. Changes away from an equilibrium position will occur only as a result of "outside events" that disturb the status quo. (81, 186)

EXCESS RESERVES are any reserves held in excess of the legal minimum. (287)

The **EXCHANGE RATE** states the price, in terms of one currency, at which another currency can be bought. (461)

An **EXPENDITURE SCHEDULE** shows the relationship between national income (GDP) and total spending. (188)

EXPONENTIAL GROWTH is growth at a constant percentage rate. (513)

An **EXPORT SUBSIDY** is a payment by the government to exporters to permit them to reduce the selling price of their goods so they can compete more effectively in foreign markets. (446)

FIAT MONEY is money that is decreed as such by the government. It is of little value as a commodity, but it maintains its value as a medium of exchange because people have faith that the issuer will stand behind the pieces of printed paper and limit their production. (278)

FINAL GOODS AND SERVICES are those that are purchased by their ultimate users. (110)

The government's **FISCAL POLICY** is its plan for spending and taxation. It is designed to steer aggregate demand in some desired direction. (251)

FIXED EXCHANGE RATES are rates set by government decisions and maintained by government actions. (469)

FIXED TAXES are tax taxes that do not vary with the level of GDP. (251)

FLOATING EXCHANGE RATES are rates determined in free markets by the law of supply and demand. (462)

A **45° LINE** is a ray through the origin with a slope of +1. It marks off points where the variables measured on each axis have equal values.[3] (24)

FRACTIONAL RESERVE BANKING is a system under which bankers keep as reserves only a fraction of the funds they hold on deposit. (282)

FRICTIONAL UNEMPLOYMENT is unemployment that is due to normal turnover in the labor market. It includes people who are temporarily between jobs because they are moving or changing occupations, or for similar reasons. (129)

GALLOPING INFLATION refers to an inflation that proceeds at an exceptionally high rate, perhaps for only a relatively brief period. Galloping inflations are generally characterized by accelerating rates of inflation so that the rate of inflation is higher this month than it was last month. (141)

GOVERNMENT PURCHASES, symbolized by the letter **G**, refers to the goods (such as airplanes and paper clips) and services (such as school teaching and police protection) purchased by all levels of government. (151)

GROSS DOMESTIC PRODUCT (GDP) is the sum of the money values of all final goods and services produced in the domestic economy during a specified period of time, usually one year. (30, 109)

An **INCOME-EXPENDITURE DIAGRAM**, also called a **45° LINE DIAGRAM**, plots total real expenditure (on the vertical axis) against real income (on the horizontal axis). The 45° line marks off points where income and expenditure are equal. (191)

INDEXING refers to provisions in a law or a contract whereby monetary payments are automatically adjusted whenever a specified price index changes. Wage rates, pensions, interest payments on bonds, income taxes, and many other things can be indexed in this way, and have been. Sometimes such contractual provisions are called *escalator clauses*. (407)

An **INDUCED INCREASE IN CONSUMPTION** is an increase in consumer spending that stems from an increase in consumer incomes. It is represented on a graph as a movement along a fixed consumption function. (214)

INDUCED INVESTMENT is the part of investment spending that rises when GDP rises and falls when GDP falls. (188)

INFLATION refers to a sustained increase in the general price level. (33, 108)

INFLATION ACCOUNTING means adjusting standard accounting procedures for the fact that inflation lowers the purchasing power of money. (362)

The **INFLATIONARY GAP** is the amount by which equilibrium real GDP exceeds the full-employment level of GDP. (195)

An **INTERMEDIATE GOOD** is a good purchased for resale or for use in producing another good. (110)

INVESTMENT SPENDING, symbolized by the letter **I**, is the sum of the expenditures of business firms on new plant and equipment and households on new homes. Financial "investments" are not included, nor are resales of existing physical assets. (151)

The **J CURVE** shows the typical pattern of response of net exports to a change in currency values. Following a depreciation or a devaluation, net exports usually decline at first and then rise. (490)

The **LABOR FORCE** is the number of people holding or seeking jobs. (128)

LABOR PRODUCTIVITY refers to the amount of output a worker turns out in an hour (or a week or a year) of labor. It can be measured as total national output (GDP) in a given year divided by the total number of hours of work performed for pay in the country during that year. That is, labor productivity is defined as GDP per hour of labor. (416)

The **LAW OF SUPPLY AND DEMAND** states that, in a free market, the forces of supply and demand generally push the price toward the level at which quantity supplied and quantity demanded are equal. (83)

A **LEADING INDICATOR** is a variable that, experience has shown, normally turns down before recessions start and turns up before expansions begin. (345)

A **LIABILITY** of an individual or business firm is an item of value that the individual or firm owes. Many liabili- ties are known as "debts." (286)

An asset's **LIQUIDITY** refers to the ease with which it can be converted into cash. (281)

The narrowly defined money supply, usually abbreviated **M1**, is the sum of all coins and paper money in circulation, plus certain checkable deposit balances at banks and savings institutions.[2] (280)

The broadly defined money supply, usually abbreviated **M2**, is the sum of all coins and paper money in circulation, plus all types of checking account balances, plus most forms of savings account balances, plus shares in money market mutual funds, and a few other minor items. (280)

The **MARGINAL PROPENSITY TO CONSUME** (or MPC for short) is the ratio of the change in consumption to the change in disposable income that produces the change in consumption. On a graph, it appears as the slope of the consumption function. (160)

A **MARKET SYSTEM** is a form of organization of the economy in which decisions on resource allocation are left to the independent decisions of individual producers and consumers acting in their own best interests without central direction. (70)

A **MIXED ECONOMY** is one in which there is some public influence over the workings of free markets. There may also be some public ownership mixed in with private property. (47)

MONETARISM is a mode of analysis that uses the equation of exchange to organize and analyze macroeconomic data. (326)

MONETARY POLICY refers to actions that the Federal Reserve System takes in order to change the equilibrium of the money market; that is, to alter the money supply, move interest rates, or both. (311)

The central bank is said to **MONETIZE THE DEFICIT** when it purchases the bonds that the government issues. (368)

MONEY is the standard object used in exchanging goods and services. In short, money is the **MEDIUM OF EXCHANGE**. (277)

A **MONEY FIXED ASSET** is an asset with a face value fixed in terms of dollars, such as money itself, government bonds, and corporate bonds. (163)

MORAL SUASION refers to informal requests and warnings designed to persuade banks to limit their borrowings from the Fed. (307)

The **MULTIPLIER** is the ratio of the change in equilibrium GDP (Y) divided by the original change in spending that causes the change in GDP. (208)

The **NATIONAL DEBT** is the federal government's total indebtedness at a moment in time. It is the result of previous deficits. (356)

NATIONAL INCOME is the sum of the incomes of all the individuals in the economy earned in the forms of wages, interest, rents, and profits. It excludes transfer payments and is calculated before any deductions are taken for income taxes. (152)

The economy's self-correcting mechanism always tends to push the unemployment rate back toward a specific rate of unemployment that we call the **NATURAL RATE OF UNEMPLOYMENT**. (394)

NEAR MONEYS are liquid assets that are close substitutes for money. (281)

NET EXPORTS, symbolized by ($X - IM$), is the difference between U.S. exports and U.S. imports. It indicates the difference between what we sell to foreigners and what we buy from them. (152)

NET WORTH is the value of all assets minus the value of all liabilities. (286)

NOMINAL GDP is calculated by valuing all outputs at current prices. (109)

The **NOMINAL RATE OF INTEREST** is the percentage by which the money the borrower pays back exceeds the money that he borrowed, making no adjustment for any fall in the purchasing power of this money that results from inflation. (137)

An economy is called relatively **OPEN** if its exports and imports constitute a large share of its GDP. An economy is considered relatively **CLOSED** if they constitute a small share. (31)

An **OPEN ECONOMY** is one that trades with other nations in goods and services, and perhaps also in financial assets. (485)

OPEN-MARKET OPERATIONS refer to the Fed's purchase or sale of government securities through transactions in the open market. (302)

The **OPPORTUNITY COST** of some decision is the value of the next best alternative which you have to give up because of that decision (for example, working instead of going to school). (7, 57)

The lower left-hand corner of a graph where the two axes meet is called the **ORIGIN**. Both variables are equal to zero at the origin. (24)

OUTPUTS are the goods and services that consumers want to acquire. **INPUTS** or **FACTORS OF PRODUCTION** are the labor, machinery, build-

ings, and natural resources used to make these outputs. (28)

The **PARADOX OF THRIFT** is the fact that an effort by a nation to save more may simply reduce national income and fail to raise total saving. (218)

A **PARTNERSHIP** is a firm whose ownership is shared by a fixed number of partners. (40)

A **PHILLIPS CURVE** is a graph depicting the rate of unemployment on the horizontal axis and either the rate of inflation or the rate of change of money wages on the vertical axis. Phillips curves are normally downward sloping, indicating that higher inflation rates are associated with lower unemployment rates. (388)

POTENTIAL GROSS DOMESTIC PRODUCT is the real GDP the economy would produce if its labor and other resources were fully employed. (126)

A **PRICE CEILING** is a legal maximum on the price that may be charged for a commodity. (91)

A **PRICE FLOOR** is a legal minimum on the price that may be charged for a commodity. (93)

The **PRINCIPLE OF INCREASING COSTS** states that as the production of a good expands, the opportunity cost of producing another unit generally increases. (61)

A **PRODUCTION POSSIBILITIES** frontier shows the different combinations of various goods that a producer can turn out, given the available resources and existing technology. (60)

PRODUCTIVITY is the amount of output produced by a unit of input. (232)

A tax is **PROGRESSIVE** if the ratio of taxes to income rises as income rises. (47)

A **PROPRIETORSHIP** is a business firm owned by a single person. (40)

The **PURCHASING POWER** of a given sum of money is the volume of goods and services it will buy. (132)

The **QUANTITY DEMANDED** is the number of units consumers want to buy over a specified period of time. (77)

The **QUANTITY SUPPLIED** is the number of units sellers want to sell over a specified period of time. (79)

A **QUOTA** specifies the maximum amount of a good that is permitted into the country from abroad per unit of time. (445)

A **RATIONAL DECISION** is one that best serves the objective of the decision maker, whatever that objective may be. Such objectives may include a firm's desire to maximize its profits, a government's desire to maximize the welfare of its citizens, or another government's desire to maximize its military might. The term "rational" connotes neither approval nor disapproval of the objective itself. (57)

RATIONAL EXPECTATIONS are forecasts which, while not necessarily correct, are the best that can be made given the available data. Rational expectations, therefore, cannot err systematically. If expectations are rational, forecasting errors are pure random numbers. (401)

A straight line emanating from the origin, or zero point on a graph, is called a ray through the origin or, sometimes, just a **RAY**. (24)

REAL GDP is calculated by valuing all outputs at the prices that prevailed in some agreed-upon year (currently 1987). Therefore, real GDP is a far better measure of changes in total production. (33, 109)

The **REAL RATE OF INTEREST** is the percentage increase in purchasing power that the borrower pays to the lender for the privilege of borrowing. It indicates the increased ability to purchase goods and services that the lender earns. (137)

The **REAL WAGE RATE** is the wage rate adjusted for inflation. It indicates the volume of goods and services that money wages will buy. (132)

A **RECESSION** is a period of time during which the total output of the economy falls. (34, 108)

The **RECESSIONARY GAP** is the amount by which the equilibrium level of real GDP falls short of potential GDP. (194)

An item's **RELATIVE PRICE** is its price in terms of some other item, rather than in terms of dollars. (134)

REQUIRED RESERVES are the minimum amount of reserves (in cash or the equivalent) required by law. Normally, required reserves are proportional to the volume of deposits. (286)

RESOURCES are the instruments provided by nature or by people that are used to create the goods and services humans want. Natural resources include minerals, the soil (usable for agriculture, building plots, and so on), water, and air. Labor is a scarce resource partly because of time limitations (the day has only 24 hours), and partly because the number of skilled workers is limited. Factories and machines are resources made by people. These three types of resources are often referred to as "land," "labor," and "capital." They are also called the inputs used in production processes or **FACTORS OF PRODUCTION**. (56)

A **REVALUATION** is an increase in the official value of a currency. (462)

A **RUN ON A BANK** occurs when many depositors withdraw cash from their accounts all at once. (275)

A **SCATTER DIAGRAM** is a graph showing the relationship between two variables (such as consumption and disposable income). Each year is represented by a point in the diagram. The coordinates of each year's point show the value of the two variables in that year. (156)

A **SHORTAGE** is an excess of quantity demanded over quantity supplied. When there is a shortage, buyers cannot purchase the quantities they desire. (81)

SPECIALIZATION means that a country devotes its energies and resources to only a small proportion of the world's productive activities. (434)

STABILIZATION POLICY is the name given to government programs designed to prevent or shorten recessions and to counteract inflation (that is, to *stabilize* prices). (119)

STAGFLATION is inflation that occurs while the economy is growing slowly ("stagnating") or having a recession. (118, 238)

A **STORE OF VALUE** is an item used to store wealth from one point in time to another. (277)

The **STRUCTURAL BUDGET DEFICIT** is the hypothetical deficit we *would have* under current fiscal policies if the economy were operating near full employment. (360)

STRUCTURAL UNEMPLOYMENT refers to workers who have lost their jobs because they have been displaced by automation, because their skills are no longer in demand, or for similar reasons. (129)

A **SUPPLY CURVE** is a graphical depiction of a supply schedule. It shows how the quantity supplied of some product during a specified period of time will change as the price of that product changes, holding all other determinants of quantity supplied constant. (79)

A **SUPPLY SCHEDULE** is a table showing how the quantity supplied of some product during a specified period of time changes as the price of that product changes, holding all other determinants of quantity supplied constant. (79)

A **SURPLUS** is an excess of quantity supplied over quantity demanded. When there is a surplus, sellers cannot sell the quantities they desire to supply. (81)

A **TARIFF** is a tax on imports. (445)

A **THEORY** is a deliberate simplification of relationships whose purpose is to explain how those relationships work. (14)

A **TIME SERIES GRAPH** is a type of two-variable diagram in which time is the variable measured along the horizontal axis. It shows how some variable changed as time passed. (32)

TRADE ADJUSTMENT ASSISTANCE provides special unemployment benefits, loans, retraining programs, and other aid to workers and firms that are harmed by foreign competition. (452)

TRANSFER PAYMENTS are sums of money that certain individuals receive as outright *grants* from the government rather than as payments for services rendered to employers. Some common examples are social security and unemployment benefits. (47, 154)

The **UNEMPLOYMENT RATE** is the number of unemployed people, expressed as a percentage of the **labor force**. (125)

The **UNIT OF ACCOUNT** is the standard unit for quoting prices. (277)

A **USURY LAW** sets down a maximum permissible interest rate for a particular type of loan. Loans at rates above the usury ceiling are illegal. (138)

A **VARIABLE** is something, such as price, whose magnitude is measured by a number; it is used to analyze what happens to other things when the size of that number changes (varies). (24)

VARIABLE TAXES are taxes that do vary with the level of GDP. (251)

VELOCITY indicates the number of times per year that an "average dollar" is spent on goods and services. It is the ratio of nominal GDP to the number of dollars in the money stock. That is:

$$\text{Velocity} = \frac{\text{Nominal GDP}}{\text{Money stock}} \quad (322)$$

The **VERTICAL (LONG-RUN) PHILLIPS CURVE** shows the menu of inflation/unemployment choices available to society in the long run. It is a vertical straight line at the natural rate of unemployment. (394)

WAGE–PRICE CONTROLS are legal restrictions on the ability of industry and labor to raise wages and prices. (405)

CREDITS

INDEX

Absolute advantage, 438
 defined, 438
Abstraction
 defined, 11
 economic aggregate as, 107
 need for, 10–13
 theory as, 14
Affluence, poverty of, 522
Africa, starvation in, 525
Age, inflation and, 137
Aggregate demand, 152
 and aggregate supply, equilibrium of, 235–36
 balancing with aggregate supply, 356–57
 composition of
  and economic growth, 518
  in planned economy, 518–19
 and currency appreciation and depreciation, 491–92
 defined, 152
 and exchange rates, 492–94
 fiscal policy and, algebraic analysis of, 272–73
 and GDP, 190
 inflation and, 384
 inflation and multiplier and, 247–48
 inflationary gap and, 240
 and international trade, 489–90
 monetarism, v. Keynesian theory, 329
 monetary policy and, 315–17
 and multiplier, 210–22
 and potential GDP, 244
Aggregate demand curve, 110, 194–95
 defined, 110
 and inflation, 240
 inflation and, and output growth, 388–89
 and multiplier, 218–20
 shifts in, 156–58
 shifts of, multiplier, 220–22
 slope of, 320
Aggregate saving, 171
Aggregate supply, 230, 318
 and aggregate demand, equilibrium of, 235–36
 balancing with aggregate demand, 356–57
 and currency appreciation and depreciation, 494
 and international trade, 494
 shifts of, and stagflation, 245–46
Aggregate supply curve, 110, 230–32
 defined, 110, 230
 inflation and, 385
  multiplier and, 246–48
  and output growth, 388–89
  unemployment and, 392–93
 shape of, 234–35, 337–39
  and resource utilization, 399
 shifts of, 232–34
  and inflationary gap, 239–40
 slope of, and money wage rate, 400–403
Aggregation, 107–108
 defined, 107
Antitrust laws, 44
Assets. See also Money fixed asset
 in banking, 288
 defined, 288
 investments as, 152
 liquidity of, 283
 purchases of physical, and demand for currency, 465
Automatic stabilizers, defined, 343
Autonomous increase in consumption, 216
 defined, 216

Balance of payments, 471–474
 adjustments under Bretton Woods system, 478–80
 defined, 474
 U.S. accounts, 474–76
Balance of payments deficit, defined, 472
Balance of payments surplus, 473
 defined, 473
Balance of trade, U.S., 474–75
Balance sheet, defined, 288
Banking
 beginnings of, 284–85
 bookkeeping in, 288
 and deposit creation, 289–94
 fractional reserve, 284
 profit v. safety in, 285–86
Bank rate. See Discount rate
Banks. See also Banking; Federal Reserve System; Excess reserves; Required reserves
 balance sheet for, 288
 deposit destruction, 294–96
 deposit insurance and, 286
 excess reserves of, 289
 loans to, and money supply, 308–309
 and money supply, 285
 net worth of, 288
 payments mechanism, efficiency of, 327
 profitability of, 284
 regulation of, 276–77, 286–88
  and improving Fed's control of money supply, 309–310
 required reserves in, 288
 controlling money supply by, 306–308
 run on, 277, 285
Barro, Robert, 374
Barter
 defined, 277
 v. money, 277
Bastiat, Frédéric, 458
Black market. See also Underground economy
 and price ceilings, 91–92
Blacks, unemployment rate of, 127–28
Bonds
 international trade in, and demand for currency, 465
 prices, and interest rates, 305–306
Booms
 budget balancing and, 357
 international, 218
 and international trade, 490
Borrowed funds. See Loans
Borrowers, inflation and, 137
Boulding, Kenneth, 521
Brain drain, 534–35
Bretton Woods system, 477–78
 exchange rate adjustments under, 478–80
Budget deficit, 4, 379–80. See also Federal budget
 burden, false claims about, 367–69
 and capital expenditure, 366
 defined, 358
 effect of recession on, 378–79
 effect of tax cuts on, 377
 and inflation, 369–70
 interest rates, and investment, 372–75
 interpreting, 361–77
 monetization and, 370–72
 v. national debt, 357–58
 partisan politics and, 356
 reduction of, 356, 379–80
 since 1543, 366–67

and state and local surpluses, 366
 structural, 361–64
 and theory of debt neutrality, 374
 and trade deficit, 502–504
Budget surplus, state and local, and federal deficit, 366
Business confidence, investment and, 184
Business cycle, 115–16. See also Economic fluctuations
 political, and stabilization policy, 350–51
Business fluctuations
 in free market, 546
 in planned economy, 547

Capital
 and aggregate supply curve shifts, 234
 earnings of, 38–39
 impediments to mobility, in international trade, 438
 sacrificing consumption for, in planned economy, 518–19
 scarcity of physical, in LDCs, 529–30
Capital equipment, economic growth and, 518
Capital expenditure, and budget deficit, 366
Capital gain
 defined, 140
 taxes on, 140
Capital good, defined, 65
Capitalism, 543–45
 defined, 543
 v. socialism, 548
  individual freedom and, 548–49
 in United States, 29–30
Central bank, 301–302
 current exchange rate system and, 482
 defined, 301
Checking deposits, 282
China
 economic growth in, 557–58
Circular flow diagram, 154–56
 and equilibrium GDP, 187–88
 simplified, 198–99
Clinton, Bill
 deficit reduction and, 356, 379–80
 and supply-side economics, 230
 and tax provision changes, 186
Clintonomics, 230
 as supply-side economics, 269, 270
Closed economy, 31. See also Economy; Open economy
 defined, 31, 497
 fiscal policy in, 497
Command economy
 five-year plans, 551–52
 one-year plans, 552
 in Soviet Union, 550
Commodity money, defined, 280
Common sense, 17–18
Comparative advantage, 439
 and cheap foreign labor, 444–45
 defined, 439
 graphing, 442–44
 math of, 439–41
 principle, 438–39
 principle of, 56
Competition
 within industries, 40–41
 international, 435
Concentration ratio, 41
 defined, 41
Constant dollars, GDP in, 111

Consumer behavior, predictability of, 168–69
Consumer expenditure, 152, 154. *See also*
    Consumption
  defined, 152
  effect of inflation, 166
  and GDP, 39
  and multiplier, 215–16
  as stabilization policy lag, 332
  and taxes, 157–58
Consumer income, and demand curve shifts,
    84–85
Consumer preferences, and demand curve
    shifts, 85–86
Consumer price index (CPI), 148–49
Consumer sovereignty, 545
  defined, 545
Consumer spending. *See* Consumer
    expenditures; Consumption
Consumption. *See also* Consumer expenditure
  autonomous increase in, 216
  and consumer behavior, 168–69
  and disposable income, 158–64
  exchange between present and future, 520
  induced increase in, 216
  sacrificing for capital, in USSR, 518–19
  and wealth, 164–65
  and wealth and income, 193–94
Consumption function, 162–64
  defined, 162
  movements along, 164
  shifts in, 164
Consumption good, defined, 65
Consumption schedule, income taxes and,
    253–56
Contour maps, 23–25
Contracts
  long-term
    and inflation, 142, 145, 410
Convergence, of productivity, 422
Coordination failure, unemployment and
    inflation as, 200–201
Corporate income tax, 46
Corporations, 40. *See also* Multinational
    corporation
  and capital, 38–39
  defined, 38
Correlation
  v. causation, 14–15
  defined, 14
Corruption, and price controls, 95
Cost, economic, rational choice and, 7–8
CPI. *See* Consumer price index
Creeping inflation, 143
  costs of, 145
  defined, 143
  and galloping inflation, 145–46
Crowding in, 373, 375
  defined, 373
Crowding out, 373, 374, 376
  defined, 373
  international, 497–99
Currency appreciation, 464
  and aggregate demand, 491–92
  and aggregate supply, 494
Currency depreciation, 464
  and aggregate demand, 491–92
  and aggregate supply, 494
Current dollars, GDP in, 111
Cyclical unemployment, 131
  defined, 131

Debt neutrality, 374
Deflating, 150
Deflation, 115–16
  defined, 115
  and recessionary gap, 241–43

Deindustrialization thesis, 427–28
Demand, 76–78. *See also* Demand curve;
    Derived demand; Derived demand
    curve
  and aggregation, 108
  for currency, 465
  level and growth of, and investment, 184–85
  in macroeconomics, 109–110
  management of, 121–23
    and trade-off between unemployment and
      inflation, 406
  for money, 311–13
  and price, 165–66
Demand curve, 19–20, 78
  defined, 78
  movement along, 164
  movements along, 84
  shift in, for domestic product, 109–110
  shifts in, 164
  shifts of, 84–87
  in supply–demand diagram, 80–81
Demand inflation, and stagflation, 240
Demand schedule, 77–78
  defined, 77
Deposit creation, 289–92
  formula for, 294, 294–97
Deposit destruction, 294–96
Deposit insurance, defined, 286
Depreciation, 176–77 *See also* Currency
    depreciation
Devaluation, 464
  defined, 464
  of fixed exchange rates, 473
Dirty float, 482
Discount rate, 308–309
  defined, 308
Discouraged worker, 130
  defined, 130
Disguised unemployment, 533
Disposable income, 153, 180–81, 594
  changes in taxes and, 253–55
  and consumption, 158–64
  defined, 153
  and movements along consumption
    function, 164
Division of labor, 68–69
  defined, 68
Domestic economy. *See* Economy, domestic
Domestic product, 107
  and national income, 154–56
Dumping, 456–57
  defined, 456

EC. *See* European Economic Community
Ecology, GDP and, 114–15
Econometric model, 344–46
  defined, 344
Economic aggregates, 107
Economic consequences of the Peace, 119
Economic fluctuations, 115–16. *See also*
    Business cycle
Economic forecasting
  accuracy of, 348–49
    and stabilization policy, 344
  econometric models, 344–46
  judgmental forecasts, 347–48
  leading indicators, 347
  survey data, 347
Economic growth
  abroad and trade deficit, 505
  in China, 557–58
  costs of in wealthy society, 522–23
  defined, 65
  desirability of, 521–22
  disembodied, 521
  education and, 532–33

embodied, 520–21
  in free market, 546
  impediments to in LDCs, 528–34
  through innovation, 520–21
  Japanese, 64–65
  in LDCs, 526–28
  measuring, 513
  payoff to, 520
  in planned economy, 547
  and population, 513
  poverty of affluence and, 522
  requirements for, 517–18
  and socialism, 548
  technical training and, 532–33
  U.S., 31–32, 33–35, 65–66
    history of, 115–18
  and unemployment, 35
Economic model, defined, 15
Economics, experimental methods of, 82
Economic systems. *See also* Capitalism; Planned
    economy; Free market; Socialism
  in transition, 550
  two distinctions, 543–45
Economic theory. *See also* Theory
  abstraction and, 11
  role of, 13–15
Economies of scale, in international trade, 436
Economy. *See also* Underground economy
  automatic stabilizers of, 343
  defined, 28
  domestic
    and fixed exchange rates and, 479–80
    and gold standard, 477
  government role in, 43–44
  history of Western, 415–17
  private enterprise, 29–30
  self-correcting mechanism
    efficiency of, 400
    Phillips curve and, 394–96
    and recessionary gap, 397
  self-correcting mechanism of, 243
  and stabilization policy and, 344
  three coordination tasks of, 68
    and market system, 70–71
    and price controls, 96–97
Education, in LDCs, 532–33
Efficiency, 66–67
Employment. *See* Full employment;
    Unemployment
EMS. *See* European Monetary System
Entrepreneurship
  and economic growth, 517
  in LDCs, 533–34
Environment. *See also* Ecology; Pollution
  damage to, economic growth and, 522–23
Equality, and output, 9
Equation of exchange, defined, 324
Equilibrium, 188–89. *See also* Gross domestic
    product (GDP), equilibrium
  of aggregate supply and demand, 235–36
  defined, 81, 188
  and demand curve shifts, 85
  demand-side, 189, 191–93
    algebraic analysis of, 207
    and full employment, 195–98
  from inflationary gap, 237–40
  and international trade pricing, 445–47
  in money market, 313–14
  of supply and demand, 80–84
  and supply curve shifts, 89
Equilibrium income, 187–88
ERM. *See* European Exchange Rate Mechanism
Essay on the Principle of Population, An, 514
European Economic Community (EC), 483–84
European Exchange Rate Mechanism (ERM),
    483–84

European Monetary System (EMS), 484
Excess reserves
  controlling money supply and, 308
  defined, 289
  interest rates and, 310–11
Exchange, 70
Exchange rates, 463–64. *See also* Fixed exchange
    rates; Floating exchange rates
  current system for, 481–82
  defined, 463
  determination of in free market, 464–67,
    470–71
  effect of inflation on, 467–69
  European mechanism for, 483–84
  fiscal policy and, 497–99
  and inflation, 494–96
  and interest rates, 469–70, 496–97
  and net exports, 490–92
  and price, 494–96
  purchasing-power theory of determination
    of, 467–69
  U.S. dollar from 1974, 482–83
Expenditure line. *See* Expenditure schedule
Expenditure schedule
  and aggregate demand curve, 193
  constructing, 189–90
  defined, 190
  graphing, 192–93
  and multiplier, 210–11
Exponential growth, 515–17
  defined, 515
Export-led growth, defined, 559
Exports. *See also* Net exports
  and relative prices, 490
Export subsidy, 448
  defined, 448
Externalities, 6–7

Factors of production, 28, 57
  defined, 28
Favoritism, and price controls, 95
FDIC. *See* Federal Deposit Insurance
    Corporation
Fed. *See* Federal Reserve System
Federal budget. *See also* Budget deficit
  balancing, 356–57
Federal Deposit Insurance Corporation (FDIC),
    286
Federal Open Market Committee (FOMC), 303
  manipulating money supply, 304–305
  and stabilization policy lags, 332
Federal Reserve System, 300
  and balance of payments deficits, 472
  control of interest rates v. control of money
    supply, 333–36
  independence of, 303–304
  Keynesians v. monetarists, 336
  loans to banks from, 308–309
  manipulating bond prices and interest rates,
    305–306
  monetization and, 370–72
  money supply control, and minimum
    required reserves, 306–308
  open-market operations of, 304–305
  origins of, 301–302
  structure, 302–303
  tightening monetary control with, 309–310
  use of moral suasion, 309
Fiat money, defined, 280
Final goods and services, 112
  defined, 112
Fiscal policy. *See also* Government purchases;
    Tax policy; Transfer payments
  and aggregate demand, algebraic analysis of,
    272–73

and budget balancing, 356–57
  in closed economy, 497
  defined, 253
  and economic stabilization, 263
  expansionary, 331
  expansive, 261–62
  inaccuracy of, 263–64
    and interest rates, 330–31
  Keynesians v. monetarists, 330–31
  monetarism and, 330–31
  v. monetary policy, 331–33
  and monetary policy, trade deficit and, 505
  in open economy, 497–99
  restrictive, 262
  spending v. taxing, 262–63
  as stimulus to economy, 253
  structural deficit and, 361–64
  and trade-off between unemployment and
    inflation, 406
  and unemployment, 396–98
Fixed exchange rates, 471–474
  and Bretton Woods system, 477–78
  defined, 471
  and gold standard, 476–77
  reasons for, 480–81
Fixed taxes, 253, 255
  defined, 253
Floating exchange rates, 464–67
  defined, 464
  problems with, 480–81
FOMC. *See* Federal Open Market Committee
Food shortages, 415
  in Africa, 525
Ford, Gerald, and tax reduction, 157
45° line, 23
  defined, 25
  diagrams, 193
Fractional reserve banking, defined, 284
Free market
  Eastern Europe and, 544
  v. planned economy, 545–48
  regulation of, 75–76
Free trade, v. protectionism, 456
Frictional unemployment, 131
  defined, 131
Friedman, Milton, 336
Full employment, 128–129, 131–32
  and demand-side equilibrium, 195–98
  and equilibrium, 198–99, 236–37
Future, expectations about, and investment,
    184

Galloping inflation, 143
  costs of, 145
  creeping inflation becoming, 145–46
  defined, 143
  in Nicaragua, 144
GDP. *See* Gross domestic product; Real gross
    domestic product
*General Theory of Employment, Interest, and
    Money, The,* 118, 174, 196
Geometric progression
  money creation and, 292
  multiplier and, 213–15
Glasnost, 553
Gold-exchange system. *See* Bretton Woods
    system
Gold standard, 476–77
Goods. *See also* specific types
  combination, 68
  distribution of, 68
  production of
    in free market, 545–46
    in planned economy, 546–47
  substitute, and demand curve shifts, 85

Gorbachev, Mikhail, 553–54
Government
  business regulation, 44
  controversy over intervention in stabilization
    policy, 778–81
  expenditures, 44
  interferences with international trade, 447–48
  in LDCs, inhibiting business activity in, 534
  policy of, and stabilization policy, 350
  ration coupons, 407
  redistribution of income, 46–47
  resource allocation and, 59
  role of in economy, 43–44
  scarcity and, 64–65
  size of, and stabilization policy, 349–50
Government purchases, 152–55, 175
  defined, 152
  and equilibrium GDP, 187
  multiplier and, 216–17, 259–60
  and shifts in aggregate demand curve,
    157–58
  taxes and, 256
  v. tax policy, 262–63
Government spending. *See* Government
    purchases
Graphs, 19–25. *See also* Time series graphs
  comparative advantage and, 442–44
  distorting trends with, 49–51
  horizontal axis, 19
  leakages and injections approach, 204–205
  origin, 19
    omitting, 51–52
    ray through, 23
  ray, 23
  two-dimensional, 19
  units of measurement and, 52–54
  vertical axis, 19
Great Depression, GDP and, 116–18
Great Leap Forward, 556
Great Proletarian Cultural Revolution, 556
Great stagflation. *See also* Stagflation
  GDP and, 119–20
Greece, quotas in, 448
Greenspan, Alan, 302
Gross domestic product (GDP), 30, 111–12, 174.
    See also Real gross domestic product;
    Potential gross domestic product
  and budget deficit, 362–65
  and consumer spending, 39
  decline of, 34–35
  decreasing, 262
  defined, 30, 111
  deflating, 150
  and demand-side v. supply-side inflation,
    384–85
  and economic well-being, 111–12
  equilibrium, 187–88. *See also* Equilibrium
    and full employment, 195–98
  growing, and aggregate supply and demand
    curves, 386–87
  housework and, 113
  increasing, 261–62
  limitations of, 113–15
  and multiplier, 210–22
    and international trade, 225–28
  and national debt, 359–60
  v. NNP, 176–77
  per capita, 418–19
  per labor hour, 418
  and population, 513
  and structural deficit, 362–65
  as sum of all factor payments, 175–76
  as sum of final goods and services, 174–75
  as sum of values added, 178–79
  taxes and, 253–56
  and total spending, 190

U.S., 31–32
and velocity of money, 324
Gross private domestic investment, 175

Hooverville, 117
Hungary, and free market, 544
Hyperinflation. *See* Galloping inflation

IMF. *See* International Monetary Fund
Imports
   demand for and exchange rates, 469
   and relative prices, 490
   relative prices and, 186–87
   variable, and leakage and injections
      approach, 206
Income
   and consumption and wealth, 193–94
   effect on saving, 171–72
   foreign, and U.S. exports, 489–90
   future, consumption and, 166–68
   GDP as sum of all, 176–77
   v. money, 301
   per capita
      in LDCs, 524
      in LDCs v. developed nations, 527
   personal, 180
   redistribution of, 46–47
      by inflation, 137–38, 410
   from saving, reduction of taxes on, 265
   of U.S. workforce, 38
Income determination, 191–93
   algebraic analysis of, 207
Income distribution
   in free market, 546
   in LDCs, 527
   in planned economy, 547
   under socialism, 548
   and supply-side economics, 268
Income-expenditure analysis, 191–95
Income-expenditure diagram, 193
   defined, 193
Income tax. *See also* Personal income tax
   changes in, and consumption, 168
   and consumption, 157
   and consumption schedule, 253–56
   corporate, reduction of, 265
   effect of reduction in, 259
   multiplier and, 256–58
Indexing, 409–410
   and costs of inflation, 410
   defined, 409
   inflation, 148–50
Index numbers, 148
Index of inequality, LDCs v. developed
   nations, 527
Induced increase in consumption, 216
   defined, 216
Induced investment, 190, 205–206
   defined, 190
Industry
   competition within, 40–41
   protecting, in international trade, 452–54
   size of, and supply curve shifts, 88–89
Inflation, 110. *See also* Demand inflation
   and aggregate demand, 122, 384
   and aggregate demand curve, output and,
      388–89
   and aggregate supply curve, 385
      output and, 388–89
   average rate of, 143
   and budget deficit, 369–70
   costs of, 133–34, 398–400
      indexing and, 410
   defined, 33, 110

and deindustrialization thesis, 429
demand-side, 387–92
demand- v. supply-side, 384–85
effect of on exchange rates, 467–69
effect on consumer spending, 166
exchange rates and, 494–96
expansionary monetary policy and, 318–19
expectations of
   and Phillips curve, 400–403, 408–409
expected, 138–39
   and interest rates, 328
loan repayments and, 364–66
measuring, 148–50
multiplier and, 246–48
and price, 142–43
price indexes and, 33
and purchasing-power myth, 134–37
redistribution of income and wealth and,
   137–38
supply-side, and Phillips curve, 392–93
taxes and, 139–40
trade-off with unemployment, 389–92, 396,
   397
   and aggregate supply curve, 392–93
   demand management and, 406
   improving, 406–407
   monetary and fiscal policy and, 406
   and rational expectations, 404–405
and unemployment, 196–98, 200–201
variability of, 143
and wages, 400–403
Inflation accounting, 364–66
   defined, 364
Inflationary gap, 197, 229, 237
   and aggregate demand, 240
   defined, 197
   inflation and, 237–40
   Phillips curve and, 395–96
Innovation
   economic growth through, 517, 520–21
   equalization of, 422–23
   growth of, 419
Input(s), 28. *See also* Labor; Capital
   defined, 28
   imported, exchange rates and, 492
   labor and capital, 35–38
   price of, and supply curve shifts, 90
   prices of, and aggregate supply curve shifts,
      233
Interest. *See also* Interest rates
   payments of, inflation accounting and,
      364–66
Interest rates. *See also* Nominal rate of interest;
      Real rate of interest
   and bond prices, open market operations
      and, 305–306
   ceilings on, 141
   and consumption, 166
   control of, 76
      v. control of money supply, 333–36
   excess reserves and, 310–11
   and exchange rates, 469–70, 496–97
   and expected rate of inflation, 328
   fiscal policy and, 330–31
   inflation and, 3–4
   and international capital flows, 496–97
   and investment, 185, 314–15
   and investment and budget deficit, 372–75
   monetary policy and, 313–14, 315–17
   v. nominal interest rates, and inflation
      accounting, 364
   trade deficit and budget deficit and, 503–504
   and velocity, 327–28
Intermediate goods, 112
   defined, 112
   and GDP, 178

International Bank for Reconstruction and
   Development, 535–36
International Monetary Fund (IMF), 477–78
International trade, 435–36. *See also*
      Protectionism
   and aggregate demand, 489–90
   and aggregate supply, 494
   and demand for currency, 465
   v. domestic, 437–38
   and foreign currencies, 438
   and impediments to mobility of labor and
      capital, 438
   interferences with, 447–48, 451–54
   and J curve, 492–94
   lags in, 492–94
   measuring, 474–75
   and multiplier, 225–28
   mutual gains from, 436–37
   political factors in, 437
   pricing equilibrium in, 445–47
   U.S.-Japanese, 506, 560
Inventory, and GDP, 174
Investment, 152, 175. *See also* Corporate
      investment; Investment spending
   as assets, 152
   domestic, and trade deficit, 504–507
   equilibrium and, 198–200
   foreign, in LDCs, 529–30
   interest rates and, 314–15
   saving and, 198–200
   as stabilization policy lag, 332
   variability of, 184–86
Investment goods, GDP, 174
Investment spending, 152, 154. *See also*
      Investment
   defined, 152
Invisible hand, 69
   interferences with, 75–76

Japan
   economic growth of, 64–65
   export-led growth in, 558–59
   industrial organization in, 559
   labor management relations in, 559–60
   manufacturing methods as U.S. import, 561
   as planned economy, 560–61
   and U.S. economic relations, 506
J curve, 492–94
   defined, 492
Johnson, Lyndon, and tax reduction, 157

Kennedy, John F.
   and full employment, 131
   and tax reduction, 157
Keynes, John Maynard, 10, 118, 119, 174, 184,
   187, 200
Keynesian model
   monetary policy and aggregate demand in,
      315–17
   money and price in, 318–20
Keynesians. *See also* Theory, Keynesian
   v. monetarists, 328–29
      at Fed, 336
      on fiscal policy, 330–31
      and shape of aggregate supply curve,
         337–39
King, Martin Luther, Jr., 127
Kuznets, Simon, 174

Labor
   and aggregate supply curve shifts, 234
   cheap, and lagging productivity, 431–32
   cheap foreign, 435, 457–59
      comparative advantage and, 444–45
   impediments to mobility, in international
      trade, 438

law of diminishing returns and, 514
U.S. workforce, 36–39
Labor force, 130
  defined, 130
Labor productivity. *See also* Productivity
  defined, 418
  growth of, twentieth century, 419–21
Law of diminishing returns, and labor, 514
Law of supply and demand, 83–84, 98
  defined, 83
  interference with, 75–76
LDCs. *See* Less developed countries
Leading indicators, 347
  defined, 347
  index of, 349
Leakages and injections approach, 204–206
Leisure, and GDP, 114
Lenders, inflation and, 137
Lenin, V.I., 550
Less developed countries (LDCs)
  aid from developed nations to, 534–35
  economic growth in, 526–28
  education in, 532–33
  entrepreneurship in, 533–34
  equalization of standard of living and
    productivity of, 423–24
  government inhibition of business activity
    in, 534
  impediments to development in, 528–34
  improvements, 536–37
  loans and grants to, 535–36
  population growth in, 527–28, 530–32
  scarcity of physical capital in, 529–30
  standard of living in, 524–25
  technical training in, 532–33
  unemployment in, 533
Lewis, W. Arthur, 532
Liability
  in banking, 288
  defined, 288
Liquidity, defined, 283
Long-run Phillips curve. *See* Phillips curve,
    vertical
Lucas, Robert E., Jr., 346

M1. *See also* Money supply
  defined, 720
M2. *See also* Money supply
  defined, 282
Macroeconomics, v. microeconomics, 107–108
Malthus, Thomas R., 512
Managed float, 482
Manufacturing, and U.S. workforce, 36
Marginal analysis, 8
Marginal propensity to consume (MPC), 162
  defined, 162
Marginal propensity to save (MPS), 171–72
Market, activity in, GDP and, 112
Market economy, saving and investment in,
    198–99
Market mechanism
  externalities and, controlling, 7
  goods served by, 71–72
  price ceilings and, 91–93
  price floors and, 93–95
Market system, 70–71
  defined, 70
Marx, Karl, and market mechanism, 72
Material incentives, 556
Medium of exchange, 279
Microeconomics, v. macroeconomics, 107–108
Minimum required reserve ratio. *See* Required
    reserves
Mixed economy, 47
  defined, 47

Model, 15
  abstract, 15
  econometric, 344–46
  Phillips machine, 16
Monetarism
  defined, 328
  and fiscal policy, 330–31
  v. Keynesian theory, 328–29
    at Fed, 336
    on monetary policy, 330–31
    and shape of aggregate supply curve,
      337–39
  from quantity theory of money, 328–29
Monetary policy, 313–114
  and aggregate demand, 315–17
  budget balancing and, 357
  defined, 313
  expansionary, and inflation, 318–19
  v. fiscal policy, 331–33
  and fiscal policy, trade deficit and, 505
  and independence of Fed, 303–304
  and interest rates, 313–14, 315–17
  monetarism v. Keynesian theory, 330–31
  in open economy, 499–500
  and trade-off between unemployment and
    inflation, 406
  and unemployment, 396–98
Monetization, 370–72
Monetize the deficit, defined, 808
Money, 279–81. *See also* Money supply
  v. barter, 277
  commodity, 280
  creation of, 289–94
  defined, 279
  demand for, 311–13
  exchange and, 70
  fiat, 280
  v. income, 301
  opportunity cost of holding, 312
  paper, 280
    banking and, 284
  and price, in Keynesian model, 318–20
  as store of value, 279
  as unit of account, 279
  value and GDP, 111–12
  on Yap, 281
Money cost, and opportunity cost, 58
Money fixed asset, 164
  defined, 165
Money GDP. *See* Nominal gross domestic
    product
Money market, equilibrium in, 313–14
Money market deposit accounts, 282
Money market mutual funds, 282
Money supply
  contracting, 294–96
  contraction of, 305
  control of
    v. control of interest rates, 333–36
    improving, 307–308
    loans to banks and, 308–309
    mechanism for, 310–11
  expansion of, 304–305
    by multiple banks, 290–94
    by single bank, 287–89
  M1, 282
  M2, 282–83
  measuring, 281–84
  need for control of, 297
  and open-market operations, 304–305
  oversimplified formula, 294, 294–97
  reserve requirements and, 306–308
Money wage rate
  and aggregate supply curve, 400–403
  and aggregate supply curve shifts, 232
Moral suasion, defined, 309

MPC. *See* Marginal propensity to consume
Multinational corporation, 40, 41. *See also*
    Corporation
  in LDCs, 530
Multiplier, 210–12
  and aggregate demand curve, 218–20
  algebraic explanation of, 214–15, 224
  calculating, 248
  consumer expenditure and, 215–16
  defined, 210
  explaining, 212–13
  and government purchases, 216–17, 259–60
  and income tax, 256–58
  and inflation, 246–48
  and international trade, 225–28
  and net exports, 217–18
  oversimplified formula for, 215
    inaccuracy of, 331
  paradox of thrift, 220
  in reverse, 219–20
  and tax policy, 258–60

National Bureau of Economic Research, 347
National debt
  v. budget deficit, 357–58
  burden, 376–77
  defined, 358, 358–61
National income, 153, 154–56, 176, 179–80
  defined, 153
  net exports and, 186
  taxes and, 254–256
National income accounting, 174
National Monetary Commission, 301
Natural disaster, GDP and, 114
Natural rate of unemployment. *See*
    Unemployment, natural rate of
Near moneys, 283
  defined, 283
Net domestic national product (NDP), 180
Net exports, 153, 155, 175. *See also* Exports
  defined, 153
  determinants of, 184–85
  and GDP, 225–28
  and multiplier, 217–18
Net national product (NNP), 176, 180
  v. GDP, 176–77
Net worth
  of banks, 288
  defined, 288
New Economics, GDP and, 118
Nicaragua, galloping inflation in, 144
Nixon, Richard, and GDP, 118
NNP. *See* Net national product
Nominal GDP, 111
  defined, 111
  monetarist theory and, 328–29
Nominal rate of interest, 139
  ceilings and, 141–42
  defined, 139
  v. real interest rates, and inflation
    accounting, 364–66

Okun, Arthur, 333
OPEC. *See* Organization of Petroleum
    Exporting Countries
Open economy, 31. *See also* Economy; Closed
    economy
  defined, 31, 487
  fiscal policy in, 497–99
  monetary policy in, 499–500
Open-market operations, 304–305
  and bond prices and interest rates, 305–306
  defined, 304
Opportunity cost, 7–8, 57–58. *See also* Scarcity
  and comparative advantage, 441, 443
  defined, 7, 57

of economic growth, 66
for governments, 64–65
of holding money, 312
for households, 64
and money cost, 58
principle of, 57
and principle of increasing costs, 61–62
and production possibilities frontier, 61
of single business firm, 59–60
Organization of Petroleum Exporting
    Countries (OPEC)
    and great stagflation, 119–20, 245–48
Origin, 19
    defined, 25
    omitting, 51–52
    ray through, 23
Output(s), 28
    defined, 28
    and equality, 9
    government, GDP and, 174
    inflation and, 388
    loss of, due to unemployment, 128–30
    per person, increase in, 420
    per person v. total, 513
    price of related, and supply curve shifts, 90
    U.S., 39–40
Output per capita. See Output(s), per person

Paradox of thrift, 220
    defined, 220
Partnership, 40
    defined, 40
Payroll tax, 46
Perestroika, 551, 553
Personal income tax, 46. See also Income tax
    as automatic stabilizer, 343
    reduction of, 265
Personal services, cost disease of, 8–9
Phillips, A.W., 390
Phillips curve
    defined, 390, 394
    demand-side inflation and, 390–92
    inflationary expectations and, 400–403,
        408–409
    restrictions of, 394–96
    shape of, and resource utilization, 399
    supply-side inflation and, 392–93
    vertical, 396
Pierce, C.S., 13–14
Planned economy
    v. free market, 545–48
    Japan as, 560–61
    saving and investment in, 199–200
    in transition, 554–55
Poland, and free market, 544
Population
    and demand curve shifts, 85
    and economic growth, 513
    exponential growth of, 515–19
    growth, 514
    in LDCs, 527–28, 530–32
Potential gross domestic product, 128–29
    and aggregate demand, 244
    defined, 128
Practical policy, v. theory, 14
Price. See also Relative prices
    and aggregate supply, 230–32
    and aggregate supply curve, shape of,
        234–35
    deflation of, 241–43
    and demand, 165–66
    and demand curve shifts, 85
    effect on aggregate demand curve slope, 320
    and equilibrium of aggregate supply and
        demand, 236
    and equilibrium of real GDP, 194–95

exchange rates and, 494–96
import, and protectionism, 456–57
increasing, and aggregate supply and
    demand curves, 386–87
and inflation, 142–43
money and, in Keynesian model, 318–20
and shifts in the consumption function, 166
and wealth and the consumption function
    and, 166
Price ceiling, 91–93, 407
    defined, 91
Price controls, 76
    favoritism and corruption with, 95
    and great stagflation, 120
    misallocation of resources and, 96
    price ceilings, 91–93
    price floors, 93–95
    unenforceability of, 96
    at Valley Forge, 75
Price floor, 93–95
    defined, 93
    and milk, 94
Price indexes, 148–50
    deflating by, 33, 149–50
Pricing, equilibrium, in international trade,
    445–47
Principle of increasing costs, 61–62
    defined, 61
Private enterprise, in United States, 29–30
Privatization, in planned economies, 554–55
Product innovation, and investment, 185
Production, resource allocation and, 59
Production possibilities frontier, 60–61
    choices and, 62–63
    defined, 60
    economic growth and, 65–66
    efficiency of, 67
Productivity
    and aggregate supply curve shifts, 233–34
    convergence of, 422
    defined, 234
    and deindustrialization thesis, 427–30
    equalization of, 422–23, 426–27
    growth of, and unemployment, 430–32
    international growth rate of, 427
    rate of growth of, 4–5
    U.S
        lag behind other industrial countries,
            426–27
        slowdown of, 424–26
Profit
    in banking, 285–86
    socialism and, 548
Profit rates, and inflation, 141
Progressive tax, 47
    defined, 47
Property tax, 46
Proprietorship, 40
    defined, 40
Protectionism, 507
    v. free trade, 456
    and infant-industry argument, 455
    and international trade, 452–54
    for national defense, 454
    strategic trade policy, 455
Public debt. See National debt
Public utilities, regulation of, and inflation, 141
Purchasing power, 134, 135–37
    defined, 134
Purchasing-power parity, 467–69
    and Big Mac, 468

Quantity demanded, 76–78
    defined, 77
Quantity supplied, 78–79
    defined, 79

Quantity theory of money
    to monetarism, 328–29
    and velocity, 324–25
Quota(s), 447–48
    defined, 447
    effects on price, 449–50, 452
    protective, 453–54
    purchasing-power parity and, 468
    v. tariff, 450–51

Rational choice, and true economic cost, 7–8
Rational decision, defined, 57
Rational expectations, 403
    defined, 403
    theory of, 403
    and trade-off between unemployment and
        inflation, 404–405
Ray, 23
Reagan, Ronald, 120–21
    and supply-side economics, 230
    and tax reduction, 158
Reaganomics, 120–21, 230
    budget deficit and trade deficit and, 503–504
    international aspects of, 500–502
Real gross domestic product, 33, 111
    defined, 33, 111
    growth rate of, 115–18
Real rate of interest, 139
    ceilings and, 141–42
    defined, 139
Real wage rate, 134–35
    defined, 134
Recession, 34–35, 110
    and aggregate demand, 122
    budget balancing and, 356–57
    defined, 34, 110
    effect on budget deficit, 378–79
    international, 218
    self-correcting mechanism for, 243
Recessionary gap, 196–97, 229, 237
    defined, 196
    deflation v. unemployment with, 241–43
    economy's self-correcting mechanism and,
        397, 400
    Phillips curve and, 394–96
Recessions
    and international trade, 490
    national debt and, 359
    unemployment insurance and, 132–33
Reich, Robert, 41
Relative prices, 136. See also Price
    defined, 136
    of exports and imports, 186–87
    exports and imports and, 490
Rent control, in New York City, 92–93
Required reserves
    controlling money supply by, 306–308
    defined, 288
Research and development. See also Innovation
Research and development
    and economic growth, 518
    tax credits for, 266
Resource allocation, 58–59
    defined, 58
    and price controls, 96–97
    and production possibilities frontier, 60–61
    in Soviet Union, 64
Resources
    defined, 56
    efficient use of, 68
    inability to utilize, 128–29
    scarcity of, 56–58
    unemployment insurance and, 133
    utilization of, and shape of aggregate supply
        and Phillips curves, 399

Revaluation, 464
  defined, 464
  of fixed exchange rates, 473–74
Ricardo, David, 439, 440
Rogers, Will, 117
Roosevelt, Franklin
  and Bretton Woods system, 477
  and Great Depression, 117
Run on a bank, defined, 277

S&Ls. See Savings and loan industry
Safire, William, 456
Sales, levels of, and investment, 185
Sales tax, 46
Saving, 154
  domestic, and trade deficit, 504–507
  effect of income on, 171–72
  equilibrium and, 198–200
  income from, reduction of taxes on, 265
  investment and, 198–200
  and U.S.-Japanese economic relations, 506
Saving function, 171
Savings accounts, 282
Savings and loan industry
  deposit insurance for, 286
  failure of, 287
  regulation of, 276
Scarcity
  economies and, 62–63
  indispensable necessity syndrome, 56
  resource allocation and, 58–59
  of resources, 56–58
Scatter diagram, 158–62
  defined, 158
Schultze, Charles, 264
Self-correcting mechanism, 243
  theory of, 244
Service economy, U.S. as, 427–28
Services. See also Cost disease of the personal
    services
  and U.S. workforce, 36
Shortage
  defined, 81
  and price ceilings, 91
Slope, 20–22
  of production possibilities frontier, 61
  of a straight line, 20–21
Smith, Adam, 69, 70, 436–37, 513
Social infrastructure
  in LDCs, 529
  in USSR, 518–19
Socialism, 543–45
  v. capitalism, 548
    and individual freedom, 548–49
  defined, 543
Social Security Act of 1935, 132
Soviet Union
  changing economic system in, 553–54
  command economy in, 550
    and perestroika, 551
  composition of aggregate demand in, 518–19
  resource allocation in, 64
Specialization, 68–69, 436
  defined, 436
  protectionism and, 453–54
Speculators
  and fixed exchange rates, 472
  and floating exchange rates, 480–81
Spending policy. See Government purchases
Stabilization policy, 121–23
  controversy over, 404–405
  controversy over government intervention,
    340–43
  defined, 121
  discretion v. rules for, 343–44
    and government policy, 350

and political business cycle, 350–51
  and size of government, 349–50
  fiscal v. monetary policy, 331–33
  lags in, 332
    difficulties presented by, 342–43
    length of, 344
    passive v. activist, 397–98
  and shape of aggregate supply curve, 337–39
Stagflation, 120, 385. See also Great stagflation
  from aggregate supply shifts, 245–47
  defined, 120, 240
  and demand inflation, 240
  1988–1990, 241
Stalin, Joseph, 550
Standard of living
  equalization of, 422–23
  history of Western, 415–17
  lagging, 431–32
  nineteenth century U.S., 416
  present U.S., 417–18
  productivity growth and, 5
  rise in productivity for, 420, 421
  U.S. v. Japan, 558
Stock market, as leading indicator, 347
Stocks, international trade in, and demand for
    currency, 465
Store of value, defined, 279
Structural budget deficit, 361–64
  defined, 362
Structural deficit. See Budget deficit; Structural
    budget deficit
Structural unemployment, 131
  defined, 131
Sum of final goods and services, GDP as,
    174–75
Sum of values added, GDP as, 178–79
Supply, 78–79
  and aggregation, 108
  of currency, 465–66
  in macroeconomics, 108–109
Supply and demand, 74–98
  equilibrium of, 80–84
  law of, 83–84, 98
    defined, 83
    interference with, 6, 75–76
Supply curve, 79
  defined, 79
  movements along, 88
  shifts of, 88–91
  in supply-demand diagram, 80–81
Supply-demand diagram, 80–81
Supply schedule, 79
  defined, 79
Supply-side economics, 9, 120–21, 230, 268–70
  Clintonomics as, 269, 270
  controversy over, 266–67
  tax cuts and, 264–66
Surplus
  defined, 81
  and price floors, 93–94
Survey data, 347

Tariff(s), 447
  defined, 447
  effects on price, 449–50, 451–52
  protective, 453–54
  purchasing-power parity and, 468
  v. quota, 450–51
Tax(es). See also specific taxes
  on capital gains, 140
  and circular flow diagram, 156
  and consumer expenditure, 157–58
  government purchases and, 256
  inflation and, 139
    costs of, 410

reduction of
  and budget deficit, 377
  effect of on consumption, 163–64
  1981, 158
  1975, 157
  1964, 157
  and supply-side economics, 264–66
  U.S., 44–46
Taxation, and individual freedom, 549
Tax policy
  and consumer behavior, 168
  and disposable income, 253–55
  failure of, 1975, 167
  v. government purchases, 262–63
  multiplier and, 258–60
Tax provisions, and investment, 185–86
Tax revenue, loss of, 268
Technology
  and aggregate supply curve shifts, 233–35
  equalization of, 422–23
  and investment, 185
  progress in and supply curve shifts, 90
  training in, in LDCs, 532–33
Teenagers
  in U.S. workforce, 36
  unemployment rate of, 127–28
Theory. See also Economic theory
  defined, 14
  Keynesian, 14
  v. practical policy, 14
Thrift, paradox of, 220
Time series graphs, 32–34. See also Graphs
  defined, 32
Total spending. See Aggregate demand
Trade adjustment assistance, 454
  defined, 454
Trade deficit
  and budget deficit, 502–504
  curing, 504–507
  problems of, 504
  U.S., 488
  and U.S.-Japanese economic relations, 506
Transfer payments, 47, 155, 260
  defined, 47, 156
  as government purchases, 175
Transition, 550, 554–55
Two-variable diagrams, 19–20

U.S. manufacturing industry
  productivity growth lag behind other
    industrial countries, 426–27
  productivity growth lag service industries,
    427–28
  productivity slowdown in, 424–26
Underground economy
  GDP and, 112, 114
Unemployment
  and aggregate demand, 122
  costs of, 398–400
    and unemployment insurance, 133
  disguised, 533
  economic costs of, 128–30
  economic growth and, 35
  effects of retraining on, 406–407
  fiscal and monetary policy to correct, 396–98
  and growth in LDCs, 533
  human costs of, 126–28
  and inflation, 196–98, 200–201
  natural rate of, 396
  and productivity growth, 430–32
  and recessionary gap, 241–43
  statistics of, 130
  trade-off with inflation, 389–92, 396, 397
    and aggregate supply curve, 392–93
    demand management and, 406

improving, 406–407
  monetary and fiscal policy and, 406
  and rational expectations, 404–405
  types of, 130–31
Unemployment insurance, 132–33
  as automatic stabilizer, 343
  and costs of unemployment, 133
Unemployment rate, 127–28
  defined, 127
United States
  economic history of, 115–18
  economy, 28–29, 42
    business in, 40–41
    business regulation in, 44
    government and, 42
    government expenditures, 44
    growth of, 31–32, 33–35
    private enterprise, 29–30
  GDP in, 31–32
  and Japanese economic relations, 506
  loans and grants to LDCs, 535–36
  population, 28–29
  population growth in, 514
  production in, 39–40
  recessions in, 34–35
  workforce, 36–39

and manufacturing, 36
  and service, 36
Unit of account, defined, 279
Usury laws, 140–41
  defined, 140

Valley Forge, price controls at, 75
Value added, 178
Variable, 19
  defined, 25
Variable taxes, 253, 254, 255
  defined, 253
Velocity
  defined, 324
  determinants of, 325–28
  monetarism and, 328–29
  and quantity theory of money, 324–25
Velocity of circulation. See Velocity
Vertical Phillips curve. See Phillips curve,
  vertical

Wage controls, and great stagflation, 120
Wage-price controls, 407–409
  defined, 407
Wages. See also Money wage rate; Real wage
  rate

and aggregate supply curve shifts, 232
  deflation of, 241–43
  inflation and, 400–403
  lagging, 431–32
  U.S. v. foreign, 435
War, and GDP, 114
War on drugs, economic aspect of, 97
Wealth
  and income and consumption, 193–94
  and consumption, 164–65
  redistribution of, by inflation, 137–38
Welfare state, 545
Women
  housework and GDP, 113
  in LDCs, 525–26
  in U.S. workforce, 36
Worker's management, 545
  defined, 545
Work ethic, and economic growth, 517
World Bank. See International Bank for
  Reconstruction and Development
World War II, GDP and, 118

Yap, money on, 281